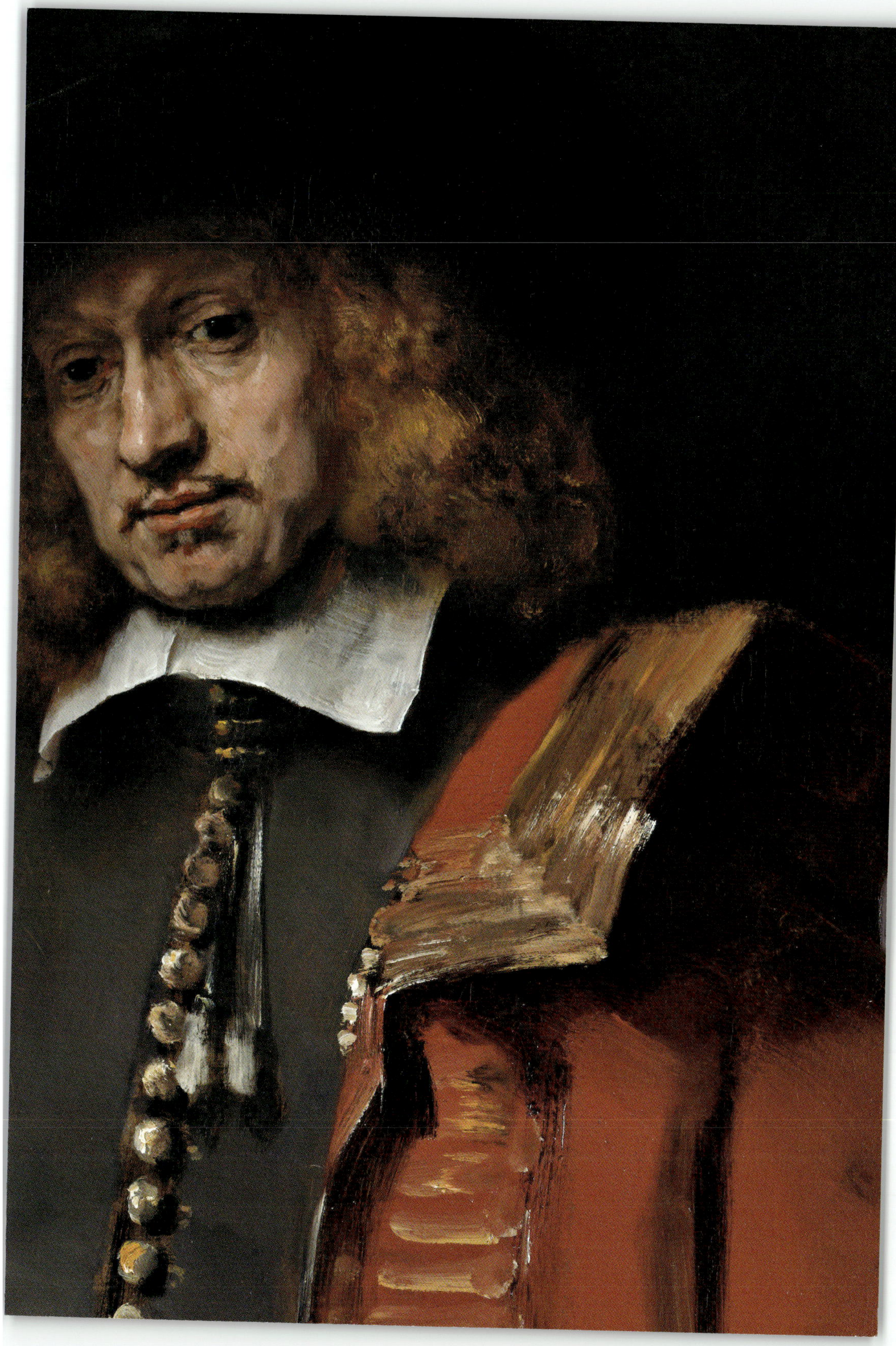

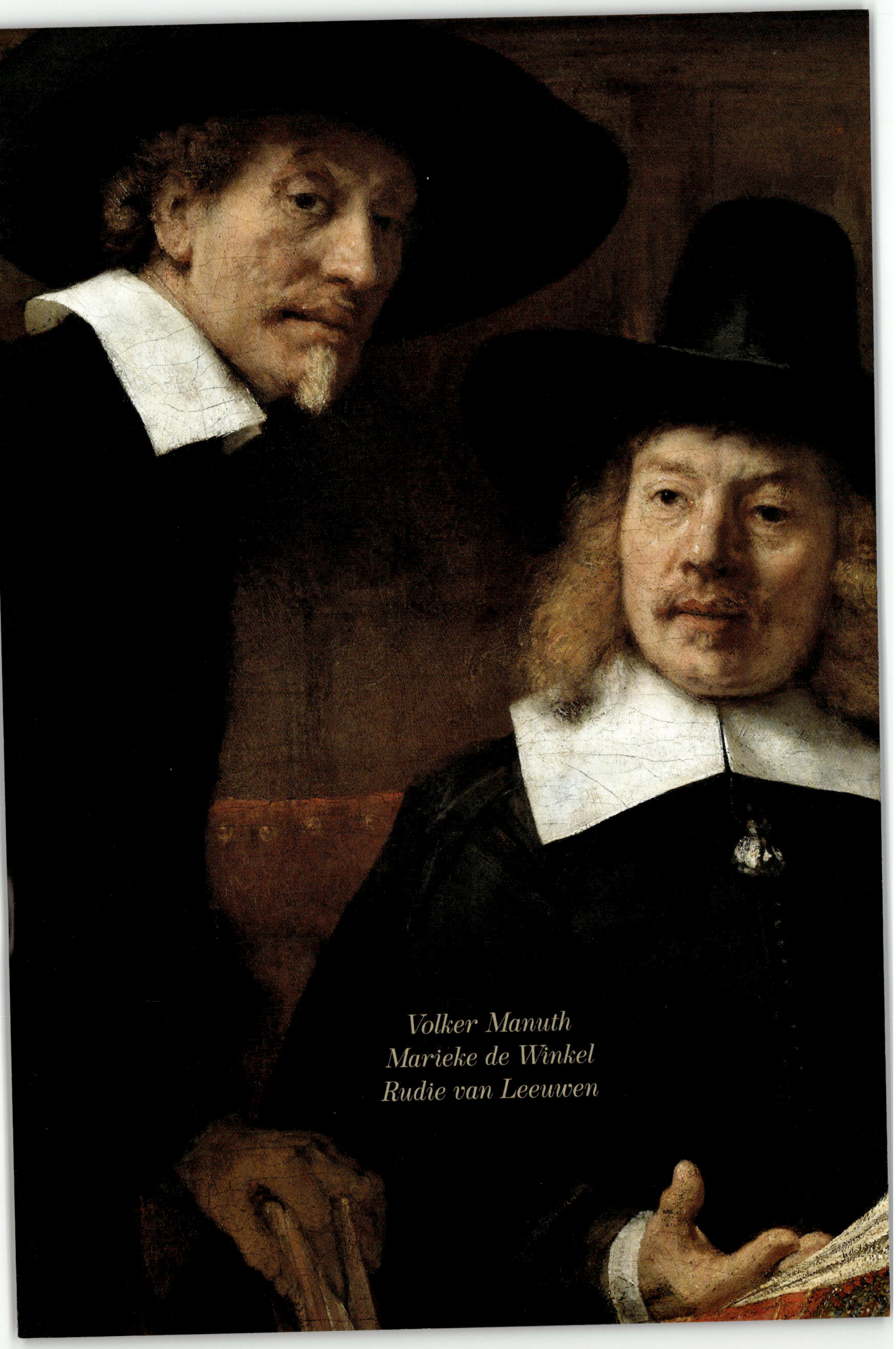

Volker Manuth
Marieke de Winkel
Rudie van Leeuwen

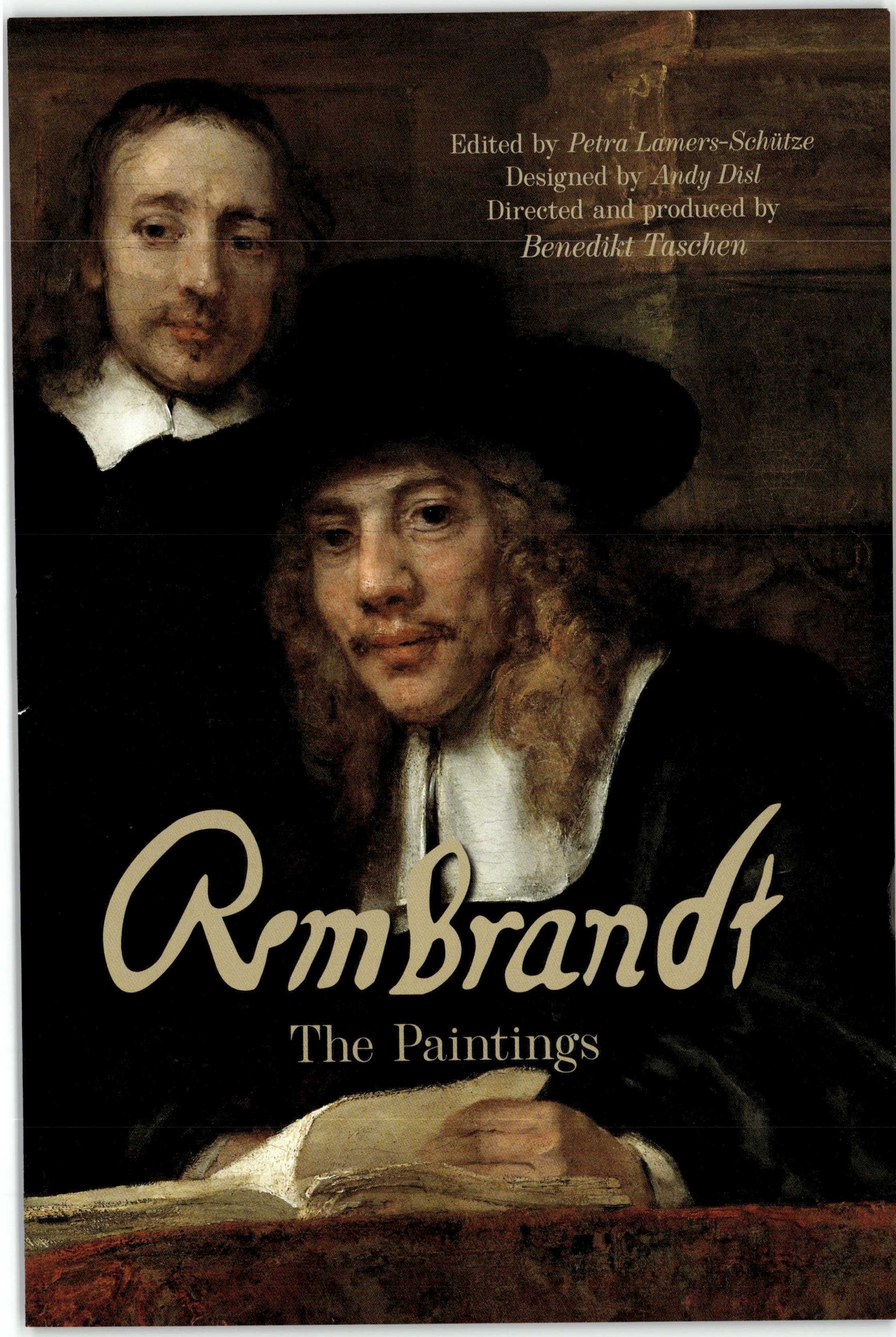
Edited by *Petra Lamers-Schütze*
Designed by *Andy Disl*
Directed and produced by
Benedikt Taschen
Rembrandt
The Paintings

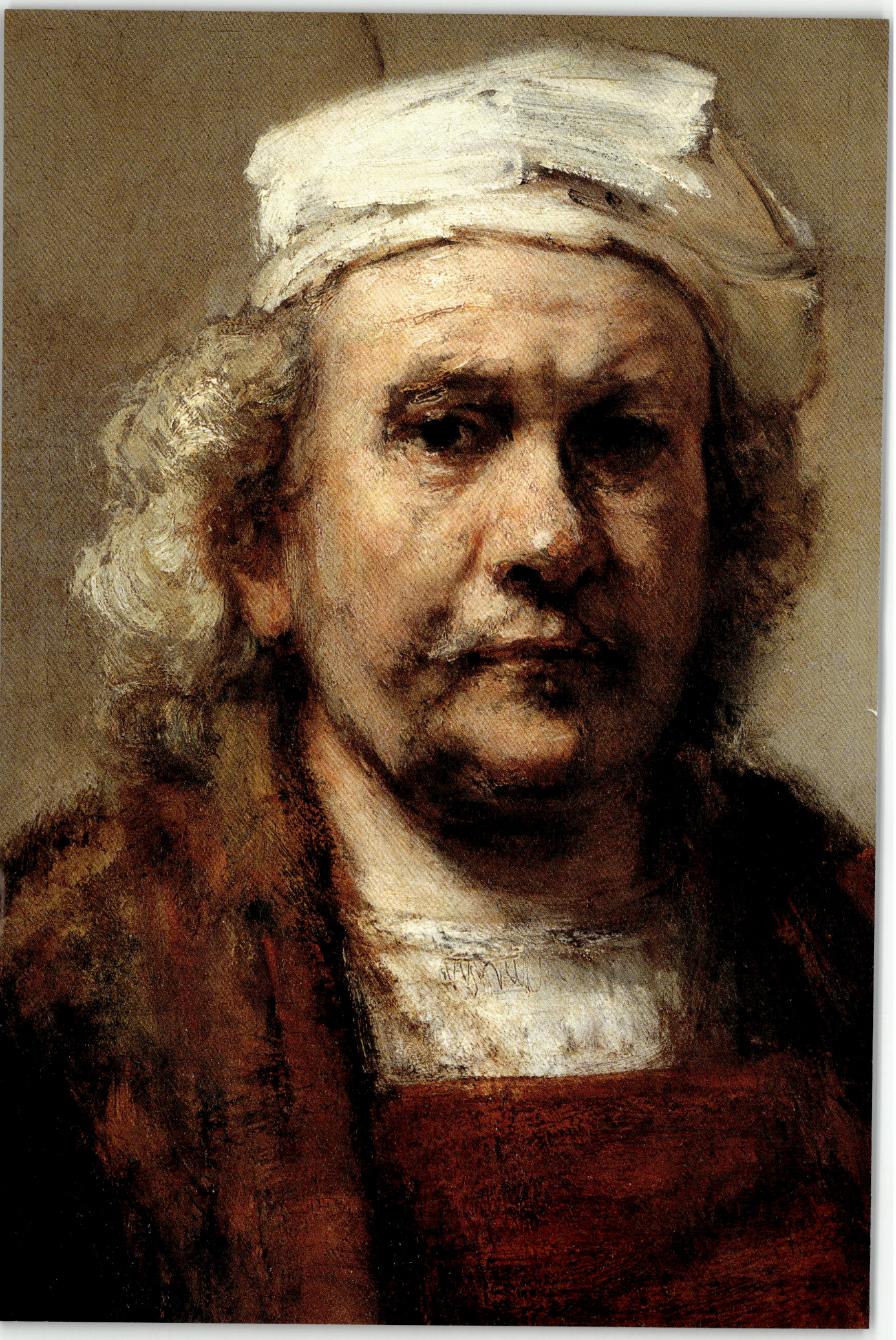

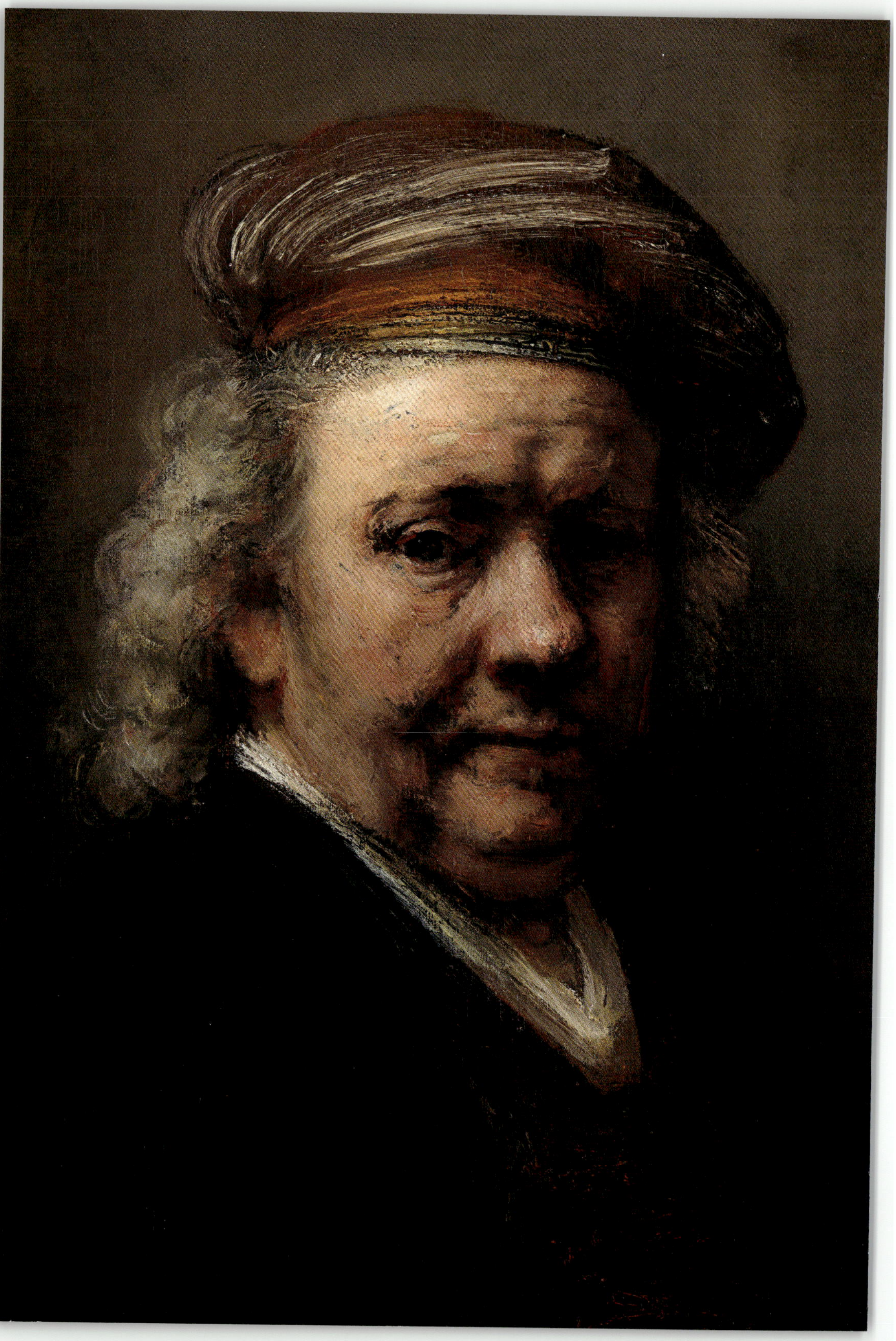

Preface

Rembrandt never vanished into obscurity. That is what sets him apart from many of the other artists of his time, whose fame faded relatively quickly after their death. They included his contemporaries in the Netherlands Frans Hals (1581/85–1666) and Johannes Vermeer (1632–1675), the two other great artists of the Golden Age of Dutch painting. Both were rediscovered only during the course of the nineteenth century, and the most important painter of the Baroque Age in Italy, Michelangelo Merisi, known as Caravaggio (1571–1610), even had to wait until the early twentieth century before being noticed again. Rembrandt was different. During his lifetime and after his death, he was praised by his fellow artists and art lovers alike, and his works were prized by collectors in the Netherlands and beyond. He remained productive even after a series of personal losses and setbacks, and his works were still sought after.

With the famous group portrait of the Amsterdam Militia Company of Captain Frans Banninck Cocq of 1642, generally known as *"The Night Watch"*, Rembrandt created a work which became the epitome of the golden age of civic culture in the Northern Netherlands and a symbol of the striving for independence in the fight against Catholic Spain. Rembrandt's history paintings and portraits reflect the new self-image of the burghers and rulers alike who helped the young emerging republic to political and economic power and prosperity. The fascination and inspiration which his works exercise on artists, art specialists and the art-loving public at large remain unbroken and extend far beyond the boundaries of culture.

Rembrandt's extensive oeuvre consists of paintings, drawing and etchings. Generations of art historians have focused on research into the aim of his works, and yet many of them continue to present us with a riddle. Rembrandt's contemporary Constantijn Huygens (1596–1687), the learned art-loving secretary of the Governor Frederik Hendrik (1584–1647), had already expressed the wish that Rembrandt, whose work he valued highly, should draw up a catalogue of his extensive oeuvre for the generations to come – in vain. The first catalogue of Rembrandt's etchings was published posthumously as early as 1751 in Paris, drawn up by the French art dealer Edmé-François Gersaint (1694–1750); but it would not be until 1836 that the Englishman John Smith (1781–1855) published the first catalogue of Rembrandt's paintings. He warned his readers not to harbour too many high expectations with regard to new knowledge about Rembrandt, "so many having already written on the subject […] so that little has been left in the field of research where so many have previously gleaned" (Smith 1829–1842, vol. 7 [1836], p. X). Smith would doubtless have been amazed at the literature that has since been published about Rembrandt, examining very different aspects of his life and work to an extent that even specialists find it virtually impossible to retain an overview.

In addition to countless books and articles, since those days more than ten catalogues raisonnés have been produced, in which the paintings thought to be by Rembrandt's own hand are listed. The number of paintings ascribed to Rembrandt varies considerably and extends from initially over 600 paintings to now around 265. By comparison, the number of works by Vermeer that for some time have been largely accepted as being by him personally scarcely exceeds about 35. The search for the "master's hand" continues to play an important part in research into Rembrandt's work, and the question as to how many of the paintings that have been attributed to him over the course of time actually are by the artist himself has continued to be discussed in recent decades, on occasion in a highly controversial manner. The publications of the Rembrandt Research Project (RRP, see Corpus I–VI, 1983–2015) have not changed much in this respect, though the six volumes that have been published without a doubt represent a milestone in the research into Rembrandt's oeuvre.

The main volumes of the Rembrandt Research Project represent the most thorough and extensive presentation of the paintings associated with Rembrandt to this day. They are aimed in particular at specialists. Both art-historical and scientific methods are used systematically and attempt above all to explain the genesis of the paintings. The present book targets a broad reading public in search of clearly presented information on the life and work of Rembrandt in line with the latest academic research. It aims to provide an overview of the artist's painterly oeuvre by means of high-quality, mostly large-format illustrations.

It should be noted here that from the very beginning it was the wish of both the authors and the publishers that the opinions represented in this book be made *à titre personnel*. Although two of the authors were briefly linked with the Rembrandt Research Project, they wish to avoid creating the impression that the present publication represents the views of the Rembrandt Research Project.

The authors of this book are aware that they – like other researchers – stand firmly on the shoulders of their predecessors and their knowledge, and that it goes without saying that new insights and results can be expected from the Rembrandt researchers of future generations. That is how it should be. Rembrandt research has been in the past, and should remain for a long time, a *work in progress*. It is important that the discussion regarding controversial research opinions should continue to be carried out in public in the future.

Volker Manuth, Marieke de Winkel, Rudie van Leeuwen

Page 10
Detail of: **Self-Portrait**, 1669
(see ill. p. 494)

I.

Rembrandt's Early Years in Leiden

1606–1631

"Rembrandt van Ryn was a meteor in art. Disdaining to acknowledge the usual laws of admission to the Temple of Fame, he boldly forged his own keys, entered, and took possession of a most conspicuous place by his own power."

JOHANN HEINRICH FUSELI, 1805

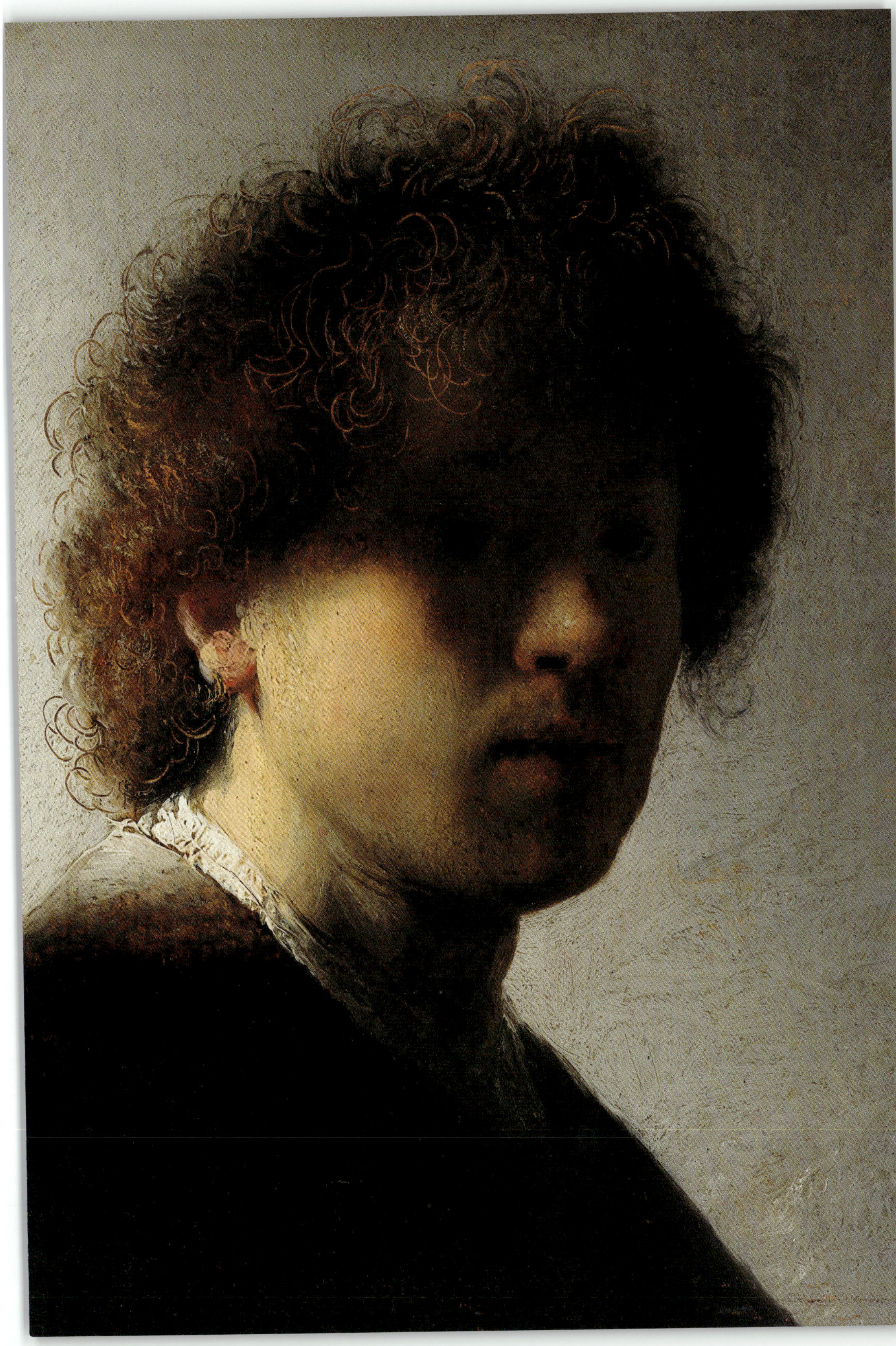

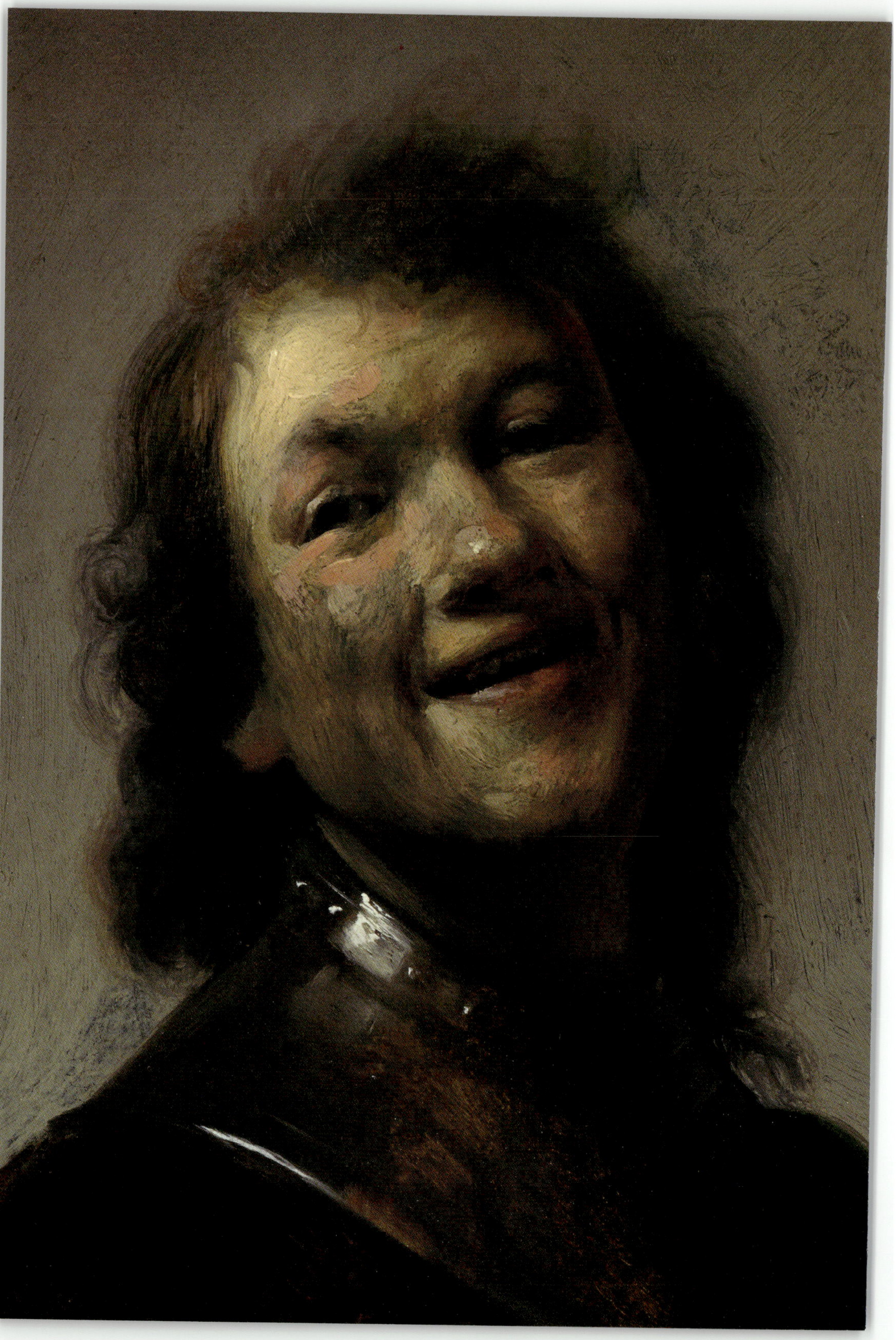

Family Background

Rembrandt's precise date of birth is not known. Probably he was born in Leiden on the 15 July 1606. That, at least, is what the burgomaster of Leiden, Jan Jansz. Orlers (1570–1646), stated in 1641 in the second edition of his *Beschrijvinge der Stadt Leyden* (Description of the City of Leiden). Apparently, Orlers was well-informed as his chapter on famous artists in Leiden shows. In his biography of Rembrandt, he notes not only the latter's date of birth but also the names of his parents and provides useful information about his early training.[1]

Rembrandt came from a family of malt millers.[2] His father, Harmen Gerritsz. (*c.* 1568–1630; p. 19, Cat. D626; p. 39, Cat. E246), adopted the surname van (den) Rijn, because the family mill in Leiden lay on the north bank of the Rhine near the Witte Poort, one of the city gates. Rembrandt's paternal grandfather, Gerrit Roelofsz., had already died 1573 and his grandmother, Lijsbeth Harmensdr. (died 1599), whose second marriage was also to a malt miller, lived with the latter and her children of her first marriage in the Weddesteeg on the north-western outskirts of Leiden. Harmen Gerritsz. married Neeltgen Willemsdr. van Zuytbroeck (*c.* 1568–1640), the daughter of a well-to-do baker on 8 October 1589 in the Pieterskerk in Leiden. In November of that year, he bought a half-share in his stepfather's mill and the neighbouring houses in Weddesteeg for 1,800 guilders. He lived there with his family for the rest of his life. It was there, too, that Rembrandt and his brothers and sisters were born.

People were dependent on malt millers in order to brew beer. Judging from their income, malt millers would have been considered to belong to the middle classes. Accordingly, Harmen Gerritsz. was not without means. Moreover, he evidently enjoyed the trust of his neighbours. In 1602, he was elected as the *buurtheer* (headman of the neighbourhood) for the Pelikaanshoek district, in which Weddesteeg lay. Like other cities within the Dutch Republic, Leiden was divided into so-called *gebuurten*,[3] semi-official organisations of inhabitants within a certain district. The *buurtheer*, who led the organisation, was a respected member of such a neighbourhood and following the nomination of his neighbours was selected by the city council from a group of three candidates (in Leiden). In addition to personal qualities, it was apparently also important, but not compulsory for the headman to be a member of the Reformed Church. The appointment

Page 15
Detail of: **Self-Portrait with a Shaded Face**, *c.* 1628
(see ill. p. 78)

Detail aus: **Self-Portrait as a Laughing Soldier**, *c.* 1628
(see ill. p. 80)

was for life and could only be ended by death, moving away, or voluntary resignation. Rembrandt's father carried out this duty for 22 years, although he was clearly in poor health. As a member of the Leiden civic militia, he had been injured at some stage during a weapons exercise. Thereafter, he retained the status of a non-active member of the militia (RD 1617/1) upon payment of six guilders per year. In 1624, and at his own request, he was permitted to retire from the position of *buurtheer* because of "impotentie" (which here means physical disability).[4] The fact that Adriaen Harmensz. van Rijn (*c.* 1597–1652), Rembrandt's elder brother, later also became *buurtheer* of Pelikaanshoek seems to indicate that the family enjoyed general respect.[5]

Harmen Gerritsz. van Rijn and his wife Neeltgen had numerous offspring. Of the ten children whose names we know, Rembrandt was the second youngest.[6] Apart from him, the only ones to reach adulthood were his elder brothers Gerrit (1589/97–1631), who worked as a malt miller's hand; Adriaen, who was initially a shoemaker and later a malt miller; and Willem (died 1655), who earned a living as a baker; and his younger sister Lysbeth (Elisabeth; died 1655). Nothing is known of Rembrandt's childhood. It was probably largely carefree, not least because his parents' mill guaranteed the family a stable income and because his elder brother, Adriaen, assumed increasing responsibility for family matters in place of his father.

Grammar School and University

Evidently, Rembrandt's parents had high expectations of their youngest son. He was to be the first in the family to attend university instead of training as a craftsman. Rembrandt was clearly a bright boy and showed signs at an early age of talents which predestined him to want more than to learn a trade. Around 1614/15, when he was eight or nine, his parents therefore sent him to the grammar school in Leiden in order "to learn the Latin language during the course of time and then to attend the Academy in Leiden [i. e. the university]".[7] From 1617 Hendrik Zwaerdecroon (*c.* 1594–1665) was Deputy Headmaster of the Grammar School.[8] He was a member of the Remonstrants and thus belonged to the more liberal wing of the Reformed Church, a fact which cost

---

Editor's note: The catalogue numbers refer to the catalogue raisonné of the paintings and the designations "Cat. D (plus no.)" and "Cat. E (plus no.)" refer to the catalogue raisonné of the drawings and etchings which were published in 2019 by TASCHEN in the following volumes: Volker Manuth, Marieke de Winkel and Rudie van Leeuwen *Rembrandt. Complete Paintings*, and Peter Schatborn and Erik Hinterding, *Rembrandt. The Complete Drawings and Etchings*. Catalogue numbers with an asterisk (*) are those for which the authors harbour doubts about the complete authorship or scope of Rembrandt's part in the execution. The abbreviation RD stands for "Rembrandt Documents", see Strauss/van der Meulen 1979 in the bibliography.

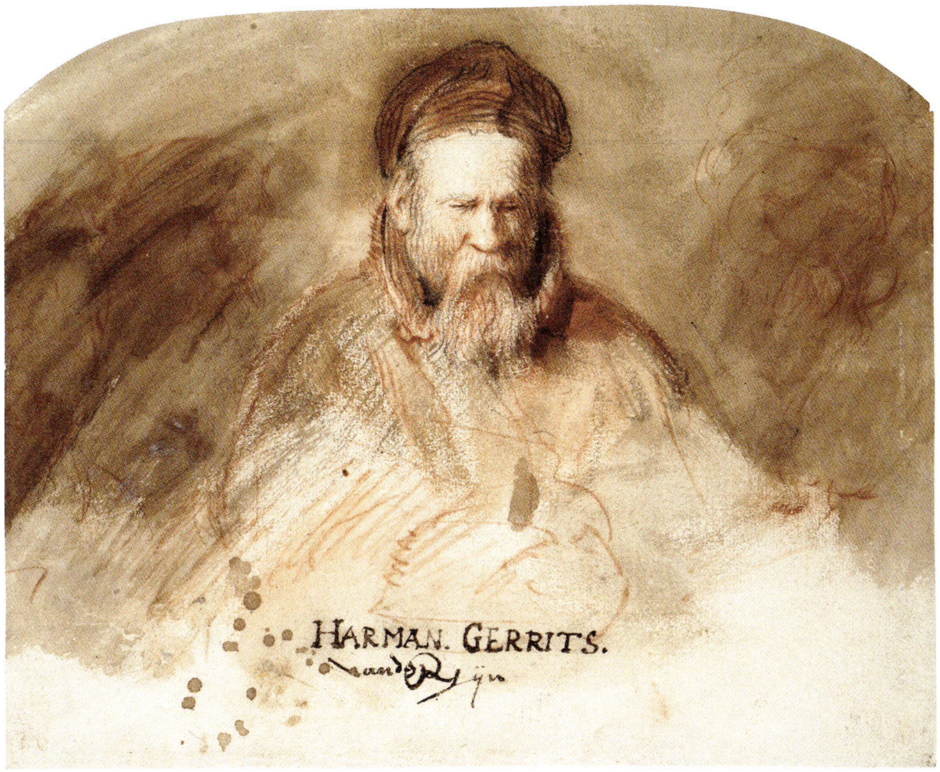

Portrait of Rembrandt's Father Harmen Gerritsz. van Rijn, *c.* 1630
Red and black chalk, brown brushwork, 19 × 24 cm (7 ½ × 9 ½ in.)
Oxford, Ashmolean Museum, Chambers Hall Collection

him his office in 1619. Already in 1618, all sympathisers with the Remonstrants in the city government of Leiden had been replaced by so-called Contra-Remonstrants. It is feasible that Zwaerdecroon, until his dismissal – he had refused to take the required oath on the decrees of the Synod of Dordrecht (1618/19) – tried to familiarise his pupils with the ideals of faith of the moderate Remonstrants. By attending grammar school, Rembrandt was prepared for study at the University of Leiden. The humanistic curriculum for the boys aged between about seven and fourteen included both religious and academic subjects.[9] In addition to the teaching of the Latin language and grammar based on the texts of classical authors including Virgil, Ovid, Terence, Aesop, Caesar, Cicero, Sallust and Livy, the pupils were also introduced to Greek. In the final grade they also received basic teaching in logic, ethics, arithmetic, geography, astronomy and calligraphy. Two days a week they studied the Catechism. Attending Sunday service with the other schoolboys

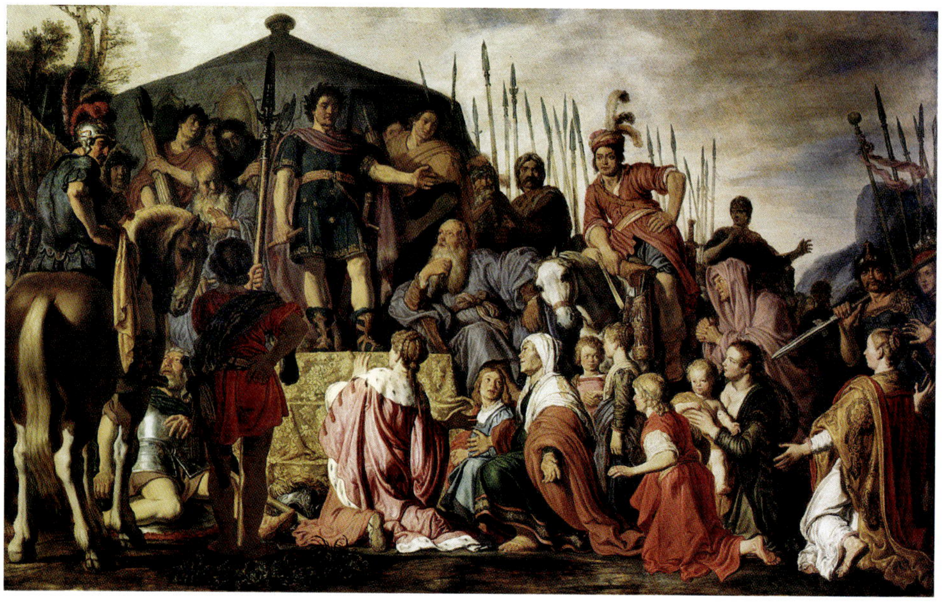

Pieter Lastman, **Coriolanus and the Roman Women**, 1625
Oil on panel, 81 × 132 cm (32 × 52 in.). Dublin, Trinity College

was compulsory. It is not certain whether Rembrandt and his fellow pupils received drawing lessons as well.[10] On 20 May 1620, Rembrandt was enrolled at the University of Leiden. The matriculation register lists the place of residence of the student, who was not quite 14 years old at the time, as "Litterarum annor[um] 14 apud parentes" (living with his parents; RD 1620/1). Rembrandt, however, did not lead a carefree student life, and it is far from certain that he ever saw the inside of a lecture theatre. For many of the pupils of the grammar school, registration in the *Album Studiosorum* of the university was apparently no more than simply a declaration of intent that they would pursue a course of study at the university at a later stage. In the meantime, the registration was associated with privileges.[11] For Rembrandt, things went no further, because, according to Orlers, "he felt no desire or wish [to study], because his natural inclination was directed exclusively towards painting and drawing; his parents therefore felt obliged to take their son out of the school [i. e. university] and according to his wishes apprenticed him to a painter, so that he could learn the first steps and the basic principles of the profession".[12] Although, by becoming an artist, Rembrandt thwarted his parents' plans, they complied willingly with their son's wishes and apprenticed him to an experienced painter in Leiden.

Jacob Isaacsz. van Swanenburg

Their choice fell on Jacob Isaacsz. van Swanenburg (1571–1638), from whom Rembrandt learned, from about 1620/21 to 1623/24, the basic principles and technical skills of the art of painting. van Swanenburg was a member of the most prominent artist dynasty in Leiden at the time; moreover, his family had also been part of the city's elite for several generations. Jacob's father, the painter Isaac Claesz. van Swanenburg (1537–1614), was the *pater familias*. Isaac had studied in Antwerp under Frans Floris (*c.* 1520–1570) and elsewhere and had returned to Leiden around 1565. He married in 1569 and worked as a successful portrait and history painter.[13] During the first decade of the seventeenth century, he also made numerous designs for stained glass windows for churches and other public buildings in Leiden and other towns in the Northern Netherlands.[14] Between 1576 and 1607, on a number of occasions, he was a member of the city council *(veertigraad)*, alderman, and burgomaster of Leiden. Isaac headed a well organised workshop and had a large number of apprentices, including three of his sons: Jacob, Claes (1572–1652) and Willem (1580–1612), who was a particularly talented engraver. The fact that Rembrandt's parents chose Jacob van Swanenburg as their son's master was no doubt also influenced by the latter's biography: he had travelled extensively and had contacts abroad.[15] After studying in his father's workshop, Jacob had travelled to Italy in 1591/92. He spent some time in Venice and Rome and lived for over 20 years in Naples, eventually converting to Catholicism.

Jacob van Swanenburg's oeuvre that has survived consists primarily of Italian townscapes and nocturnal scenes of Hell and conflagrations. But he seems to have been more versatile than that and apparently also occasionally painted history scenes and portraits.[16] Nonetheless, neither the subjects nor the style of Rembrandt's first teacher left visible traces in the latter's work. Much more important was probably that he learned a great deal about Italian artists and current developments in art in Venice, Rome and Naples from conversations with van Swanenburg, who had lived and worked in Italy for over 20 years.

Pieter Lastman

Far more important for Rembrandt's further development was his apprenticeship with his second teacher, Pieter Lastman (1583–1633).[17] Lastman was a son of Catholic parents who were members of the middle classes. Pieter Lastman's father, Pieter Segersz. (1548–1620?), earned a living as city messenger and administrator of the property of orphans and widows. In 1578, when Catholics were excluded from all official posts in the city government and were replaced by members of the Reformed Church, Lastman's father also lost his position and was even exiled from Amsterdam for a short while. During this time, the family profited not least from the business acumen and competence of Lastman's mother,

Barber Jacobsdr. (1549–1624). She traded in used goods and also worked on behalf of the city as an expert assessor of estates, which frequently also included paintings, drawings and engravings. Her expertise in these areas ensured a regular income for the family and probably she was the one who introduced her sons Pieter, Claes (1586–1625) and Seger (1578–1650), to art. Claes also became a painter and engraver, while Seger worked as a goldsmith. Pieter, however, was the most successful of the three. Before travelling to Italy, he served an apprenticeship under Gerrit Pietersz. Sweelinck (1566–after 1608).

It would be hard to overestimate Lastman's importance for the development of history painting in the first three decades of the seventeenth century in Amsterdam in particular. He, too, had spent some years in Italy and had had the opportunity of studying the new developments in painting at close quarters in Venice and Rome. As early as 1604, the painter, poet and art historiographer Karel van Mander (1548–1606) had described Lastman in his *Schilder-Boeck* as a "very promising" painter who was currently sojourning in Italy.[18] Lastman's journey lasted from about 1602 until 1606/07 and seems to have taken him to Naples as well. He knew the classical compositions of the Carracci brothers Agostino (1557–1602) and Annibale (1560–1609), whose works were based on the art of the Renaissance, and he was familiar with the religious scenes of Michelangelo Merisi, known as Caravaggio, whose shockingly realistically painted figures in strong chiaroscuro provoked passionate and controversial discussions in Rome amongst artists and art lovers. The artist who made the greatest impression on Lastman, however, was Adam Elsheimer (1578–1610), from Frankfurt am Main.[19] His oeuvre consisted of small-size religious and mythological scenes in poetic landscapes, mostly painted on copper. In his pictures, Elsheimer succeeded in linking the story with a new approach to the landscape, thereby creating an atmospheric whole. Landscape no longer served him as a backdrop for his scenes, but became an integral part of his compositions, into which he convincingly integrated the figures. Another admirer of Elsheimer was Peter Paul Rubens (1577–1640), whose compositions and dramatic pictorial language with powerfully built muscular figures evidently also impressed Lastman.

After his return from Italy, Lastman became the most important and influential reformer of Dutch history painting. He set the tone in a group of painters who were in some cases also related to each other and who clearly based their work in his narrative and painting style. Among them were François Venant (1590/91–1636), who married Lastman's sister, Agnietje, in 1625, Claes Cornelisz. Moyaert (1592/93–1655), the brothers Jan (1581–1631) and Jacob Pynas (1592/93–after 1650), and their brother-in-law, Jan Tengnagel (1584–1635). Literature refers to this group of artists as the "Pre-Rembrandtists", a term which is rightly criticised since it characterises the painters as forerunners and at the same time as followers of Rembrandt.

Pieter Lastman was highly esteemed and praised by his contemporaries. The poet Theodoor Rodenburgh (1592–1641) refers to him in his drama *Mélibea* (1618) as being among the best painters in Amsterdam, and long after Lastman's death (in 1633), the poet Joost van den Vondel (1587–1679) called him "the Apelles of our century", placing him on the same level as Peter Paul Rubens.[20]

The Earliest History Paintings

According to Orlers, Rembrandt spent only six months working in Lastman's Amsterdam workshop.[21] The paintings of his second master show the diversity of subject matter and the wealth of dramatic narrative of the Bible, which would also remain Rembrandt's most important source of inspiration throughout his life. Like Lastman, Rembrandt specialised in the most demanding genre of painting: history painting. It includes scenes from the Bible and other religious sources, from classical mythology, and from history. These subjects enjoyed the highest regard in the hierarchy of the various genres of painting. While painters of portraits, landscapes and still lifes could imitate nature with greater or lesser accuracy, the history painter needed in each case a good knowledge of the relevant literary source. So in order to reproduce the precise circumstances of these fictitious subjects, he was dependent on excellent imaginative powers; after all, no painter knew what it had looked like in the Holy Land when Jesus lived and taught there.

Rembrandt's earliest dated history painting is *The Stoning of St Stephen* (p. 43, Cat. 30), dated 1625. Exactly ten years later, in 1635, Rembrandt took up the scene again in an etching (p. 26, Cat. E34). The choice of subject matter, the martyrdom of a saint, seems surprising when we consider that the Reformed Church rejected the veneration of the saints. However, the stoning of this saint is described in the Bible (Acts of the Apostles 7: 56) and therefore was also accepted by the Protestants as trustworthy. The drama of the stoning is reflected especially in the emotions on the faces of those directly involved. Immediately above the head of the saint, among the spectators, can be seen a young man with his face distorted in anguish; it is very likely that Rembrandt portrayed himself in this figure. Since it was painted a year before the self-portrait in the so-called *History Piece* (pp. 48/49; Cat. 124) in Leiden, this is probably the earliest known self-portrait by the artist, who later frequently depicted himself in history paintings. Jacob Pynas had already chosen the subject of the stoning in 1617, basing himself on Elsheimer's painting which is now in the Scottish National Gallery in Edinburgh (p. 26).[22] Apart from the choice of subject matter, there is evidence that Rembrandt was familiar with this particular painting by Pynas because of the similarity between the man throwing a stone on the right and the corresponding figure in Pynas' work. In this context the observation by the painter and art biographer Arnold Houbraken (1660–1719) gains in credibility. In his biography of Rembrandt of 1718 he stated that the latter had undergone a short apprenticeship with Jacob Pynas.[23] Rembrandt's painting was possibly made on commission, but on whose behalf remains unknown.

Rembrandt returned to Leiden from Amsterdam, probably by the end of 1625. The following year was particularly productive, with pictures which are clearly inspired by Lastman's history paintings. Characteristic of Rembrandt's early paintings is the wide differentiation in the application of the paint, a great wealth of details and – compared with his later works – a noticeable colourfulness (including shades of bright green, violet and pink). Rembrandt's mostly small-size paintings often depict the same rarely depicted subjects which also occur in Lastman's oeuvre, so that they look like variants of the works by his teacher. For example, Rembrandt drew on Lastman's painting from 1622 (p. 33) for his painting *Balaam and the Ass* (p. 45, Cat. 1), dated 1626. However, in comparison to Lastman, Rembrandt heightened the dynamism and drama of his compositions by choosing an upright format instead of Lastman's horizontal format. This can also be seen in *The Baptism of the Eunuch* (p. 47, Cat. 32), also dated 1626. The painting again shows a clear relationship with Lastman's version of the subject, which had been made roughly between 1615 and 1620 (p. 46). Moreover, in his pyramidal compositions, Rembrandt reduces the number of figures and concentrates more strongly on the protagonists. Here and there he seems to want to correct his former teacher. Mostly it is a matter of details, which, however, correspond more closely with the information provided by the Bible text with regard to the context of the story. Thus in his *Baptism of the Eunuch*, Rembrandt replaces Lastman's lush vegetation of oak trees with a single palm tree because according to the Acts of the Apostles (8: 26) the scene took place on the road between Jerusalem and Gaza, "which is desert".[24] Objects relevant to the content of the story, such as the chariot of the eunuch and the book with the texts of Isaiah (Acts 8: 28) are emphasised more strongly. Even in these early works Rembrandt was able to separate the elements which were important for the narrative context from mere decorative accessories and to allocate them a more prominent place in his compositions.

To this day, it has not been possible to identify unequivocally the subject of all of Rembrandt's early history paintings. This applies, for example, to the so-called "Leiden History Piece" from 1626 (pp. 48/49, Cat. 124), which is still regarded as one of the most puzzling paintings in his entire oeuvre. It is also one of the few multi-figured history paintings from Rembrandt's Leiden period. The attempts to identify the subject which have been adduced are as numerous as they are diverse. Does the scene take place in antiquity, in the Christian Middle Ages or in early modern times? Is the subject taken from the Bible or does it depict a scene from secular legend or from contemporary litera-

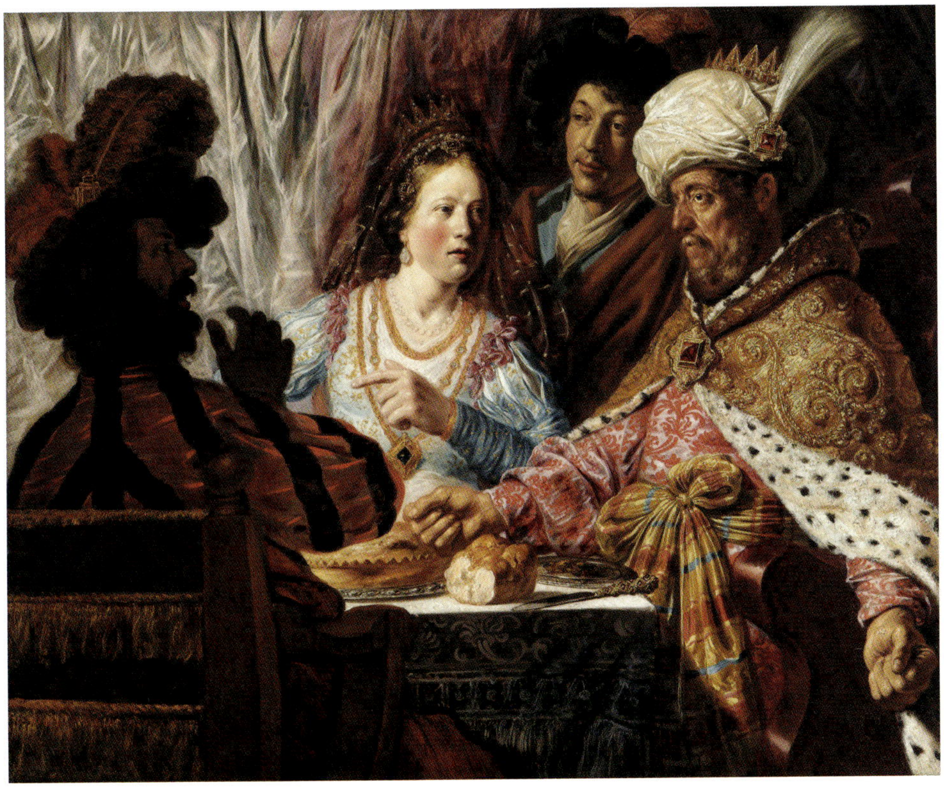

Jan Lievens, **The Feast of Esther**, *c.* 1625
Oil on canvas, 130.8 × 163.8 cm (51 ½ × 64 ½ in.)
Raleigh, North Carolina Museum of Art

ture? Who is the ruler with crown and sceptre who is standing in an elevated position? Some details of his costume recall the clothing of Roman officers, who, however, did not wear a crown and only occasionally wore trousers. And who are the men he is addressing? Is he granting them forgiveness or is he receiving their oath of allegiance? One of the key figures seems to be the man standing with a yellow buff coat, a sleeveless jerkin made of ox hide of the kind worn by soldiers and officers during the seventeenth century. His gaze is directed towards the viewer. To date there has been no agreement as to whether this is a portrait. Also the subject of much debate is the four-legged animal on the column in the background, which so far has been identified as either a sheep (lamb) or as a wolf. A sheep or a lamb could point to Christ as *Agnus Dei* (The Lamb of God) and hence to a Christian context, while a wolf would indicate Roman antiquity *(Lupa Romana)*. It is also

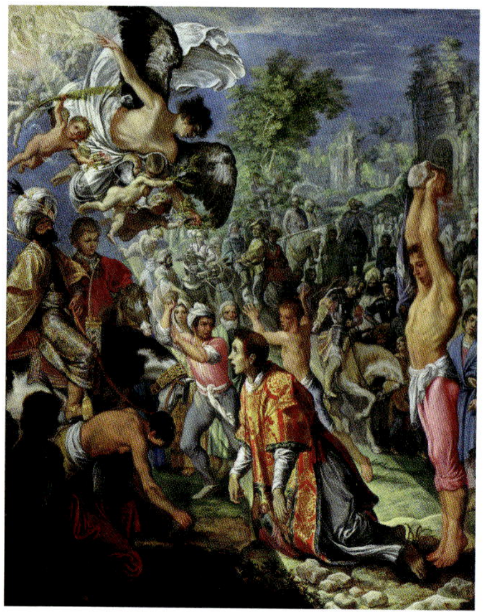

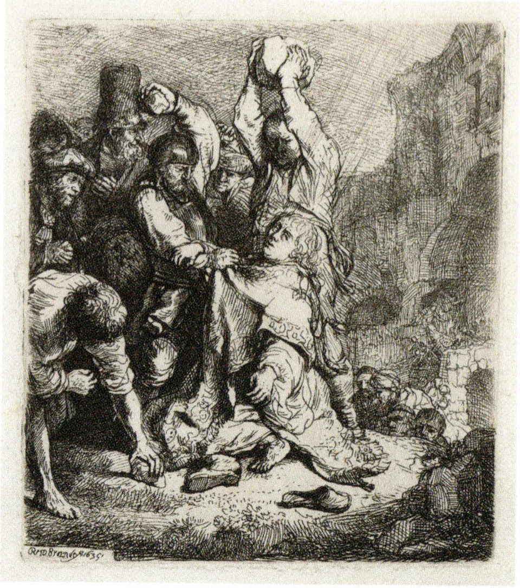

not clear whether there are contemporary long-barrelled firearms amongst the weapons in the foreground in addition to the archaic shields, pikes and halberds.

It is noticeable that the Leiden history painting has almost exactly the same measurements as *The Stoning of St Stephen* (p. 43, Cat. 30), which was completed one year earlier. It is not known whether they are companion pieces or two paintings originally planned for a larger series. The same also applies to the patron who commissioned the pictures. It is remarkable, on the other hand, that the Leiden picture also contains an early self-portrait of Rembrandt. Overlapped by the ruler's sceptre, he gazes out towards the viewer from the background with an alert expression.

The basic features of the composition with the main figure on a dais gazing at the figures kneeling or standing before him are of classical origin (*adlocutio*, the stance taken when delivering a public address). They were clearly borrowed from Pieter Lastman's principal work *Coriolanus and the Roman Women* (p. 20), which was executed in 1625; the

Adam Elsheimer, **The Stoning of St Stephen**, *c.* 1603/04
Oil on silver-plated copper, 34.7 × 28.6 cm (13 ¾ × 11 ⅜ in.)
Edinburgh, Scottish National Gallery

The Stoning of St Stephen, 1635
Etching with some burin, 9.5 × 8.5 cm (3 ¾ × 3 ⅜ in.)
Amsterdam, Rijksmuseum

very year of Rembrandt's apprenticeship. Just one year later, he referred to his teacher's *Coriolanus* in the Leiden history painting, probably having seen its creation with his own eyes during his time in Lastman's workshop.

Just as puzzling as the Leiden history painting is the subject of the *Musical Company* (*Allegory of Music*; p. 51, Cat. 121), which was also painted in 1626. The interior shows a young woman singing and beating time with her right hand. She is accompanied by a man in Oriental dress wearing a turban, who is playing a viola da gamba. Behind him stand a young man with a harp and an elderly woman wearing a headscarf who is listening intently. Scattered in the foreground are books, manuscripts and musical instruments. The precious costumes look both Oriental and antique, indicating that this is not an everyday genre scene. The picture-within-a-picture very probably plays a key role in the identification of the subject of Rembrandt's painting. On the left against the back wall we can recognise the framed representation of a group of figures in a landscape. There is no doubt that the subject of this picture is the flight of Lot and his family from Sodom (Genesis 19: 15–26), which is described in the Old Testament. It is not yet clear in which context the musical company stands to the biblical scene of the destruction of the sinful city of Sodom and the punishment of Lot's wife, who was turned by God into a pillar of salt because of her disobedience. The painting is probably an allegory of music, in which the musicians and their activities symbolise man's sense of hearing or harmony, which Rembrandt's contemporaries believed to be essential not only for making music, but also for the relation between the sexes. Although Rembrandt was only 20 years old when he made this work, the painting technique already demonstrates a great differentiation in the application of the paint. He constantly varied the brushstrokes in order to achieve a convincing rendering of different materials such as textiles, metal, wood, skin and hair, thereby giving the illusion of either smooth or rough surfaces. This is particularly visible in the golden threads of the kerchief of the young woman and in the contrast between the lacquer-like smooth outer surface of the lute and the matt paper surfaces of the books. Rembrandt had mastered the manipulation of the paint and clearly experimented constantly with new solutions in order to arrive at a convincing illusion.[25]

No less unusual, but easier to identify is the subject of Rembrandt's painting *Tobit and Anna with the Kid* (p. 52, Cat. 2), also created in 1626. It shows a scene from the story of the pious but impoverished blind Tobit, whose wife Anna earns a living by spinning. Tobit wrongly accuses her of the theft of a kid that she had received as a gift. In the ensuing quarrel, Anna mocks her husband on account of his piety. Tobit bemoans his fate and begs God to forgive him his sins and allow him to die. "Then I being grieved did weep, and in my sorrow prayed" (Tobit 3: 1). It is this moving moment which Rembrandt portrays.

The scene is set in a scantily furnished room, illuminated by light through a window and by an open wood fire. Tobit is sitting on a roughly made chair with his hands folded imploringly, gazing upwards. Rembrandt characterises him as a poor man whose gown, lined with fur and once valuable, and whose shoes show evident signs of wear. Anna, speechless and clinging firmly to the kid, looks at Tobit in astonishment. The figure of Tobit is a particularly fine example of Rembrandt's enormous talent for reproducing human emotions and feelings. The expressiveness and dignity of the old man is remarkable for an artist who was just 20 years old: Tobit's face is deeply lined with age and his empty eye sockets characterise his blindness as he folds his hands in a gesture of despair.

If we look at the large number of Old Testament scenes in Rembrandt's oeuvre, it is noticeable that a comparatively large number of episodes are taken from the apocryphal Book of Tobit.[26] In contrast to the Catholics, the Protestants include the book amongst the so-called Apocrypha and so it does not belong to the canonical and thus accepted books of the Holy Scriptures. Nonetheless, the stories of Old Tobit and his son, Tobias, were very popular amongst artists and their clients in the Northern Netherlands during the seventeenth century. This was due to the fact that Christian convictions whose moral value were uncontested by the members of the different religious denominations were expressed in a simple manner in the Book of Tobit in particular. The ministers of the Reformed Church were forbidden to read the text of the Book of Tobit to their congregation during services. However, since in the opinion of the Reformed theologians the books of the Apocrypha contained "useful exhortations and examples" they considered it to be "not entirely useless that it should also be read [outside the church], [but] it had to be constantly examined according to the touchstone of divine doctrine".[27] The immense popularity of the Book of Tobit apparently did not suffer as a result of the warnings of the Church authorities, as Rembrandt's painting also shows. In the interpretation of Protestant theologians in particular during the sixteenth and seventeenth centuries, the good fortune and misfortune of Old Tobit were linked with the fate of the simple believers.[28] He became a model of everyday piety and trust in God and his marriage with Anna served as an example of the state of marriage, which stood under divine protection.

For the composition of his painting, with its rarely depicted subject, Rembrandt had clearly been inspired by an etching by Jan van de Velde II (*c.* 1593–1641) after a design by Willem Buytewech (1591/92–1624) from around 1619/20 (p. 53). The sheet shows an earlier

Detail of: **Self-Portrait**, 1629
(see ill. p. 79)

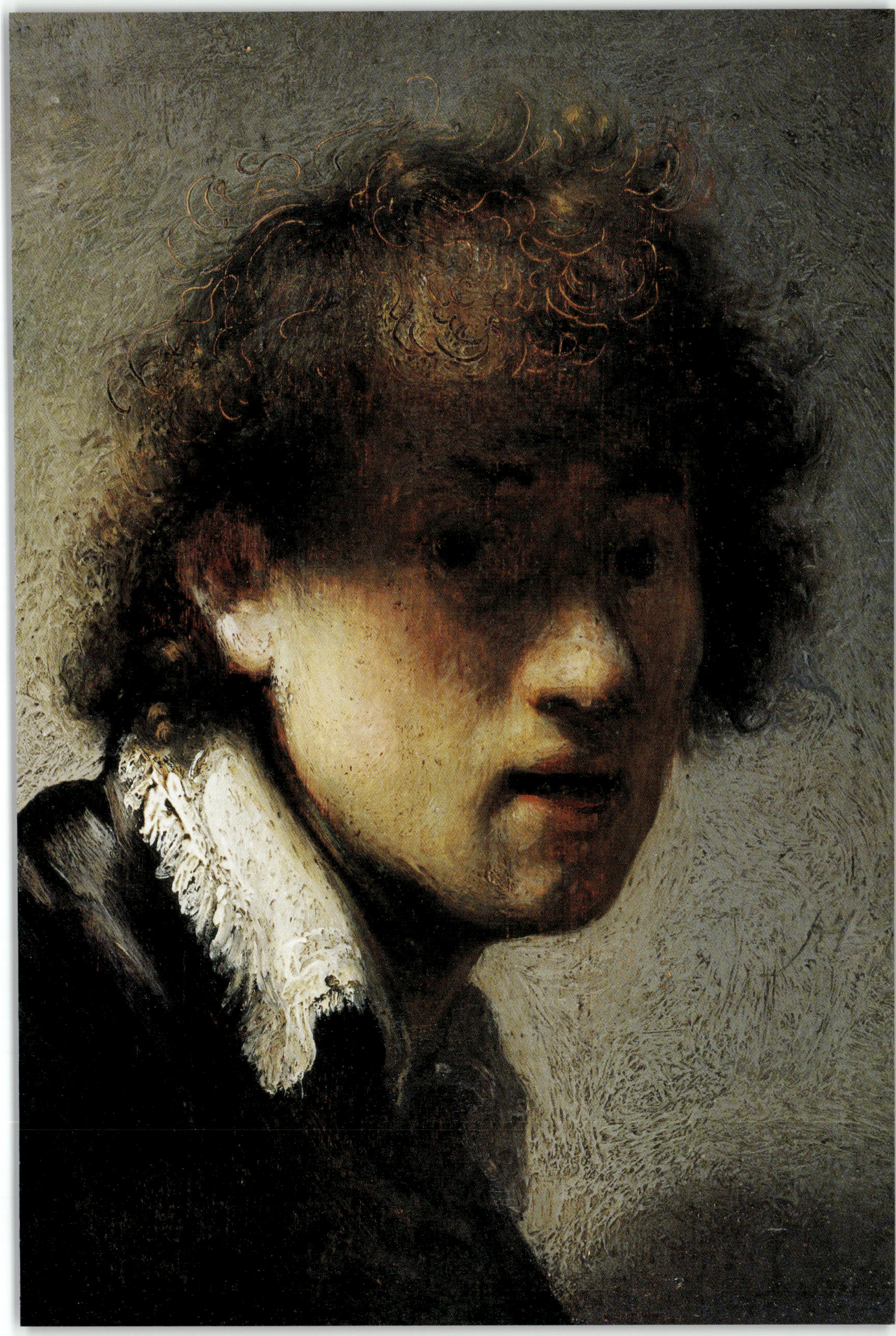

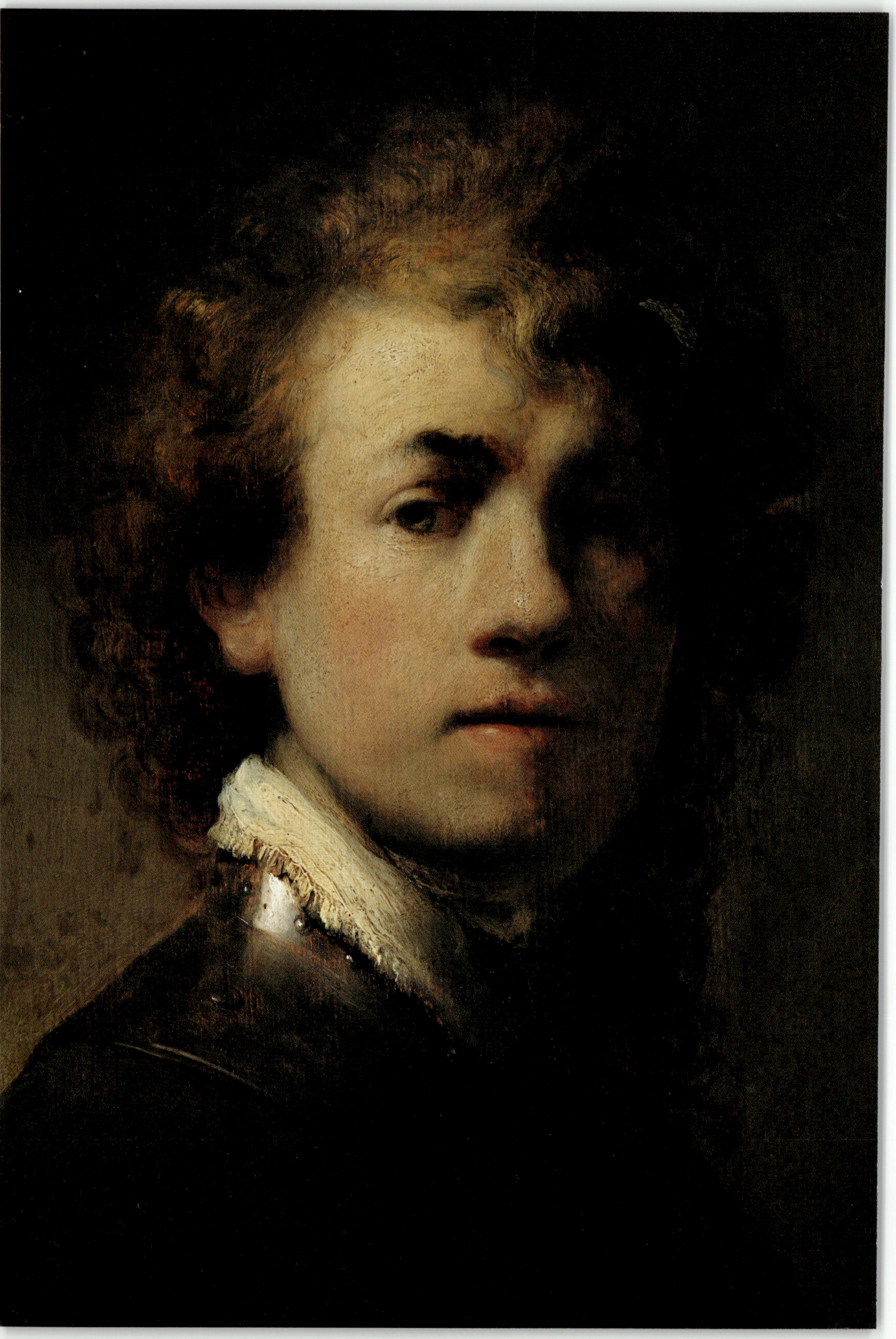

moment in the story, when Tobit accuses Anna and she reacts angrily. Clear parallels in the arrangement of the figures, the depiction of the interior with the window on the left, and also details like the string of onions and the birdcage show that the etching served as a model for Rembrandt. We can already see here that Rembrandt was very familiar with the older pictorial tradition. For a long time, it was incorrectly assumed that the composition of the picture and its iconography were the result simply of his prodigious talent and inexhaustible creativity. It was believed that a genius like Rembrandt created his pictures solely from his own imagination and would more or less ignore the works of other artists. It has since become clear, however, that Rembrandt also stood firmly on the shoulders of his predecessors and that he frequently sought ideas with regard to content especially in old prints, which he collected, studied and modified but never copied.[29] At the latest after he moved to Amsterdam in 1631/32, Rembrandt repeatedly purchased prints at auctions and built up his collection in a purposeful way and with a not inconsiderable financial investment.

Rembrandt and Lievens

After his short apprenticeship with Lastman, Rembrandt returned to Leiden, where he had close contact with his contemporary Jan Lievens (1607–1674) between 1625 and 1631. For a long time, it was incorrectly assumed that Rembrandt was Jan Lievens' teacher. Rather, the two artists worked in competition in a mutually stimulating atmosphere. Lievens, who was one year younger that Rembrandt, was initially apprenticed to Joris van Schooten (1587–1651), a native of Leiden, and then continued his training under Pieter Lastman in Amsterdam, probably between about 1617/18 and 1619/20. In his early history paintings and his single figures, Jan Lievens experimented with various styles. When Rembrandt returned from Amsterdam, Lievens had already been working for some time as an independent master-painter in Leiden. Rembrandt and Lievens were linked there by a sort of artistic symbiosis: they stimulated and inspired each other, evidently sharing certain views regarding their ideas and therefore also agreeing on certain artistic ideals and ambitions. The two youthful talents both owed a great deal to Pieter Lastman, the teacher they had shared. This applies not only to the colour schemes of their early works but also to their narrative style. Both were increasingly fascinated above all by the effect of light in their paintings. They were especially interested in the works of the Caravaggisti who had returned to Utrecht from Rome: Hendrick ter Brugghen (1588–1629), Dirck van Baburen (*c.* 1595–1624) and Gerard van Honthorst (1592–1656).[30] This group of painters

Detail of: **Self-Portrait with a Gorget**, *c.* 1629
(see ill. p. 81)

had been inspired in Rome by the dramatic chiaroscuro and merciless realism of the paintings by Michelangelo Merisi da Caravaggio, and after their return they also influenced many of their fellow artists. The Dutch painter and art historiographer Karel van Mander had already reported about Caravaggio and his fascinating naturalism in his *Schilder-Boeck* from 1604. Lievens evidently developed an interest before Rembrandt in compositions in the style of Caravaggio, with the typical half- or three-quarter-length figures shown with strong contrasts of light and shadow close to the picture plane. Lievens' *Feast* of *Esther* (p. 25), created around 1625, was long thought to be a work by Rembrandt. When examining Rembrandt's paintings created between 1627 and 1631, one can observe that he, too, was increasingly interested in strong chiaroscuro effects. However, in most cases his paintings were smaller than those of Lievens.

Rembrandt's *The Parable of the Rich Man* (pp. 64/65, Cat. 34) dates from 1627. In St Luke's Gospel (12: 13–21), Jesus tells of the rich grain farmer who stored increasing stocks in his barns without leading a God-fearing life. So God punished him with death. "Thou fool, this night thy soul shall be required of thee: then whose shall these things be, which thou has provided? So is he that layeth up treasure for himself, and is not rich toward God" (Luke 12: 20–21). In Rembrandt's painting, an old man is holding a coin against the light of a candle in his right hand; the flame is shielded from the beholder's view, so that the light which is reflected into the depths of the picture illuminates details of the man's immediate surroundings. He and the papers with which he is surrounded are bathed in contrasting light and shadow. For a long time, the nocturnal scene was interpreted as an allegory of avarice *(avaritia)*, though this is usually personified as a woman. Since the letters on the document on the right-hand edge of the picture, though illegible, are recognisably Hebraistic, the painting has since been interpreted as a history painting depicting the Parable of the Rich Man from the New Testament.[31]

The real theme of Rembrandt's nocturnal scene is, however, the effect of the shielded candle as an artificial source of light within the picture. It is very unlikely that Rembrandt had ever seen an original painting by Caravaggio.[32] He owed his knowledge of Caravaggio's chiaroscuro and the effect of artificial light sources to the paintings of Gerard van Honthorst. When in Rome, the latter had specialised in night pieces with artificial light under the impression of works by Caravaggio and especially his early successors, the Caravaggisti; after his return to the Netherlands in 1620, he caused a sensation. *The Parable of the Rich Man* shows that Rembrandt, too, was particularly interested in Honthorst's night scenes lit by candlelight, even during his years in Leiden. It was only during the 1630s in Amsterdam that Rembrandt resumed his study of Caravaggio and his realistic and dynamic compositions.

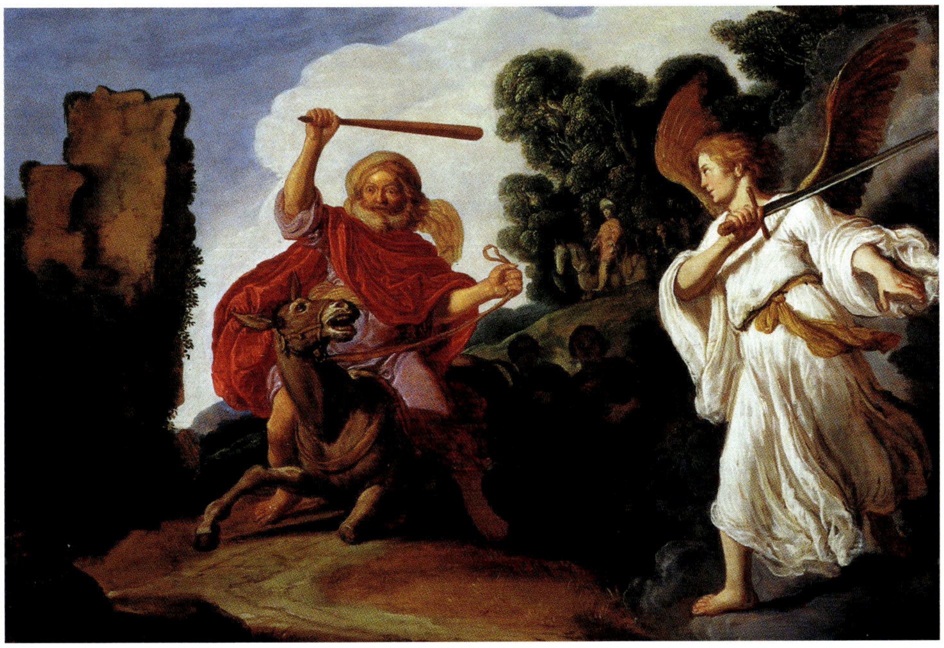

Pieter Lastman, **Balaam and the Ass**, 1622
Oil on panel, 41.3 × 60.4 cm (16 3/8 × 23 7/8 in.)
Jerusalem, The Israel Museum

Constantijn Huygens' Visit to Rembrandt and Lievens

Towards the end of 1628, Rembrandt and Lievens were visited in Leiden by one of the most exceptional personalities of the Stadtholder's court in The Hague. A lawyer, poet, and diplomat, Constantijn Huygens was a loyal servant of the House of Orange, and from 1625 he had been the secretary of the stadtholder, Prince Frederik Hendrik. One of Huygens' sons was the famous scientist Christiaan Huygens (1629–1695). Constantijn and his brother Maurits (1595–1642) had received a wide-ranging education at the hands of private tutors. In addition to the classics, the brothers received lessons in riding, fencing, modelling and drawing before they studied law at the University of Leiden. Widely travelled and well-read, Constantijn Huygens corresponded and wrote poetry in several languages. He also proved himself to be a talented composer. Throughout his life, Huygens had been interested in painting and he followed attentively and in a well-informed manner the developments in art. In his opinion, the works of Peter Paul Rubens were unequalled. From the fragments of his diary for the years 1628/30, we know that Huygens met Rembrandt and Lievens during a visit to Leiden. He reports in detail on the meeting. Huygens describes the two young painters as "still beardless" and "closer to childhood than youth as regards build and facial features". He praises their diligence and talent, to which in his view they owe everything – not to their teachers, whom he fails to name. Comparing the two, Huygens is of the opinion that "Rembrandt surpasses Lievens in his ability to pick out the quintessence of his subjects and in the natural power with which he is able to move the spirit of his subjects. Conversely, Lievens is superior in invention and a certain grandeur of his daring themes and forms [...] whereas, Rembrandt, since he gives himself wholly over to dealing with what he wants to express from within himself, prefers to concentrate [his work] in a smaller picture, and to seek compactness to bring about an effect that one may seek in vain in the largest pieces by others."[33]

The visitor from The Hague must have called on Rembrandt in his studio. Supporting this assumption is the fact that he describes in detail the figure of Judas in the painting created in 1629, in which Judas is shown returning the pieces of silver (pp. 68/69, Cat. 38), characterising it vividly and praising it effusively: "his painting of the repentant Judas returning to the high priest the silver coins which were the price for our innocent Lord. Compare this with all Italy, indeed, with all the wondrous beauties that have survived from the most ancient of days. The gesture of that one despairing Judas (not to mention all the other impressive figures in the painting), that one maddened Judas, screaming, begging for forgiveness, but devoid of hope, all traces of hope erased from his face; his gaze wild, his hair torn out by the roots, his garments rent, his arms contorted, his hands clenched until they bleed; a blind impulse has brought him to his knees, his whole body writhing in pitiful hideousness. All this I compare with all the beauty that has been produced throughout the ages. This is what I would have those naïve beings know, who claim (and I have rebuked them for it before) that nothing created or expressed in words today has not been expressed or created in the past. I maintain that it did not occur to Protogenes, Apelles or Parrhasius, nor could it occur to them, were they to return to earth, that a youth, a Dutchman, a beardless miller, could put so much into one human figure and depict it all. Even as I write these words I am struck with amazement. All honour to thee, Rembrandt!"[34]

This judgment by a connoisseur and scholar is remarkable for a number of reasons. It confirms the high esteem and considerable reputation which Rembrandt and Lievens enjoyed even at the beginning of their careers. It also shows that Rembrandt's contemporaries valued in particular his talent in rendering emotions and moods in physiognomy and gestures. If we examine Rembrandt's further development as a portraitist, it is surprising that it was Jan Lievens and not Rembrandt who painted a portrait of Huygens. However, according to Huygens, Lievens had more or less forced his offer on

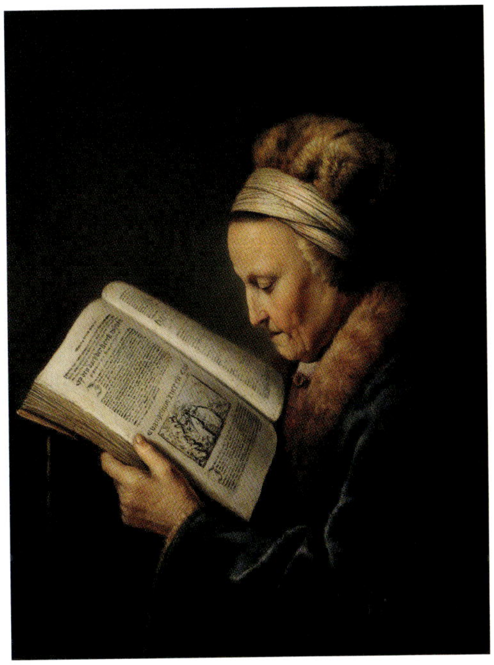

him, and he had then accepted it. We should also bear in mind that at this time Rembrandt had painted and etched self-portraits and *tronies*, but as far as we know no commissioned portraits. The start of his stellar career as a portraitist only started after he moved from Leiden to Amsterdam, where he initially worked in the studio of the art dealer Hendrick Uylenburgh (*c.* 1584/89–1661), who procured commissions for portraits for him.

First Apprentices

One result of Rembrandt's extraordinary talent was that already in Leiden he trained young painters in his workshop (pp. 70/71, Cat. 126). These were not beginners, but rather advanced apprentices who had already received initial training in the workshop of another artist. One of the first was Gerard Dou (1613–1675), the son of a stained-glass artist and glass engraver from Friesland.[35] Orlers reports that Dou had completed two apprenticeships, one with the Leiden etcher Bartholomäus Dolendo (*c.* 1571–after 1629) and the other with the glass engraver Pieter Kouwenhorn (1599–1654), before he became a pupil in Rembrandt's studio in 1628 (RD 1641/9). By 1632 he was independent and ran his own workshop. Dou was a highly talented 15-year-old when he came to Rembrandt. The precision of his fine painting and his imitation of nature were outstanding from an early stage. His genre paintings, often with emblematic references, are staged and frequently presented through a trompe-l'oeil window. During his time in Rembrandt's workshop, he used the same models for some of his paintings that we also find in some of Rembrandt's pictures. Dou's *Old Woman Reading* from around 1631/32 is a good example of this (p. 35). For the old woman shown in profile, Dou used the same model as in Rembrandt's *Old Woman Reading a Book* (p. 223, Cat. 43). The painting captivates us with its virtuoso

Gerard Dou, **Old Woman Reading**, *c.* 1631/32
Oil on panel, 71.2 × 55.2 cm (28 × 21 ¾ in.)
Amsterdam, Rijksmuseum

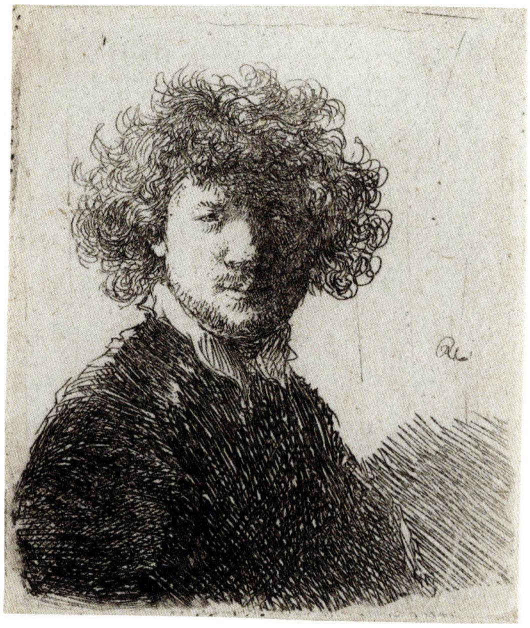

rendition of the different materials: paper, fur, skin, wool. Dou became the leading artist of the so-called Leiden Fine Painters. Even during his lifetime, his paintings were sold for exorbitant prices which in some cases were higher than the prices fetched by Rembrandt's pictures. Amongst Dou's many pupils were Frans van Mieris the Elder (1635–1681) and Godefridus Schalcken (1643–1706).

Isaac de Jouderville (1612/13–1645/48), who is also documented as a pupil of Rembrandt's in Leiden, served an apprenticeship in his workshop from 1629 until 1631. Jouderville's parents died shortly after each other in 1629, and his guardians paid for his training under Rembrandt, as the latter acknowledged several times. The receipts, which have been preserved in the archive in Leiden (RD 1630/2; 1630/4; 1631/3; 1631/7; 1631/9; 1631/10),[36] indicate that Rembrandt received 100 guilders per year for teaching Jouderville. He probably accompanied his master when the latter moved to Amsterdam in 1631/32. Isaac de Jouderville's oeuvre is small and shows him primarily as an imitator of Rembrandt's *tronies*. The small number of genre pictures show a distant resemblance to those of his fellow student Gerard Dou. It was not until Rembrandt's move to Amsterdam that a stream of young and experienced painters flocked to his studio, hoping to gain inspiration, a substantial knowledge of artistic solutions and painting techniques. The painter and art historiographer Joachim von Sandrart (1606–1668) would later observe in his biography of Rembrandt in the *Teutsche Academie der Edlen Bau-, Bild- und Mahlerey-Künste* (The German Academy of the Nobel Arts of Architecture, Sculpture and Painting; 1675), that his house in Amsterdam "[was] filled with almost innumerable genteel children who paid him 100 guilders a year for instruction and apprenticeship".[37]

Self-Portrait with Curly Hair and White Collar, Bust, *c.* 1630
Etching, 5.7 × 5 cm (2 ¼ × 2 in.)
Amsterdam, Rijksmuseum

Tronies

In addition to history painting, in Leiden both Rembrandt and Jan Lievens had specialised in a relatively new genre: the character head.[38] These pictures were often small in size and were known as *"tronies"*, derived from the mediaeval French *trogne*, which means face or (grotesque or comic) head. *Tronies* were probably created as "study heads" in the workshop in order to practise the portrayal of moods, temperament and different ages. They originally also served as model studies of facial features and expressions in preparation for history paintings. Over time these head studies acquired the status of independent works of art, produced for sale on the open market. Thus these relatively inexpensive character heads found their way not only into art collections, but also into the homes of ordinary people, where they served as popular wall decorations. *Tronies* showed certain clearly recognisable stereotypes who sparked the imagination – such as the fierce-looking soldier (Cat. 270, 272; p. 75, Cat. 277), the exotic Oriental (Cat. 271) or the wrinkled old granny (Cat. 311). In some ways, they can be compared with the little boy with the tear on his cheek or the "gypsy girl" of modern times. As the description *"tronie naer 't leven"* (*tronie* from life), a comment frequently found in seventeenth-century inventories, indicates such studies were almost always painted after a live model. But unlike the portrait, here the identity of the subject was of secondary importance. What mattered was the often exotic, "picturesque" clothing of the figures, which, however, did not coincide with contemporary fashion.

A further aspect which doubtless contributed to the popularity of the *tronies*, was the often virtuoso, apparently casual style. A good example of this is Rembrandt's *tronie Old Man (Rembrandt's Father?)* from around 1630/31 (p. 77, Cat. 275), in which the wrinkled face is rendered with loosely applied licks of paint. *Old Man with a Fur Hat* (p. 76, Cat. 273) was painted at about the same time. Here the wrinkled face of the old man is worked out in a particularly delicate and detailed manner with opaque paint, while the clothing and the background have been executed in a much freer style. The shaggy texture of the fur, for example, is suggested by small brushstrokes in thin black paint, leaving a large part of the warm brown ground intentionally visible. The way the coloured ground shines through also plays an important role in the rough wall in the background. The black hat the man is wearing, with an oriental scarf around it, was unusual in Rembrandt's time and was intended to create the impression that the figure showed a Polish man or an Oriental.

In Rembrandt's time, people were fascinated by the appearance and habits of foreigners. This explains the popularity of the genre of the exotic *tronie*. Rembrandt painted heads of this kind throughout his career. Initially, they were in small format, but later he also created large three-quarter-length figures. The demand for such pictures can be seen in a series of etchings which were published in 1633/34 by the Leiden etcher Jan Gillisz. van Vliet (*c.* 1605–1668) after Rembrandt's images.

Early Self-Portraits

Rembrandt painted his own face more frequently than any other artist before him. By the time he died he had recorded his own characteristic features in paintings, etchings and drawings more than 80 times.[39] Initially, he appears with his unruly curls only as a bystander in his history paintings (e.g. pp. 48/49 Cat. 124), but at the end of the Leiden years he started to produce his first autonomous self-portraits. At the beginning, they served primarily as experiments regarding the effect of light. The etched self-portraits from this period, by contrast, are exercises in the reproduction of different emotions and expressions (Cat. E192–207, e.g. p. 36). These studies are of modest size and could be used later in larger works such as history paintings or *tronies*.

One of Rembrandt's first autonomous self-portraits was created about 1628; he was roughly 22 years old at the time (p. 78, Cat. 144). A strong beam of light illuminates just the neck, part of the cheek, the ear lobe and the tip of the nose. The other parts of the face are lost in deep shadow, so that the recognisability of his features seems to have been of secondary importance. The head rises darkly against the partly illuminated wall behind him. This creates an increased impression of depth and the face acquires a mysterious, almost dramatic feel. In this small painting, Rembrandt repeatedly changed his painting style in order to reproduce the different effects of the light. Areas which capture most light, like the collar or the little highlight on the nose, are painted in opaque white or yellow brushstrokes and thus literally stand out. By contrast, the dark colour (for example on the shoulder) is applied so thinly that the warm brown ground appears through it. A similar coloured ground was also used for the hair. The curls have been scratched out of the wet, dark paint using a reed pen and thereby seem to shine. Under the light-grey background, and in the curls around the neck, by contrast, Rembrandt applied a dark layer which comes through faintly on the right. This light-grey paint was applied with short, small brushstrokes in all directions in order to give the impression of a coarsely plastered wall across which the light is falling. Thus this little panel provides an example of the painterly means which Rembrandt explored in order to record different light effects.

In the little self-portrait which Rembrandt painted slightly later (p. 79, Cat. 146), we can recognise similar light effects, but here he has introduced more movement by turning the face sharply. The wildly scratched out hairs emphasise the agitation. The expression of astonishment created by the raised eyebrows makes the painter look as if he has been surprised by something. In addition to a study of light effects, this is also an exercise in

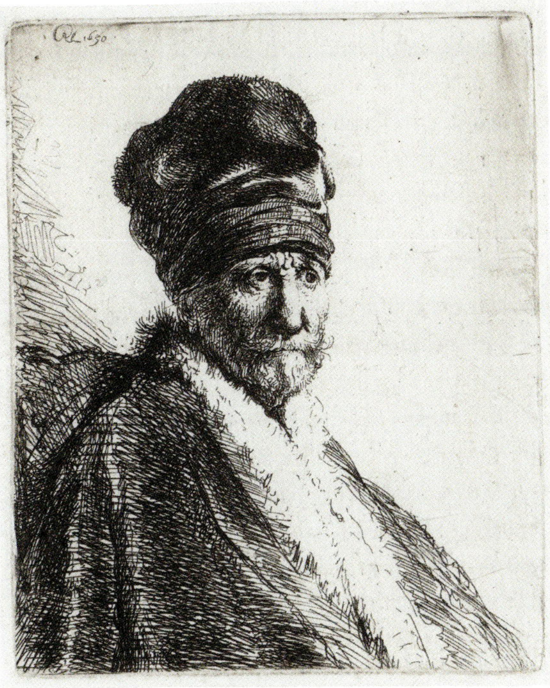

recording a fleeting moment, a sort of snapshot effect which Rembrandt would later use frequently in his history pieces and portraits.

These small early self-portraits with scarcely recognisable features or expressions distorted by emotion deviate strongly from the self-portraits of his predecessors and contemporaries, who generally portrayed themselves in a clearly recognisable manner and wearing their smartest clothes. Rembrandt's early self-portraits demonstrate the characteristics of a *tronie* rather than those of a conventional self-portrait. This also applies to the picturesque costumes in which the young Rembrandt portrayed himself (Cat. 142–148). For example, on a number of occasions he depicted himself in the role of a soldier with a gorget (pp. 80, 81, 85, Cat. 142, 143, 145), as in the little self-portrait on copper from about 1628 (p. 80), in which he shows himself with a challenging laugh, his head thrown back and his hand on his hip. In the self-portrait from about 1629 (p. 81), on the other hand, he is looking almost arrogantly over his shoulder. Above the shining gorget, he wears a long lock of hair which falls onto his left shoulder. It is relatively unlikely that Rembrandt actually wore his hair in this fashion. These "lovelocks", also known as *cadenettes*, were exclusively reserved for (foreign) aristocrats and soldiers from the international retinue of the King of Bohemia in The Hague.[40] As far as we know, Rembrandt was never a member of the civic militia. There has therefore been a great deal of speculation as to why he portrays himself here as a soldier. Some scholars have thought that the gorget is a symbol of vanity, or a display of militant patriotism.[41] But in view of his great interest in the effect of light, it is

Bust of a Man Wearing a High Cap, Three-quarters Right (The Artist's Father?), 1630
Etching with some drypoint, 10.2 × 8.4 cm (4 × 3⅜ in.). Amsterdam, Rijksmuseum

also feasible that Rembrandt introduced the gorget because the gleaming collar provided him with an opportunity to show the light reflecting on the metal and thus illuminating more of the face. On other self-portraits, he has always painted another light accent on the shoulder, mostly a small white collar, which fulfilled a similar purpose. Perhaps it is significant that Rembrandt never portrayed himself with a gorget in his etchings or drawings, in which the effect of such light reflections are not important.

It was long assumed that Rembrandt produced such studies for his own use and painted his face for purely practical reasons, because in this way he was not dependent on a model. Nonetheless, in the period around 1629, Rembrandt was already aware of the circumstance that he was no longer a stranger amongst art experts, and that there was a market for his self-portraits. Self-portraits provided an ambitious artist with an excellent means of self-advertisement. Giorgio Vasari (1511–1574), and van Mander repeatedly recorded in which works self-portraits by artists were to be found. Rembrandt's later biographer Houbraken also reports on the pleasure that "well-read art lovers" experienced when they recognised self-portraits in history pieces.[42] It is remarkable that in Rembrandt's workshop good-quality copies of his self-portraits were made from very early on (for example of Cat. 144, 145, pp. 78 and 81).

Detail of: **Self-Portrait with a Feathered Cap**, 1629
(see ill. p. 82)

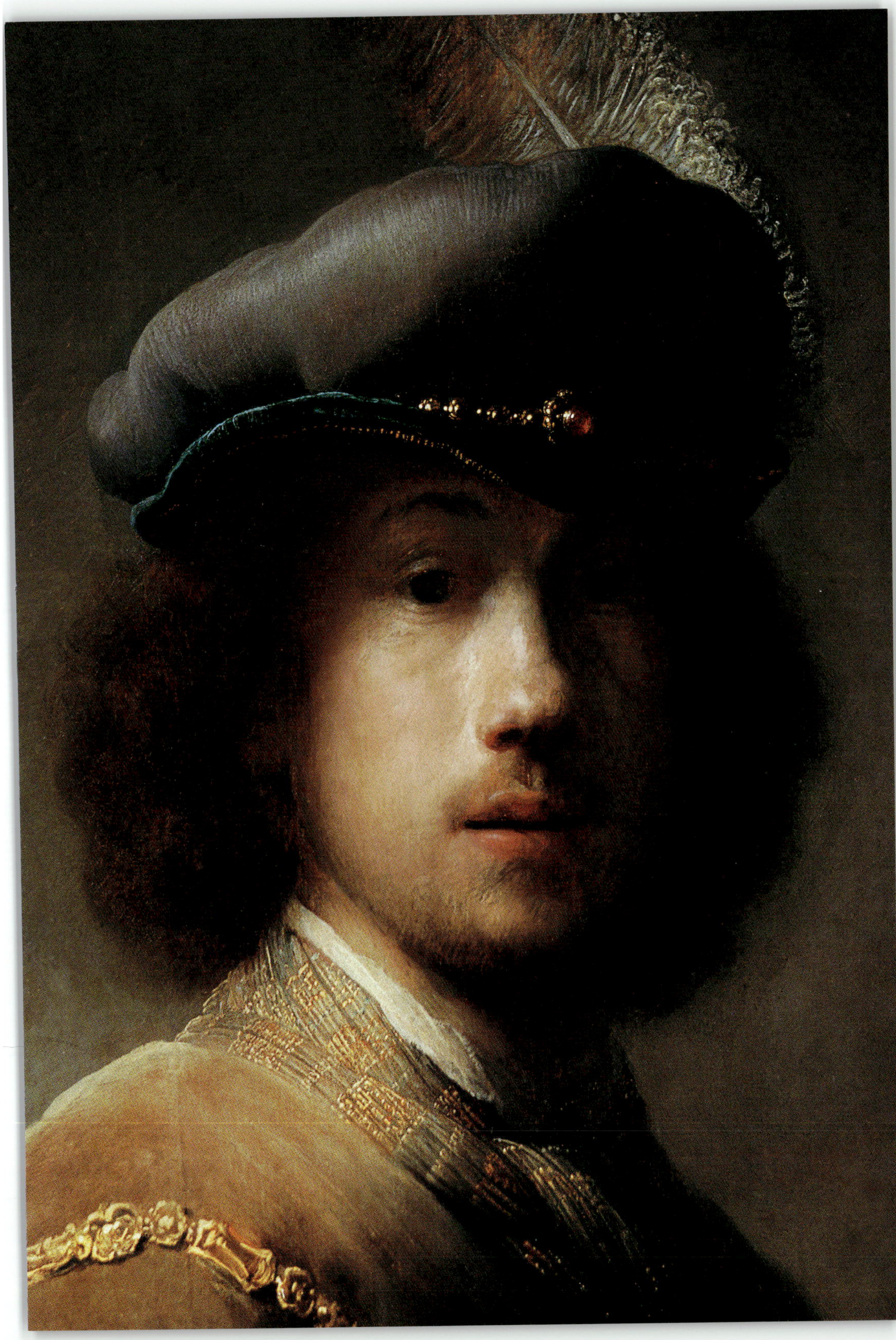

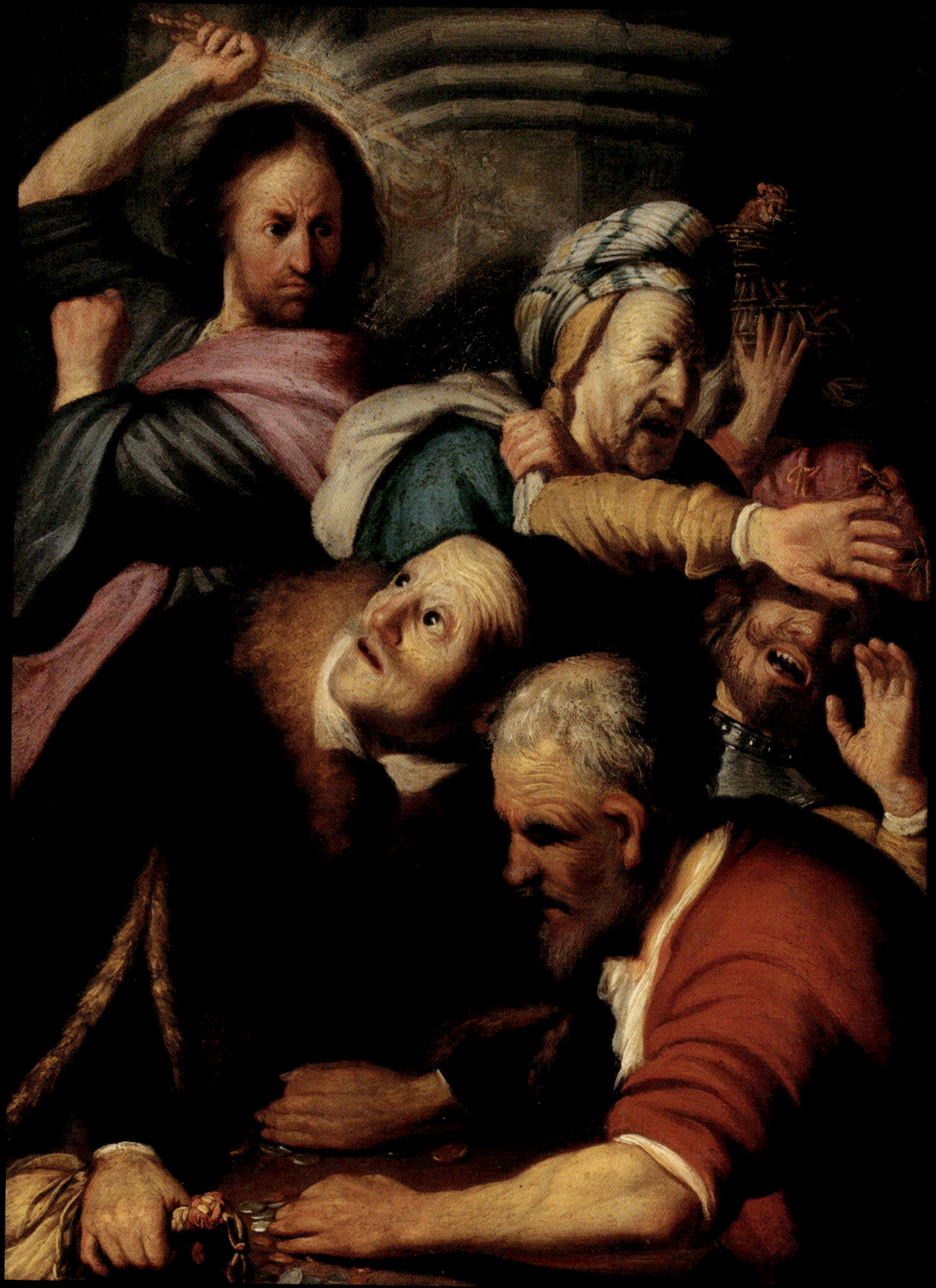

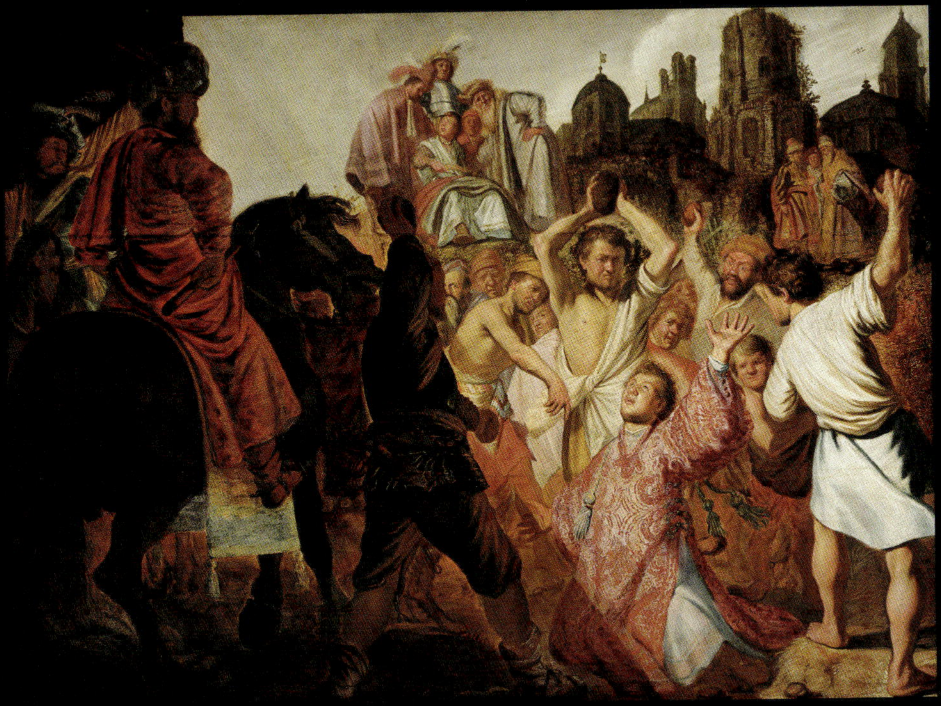

Christ Driving the Money Changers from the Temple, 1626
Oil on panel, 43.1 × 32 cm (16 ¾ × 12 ⅝ in.)
Moscow, Pushkin Museum

The Stoning of St Stephen, 1625
Oil on panel, 89.5 × 123.6 cm (35 ¼ × 48 ⅔ in.)
Musée des Beaux-Arts de Lyon

Balaam and the Ass, 1626
Oil on panel, 63.2 × 46.5 cm (24 ¾ × 18 ¼ in.)
Paris, Musée Cognacq-Jay

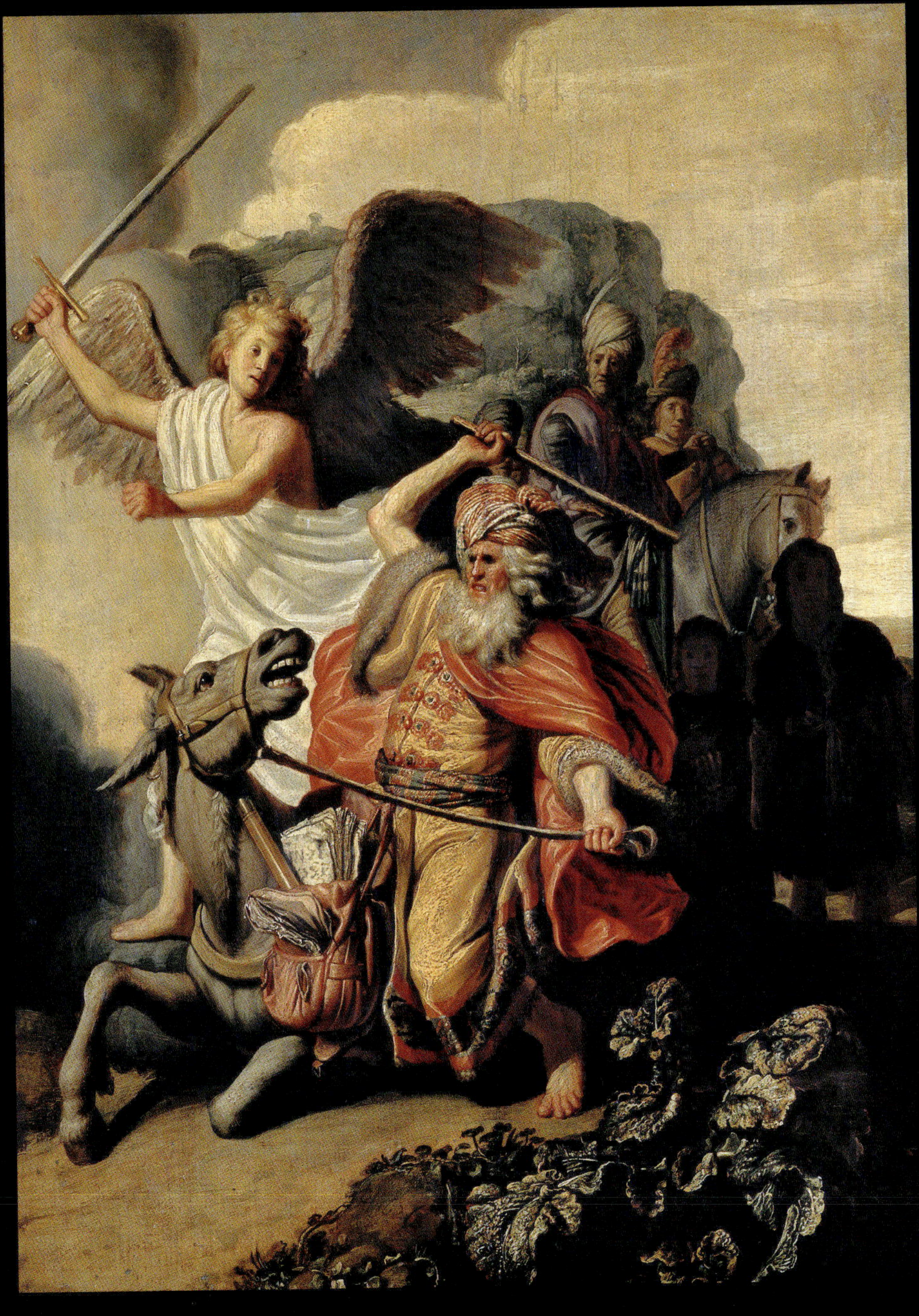

Pieter Lastman
The Baptism of the Eunuch, *c.* 1615–1620
Oil on panel, 63.5 × 98.8 cm (25 × 39 in.)
Paris, Fondation Custodia

The Baptism of the Eunuch, 1626
Oil on panel, 63.5 × 48 cm (25 × 18 ¾ in.)
Utrecht, Museum Het Catharijneconvent

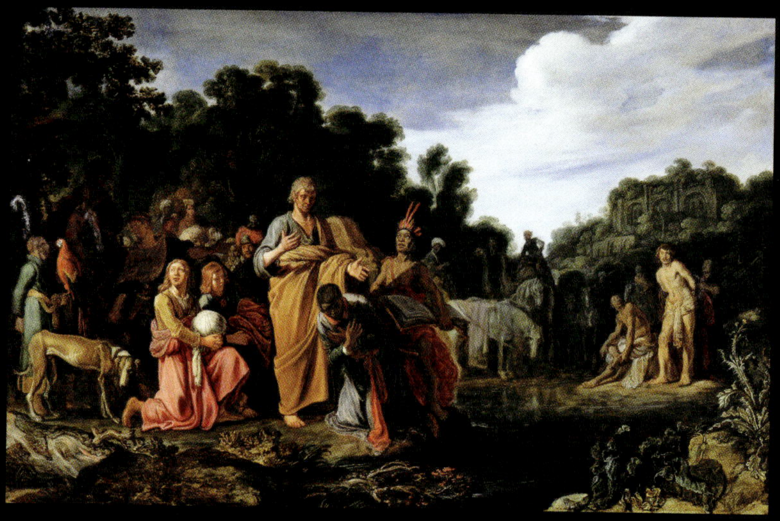

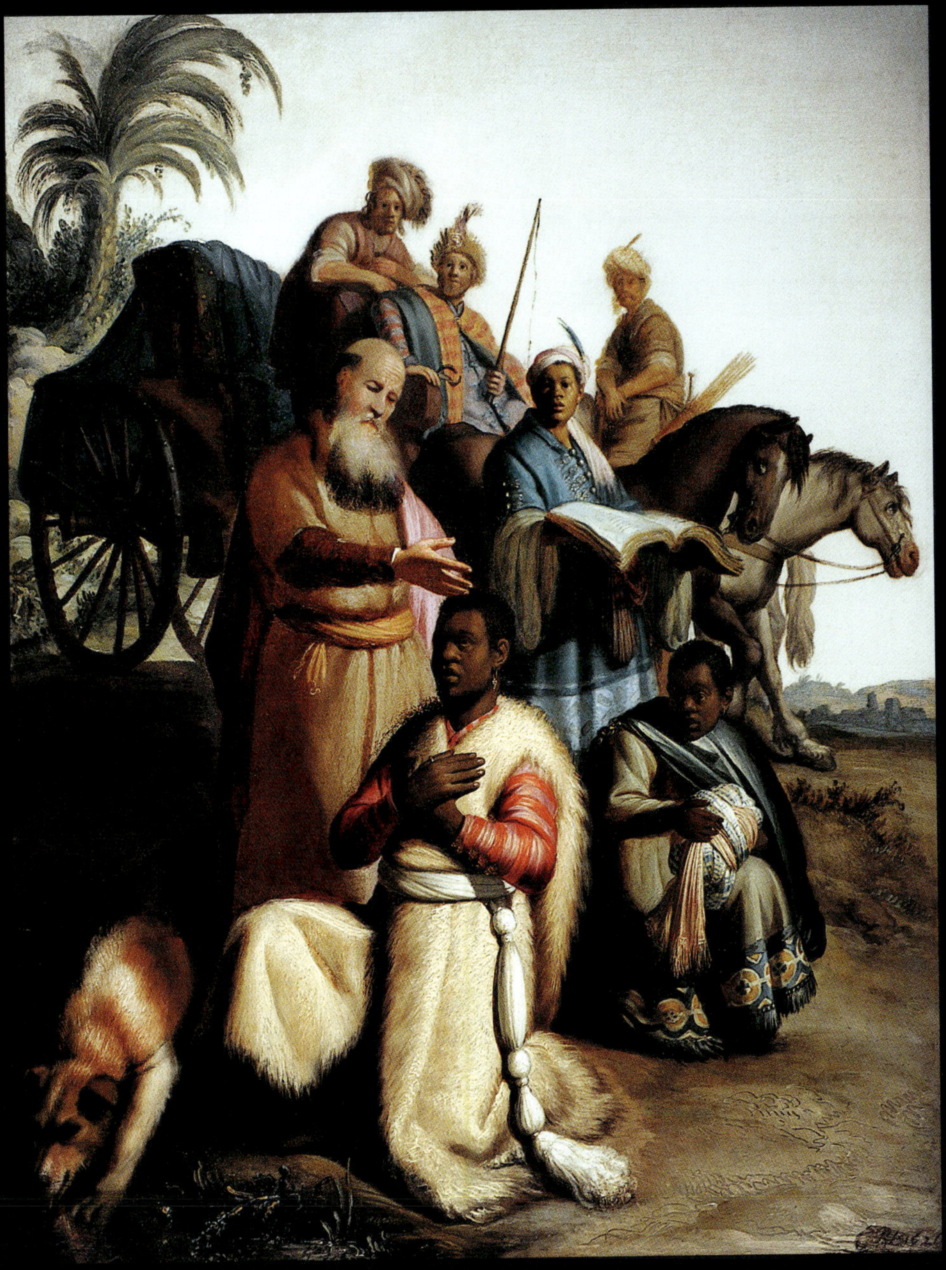

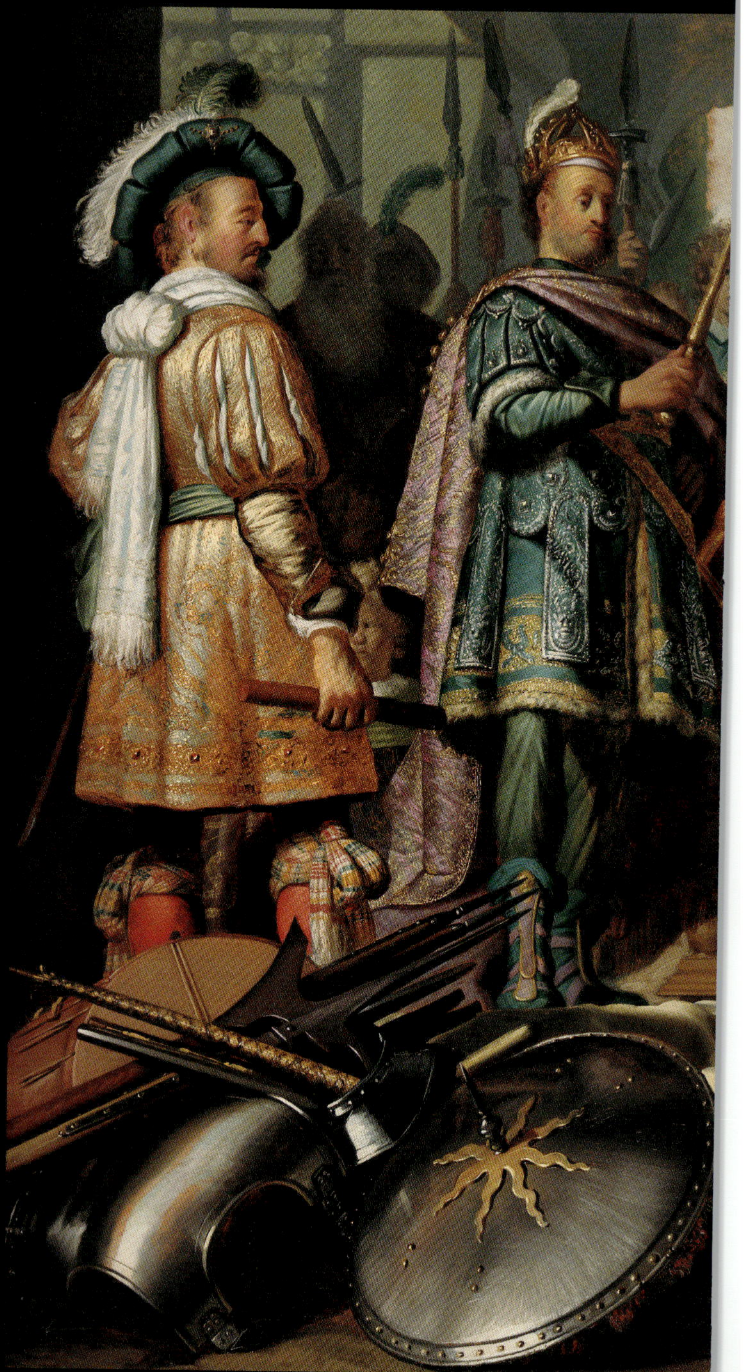

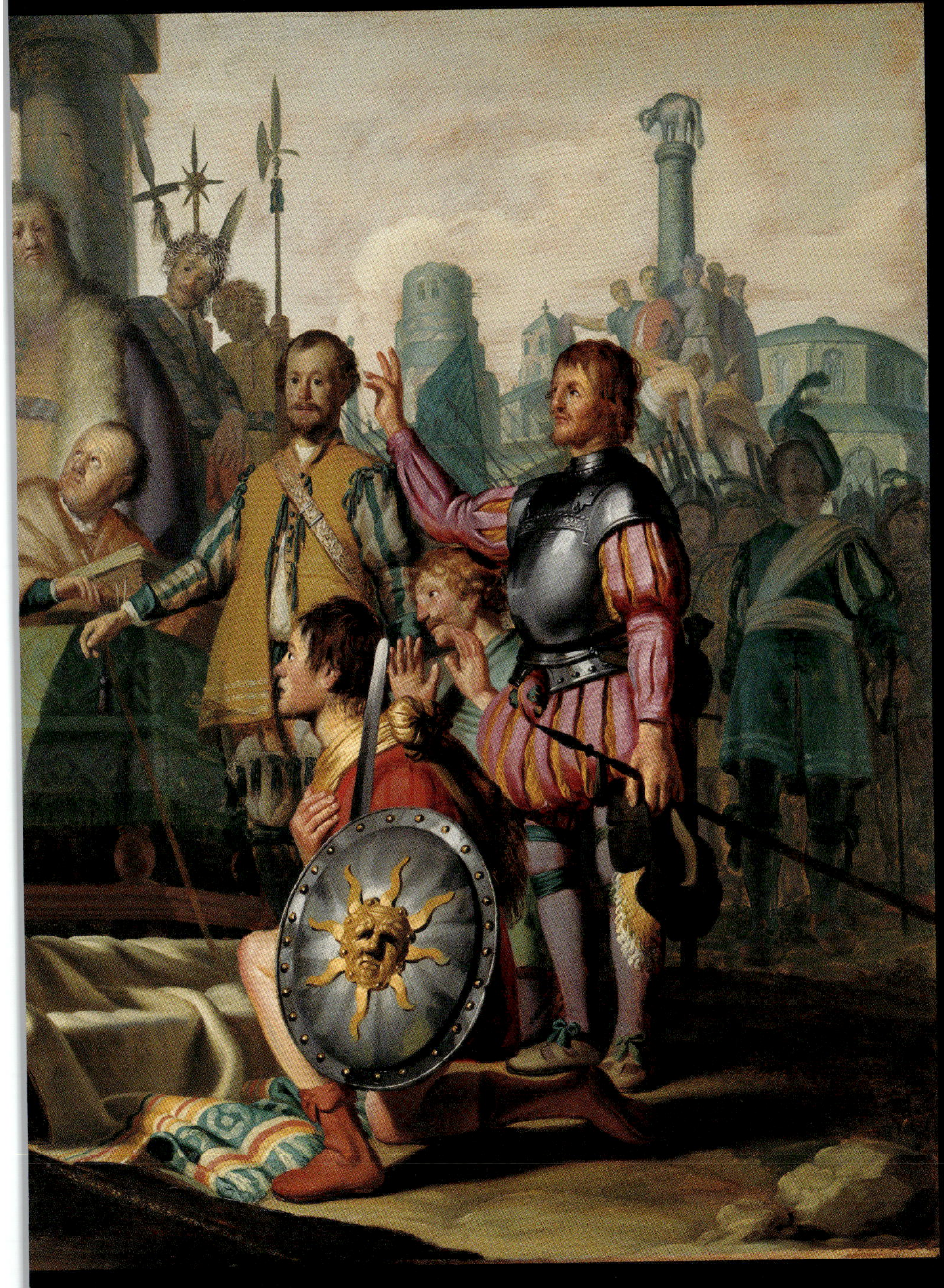

Pages 48/49
History Piece (with Unknown Subject), 1626
Oil on panel, 90.1 × 121.3 cm (35 ½ × 47 ¾ in.)
Leiden, Museum De Lakenhal, on permanent loan from the Collection Cultural Heritage Agency of the Netherlands

Musical Company (Allegory of Music), 1626
Oil on panel, 63.4 × 47.6 cm (24 ¾ × 18 ¾ in.)
Amsterdam, Rijksmuseum

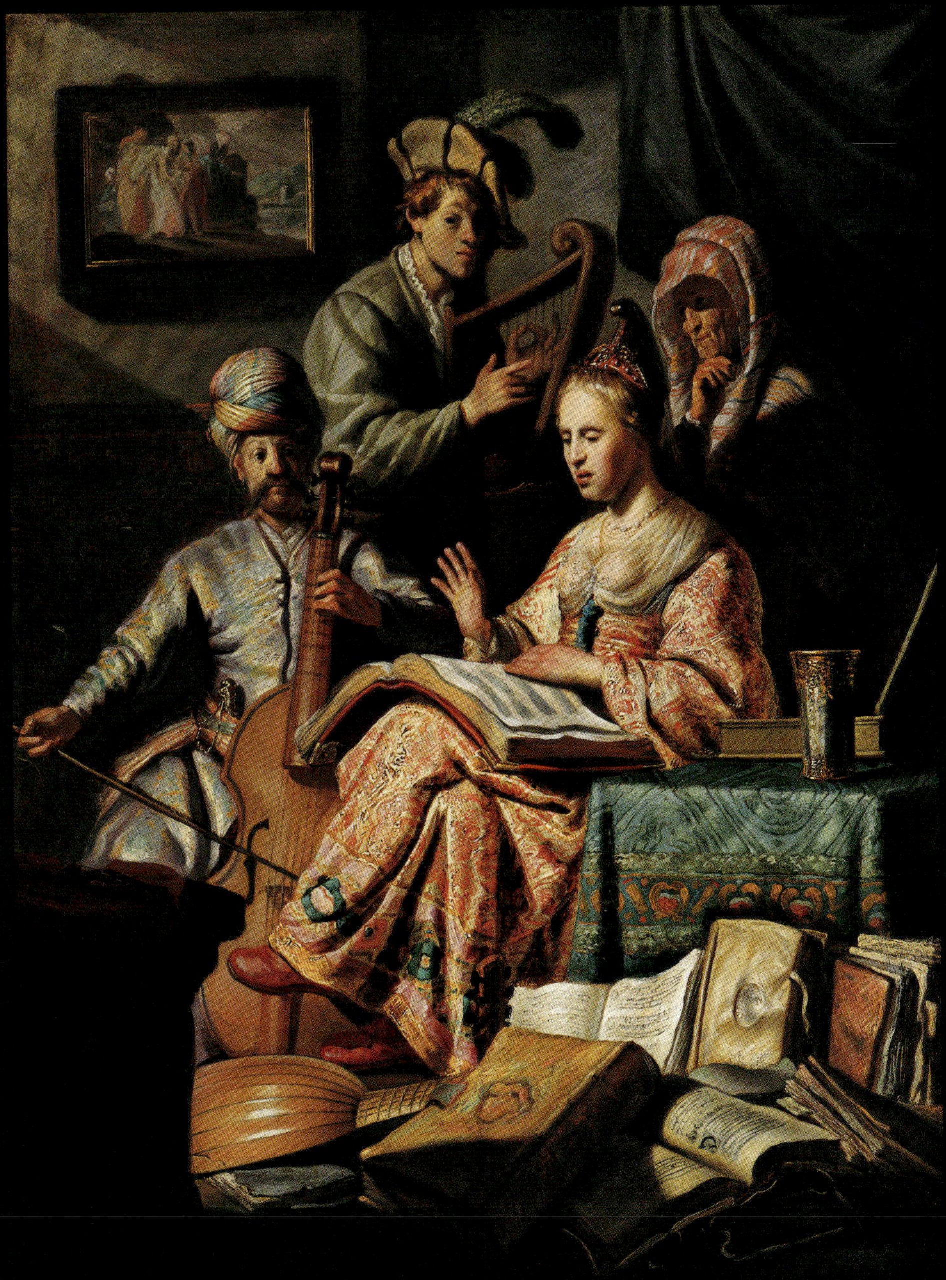

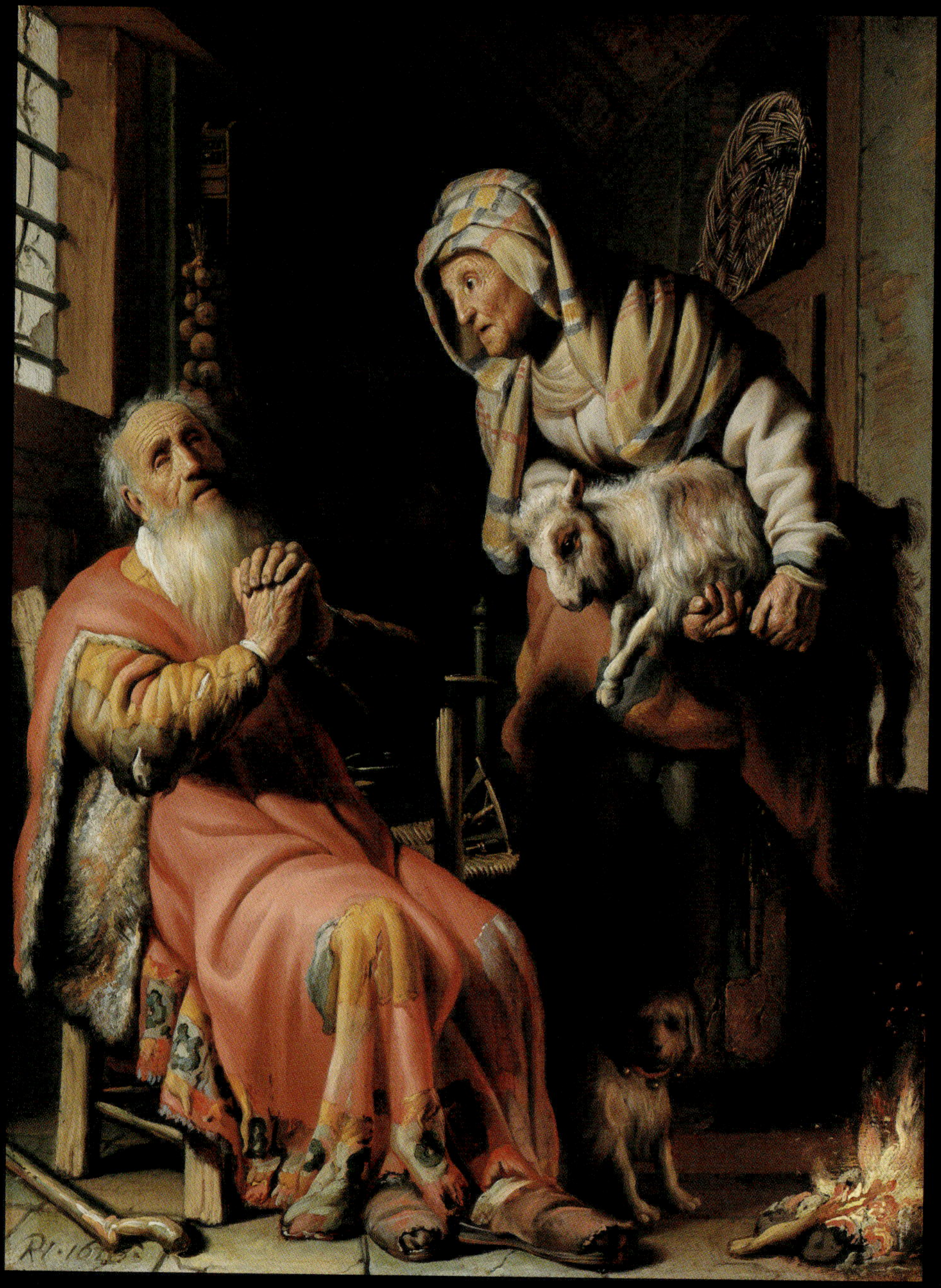

Tobit and Anna with the Kid, 1626
Oil on panel, 39.5 × 30 cm (15 ½ × 11 ¾ in.)
Amsterdam, Rijksmuseum

Jan van de Velde II after Willem Buytewech
Tobit and Anna with the Kid, *c.* 1619/20
Etching, 19.4 × 11.2 cm (7¾ × 4½ in.)
Amsterdam, Rijksmuseum

Pages 54/55
David with the Head of Goliath before Saul, 1627
Oil on panel, 27.4 × 39.7 cm (10 ¾ × 15 ⅝ in.)
Kunstmuseum Basel, Max Geldner Bequest 1958

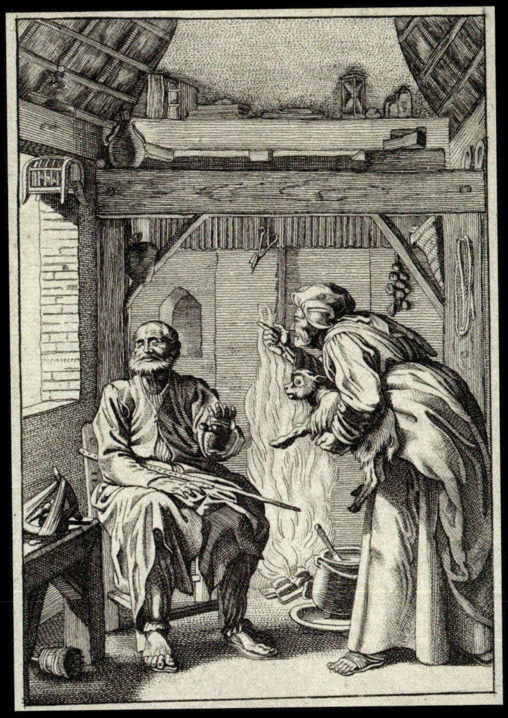

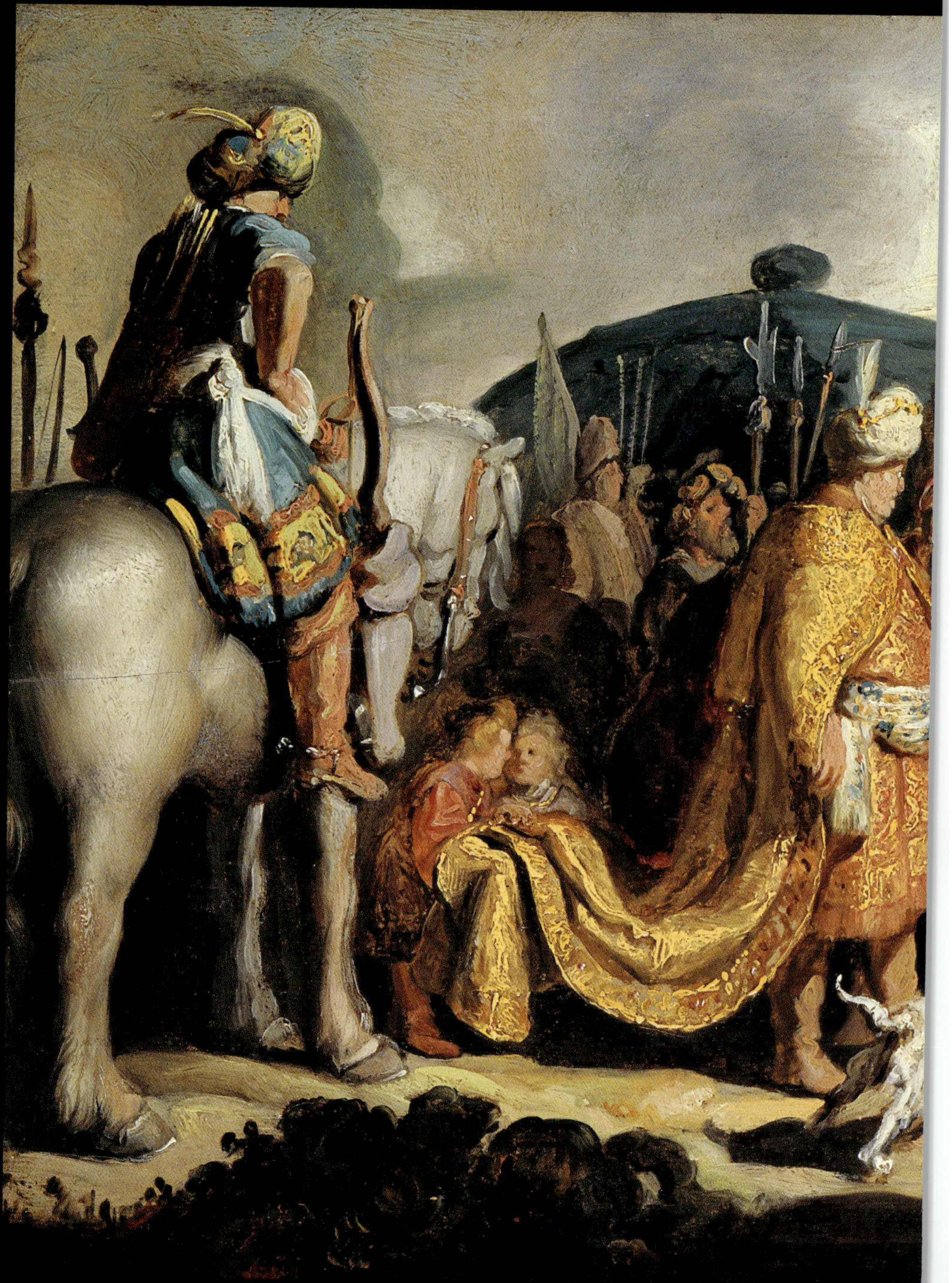

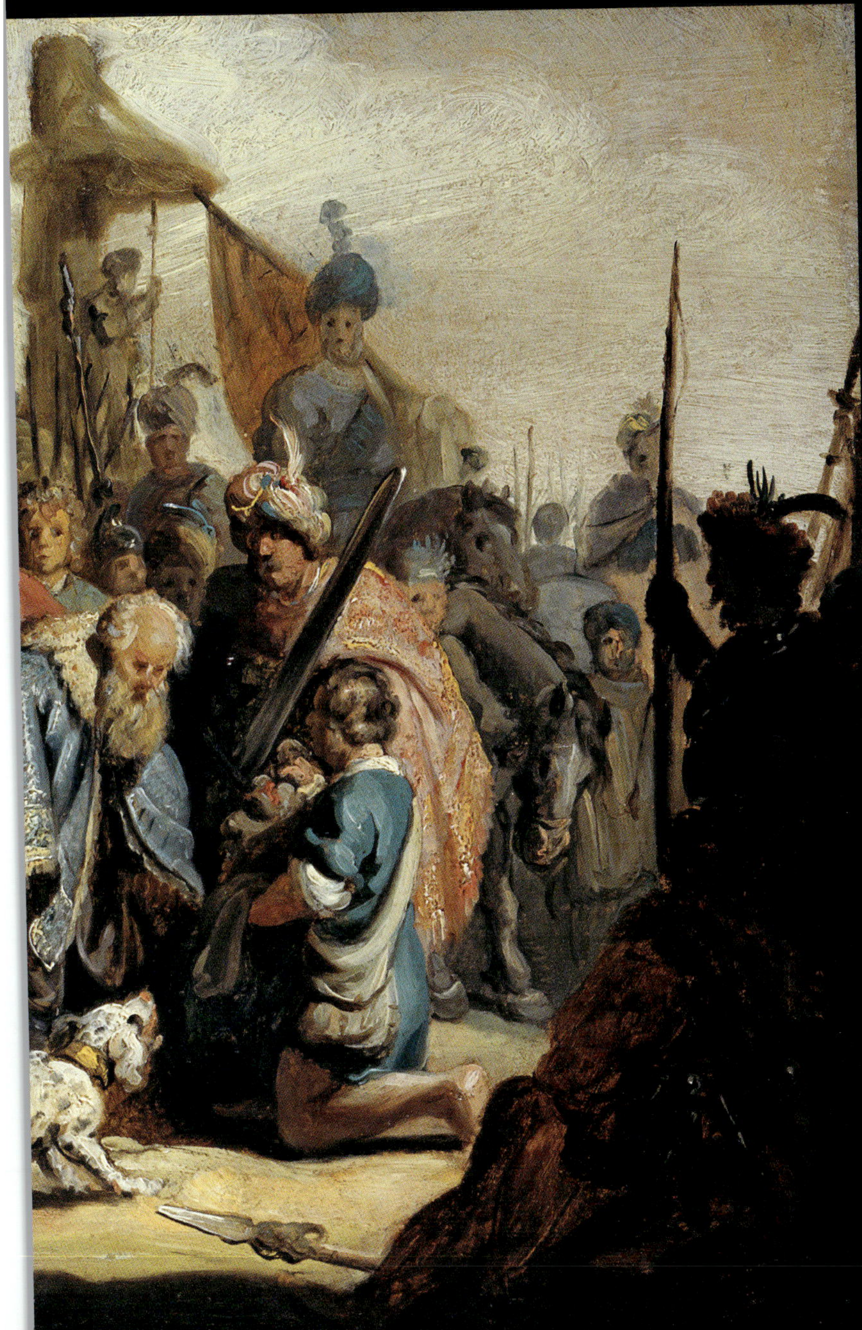

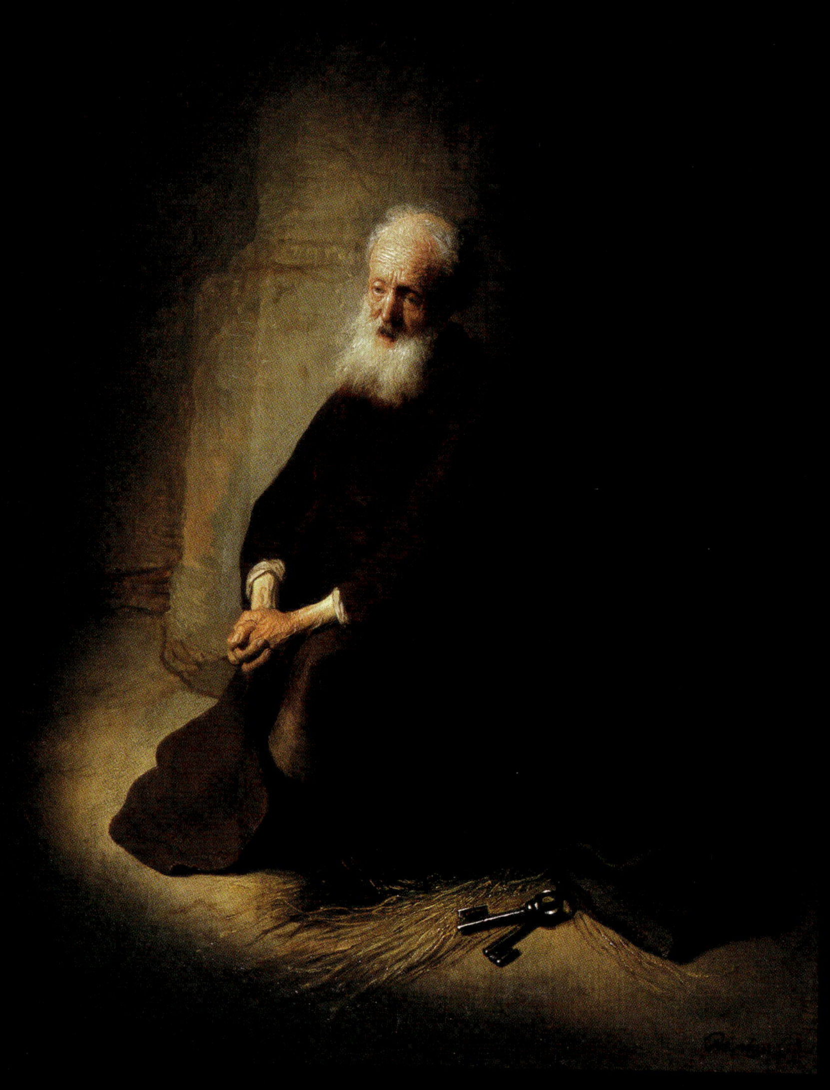

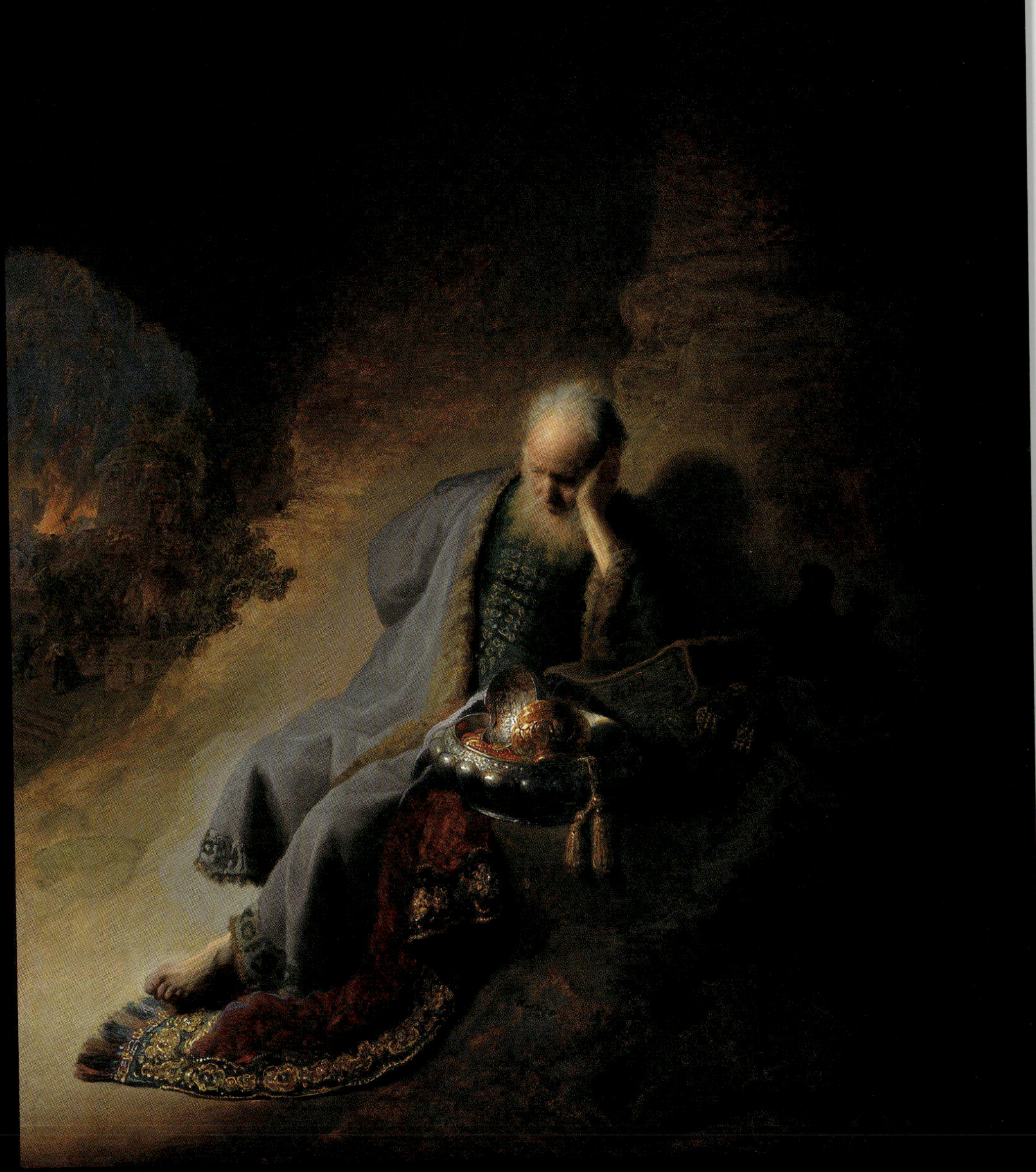

Page 56
St Peter Repentant, 1631
Oil on panel, 59.1 × 47.8 cm (23 ¼ × 18 ¾ in.)
Jerusalem, The Israel Museum

Page 57
Jeremiah Lamenting the Destruction of Jerusalem, 1630
Oil on panel, 58.3 × 46.6 cm (22 ¾ × 18 ⅓ in.)
Amsterdam, Rijksmuseum

The Apostle Paul at His Desk, *c.* 1629/30
Oil on panel, 47.2 × 38.6 cm (18 ⅝ × 15 ¼ in.)
Nuremberg, Germanisches Nationalmuseum

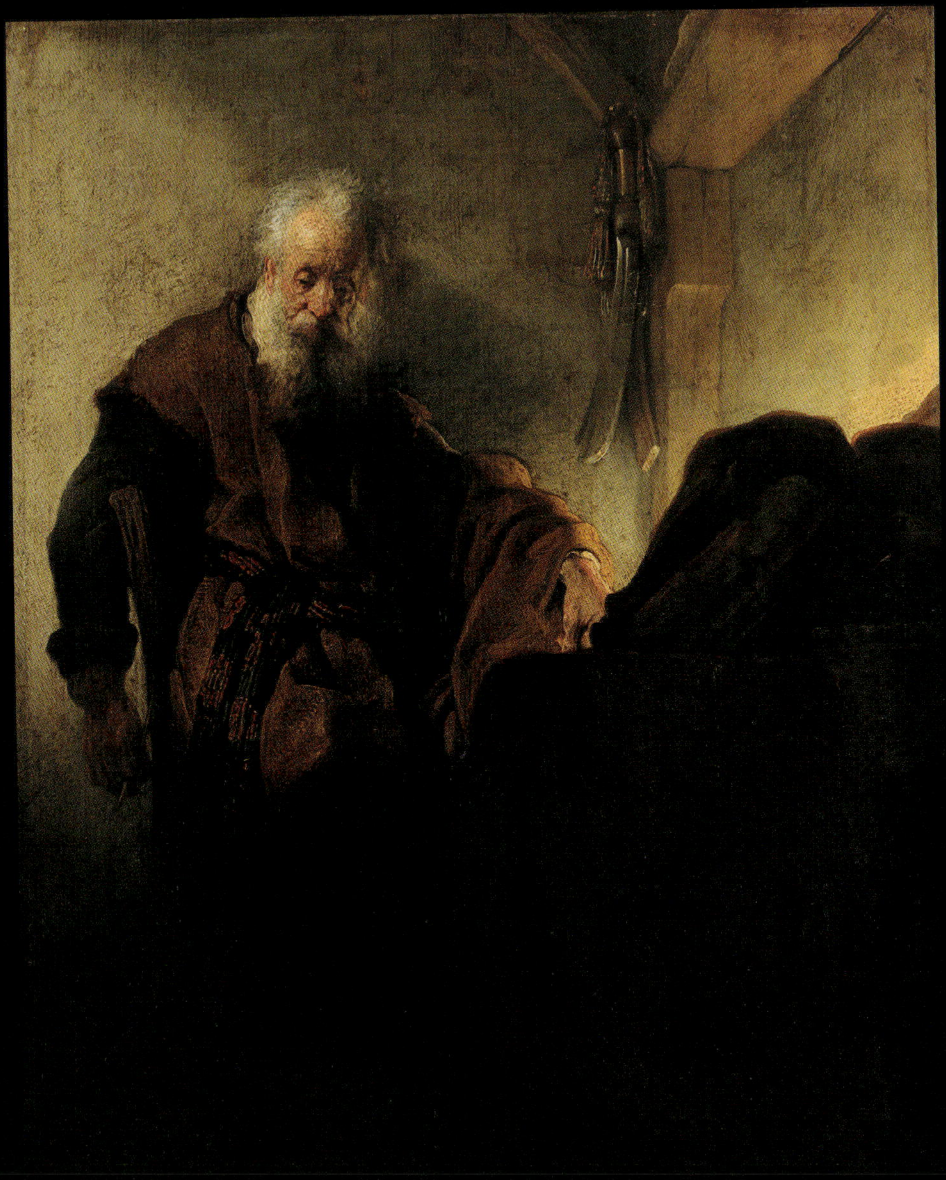

Lucas van Leyden
St Paul and St Peter Seated in a Landscape, 1527
Copper engraving, 9.7 × 14.8 cm (3 7/8 × 5 7/8 in.)
Amsterdam, Rijksmuseum

Two Old Men Disputing
Probably the Apostles Peter and Paul, 1628
Oil on panel, 72.4 × 59.7 cm (28 ½ × 23 ½ in.)
Melbourne, National Gallery of Victoria,
Felton Bequest 1936

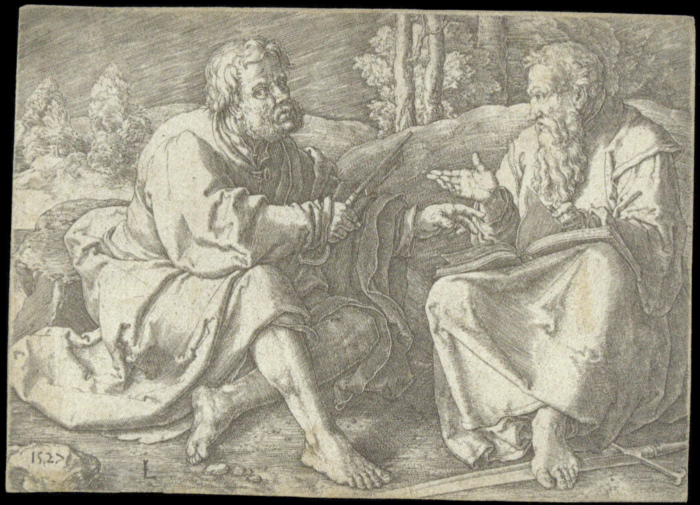

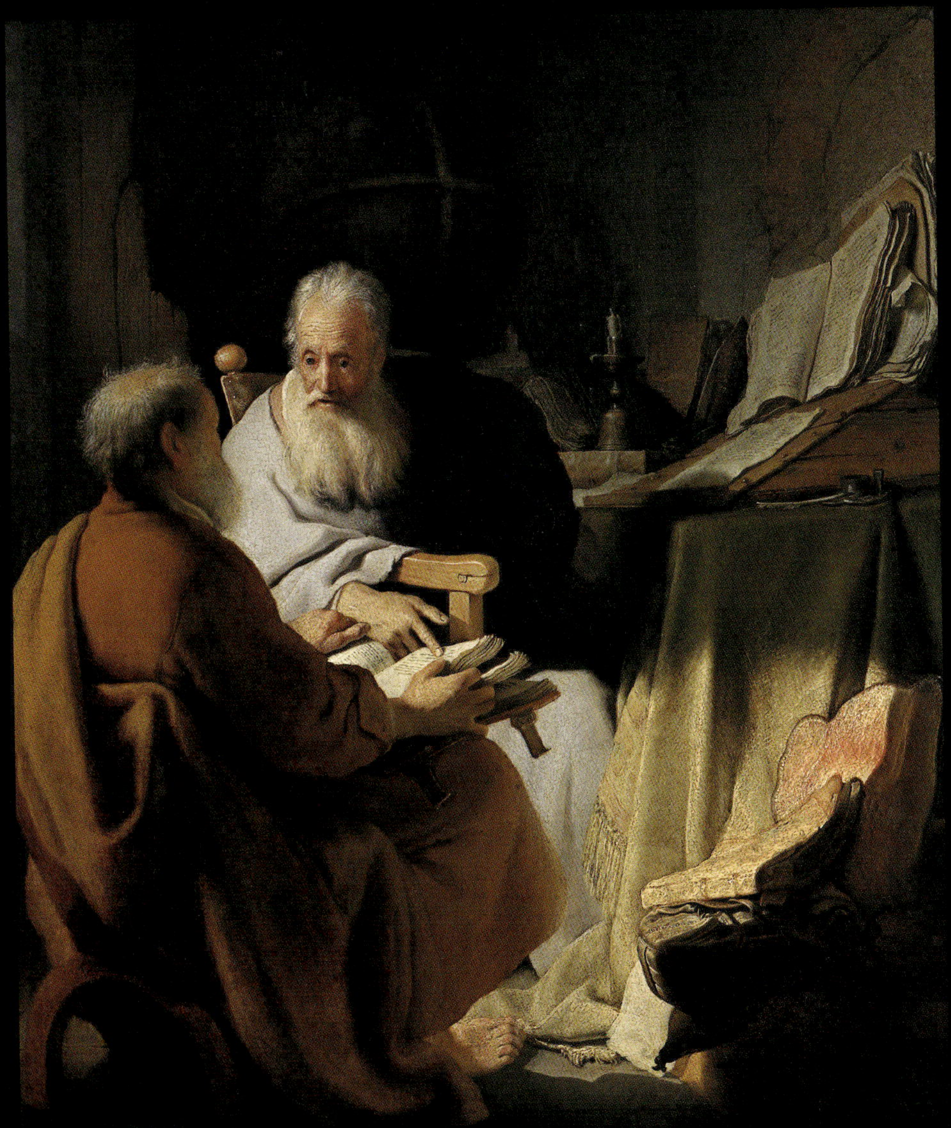

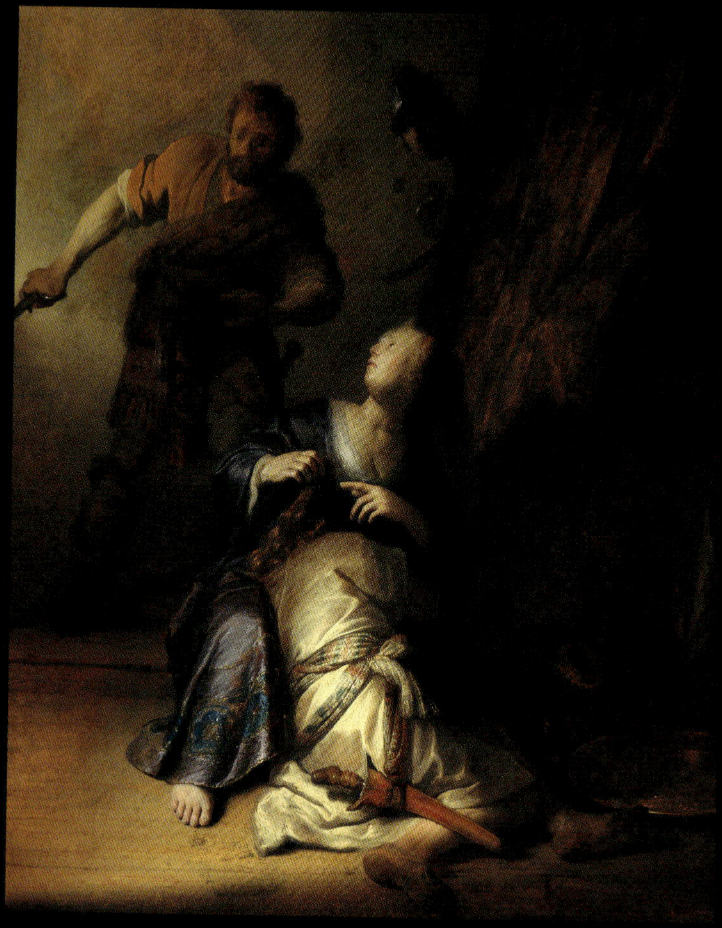

Samson and Delilah, 1628
Oil on panel, 61.3 × 50.1 cm (24 ⅛ × 19 ¾ in.)
Staatliche Museen zu Berlin, Gemäldegalerie

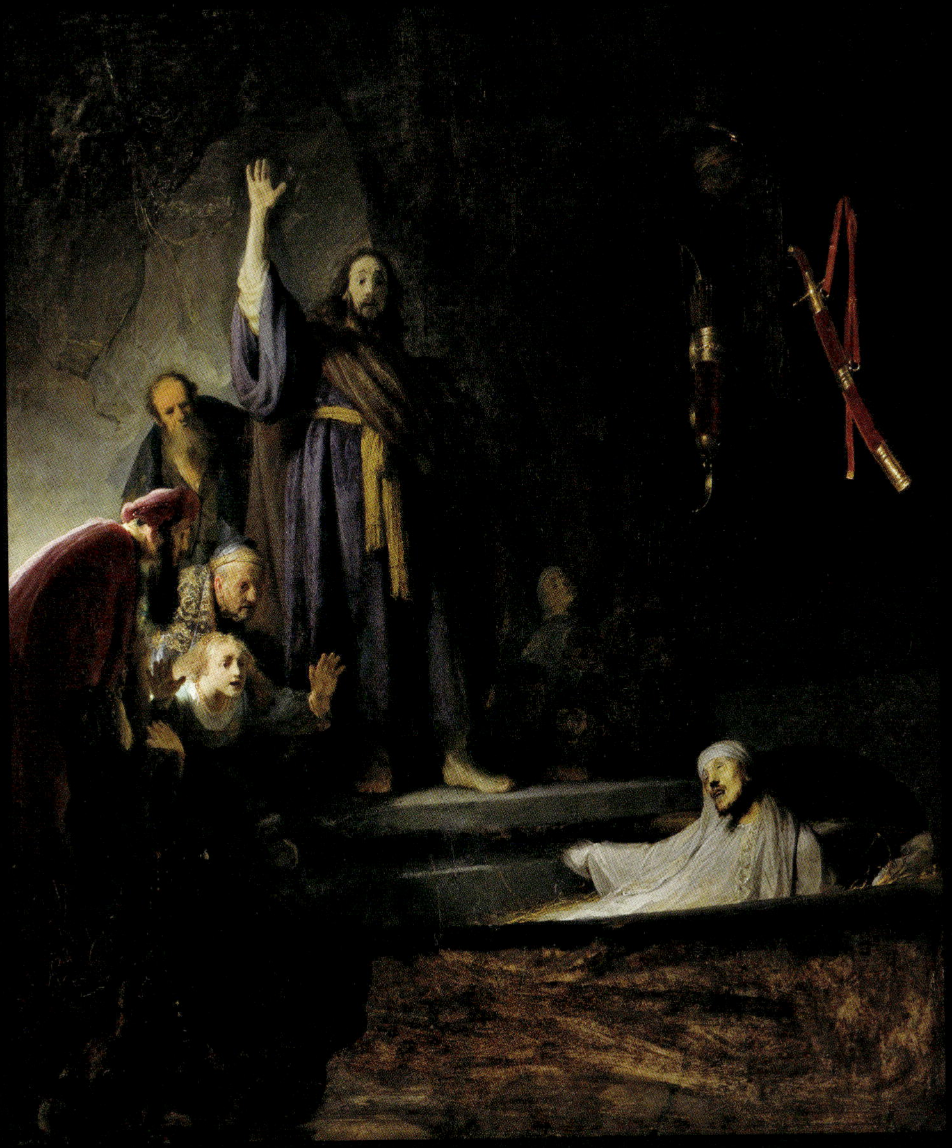

The Raising of Lazarus, 1630/31
Oil on panel, 96.2 × 81.5 cm (37 ¾ × 32 ⅛ in.). Los Angeles County Museum of Art, Gift of H. F. Ahmanson and Company, in memory of Howard F. Ahmanson

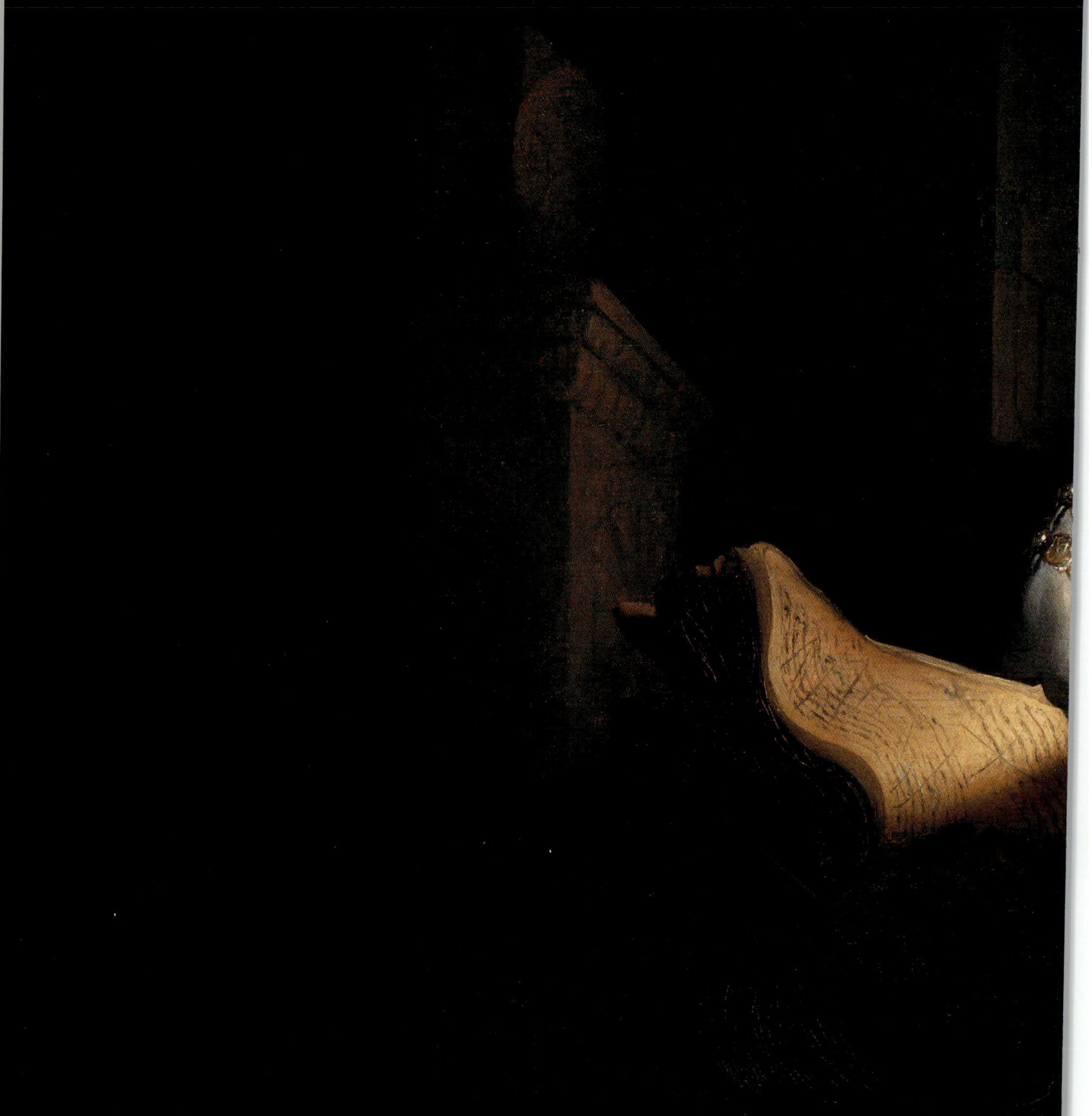

The Parable of the Rich Man, 1627
Oil on panel, 32 × 42.5 cm
(12 5/8 × 16 3/4 in.)
Staatliche Museen zu
Berlin, Gemäldegalerie

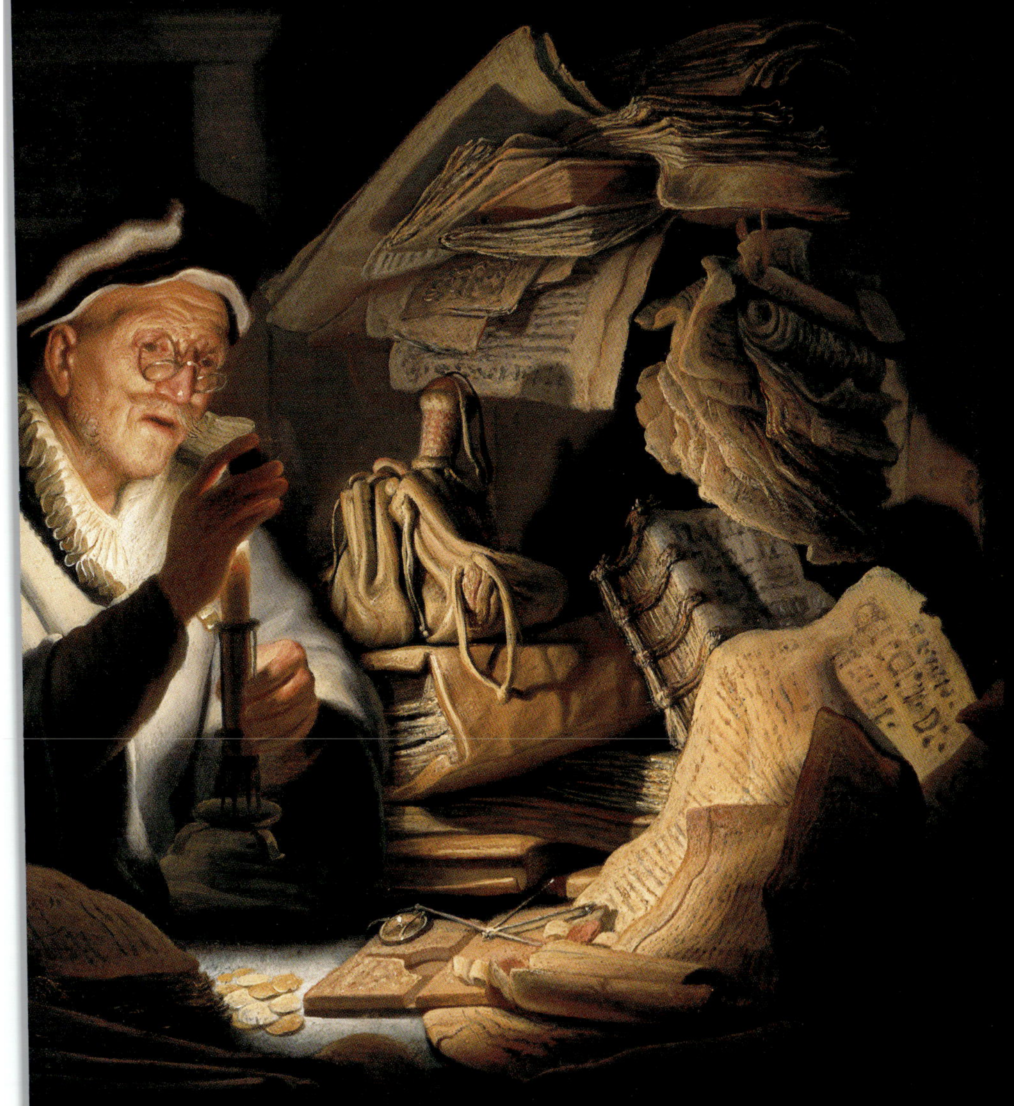

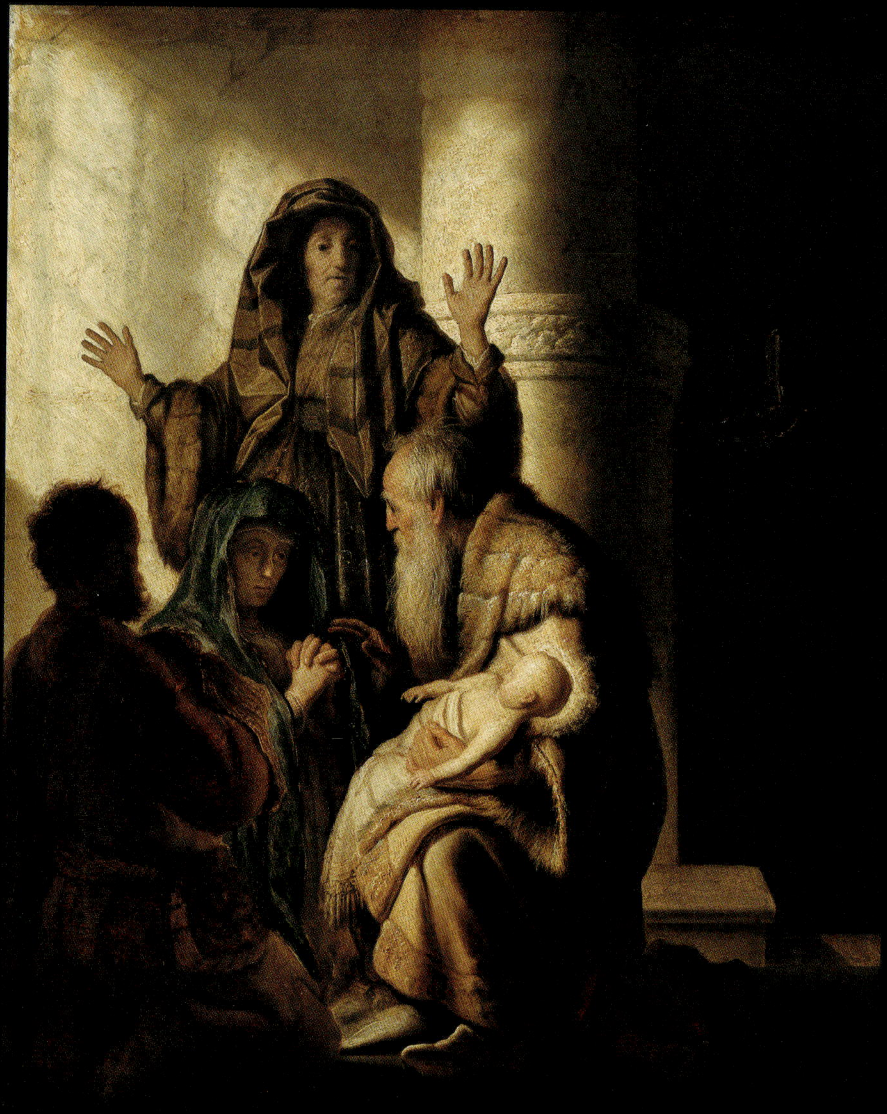

The Presentation in the Temple, *c.* 1628
Oil on panel, 55.4 × 43.7 cm (21 ¾ × 17 ¼ in.)
Hamburger Kunsthalle

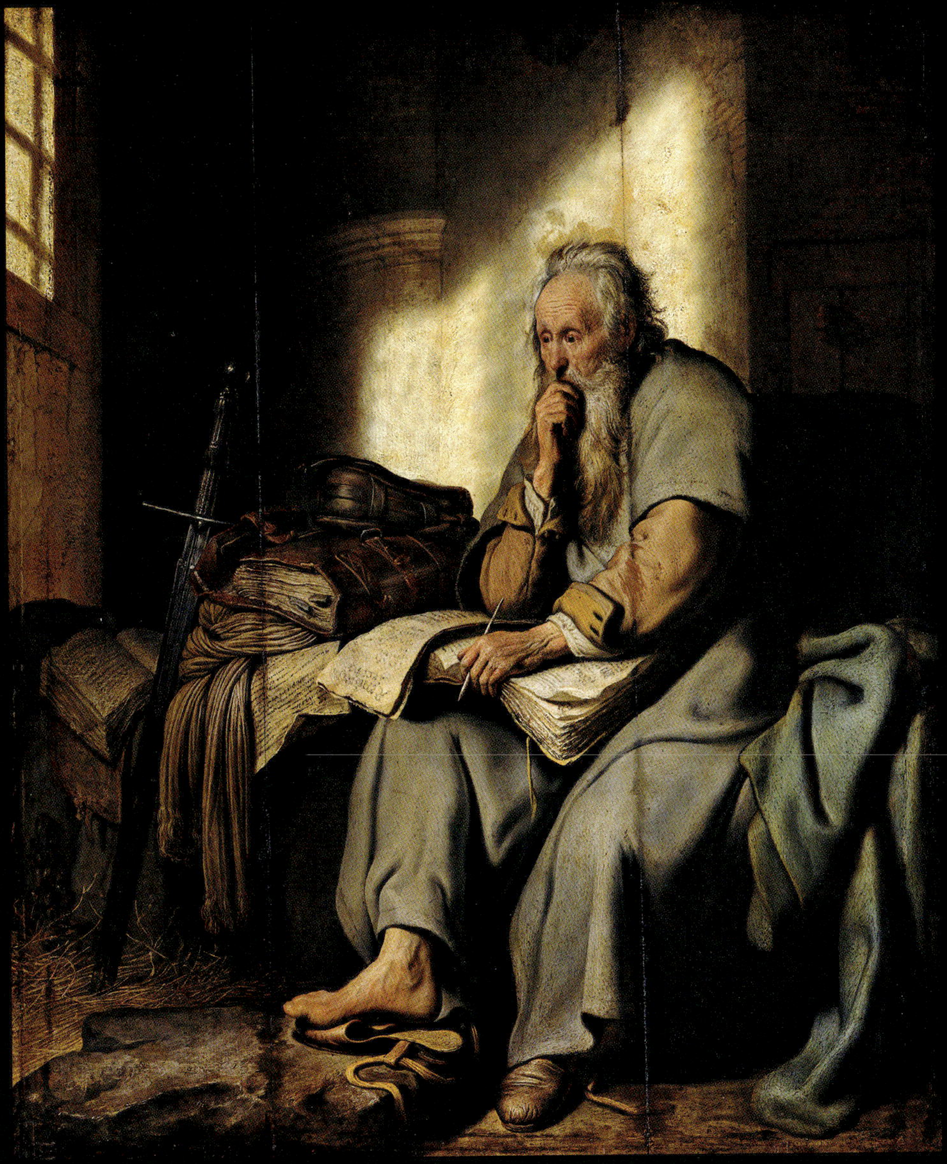

St Paul in Prison, 1627
Oil on panel, 72.8 × 60.2 cm (28 2/3 × 23 3/4 in.)
Staatsgalerie Stuttgart

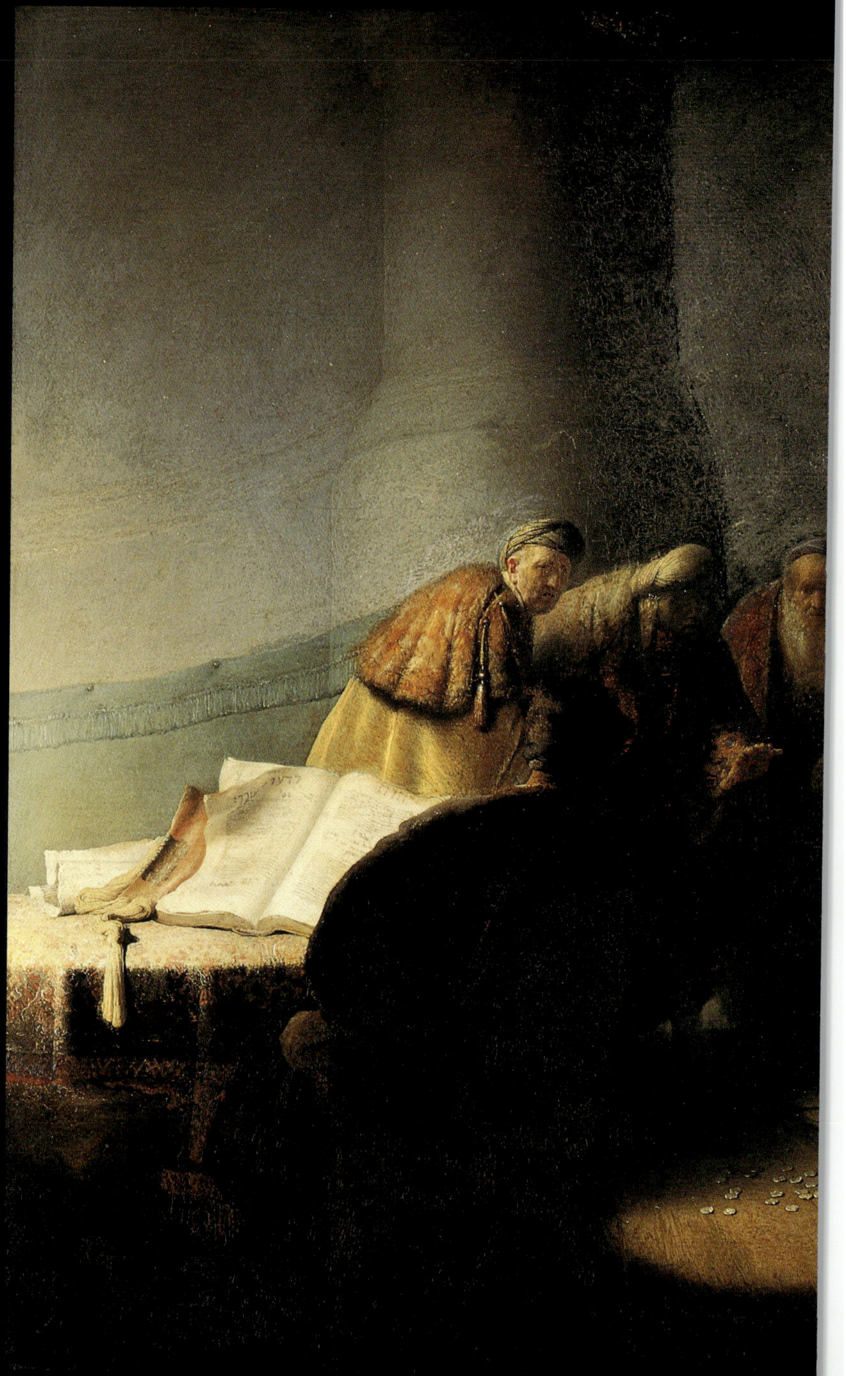

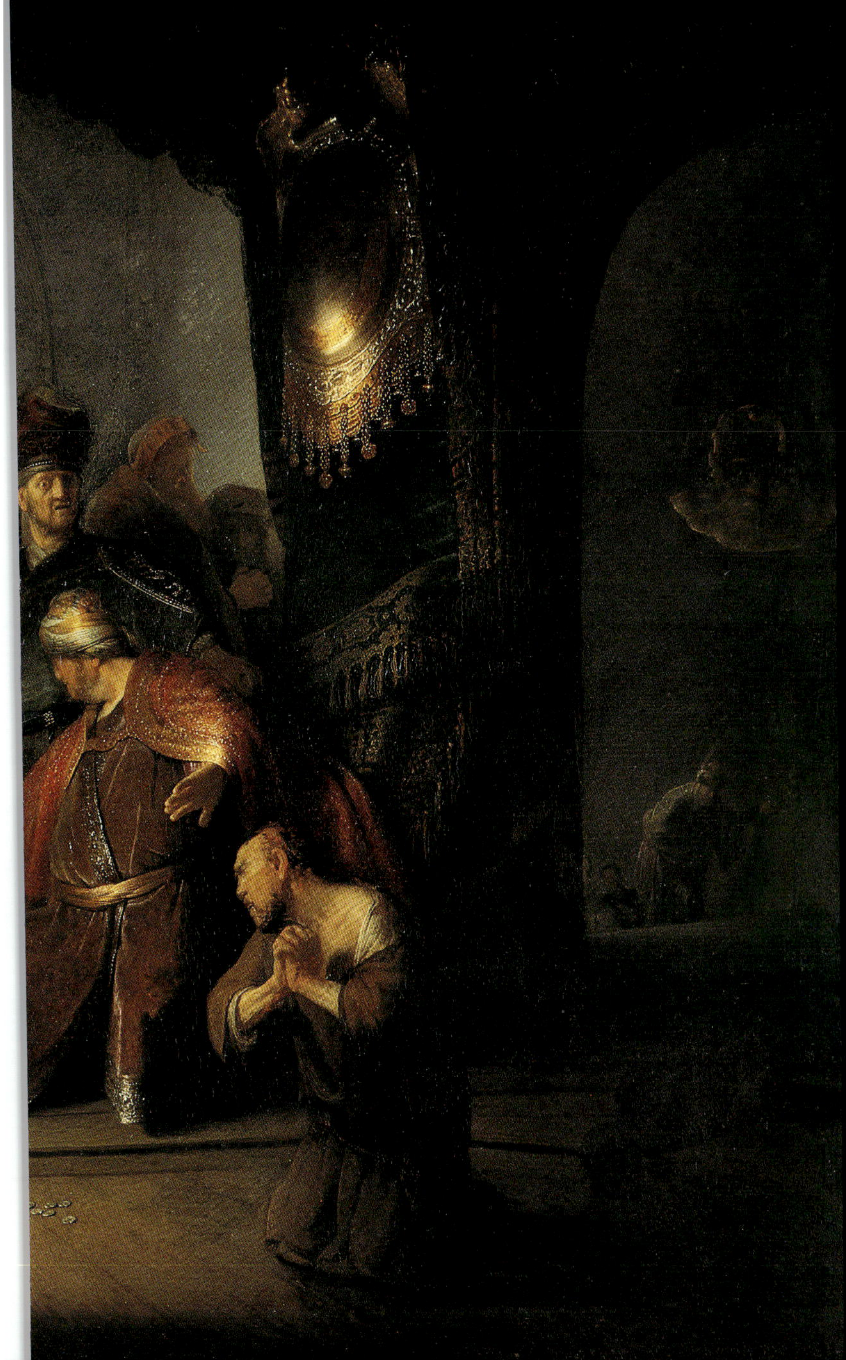

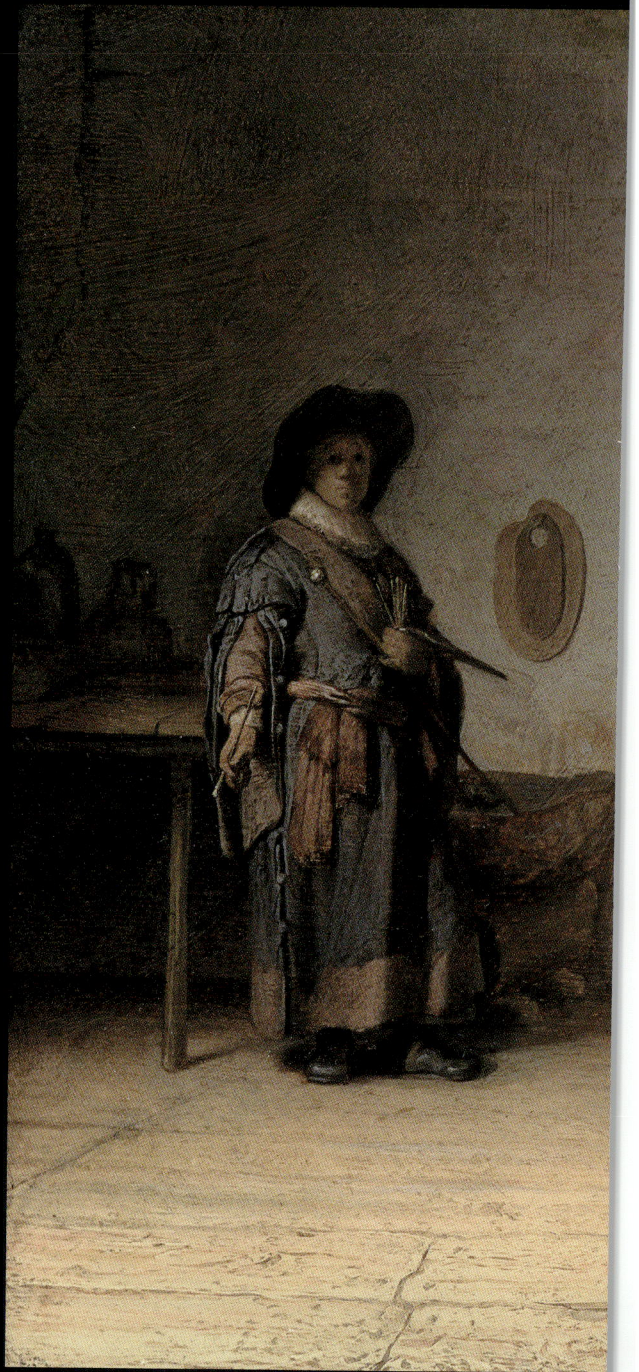

Pages 68/69
The Repentant Judas Returning the Pieces of Silver, 1629
Oil on panel, 79 × 102.3 cm
(31 ⅛ × 40 ¼ in.)
Private Collection

The Artist in His Studio, *c.* 1628
Oil on panel, 24.8 × 31.7 cm
(9 ¾ × 12 ½ in.)
Boston, Massachusetts,
Museum of Fine Arts,
Zoë Oliver Sherman Fund in
Memory of Lillie Oliver Poor

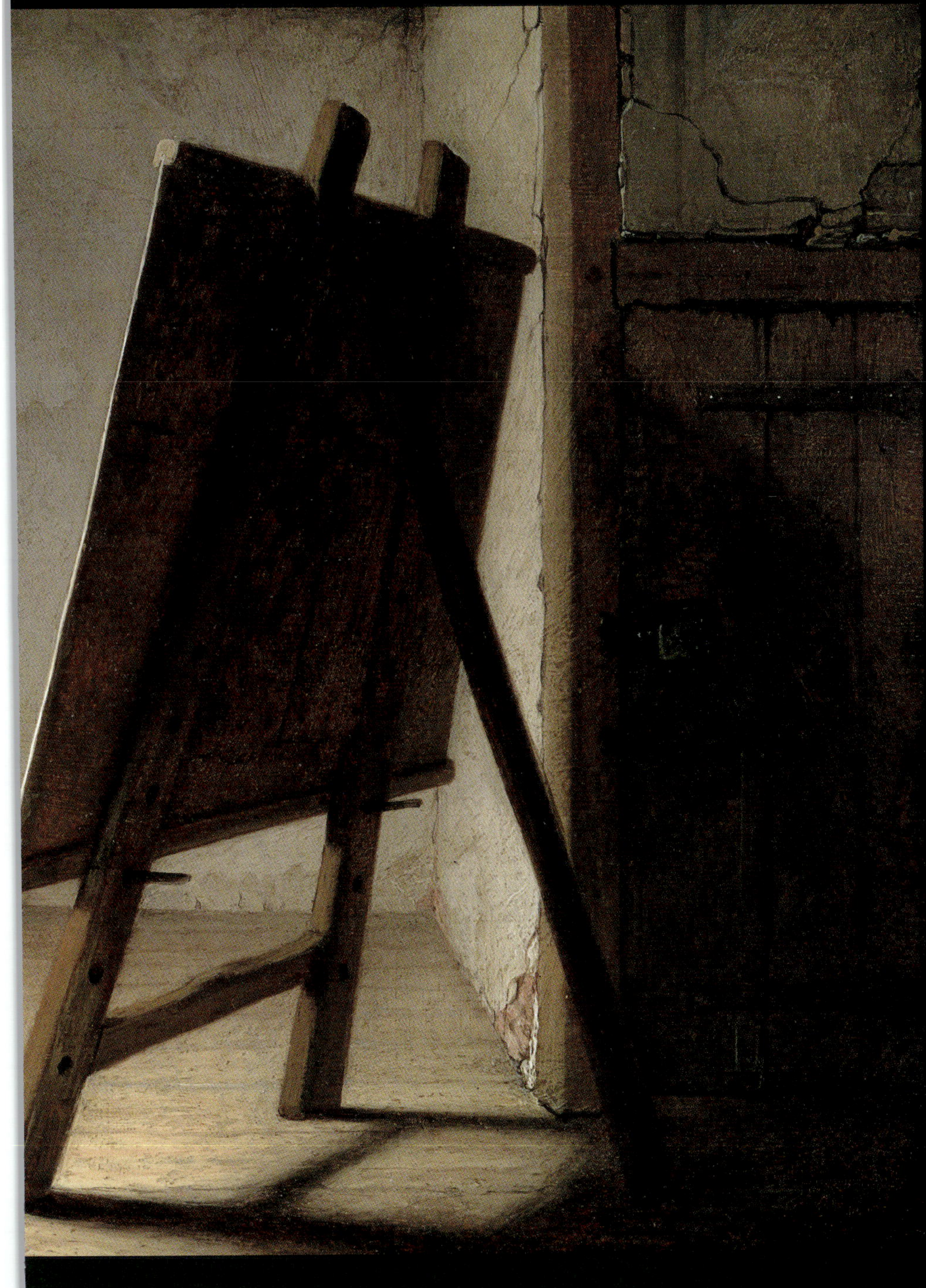

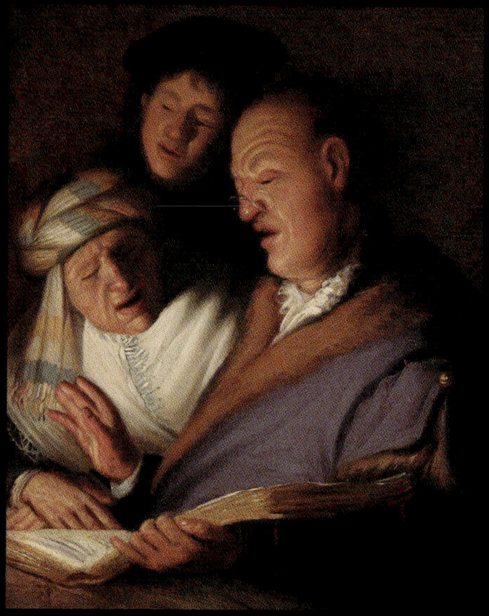

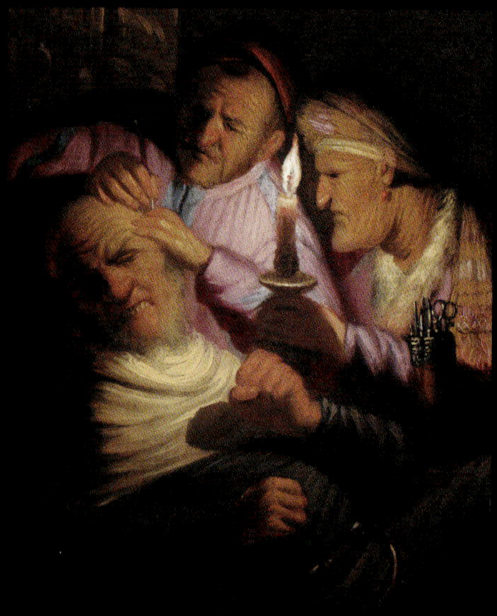

Three Singers (Allegory of Hearing), 1624/25
Oil on panel, 21.6 × 17.6 cm (8 ½ × 6 ¾ in.)
New York, The Leiden Collection

The Operation (Allegory of Touch), 1624/25
Oil on panel, 21.5 × 17.6 cm (8 ½ × 6 ¾ in.)
New York, The Leiden Collection

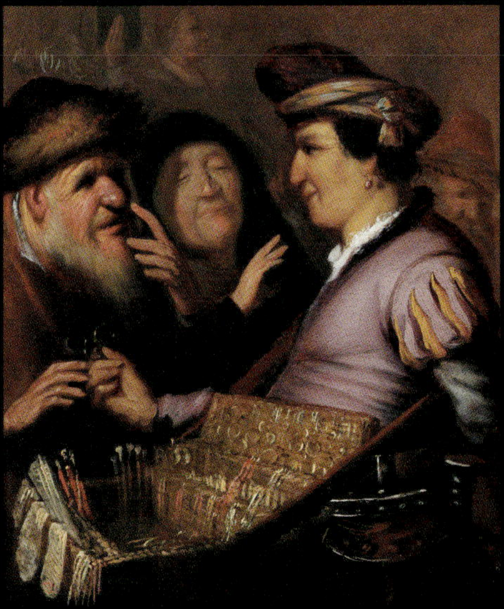

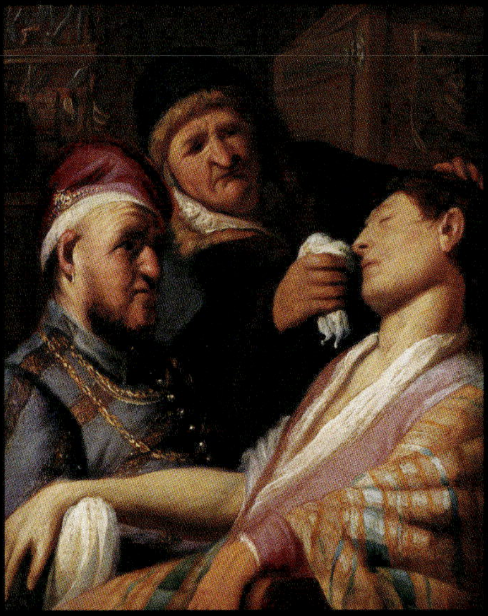

The Spectacles Pedlar (Allegory of Sight), 1624/25
Oil on panel, 21 × 17.8 cm (8 ¼ × 7 ⅛ in.)
Leiden, Museum De Lakenhal

The Unconscious Patient (Allegory of Smell), 1624/25
Oil on panel, 31.8 × 25.4 cm (12 ½ × 10 in.)
New York, The Leiden Collection

Old Man with a Feathered Beret and a Gorget, *c.* 1630/31
Oil on panel, 65.7 × 51.8 cm (25 ¾ × 20 ⅜ in.)
Los Angeles, The J. Paul Getty Museum

Page 76
Old Man with a Fur Hat, 1630
Oil on panel, 22.2 × 17.7 cm (8 ¾ × 6 ¾ in.)
Innsbruck, Tiroler Landesmuseum Ferdinandeum

Page 77
Old Man (Rembrandt's Father?), *c.* 1630/31
Oil on panel, 24.3 × 20.3 cm (9 ⅝ × 7 ¾ in.)
Kingston, Ontario, Queen's University, Agnes Etherington
Art Centre, Gift of Alfred and Isabel Bader, 2003

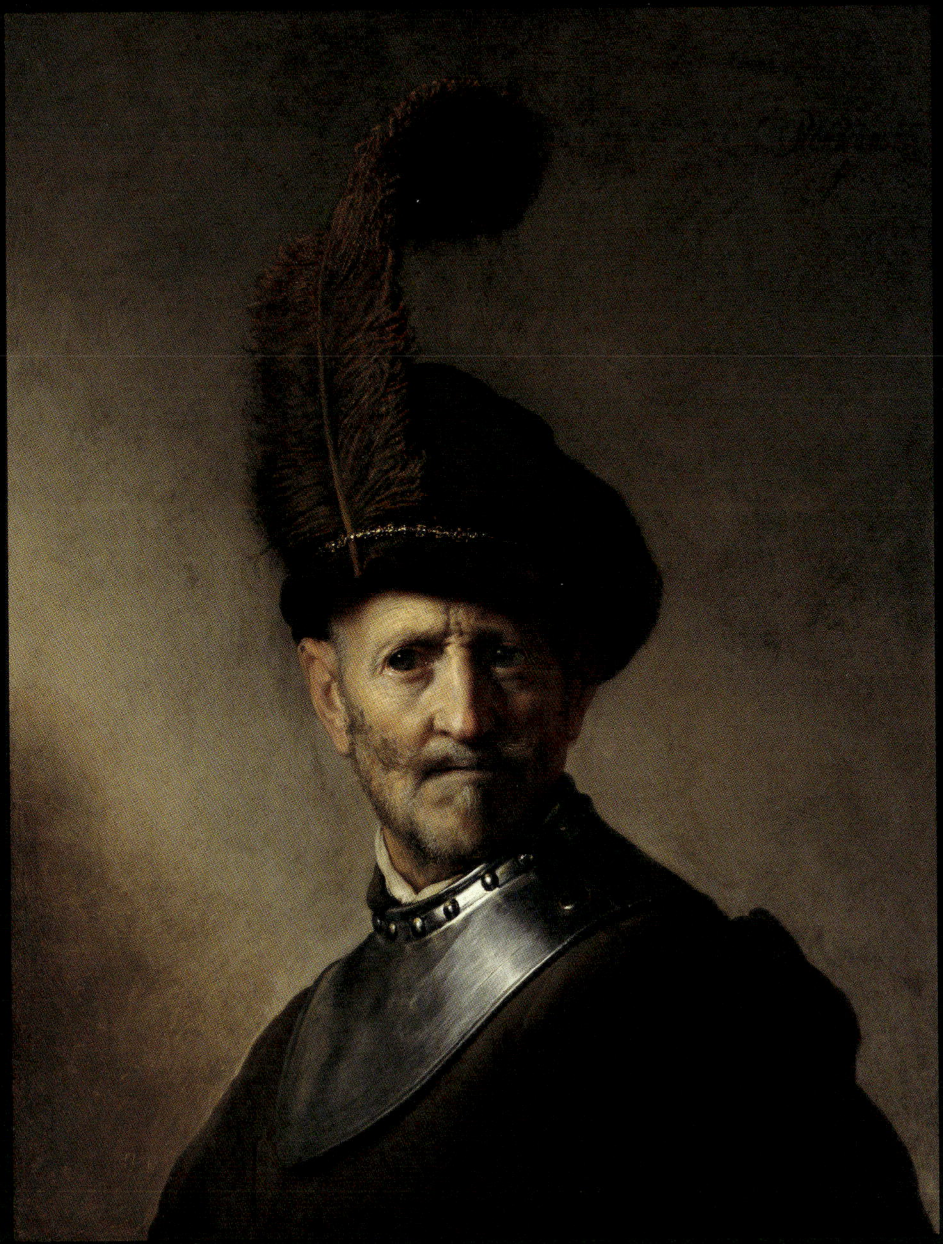

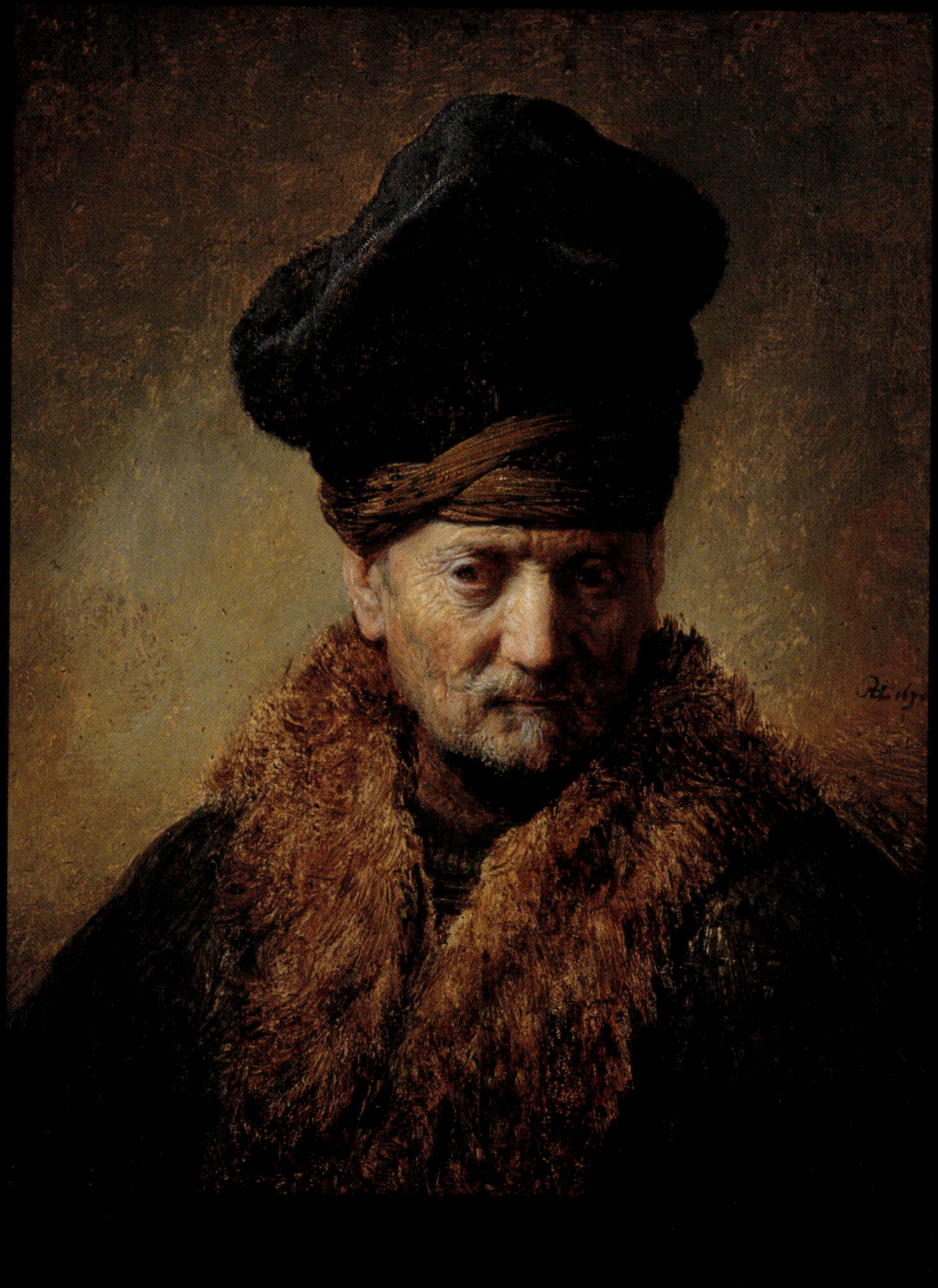

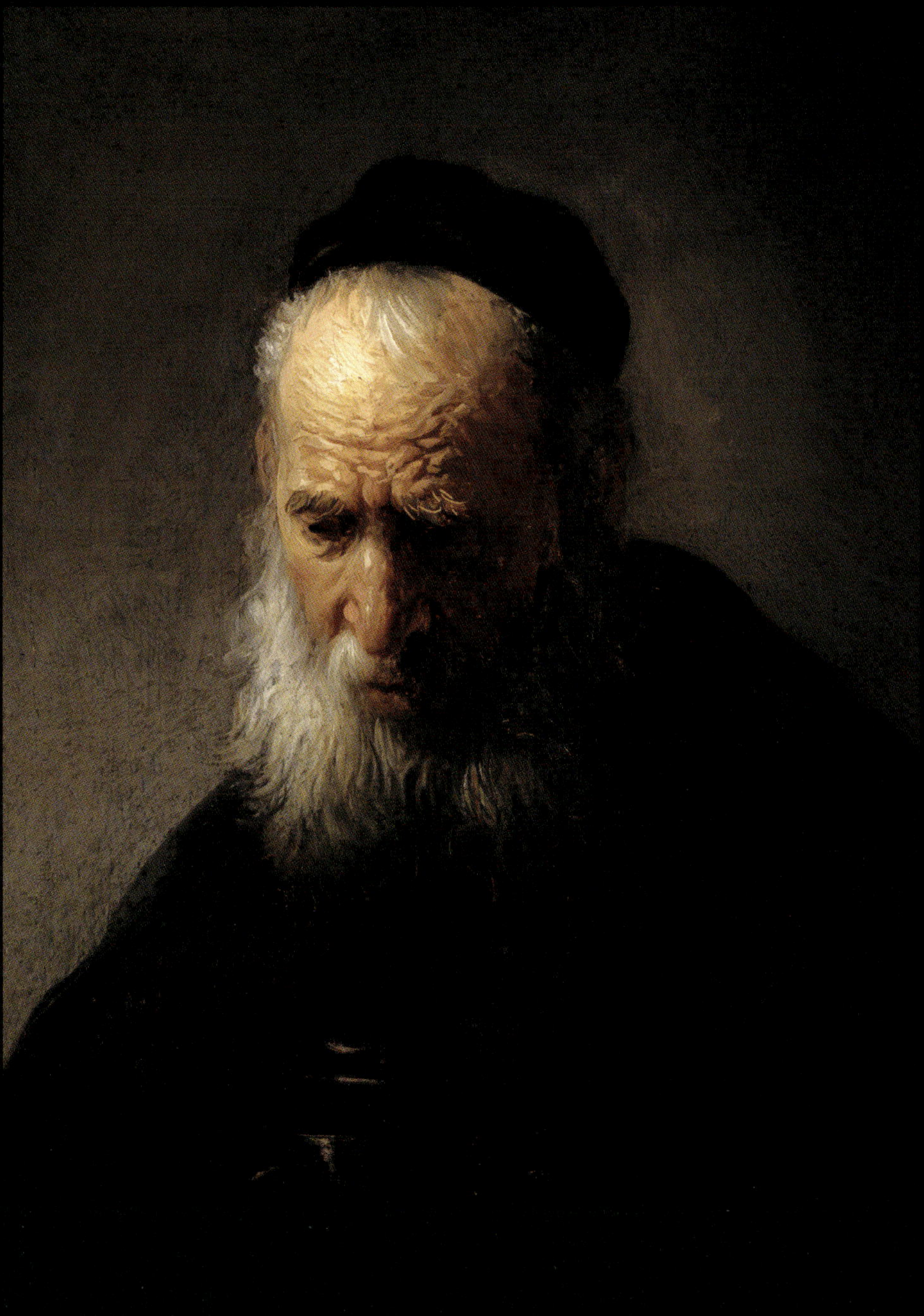

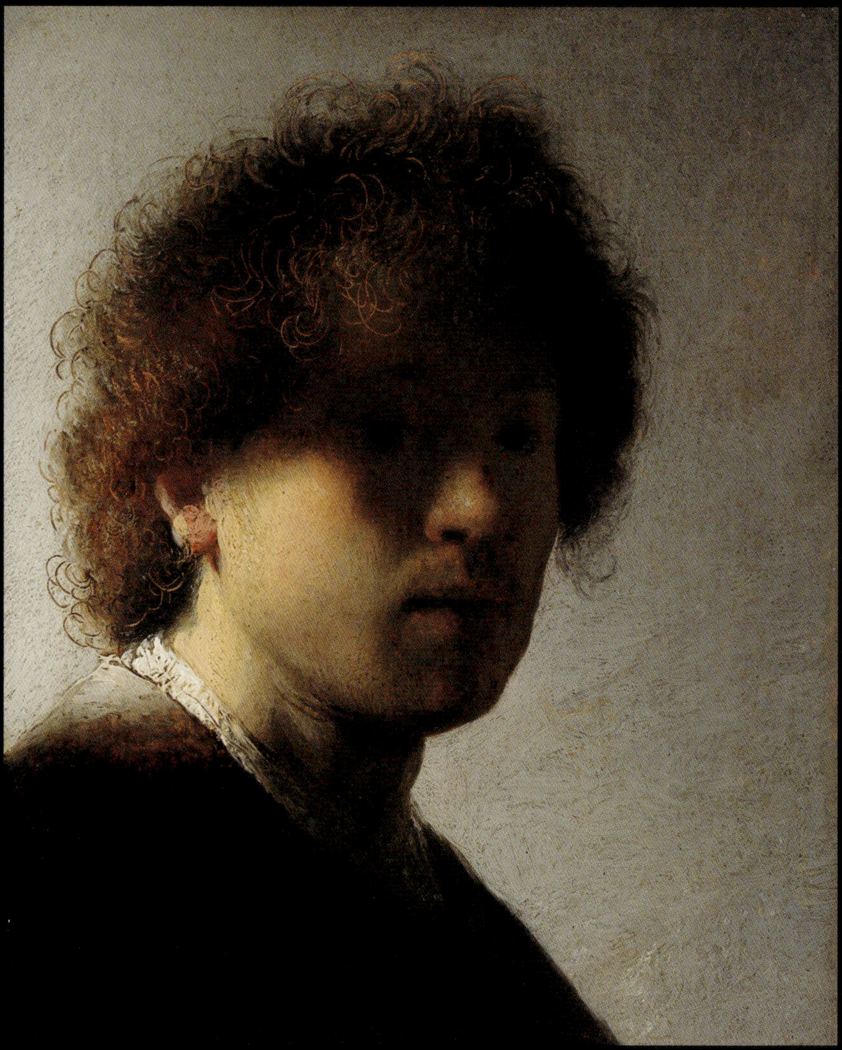

Self-Portrait with a Shaded Face, *c.* 1628
Oil on panel, 22.6 × 18.7 cm (8 ¾ × 7 ⅜ in.)
Amsterdam, Rijksmuseum

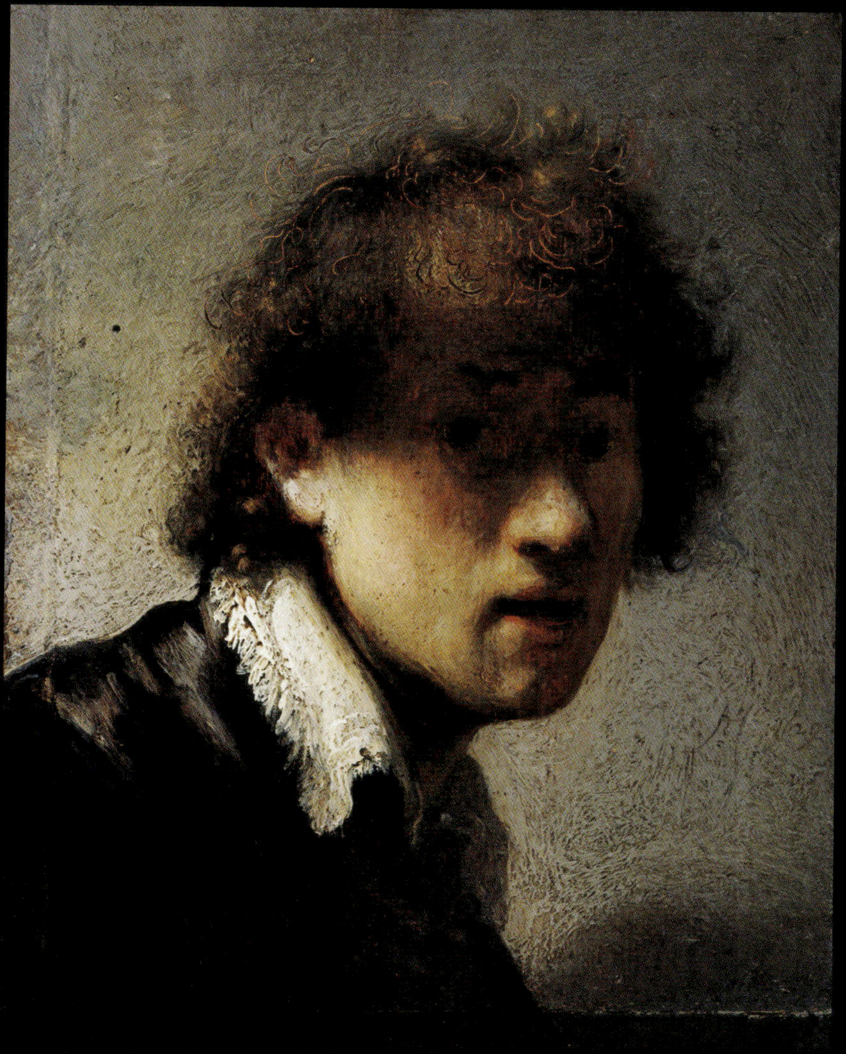

Self-Portrait, 1629
Oil on panel, 15.5 × 12.7 cm (6 1/8 × 5 in.)
Munich, Bayerische Staatsgemäldesammlungen, Alte Pinakothek

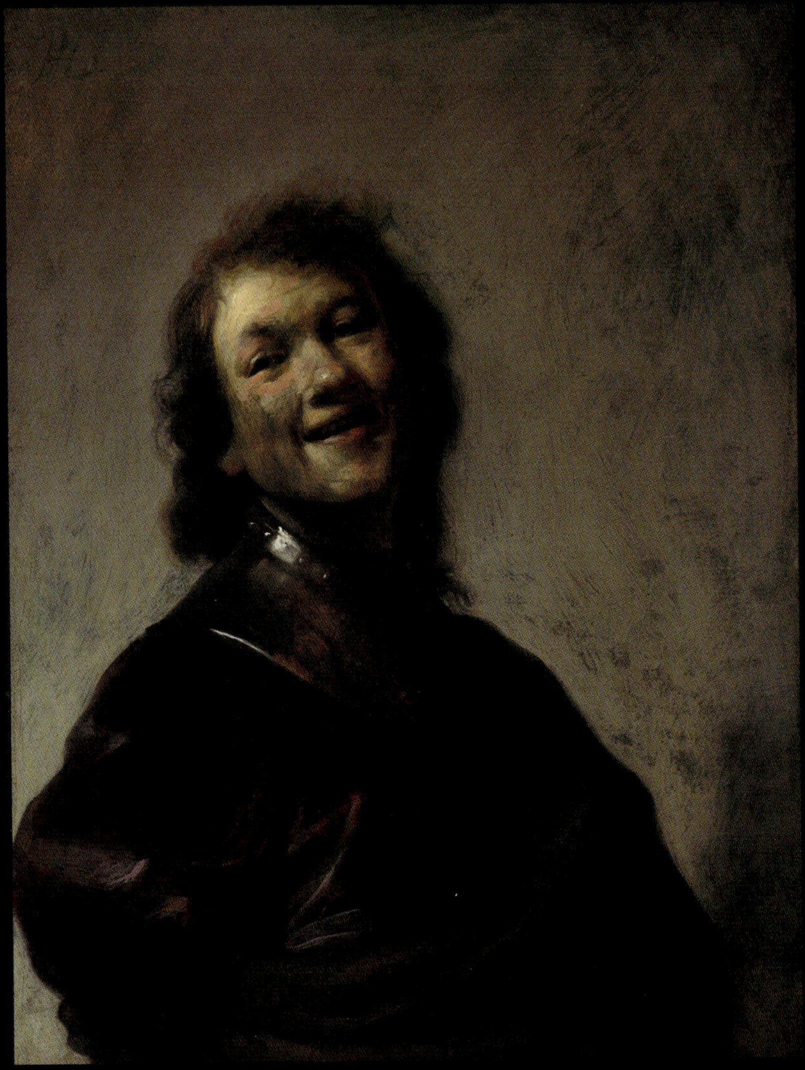

Self-Portrait as a Laughing Soldier, *c.* 1628
Oil on copper, 22.2 × 17.1 cm (8 ¾ × 6 ¾ in.)
Los Angeles, The J. Paul Getty Museum

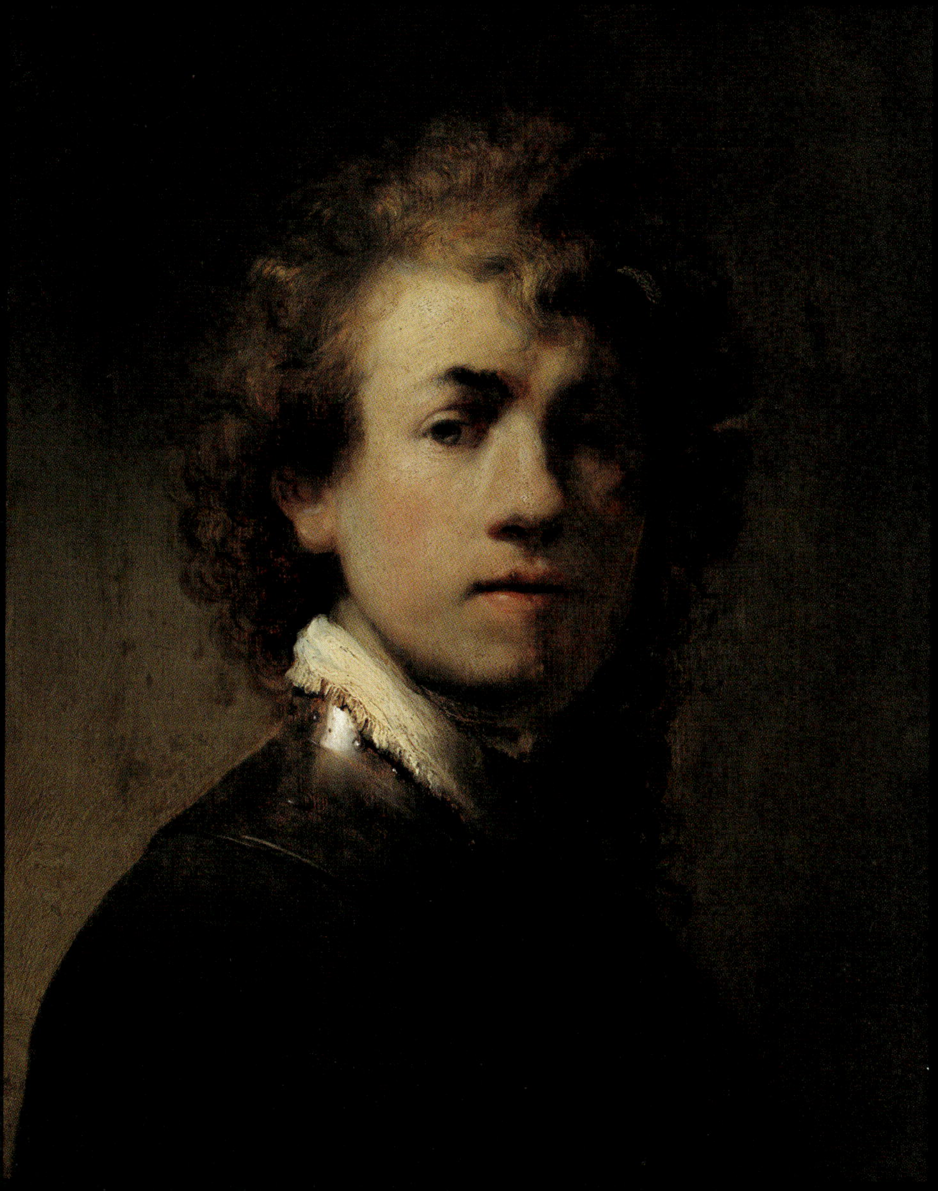

Self-Portrait with a Gorget, *c.* 1629
Oil on panel, 38.2 × 31 cm (15 ⅛ × 12 ¼ in.)
Nuremberg, Germanisches Nationalmuseum

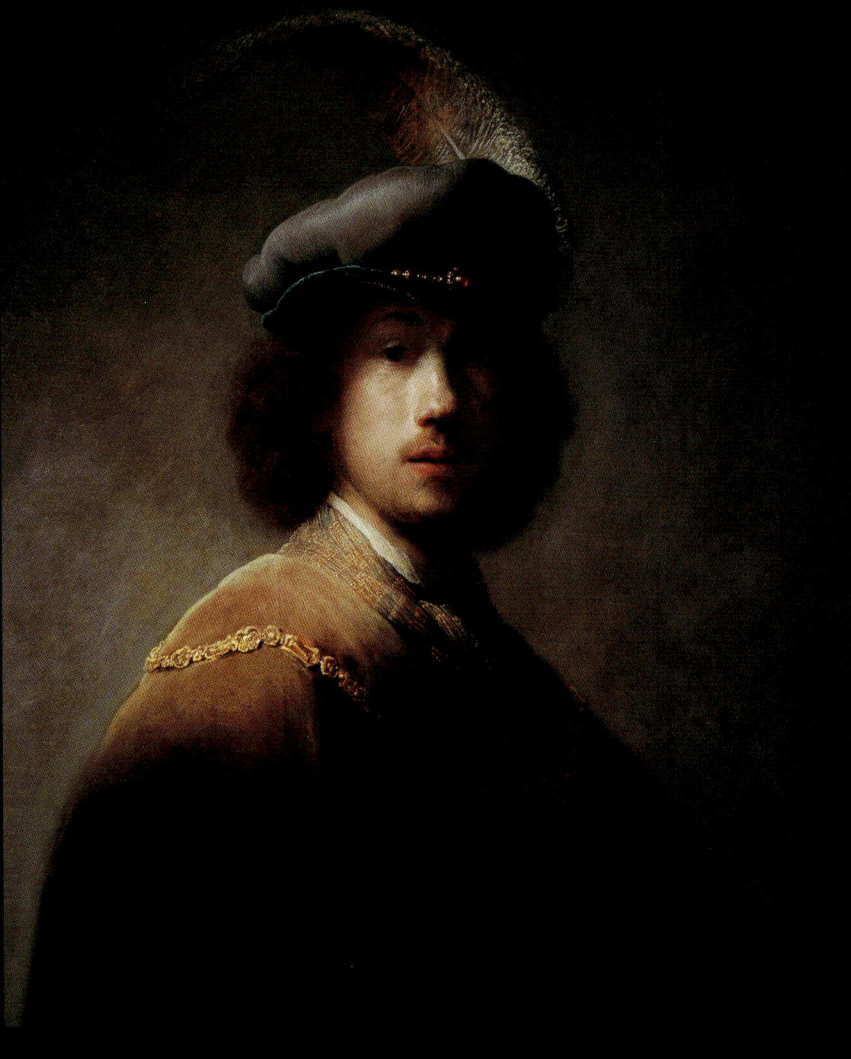

Self-Portrait with a Feathered Cap, 1629
Oil on panel, 89.7 × 73.9 cm (35 ⅓ × 29 ⅛ in.)
Boston, Massachusetts, Isabella Stewart Gardner Museum

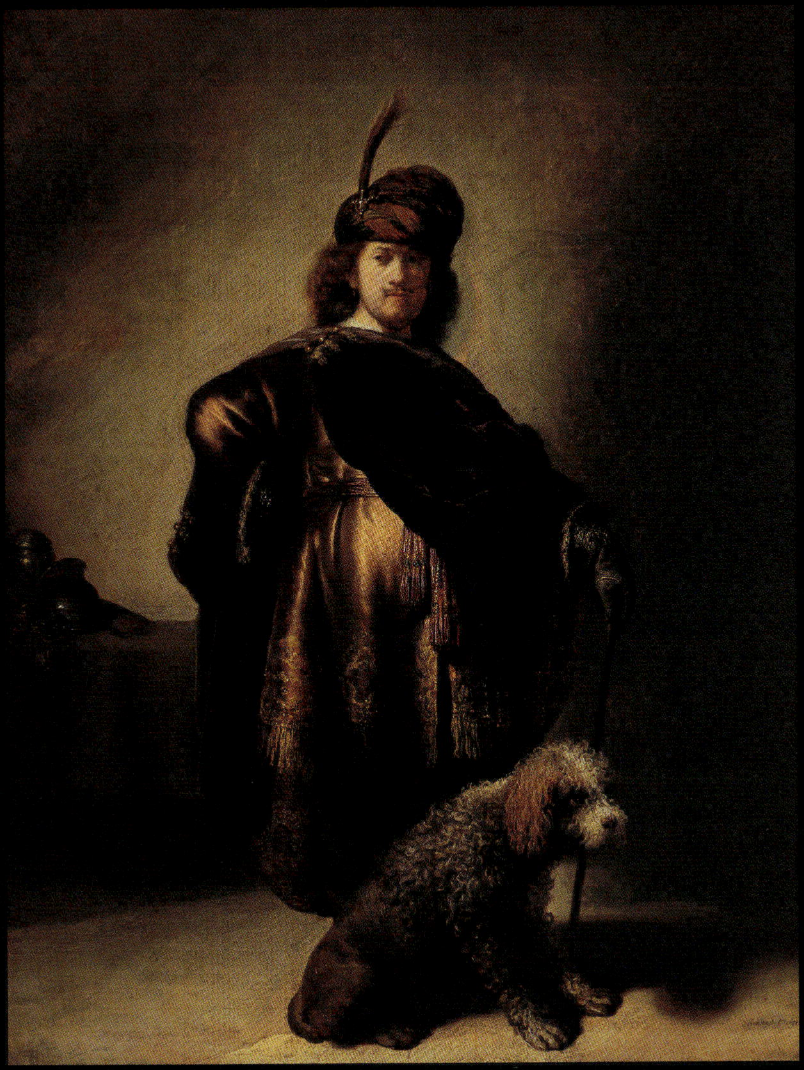

Self-Portrait in Oriental Costume with a Spanish Water Dog, 1631
Oil on panel, 66.5 × 52 cm (26 ⅛ × 20 ½ in.)
Paris, Musée du Petit Palais

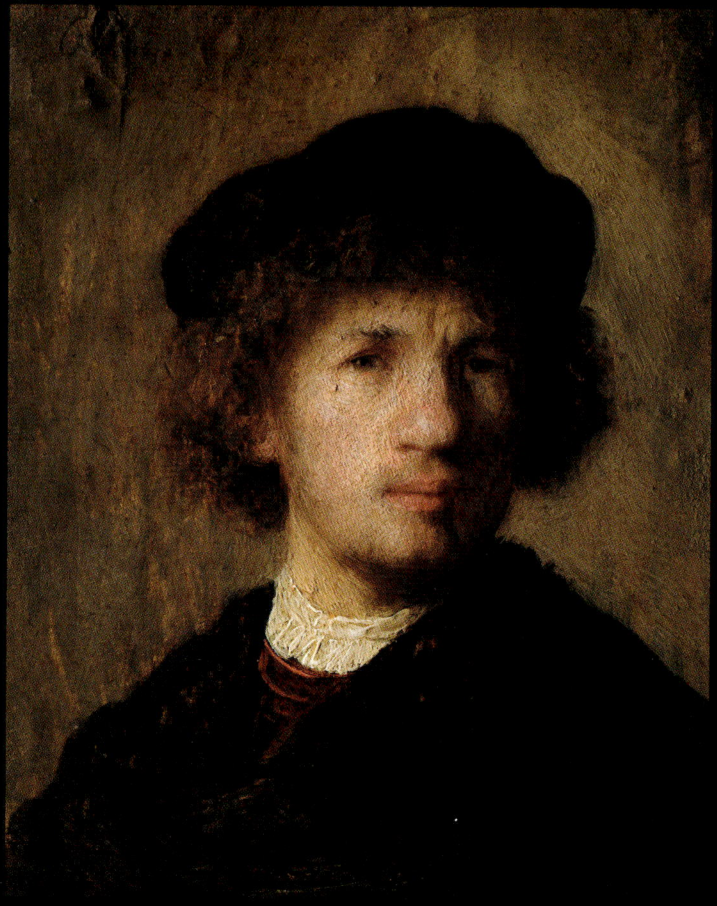

Self-Portrait, 1630
Oil on copper, gilded with gold leaf, 15 × 12.2 cm (5 ¾ × 4 ¾ in.)
Stockholm, Nationalmuseum

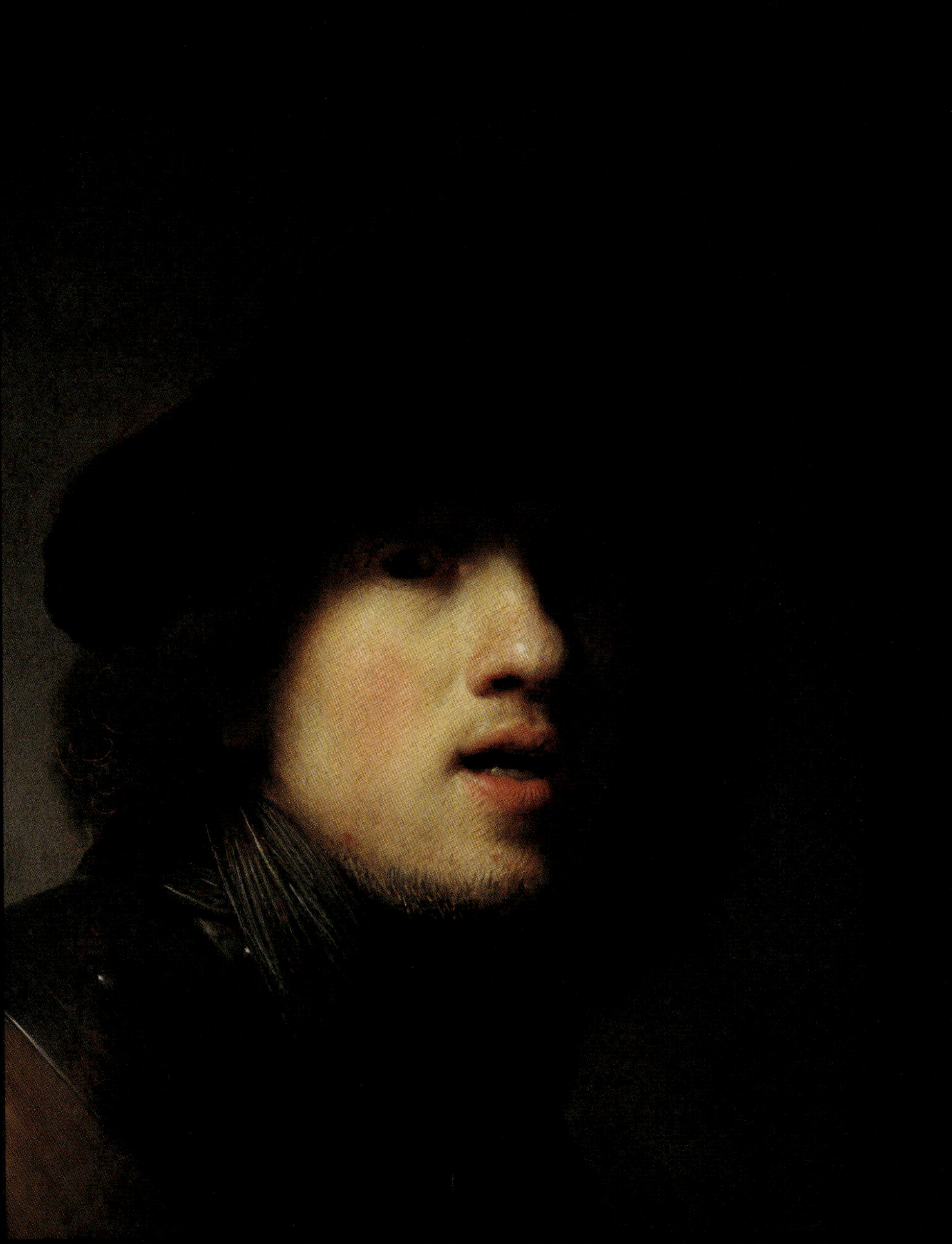

Self-Portrait with an Open Mouth, *c.* 1628
Oil on panel, 42.8 × 33 cm (16 ¾ × 12 ¾ in.)
Indianapolis Museum of Art, Courtesy of the Clowes Fund

II.

Amsterdam

1631–1639

"The mellow brilliancy of his lights, the breadth and harmony of his middle tints, and the rich depth of his shadows, give to his pictures an effect which seems to be the work of enchantment."

DANIEL DAULBY, 1797

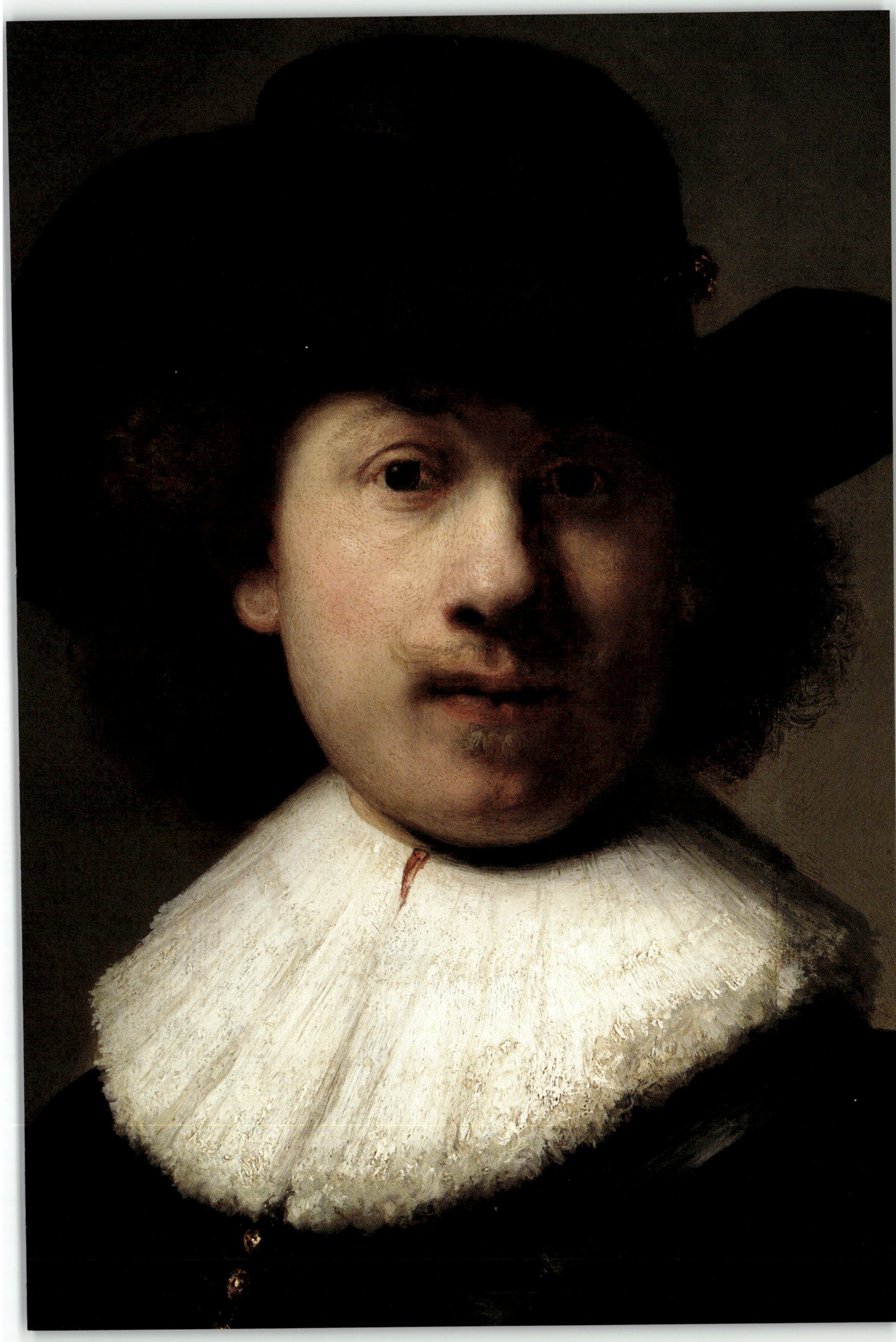

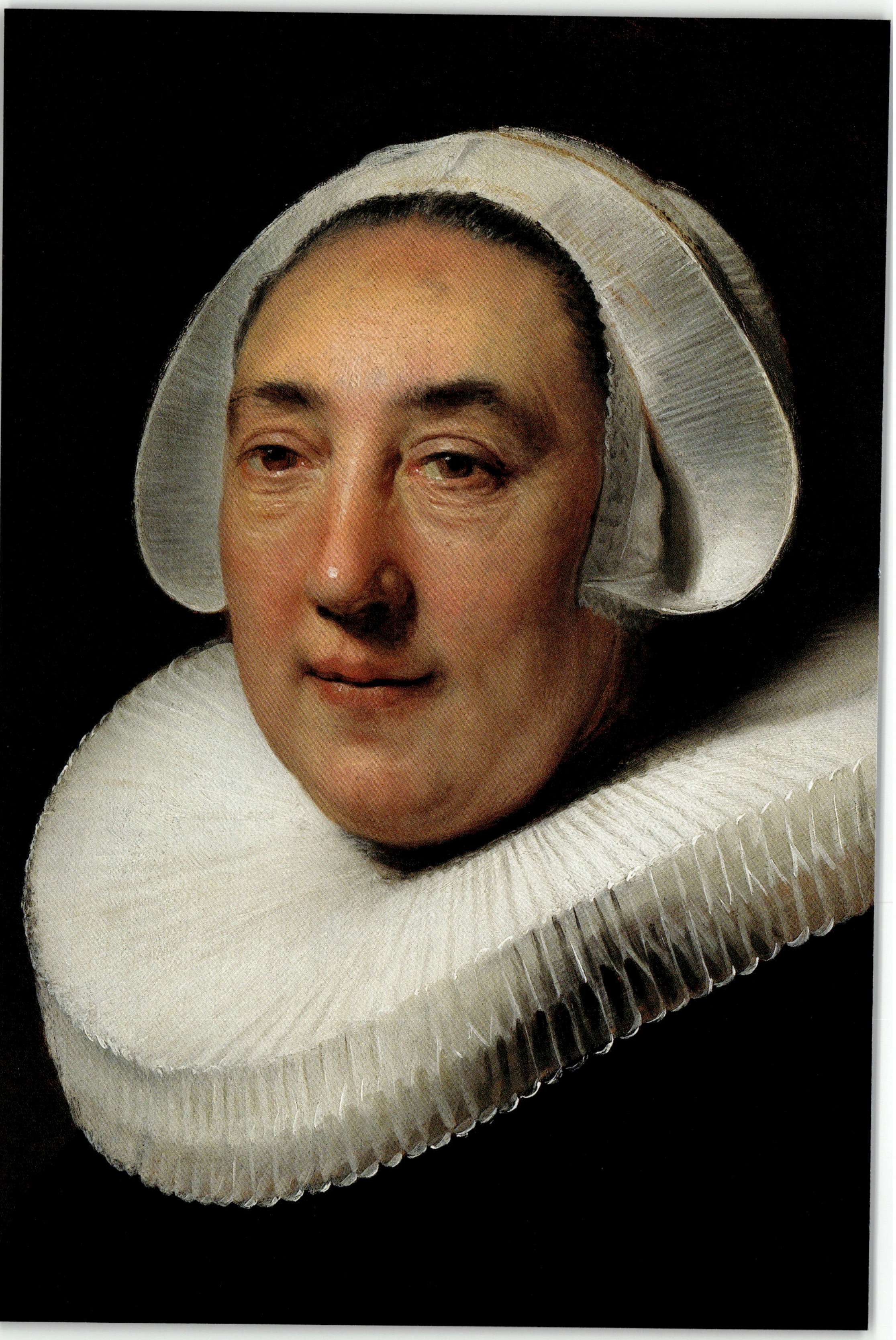

Hendrick Uylenburgh

For Rembrandt, the beginning of the new decade brought fundamental changes in every respect. As the burgomaster of Leiden, Jan Orlers, reports, Rembrandt's paintings became so popular in Amsterdam that he was requested on a number of occasions to "make portraits or other pictures in that city". He therefore decided "in the year 1630 or thereabouts", to exchange the relatively small city of Leiden for the international metropolis of Amsterdam, where he was "overwhelmed with work from all sides" (RD 1641/8).[43] Certainly, on 26 July 1632 a notary found Rembrandt to be living in the house of the art dealer Hendrick Uylenburgh, on the corner of Sint Antoniesbreesstraat in Amsterdam (RD 1632/2). Uylenburgh had settled there in 1625 more or less as a neighbour of Pieter Lastman, under whom Rembrandt served an apprenticeship at the time; it is thus quite possible that the two men already knew each other. Since Rembrandt's move to Amsterdam was probably a gradual process, in 1631 he would have continued to travel regularly back and forth between Leiden and Amsterdam. In any case, in June 1631, when Rembrandt lent the considerable sum of 1,000 guilders to Uylenburgh, he was still "resident in Leiden" (RD 1631/4). It was only three years later, in 1634, that he entered the Amsterdam Guild of St Luke as an independent master artist (RD 1634/10). To achieve this status, it was necessary to have been registered as a citizen *(poorter)* of Amsterdam for at least one year. Until then Rembrandt headed Uylenburgh's workshop.

Uylenburgh was more than 20 years older than Rembrandt. He was a Mennonite and an international art dealer and was running a famous "painting academy" in which young artists worked and also produced copies.[44] Uylenburgh had at his disposal a wide-ranging network of trading contacts in Antwerp, Poland and Leiden from which Rembrandt could benefit. At the time, there was a considerable demand for portraits in Amsterdam, but very few portrait painters.[45] The young and ambitious artist from Leiden took advantage of this opportunity, and the cooperation with the older art dealer, which lasted for over four years, will have been highly profitable for both of them. It is surprising that Rembrandt, who had painted only small-size history paintings and other figure pieces while in Leiden, should suddenly – perhaps at Uylenburgh's suggestion – have applied himself to a genre that was completely new to him, but nonetheless lucrative: the painting of often life-size portraits.

Page 87
Detail of: **Self-Portrait with a Wide-Brimmed Hat**, 1632
(see ill. p. 195)

Detail of: **Portrait of Haesje Jacobsdr. van Cleyburg**, 1634
(see ill. p. 163)

Contemporaries regarded the sheer "conterfeyten naer 't leven" (painting portraits from life) as merely a "sijd-wegh der Consten" (side-road of the arts), an excellent exercise but also a mechanical task which was unworthy of a true history painter.[46] Rembrandt's pupil Samuel van Hoogstraten (1627–1678), however, subdivided the genre into two categories. In the lower category, the portraitist could succeed in copying a face realistically and "imitating eyes, nose and mouth in a skilful manner", but he only achieved the utmost if he was also able to show (as in history paintings) the "reedewikkingen of menschelijke zielen" (considerations or human souls) of his sitters.[47] Statements by Rembrandt's contemporaries indicate that he was not always successful in recording a good likeness. Constantijn Huygens, for example, wrote a series of mocking verses in 1633 about the fact that Rembrandt's portrait scarcely resembled his friend Jacques de Gheyn III (1596–1641; p. 171, Cat. 181; RD 1633/1); and in 1654 Rembrandt was involved in a dispute with a client because of a similar complaint (RD 1654/4). However, in the second aspect, the rendition of the "reedewikkingen of menschelijke zielen" (what we would describe today as psychological insight) of his sitters, Rembrandt is still regarded as unsurpassed.

Portraits 1631–1635

Rembrandt's first portrait, the likeness of the Amsterdam merchant Nicolaes Ruts (1573–1638) from 1631 (p. 132, Cat. 176), was a masterpiece which gave no indication that it was the work of a painter who had never painted a portrait before. The 58-year-old fur merchant is shown at half-length looking directly at the viewer with a penetrating gaze. He seems to direct himself to the viewer to hand over a letter. His other hand is resting on the back of a chair which functions as a sort of barrier in the foreground. Through the simple outline the figure stands out darkly against the partly illuminated background. These are visual devices which Rembrandt used not only to suggest more depth but also to give the illusion of direct interaction with the sitter. Through the active pose, the gaze and the dramatic lighting, the sitter shows a sort of liveliness and a "presence" which is typical of Rembrandt's portraits. The artist took great pains to render the texture of the different materials as convincingly as possible, for example the crisply starched white ruff and the fluffy hairs of the fur.

Nicolaes Ruts was a Remonstrant, but had a Mennonite background. Despite their common principle of defencelessness and pacifism, the Mennonite movement was constantly divided into various factions and splinter groups. Hendrick Uylenburgh belonged to the more liberal *Waterland* faction and received financial support on repeated occasions from the tightly-knit circle of his fellow brethren.[48] Some of Rembrandt's portrait commissions also seem to have come from this Mennonite connection. In January

1632, for example, he completed the portrait of the Mennonite merchant Marten Looten (1586–1649; p. 133, Cat. 178), who in the year in which Rembrandt painted him, converted from the dogmatic "Oude Vlamingen" (Old Flemings) to the somewhat more moderate "Jonge Vlamingen" (Young Flemings).[49] His austere clothing was an expression of the Mennonite principle of "world avoidance" and rejection of worldly pomp. Looten's right hand is placed on his heart, a gesture which expresses his piety. This gesture can also be seen in Rembrandt's portraits of clergymen (p. 134, Cat. 243; p. 159, Cat. 184), albeit with the left hand.[50] In a novel published at a later date, sanctimonious proselytes are mocked, who always "walk with their right hand on their heart", since "it seems not to be godliness, but rather foolishness, that people are to be forbidden merriment and laughing through melancholy gestures of this kind".[51] Looten's plain appearance and pious gesture do not betray his immense wealth; only the knowledge that a portrait painted by Rembrandt like this one was a valuable luxury object which not everyone could afford, gives an indication of his position.

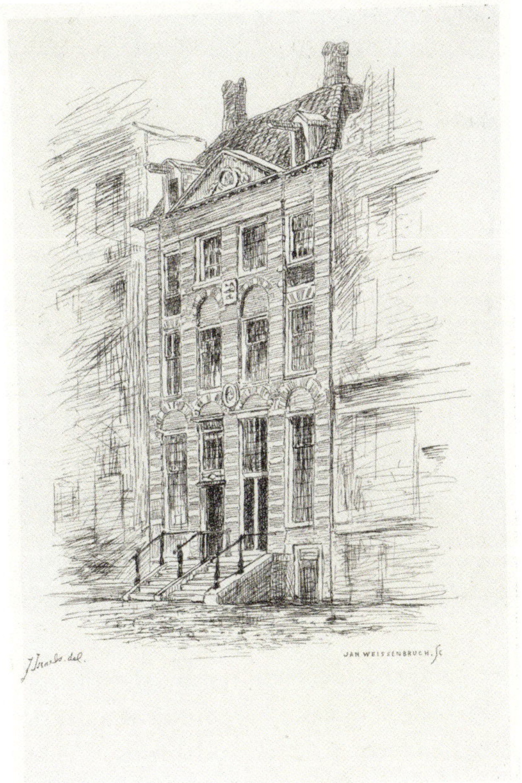

Portraits as lively as these, with their strong emphasis on the physical presence of the sitter, were something totally new and must have deeply impressed the Amsterdam public. Before long, the newcomer, who had proved that he was able to work on a large scale, received an important commission: he was to paint the group portrait of the Amsterdam surgeons. In *The Anatomy Lesson of Dr Nicolaes Tulp* (pp. 136/137, Cat. 261) from 1632, the surgeons are sitting and standing around the dissecting table

Jan Weissenbruch after Jozef Israëls, **Rembrandt's House**, 1837–1880
Etching, 21.1 × 13.6 cm (8 3/8 × 5 3/8 in.). Amsterdam, Rijksmuseum

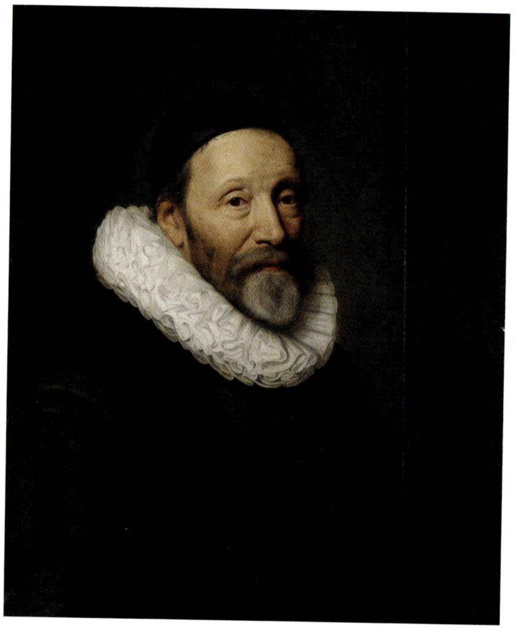

with the corpse. Nicolaes Tulp (1593–1674) is holding up a bunch of arm muscles and tendons with a pair of forceps; his other hand is raised in a lecturing gesture. For Rembrandt, trained in the composition of history paintings with many figures, the painting of this group portrait must have presented a particular challenge. The knowledge that this picture was to be hung in the guild chamber amongst the works by other artists must have challenged the ambition of the young artist even more. Such group portraits were generally rather stiff compositions, nothing more than a row of individual portraits; that will doubtless have spurred Rembrandt to make sure the comparison worked in his favour. What was completely new about his portrait was that he did not show the surgeons posing, but presented them as active participants in the action. Arranged in three rows, they lean forward interestedly to hear Dr Tulp's explanations. The dramatic lighting shifts the focus onto the pale corpse and is reflected in the faces of the surgeons and the *praelector* as they lean forward. The illusion of three-dimensionality is heightened to the extreme in the illuminated faces in the foreground. By comparison, the ruffs and faces of the surgeons at the back are painted in less detail and in a shade of bluish-grey. Here Rembrandt uses the principle of atmospheric perspective, whereby things that are further away look more blurred and acquire a bluish tinge. Rembrandt's pupil Samuel van Hoogstraten would later describe this principle as the *"dikte van de locht, een zacht verblaeuwen"* (density of the air, a gradually increasing shade of blue).[52] Landscape painters had long followed this principle, but Rembrandt was the first to employ it in an interior in order to create an illusion of great depth (which in reality was not present) in his composition.[53]

The clientele of Uylenburgh and Rembrandt was very diverse. It included wealthy merchants and craftsmen, as well as poets and also clergymen from a variety of denomin-

Workshop of Michiel Jansz. van Mierevelt, **Portrait of Johannes Wtenbogaert**, 1632
Oil on panel, 69.6 × 58.6 cm (27 ½ × 23 in.). Amsterdam, Rijksmuseum

ations. During the first half of the 1630s, Rembrandt was the most sought-after and productive portrait painter in Amsterdam. From 1631 until 1635, he painted almost 50 portraits, in other words an average of one portrait per month. Yet, there is no sign of any mechanical repetition; instead, he kept searching for new pictorial solutions in his pursuit of greater plasticity, liveliness and the impression of depth. There are also clear differences in the execution and in the degree of detail. Some portraits Rembrandt painted thinly and smoothly (p. 142 and 143, Cat. 223 and 224), while in others he used a more fluent, loose painting style (p. 164, Cat. 213), which contributes greatly to the remarkably lively appearance of the paintings.

In Rembrandt's early portraits, it is not only the way the paint is applied that is remarkably lively; so, too, is the pose of his sitters. They often look as if they have been interrupted during some activity, as in the early *Portrait of a Man Writing at His Desk* from 1631 (p. 141, Cat. 177), in which the man is looking up from his writing. In some likenesses, Rembrandt simply captures a fleeting moment, as in *Portrait of a Man Trimming a Quill* from 1632 (p. 142, Cat. 223) and that of his young wife (p. 117, Cat. 224), getting up from her chair. This dramatic effect acquires an almost anecdotal character in *Double Portrait of the Shipbuilder Jan Rijcksen and His Wife Griet Jans* from 1633 (pp. 144/145, Cat. 263), where the excited Griet Jans storms into the room with a letter for Jan Rijcksen (*c.* 1561–1637), who looks up in mild consternation from his construction drawings. Her arm, extended sideways, enhances the dramatic effect. In many companion pieces, Rembrandt suggests interaction between the husband and wife, whereby the man extends his hand sideways towards his wife in a gesture of introduction. In contrast to the dynamic man, the woman is often shown frontally and more balanced, with closed contours. This contrast between the active man and his passive counterpart can also be observed in the intriguing unknown couple whose portraits Rembrandt painted in 1633 (pp. 148 and 149, Cat. 233, 234). Here the man is just rising from a chair and gestures by way of introduction towards his wife, seated with her legs straddled. In order to create depth, Rembrandt painted her face unusually thin – almost diffuse – while her clothing has been recorded with all the latest fashionable details. Both sitters are dressed in the latest French fashion, with an exquisite Flemish lace collar and cuffs. In the woman's portrait in particular, the folds of the skirt, the overlapping layers of the collar and the slightly curled edge of the cuff give an impression of three-dimensionality.

The portraits of Marten Soolmans (1613–1641) and Oopjen Coppit (1611–1689; pp. 154 and 155, Cat. 241 and 242) from 1634, which measure more than two metres high, resemble those of the unknown couple in many respects. In the case of these young sitters, too, the fashionable details of their clothing seem to be more important than their faces. Marten, who is lavishly dressed, is also extending his hand as he presents his wife. She is lifting her skirt slightly as she takes a small step towards him. These life-size, full-length companion pieces are the only wedding portraits which Rembrandt ever painted in this aristocratic format.[54] Oopjen and Marten married on 28 June 1633, and because the young couple is shown in summer dress (in light silk with a fan and sun veil), they must have posed for Rembrandt during this same summer. Marten's portrait is dated 1634, an indication that this pair of portraits was completed only during the year following their marriage.[55] In view of the large number of portraits that Rembrandt was working on during that year, it is not surprising that it took him more than six months to finish such monumental works. This procedure was confirmed by Houbraken, Rembrandt's biographer: "For a number of years in succession his painting kept him so occupied that the people had to wait a long time for their works, regardless of the fact that he was working so rapidly."[56] We know from documents that Rembrandt sometimes began a painting and then left it standing for some time before finishing it (RD 1639/1, 1662/11, 1665/17).

In 1633 Rembrandt had the honour of receiving a commission to paint a life-size portrait of the famous minister Johannes Wtenbogaert (1557–1644; p. 92; p. 159, Cat. 184). Wtenbogaert was one of the most important and controversial religious leaders of the Dutch Golden Age. As the head of the liberal Remonstrant Brotherhood, he was an advocate of religious tolerance. His followers revered him almost as a saint, and it was one of Wtenbogaert's Amsterdam supporters who commissioned Rembrandt to paint the portrait.[57] The theologian, who was 76 years old at the time, is shown standing by a table on which his hat and an open manuscript are lying. The light falls on his ruff and his wrinkled skin, both of which have been worked out in great detail. The crisply starched ruff contrasts with the soft grey and brown hairs of Wtenbogaert's beard and the fluffy fur. The hands and the manuscript on the table, by contrast, are painted more diffusely. The black cloak and the closed contours ensure that the figure stands out like a dark block against of the illuminated background. These artistic devices are intended to focus our attention entirely on the sitter's face and his penetrating gaze. Compared with the portrait of Wtenbogaert (p. 92) from the workshop of Michiel Jansz. van Mierevelt's (1567–1641) it is noticeable above all that there are few similarities between the two likenesses. In van Mierevelt's portrait, the great strength of mind and character which are evident in Rembrandt's portrait are missing, and van Mierevelt shows the elderly theologian rather as a tired-looking man. van Mierevelt, however, had an excellent reputation

Detail of: **Portrait of Johannes Wtenbogaert**, 1633
(see ill. p. 159)

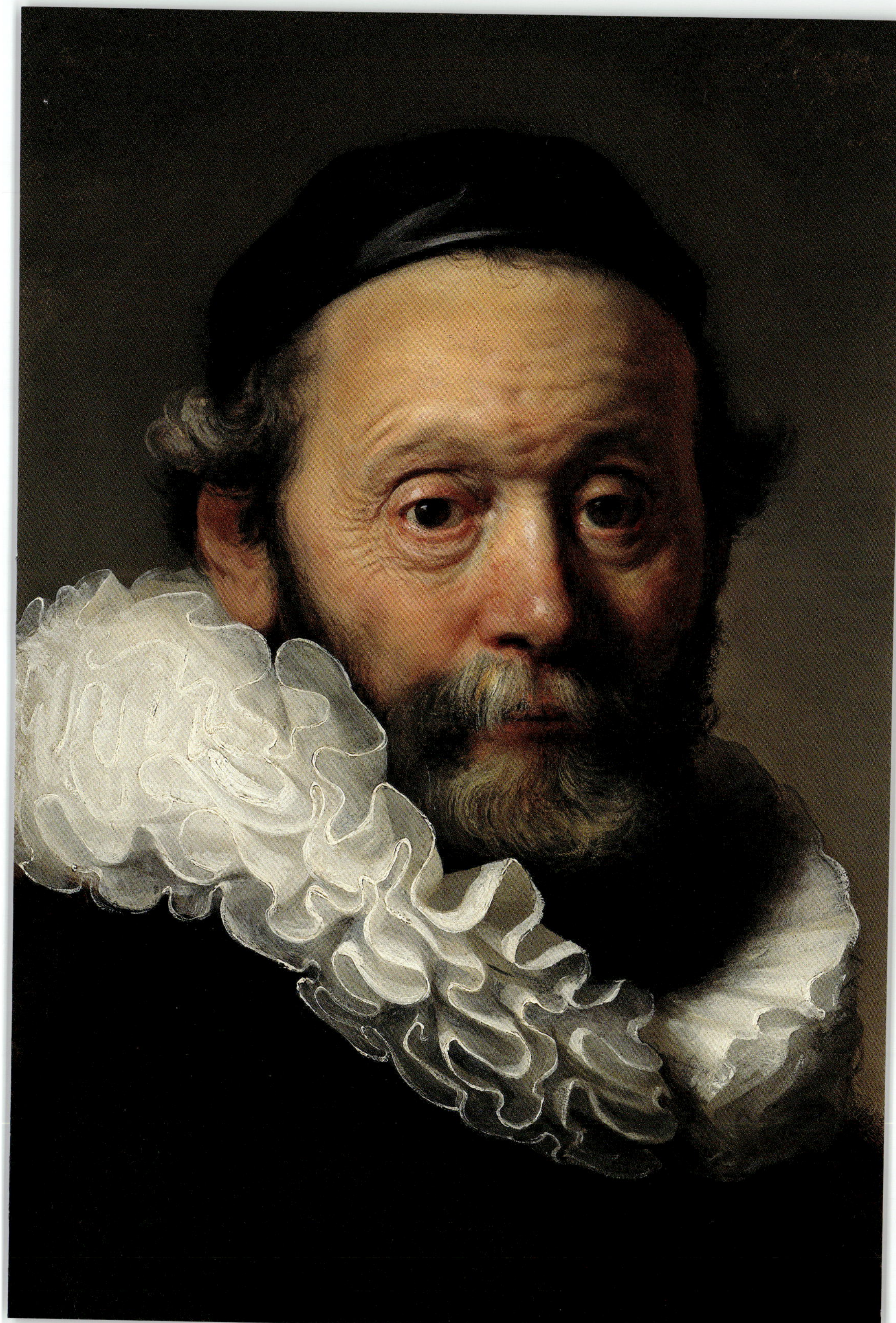

with regard to the likeness of his portraits, while this seems not to have been Rembrandt's forte. Possibly the expression of character which Rembrandt achieved in his portraits was at the expense of physical likeness.

On 13 April 1633, the elderly theologian noted in his diary that he had been "painted by Rembrandt" on that day (RD 1633/2). He makes no mention of further sittings, which seems to indicate that Rembrandt may have completed the portrait on the basis of a single session. He probably painted (or drew) only the face on that occasion. He could have worked out the fur cloak and the pose with the help of a lay figure in his workshop. The hands differ stylistically from the rest of the painting to such an extent that they were probably the work of one of the assistants in his workshop. At that time, it was not unusual – also in other workshops – for assistants to participate in the execution of portraits. The great demand for portraits by Rembrandt will have resulted in his workshop assistants taking over various parts of his portrait production (see, for example, Cat. 222*, 245*, 246*).

In addition to these large, expensive portraits, Rembrandt especially painted smaller bust portraits, in the oval format fashionable at the time, which would have been less expensive. The faces are often painted with remarkable expressiveness, as in the bust portrait of an unknown 40-year-old man (p. 160, Cat. 182). The wrinkles, recorded in detail, underline his ironic gaze and give the gently smiling man an expressive air which betrays Rembrandt's extensive experience in painting character heads *(tronies)*. The detailed execution, the expressiveness and the way the man has been placed in the picture plane make this likeness very comparable to the *Portrait of a 62-Year-Old Woman* (p. 161, Cat. 211). Both are wearing similarly plain, somewhat old-fashioned clothing; both panels have the same measurements and are both dated 1632. The *Portrait of a 62-Year-Old Woman* is generally identified as a portrait of Aeltje Pietersdr. Uylenburgh (*c.* 1571–1644), who was (approximately) this age.[58] The problem is, however, that the woman's clothing seems too simple, because Aeltje was of a good family and the wife of a prominent Reformed clergyman. If the two portraits are companion pieces, we would have to think of them perhaps as a man and his mother, who was 22 years older.

By comparison, the portraits of the 51-year-old Haesje Jacobsdr. Cleyburg (1583–1642; p. 163, Cat. 238), her husband, the wealthy brewer Dirck Jansz. Pesser (1587–1651; p. 162, Cat. 237), and the latter's 83-year-old mother, Aechje Claesdr. van der Horst (1551–1636; p. 164, Cat. 213), were painted much more rapidly and fluently. In July 1634, shortly after his wedding, Rembrandt travelled to Rotterdam (RD 1634/7) to paint these three portraits. The deeply wrinkled face of the family's matriarch prompted Rembrandt to make use of an extreme form of his summary, open painting style. Portraits like these

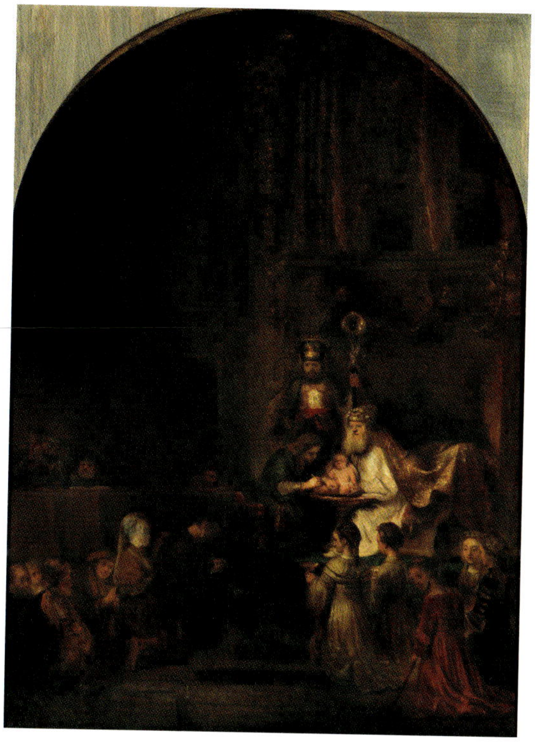

clearly show why Rembrandt was famous as a painter of elderly men and women.

The Pessers were prominent supporters of the Remonstrant Brotherhood, whose leader, Johannes Wtenbogaert, Rembrandt had painted the previous year. Wtenbogaert was a close friend of the widow Pesser and stayed regularly at her house or the homes of her sons and sons-in-law at the Leuvehaven. In 1630, for example, he was invited to the wedding of her daughter, Maria Pesser (1595–1641), to the "second-in-command" of the Remonstrants, Simon Episcopius (1583–1643). It is possible that the unknown 41-year-old man (p. 166, Cat. 235) and his 40-year-old wife (p. 167, Cat. 236), whose portraits Rembrandt painted in 1633 and 1634 respectively, belonged to this same circle of wealthy Rotterdam Remonstrants. Their clothing is not only identical with that of the Pessers, but is also the same as that of other citizens of Rotterdam who belonged to the same circle, such as, for example, Eeuwout Eeuwoutsz. Prins (died 1636) and his wife Catharina de Keyser (1597–1665) in Jan Daemen Cool's (1589–1660) portrait from around 1635 (p. 103). In particular the unusual manner in which the women wore their caps seems to have been typical of this group of Remonstrants in Rotterdam.

Possibly by the end of 1634, Rembrandt was admitted to the Amsterdam Guild of Saint Luke as an independent master painter (RD 1634/10). The fact that the young couple moved into the Nieuwe Doelenstraat in May 1635 meant that Rembrandt could now establish his own workshop. This brought, at least temporarily, an abrupt end to his large production of portraits. The talented and ambitious Mennonite Govert Flinck

Workshop of Rembrandt, **The Circumcision in the Temple**, 1646
Oil on canvas, 97.8 × 72 cm (38 5/8 × 28 3/8 in.)
Braunschweig, Herzog Anton Ulrich-Museum

(1615–1660), one of Uylenburgh's assistants, who had moved from the latter's branch in Leeuwarden to Amsterdam at the beginning of 1634, took over the direction of the portrait workshop in Rembrandt's stead.[59] During the year 1635, only the oval portraits of the East India Company Commander Philips Lucasz. (before 1600–1641; Cat. 245*) and his bride, Petronella Buys (1605–1670; Cat. 246*), appear to have been largely from Rembrandt's hand. Since they set sail for Batavia (present-day Jakarta) on 2 May 1635, the likenesses must have been completed during the first months of the year. The only other portraits signed and dated by Rembrandt in 1635 (Cat. 247*, 248*) were largely the work of one of Uylenburgh's workshop assistants.

Commissions from The Hague

Even before he finally moved to Amsterdam, Rembrandt clearly had good contacts with the court of the stadtholder, Prince Frederik Hendrik. According to an inventory, in 1632 the prince already owned four of Rembrandt's small-figure history paintings of the kind that his secretary Constantijn Huygens had praised so effusively: *Samson and Delilah*

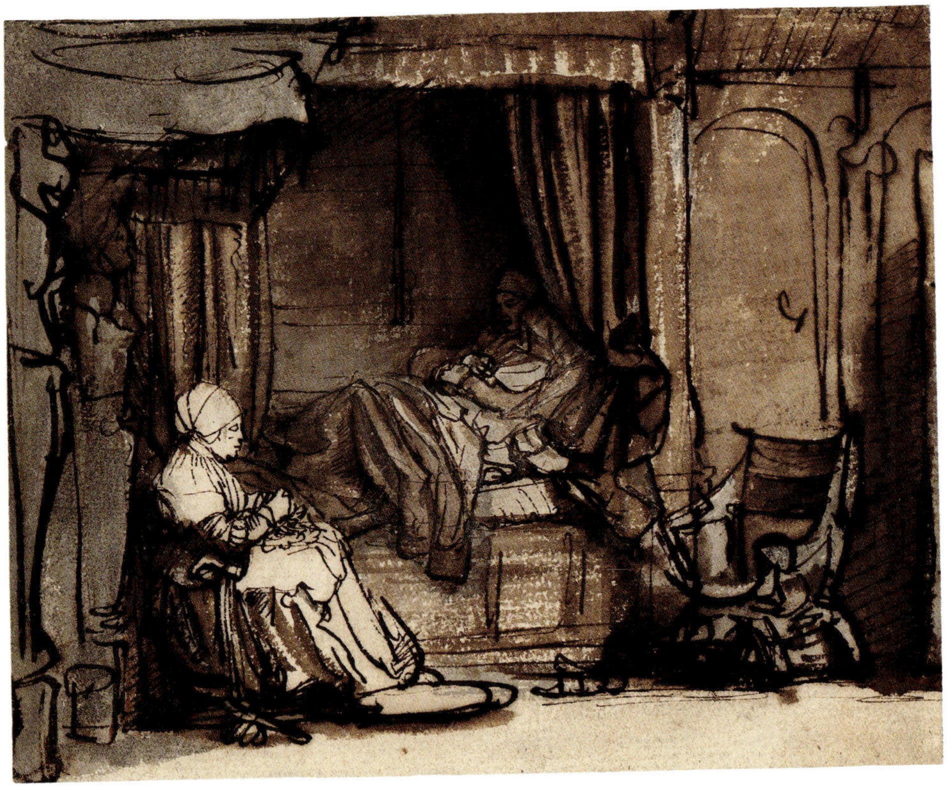

from 1628 (p. 62, Cat. 5), *Minerva in Her Study* (p. 213, Cat. 95), *The Rape of Proserpina* (p. 210, Cat. 96), and *Simeon's Song of Praise* (p. 207, Cat. 44). The last three had been painted around 1631. During the following year, Rembrandt travelled to the stadtholder's court in The Hague in order to paint the Prince's wife. This *Portrait of Amalia of Solms* (p. 169, Cat. 210) is quite unusual in Rembrandt's oeuvre because of its painted scrollwork frame and the sitter's pose in profile. These characteristics were probably linked to the specific terms of the commission: the portrait had to match a profile portrait of Frederik Hendrik with the same measurements and scrollwork frame by the court painter Gerard van Honthorst of 1631 (p. 168).[60] Even if we allow for the fact that Rembrandt's portrait has suffered from wear and is now only a pale shadow of its original condition, the sitter makes a somewhat graceless impression. She bears little resemblance to Amalia of Solms (1602–1675) as we know her from portraits by other artists, especially in comparison with the much more flattering likeness by Anthony van Dyck (1599–1641) from the same year.[61] The two companion pieces were never hung side by side in the apartments of the princess; in later years, a much more elegant profile portrait of Amalia painted by van Honthorst (p. 168) took the place of Rembrandt's portrait as the companion piece of the portrait of Frederik Hendrik.

This does not necessarily mean that his patrons did not like Rembrandt's paintings anymore. During the following year, 1633, Rembrandt delivered two history paintings to the court: a *Raising of the Cross* (p. 183, Cat. 49) and *The Descent from the Cross* (p. 185, Cat. 50). It is not clear whether these works were commissioned or purchased from Rembrandt's stock of pictures. The latter seems feasible, at least for *The Descent from the Cross*, which is painted on panel and was probably already finished somewhat earlier (possibly as early as 1631). *The Descent from the Cross*, which is almost one metre high, was quite clearly an ambitious work. Rembrandt created a large-scale etching after it in 1633 (Cat. E27 and E28) that was published by Uylenburgh. The format of the panel, an upright format rectangle with an arched top, was also unusual. The format had been popular in the Netherlands around 1500 in particular and was only used occasionally in Rembrandt's time, predominantly for religious works.

The composition of *The Descent from the Cross* was clearly a response to Rubens' famous Antwerp altarpiece with the same subject (p. 184). It no doubt appealed to both Huygens' taste and that of the prince, who were both great admirers of the Flemish master. Well-thought-out details express the suffering even more poignantly in Rembrandt's

Interior with Saskia in Bed and a Woman Doing Needlework, *c.* 1641
Pen and brown ink, brushwork in brown and grey, some red and black chalk, 14.2 × 17.7 cm (5 ⅝ × 7 in.). Paris, Fondation Custodia, Collection Frits Lugt

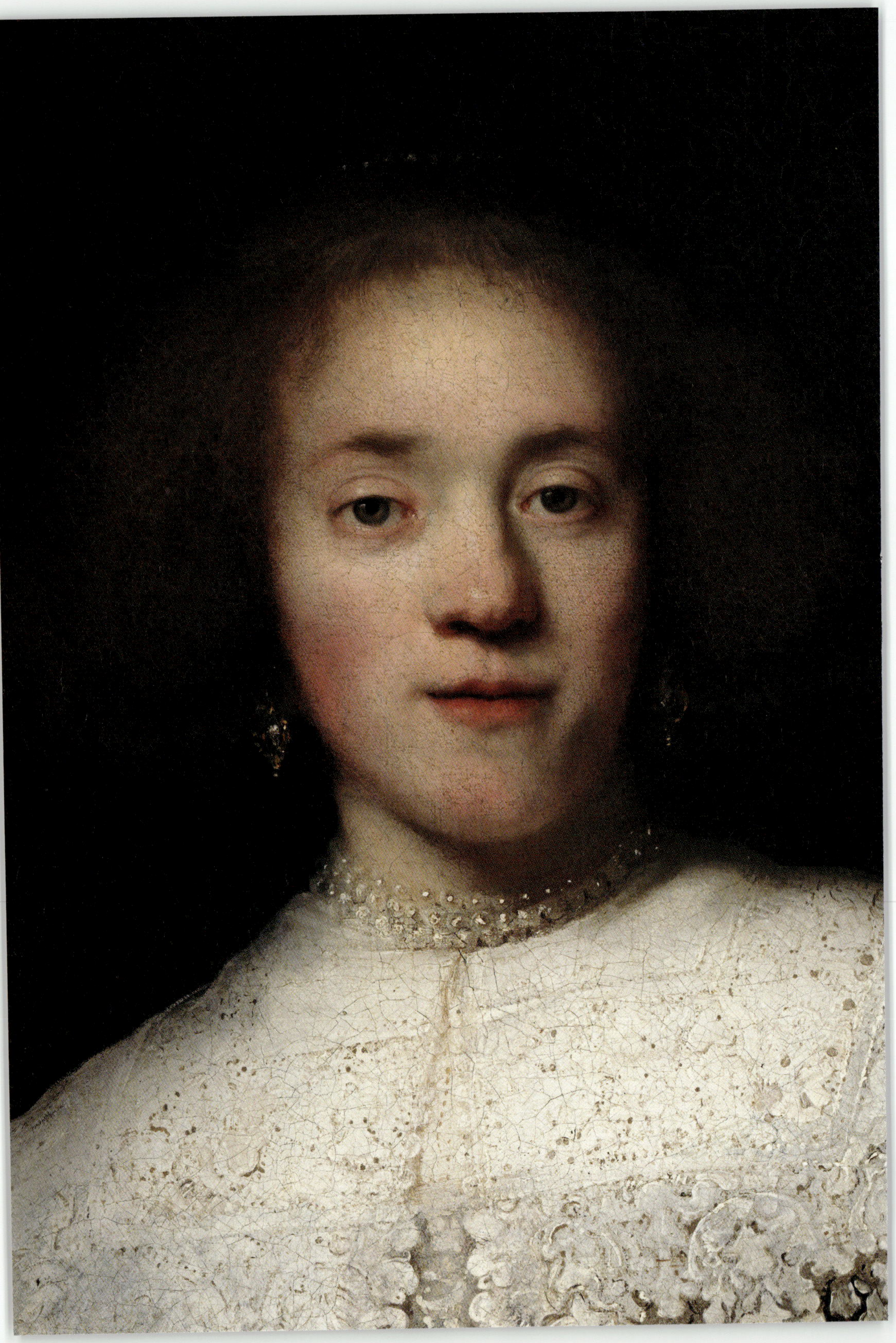

much smaller version. In the Rubens painting, the lifeless body of Christ is still suspended with a degree of grace, but in Rembrandt's version he is bereft of all worldly glory: his emaciated body is broken, his belly swollen. Another haunting detail forms the empty Cross with its large bloodstains recalling Christ's wounds. Perhaps more strongly than Rubens' Baroque pathos, these painfully realistic, carefully considered details arouse in the viewer a deep empathy with the suffering of Christ.[62] Rembrandt may have painted the *Raising of the Cross* on canvas in 1633 at the request of the stadtholder as a companion piece. What is remarkable here is that the artist has portrayed himself in the middle of the picture as one of Christ's tormentors who is helping to raise the Cross. Although it is disconcerting that Rembrandt has painted himself in this negative role, the idea can be explained by the Protestant belief that it was the inherent sinfulness of mankind (in other words, also of Rembrandt himself) which led to Christ being crucified.[63] But Rembrandt would also have been well aware that connoisseurs – like Huygens and the stadtholder – would appreciate such recognisable (self-)portraits and would point out details like these to each other.[64]

Sometime before 1636 Rembrandt had the honour of being commissioned to paint three further works which would match the two earlier paintings as regards both format and subject. Seven letters written by Rembrandt to Huygens – the only ones in his own hand that are known today – discuss the further course of the project and give us a rare and fascinating insight into the painter's artistic and commercial thinking. In early 1636 he wrote to Huygens that he was working "diligently" on another three "Passion pieces", which "His Excellency [the Prince] has ordered personally", namely an "Entombment, a Resurrection and an Ascension of Christ"; RD 1636/1). Two of the works were only half-finished, but Rembrandt asked whether the Prince would like to have the *Ascension* (p. 187, Cat. 61), which was already completed, immediately. Apparently, this was the case, because in an undated letter (RD 1636/2) to Huygens, the artist wrote that he was planning to travel to The Hague shortly to see whether his picture would go with the others. His comment is remarkable: "it will be best shown in the gallery of H[is] Exc[e] ll[ency], because the light there is strong." This gallery, which ran along the side of the prince's private apartments, lay on the first floor of the stadtholder's residence.[65] The artist also felt that the work was most certainly worth 200 Flemish pounds (= 1,200 guilders), but he wanted to leave his payment to the Prince's judgement.

The completion of the *Entombment* (p. 189, Cat. 59) and the *Resurrection* (p. 191, Cat. 60), however, took a long time, but on 12 January 1639 (RD 1639/1) Rembrandt

Detail of: **Seated Woman with a Fan**, 1633
(see ill. p. 149)

wrote about the "great pleasure and devotion that I have put into the execution of the two pieces", and that they were now also finished thanks to his *"stuijdiose vlijt"* (studious diligence). Rembrandt claimed that the reason why he had been working on the paintings for so long was that in them "die meeste ende die naetuereelste beweechgelickheijt in geopserveert is" (the greatest and most natural movement has been observed). It is not certain whether he understood the greatest and "most natural movement" of his figures to mean the depiction of emotions or of physical motion – he probably meant both. In the *Resurrection*, the soldiers stagger and fall in all directions in consternation, so that here we can imagine that he was thinking primarily of physical motion.[66] But in the passage referred to, Rembrandt speaks of "these two" paintings, and in the much more restrained *Entombment* the focus lies mainly on the pitiful Marys, moved by grief. After all, it was exactly Rembrandt's skill in convincingly rendering the "liveliness of emotions" in his history paintings that Huygens had admired most. Likewise, Samuel van Hoogstraten writes that the essence of Rembrandt's mastery lay in the portrayal of "de lijdingen des gemoeds" (the inner passions).[67] In contemporary art theory, great importance was attached to the correct portrayal of human emotions such as surprise, joy, fear or grief. Thus the viewer could better empathize with the story, which led to reflection on human behaviour and the (moral) decisions leading to these actions.

We gather from the invoice accompanying the letter that Rembrandt was of the opinion that each of the works was worth (the exorbitant sum of) 1,000 guilders, plus 44 guilders which he had advanced for frames and packaging (RD 1639/3). In a letter of 27 January 1639 which he had dashed off in haste, Rembrandt brazenly urges that payment should be prompt because he could well use the money (RD 1639/4). In February he answered that he was satisfied that the Prince was prepared to pay 600 guilders per picture (RD 1639/5). Rembrandt's sudden pressing need was probably connected to the down payment for the house in Sint Antoniesbreestraat, which he had purchased a few weeks previously. Apparently, he had also sent Huygens another painting as a personal gift. For this (unknown) picture he likewise advised emphatically that it should be hung in "strong light", so that viewed from a distance, "salt best voncken" (it will glow best).

In 1646 the five-part series of the Passion of Christ was extended further by two scenes from the childhood of Christ: *The Adoration of the Shepherds* (p. 188, Cat. 70) and a *Circumcision in the Temple*, for which Rembrandt did in fact receive the amount of 1,200 guilders which he had asked previously (RD 1646/6). The last-mentioned painting was already lost by the end of the seventeenth century and we know it only through a good workshop copy (Corpus V, 10; p. 97).[68] The surviving paintings from this series – often incorrectly described as a "Passion series" – were also treated in a negligent manner

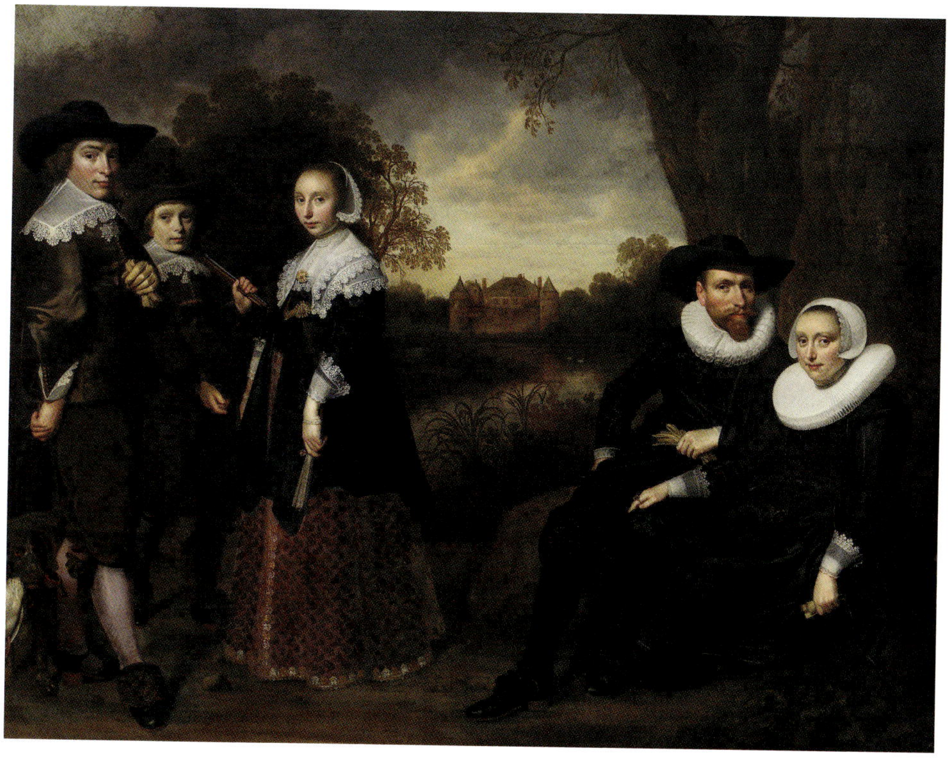

Jan Daemen Cool, **Portrait of Eeuwout Eeuwoutsz. Prins and his Family**, *c.* 1635
Oil on panel, 173 × 222 cm (68 ⅛ × 87 ½ in.). Rotterdam, Het Schielandshuis

in later years. They were damaged during the mid-eighteenth century as a result of an unknown incident, and following repeated vigorous restorations little of Rembrandt's original brushwork can now be detected.

Already during his time in Leiden, Rembrandt had contact with art lovers in The Hague. Houbraken reports that the young Rembrandt walked from Leiden to The Hague to present a painting to a certain gentleman there, and that he was paid 100 guilders for the work.[69] In 1632 he will have spent a considerable amount of time in The Hague for the painting of the portrait of Amalia of Solms. During this time, he also painted at least four further portraits of persons who lived there: the small pendants of Maurits Huygens (p. 170, Cat. 180) and his friend Jacques de Gheyn III (p. 171, Cat. 181), the knee-length *Portrait of Joris de Caullery* (p. 173, Cat. 179) and a likeness of the latter's little son, which has been lost (RD 1661/7). The small friendship portraits of Huygens' elder brother Maurits and his friend Jacques de Gheyn are not companion pieces in the usual sense because they initially did not hang side by side; they were only united after the death of the two friends. De Gheyn, an art lover and engraver, was evidently one of Rembrandt's first clients, because he owned two of the artist's early works, *Two Old Men Disputing, Probably the Apostles Peter and Paul* from 1628 (p. 61, Cat. 37) and *Sleeping Old Man in a Chair (Sloth)* from 1629 (Cat. 122). It was possibly the artist De Gheyn who first drew the attention of the Huygens brothers to the qualities of the young Rembrandt.

If the two large companion pieces (Cat. 225, 226*) from the same year 1632 do in fact show Thomas Brouart (1584–1635) and Johanna van Clootwijck (1584–after 1657), then the two of them must also have sat for Rembrandt in The Hague.[70] As Frederik Hendrik's treasurer, Brouart belonged to the same circle as the Huygens family. Moreover, Brouart was an art lover who according to Huygens owned a *tronie* of an old man by Jan Lievens (already before 1630).[71] Surely, the man's portrait shows a number of formal similarities to the portrait of Joris de Caullery (*c.* 1600–1662/69; p. 173, Cat. 179), who is shown in a confident pose and wearing military dress in his function as "appoincté" (a sort of temporary officer) in the navy of the Dutch States General.[72] De Caullery seems to have possessed a choleric temperament, because in the same year in which Rembrandt painted him he was arrested in Rotterdam after he had stabbed a seaman in the cheek for no reason. The matter was dealt with benevolently by Admiral Philips van Dorp (1587–1652), under whom the accused served, and De Caullery paid a fine in order to avoid prosecution.[73] De Caullery was also the owner of a well-known and elegant inn, "De grote Zwaan" (The Big Swan), opposite the Buitenhof. It is possible that Rembrandt stayed here during his sojourn in The Hague.[74]

The artist placed De Caullery mainly in the shadows, with only a bright beam of light falling onto his shoulder. The shiny gorget and the embroidered baldric are painted in a detailed and pastose manner, while the face is executed smoothly. Rembrandt was experimenting here with a new stylistic device to achieve greater depth. This principle would later be described by his pupil van Hoogstraten as "kenlijkheyt": that things with a rough, "recognisable" surface appear optically closer than things without a recognisable structure, which thus seem to be further away.[75]

Detail of: **Portrait of Nicolaes Ruts**, 1631
(see ill. p. 132)

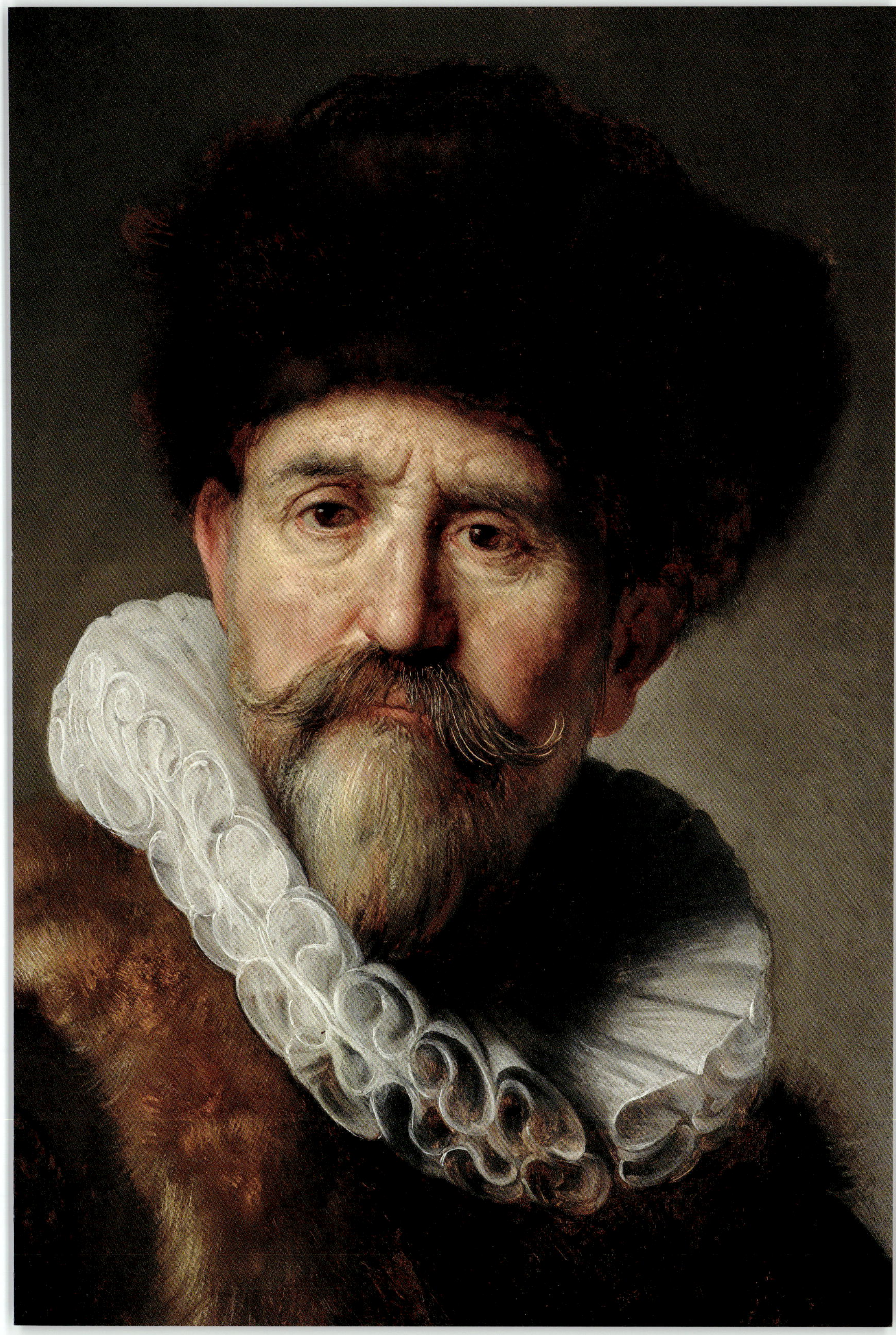

Signatures

The way in which Rembrandt signed his works was the result of an extended process. His very first monogram appears on a work from 1624/25 (p. 73, Cat. 120a). It reads *RHF*, the abbreviation for Rembrant Harmenszoon – as he was known in everyday life – followed by *F* for *fecit* (made it). In 1625, he simply signed his works with the monogram *R.*; the following year he extended it to the initials *RH.*[76] From 1628 on he added an *L*: *RHL*, the *L* standing for *Leidensis* (from Leiden). This addition was most unusual and will partly have been an expression of pride in his home town; it was, however, also a deliberate reference to famous artists from Leiden such as Lucas van Leyden (1494–1533) and Aertgen van Leyden (*c.* 1498–*c.* 1564). In 1632 in Amsterdam, he experimented briefly with *RHL van Rijn* and on a single occasion with *Rembrant van Ryn* (Cat. E1). On his ambitious *Anatomy Lesson of Dr Nicolaes Tulp* (pp. 136/137, Cat. 261), which he probably painted at the end of 1632, he confidently signed his name for the first time with only his first name: *Rembrant.* From 1633 until his death, for some unknown reason he suddenly started spelling his name (both on his works and in documents) with *dt* as *Rembrandt.* Even earlier than this, others had already started to refer to him only by his first name, as we learn from a note by Johan Huydecoper (1599–1661), who was able to call a *tronie* by "Rembrant" his own as early as 1628.[77] In his Latin eulogy from about 1630, Constantijn Huygens likewise calls him "Rembrantio" (in contrast to "Livio" and "Rubenio"). Signing works simply with one's first name was without any precedent in the Northern Netherlands. Knowingly or unknowingly, Rembrandt was following in the footsteps not only of famous Italian precursors such as Leonardo (1452–1519), Raphael (1483–1520), Michelangelo (1475–1564) and Titian (*c.* 1488/90–1576), but also of northern artists such as Lucas (van Leyden) and Albrecht (Dürer; 1471–1528), who were also referred to by their first names in van Mander's *Schilder-Boeck.*

Saskia

The close professional relationship to Hendrick Uylenburgh also had far-reaching consequences for Rembrandt's private life. It was probably through the latter that he made the acquaintance of Uylenburgh's cousin, Saskia Rommertsdr. (van) Uylenburgh (1612–1642), the youngest daughter of the pensionary, burgomaster and councillor of Leeuwarden, Rombartus Uylenburgh (1554–1624). Saskia was an orphan; her mother had died when she was six and her father when she was twelve years old.[78] She grew up in the family of her elder sister, Hiske, in the Frisian village of Sint-Annaparochie. Possibly in 1632 or at the beginning of 1633, she must have visited Amsterdam, where not only her cousin, Hendrick, but also her (much older) cousin, Aeltje Pietersdr. Uylenburgh, lived. The latter was married to the famous Reformed minister Jan Cornelisz. Sylvius

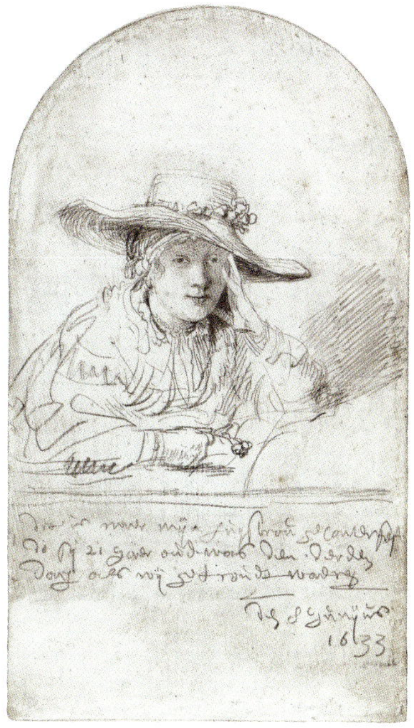

(1564–1638). The *Portrait of a 62-Year-Old Woman* (p. 161, Cat. 211) is thought to be a likeness of Aeltje, because she was (approximately) the same age. Saskia probably stayed in Amsterdam with her cousin, Aeltje, and will have met Rembrandt during this time. However it came to pass, in June 1633 the artist visited Saskia in Sint-Annaparochie. It was here that Rembrandt, who was evidently in love, drew the silverpoint portrait of a smiling Saskia with a flower, under which he (later) noted that this had been the third day after their engagement (p. 107, Cat. D629). Here Rembrandt has recorded exactly what she looked like at that time, on a sunny day in June in rural Friesland. On her head she is wearing a white cap and on top of that a sun hat; draped around her shoulders is a so-called *nachthalsdoek* (night rail), a kind of informal house dress which was also sometimes worn outside the home.[79] From their betrothal, the blonde Saskia acted as Rembrandt's model and muse. In contrast to the drawing, in his paintings and etchings we are introduced to another, much more idealised Saskia in imaginative costumes or in historical or mythological roles (p. 193, Cat. 58; p. 194, Cat. 315; Cat. 316; p. 201, Cat. 317; p. 259, Cat. 318; Cat. E283, E285, E286).

In June 1634, Rembrandt travelled to Sint-Annaparochie once more in order to marry Saskia. His family did not join him on the journey to faraway Friesland, but his mother had given her permission for the marriage in a notarial deed, declaring that her son's choice was "extremely pleasing and suited her well" (RD 1634/3). Initially, the young couple continued to live with Cousin Hendrick Uylenburgh on the Sint Antoniesbreestraat, but on 1 May 1635 they rented a new house in the elegant Nieuwe Doelenstraat for 600 guilders a year (RD 1635/1). In the meantime, Rembrandt had entered the Guild of St Luke and was therefore permitted to take on his own pupils. That house was possibly too small for him also to be able to work there, which is why, two years later, they moved into a house in a more industrial district: the *Suycker-backerij*

Portrait of Saskia Uylenburgh, 1633
Silverpoint on white prepared parchment, 18.5 × 10.6 cm (7 3/8 × 4 1/4 in.)
Staatliche Museen zu Berlin, Kupferstichkabinett

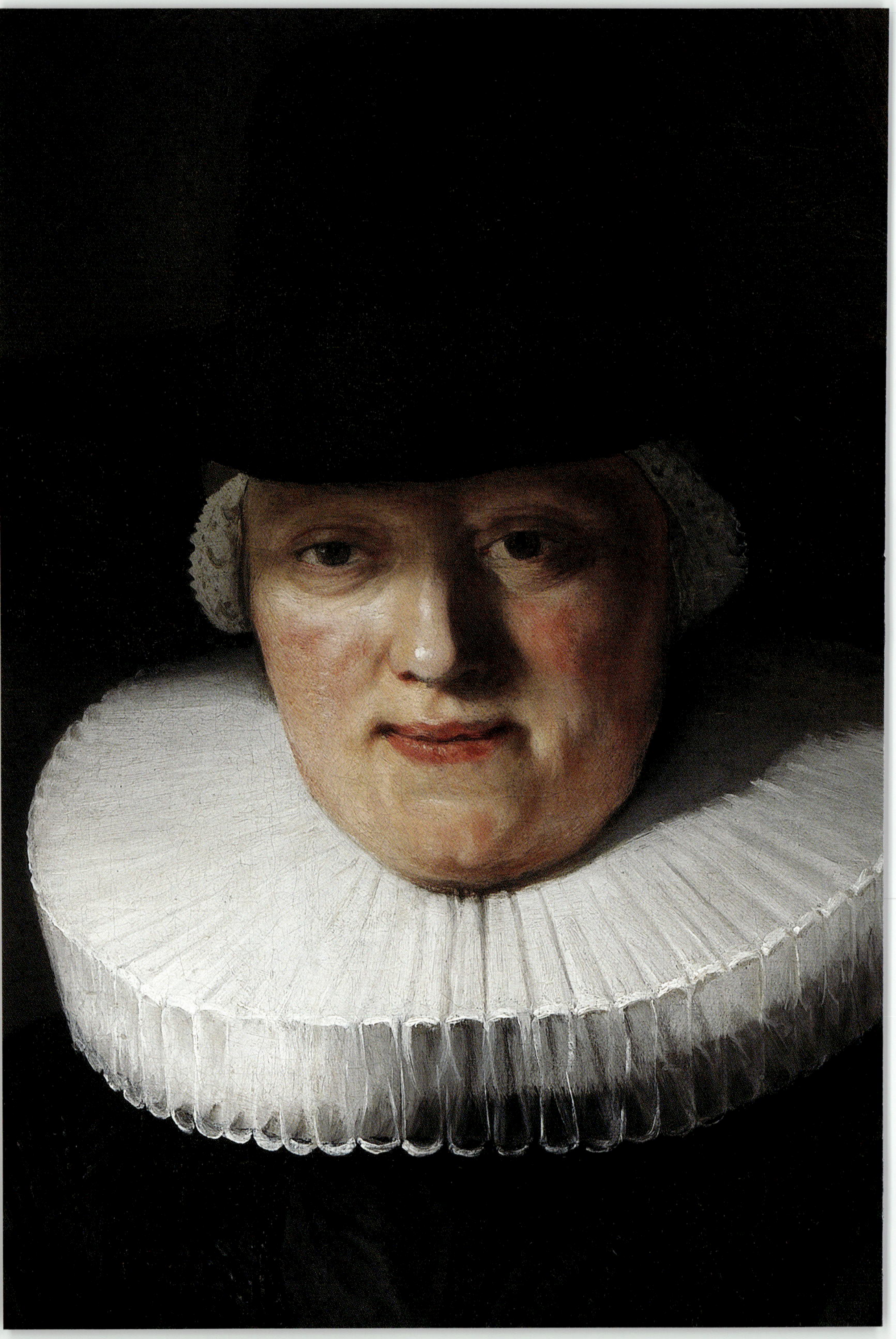

on the Binnen Amstel (Zwanenburgerstraat; RD 1637/7). In January 1639, Rembrandt returned to Sint Antoniesbreestraat (present-day Jodenbreestraat 4), to the place where he had begun his career in Amsterdam. He purchased an imposing merchant's house (today the Museum Het Rembrandthuis; RD 1639/1) on the corner of the Sint Antoniesluis for 13,000 guilders, an enormous sum in those days. He was to live and work there for almost 20 years.[80]

It has often been assumed that Rembrandt's marriage to the burgomaster's daughter brought him a great deal of money and numerous contacts in higher circles. However, although Saskia's family surely was more distinguished than his, she had to share her parents' inheritance with seven brothers and sisters. Conversely, the ambitious young artist from cosmopolitan Amsterdam, who was earning a good living, would have been an attractive match for the orphan girl from rural Friesland. There is also the question as to why her family (of lawyers) did not insist on a marriage contract, which they would certainly have done if Saskia had had (many more) possessions to bring into the marriage. Rembrandt and Saskia had community of property, which meant that she became the owner of half of Rembrandt's earnings. Saskia's network seem to have been limited above all to her immediate family circle.[81] After she moved to Amsterdam, her relationship with the family of her cousin Aeltje and the Reverend Sylvius (who had already represented Saskia during the banns), remained cordial. Sylvius baptised Rembrandt and Saskia's two oldest children. Rembrandt must have painted (unknown) portraits of husband and wife, and he also made a portrait etching of Sylvius on two occasions (Cat. E219 and E226). In both cases, the godparents were Saskia's elder sister, Titia Uylenburgh (1605–1641), and/or the latter's husband, François Coopal (*c.* 1600–1658), who lived in Vlissingen.[82] Only a small, informal drawing of Titia by Rembrandt from 1639 (Cat. D635) has survived. They also had contact with the family of Saskia's sister, Hiske. In 1641, her husband, Gerrit van Loo (*c.* 1580–1641), acted as godfather to Titus, together with his brother-in-law, Coopal. Rembrandt and Saskia were also "very good acquaintances" of van Loo's brother, the silversmith Jan van Loo (*c.* 1590–1659; RD 1659/13). There must once have been an (unknown) portrait by Rembrandt of the latter's wife, Anna Huybrechts, who eventually was to become Titus' mother-in-law in 1668 (RD 1668/10).

The many portrait commissions which Rembrandt had received in the preceding years had brought the young couple great material prosperity, and they probably showed it, too. In faraway Friesland, at any rate, it was rumoured amongst Saskia's distant relations that she had squandered her father's inheritance with "proncken ende praelen"

Detail of: **Portrait of Maria Bockenolle**, 1634
(see ill. p. 135)

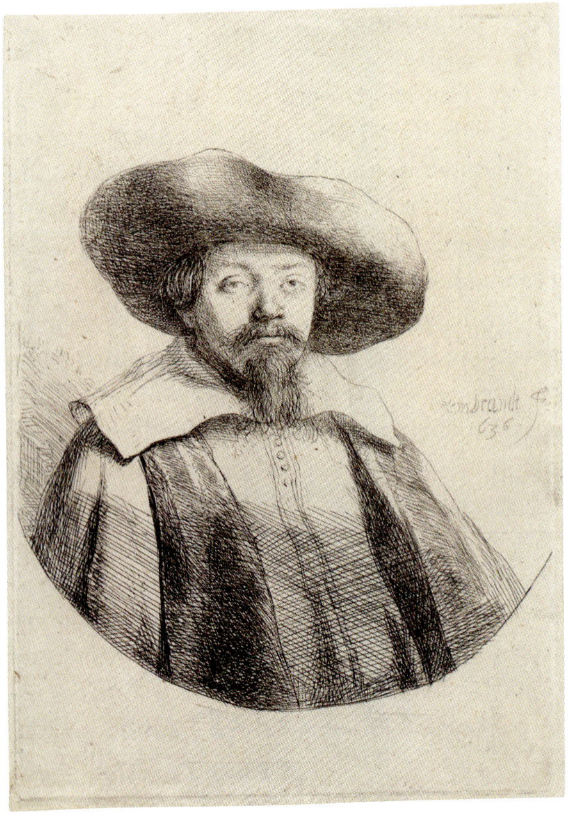

(flaunting and showing off; RD 1638/7). Rembrandt regarded this accusation as malicious gossip and answered in 1638 in a notarial deed that nothing had been squandered, but that they were now "plentifully and abundantly provided for [for which they would never be able to thank the Almighty adequately]" (RD 1638/7). The accused found Rembrandt's claim for compensation excessive, after all it concerned "only an artist or an artist's wife". According to the declaration by the silversmith Jan van Loo and his wife, their worldly goods included in addition to "many pewter, copper and iron objects" also ostentatious banqueting dishes, plates and jugs of silver. van Loo continued that Saskia owned two necklaces of large pearls, two drop-shaped pearls (as earrings), a ring with a large diamond, two diamond (ear)rings, enamelled bracelets and a string of pearls for her hair (RD 1659/13).

Rembrandt mostly painted his young wife wearing these drop-shaped earrings, but never in everyday fashionable dress. Without exception he showed her in imaginative or historical costumes in a succession of different roles.[83] In both 1634 (p. 202, Cat. 101) and 1635 (p. 203, Cat. 103), Saskia served as model for a large half-length figure representing Flora, the goddess of youth, spring and flowers. The X-ray of the latter painting shows that this work showing Saskia with a sweet smile on her lips initially had a much more bloodthirsty subject, namely the Old Testament heroine Judith holding the decapitated head of the general Holofernes. Only at a relatively late stage did Rembrandt change the

Menasseh ben Israel, 1636
Etching, 14.9 × 10.3 cm (5 7/8 × 4 in.). Vienna, Albertina

subject of the picture radically by transforming the bloody sword in Judith's hand into a staff, and the decapitated head into a large bouquet of flowers.[84]

In spite of all their material prosperity, Rembrandt and Saskia were faced with the inevitable strokes of fate. Between 1636 and 1640 they had to bury three small children: their firstborn, Rumbartus, on 15 February 1636 (RD 1636/3) and two little daughters, both called Cornelia, the first on 14 August 1638 (RD 1638/9) and the second daughter on 12 August 1640 (RD 1640/6). As we learn from their baptismal records, the children (in this order) were just three months, three weeks, and two weeks old (RD 1635/3; 1638/8; 1640/5). Rembrandt's mother, Neeltgen (Cornelia) Willemsdr. van Zuytbroeck (RD 1640/8), after whom the two girls had been named, also died one month after the youngest child, in September 1640. Rembrandt received almost 2,500 guilders, as his share of the considerable inheritance (RD 1640/9). His contacts with his relatives in Leiden seem to have eased a little during these last years. Earlier in 1640, the painter had sold his property in Zoeterwoude (a plot of land not far from the city gate of Leiden which was adjacent to that of his mother) to his brother Willem at a loss (RD 1640/3).

One year later Rembrandt and Saskia were able to rejoice at the birth of their son Titus (1641–1668), who was baptised on 22 September (RD 1641/4). He was named after his aunt Titia, who had died a short while before (RD see 1642/3). Also Saskia's health was not good. She was apparently confined to her bed for a long time, because Rembrandt drew her in her sickbed on several occasions (Cat. D265–267, 269, 297, 308). Around 1641, he drew Saskia during her confinement in the large room of their new house; she is holding a baby (Titus?) in her arms, and a nurse doing needlework is sitting beside her (p. 98, Cat. D364). After the birth of Titus, Saskia probably remained in poor health. On the morning of 5 June 1642, she summoned a notary in order to draw up her will. In it she named little Titus as her heir (RD 1642/2). She clearly had complete confidence in Rembrandt, because she appointed him as sole guardian. Nine days later, on 14 June, Saskia was laid to rest in the Oude Kerk in Amsterdam. She was 29 years old (RD 1642/4).

Landscapes and Still Lifes

At the end of the 1630s, Rembrandt suddenly began to show an interest in two genres which he had hitherto only studied as a part of his history paintings: still lifes and landscapes. Although his landscapes represent only a small part of his oeuvre (he painted only seven of them, Cat. 135–141, pp. 218/219, 220/221, 334/335, 350/351), they nonetheless occupy a special place in Dutch landscape painting. Unlike Jan van Goyen (1596–1656) and Salomon van Ruysdael (1600/03–1670), the artists who were his important sources of inspiration, and different from his drawings, Rembrandt almost never portrayed the typical Dutch landscape of the Netherlands in his paintings. He mostly depicted imaginary, exotic or stormy panoramas. He shared his preference for panoramic distant views with ominous and menacing skies and contrasting colours with the influential landscape artist Hercules Segers (1589/90–*c.* 1638; p. 94). Although Rembrandt's *Landscape with a Stone Bridge* (pp. 218/219, Cat. 137) from about 1638 shows unmistakably Dutch features, even here the everyday elements are strongly dramatised by the extreme light, and the work contains more imaginative than realistic elements. Rembrandt created the landscape in a reduced colour scheme of shades of grey, brown and green. In order to suggest turbulent weather, he added short brushstrokes in all directions to the heavy blanket of clouds in thin black paint. He intentionally left the light colour of the ground layer shining through in places. The strongly lit group of trees in the middle has been added on top of the green by means of short yellow brushstrokes so that they literally seem to loom out of the picture. Nowhere else in Rembrandt's works is the light heightened to such an extreme, so that it is hard to imagine that this highly charged landscape does not have a symbolic meaning. It has been suggested, for example, that the stooping man on the far left in the picture could be interpreted as a symbolic representation of the "Pilgrim of Life".[85] He is walking alone on the "true path of life" from the inn on the far left towards the church in the background. But Rembrandt rarely used such obvious symbolism; it is therefore very likely that in this little painting his decision in favour of the extreme weather conditions and the dramatic light was based purely on artistic considerations.

Girl with Dead Peacocks (p. 205, Cat. 133) from around 1639 is also unusual; as a still life it is unique in Rembrandt's work and also in seventeenth-century Dutch painting. With the dead birds and the fruit basket in the foreground, the painting indeed looks at first sight like a still life. The young girl in sixteenth-century dress, depicted in a summary manner, looks primarily as if she is intended to contrast with the birds, which are rendered in a more detailed, illusionistic way. One of them is hanging by its feet from a shutter. The birds, once strutting proudly around, are dead and robbed of their wonderful tail feathers, laid out or hung up to mature before ending up on the dinner table. Incidentally, Rembrandt had the idea of removing the display feathers only while he was painting the picture. In the X-ray of the painting, and in the top layer of the paint, we can see that initially Rembrandt painted the long tail feathers hanging above the girl and then decided to paint them out. Substantial changes to the composition of this kind during the painting process were typical of Rembrandt's working method. We can no longer ascertain whether he decided on this change for compositional reasons or in order to make the desolate state of the dead birds even more moving. Over the course of time an attempt was made to mitigate the ghastly sight of the dead birds by covering the small puddle of blood. When this overpainting was removed in 1930, the illusionism of the stone ledge and the peacock's head sticking out became even stronger.

In *Hunter with a Dead Bittern* (p. 204, Cat. 132) from 1639, it is once again a dead bird which plays the main role. Because the outstretched wings of the bittern catch the light, our entire attention is directed towards the deceptively realistic portrayal of the plumage. This startling illusionism is further heightened by the wooden bracket from which the bird is suspended and which runs parallel to the picture-plane. In this painting, too, the dead creature is accompanied by a figure in historic dress who has been rendered in a sketch-like manner. The way Rembrandt plays with deceptively realistic elements and a figure leaning on a windowsill anticipates the illusionistic figure pieces with an architectural framework from the early 1640s (pp. 318, 357, 358, Cat. 320, 322, 323).

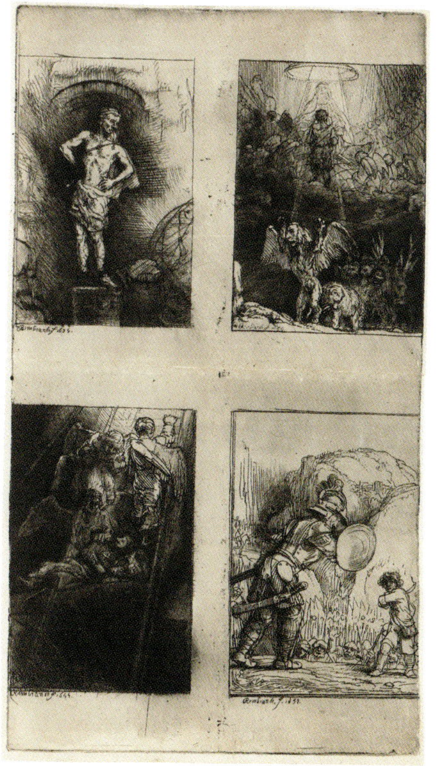

History Pieces in Amsterdam

In spite of the numerous portraits which he painted from 1631 onwards, Rembrandt would have seen himself primarily as a history painter. It is quite possible that he had reached an agreement with Uylenburgh that in addition to the portraits – for which the commissions were handled via Uylenburgh's business – he would continue to create history paintings on his own account. In the case of the history pieces for the stadtholder, this was certainly the case (see pp. 98–99, 101–104). The prestigious commission for the painting of the series of scenes from the Life of Christ seems to have evolved from the purchase of *The Descent from the Cross* (p. 185, Cat. 50), an ambitious composition

Four illustrations for a Spanish book (Menasseh ben Israel, Piedra Gloriosa): Nebuchadnezzar's Dream, Daniel's Vision of the Four Beasts, Jacob's Ladder, David and Goliath, 1655
Etching, drypoint and burin, with surface tone on Japan paper, 28 × 16 cm (11 × 6 3/8 in.)
Amsterdam, Rijksmuseum

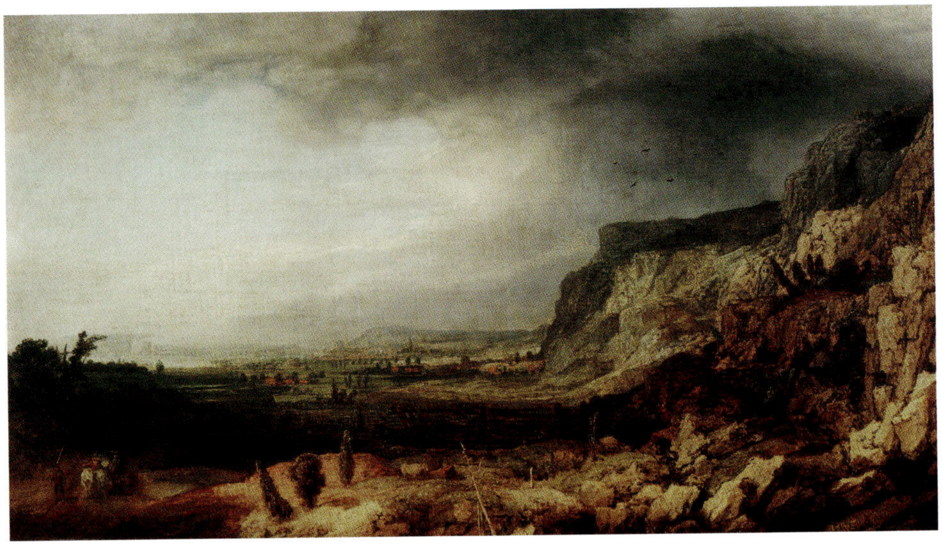

which Rembrandt seems to have initiated himself. With certain exceptions (pp. 474/475, Cat. 115), there is growing evidence that Rembrandt chose the subjects of his history pictures himself. For the artist the painting of portraits brought an additional advantage: that he could tempt the clients to purchase one of the history or figure pieces which was perhaps on the easel in the studio.[86] Thus Marten Looten, whom Rembrandt painted in 1632 (p. 133, Cat. 178), very probably also owned the magnificent single figure of an *Man in Oriental Costume* (p. 253, Cat. 281) from the same year. Dirck Jansz. Pesser and his wife, Haesje Jacobsdr. van Cleyburg (pp. 162 and 163, Cat. 237 and 238), possibly possessed in addition to their own portraits a large "Paracelsus" (see p. 251, Cat. 285); and Marten Soolmans and his wife (pp. 154 and 155, Cat. 241 and 242) owned *The Holy Family* (p. 177, Cat. 54), all works from the same year, 1634. All these were wealthy occasional purchasers (the Soolmans had just married and were in the process of furnishing their new home), but Rembrandt will have had his eye above all on art connoisseurs and art collectors with his ambitious history paintings. One of them was Jacques Specx (1585–1652), who had returned to Amsterdam in July 1633 with vast wealth acquired as the Governor General of Batavia and who had started to collect paintings immediately after his arrival. According to his inventory (RD 1653/4), his exquisite collection included

Hercules Segers, **Rocky Landscape**, 1620–1625
Oil on canvas, 55 × 99 cm (21 ¾ × 39 in.)
Florence, Galleria degli Uffizi

five paintings by Rembrandt, including a St Paul (probably Cat. 40 from 1629/30, p. 59), *The Rape of Europa* (pp. 216/217, Cat. 97) from 1632, the impressive *Christ in the Storm on the Sea of Galilee* (p. 227, Cat. 48) from 1633, as well as the portraits of his sister-in-law Petronella Buys and her husband (Cat. 245*, 246*) from 1635. Because some of these works had already been completed before Specx returned it seems plausible that Rembrandt had a stock of history paintings and single figures from which interested purchasers could choose. In view of the high prices which he asked for his works, only the very wealthiest art lovers would have been in a position to buy them.

In his letter of 12 January 1639 to Constantijn Huygens (RD 1639/1), Rembrandt justified the high price and long waiting time with the "greatest and most natural movement" of his figures and the extraordinary "studious diligence" which he invested in his history pictures. According to the art theory of the time, this "studious diligence" is essential for a good history piece. The artist must read and make a thorough study of the sources on which his story was based. According to Rembrandt's artist colleague and fellow citizen Philips Angel (1616–1683) it was "to be prized above all [...] to occupy ourselves by diligently scouring the musty old books to acquire a knowledge of histories".[87]

Although today Rembrandt is seen primarily as an intuitive artist and not so much as a learned painter, he had a thorough knowledge of the writers of antiquity. His humanist education at grammar school provided him with the required knowledge to a greater extent than was the case with other history painters. Rembrandt's history paintings reveal that he really had studied the sources scrupulously. In addition to the correct depiction of the actual story, it was considered admirable for an artist to "amplify" or enrich the story by adding additional elements which were the result of his imagination *(imaginatio)*.[88] Angel wrote that it was above all due to his "lofty and profound reflection" and his vivid imagination that "the far-famed Rembrant" was superior to all other history painters.

In the years around 1631, when Rembrandt painted his first portraits and travelled back and forth between Leiden and Amsterdam, he also made a large number of history paintings. Unlike the large-size Amsterdam portraits which suddenly and surprisingly appeared, his history pictures show a much more gradual development as he moved from Leiden to Amsterdam. With their medium-size format, the amount of detail and the bundled light they seem to have evolved from *The Repentant Judas Returning the Pieces of Silver* (pp. 68/69, Cat. 38) from 1629.[89] A number of small figures show the "greatest and most natural observation of movement", referred to in Rembrandt's letter to Huygens, in the sense of both physical movement and moved by strong emotions. In *Simeon's Song of Praise* from 1631 (p. 207, Cat. 44) Rembrandt focuses predominantly on the different range of emotions, while in *The Rape of*

Europa (pp. 216/217, Cat. 97) from 1632 and the later *Diana Bathing* (pp. 214/215, Cat. 99) from about 1634 it is the physical agility and the gestures of the figures. In the dynamic *Rape of Proserpina* (p. 210, Cat. 96) from 1631, Rembrandt expresses both physical motion and emotion. There is nothing classical about this goddess from antiquity: her face distorted with fear and horror, Proserpina claws and scratches like a cat. Her shocked companions pull so hard at her precious cloak that it is about to rip. Rembrandt here tried to put himself in the position of the girl who is being forcibly abducted, and instead of the classical, graceful beauty of antiquity he choose a much more "natural", credible depiction of the terrified goddess. He summarised all the emotions associated with the story in Proserpina's desperate gestures into what Samuel van Hoogstraten later described as "only a single instantaneous movement *[oogenblikkige beweging]* which expresses the essence of the story".[90]

In addition to these multi-figured historical compositions *(ordonnantien)* full of (e)motion, during these years Rembrandt began to concentrate on painting scenes in which the essence of the whole story was reduced to just one single figure. It seems as if he had been spurred on by Karel van Mander's observation that "Great masters teach us to pay great attention to solitude, and know that with few figures their works will gain in beauty and gracefulness".[91] Illuminated by a bright beam of bundled light, the solitary figure "glows" out of the darkness surrounding him or her, for example like *St Peter Repentant* (p. 56, Cat. 45) kneeling in the dungeon or the naked *Andromeda* (p. 211, Cat. 94) chained to a rock. His extreme focus on the frightened, helpless Andromeda lead Rembrandt to omit not only the monster that is usually included in the pictorial tradition, but also Andromeda's rescuer, Perseus. This isolation of the main figure by dispensing with further protagonists or the usual attributes would become an important characteristic of Rembrandt's history paintings. This principle of extreme concentration on the main figure, which is sometimes referred to as "Herauslösung" (singling out), was also the reason that in the literature there is so much discussion about the precise subject matter of Rembrandt's history pieces.[92] Also the subject of *Jeremiah Lamenting the Destruction of Jerusalem* (p. 57, Cat. 7) from 1630 gave rise to lengthy debates because the subject was a very rare one. Illuminated by bright light, the aged prophet emerges mysteriously from the intense darkness. He is sitting against a crumbling pillar, his head resting on his hand, mourning the fall of Jerusalem, which is burning behind him. He had prophesied that it would happen but had been unable to prevent it. In the illuminated areas, the texture of the various materials is rendered in great detail, for example the wrinkled skin, the fur of the gown, the red rug and the gleaming vessels beside Jeremiah. Here Rembrandt drew on more than one source. He could read the story of the prophet Jeremiah in the Old Testament (Jeremiah 32 and 33). But the Bible says nothing of the

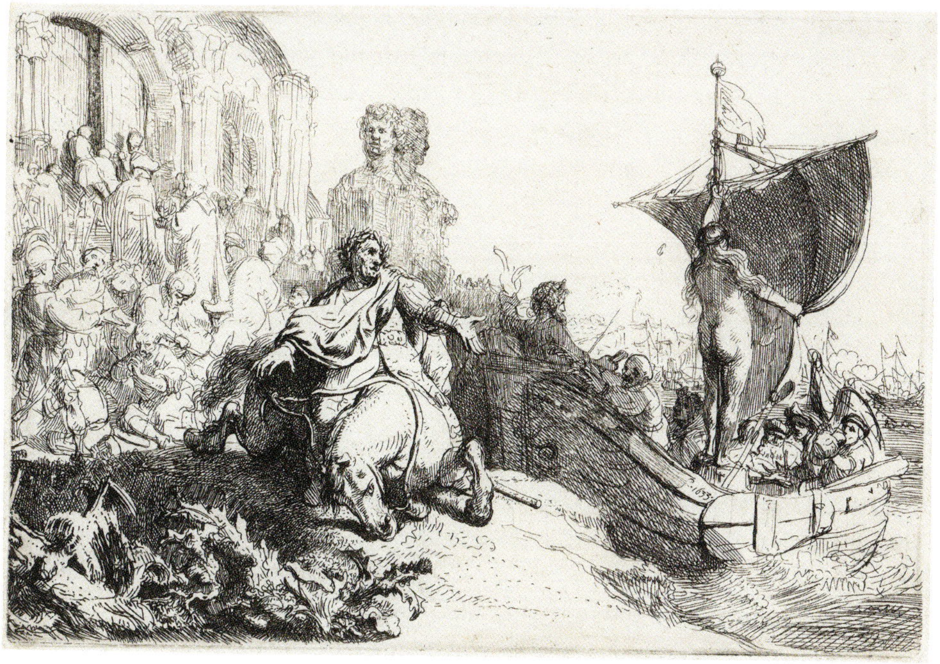

The Ship of Fortune, 1633
Etching, 11.3 × 18.4 cm (4 ½ × 7 ¼ in.)
Amsterdam, Rijksmuseum

crumbling pillar against which Jeremiah is leaning, nor does it mention the golden vessels shown so prominently beside him. For that Rembrandt must have read the *Antiquities of the Jews* by the Jewish historian Flavius Josephus (37–after 95 CE); he owned a copy of an illustrated German edition published in 1574. This relates that instead of moving to Babylon, Jeremiah preferred to spend his last days in the ruins of Jerusalem, in order to "remain amongst the ruins of his native city and its miserable remains". Thereupon, the old man was presented "with rich gifts" (Book X, chap. 9, v. 1). Rembrandt reproduced these in the form of the golden vessels. However, neither the Bible nor Flavius Josephus reports that Jeremiah sat in the ruins and grieved. This logical extrapolation was the result of Rembrandt's "lofty and profound reflection" on the story which had been so highly praised by Philips Angel.

The *Old Woman Reading a Book* (so-called *Prophetess Anna*; p. 223, Cat. 43) is also very difficult to allocate to a category with accuracy, because the picture has characteristics of a *tronie*, but also those of a biblical figure like the pious prophetess Anna, who spent her days praying and reading. In this famous and popular single figure from 1631, the light falls from behind on the Bible and on the wrinkled hand which looks as if it has been modelled from paint. Particularly noticeable are the portrayal of the gleaming gold threads in her hood and the shawl that was laced through it. The light seems to graze, as it were, the velvet pile of Anna's reddish-brown cloak. In this painting, the rendering of the texture of the skin, velvet and gold threads seems to be the main focus. The convincing depiction of velvet in particular was supposed to be very difficult, and Angel maintains that it was rare to see the "luyster" (lustre) of velvet depicted well. Here we have the impression that Rembrandt wanted to demonstrate his virtuosity in the reproduction of various types of textiles.[93] In his *Minerva in Her Study* (p. 213, Cat. 95) from the same year, and especially in the *Heroine of the Old Testament at Her Toilet* (p. 212, Cat. 8) from 1632/33, it also seems as if the velvet cloak with its border of gold threads was the real subject.

Now faded, King Saul's cloak in *David Playing the Harp to Saul* (p. 225, Cat. 6) from 1629–1631 was probably originally also a reddish-brown velvet. Today, the "luyster" has completely disappeared because the paint is abraded due to vigorous cleaning in the past. Although he is accompanied by David, who is playing his harp in the shadows at the bottom of the picture, the surly king appears to be completely alone, consumed by his envy of the boy (1 Samuel 18: 11). He stubbornly stares past David, his eyes glaring, and in the centre of the picture we see his fist clenched around the javelin that he will throw at David in his rage. The composition of the picture is a variation of an engraving with the same subject by Lucas van Leyden, whom Rembrandt greatly admired (p. 224). The fact that Karel van Mander praises the engraving as the epitome of an apt representation of violent emotion, or "frenzy", may well have prompted Rembrandt to surpass this frenzy himself.[94]

During the course of the years 1633 and 1634, the format of Rembrandt's history paintings grew progressively larger. His ambitious *Christ in the Storm on the Sea of Galilee* (p. 227, Cat. 48) from 1633 is the first large-size history painting and Rembrandt's only seascape. The small figures show a wide range of variations of emotions and attitudes, especially the sailors who are struggling against the storm. At the same time Rembrandt also started to paint large-size histories with formidable female single figures. His first attempt was the knee-length depiction of *Bellona* (Cat. 98), which seems mainly to have been an exercise in the portrayal of light reflections on the metal armour. The majestic *Minerva* (p. 229, Cat. 104) and *Artemisia* (*Sophonisba?*; p. 228, Cat. 113) from 1635 and 1636 were more successful. In these life-size history paintings, Rembrandt's concern is less with violent emotions than the portrayal of the three-dimensionality of the splendid figures, the shimmering texture of the fabrics and the precious jewels.

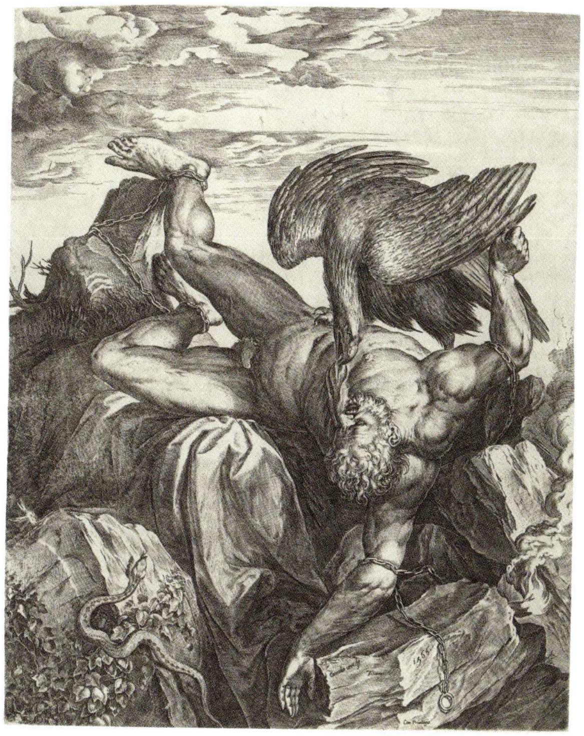

In 1635, after he had moved to the Nieuwe Doelenstraat and established himself as an independent master, Rembrandt began to paint large dramatic history paintings with life-size figures. In these ambitious Baroque works – in which he seems to be competing with Rubens and Caravaggio (p. 230) – Rembrandt's protagonists extend their arms in sweeping gestures, as in *Abraham's Sacrifice* (p. 231, Cat. 11). For *Belshazzar's Feast* (pp. 236/237, Cat. 13), Rembrandt used the large horizontal format for the first time. This night scene owes its vitality to its Baroque drama and pathos. The painting shows the King of Babylon, Belshazzar, celebrating a banquet with his retinue. He is having the wine served from the sacred vessels which his father, Nebuchadnezzar, had looted in Jerusalem (Daniel 5: 1–6). The feast is suddenly interrupted by a hand which writes a sinister prophecy for Belshazzar on the wall which only the hastily summoned prophet Daniel can read (Daniel 5: 26–28). The reason for this is the way the Hebrew inscription has been written – not only from right to left, as is usual, but also from top to bottom. Rembrandt, who frequently uses Hebrew and pseudo-Hebrew letters in his paintings, could not read Hebrew; he copied printed and written sources. This was also the case here. The written form of the inscription derives from the model of the Jewish rabbi, scholar and printer of books Menasseh ben Israel (1604–1657), of whom Rembrandt made a portrait etching in 1636 (p. 110, Cat. E222) and for whose book *Piedra Gloriosa* he would etch four illustrations in 1655 (p. 113, Cat. E13). Rembrandt adopted the inscription from Menasseh's book *De termino vitae*, which, however, was published only in 1639.[95] Since his Belshazzar must

Cornelis Cort after Titian, **Tityos Punished in Hell**, 1566
Copper engraving, 38 × 31.2 cm (15 × 12 3/8 in.). Amsterdam, Rijksmuseum

have been painted around 1635, however, we must assume that Rembrandt had access to Menasseh's very specific way of writing the inscription before publication. It is possible that the Jewish scholar provided Rembrandt with a handwritten template which he then copied – albeit with some mistakes.

Rembrandt concentrates on the moment when Belshazzar and his courtiers discover the mysterious hand, surrounded by a cloud and writing on the wall. The king is filled with panic and leaps to his feet, his eyes staring wildly at the inscription behind him. A woman in red, shown from behind, leans backwards towards the viewer, spilling wine from a golden goblet. On the left, other participants in the feast gaze in horror at the ominous apparition. The picture format and the almost life-size half-length and three-quarter-length figures in action at the very front edge of the picture, under the eyes of the viewer, clearly recall compositions by Caravaggio and his followers. Rembrandt was evidently particularly fascinated by the depiction of a very fast-moving object which changes position in a fraction of a second. In his picture of Belshazzar, he portrays two overturned drinking vessels in the very moment in which the content cascades over the brim. These "snapshots" of falling objects recall *Abraham's Sacrifice*, which is dated 1635 (p. 231, Cat. 11), in which the knife slips out of the patriarch's hand and falls to the ground as a result of the angel's intervention. Rembrandt's figure of Belshazzar can be compared with that of Artemisia (p. 228, Cat. 113) from 1634 and Minerva (p. 229, Cat. 104) from 1635 with regard to the execution of painterly details and especially the way the main figure dominates the centre the picture.[96] The same also applies to the way Rembrandt has painted the precious fabrics and jewels.

The dimensions of *Belshazzar* were exceeded by *The Blinding of Samson* from 1636 (pp. 238/239, Cat. 15). It was a work which doubtless caused considerable amazement in Amsterdam. At the time of its completion, the painting was not only the most monumental of all Rembrandt's pictures, alongside his *Danae* (pp. 241/242, Cat. 105), which was subsequently reduced in size; with regard to the staging of emotions and Baroque drama, it was also the most shocking.[97] Nobody before him had depicted with comparable ruthlessness the fatal consequences of the Old Testament hero's night of love with Delilah. She had persuaded Samson, intoxicated with wine and love, to reveal his secret to her which she then betrayed to the Philistines. The reason for his supernatural strength lay in his uncut hair (Judges 16: 4–20). However, unlike other painters, Rembrandt did not choose the scene in which Delilah or a barber she has summoned cuts off Samson's long locks; but the next moment, when he is blinded by the Philistines (Judges 16: 21). Thus

Detail of: **Portrait of a Young Woman**, 1633
(see ill. p. 147)

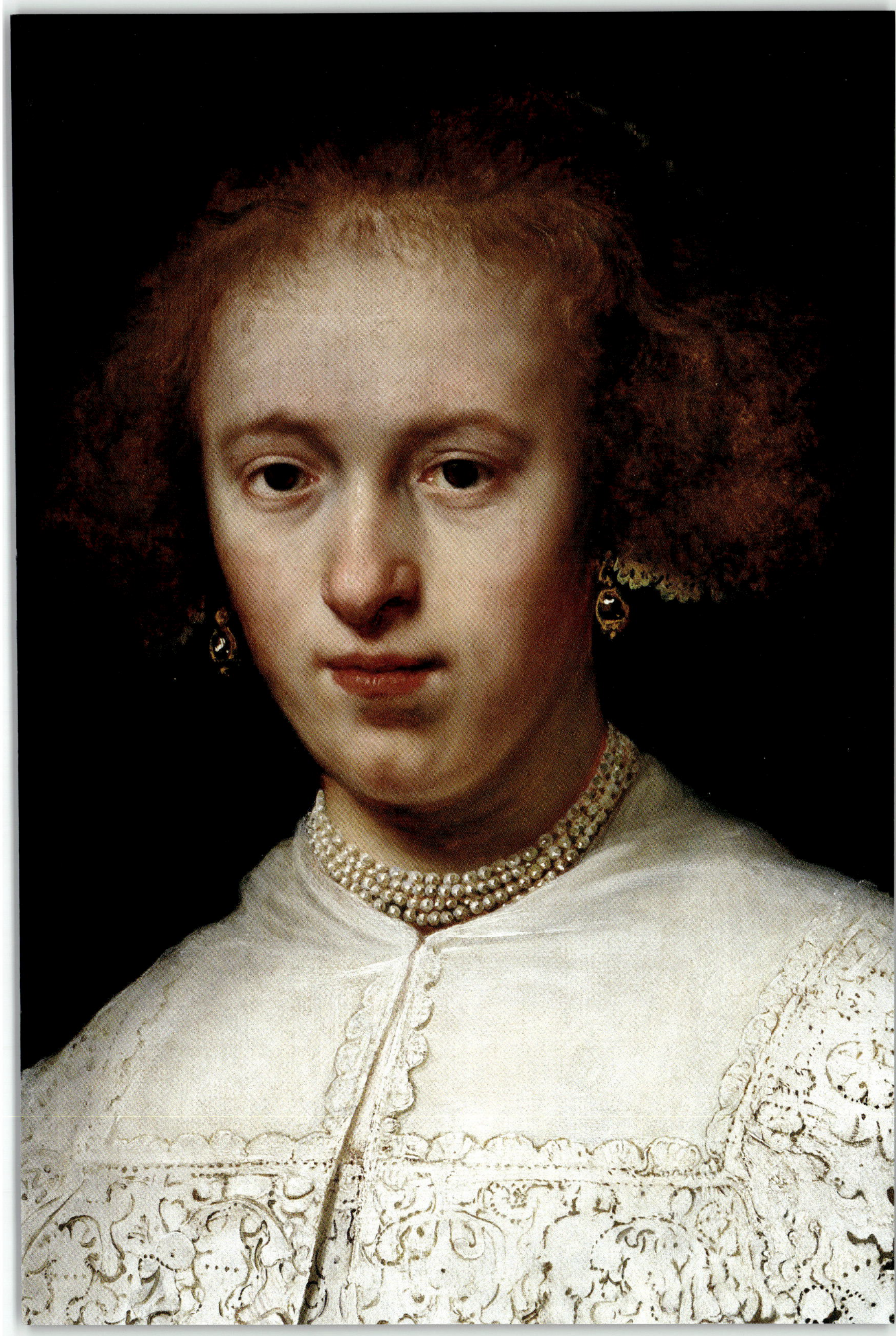

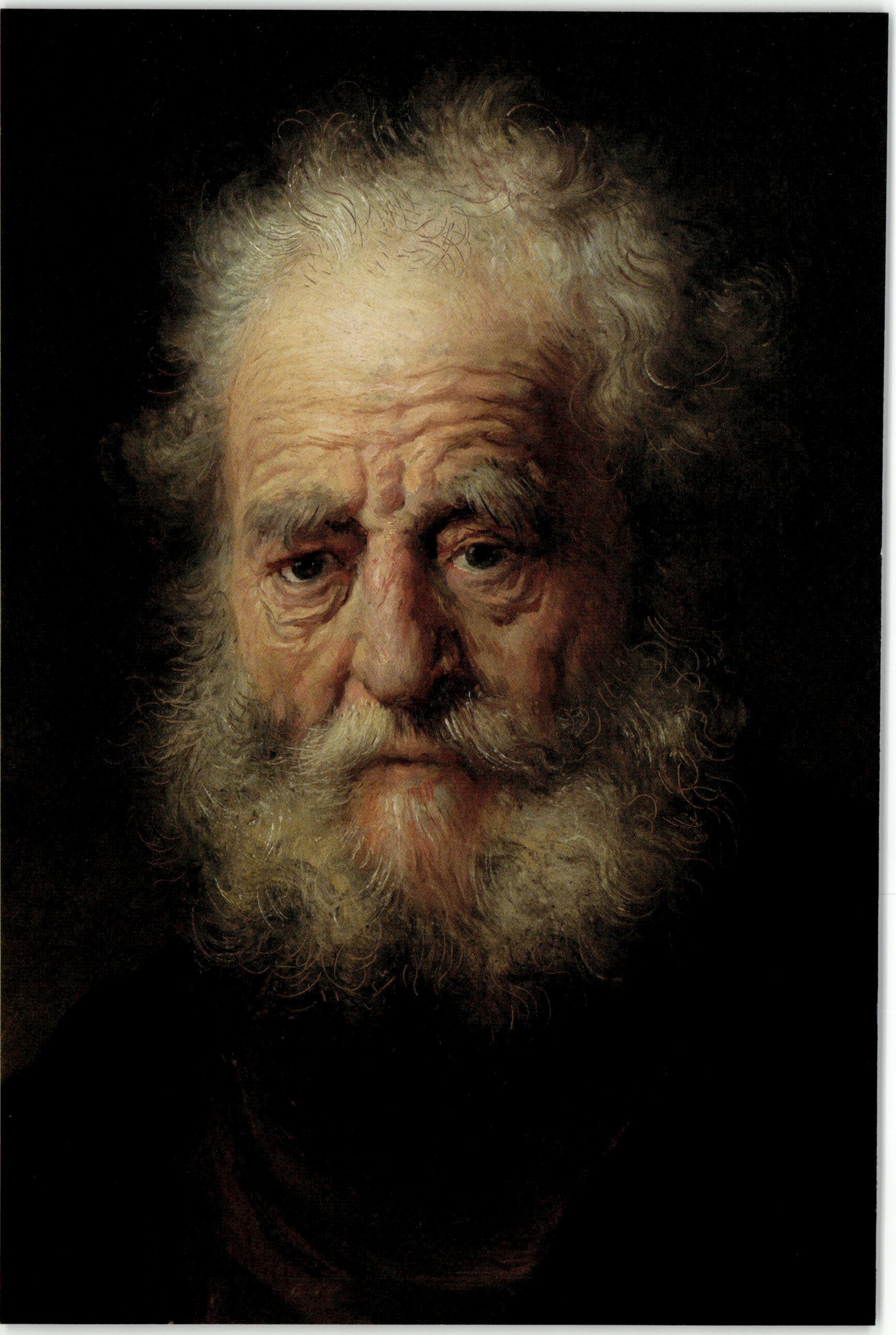

Rembrandt decided on a narrative moment which is extremely rare in post-medieval pictorial tradition. Samson, powerless as a result of the deception, his own lust and gullibility, is overpowered by a total of five armed Philistines and is thrown to the ground. In the background Delilah exits the scene, triumphantly carrying the hero's curls she has cut off. She demonstratively holds them out towards the viewer. In the centre of the scene, one of the Philistines is plunging a dagger into Samson's right eye. It is, in fact, a *kris*, an exotic thrusting weapon which in Rembrandt's day was imported from Indonesia by the Dutch East India Company (VOC). It is very likely that Rembrandt owned such a weapon. His teacher, Pieter Lastman, also owned a *kris*, which is referred to in his inventory from 1632 as "pongiaert" (dagger) in an "Oostindische kist" (chest from the East Indies) and which can be seen in several of his paintings.[98] Masterfully Rembrandt uses the fall of light to emphasise the staging and the tragic moment of the action. Samson is being dragged from the brightly lit part of the room into the darker foreground, which belongs to his enemies, the Philistines. This corresponds to the act of blinding the biblical hero, who will thus be condemned to a life in darkness. "Everything is concentrated on this act of torture and the terrible suffering this causes", as Weisbach writes.[99]

Large-size paintings with scenes from the story of Samson and Delilah are to be found during the first half of the seventeenth century with particular frequency in the art of Rubens and his circle in the Southern Netherlands.[100] The preferred subjects were either the cutting off of Samson's hair by Delilah or a Philistine summoned by her, or the scene when the hero is taken prisoner immediately before being blinded. Rembrandt clearly wanted to compete here against Rubens. The latter had portrayed both Samson having his hair cut off by a Philistine (London, The National Gallery), a work that was known through a mirror-image engraving by Jacob Matham (1571–1631); and also – in two oil sketches – his capture immediately before the blinding, which, however, had not yet been carried out (The Art Institute of Chicago and Madrid, Museo Nacional Thyssen-Bornemisza). Unlike Rubens, Rembrandt goes a step further in his painting and shows the gouging out of Samson's eyes in all its brutality.

There has been much speculation about the possible source of inspiration for Rembrandt's figure of Samson. The suggestions range from Raphael and Caravaggio to Titian, Jusepe de Ribera (1591–1652) and Indian miniatures.[101] One of the most frequently mentioned suggestions is above all Rubens' painting *Prometheus Bound* from around 1611/12 (Philadelphia Museum of Art), which until 1625 hung in the house of the English envoy Sir Dudley Carleton (1573–1632) in The Hague. It is not known whether

Detail of: **Old Man with a Gold Chain**, *c.* 1632
(see ill. p. 257)

Rembrandt knew the Rubens painting (or one of the few copies). Rubens in turn had been influenced by a painting by Titian depicting Tityos from about 1549/50 (Madrid, Museo Nacional del Prado), which Cornelis Cort (1533–1578) had engraved in 1566 (p. 119). The engraving was widely known, and Rembrandt doubtless would have found it easier to access the Cort engraving than the Rubens painting. Moreover, in addition to the formal parallels there are also similarities of content with regard to the figure of Tityos. As Karel van Mander writes in his interpretation of the *Metamorphoses* of Ovid (43 BC–17/18 CE), Tityos was punished in Hades for his unbridled lasciviousness, for he had attempted to violate Leto, the mother of Diana and Apollo.[102] Tityos therefore symbolises the agonies of sensuous passion, for which the gods decreed he would have to atone. In the exegeses of the story of the Old Testament champion, the writings of the Reformed theologians, with which Rembrandt and his contemporaries were doubtless familiar, contained remarkable similarities.[103] Samson, too, had been unable to curb his passion and had committed fornication with Delilah. It was for this that God punished him. Rembrandt was very probably inspired in his representation of the violent emotions and unbridled brutality by Rubens' hunting scenes, which the latter made from 1615 onwards and which frequently showed a creature that had been cornered and was forced to fight for its life. We can see a clear parallel between the composition of Rembrandt's Samson and Rubens' *Calydonian Boar Hunt*.[104] Figures like the man with the spear at the left of the picture also recall related hunting scenes by Antonio Tempesta (1555–1630).[105] *The Blinding of Samson* represents simultaneously the high point and the end of Rembrandt's monumental history paintings. *Belshazzar's Feast* from about 1635 and *The Blinding of Samson* from 1636 would remain Rembrandt's largest history paintings until *The Conspiracy of the Batavians under Claudius Civilis* (pp. 474/475, Cat. 115) from 1661/62, the dimensions of which were dictated by his patrons.

This experiment with life-size figures involved in a dramatic action proved to be short-lived. In his *Danae* (pp. 240/241, Cat. 105) from 1636–1643 (which was originally as large as the *Samson*), we can discern a change to much more intimate, atmospheric scenes with small female figures and a warm colour scheme. In the two versions of Susanna bathing from 1636 (p. 243, Cat. 14) and 1638–1647 (pp. 244/245, Cat. 18), Rembrandt concentrates to a greater extent on the inner emotions of the vulnerable-looking nude female figures.

For unknown reasons, Rembrandt painted very little in 1637, but then in 1638 he completed another large composition, albeit with much smaller figures than in 1636. Philips Angel presents this painting, *The Wedding of Samson* from 1638 (pp. 248/249, Cat. 17), to all other artists as a model: "Behold, this fruit of true, natural depiction came from reading the story properly and examining it with lofty and profound reflection."[106]

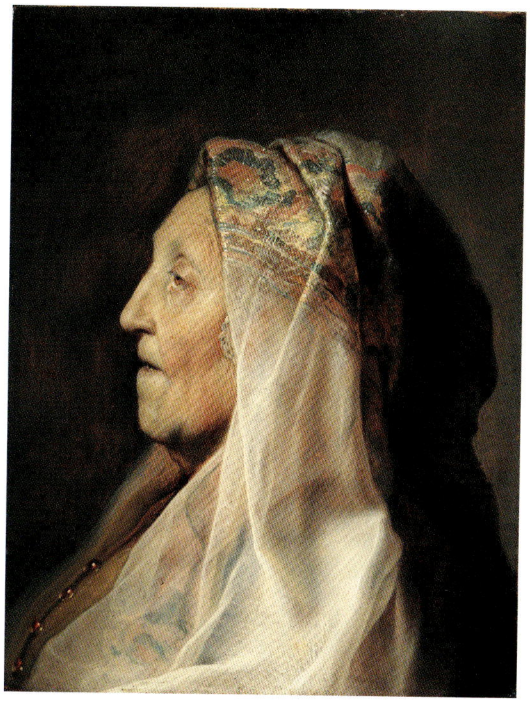

By painting the Old Testament hero with long, curly hair, Rembrandt showed that he had read the Bible text carefully (Judges 16: 17), because the Bible relates that Samson could not cut his hair because this was said to be the source of his superhuman strength. Furthermore, the artist had also gathered information about the customs of classical antiquity and of the Orient: he shows the guests reclining at the table instead of sitting. Rembrandt's "lofty and profound reflection" and his "naturalness" can also be seen in Samson's gesture, with which he clearly shows that he is presenting the wedding guests, who are listening attentively, with a riddle. The complacent pose of the smiling bride speaks volumes: she will soon reveal the answer and thus betray her bridegroom. By "natural", Angel also means the way in which other wedding guests are clearly not interested in the riddle and are simply celebrating merrily, as is the custom at weddings.

Indeed, the work can be seen as a summary of Rembrandt's strengths as a history painter. The well-thought-out narrative demonstrates his tremendous powers of imagination, linked with his archaeological interest and a convincing portrayal of reality (naturalness). Rembrandt always placed particular emphasis on the human aspect of the story. His view is not so much moralising, but rather an emphatic observation of human emotions.

Tronies and single figures

The move from Leiden to Amsterdam was also accompanied by a change in the *tronies*: the character heads were enlarged into impressive single figures, in some cases with the size of the large portraits of these years – like the *Old Man with a Gold Chain* (p. 255,

Jan Lievens, **Head of an Old Woman in Profile ("Rembrandt's Mother")**, *c.* 1630
Oil on panel, 43.2 × 33.7 cm (17 × 13 3/8 in.)
Kingston, Ontario, Queen's University, Agnes Etherington Art Centre

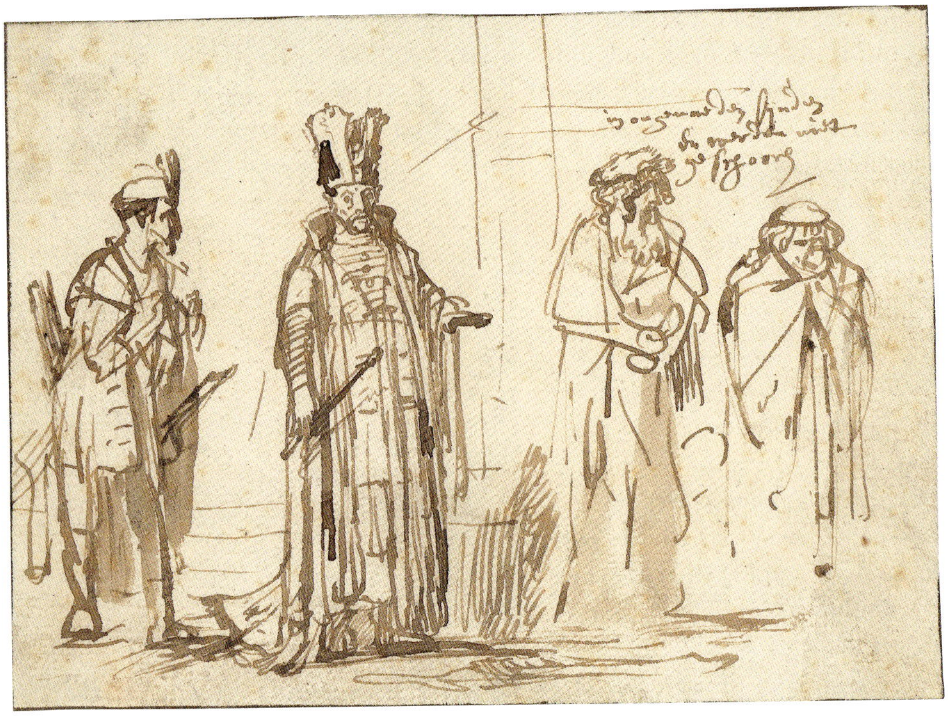

Cat. 280) from 1631/32. The wrinkled character head with the penetrating gaze is shown in great detail. The same model can be found on several occasions in Rembrandt's early works. His picturesque accoutrements are an amalgam of various historical and military elements. In this painting the light takes on an important role because of the way the various materials are reflected. The gleaming gold chain and the steel gorget stand out strongly against the opulent dark of the black velvet.

In the *Scholar in His Study* (p. 251, Cat. 285) from 1634, too, the entire focus is on the virtuoso portrayal of the wrinkled skin, the sheen of the tablecloth and the gold on the black velvet cloak. As in the case of the *Old Woman Reading a Book* (so-called *Prophetess Anna*; p. 222, Cat. 43), this large-size figure is very difficult to catagorise. The character head and the picturesque clothing recall the type of the *tronie*, but the large format and the numerous scholarly attributes suggest that this may in fact be a history painting.

A Russian Archer, a Nobleman and Two Bearded Russians, *c.* 1636
Pen and brush in brown, 14.3 × 20 cm (5 ¾ × 7 ⅞ in.)
New York, The Morgan Library & Museum

In the impressive life-size *Man in Oriental Costume* (so-called *Noble Slav*; p. 253, Cat. 281) from 1632 the colourfulness was sacrificed in favour of the convincing suggestion of light. Here, too, the illuminated parts like the golden yellow fabric of the cloak and the aged features of the man are depicted in great detail, while the hand and the shaded part of his costume are only hinted at in a summary manner. At the time, people were fascinated by the absolute power and enormous wealth of Oriental princes. For Rembrandt, painting such exotic figures was attractive because he could allow his fantasy free rein in the depiction of richly patterned fabrics, jewels and picturesque heads. As a history painter he already had experience with the portrayal of such types; his oriental *tronies* seem to be a logical continuation.

The work seems to be a reaction to the single figure of an Oriental prince (Potsdam, Sanssouci) which Jan Lievens had painted earlier for the stadtholder and of which Huygens reported that the artist had taken a Dutchman as model (p. 252).[107] Lievens used cool, greyish-blue colours for his Oriental ruler, while Rembrandt's prince appears out of the darkness in shining gold. The exotic clothing, the pearl earrings and the *aigrettes* on the tall turban are almost identical in the two paintings. Rembrandt's Oriental wears around his neck a scarf of many colours with gold threads that is almost iridescent. Lievens was also a brilliant master of the reproduction of iridescent fabrics, as his *Man in Oriental Costume* and *Head of an Old Woman in Profile* from about 1630 prove (p. 125). In Rembrandt's *Man in Oriental Costume* (p. 254, Cat. 286) from 1633/34 the many-coloured scarf was used as a turban. The contrast between the detailed execution of the illuminated parts and the sketch-like treatment of the hands and costume in the shadows is heightened still further here.

The *tronie* of the *Young Woman with Pearl Earrings* (p. 264, Cat. 312) shows the model more or less frontally and more evenly illuminated. This lighting is probably chosen as a result of the subject, because here the main focus is on the portrayal of the smooth young skin with the delicate pink of the cheeks and the golden hair. During these years, Rembrandt painted *tronies* of young women in profile on two occasions (Cat. 314; p. 201, Cat. 317). The pose shows a resemblance with the *Portrait of Amalia of Solms* from 1632 (p. 169, Cat. 210).

The realistic portrayal of the heads and the convincing depiction of the fabrics might give the impression that Rembrandt dressed live models in these picturesque accoutrements. In fact, a significant number of his historical or exotic costumes derived from prints. A good example of this approach is his *Standard Bearer* from 1636 (p. 262, Cat. 289), a work that is praised for its remarkable three-dimensionality, the successful use of shadows and the convincing shiny highlights on the arm.[108] This highly life-like figure has even been interpreted as a (self-)portrait on more than one occasion. Nonetheless, this martial figure is based almost literally on a small woodcut after Jörg Breu the Younger (*c.* 1510–1547) from about 1530 (p. 129). It shows clearly how experienced Rembrandt was in rendering a deceptively realistic-looking figure, even when he based the work on a two-dimensional source. The woodcut also puts into perspective the heroic meaning which has been given to Rembrandt's standard bearer. The corpulent mercenary who served as a model, on the other hand, had a humorous character and bore the title *Stoffel Allweg Vol* (Stoffel Always Drunk).

The loosely painted *Russian Boyar* (p. 263, Cat. 290) from 1637 is sometimes also thought to be a portrait because of its lively features. The deeply furrowed brow speaks against this idea, however. Rembrandt's fascination during these years with Russian dress and the foreign customs at the Muscovite court is demonstrated in a drawing from about 1637 (p. 126, Cat. D46), in which a tsar is dismissing two courtiers who have fallen into disgrace (*opala*). As in many of his "oriental" *tronies*, Rembrandt was inspired here, too, by costume plates and print series of princely portraits (real or imaginary) when portraying elements of the dress.

Pupils

As has already been indicated, the enormous number of portraits which were produced in Uylenburgh's workshop under Rembrandt's guidance could only be realised because studio collaborators and assistants carried out parts of the works to a greater or lesser degree. Thus the *Portrait of a Seated Man* from around 1632 (Cat. 221) was very probably painted by Rembrandt himself, but the companion piece, *Portrait of a Seated Woman* (Cat. 222*), was probably laid out by Rembrandt but executed by another painter. There can be no doubt that the portraits belong together because both are painted on panels of (rare) walnut wood with the same measurements.

There seems to have been no fixed division of work in Uylenburgh's workshop. The assistants did not specialise in certain details, such as the clothes or jewels, as was usual, for example, in the large Rubens workshop in Antwerp or in the "portrait factory" of Michiel Jansz. van Mierevelt in Delft.[109] In Uylenburgh's workshop, the (anonymous) assistants took over varying parts of the portraits. Thus, there is a difference in the way Rembrandt painted lace patterns and the lace which the assistants executed.[110] It seems that only small parts of the portrait were painted by one of Rembrandt's assistants, like the hands in the *Portrait of Johannes Wtenbogaert* from 1633 (p. 159, Cat. 184) or the lace pattern on the collar in the *Portrait of Philips Lucasz.* from 1635 (Cat. 245*).

During these years, Uylenburgh's workshop appears to have attracted a large number of young artists who wanted to work under the direction of Rembrandt in order to

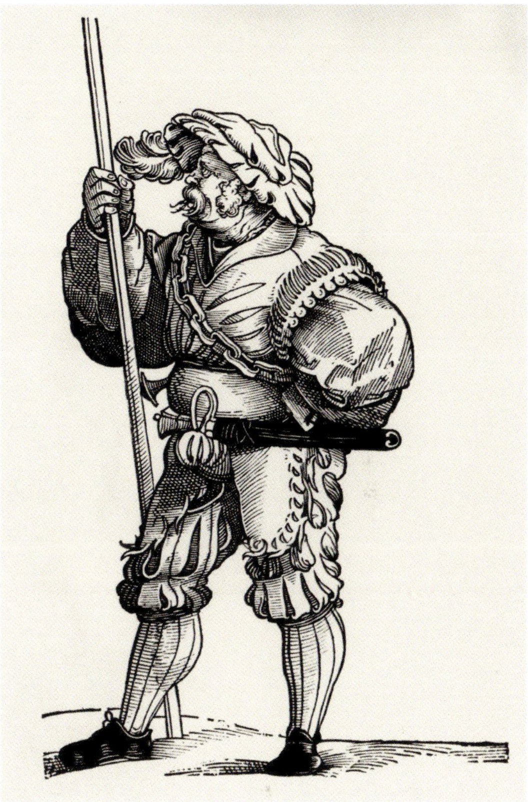

learn how to paint in his style. They included talented young artists like Govert Flinck from Cleves, who completed his training in the workshop of Lambert Jacobsz. (*c.* 1598–1636) in Leeuwarden. Houbraken reported that Flinck had moved because at the time "Rembrandt's manner was generally praised, so that everything had to be tailored to fit this same pattern if it was to find favour with the world". Flinck even succeeded within a short space of time in "imitating [Rembrandt's way of working], so that some of his pictures were taken for authentic paintings by Rembrandt and were sold as such".[111]

The fact that workshop assistants were actually able to imitate Rembrandt's style with such skill is evidenced by the fact that discussions continue today regarding the attribution of some works. In May 1635, Flinck took Rembrandt's place as the head of Uylenburgh's workshop and remained there until 1644. In later years he had a highly successful career as a portraitist and history painter and became one of Rembrandt's important rivals.[112] The same applied to Ferdinand Bol (1616–1680), who moved to Amsterdam from Dordrecht in 1636 in order to serve an apprenticeship under Rembrandt. Rembrandt was just establishing his own workshop at that time. In order to contribute to the workshop production, Rembrandt's apprentices made copies of his works. On the back of a drawing Rembrandt noted in 1637 the prices which he received for these workshop copies (RD Undated Doc. 3, pp. 594–595). He was referring to copies by Bol and by another painter, Leendert Cornelisz. van Beijeren (1619–1649), after his *Flora* (p. 203, Cat. 103) from 1635 and *The Standard Bearer* (p. 262, Cat. 289) from 1636.

Jost de Negker after Jörg Breu the Younger, **Stoffel Always Drunk**, *c.* 1530
Woodcut, 30.5 × 9.7 cm (12 × 3 7⁄8 in.). Hulton Archive

Detail of: **Self-Portrait**, *c.* 1638
(see ill. p. 199)

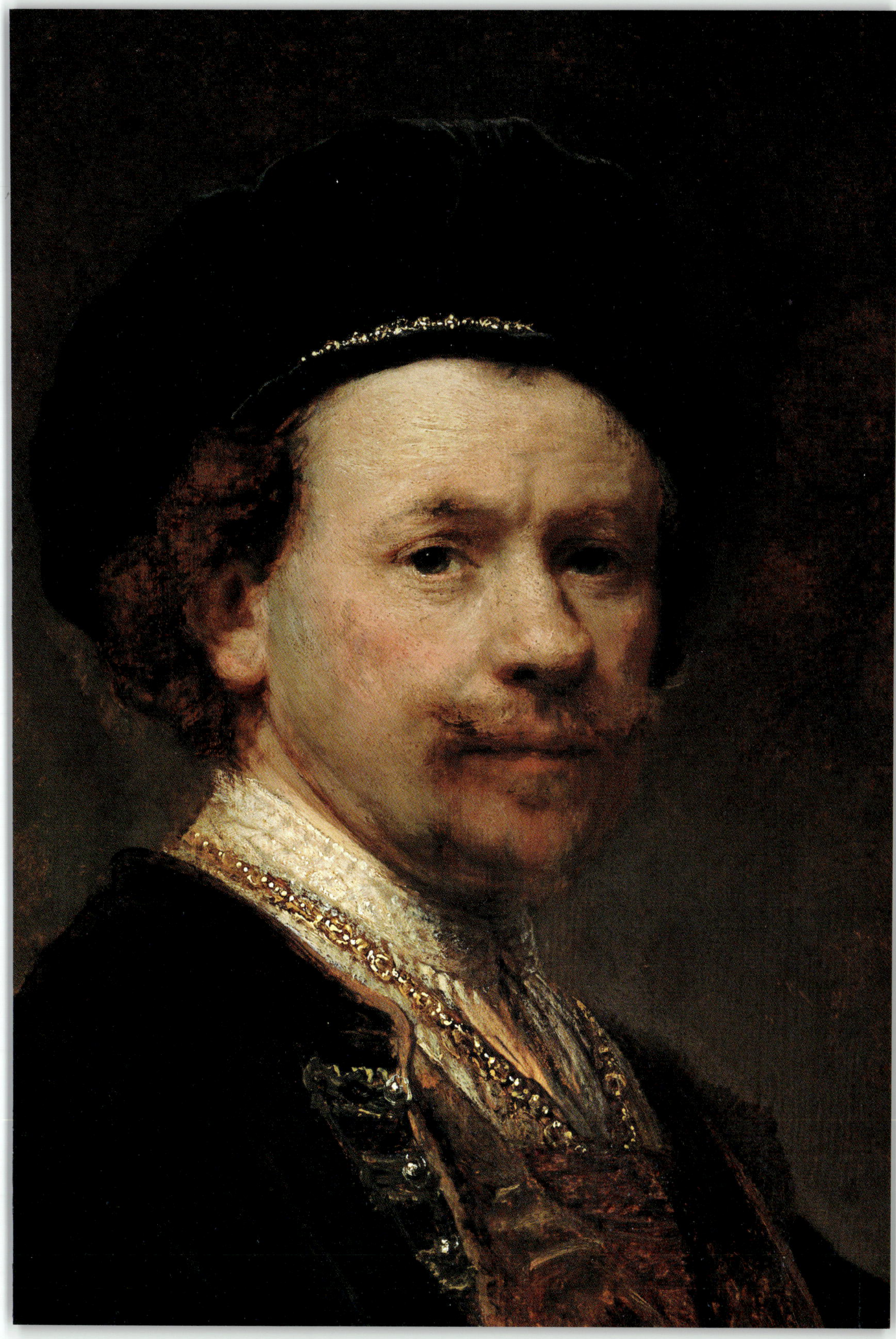

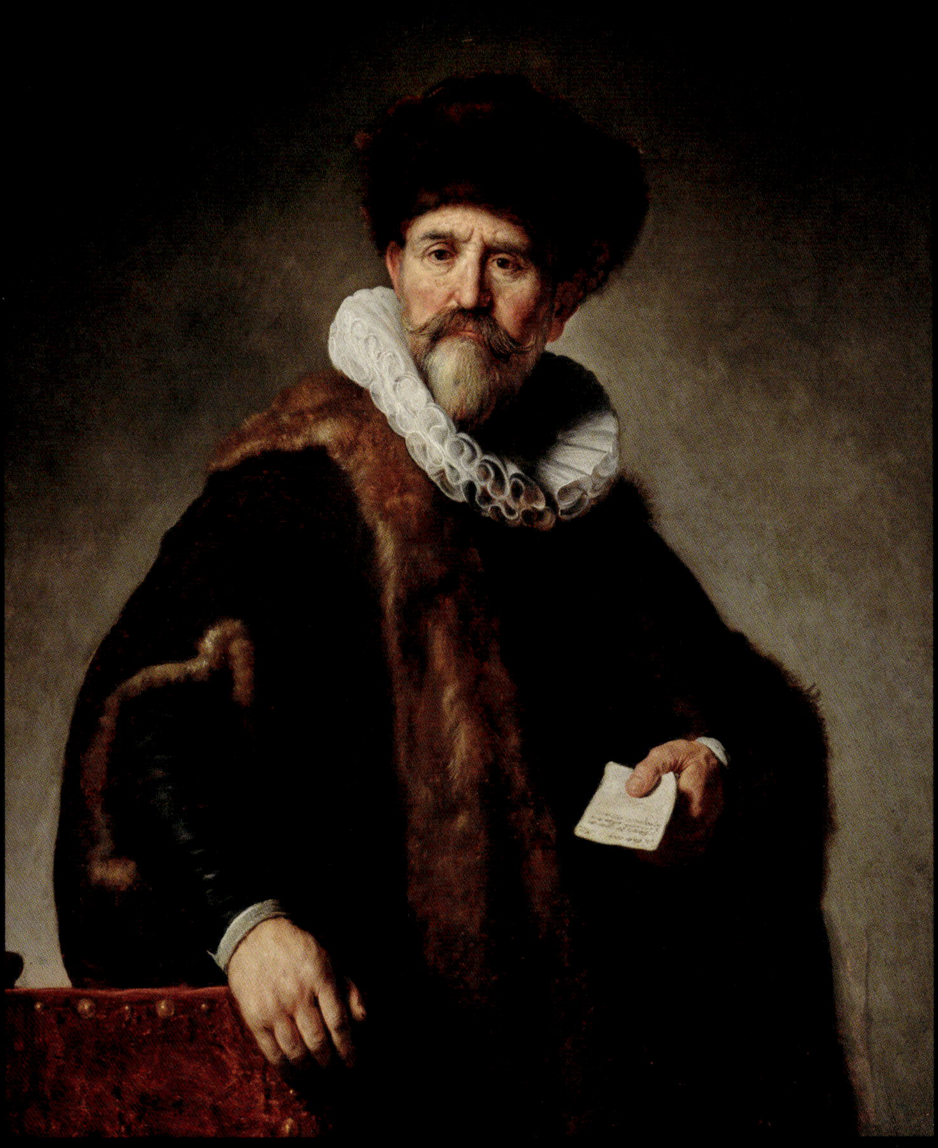

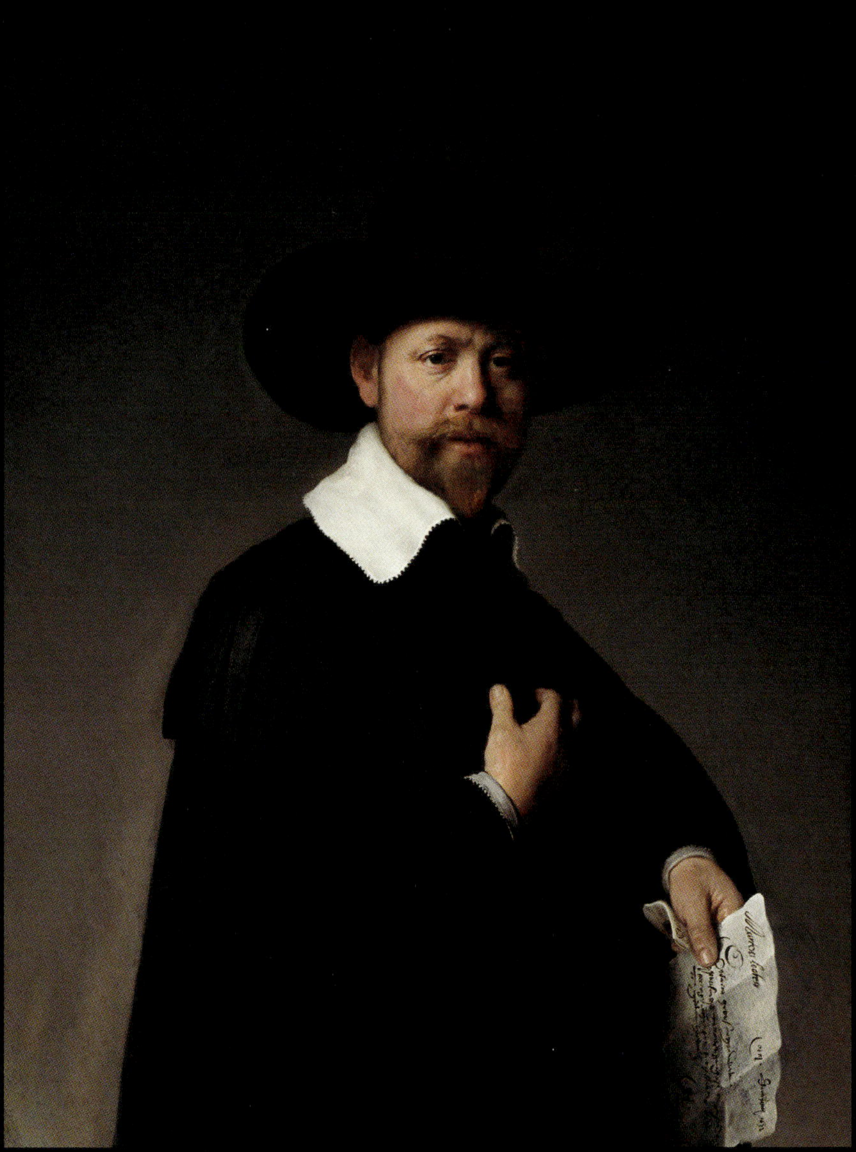

Portrait of Nicolaes Ruts, 1631
Oil on panel, 116.8 × 87.3 cm (45 ¾ × 34 ⅜ in.). New York, The Frick Collection

Portrait of Marten Looten, 1632
Oil on panel, 92.7 × 76.2 cm (36 ½ × 30 in.). Los Angeles County Museum of Art

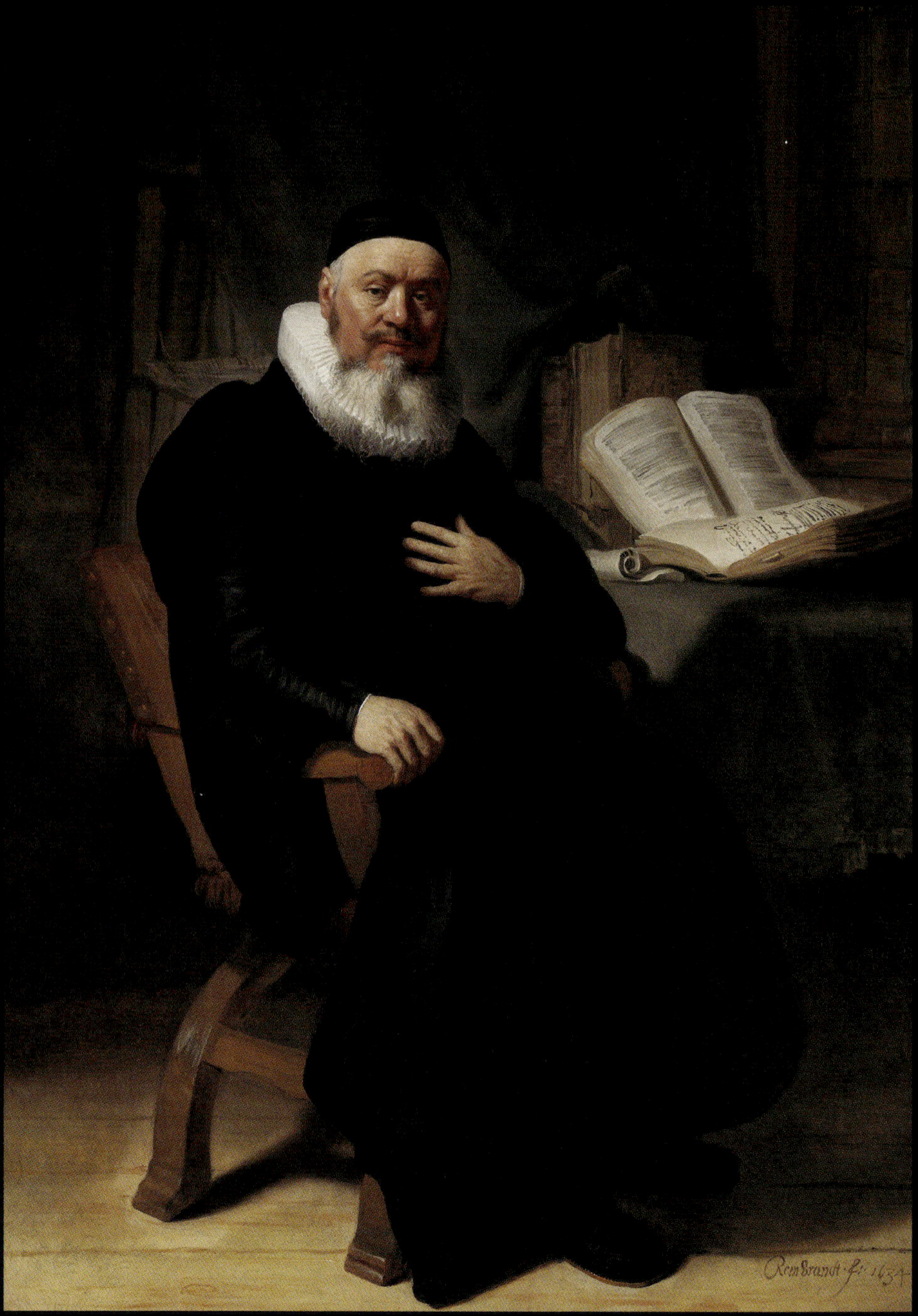

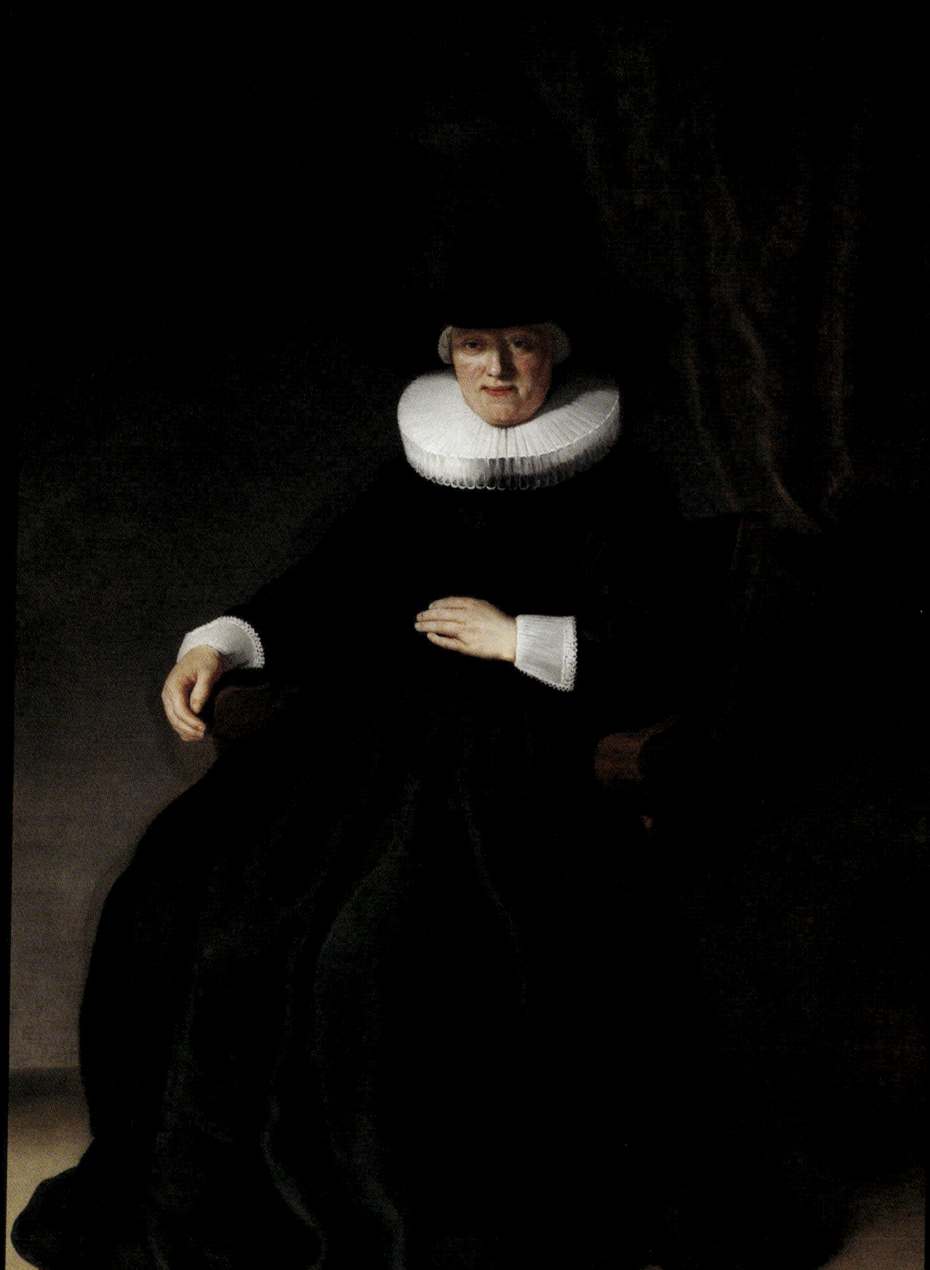

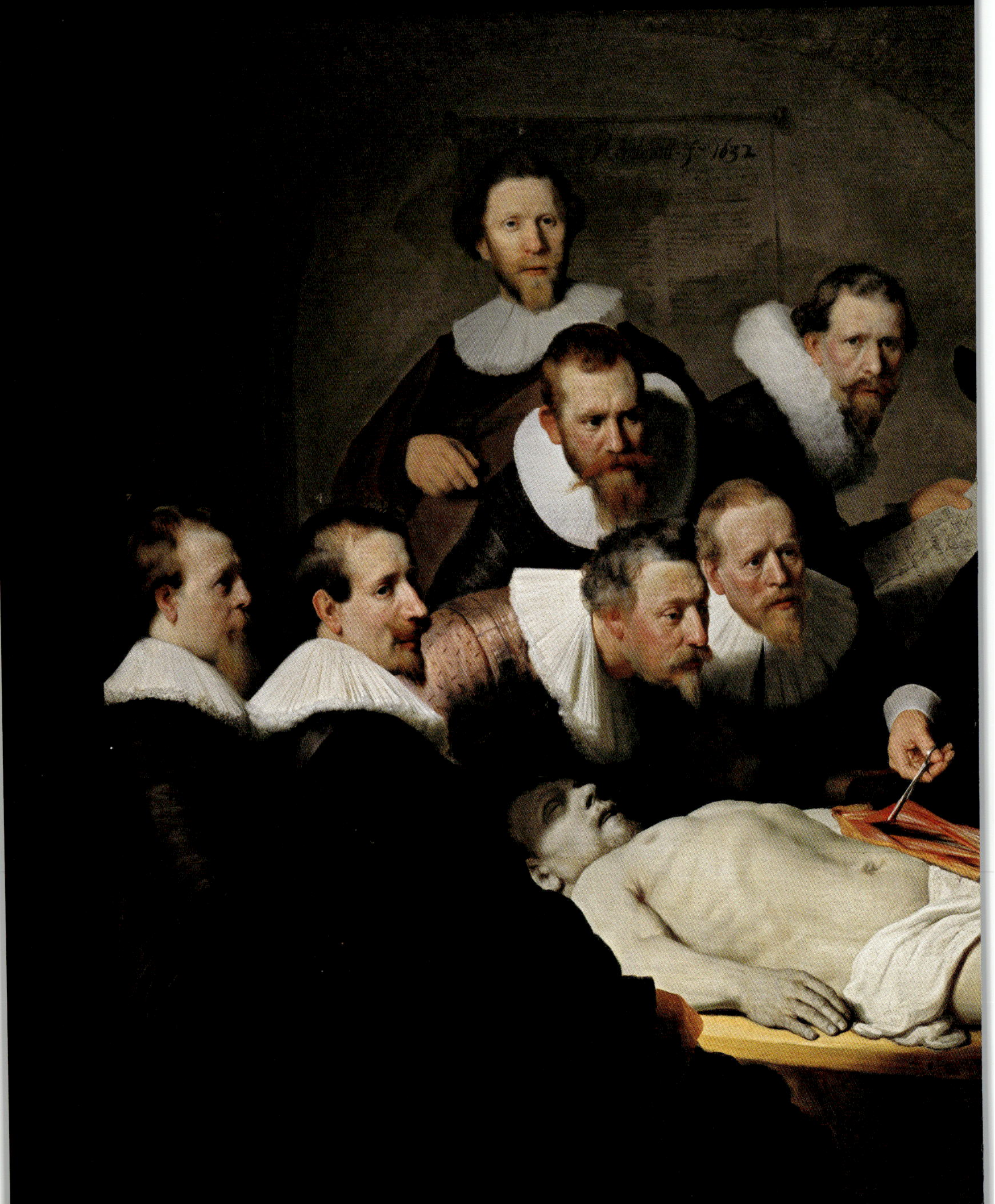

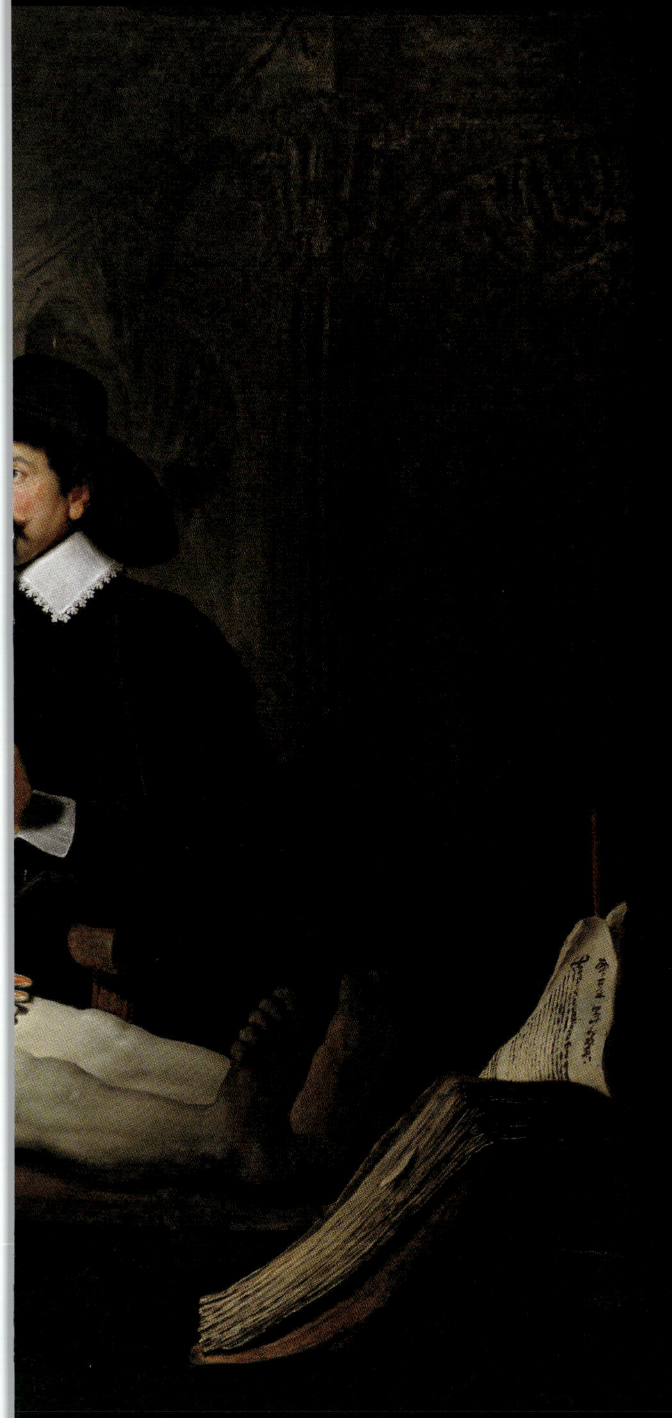

Page 134
Portrait of
Johannes Elison, 1634
Oil on canvas, 174 × 124.5 cm
(68 ½ × 49 ⅛ in.)
Boston, Massachusetts,
Museum of Fine Arts,
William K. Richardson Fund

Page 135
Portrait of
Maria Bockenolle, 1634
Oil on canvas, 174.5 × 123 cm
(68 ¾ × 48 ⅜ in.)
Boston, Massachusetts,
Museum of Fine Arts,
William K. Richardson Fund

The Anatomy Lesson of
Dr Nicolaes Tulp, 1632
Oil on canvas,
169.5 × 216.5 cm
(66 ¾ × 85 ¼ in.)
The Hague, Mauritshuis
(detail pages 138/139)

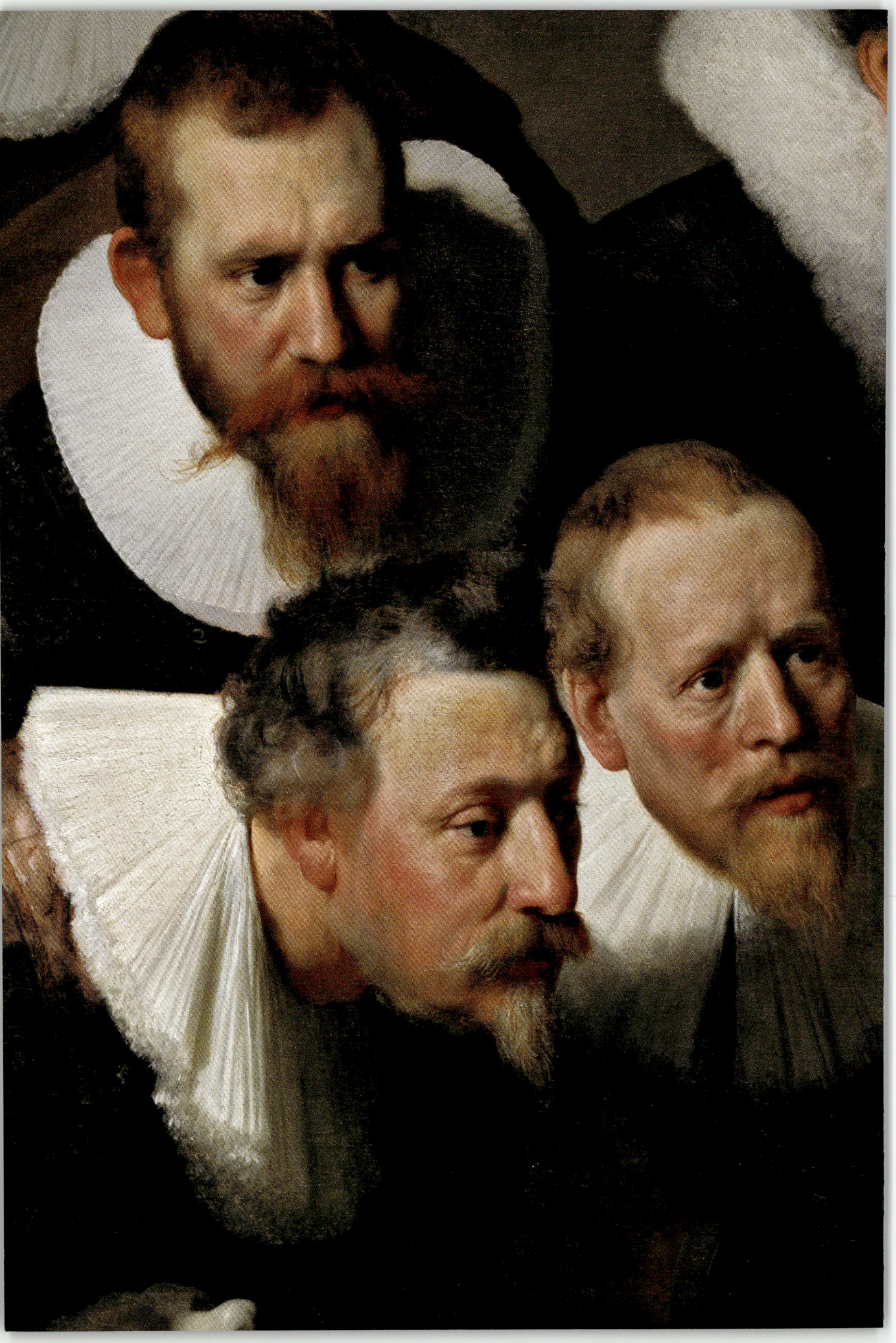

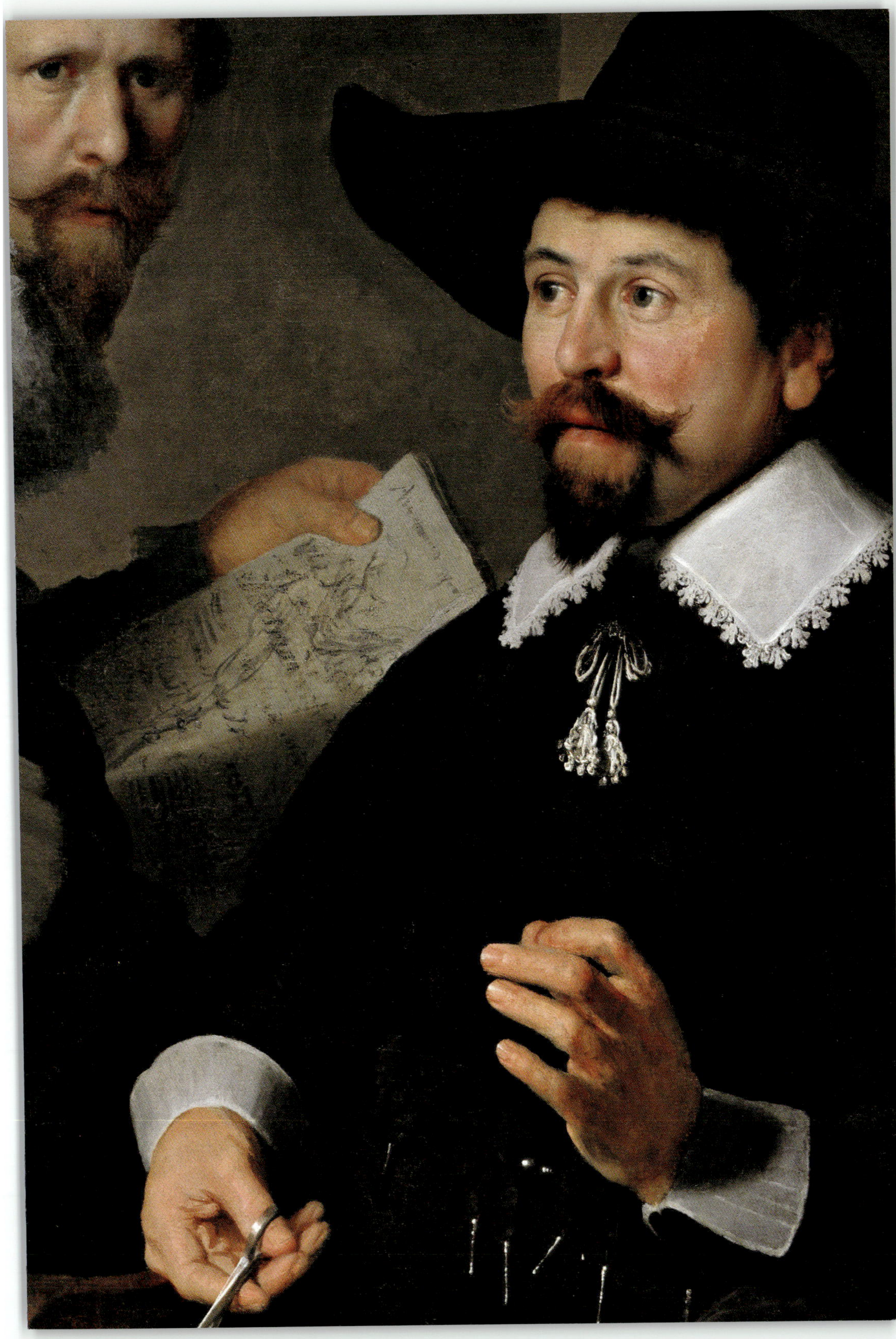

Portrait of a Man Writing at His Desk, 1631
Oil on canvas, 104.5 × 92 cm (41 ⅛ × 36 ¼ in.)
St Petersburg, The State Hermitage Museum

Page 142
Portrait of a Man Trimming a Quill, 1632
Oil on canvas, 105 × 85 cm (41 ⅓ × 33 ½ in.)
Hessen Kassel Heritage, Gemäldegalerie Alte Meister

Page 143
Portrait of a Seated Young Woman, 1632
Oil on canvas, 92 × 71 cm (36 ¼ × 27 ¾ in.)
Vienna, Gemäldegalerie der Akademie der bildenden Künste Wien

Pages 144/145
Double Portrait of the Shipbuilder Jan Rijcksen and His Wife Griet Jans, 1633
Oil on canvas, 113.8 × 169.8 cm (44 ¾ × 66 ¾ in.)
London, Royal Collection

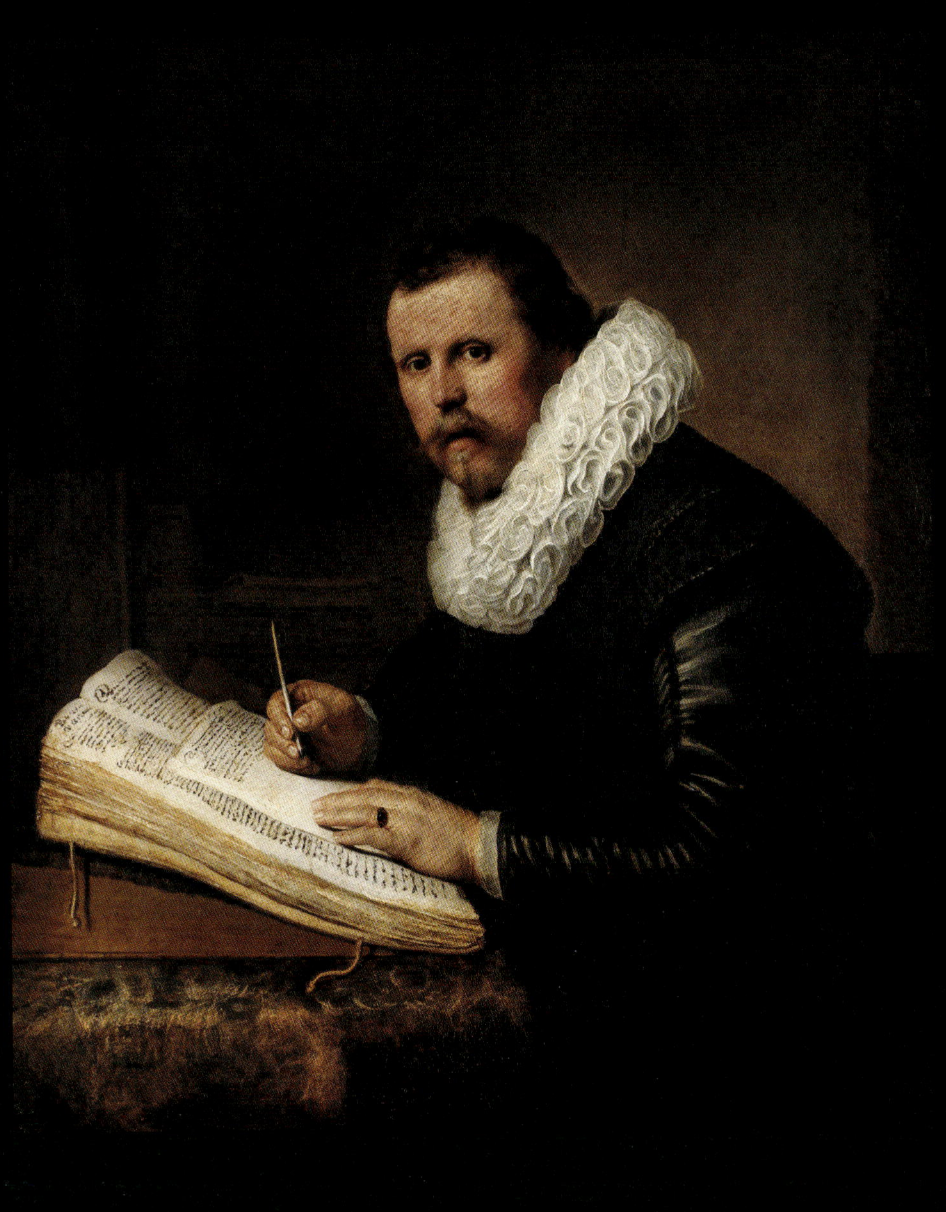

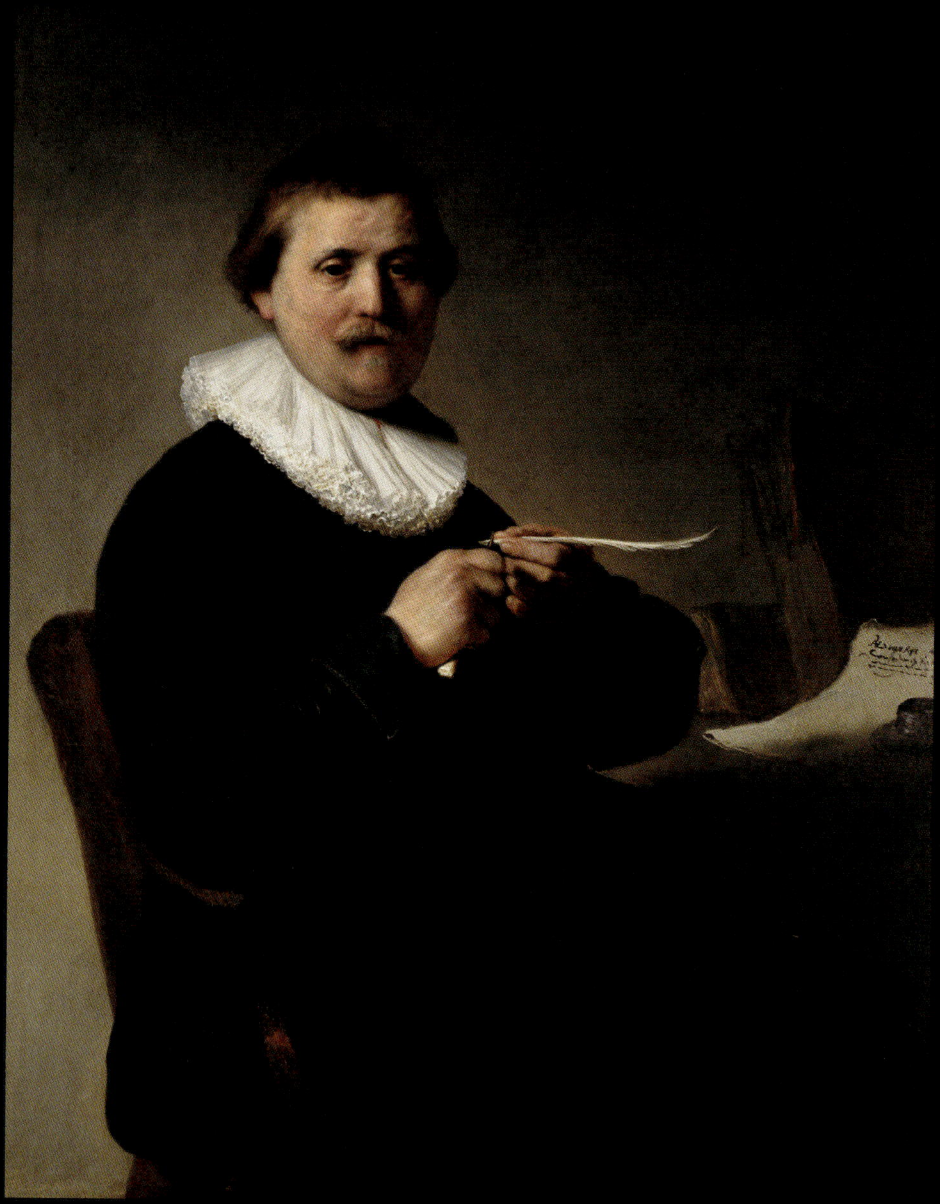

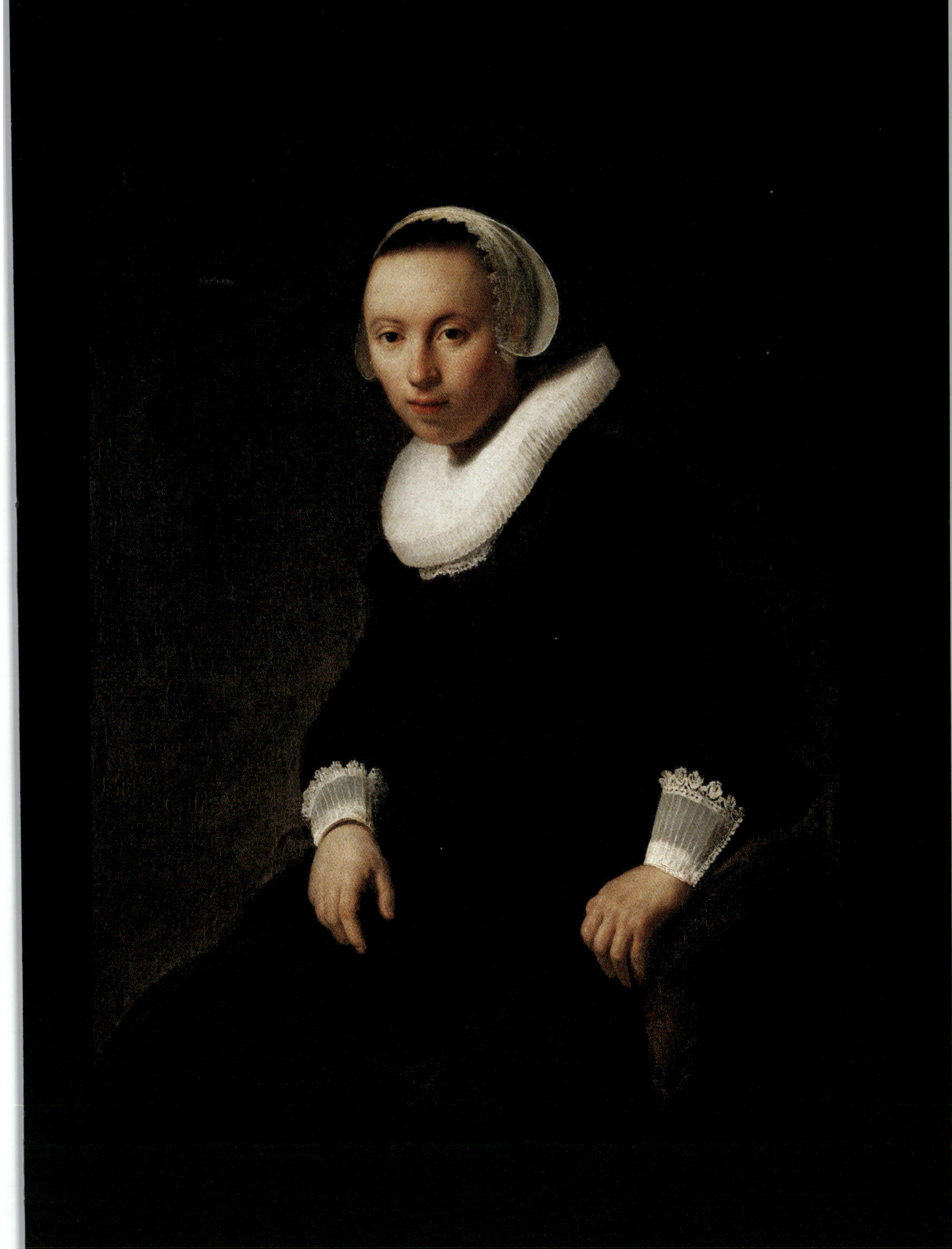

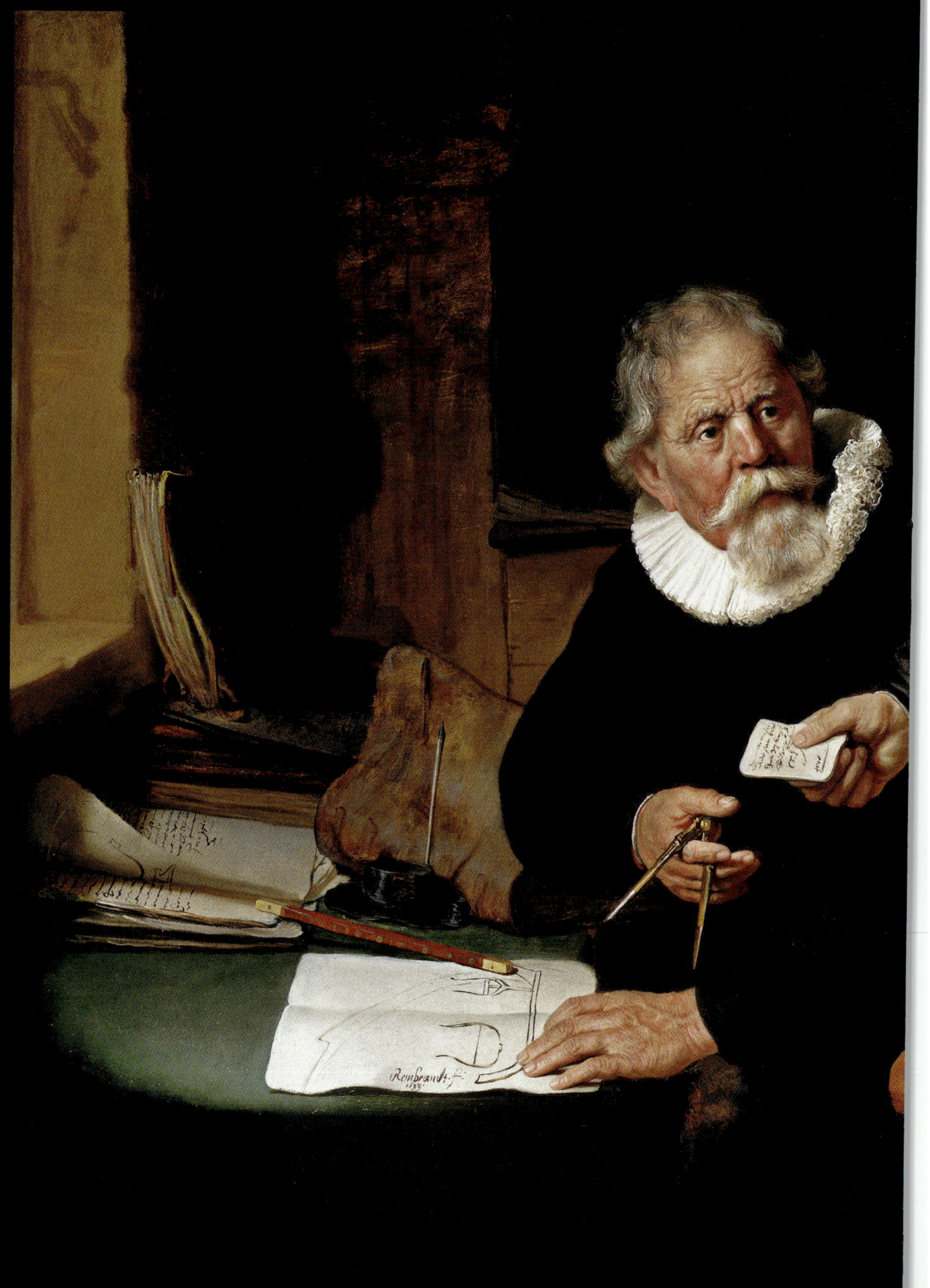

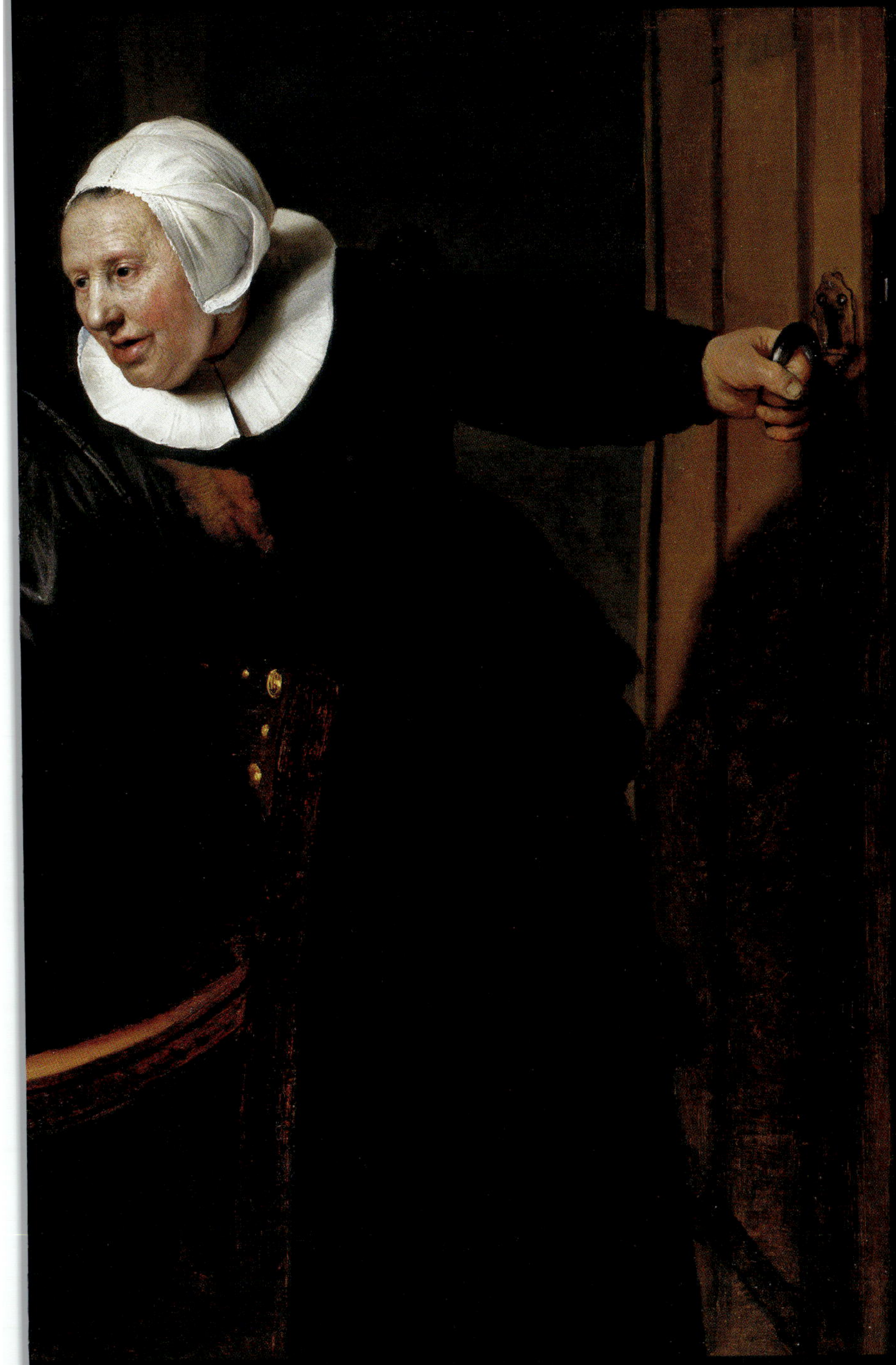

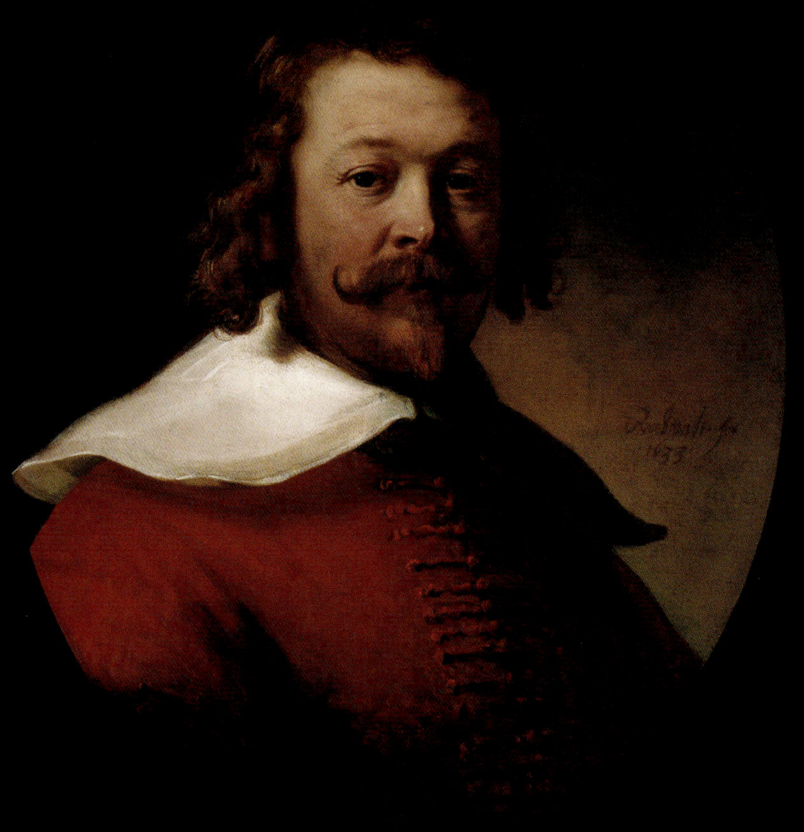

Portrait of a Man in a Red Coat, 1633
Oil on panel, 63.7 × 50.8 cm (25 ⅛ × 20 in.)
New York, The Leiden Collection

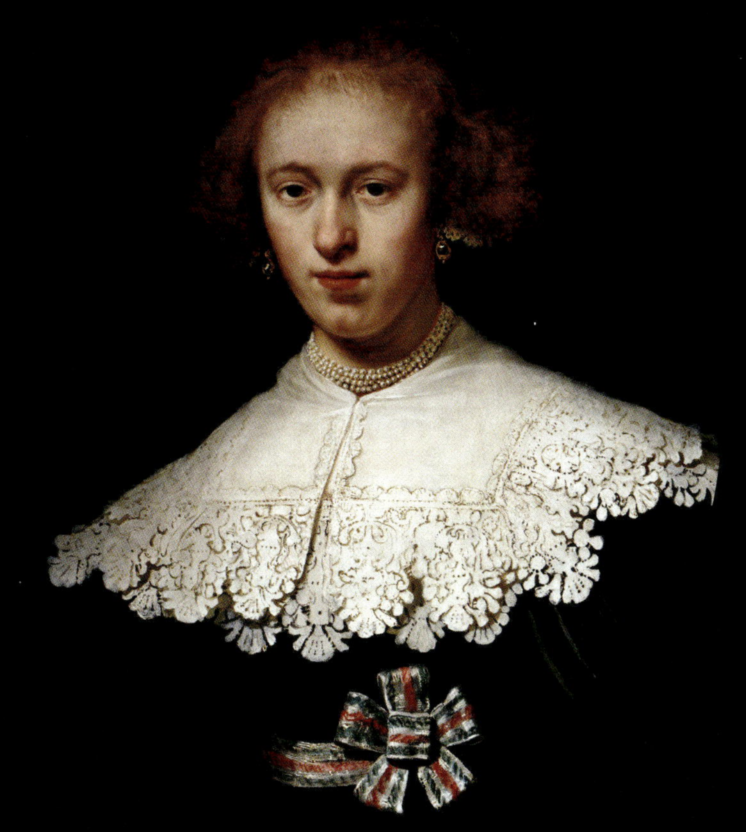

Portrait of a Young Woman, 1633
Oil on panel, 65.4 × 48.9 cm (25 ¾ × 19 ¼ in.)
Houston, Texas, The Museum of Fine Arts

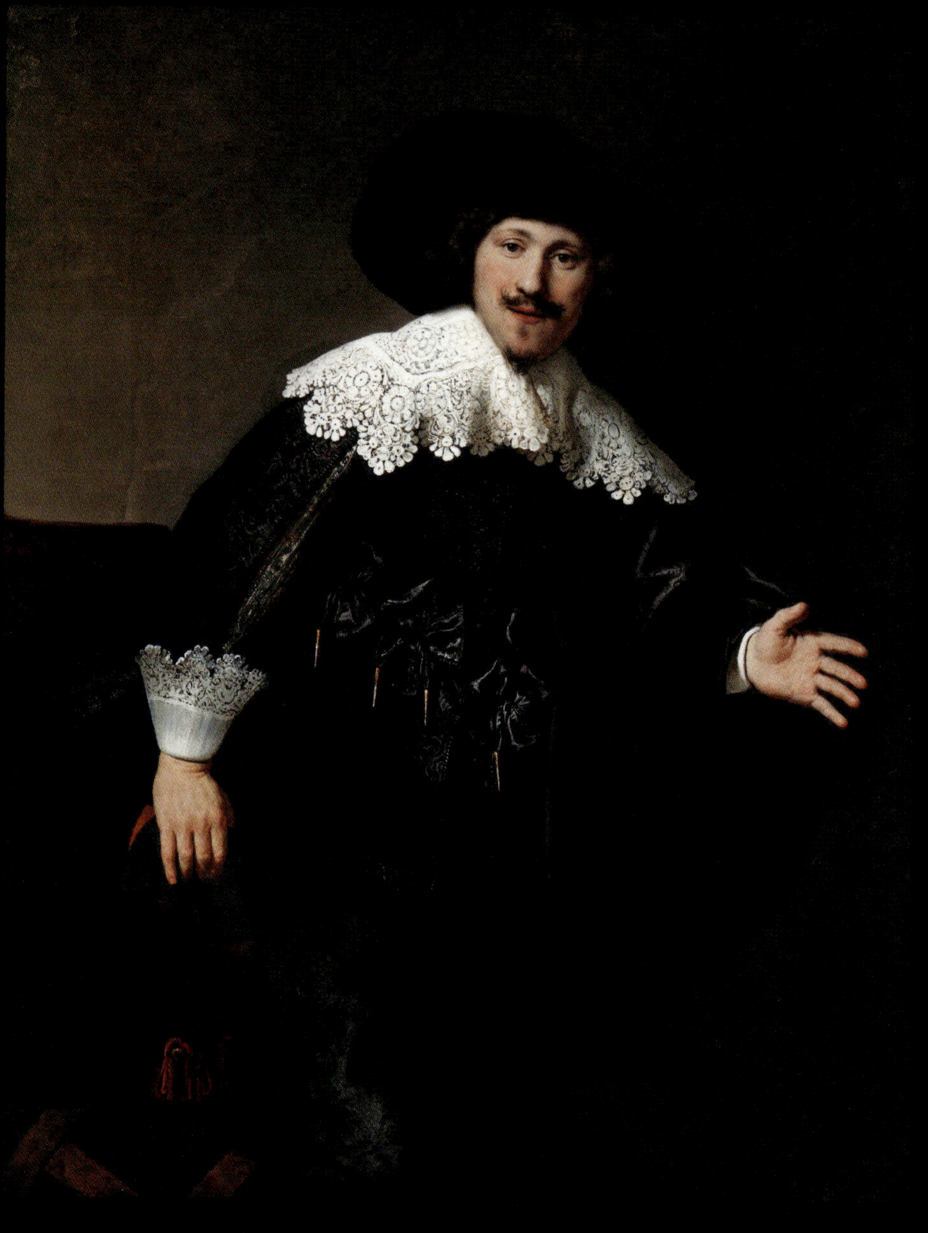

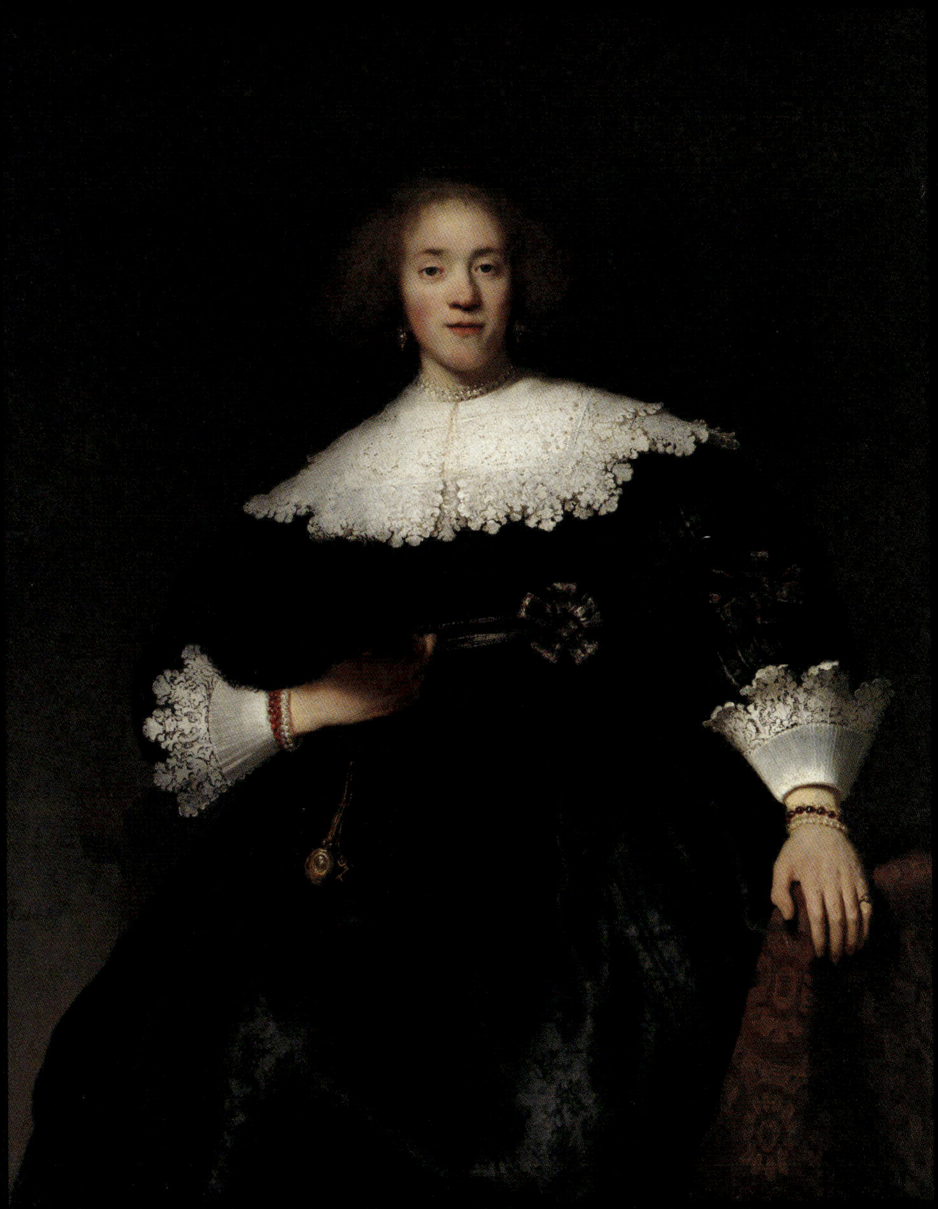

Page 148
Portrait of a Man Rising from His Chair, 1633
Oil on canvas, 124 × 98.5 cm (48 ¾ × 38 ¾ in.)
Cincinnati, Ohio, The Taft Museum

Page 149
Seated Woman with a Fan, 1633
Oil on canvas, 125.7 × 101 cm (49 ½ × 39 ¾ in.)
New York, The Metropolitan Museum of Art,
Gift of Helen Swift Neilson, 1943
(detail page 151)

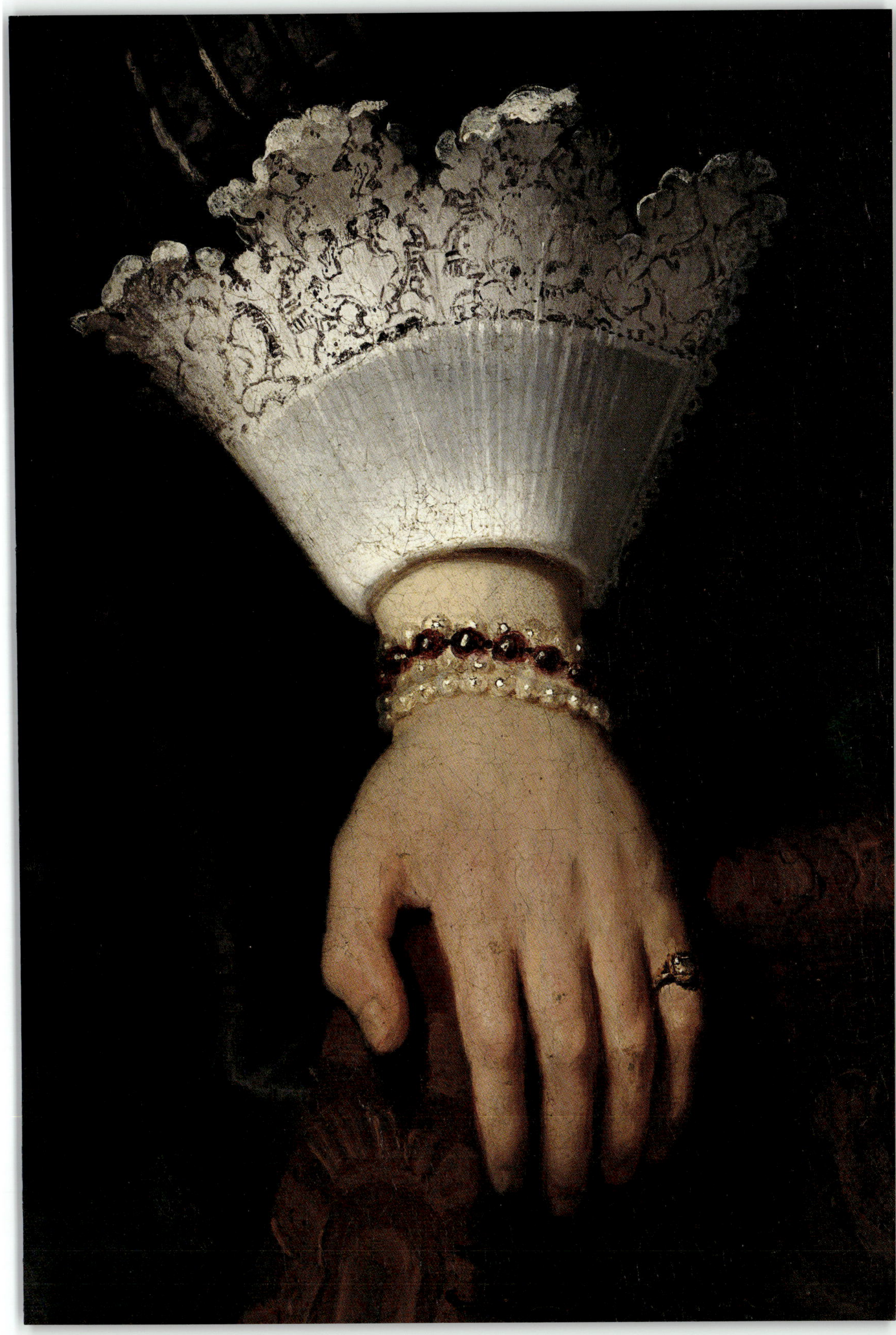

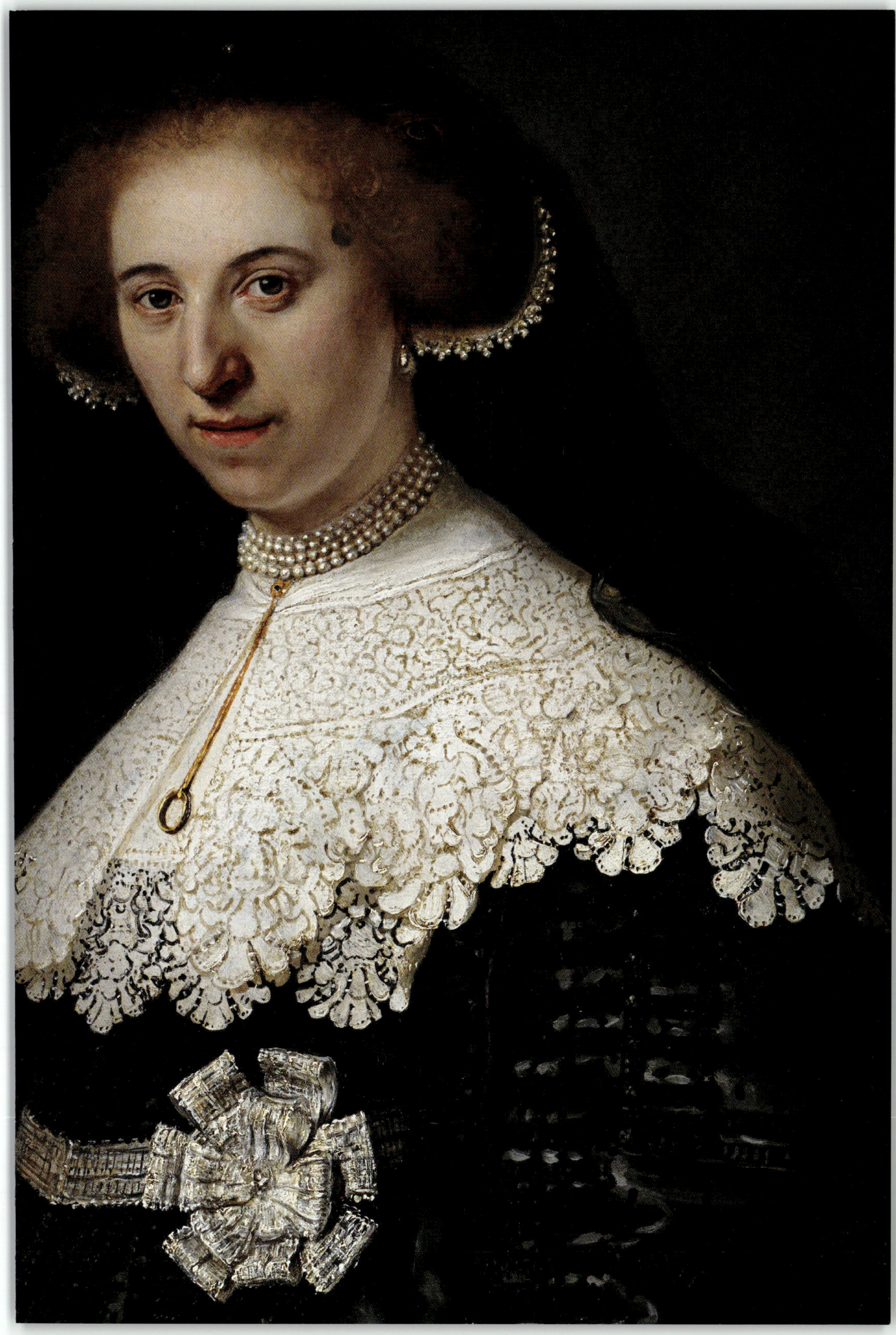

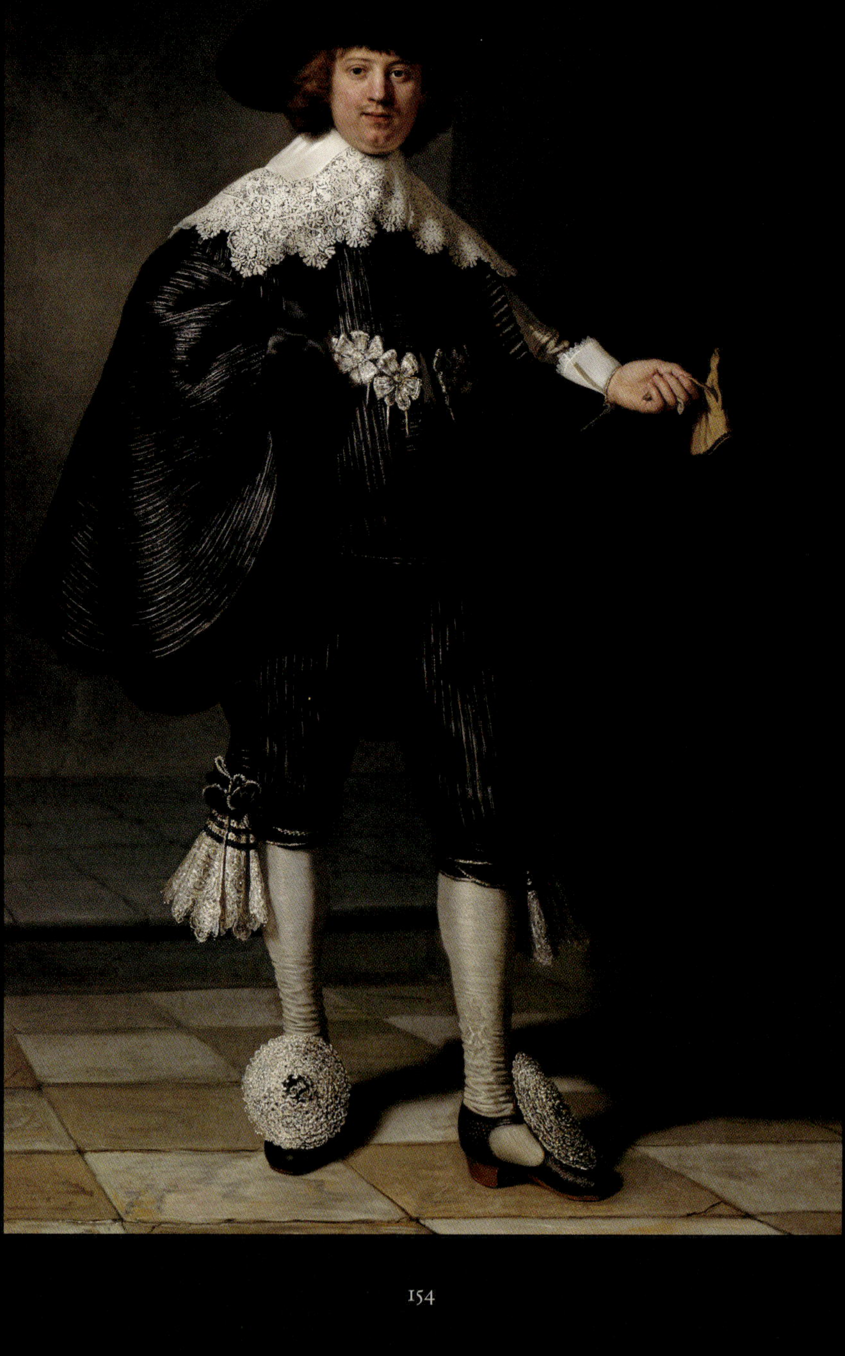

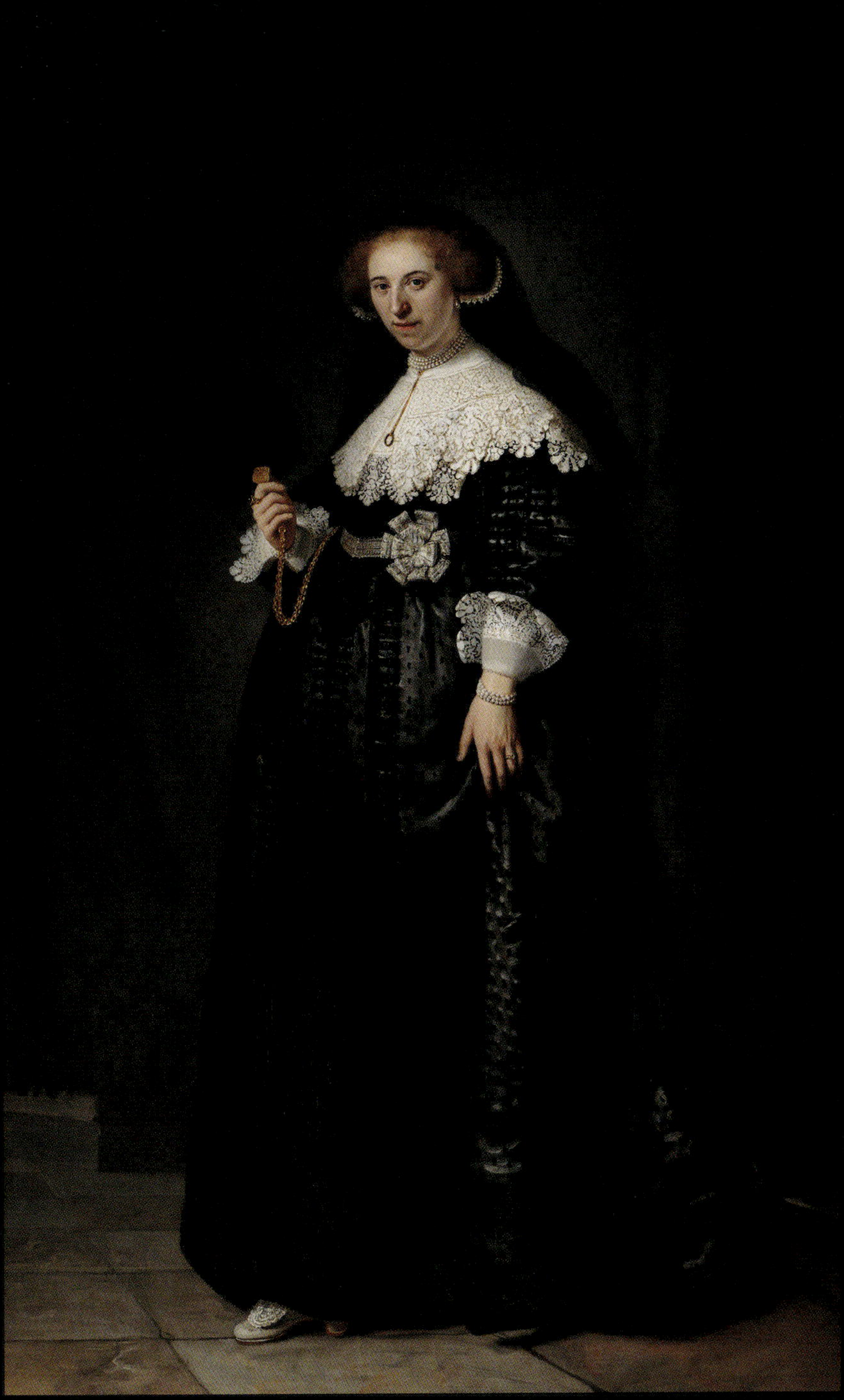

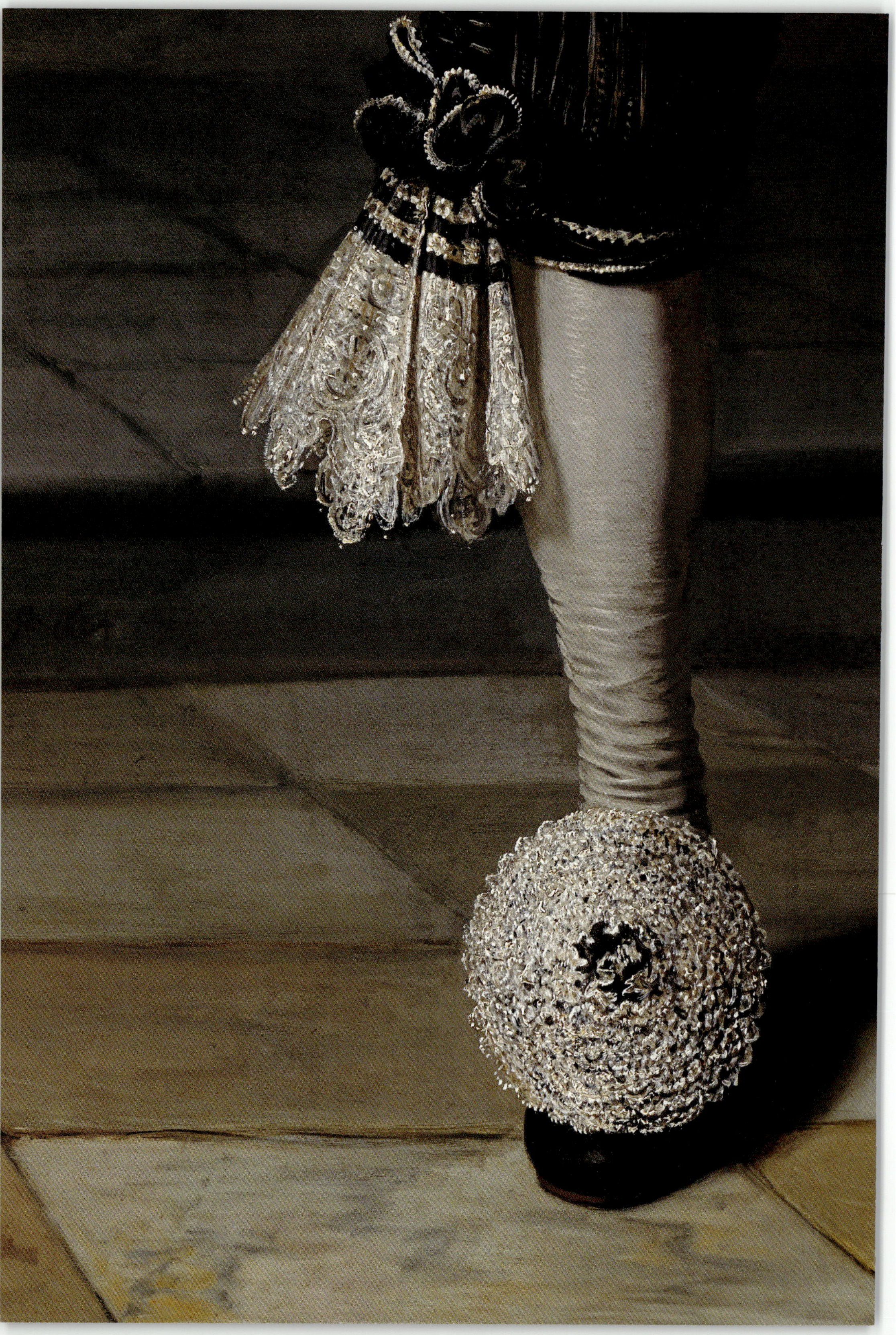

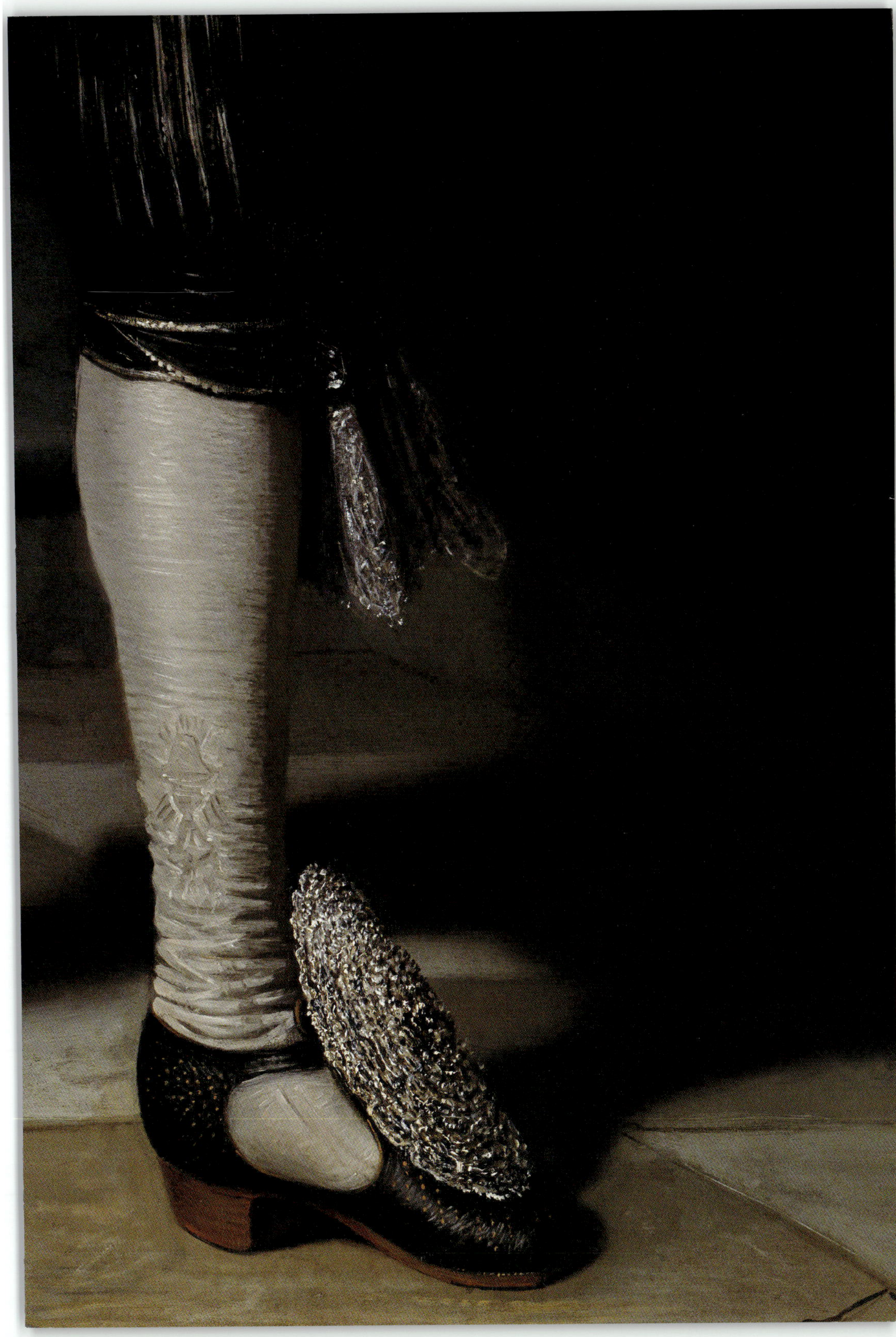

Page 154
Portrait of Marten Soolmans, 1634
Oil on canvas, 207 × 132.5 cm (81 ½ × 52 ⅛ in.)
Amsterdam, Rijksmuseum. Paris, Musée du Louvre
(detail pages 156/157)

Page 155
Portrait of Oopjen Coppit, *c.* 1634
Oil on canvas, 207 × 132 cm (81 ½ × 51 ¾ in.)
Amsterdam, Rijksmuseum. Paris, Musée du Louvre
(detail pages 152/153)

Portrait of Johannes Wtenbogaert, 1633
Oil on canvas, 130 × 103 cm (51 ⅛ × 40 ½ in.)
Amsterdam, Rijksmuseum

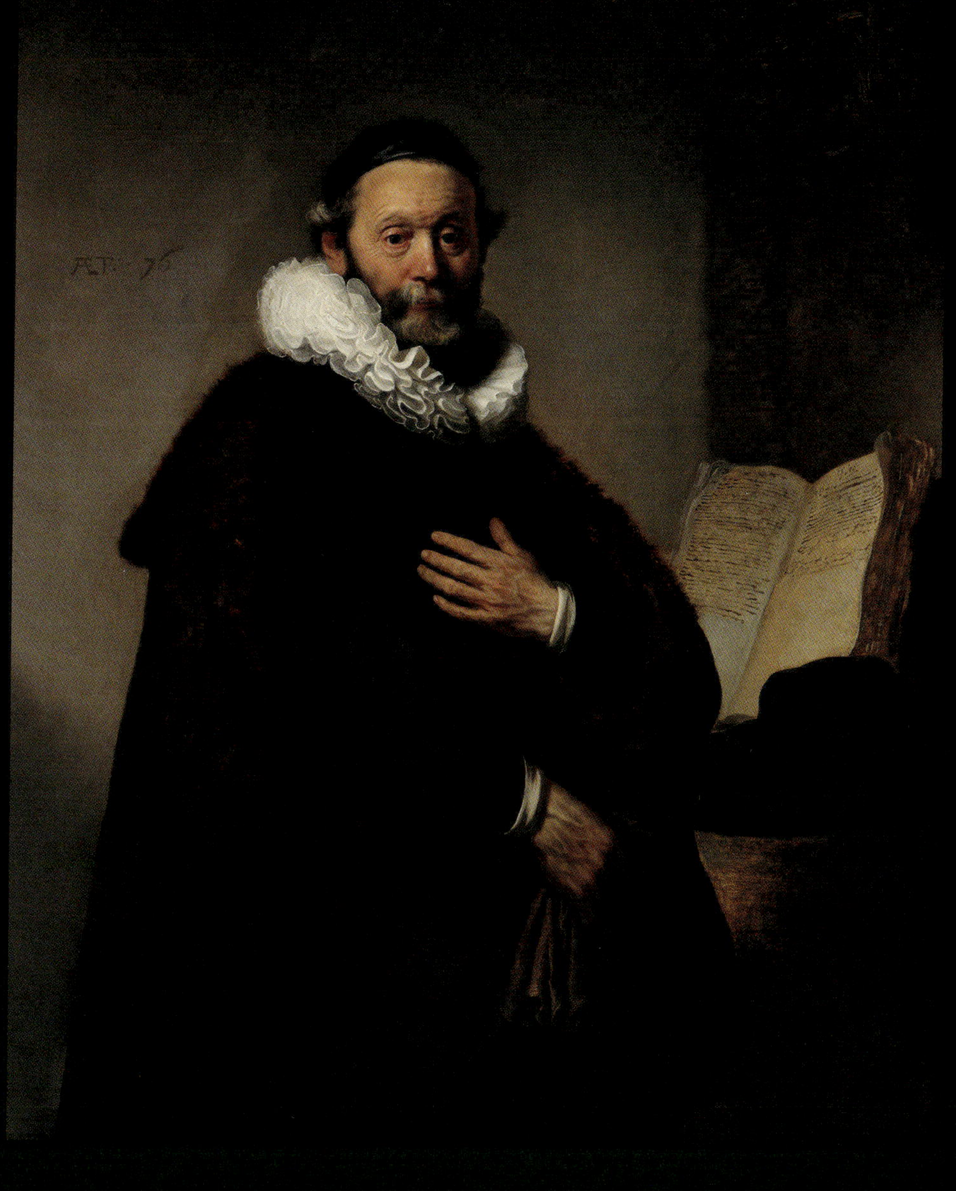

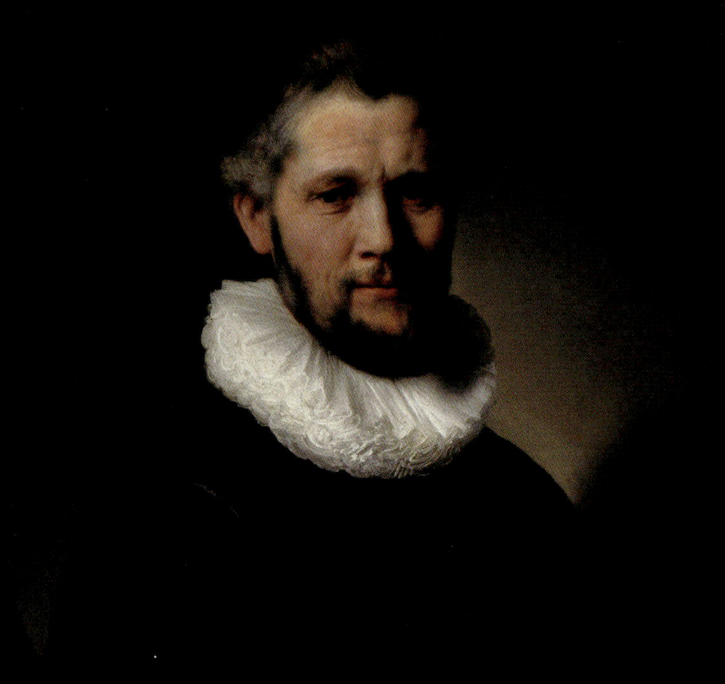

Portrait of a 40-Year-Old Man, 1632
Oil on panel, 75.6 × 52.1 cm (29 ¾ × 20 ½ in.)
New York, The Metropolitan Museum of Art, Gift of
Mrs Lincoln Ellsworth, in memory of Lincoln Ellsworth, 1964

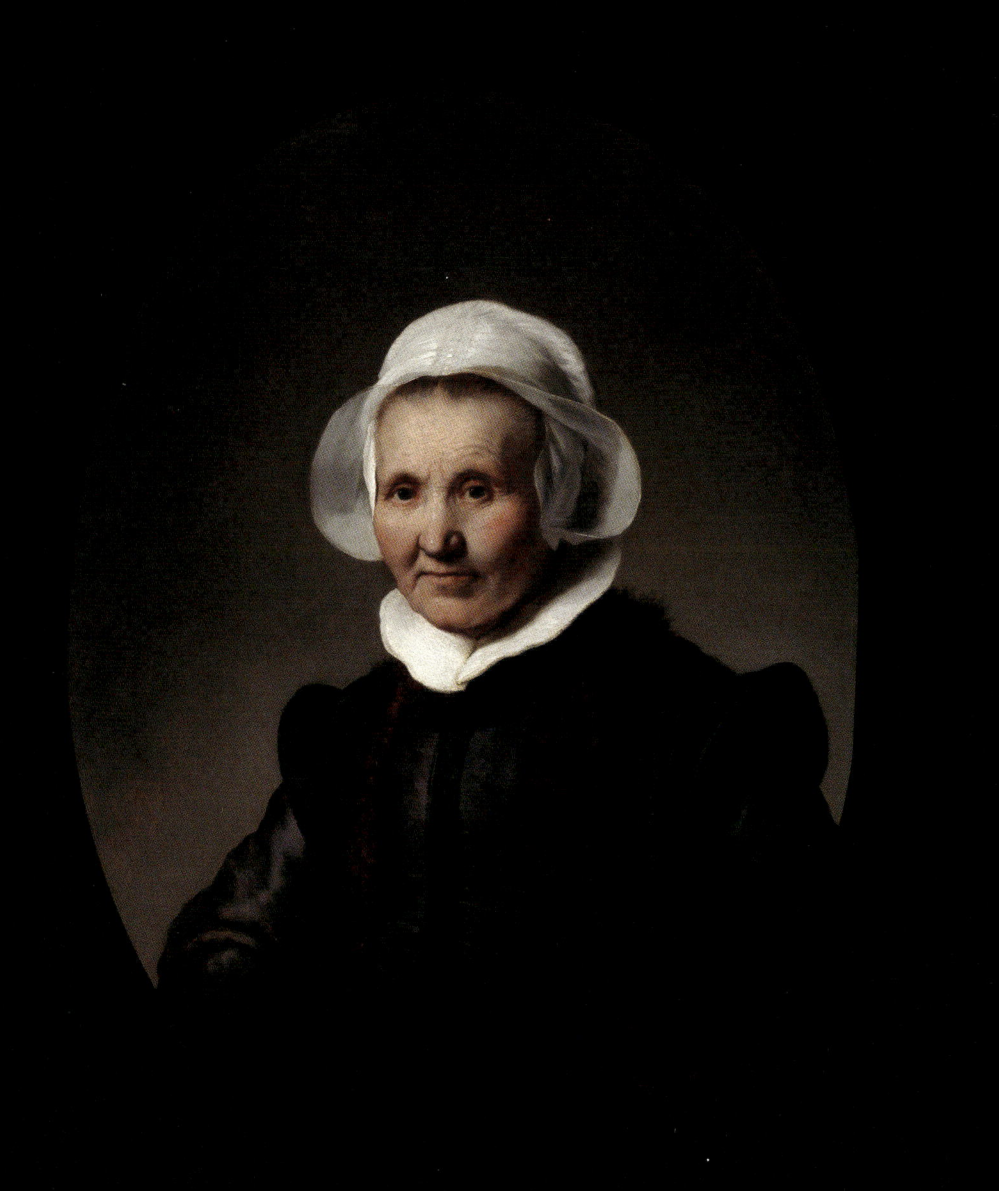

Portrait of a 62-Year-Old Woman (Aeltje Pietersdr. Uylenburgh?), 1632
Oil on panel, 73.7 × 55.8 cm (29 ⅛ × 21 ¾ in.)
Boston, Massachusetts, Museum of Fine Arts, promised gift of Rose-Marie & Eijk van Otterloo in support of the Center for Netherlandish Art

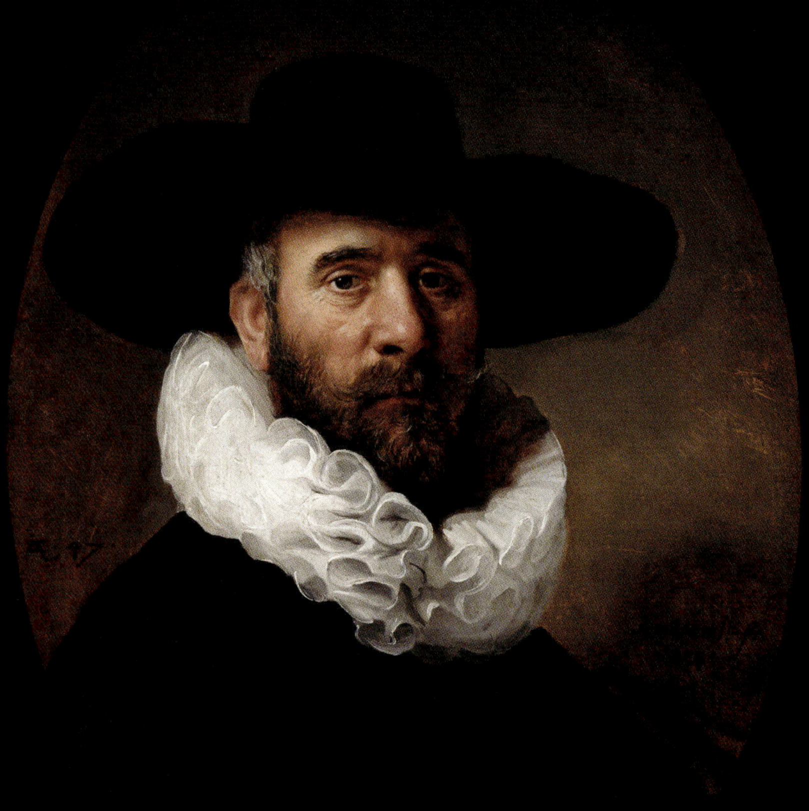

Portrait of Dirck Jansz. Pesser, *c.* 1634
Oil on panel, 64.8 × 50.5 cm (25 ½ × 19 ¾ in.)
Los Angeles County Museum of Art,
Frances and Armand Hammer Purchase Fund

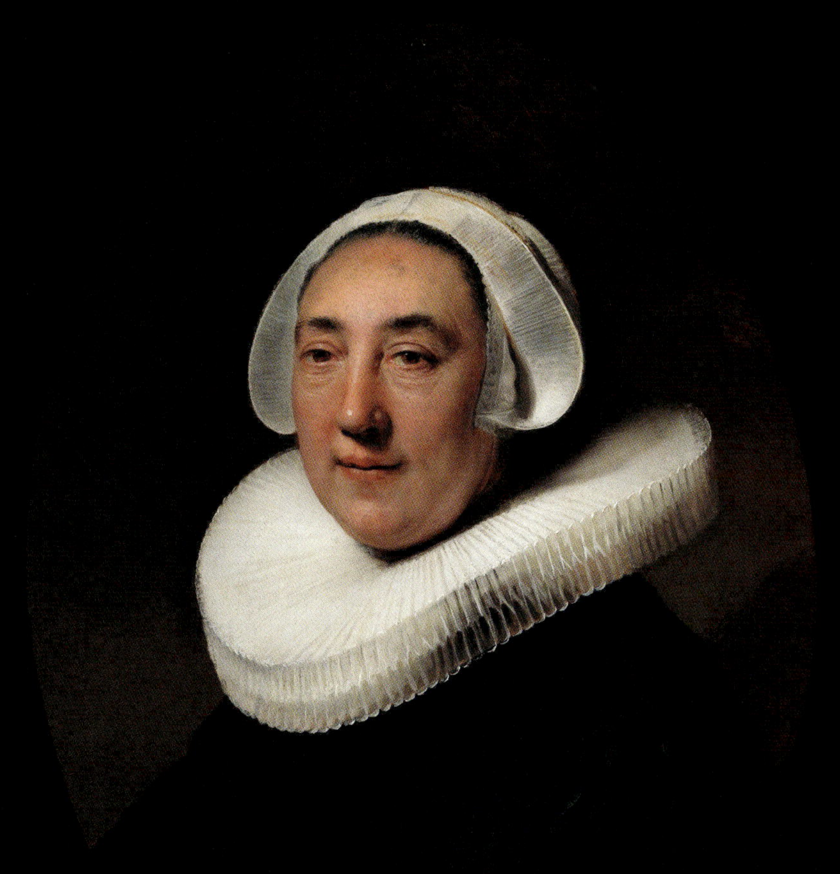

Portrait of Haesje Jacobsdr. van Cleyburg, 1634
Oil on panel, 68.6 × 53.4 cm (27 ⅛ × 21 ⅛ in.)
Amsterdam, Rijksmuseum

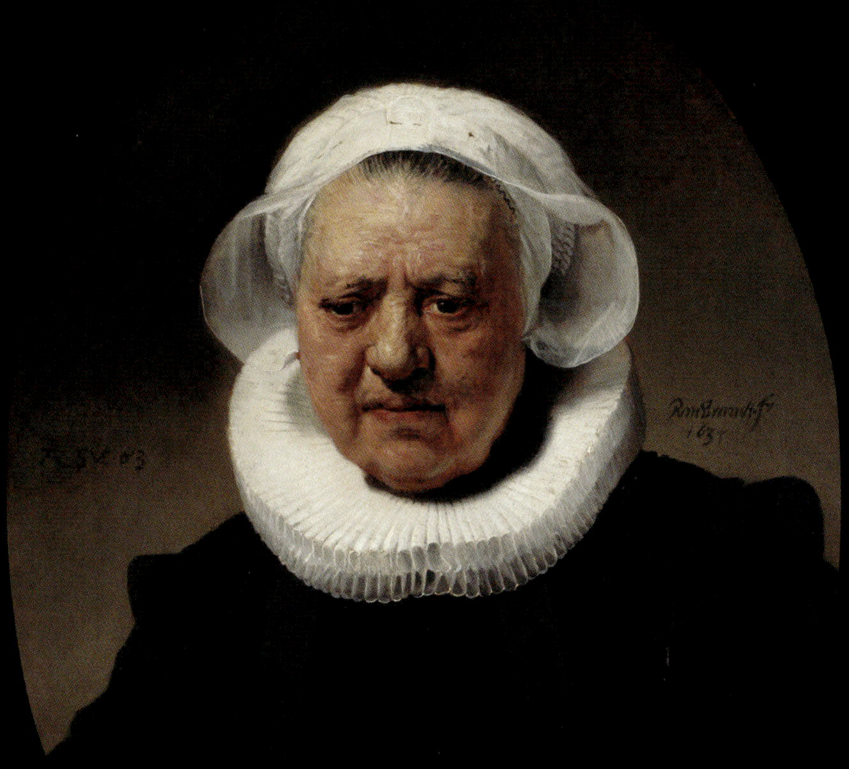

Portrait of Aechje Claesdr. van der Horst, 1634
Oil on panel, 71.1 × 55.9 cm (27 ¾ × 22 ⅛ in.)
London, The National Gallery

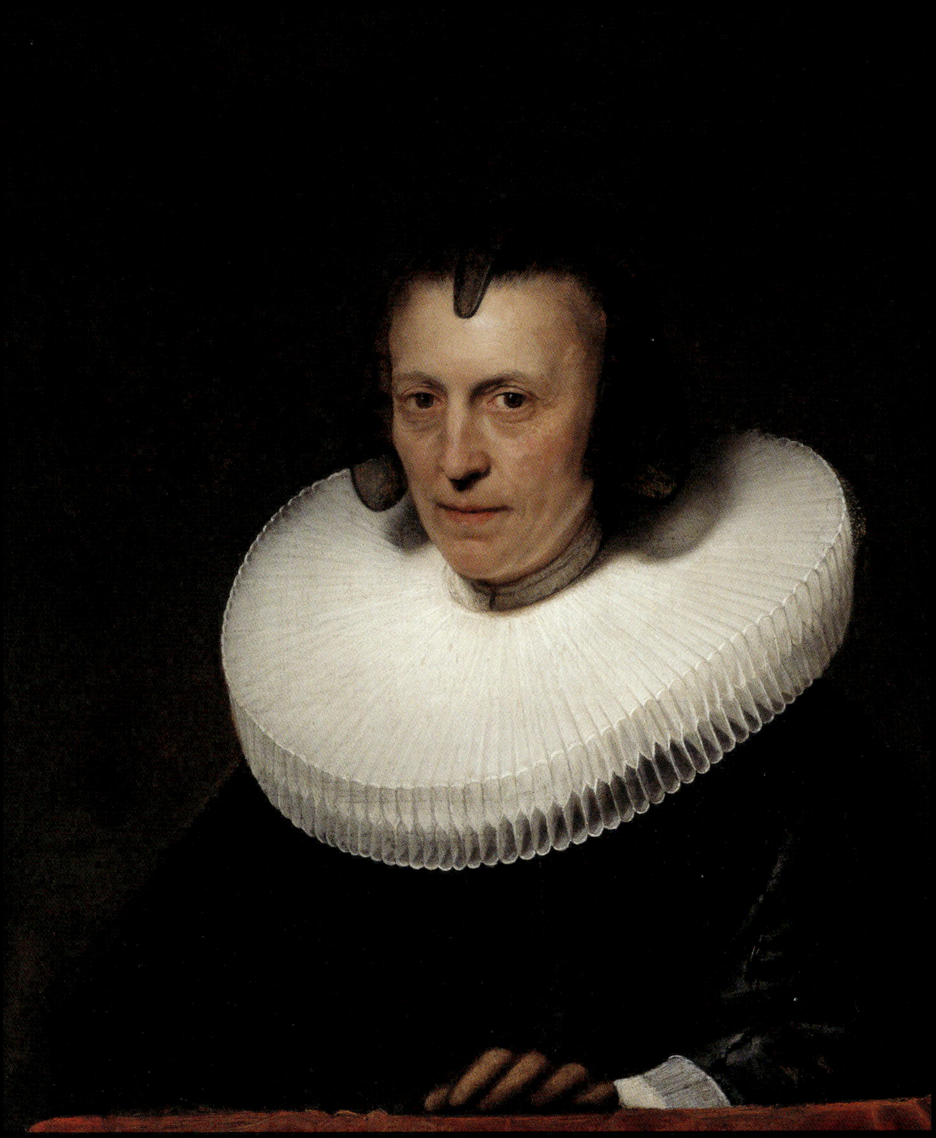

Portrait of Aletta Adriaensdr., 1639
Oil on panel, 65.5 × 55.5 cm (25 ¾ × 21 ¾ in.). Rotterdam, Museum Boijmans Van Beuningen, on loan from Stichting Willem van der Vorm

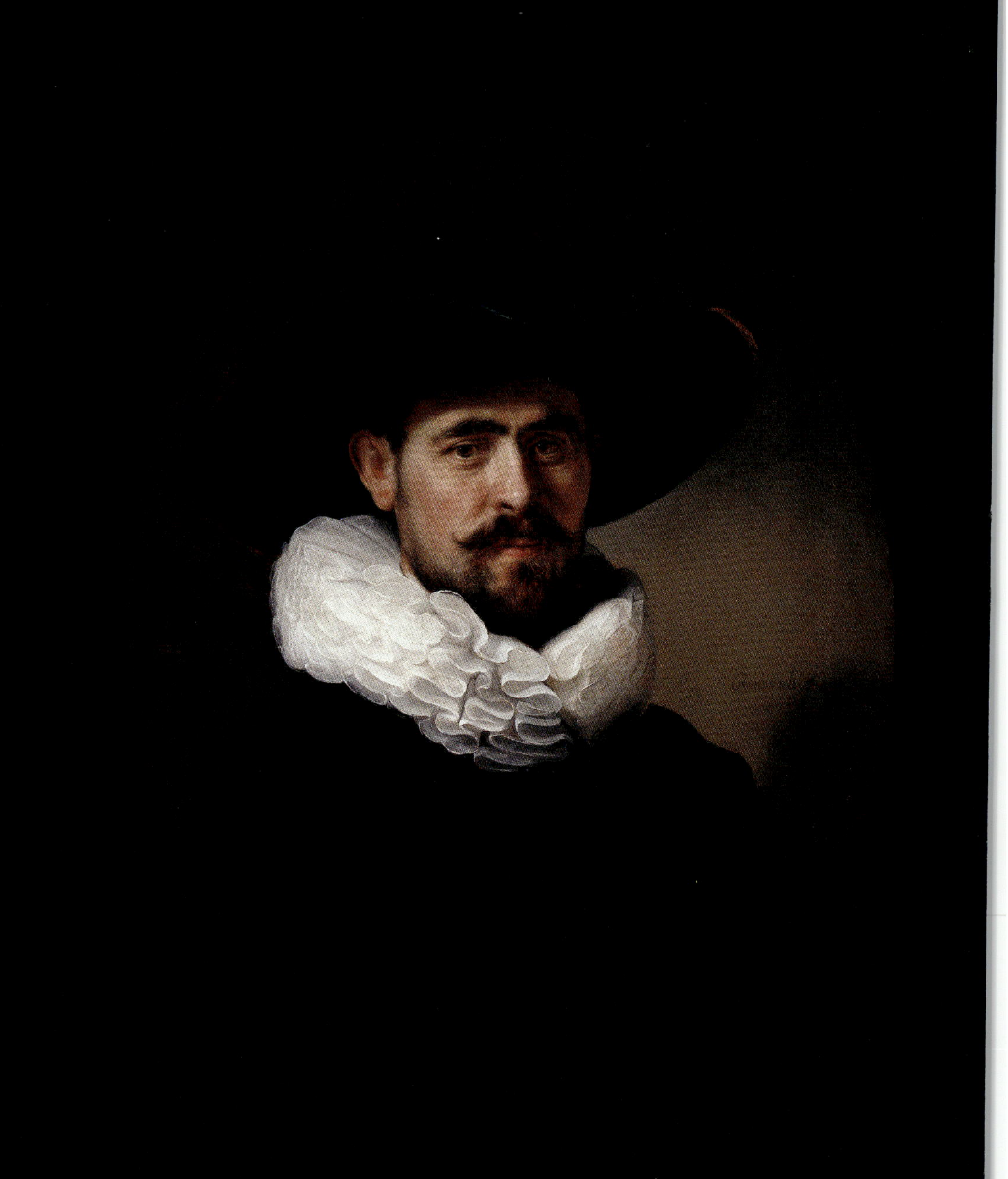

Portrait of a 41-Year-Old Man, 1633
Oil on panel, 69.5 × 54.7 cm (27 3/8 × 21 1/2 in.)
Pasadena, California, Norton Simon Art Foundation

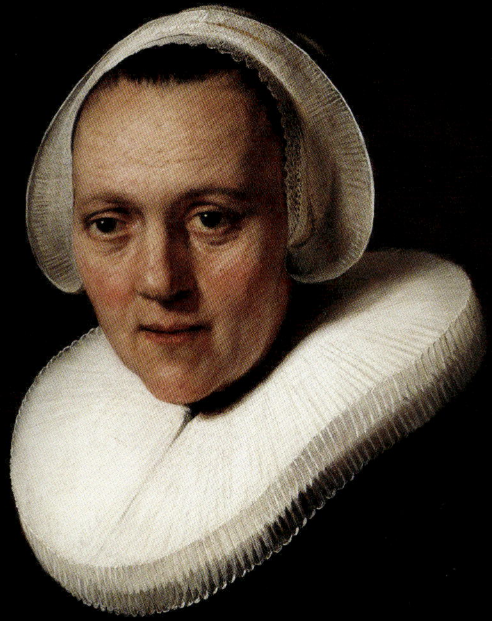

Portrait of a 40-Year-Old Woman, 1634
Oil on panel, 69 × 55 cm (27 ⅛ × 21 ⅔ in.)
Louisville, Kentucky, Speed Art Museum

Gerard van Honthorst
Portrait of Frederik Hendrik, 1631
Oil on panel, 77 × 61 cm (30 3/8 × 24 in.)
Den Haag, Mauritshuis, on permanent loan from Stichting Historische Verzamelingen van het Huis Oranje-Nassau

Gerard van Honthorst
Portrait of Amalia of Solms, 1630s
Oil on panel, 75 × 60 cm (29 5/8 × 23 5/8 in.)
Den Haag, Stichting Historische Verzamelingen van het Huis Oranje-Nassau

Portrait of Amalia of Solms, 1632
Oil on canvas, 69.5 × 54.5 cm (27 3/8 × 21 1/2 in.)
Paris, Musée Jacquemart-André

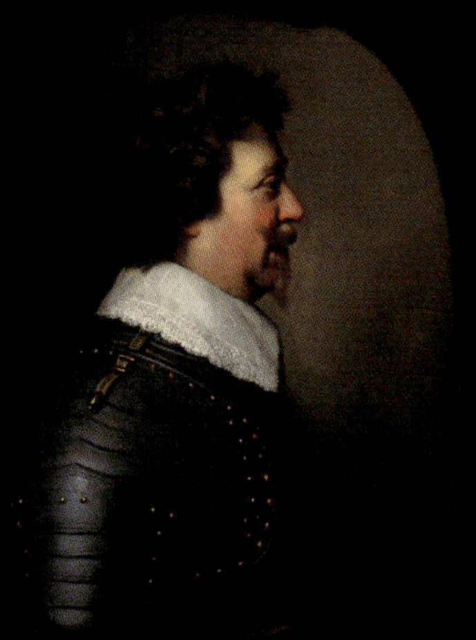

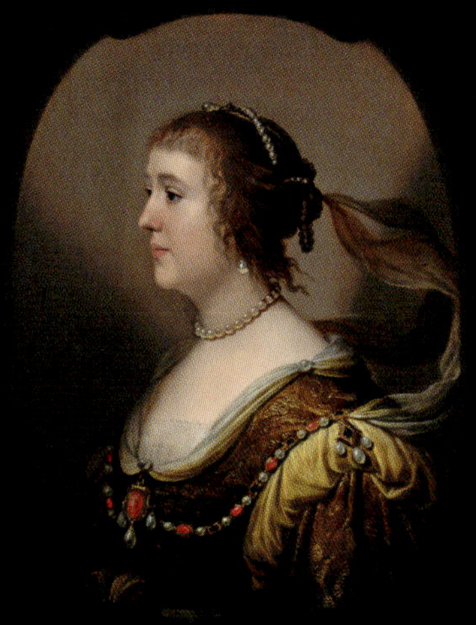

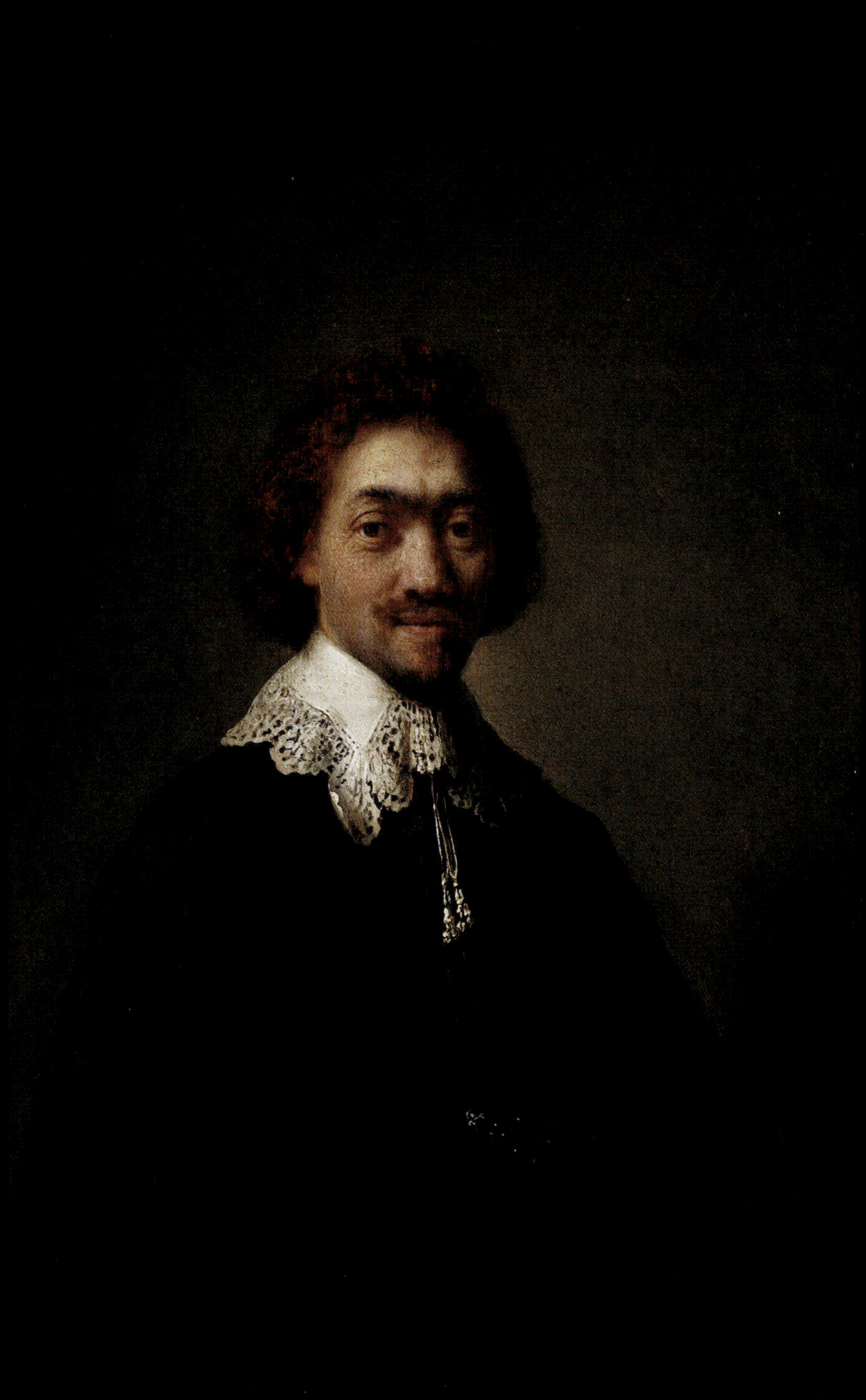

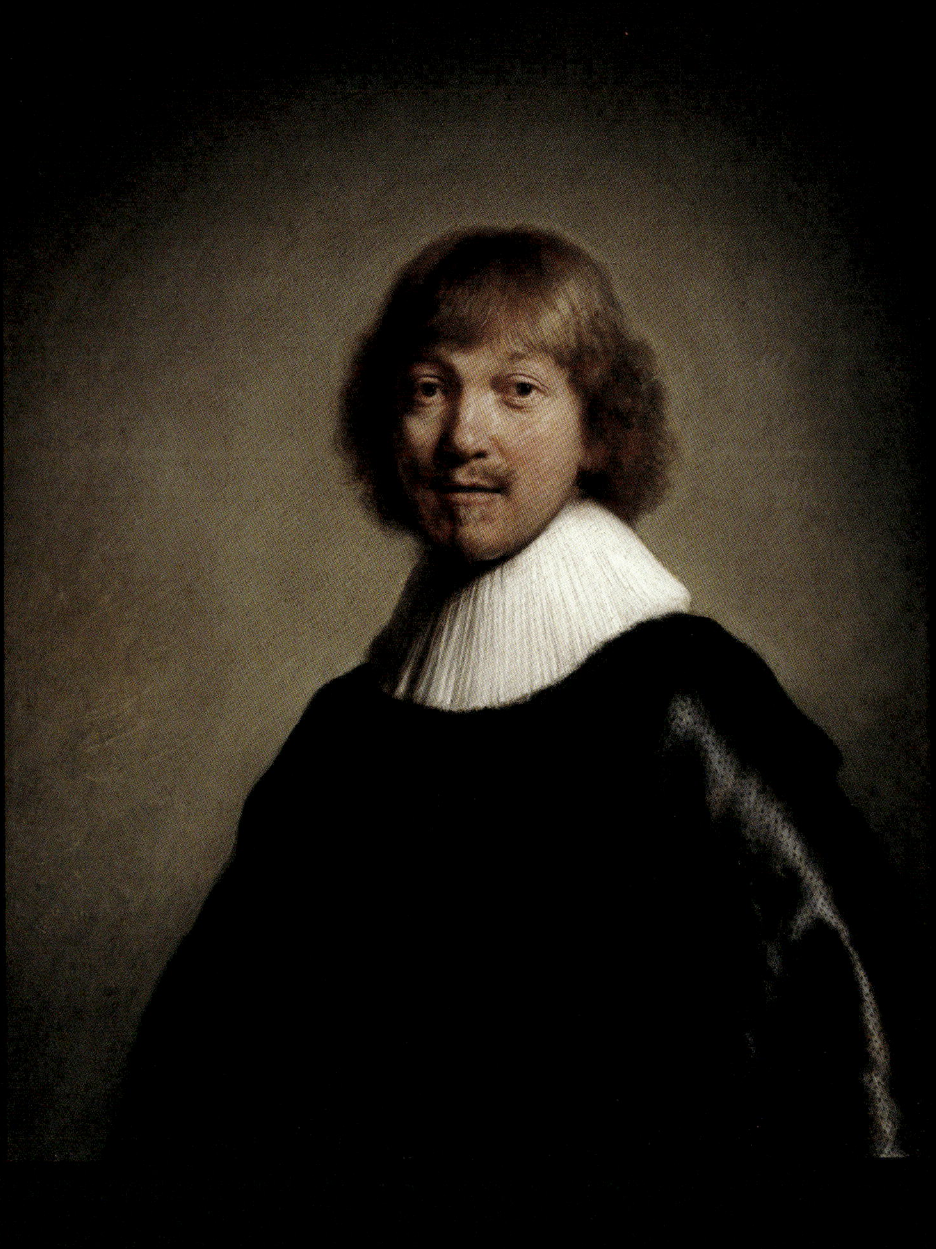

Page 170
Portrait of Maurits Huygens, 1632
Oil on panel, 31.1 × 24.5 cm (12 ¼ × 9 ⅝ in.)
Hamburger Kunsthalle

Page 171
Portrait of Jacques de Gheyn III, 1632
Oil on panel, 29.9 × 24.9 cm (11 ¾ × 9 ¾ in.)
London, Dulwich Picture Gallery

Portrait of Joris de Caullery, 1632
Oil on canvas, mounted on panel, 102.9 × 84.3 cm (40 ½ × 33 ¼ in.)
Fine Arts Museums of San Francisco, Legion of Honor Museum

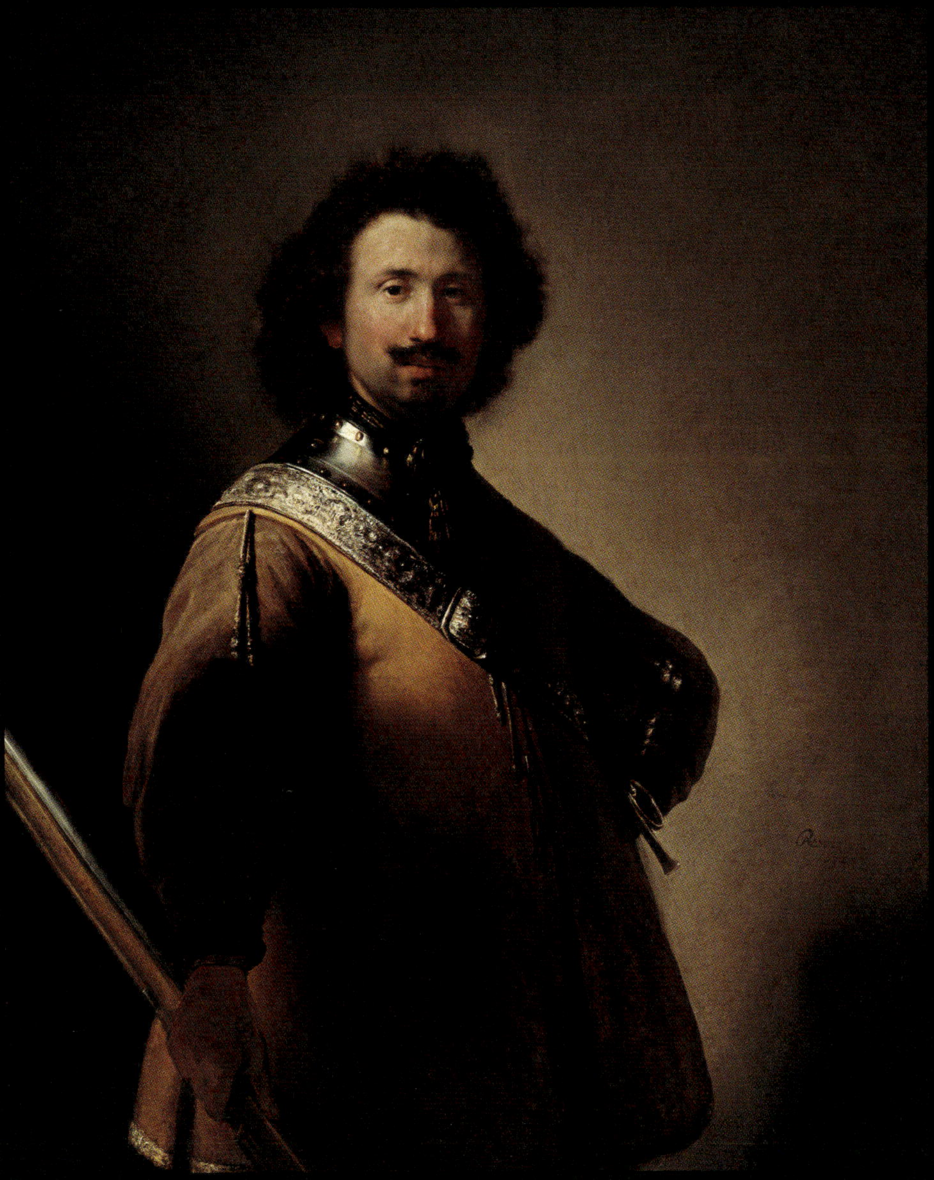

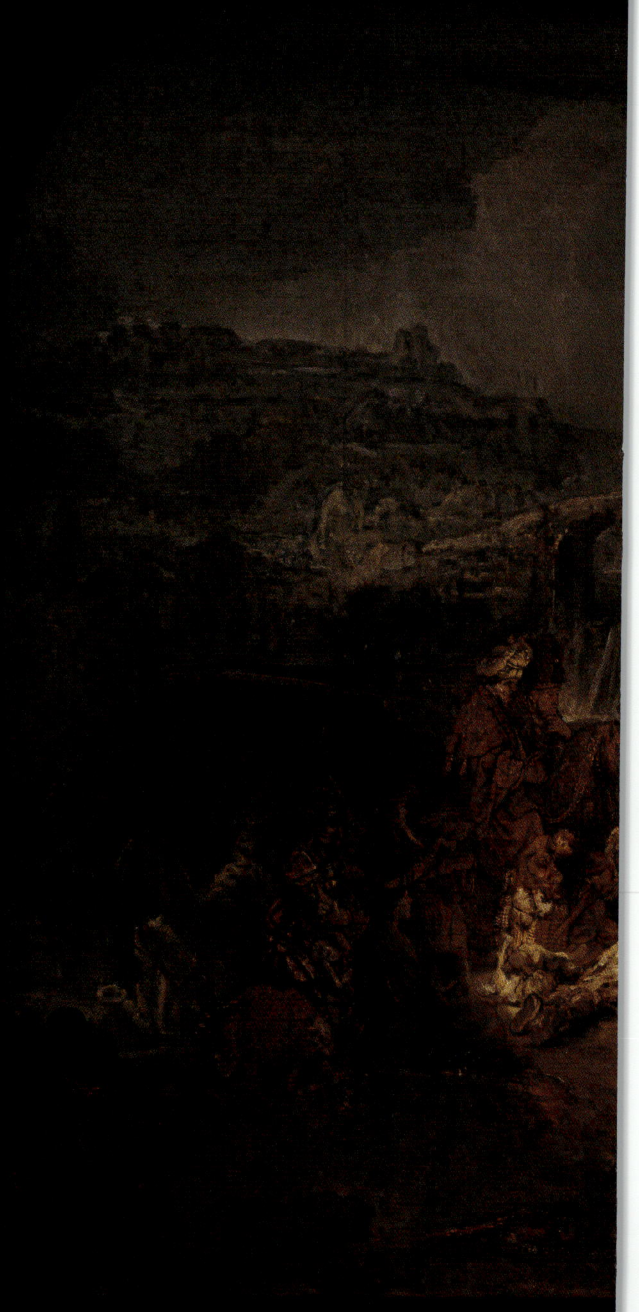

John the Baptist Preaching, 1634/35
Oil on canvas, transferred to wood, 62.7 × 81.1 cm (24⅔ × 31¾ in.)
Staatliche Museen zu Berlin, Gemäldegalerie

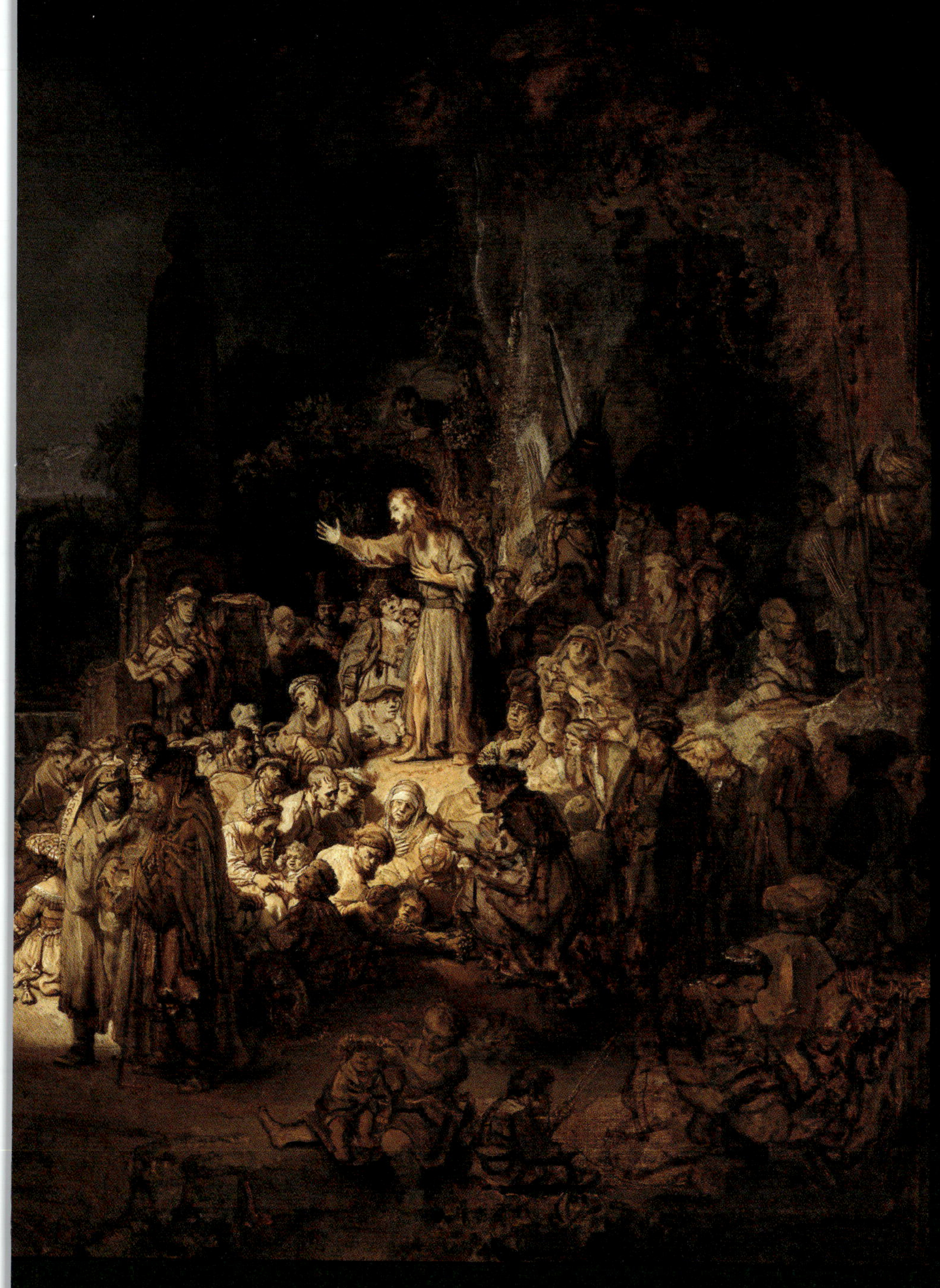

The Holy Family, *c.* 1634
Oil on canvas, 183.5 × 123.5 cm (72 ¼ × 48 ⅝ in.)
Munich, Bayerische Staatsgemäldesammlungen,
Alte Pinakothek

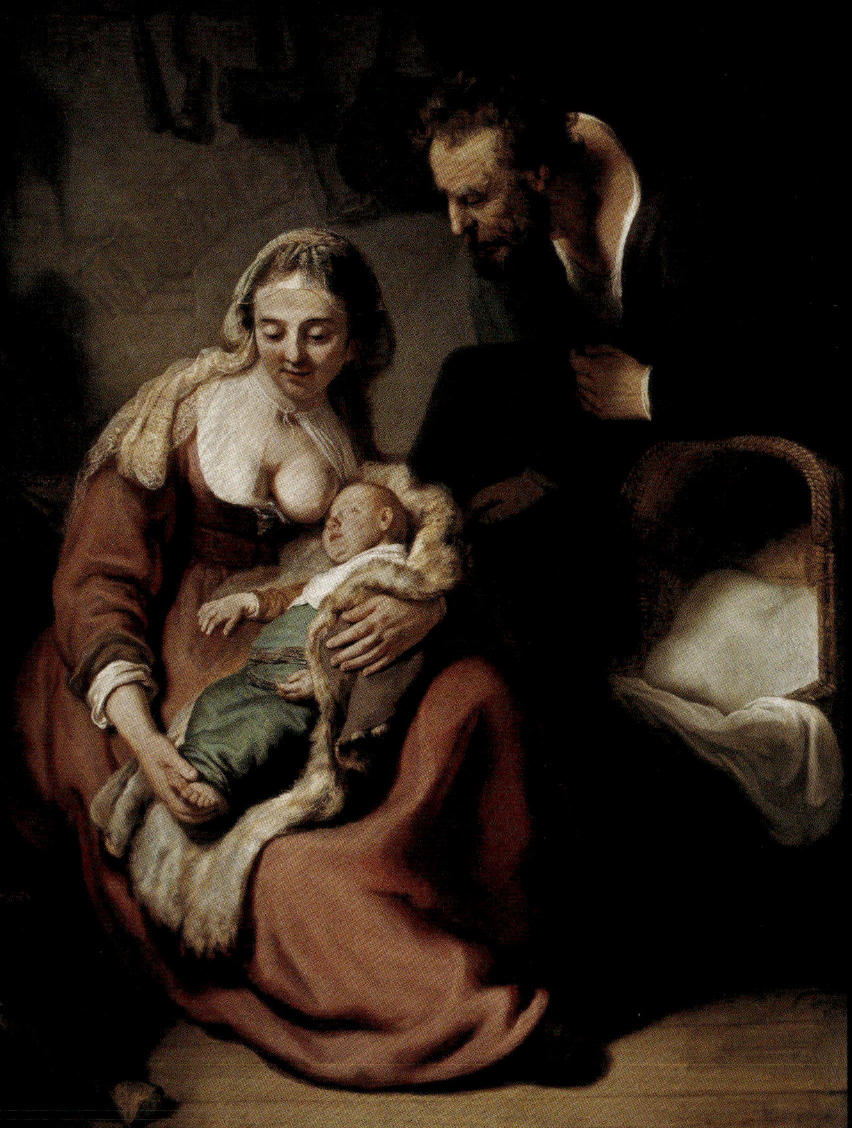

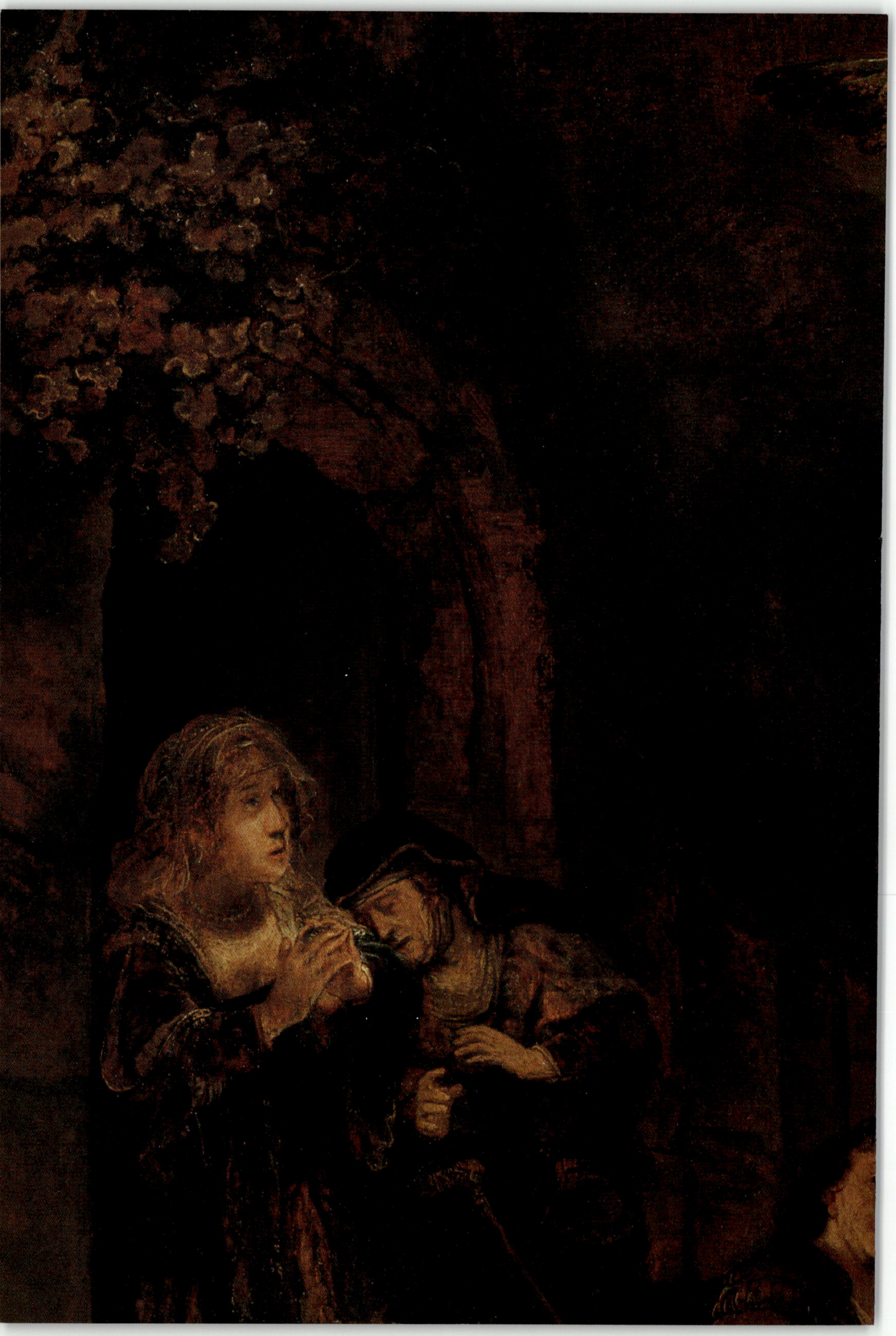

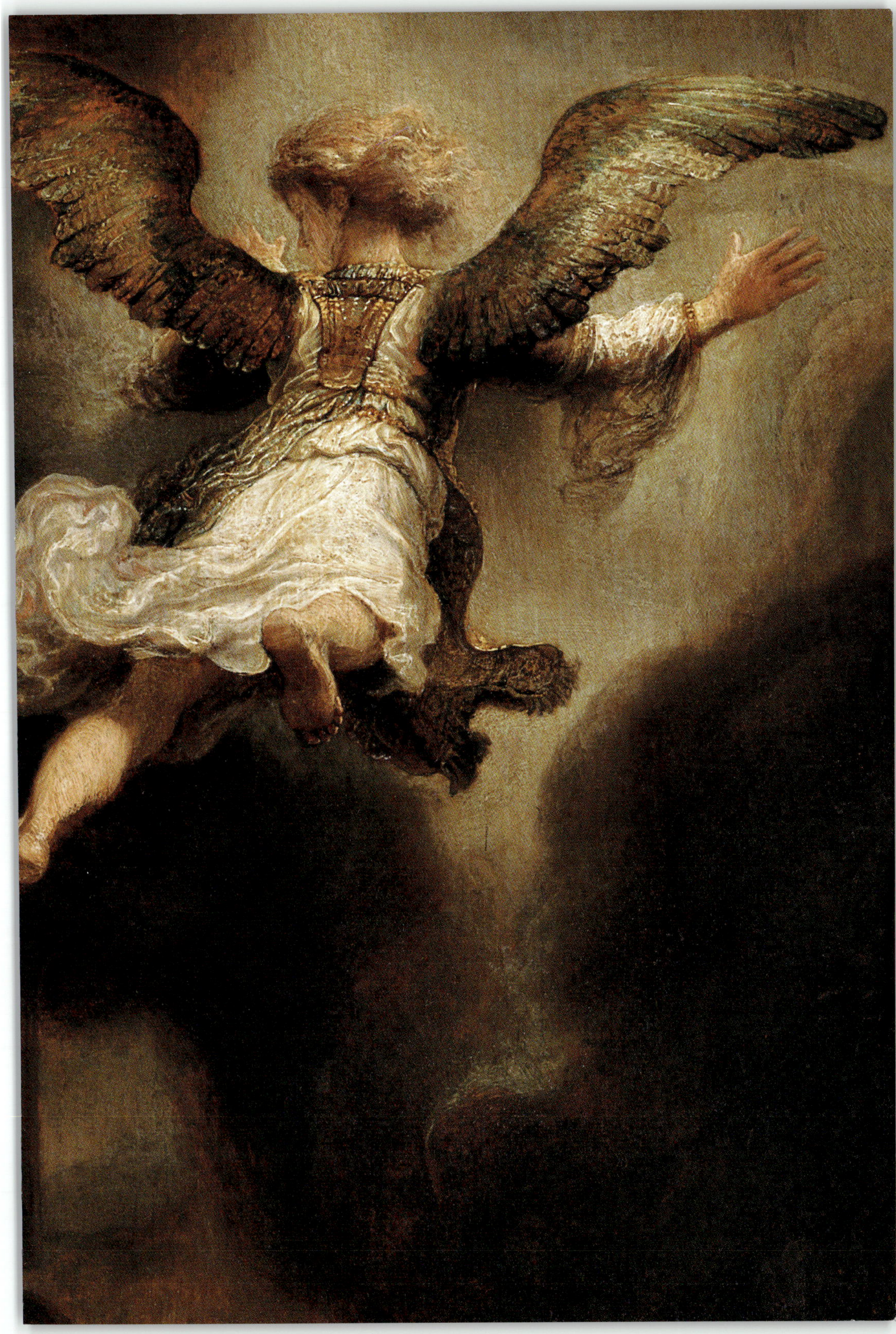

The Angel Raphael Leaving Tobit and His Family, 1637
Oil on panel, 68 × 52 cm (26 ¾ × 20 ½ in.)
Paris, Musée du Louvre
(detail pages 178/179)

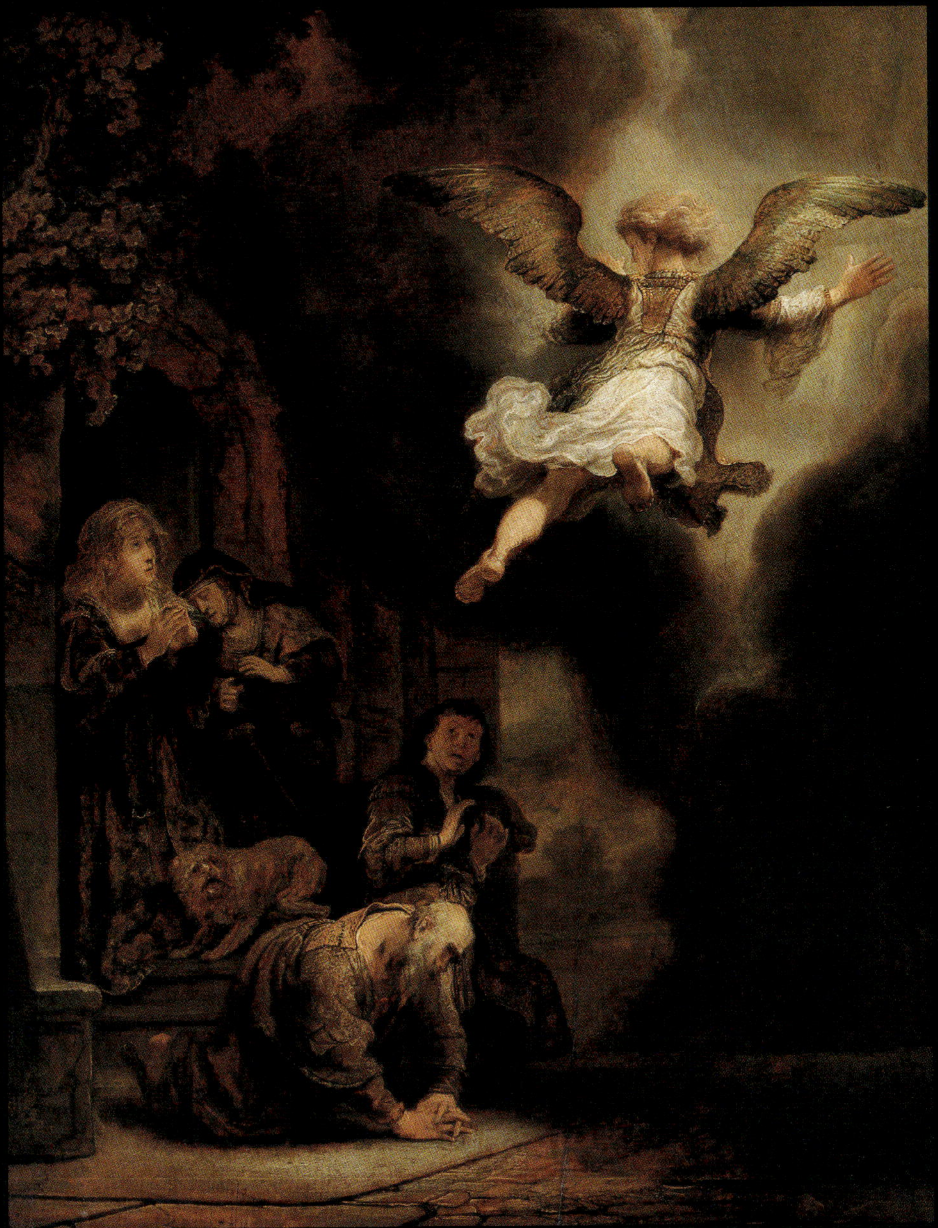

The Raising of the Cross, *c.* 1633
Oil on canvas, 95.7 × 72.2 cm (37 ⅔ × 28 ⅜ in.)
Munich, Bayerische Staatsgemäldesammlungen,
Alte Pinakothek

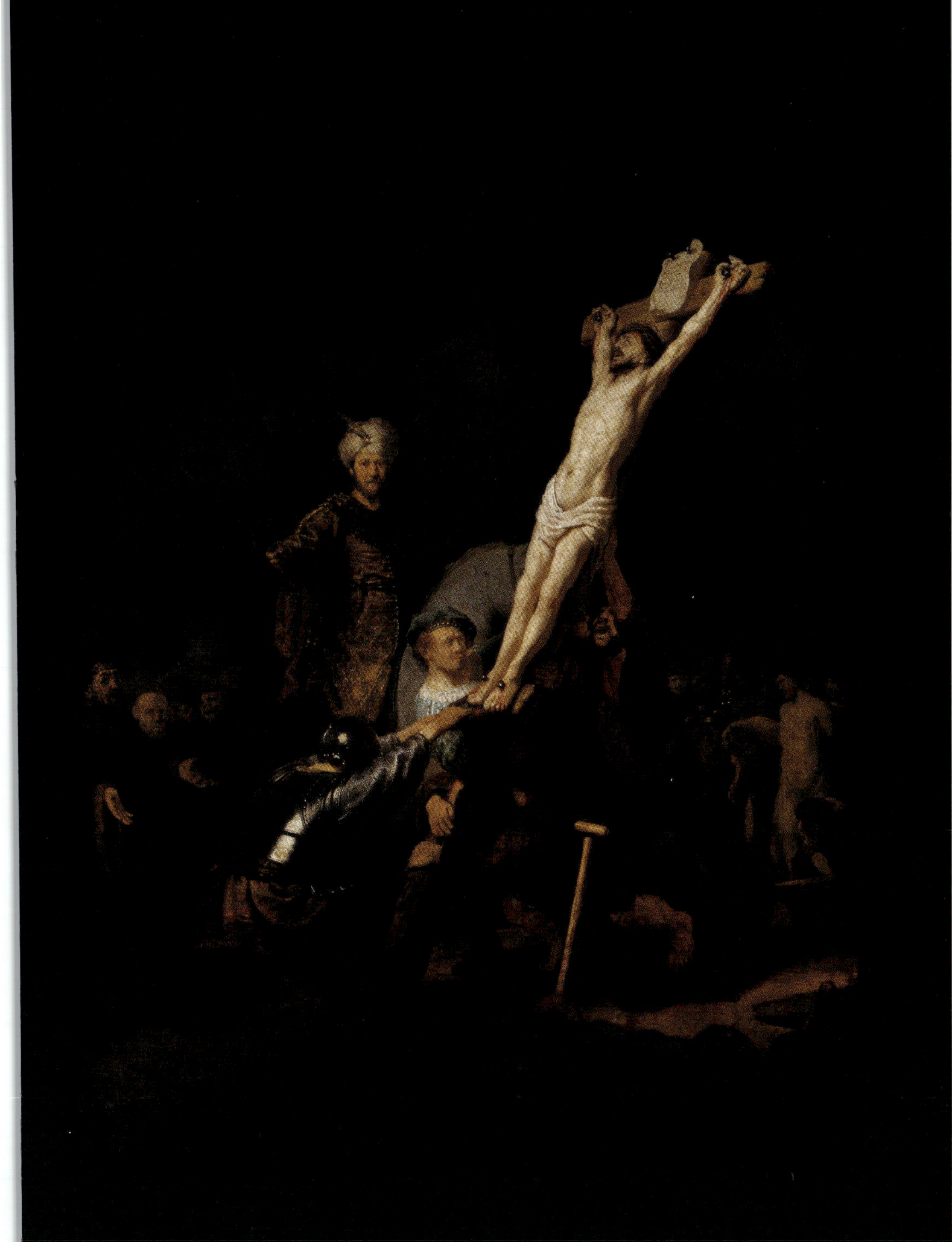

Peter Paul Rubens
The Descent from the Cross, 1611–1614
Oil on panel, 421 × 311 cm (165¾ × 122½ in.)
Antwerp, Cathedral of Our Lady

The Descent from the Cross, *c.* 1633
Oil on panel, 89.6 × 65 cm (35¼ × 25⅝ in.)
Munich, Bayerische Staatsgemäldesammlungen,
Alte Pinakothek

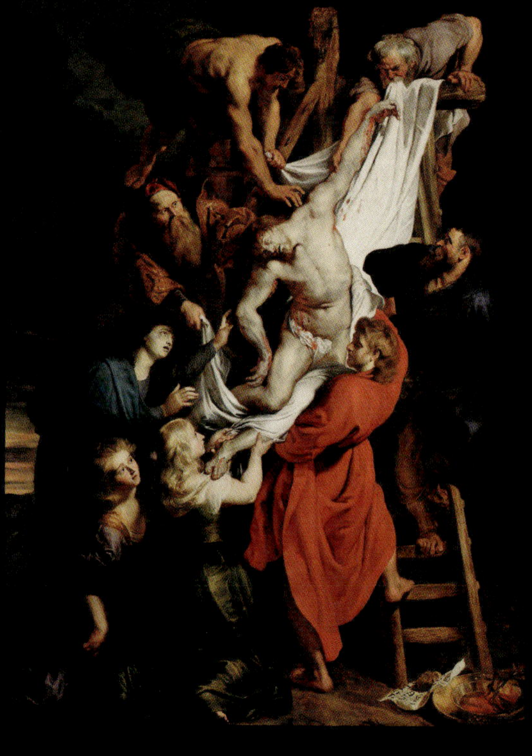

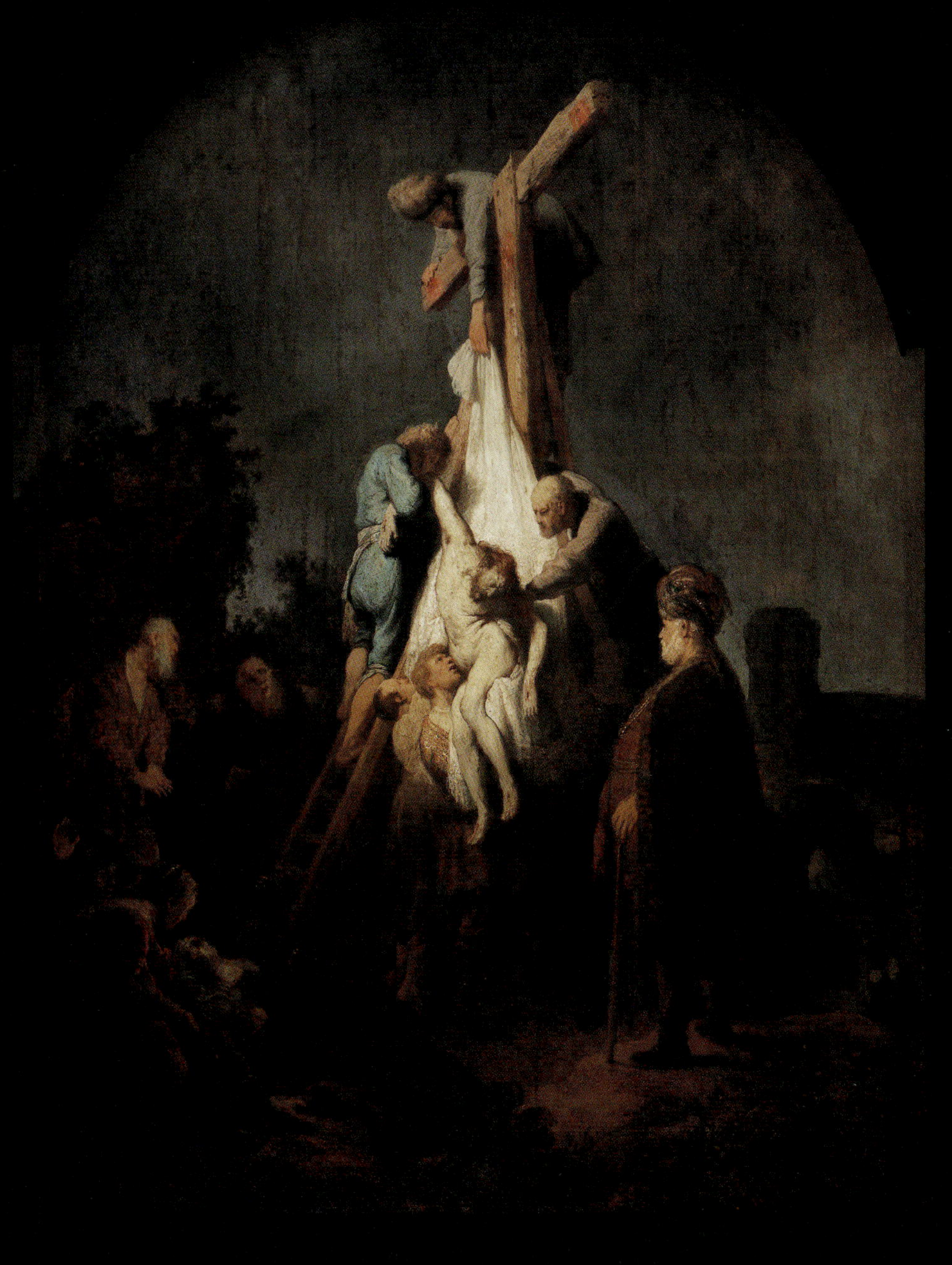

Titian
The Assumption of the Virgin Mary (Assunta), 1516–1518
Oil on panel, 690 × 360 cm (271 ¾ × 141 ¾ in.)
Venice, Santa Maria Gloriosa dei Frari

The Ascension, 1636
Oil on canvas, 93 × 68.7 cm (36 ⅝ × 27 ⅛ in.)
Munich, Bayerische Staatsgemäldesammlungen, Alte Pinakothek

Page 188
The Adoration of the Shepherds, 1646
Oil on canvas, 97 × 71 cm (38 ¼ × 27 ¾ in.)
Munich, Bayerische Staatsgemäldesammlungen, Alte Pinakothek

Page 189
The Entombment, 1635–1639
Oil on canvas, 92.6 × 68.9 cm (36 ½ × 27 ⅛ in.)
Munich, Bayerische Staatsgemäldesammlungen, Alte Pinakothek

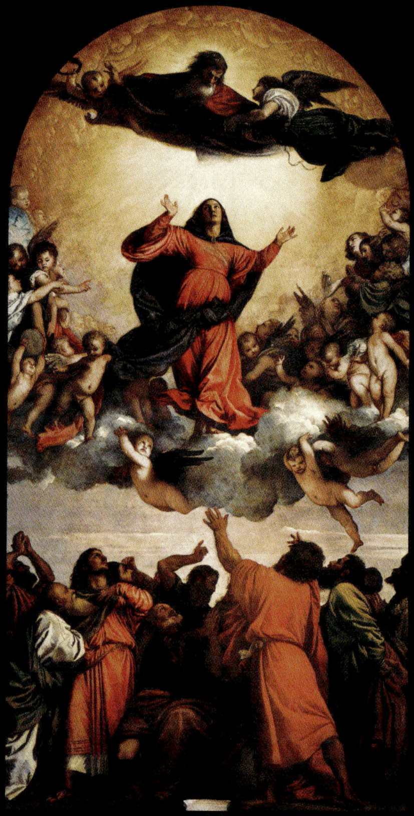

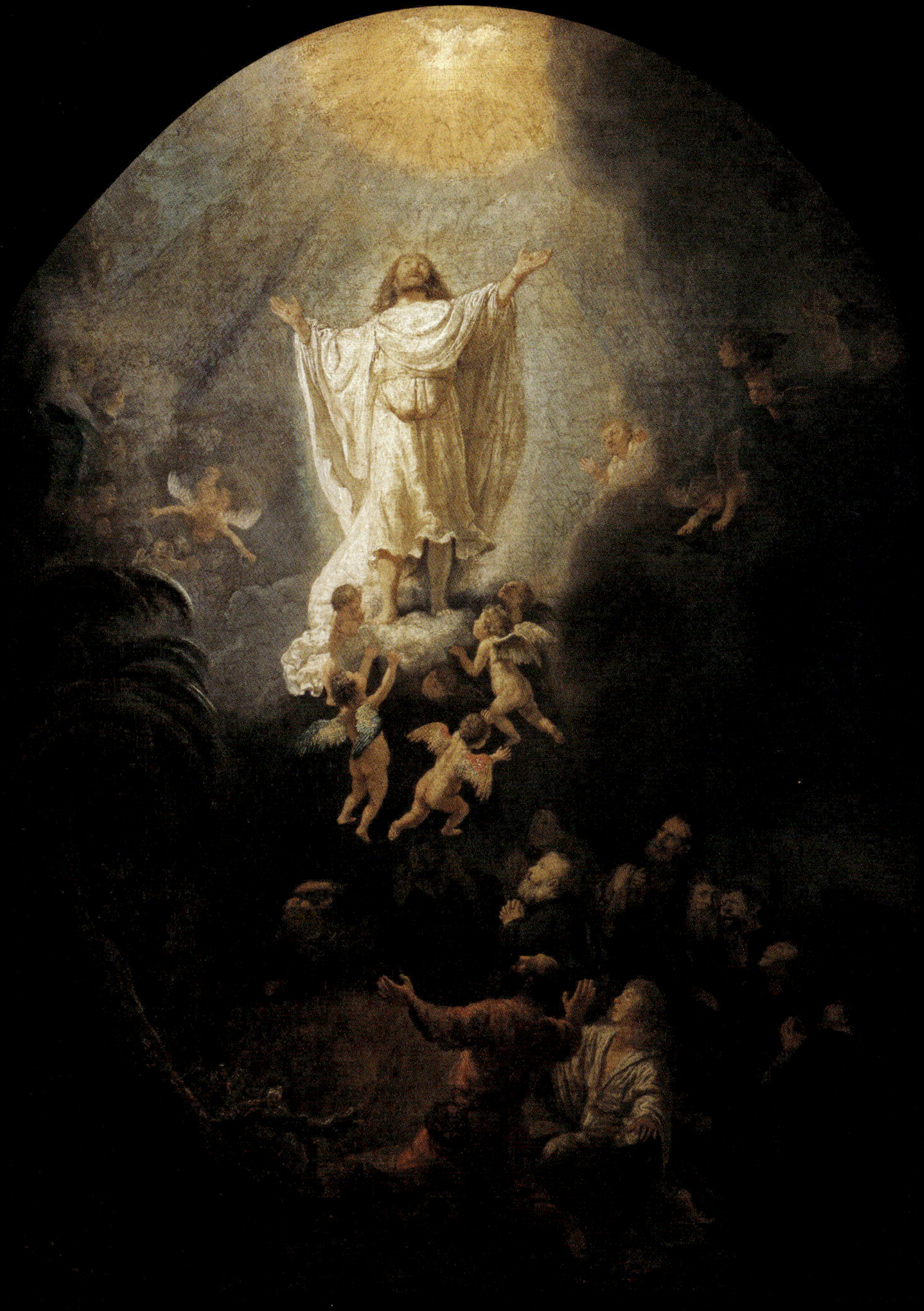

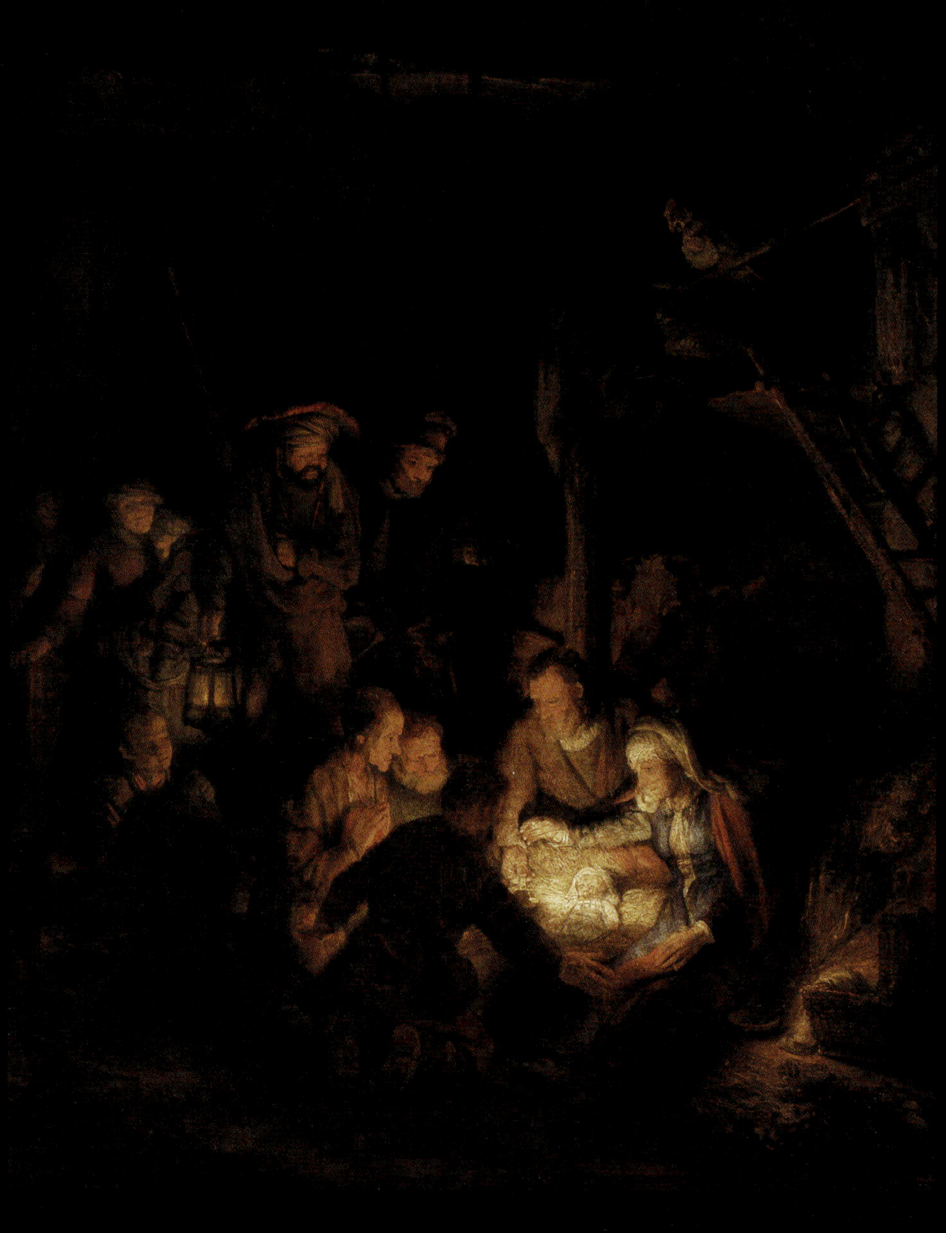

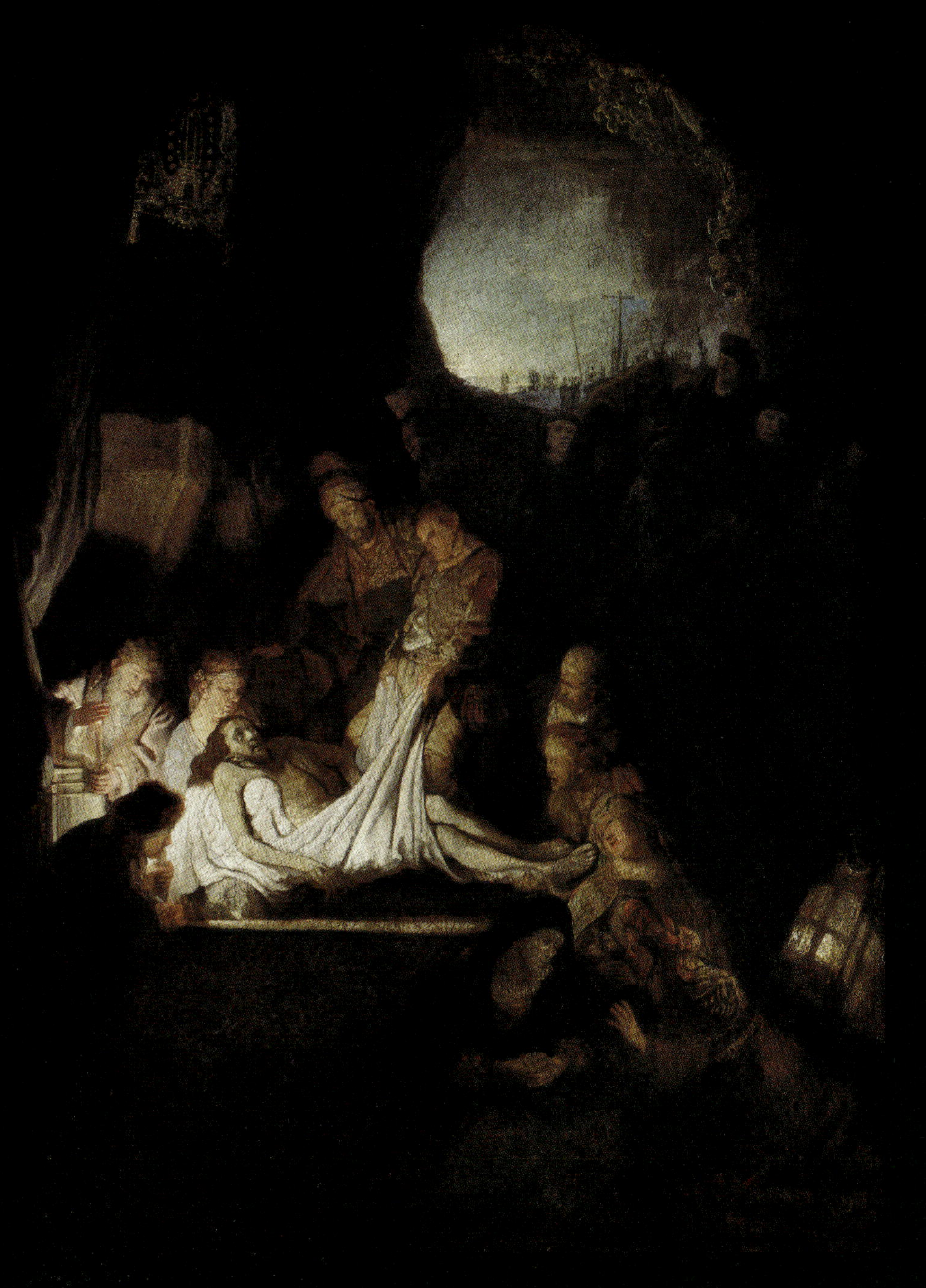

The Resurrection, 1635–1639
Oil on canvas, attached to a wooden panel, 91.9 × 67 cm (36 1/8 × 26 3/8 in.)
Munich, Bayerische Staatsgemäldesammlungen, Alte Pinakothek

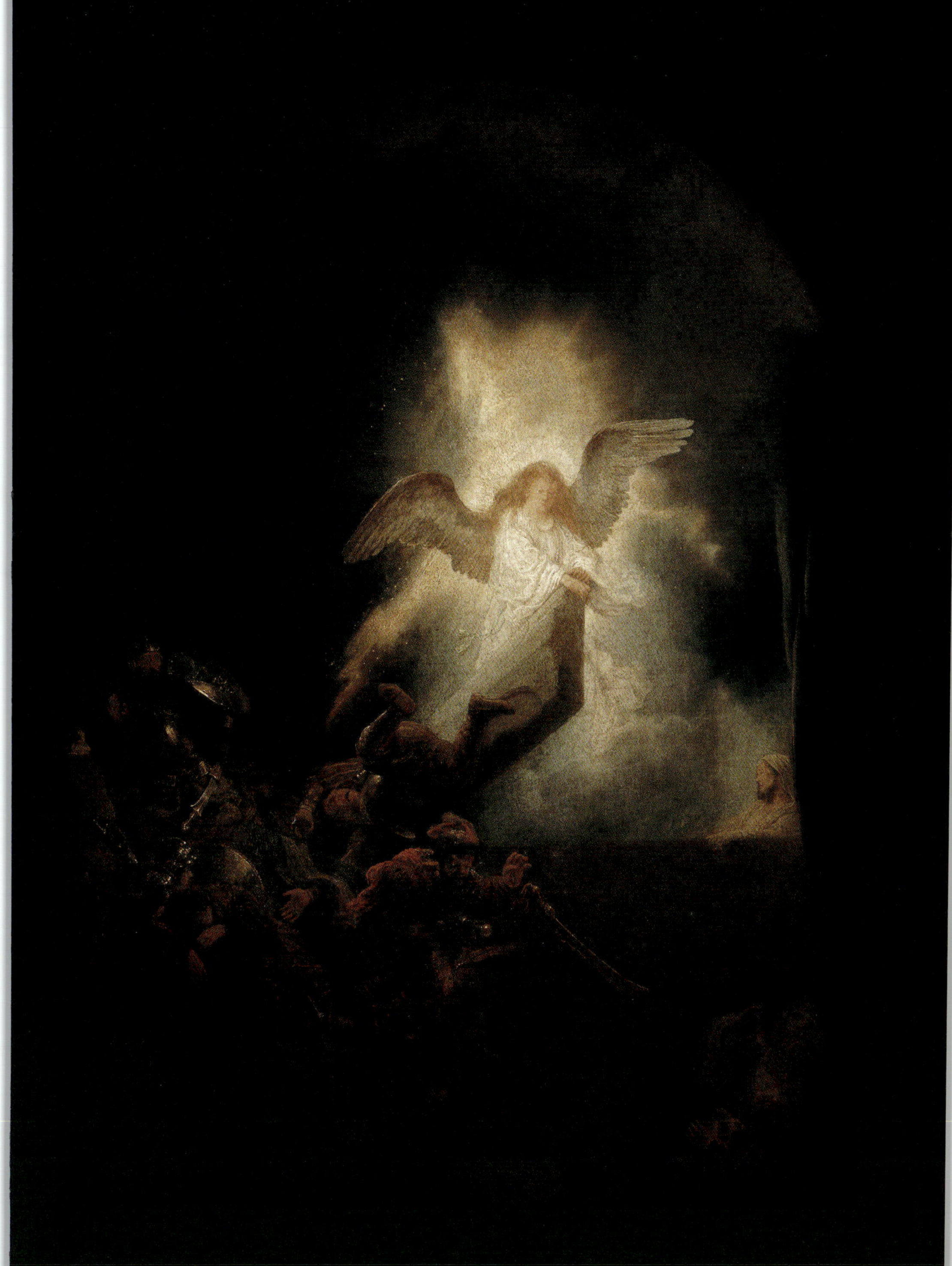

The Prodigal Son in the Inn
(Self-Portrait with Saskia), *c.* 1635
Oil on canvas, 161 × 131 cm (63 3/8 × 51 5/8 in.)
Staatliche Kunstsammlungen Dresden,
Gemäldegalerie Alte Meister

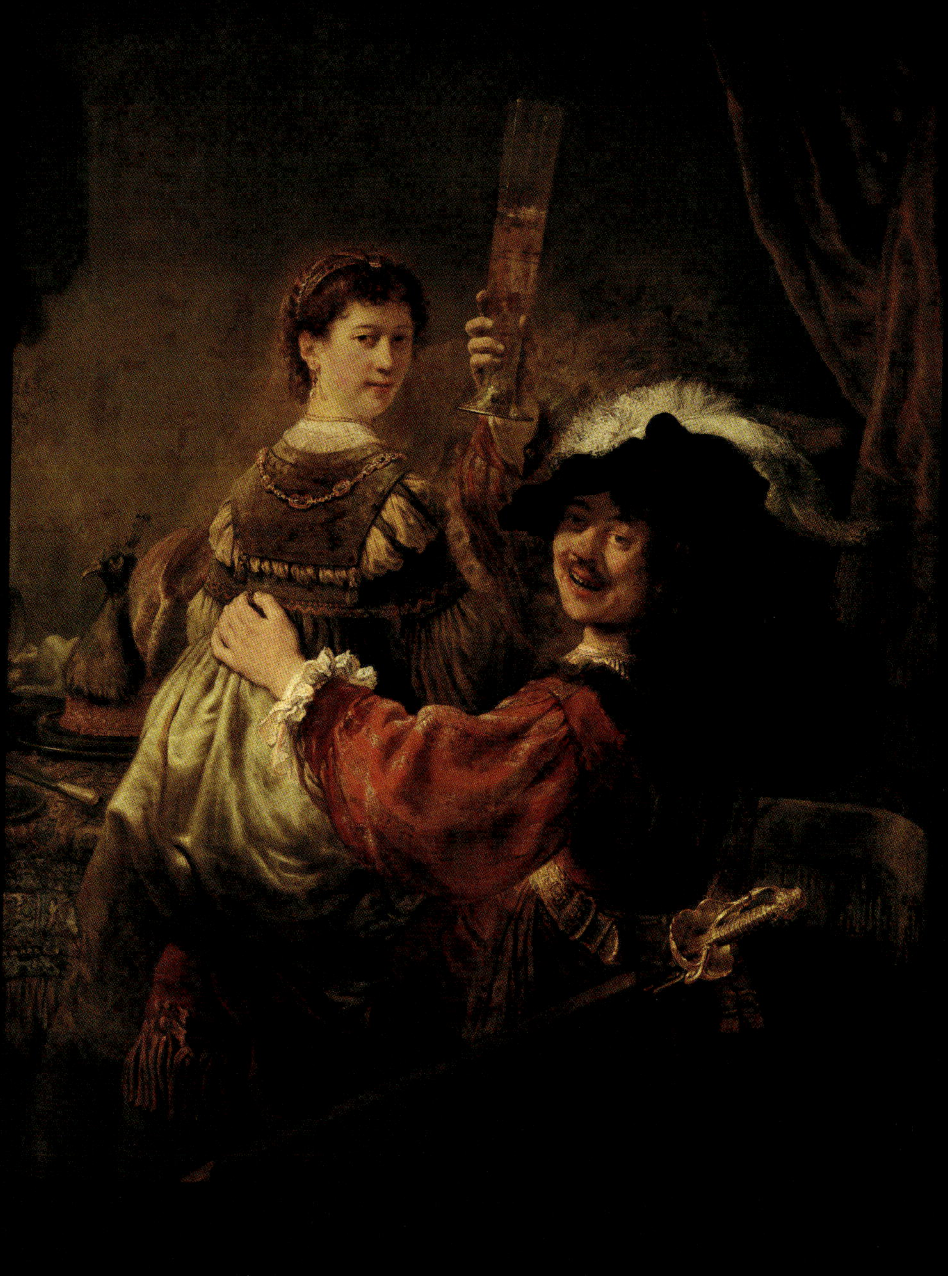

Young Woman in Fantasy Costume (Saskia?), 1633
Oil on panel, 65 × 48 cm (25 ⅝ × 18 ¾ in.)
Amsterdam, Rijksmuseum

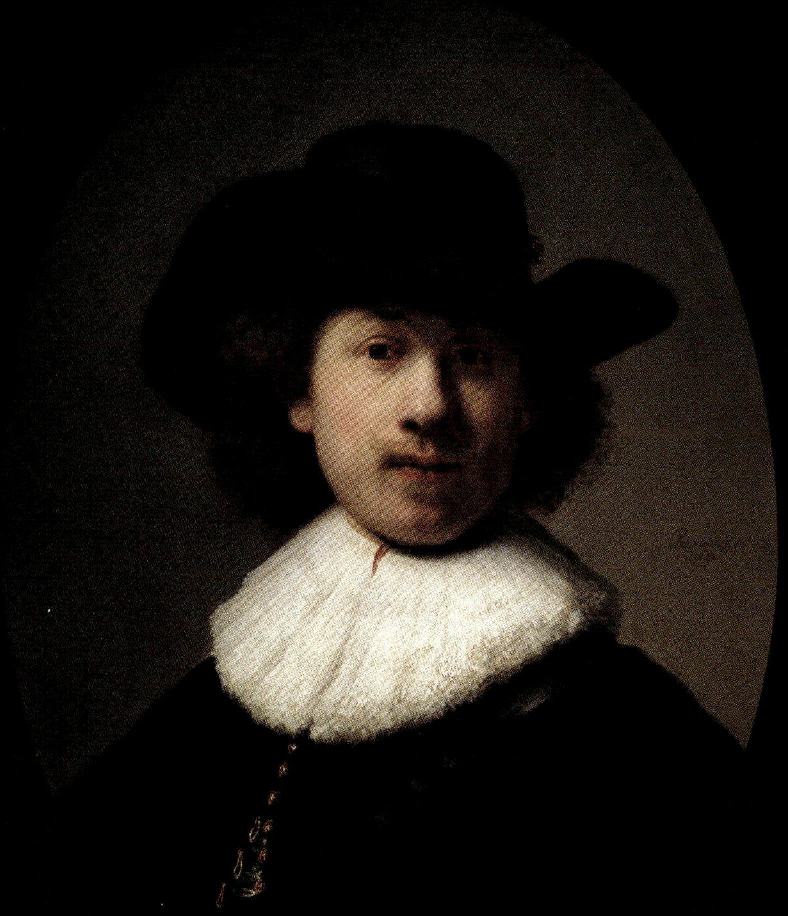

Self-Portrait with a Wide-Brimmed Hat, 1632
Oil on panel, 64.4 × 47.6 cm (25 3/8 × 18 3/4 in.)
Glasgow Museums, The Burrell Collection

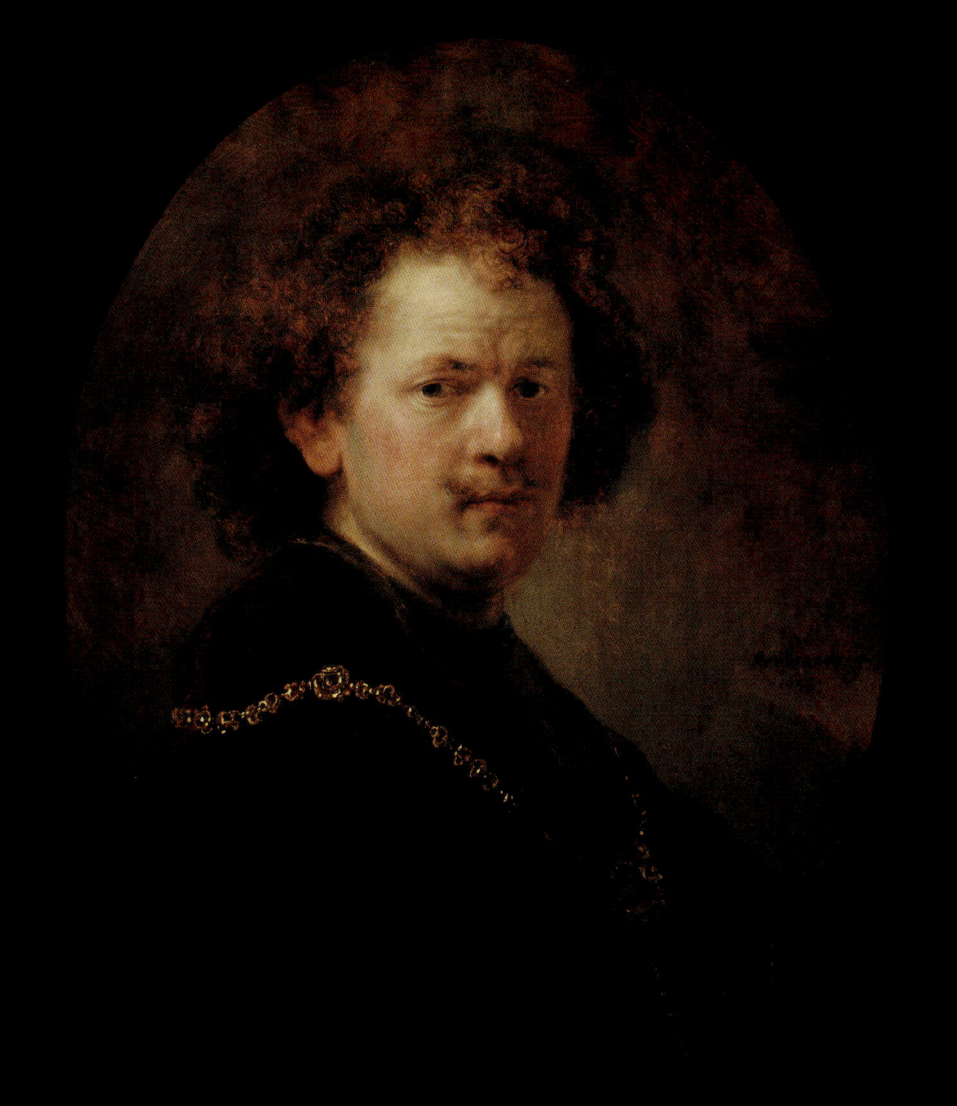

Self-Portrait with a Gold Chain, 1633
Oil on panel, 61 × 48.1 cm (24 ⅛ × 18 ¾ in.)
Paris, Musée du Louvre

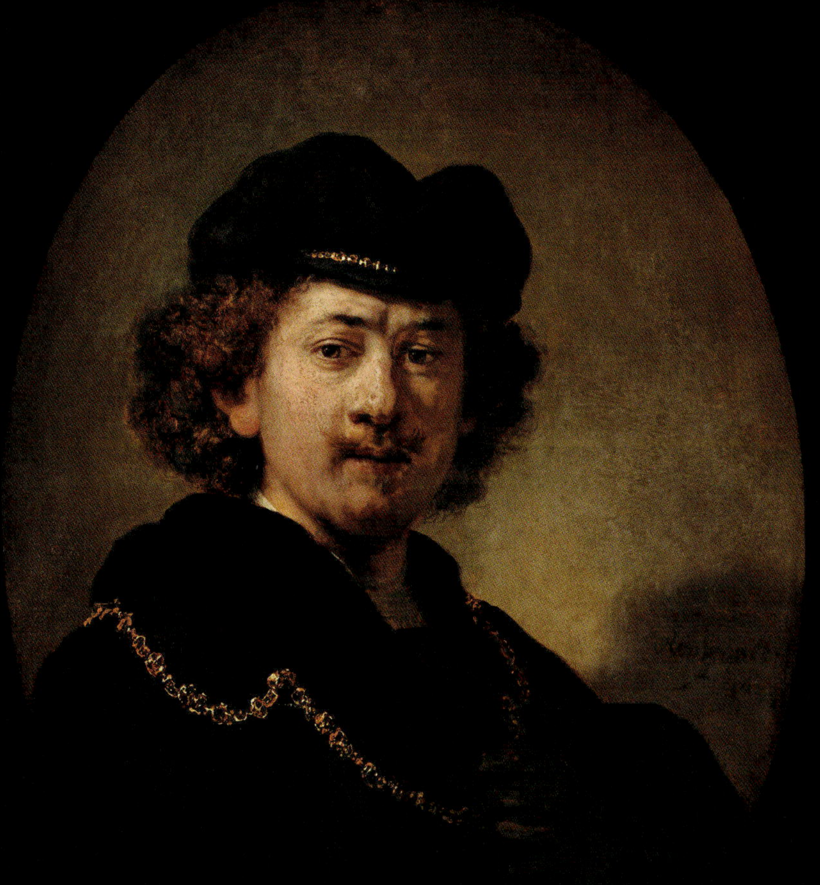

Self-Portrait with a Cap, 1633
Oil on panel, 70.4 × 54 cm (27 ¾ × 21 ¼ in.)
Paris, Musée du Louvre

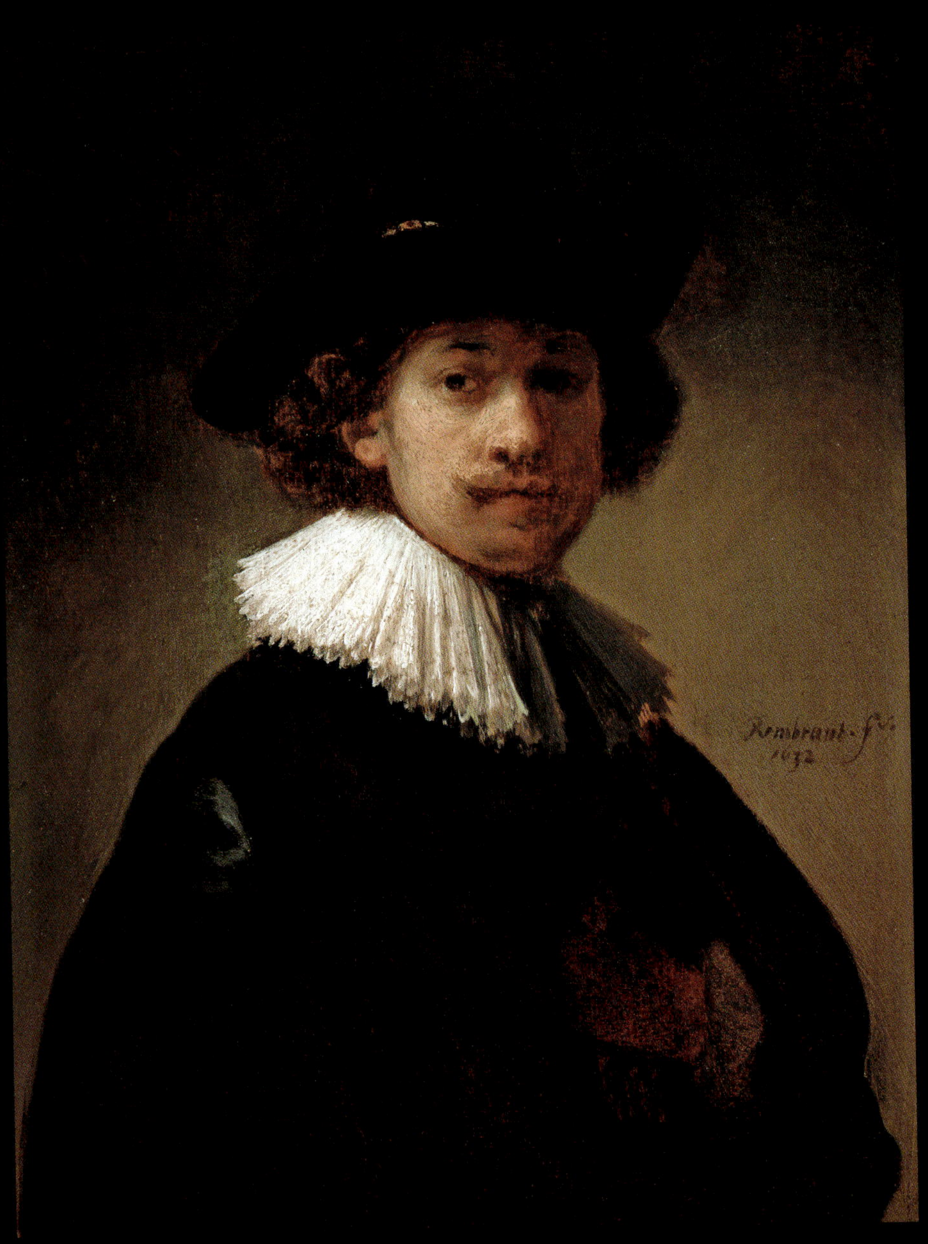

Self-Portrait with a Wide-Brimmed Hat, 1632
Oil on panel, 21.8 × 16.3 cm (8 5/8 × 6 3/8 in.)
Private Collection

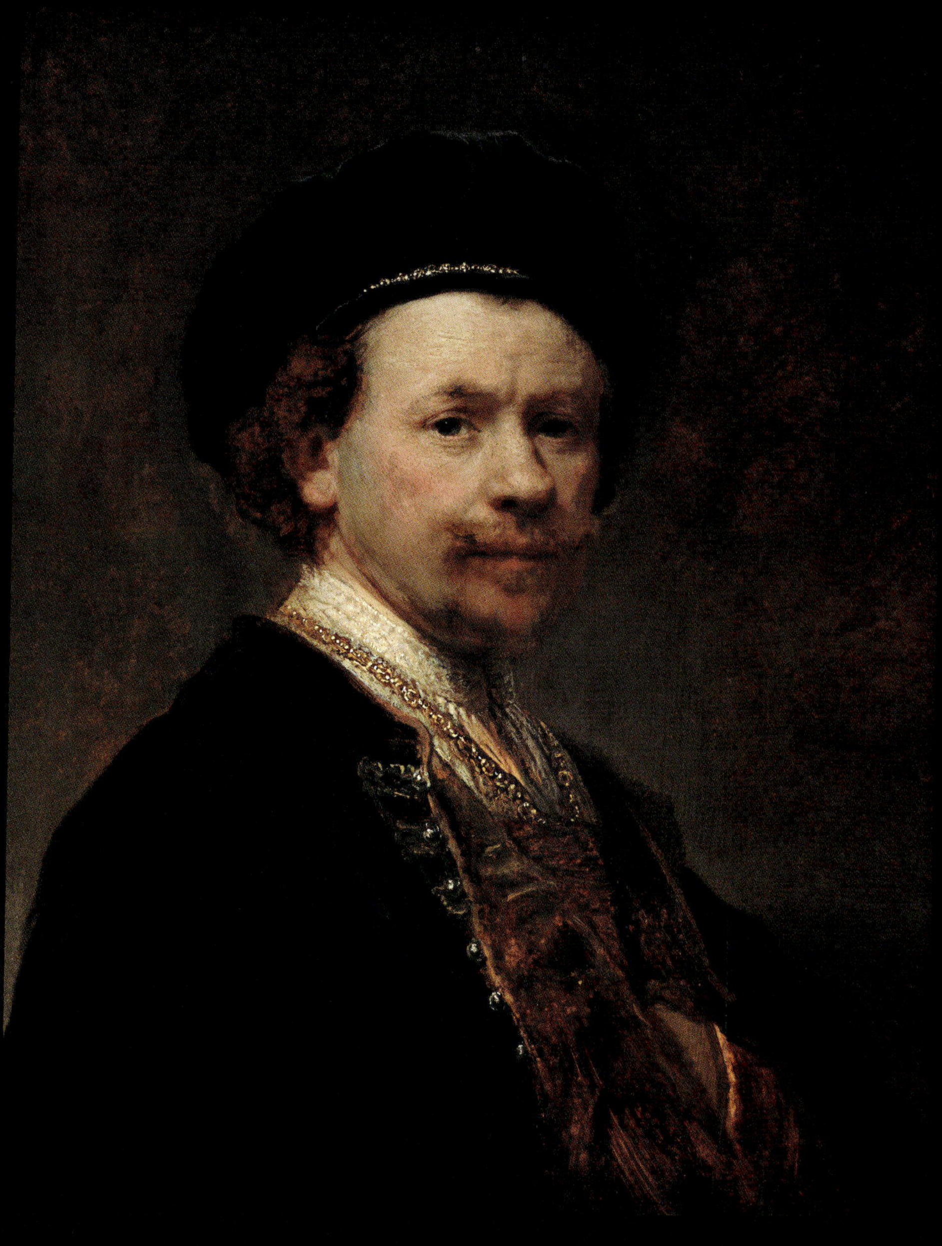

Self-Portrait, *c.* 1638
Oil on panel, 63.2 × 50.5 cm (24 ¾ × 19 ¾ in.)
Pasadena, California, The Norton Simon Foundation

Saskia Uylenburgh in Sixteenth-Century Costume, 1633/34–1642
Oil on panel, 99.5 × 78.5 cm (39 ⅛ × 30 ¾ in.)
Hessen Kassel Heritage, Gemäldegalerie Alte Meister

Page 202
Flora, 1634
Oil on canvas, 124.7 × 100.4 cm (49 ⅛ × 39 ½ in.)
St Petersburg, The State Hermitage Museum

Page 203
Flora, 1635
Oil on canvas, 123.5 × 97.5 cm (48 ⅝ × 38 ⅜ in.)
London, The National Gallery

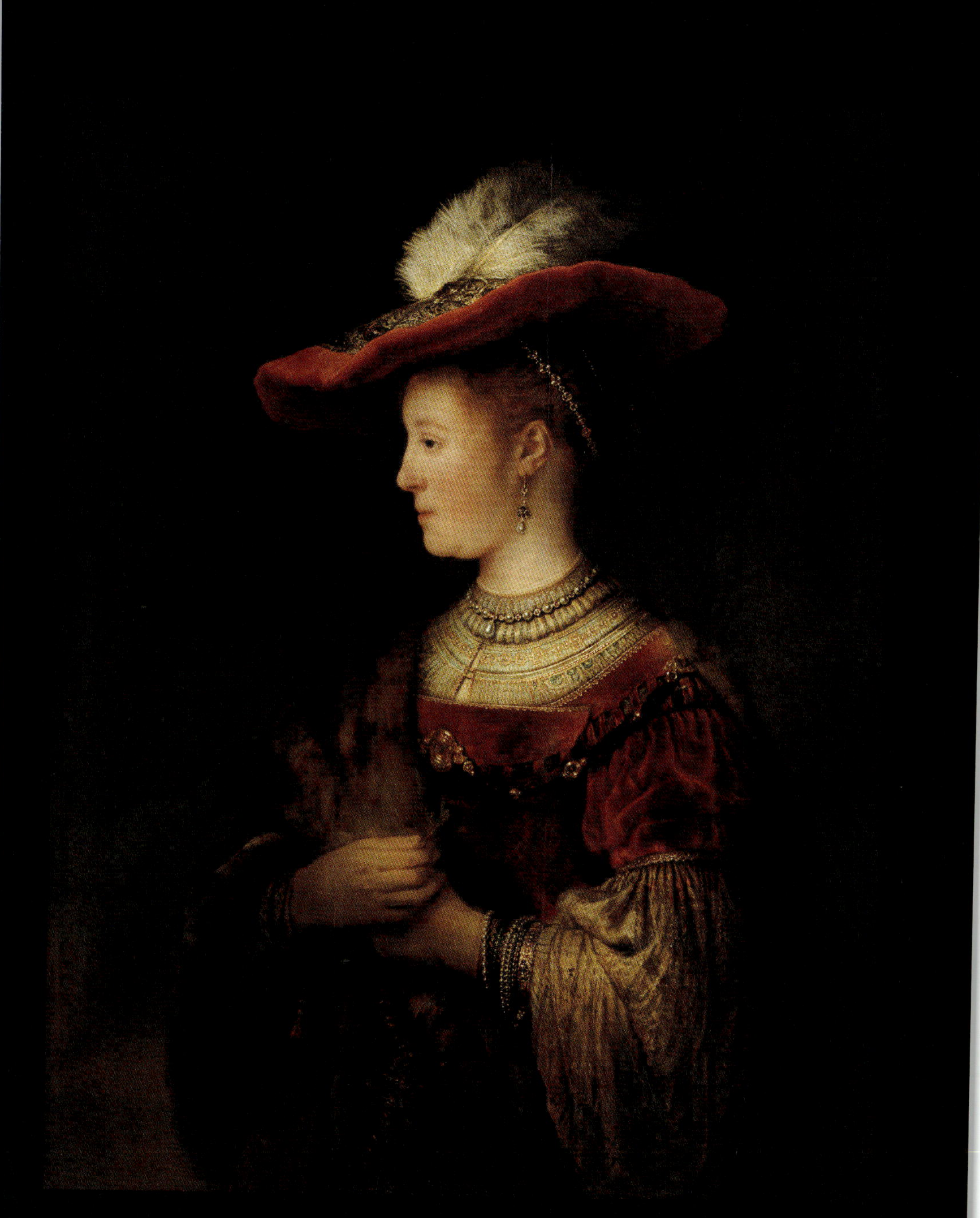

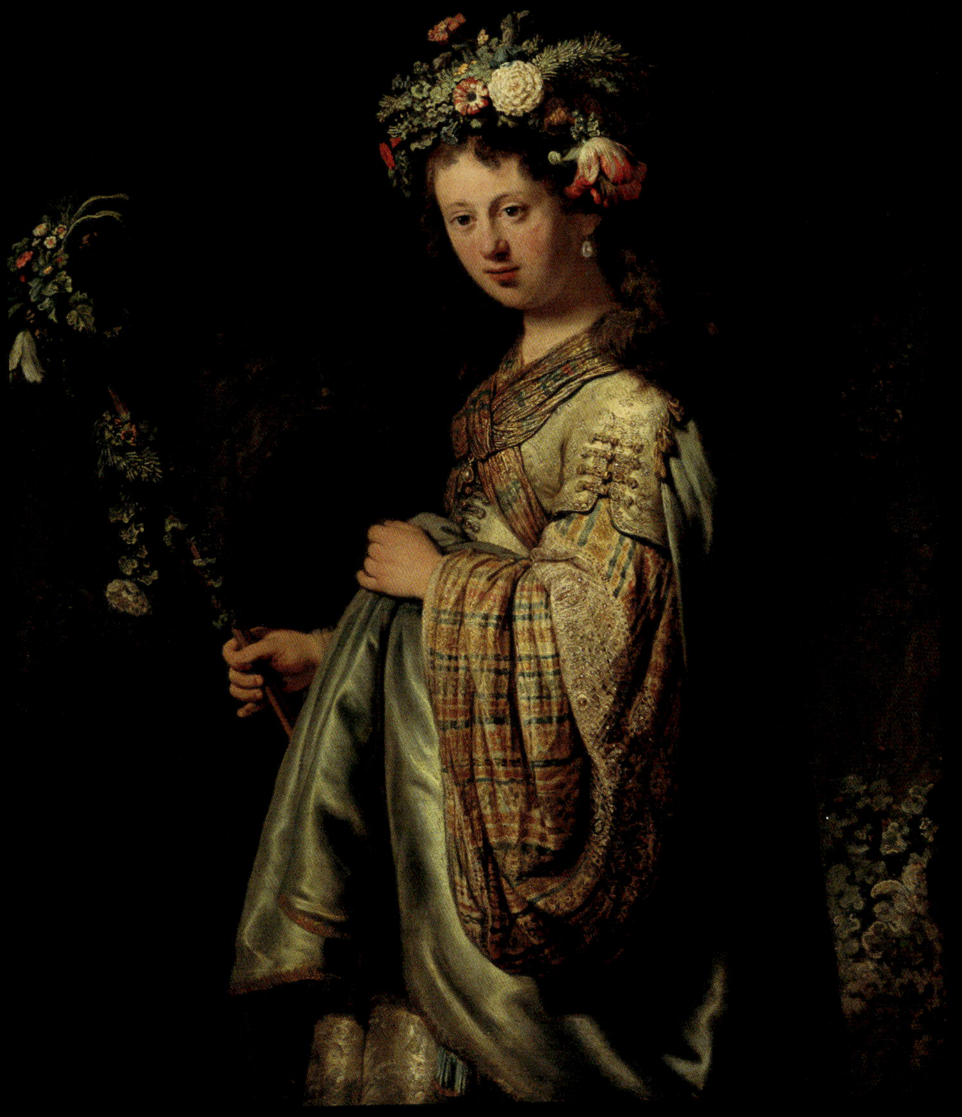

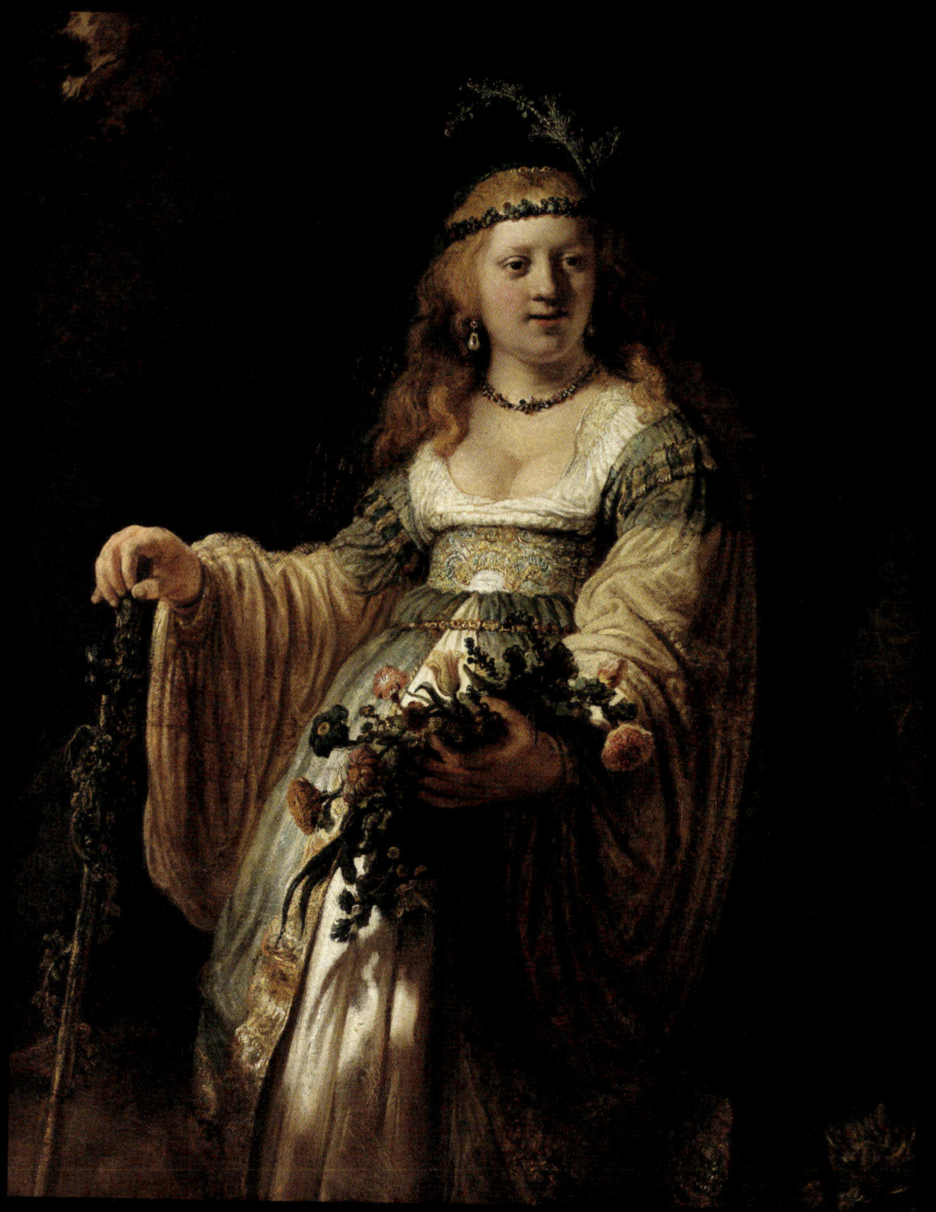

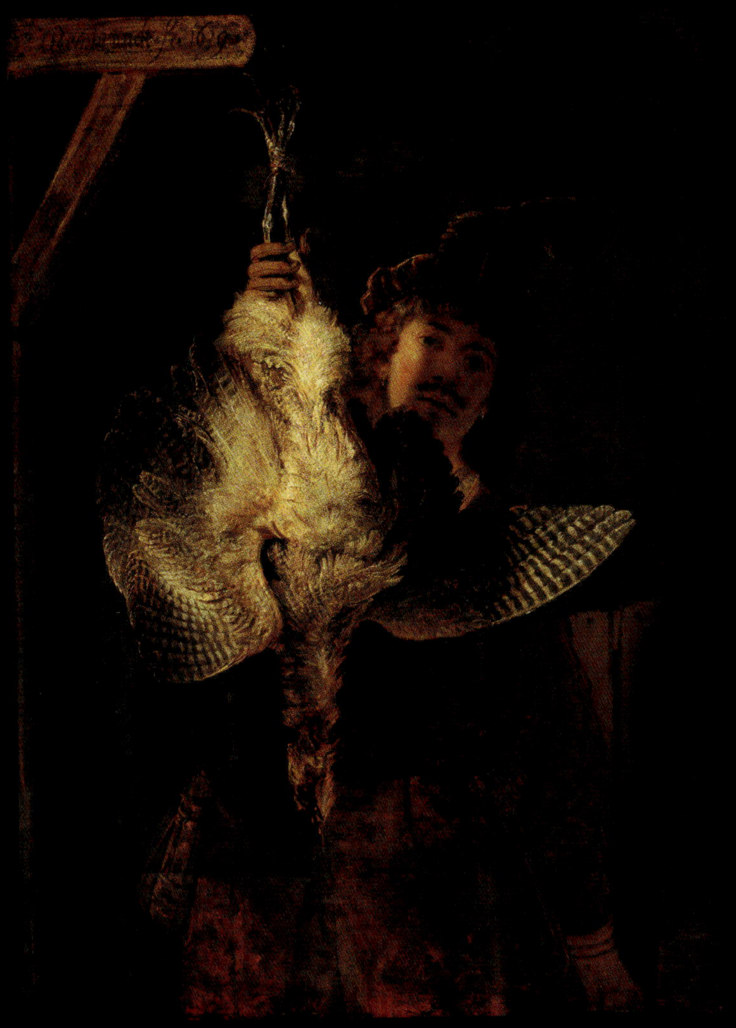

Hunter with a Dead Bittern, 1639
Oil on panel, 120.7 × 88.3 cm (47 ½ × 34 ¾ in.)
Staatliche Kunstsammlungen Dresden,
Gemäldegalerie Alte Meister

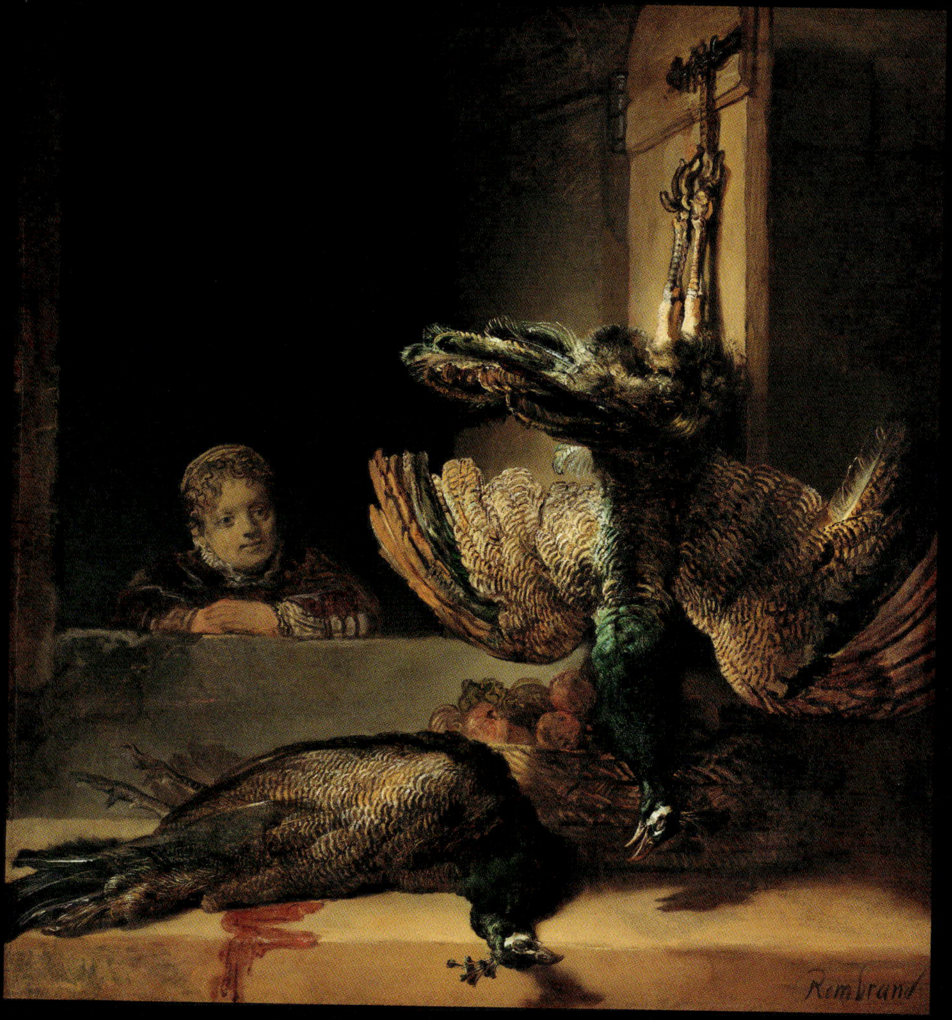

Girl with Dead Peacocks, *c.* 1639
Oil on canvas, 145 × 135.5 cm (57 ⅛ × 53 ⅓ in.)
Amsterdam, Rijksmuseum

Simeon's Song of Praise, 1631
Oil on panel, 60.9 × 47.9 cm (23 ¾ × 18 ¾ in.)
The Hague, Mauritshuis

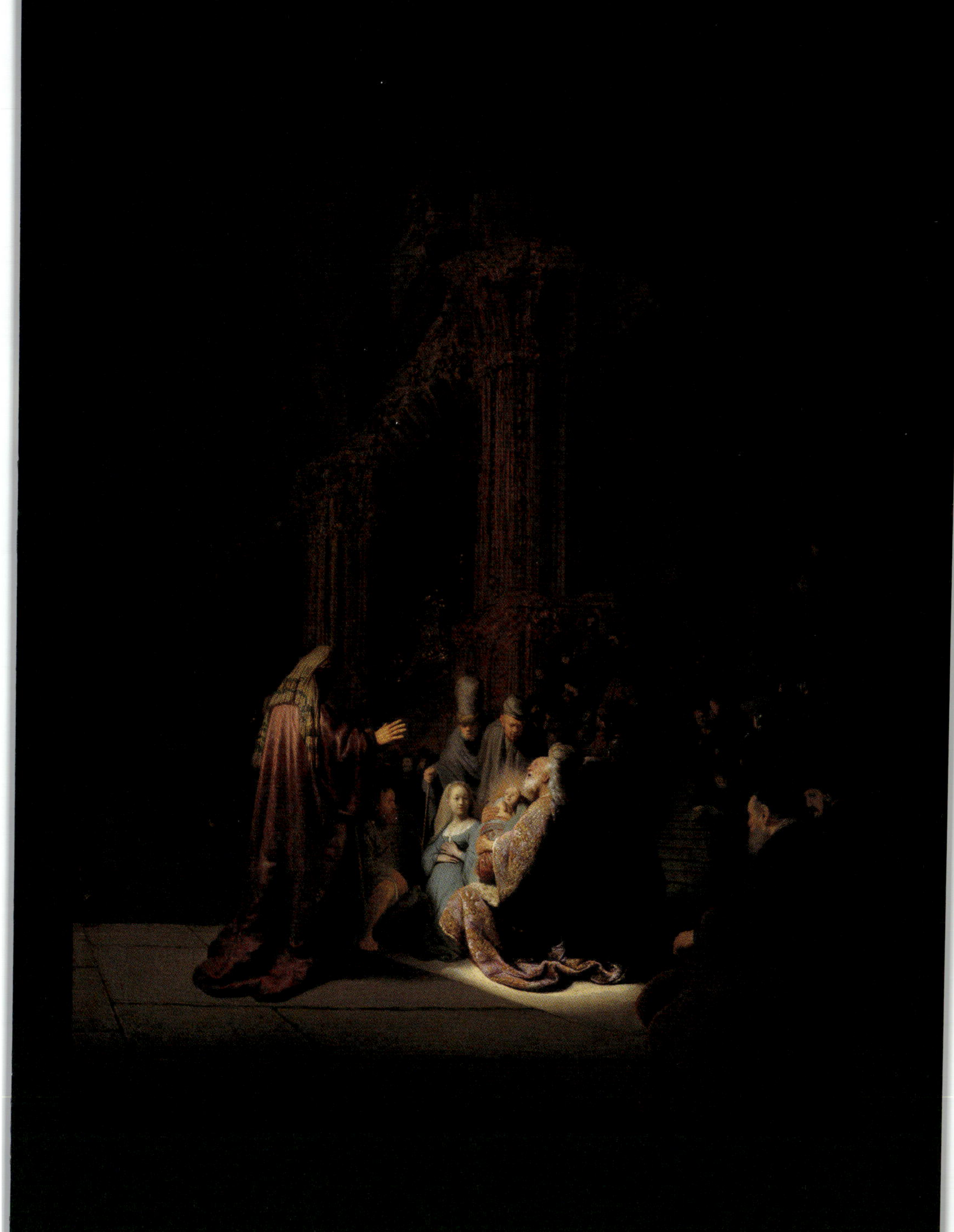

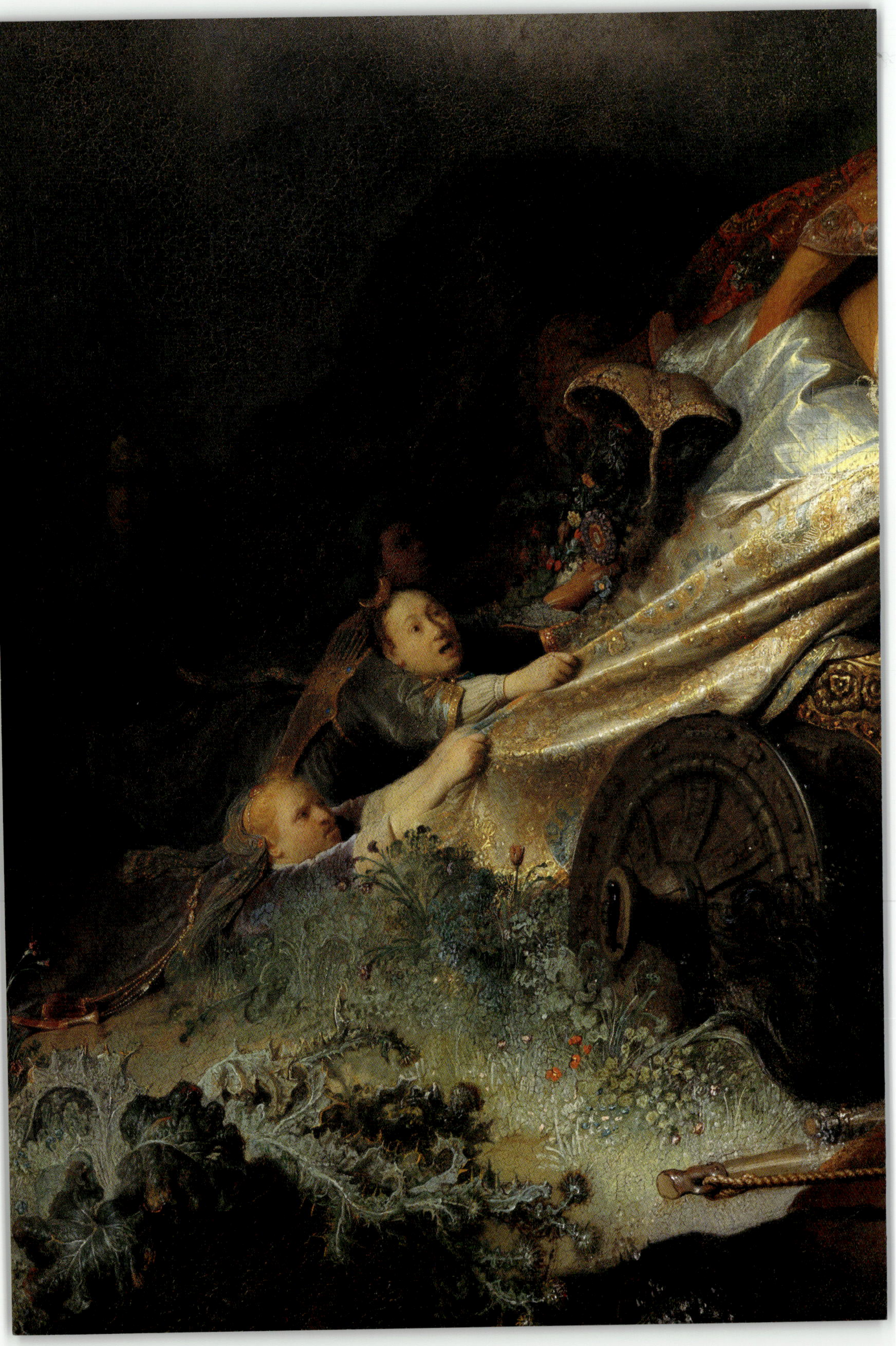

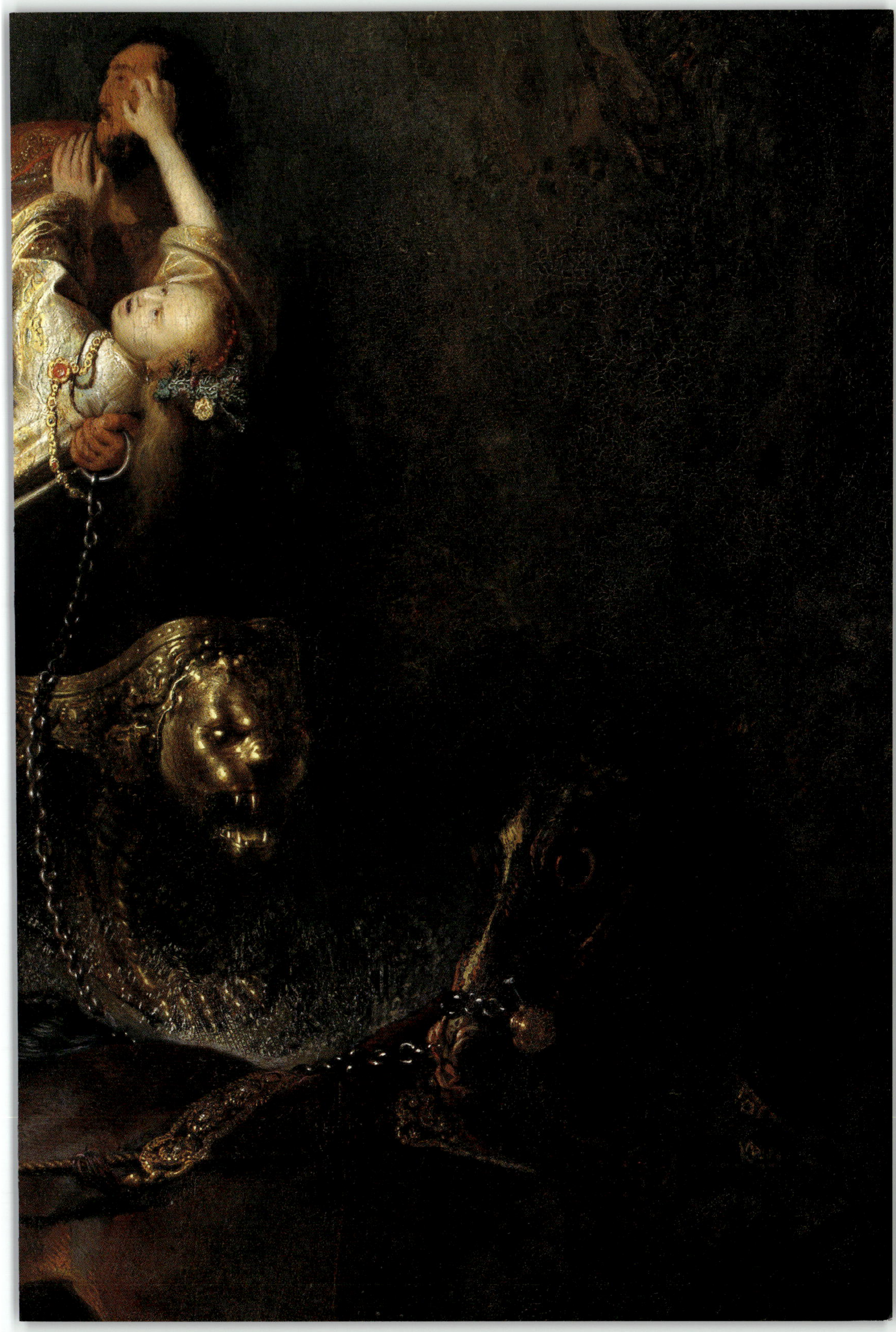

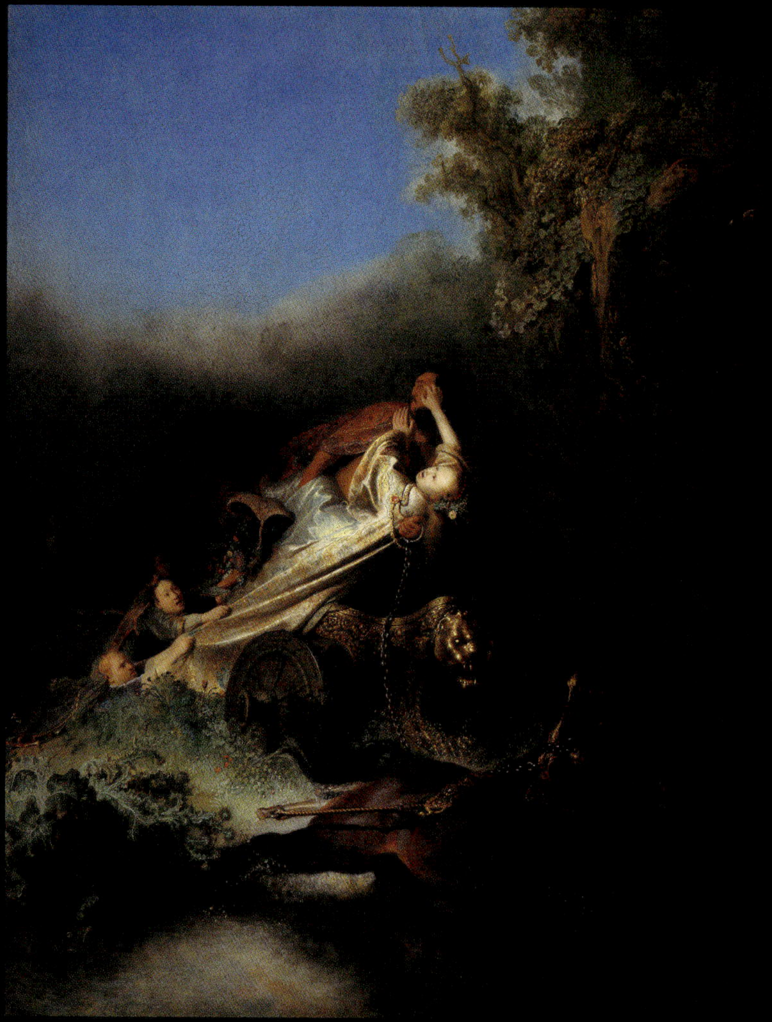

The Rape of Proserpina, *c.* 1631
Oil on panel, 84.8 × 79.7 cm (33 3/8 × 31 3/8 in.)
Staatliche Museen zu Berlin, Gemäldegalerie
(detail pages 208/209)

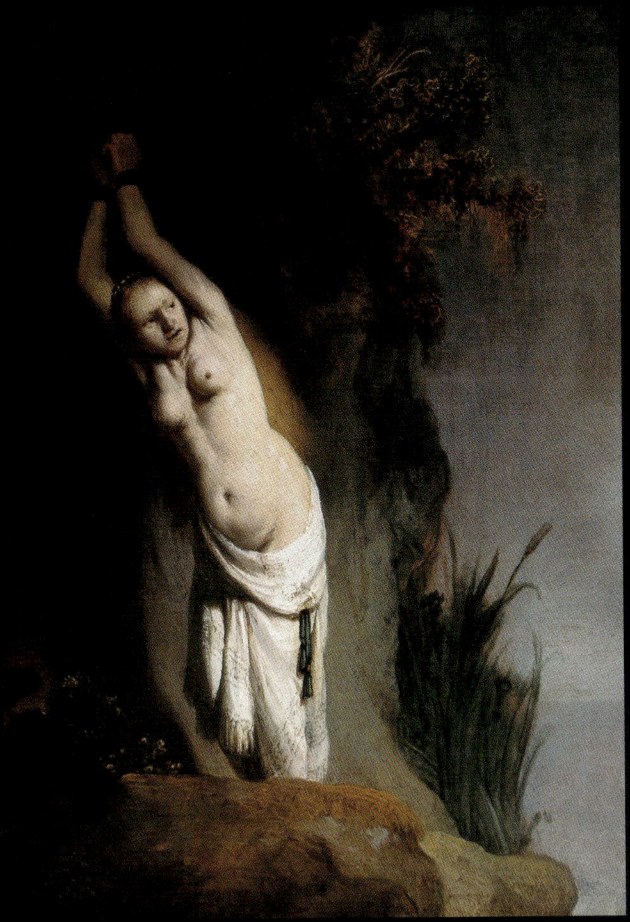

Andromeda, *c.* 1630/31
Oil on panel, 34 × 24.5 cm (13 3/8 × 9 5/8 in.)
The Hague, Mauritshuis

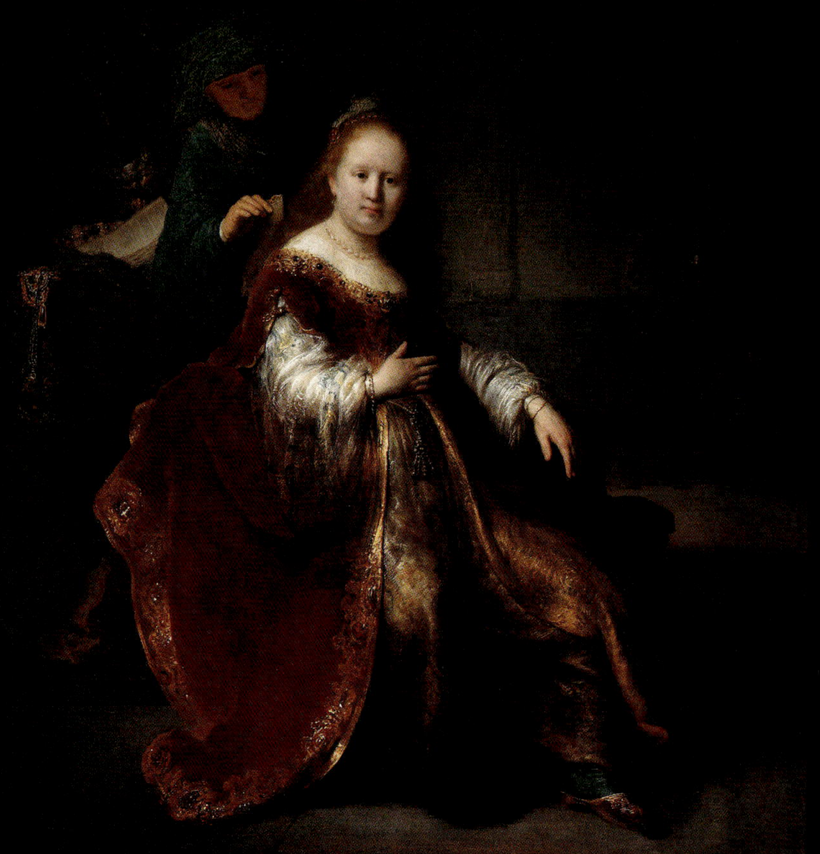

Heroine of the Old Testament at Her Toilet, 1632/33
Oil on canvas, 109.2 × 94.4 cm (42 ¾ × 37 ⅛ in.)
Ottawa, National Gallery of Canada

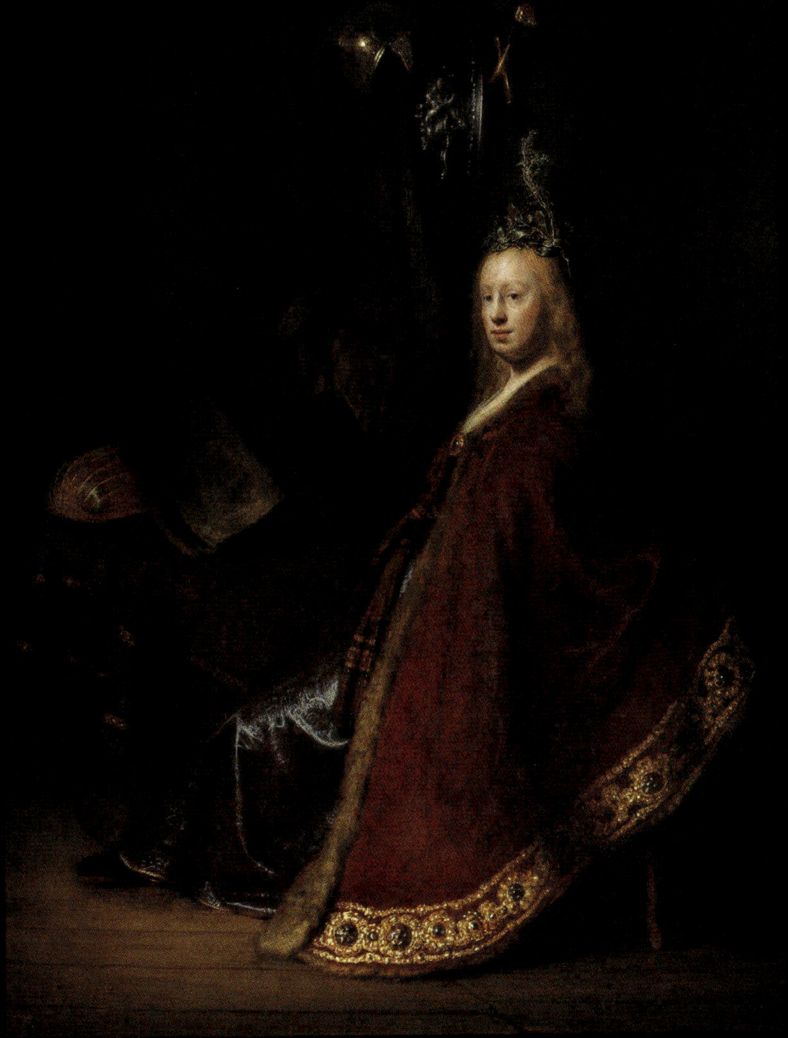

Minerva in Her Study, *c.* 1631
Oil on panel, 60.5 × 49 cm (23 ¾ × 19 ¼ in.)
Staatliche Museen zu Berlin, Gemäldegalerie

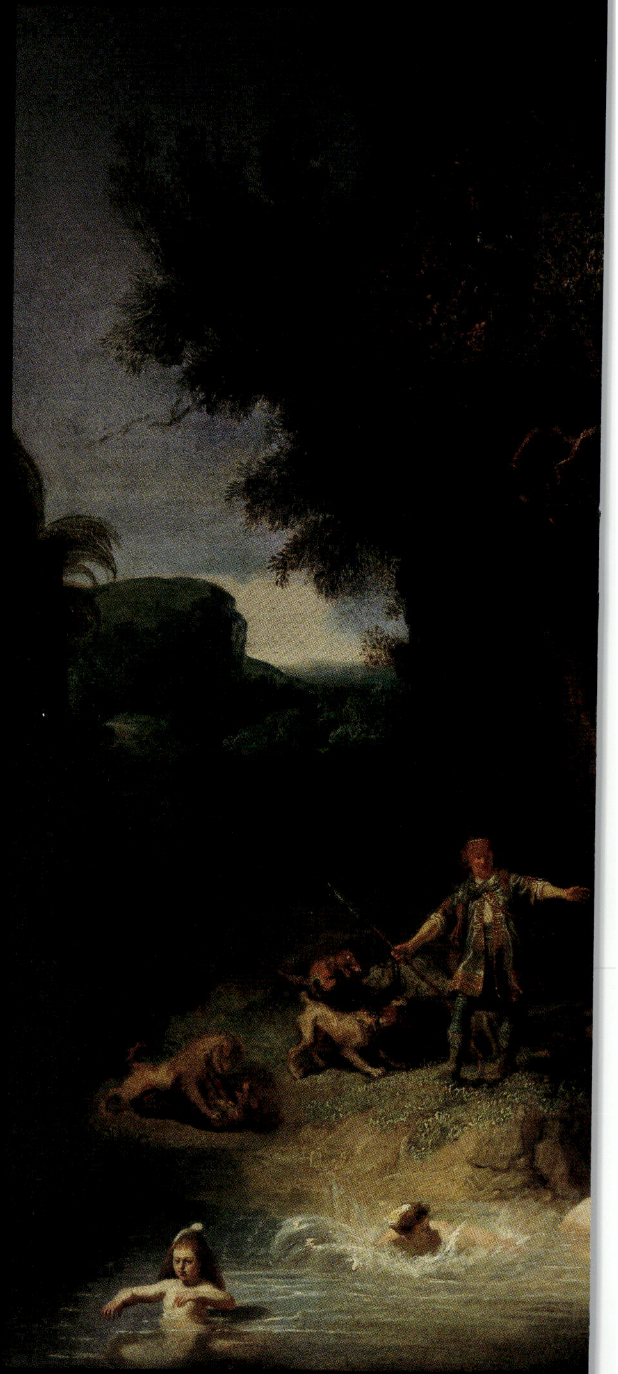

Diana Bathing, with Actaeon and Callisto, *c.* 1634
Oil on canvas, 73.5 × 93.5 cm
(28 ¾ × 36 ¾ in.)
Anholt (Isselburg),
Museum Wasserburg Anholt,
Prince of Salm-Salm Collection

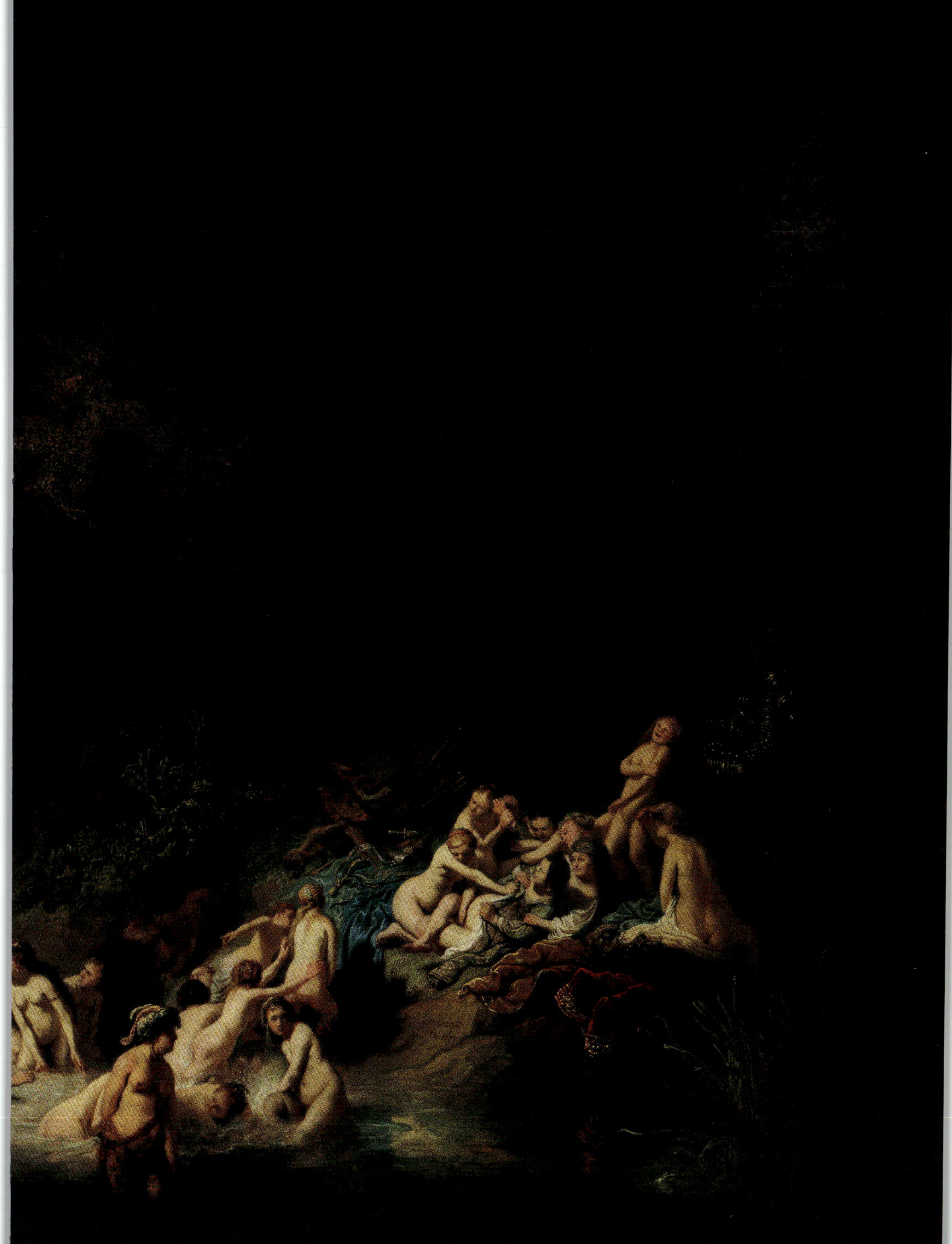

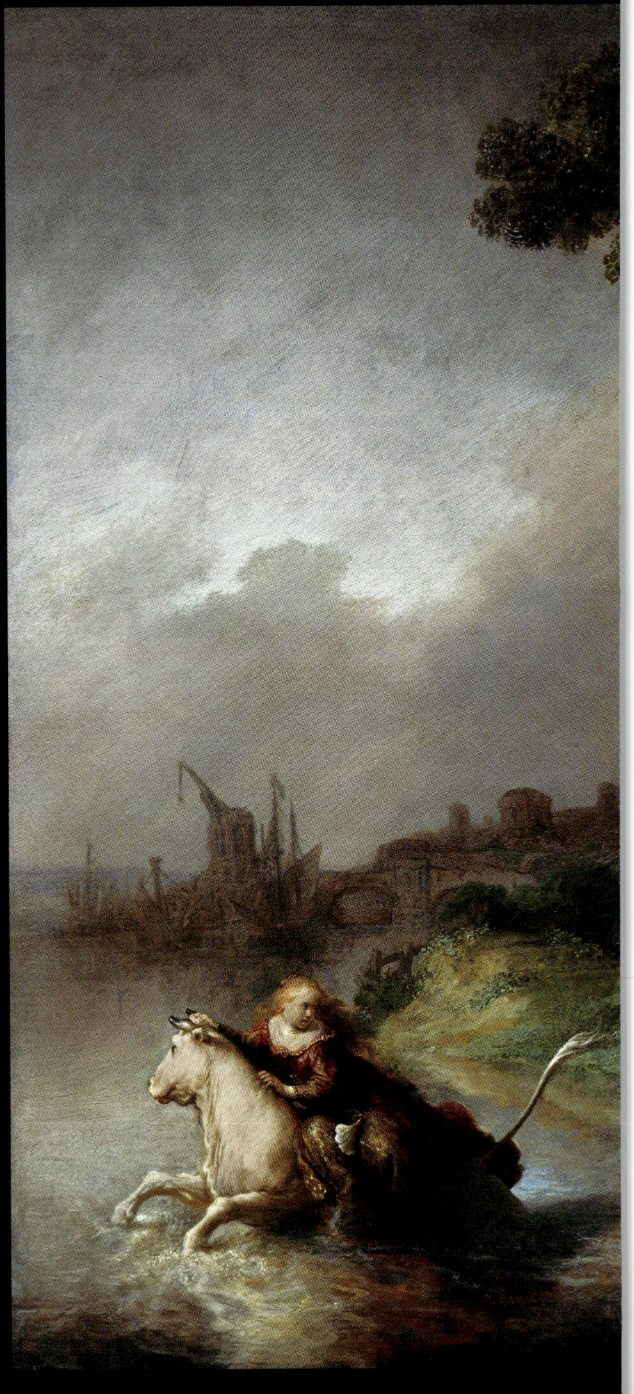

The Rape of Europa, 1632
Oil on panel, 64.6 × 78.7 cm
(25 3⁄8 × 30 3⁄4 in.)
Los Angeles, The J. Paul
Getty Museum

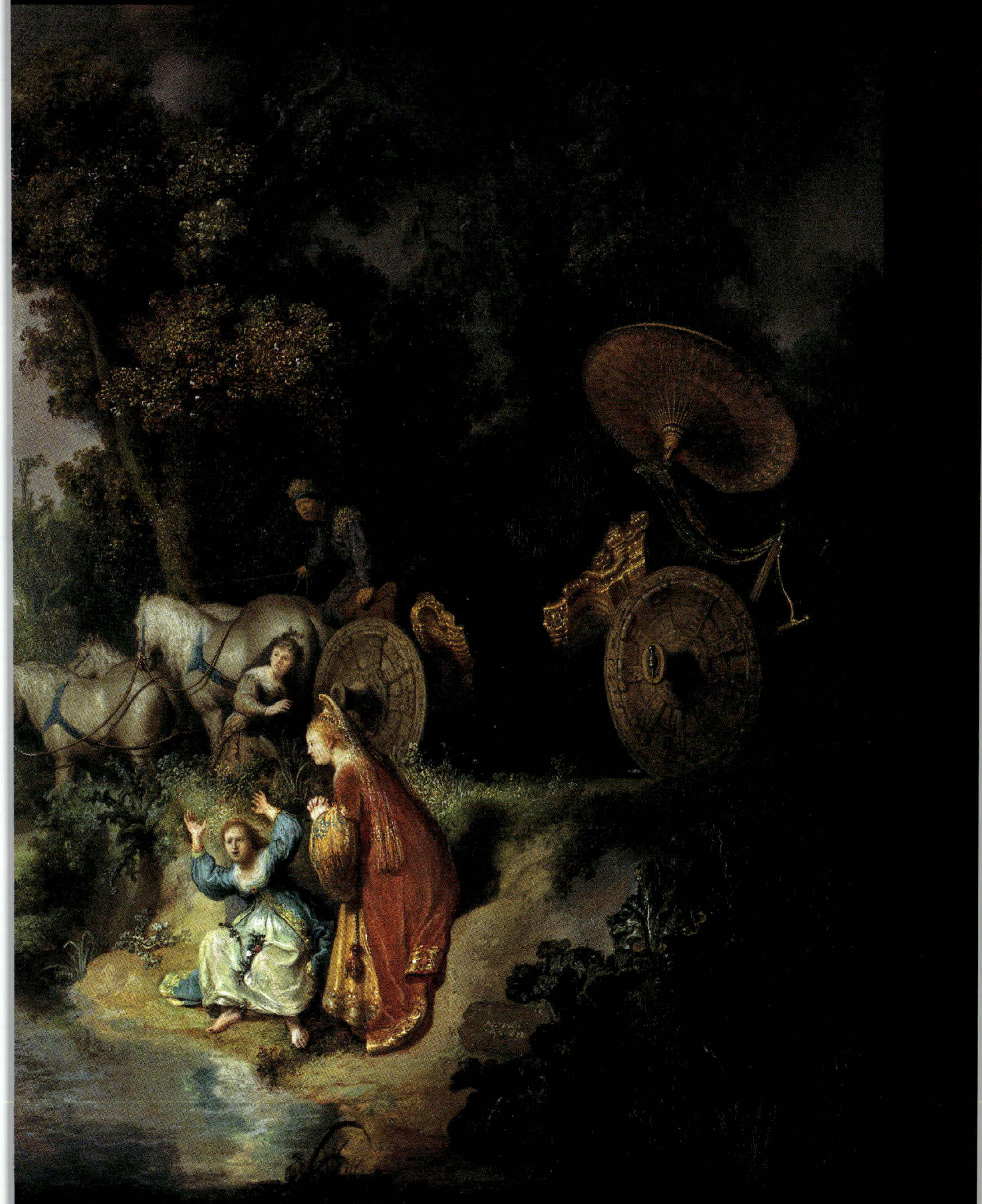

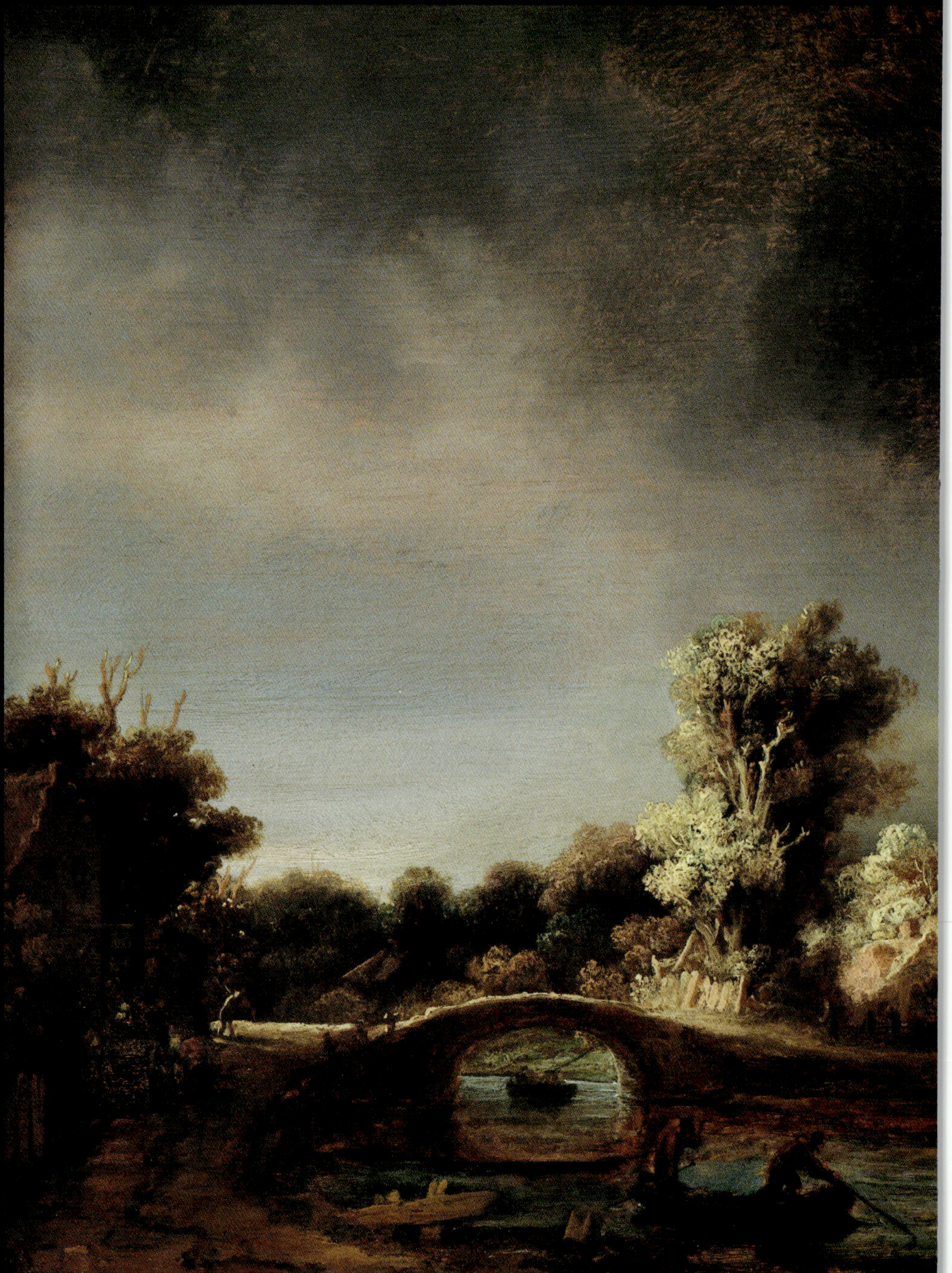

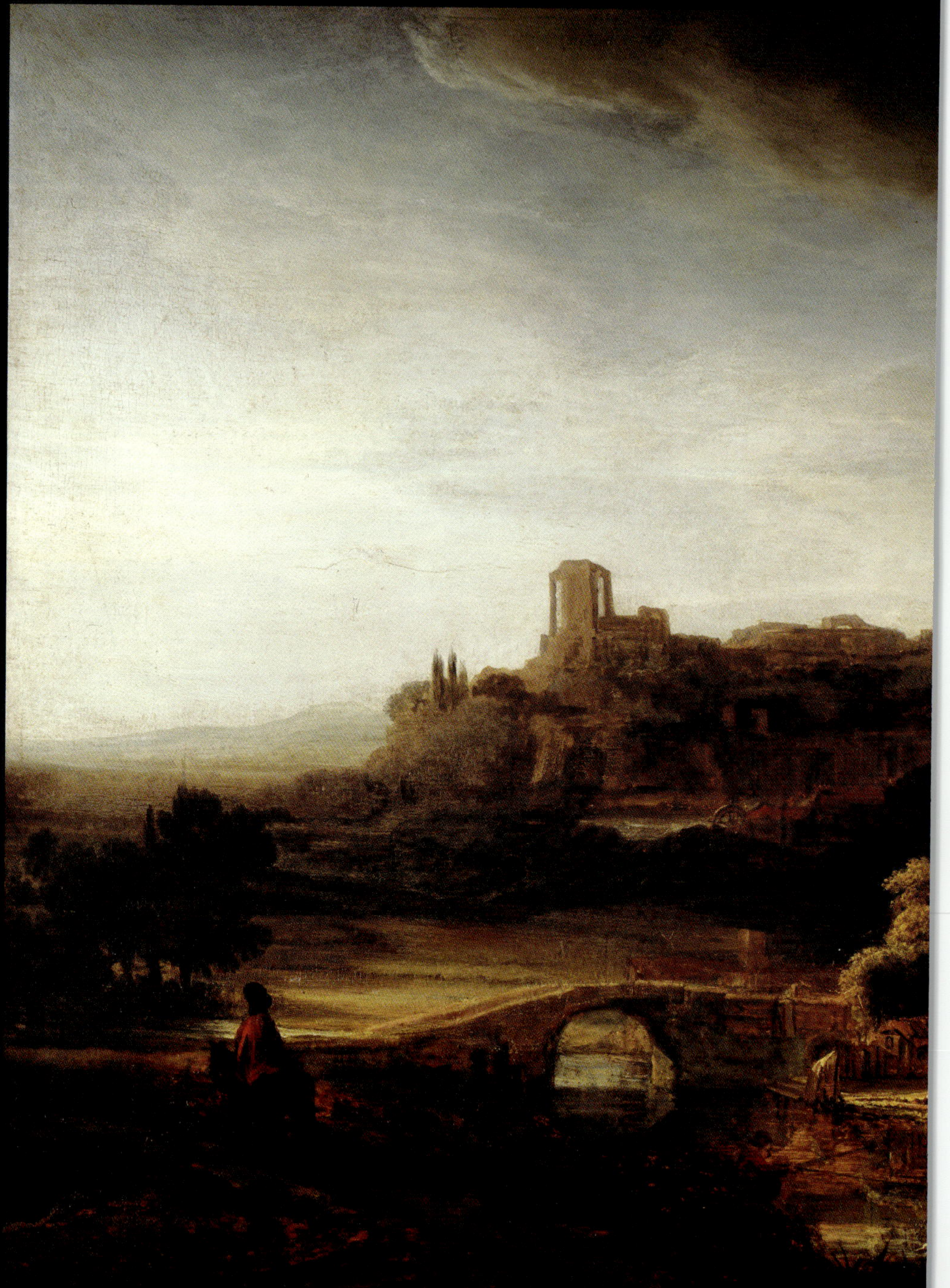

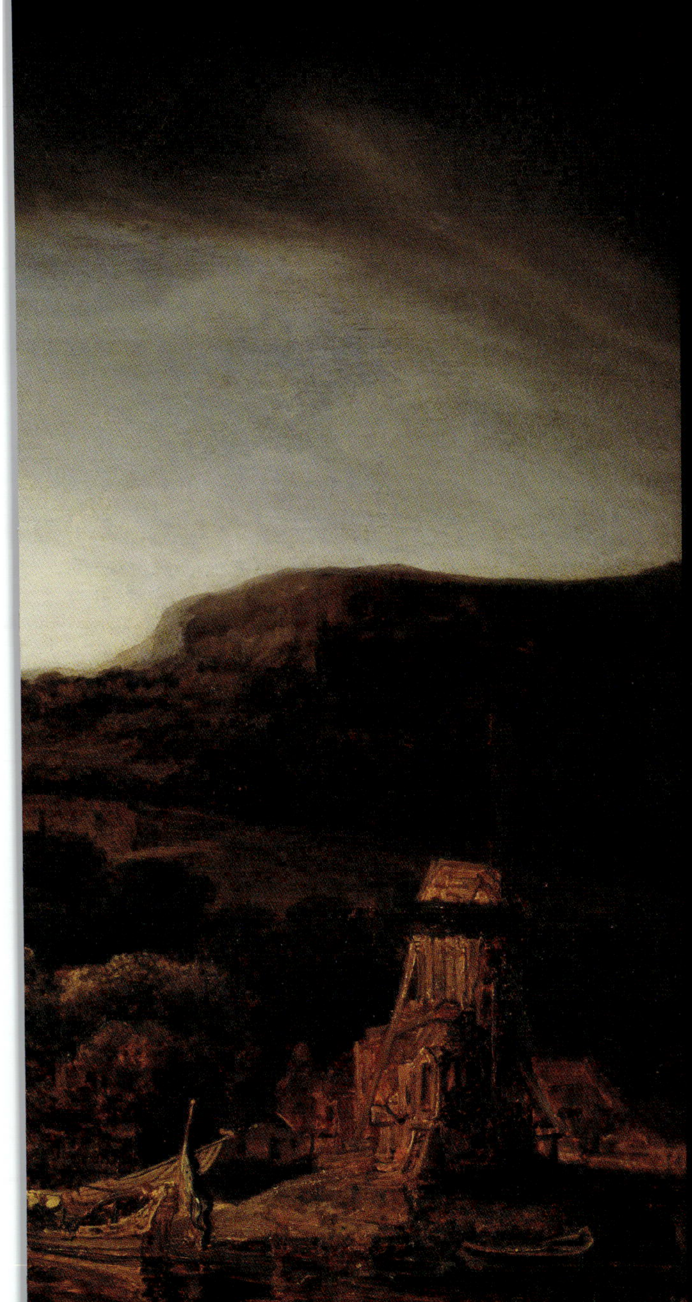

Pages 218/219
Landscape with a Stone Bridge, *c.* 1638
Oil on panel, 29.5 × 42.5 cm (11 ⅝ × 16 ¾ in.)
Amsterdam, Rijksmuseum

Pages 220/221
River Landscape with Windmill and Ruins, *c.* 1637–1645
Oil on panel, 67 × 87.5 cm (26 ⅜ × 34 ½ in.)
Hessen Kassel Heritage, Gemäldegalerie Alte Meister

Old Woman Reading a Book (so-called **Prophetess Anna**), 1631
Oil on panel, 59.8 × 47.7 cm (23 ⅝ × 18 ⅞ in.)
Amsterdam, Rijksmuseum

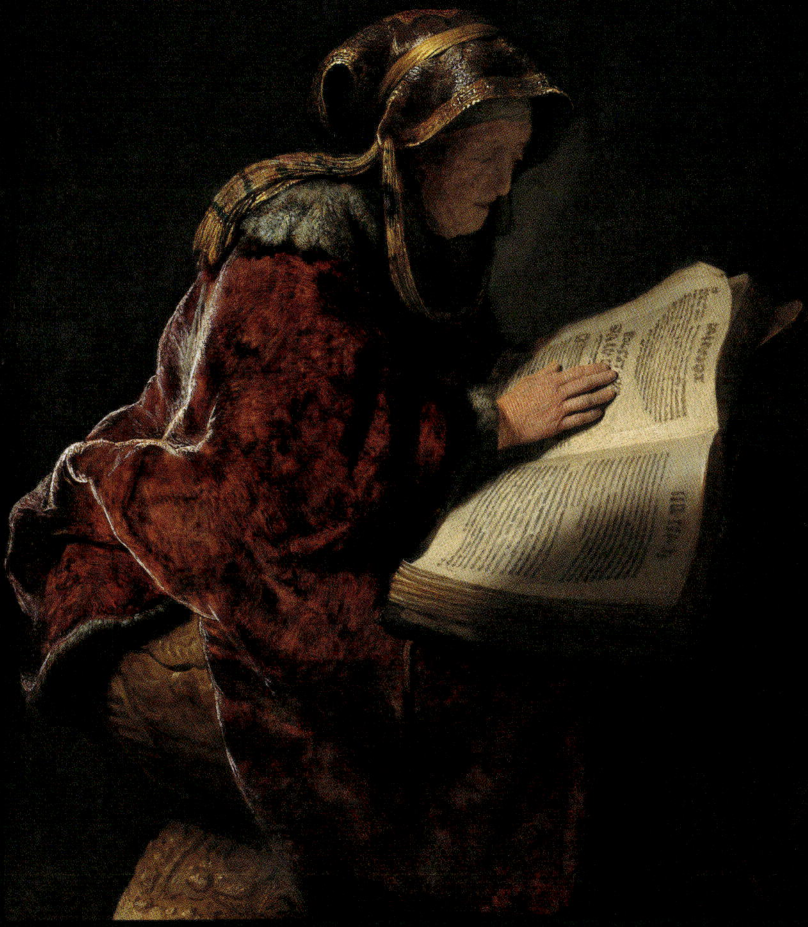

Lucas van Leyden
David Playing the Harp to Saul, 1506–1510
Copper engraving, 25.2 × 18.5 cm (10 × 7 3⁄8 in.)
Amsterdam, Rijksmuseum

David Playing the Harp to Saul, *c.* 1629–1631
Oil on panel, 62.0 × 50.1 cm (24 3⁄8 × 19 3⁄4 in.)
Frankfurt am Main, Städel Museum

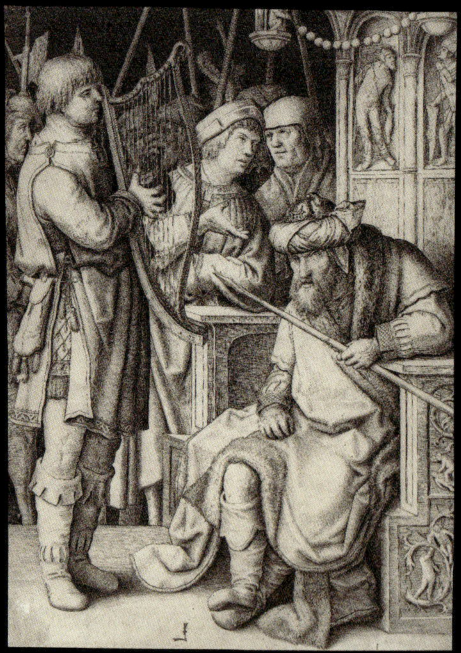

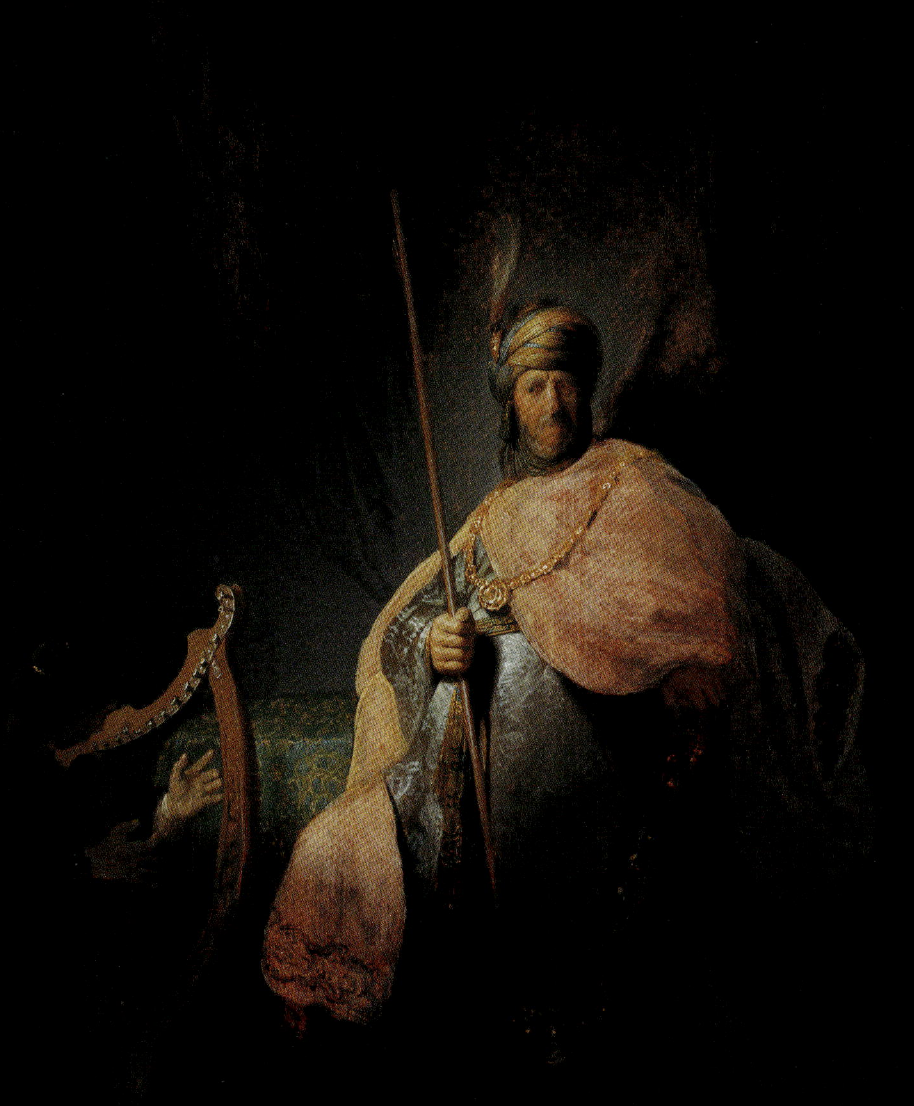

Christ in the Storm on the Sea of Galilee, 1633
Oil on canvas, 160 × 128 cm (62 ¾ × 50 ⅜ in.)
Formerly Boston, Massachusetts,
Isabella Stewart Gardner Museum

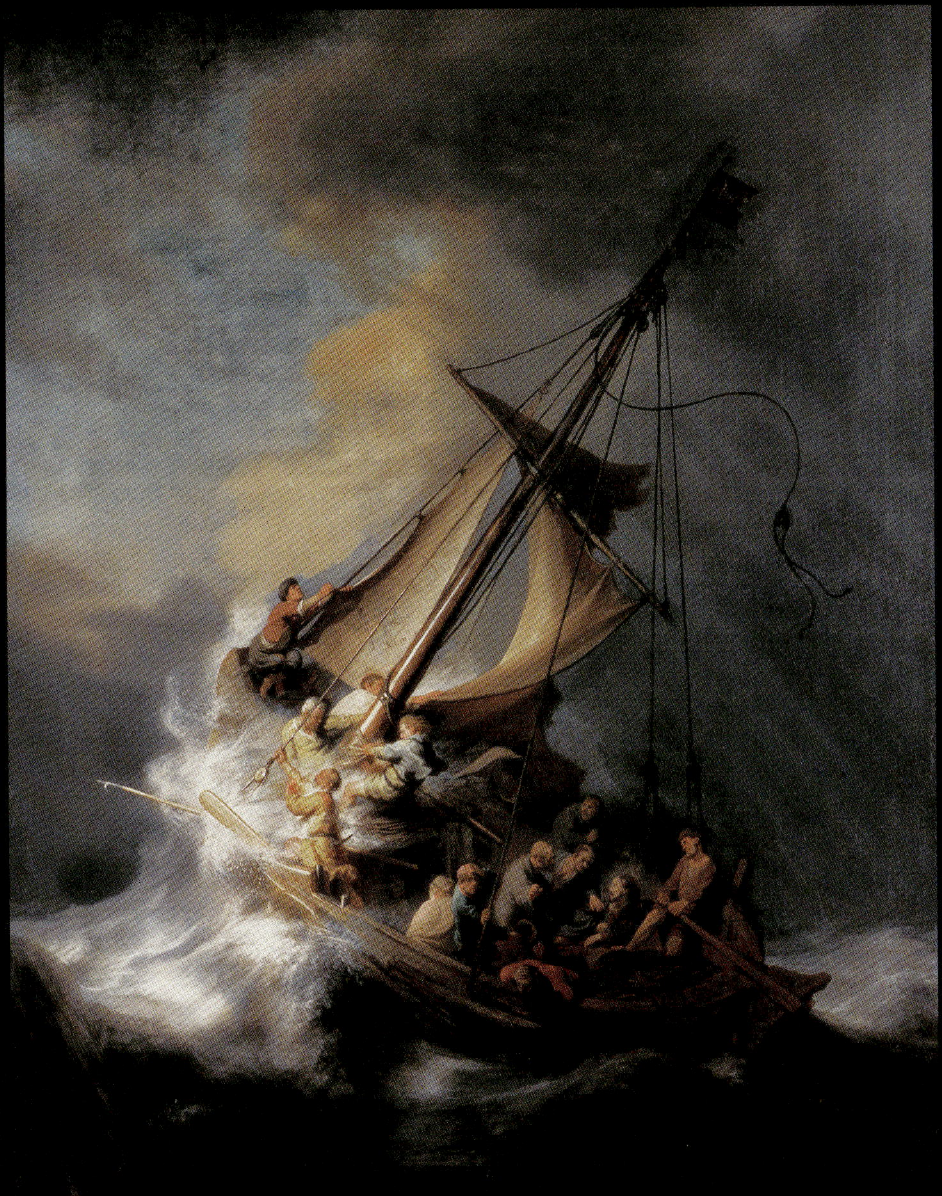

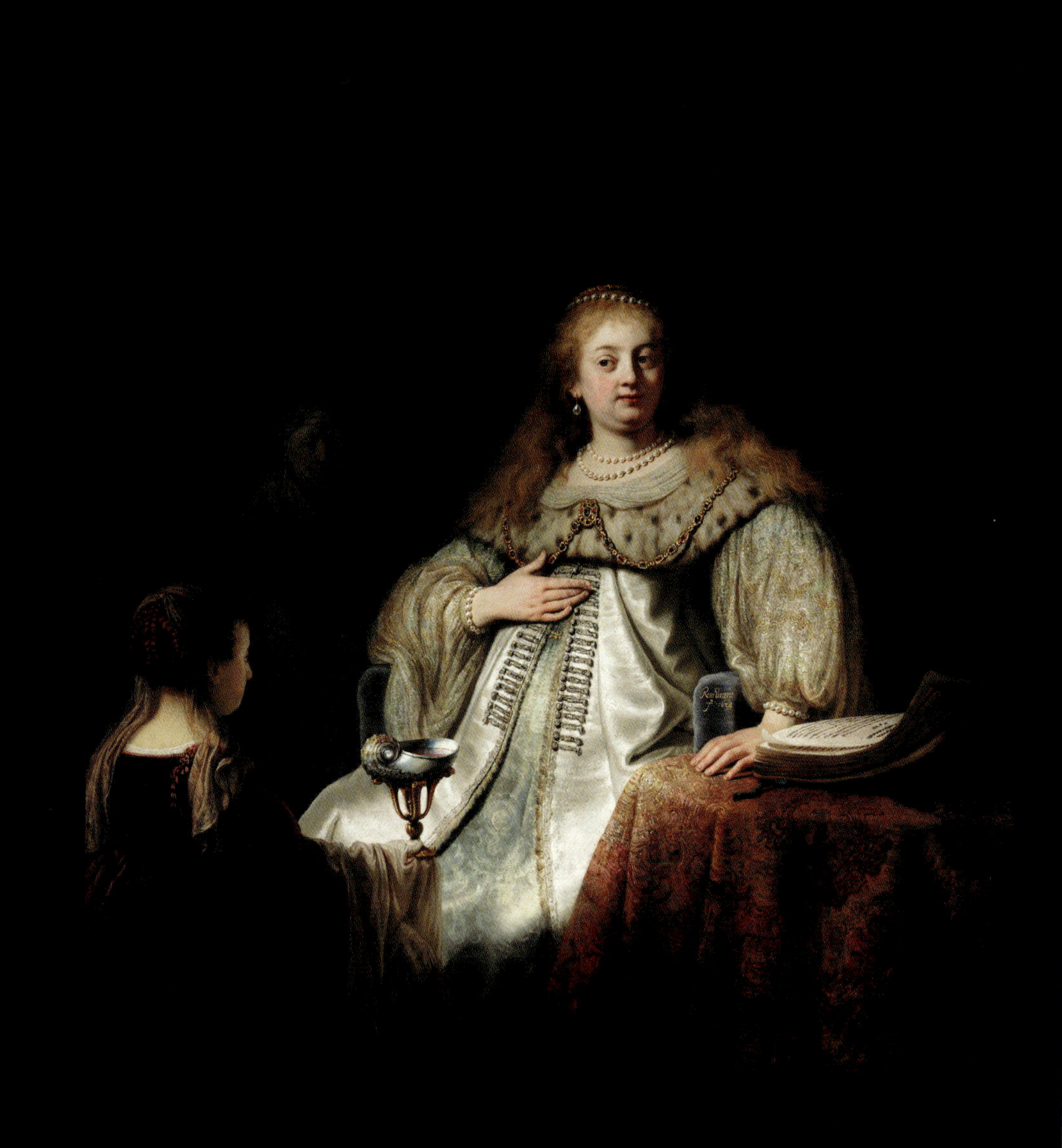

Artemisia (Sophonisba?), 1634
Oil on canvas, 142 × 153 cm (55 ¾ × 60 ¼ in.)
Madrid, Museo Nacional del Prado

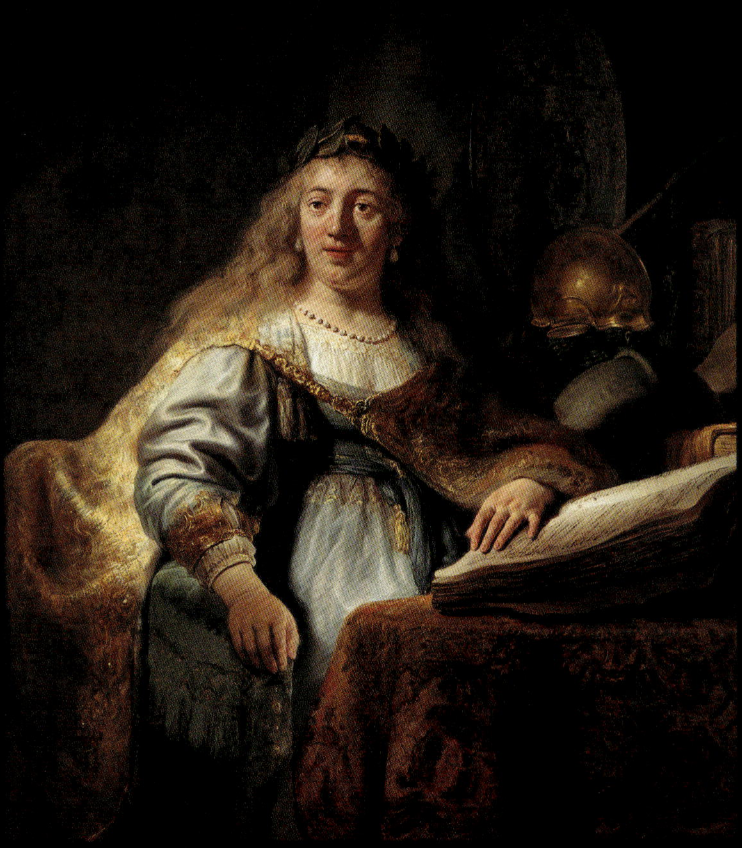

Minerva in Her Study, 1635
Oil on canvas, 137.2 × 116 cm (54⅛ × 45⅔ in.)
New York, The Leiden Collection

Michelangelo Merisi da Caravaggio
The Sacrifice of Isaac, *c.* 1603
Oil on canvas, 104 × 135 cm (41 × 53 ¼ in.)
Florence, Galleria degli Uffizi

Abraham's Sacrifice, 1635
Oil on canvas, 193.5 × 132.8 cm (76 ⅛ × 52 ¼ in.)
St Petersburg, The State Hermitage Museum

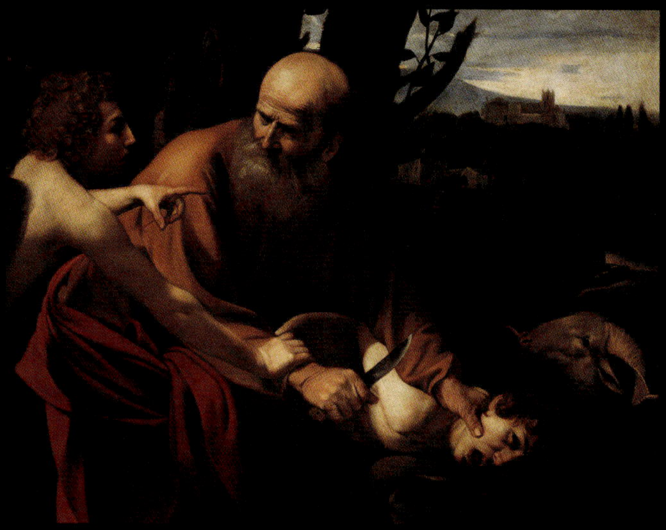

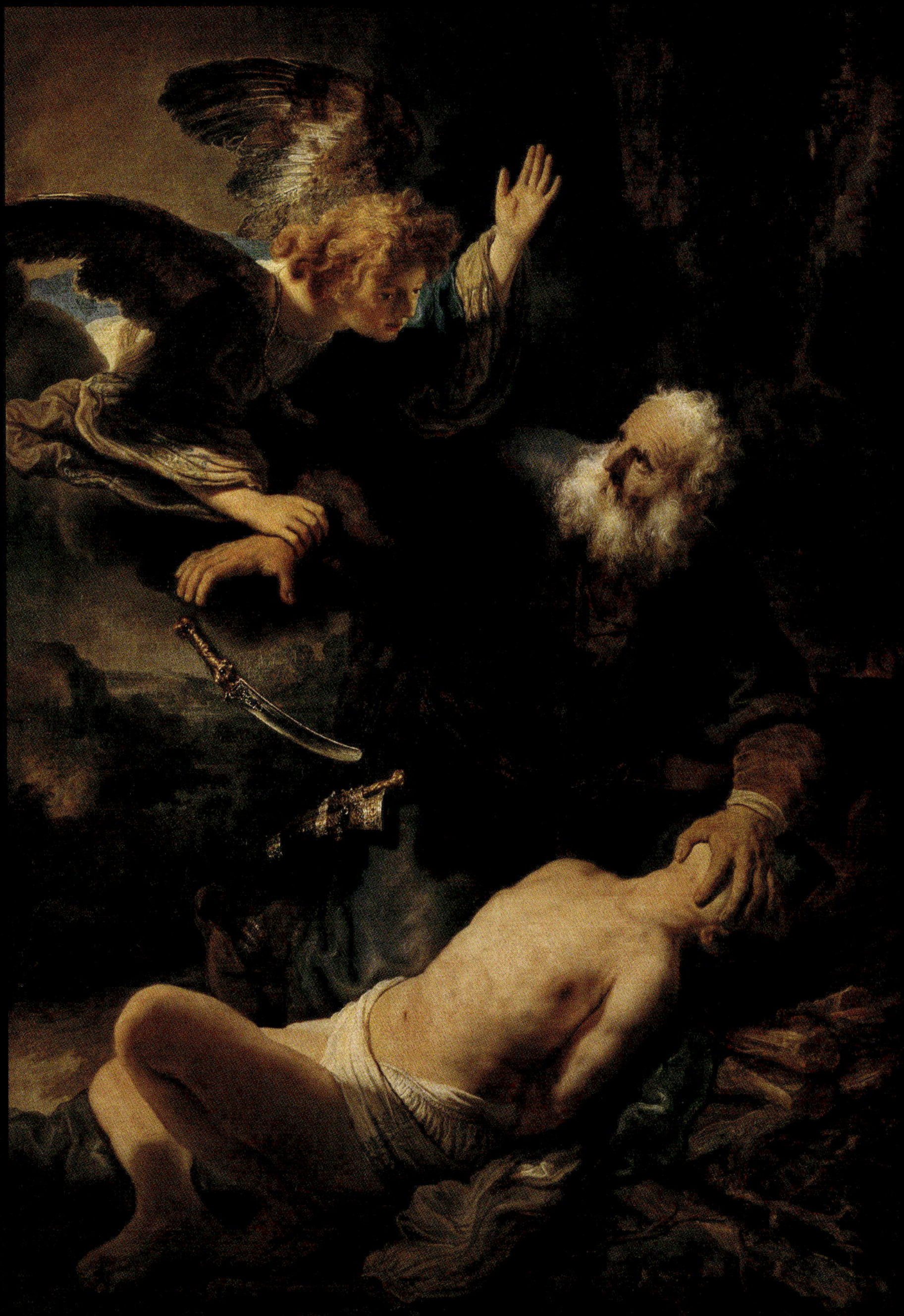

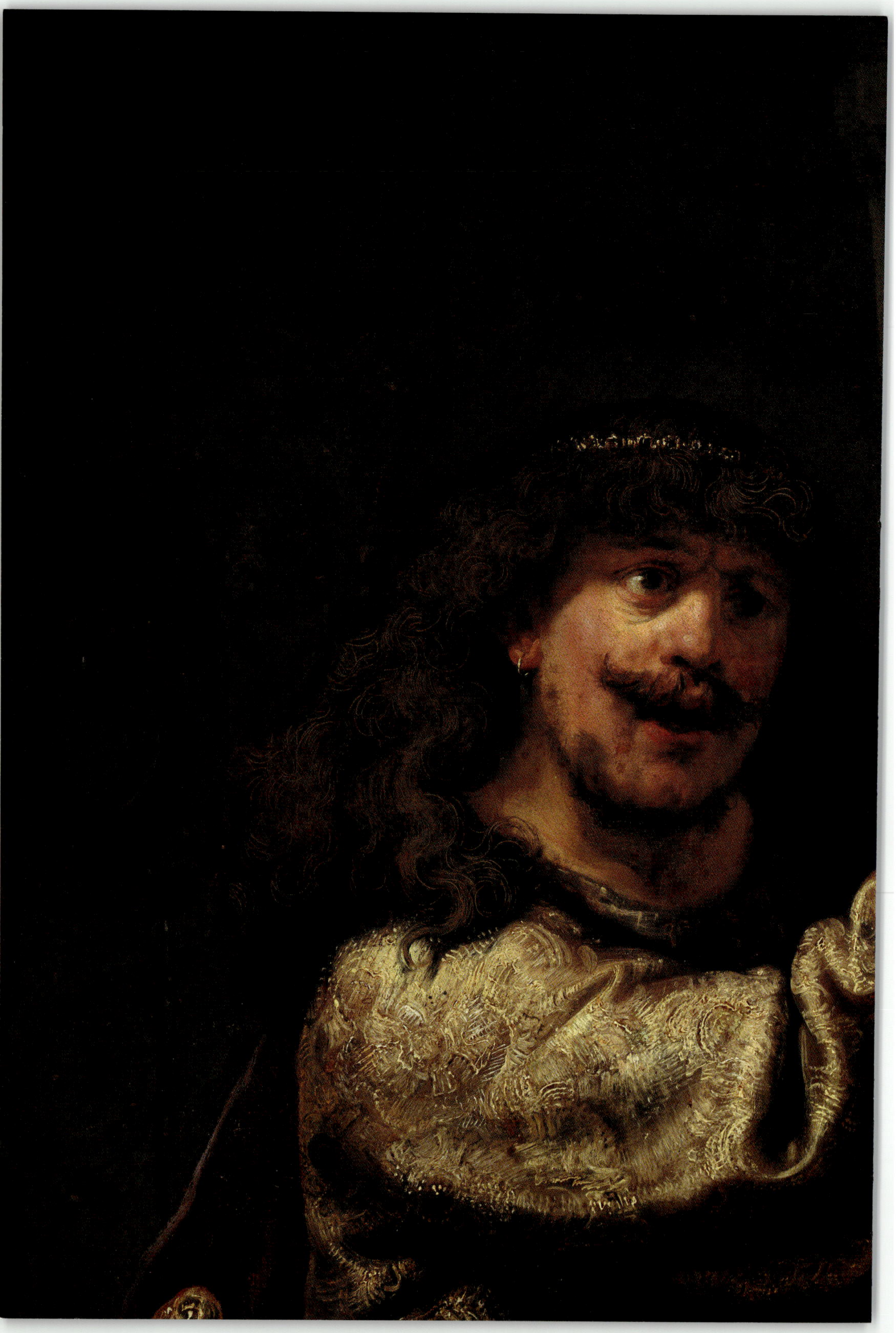

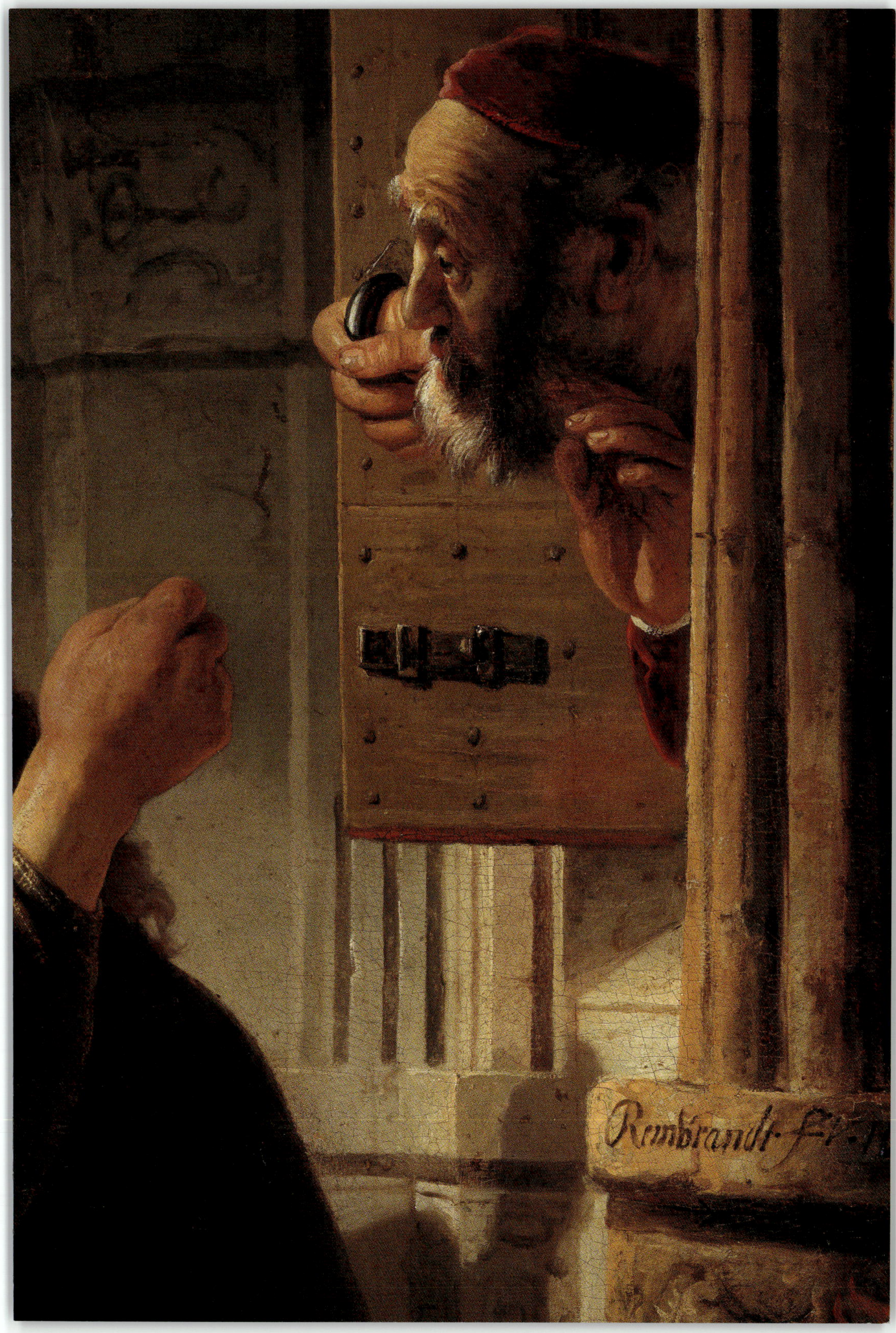
Rembrandt

Samson Threatening His Father-in-Law, *c.* 1635
Oil on canvas, 158.5 × 130.5 cm (62 3/8 × 51 3/8 in.)
Staatliche Museen zu Berlin, Gemäldegalerie
(detail pages 232/233)

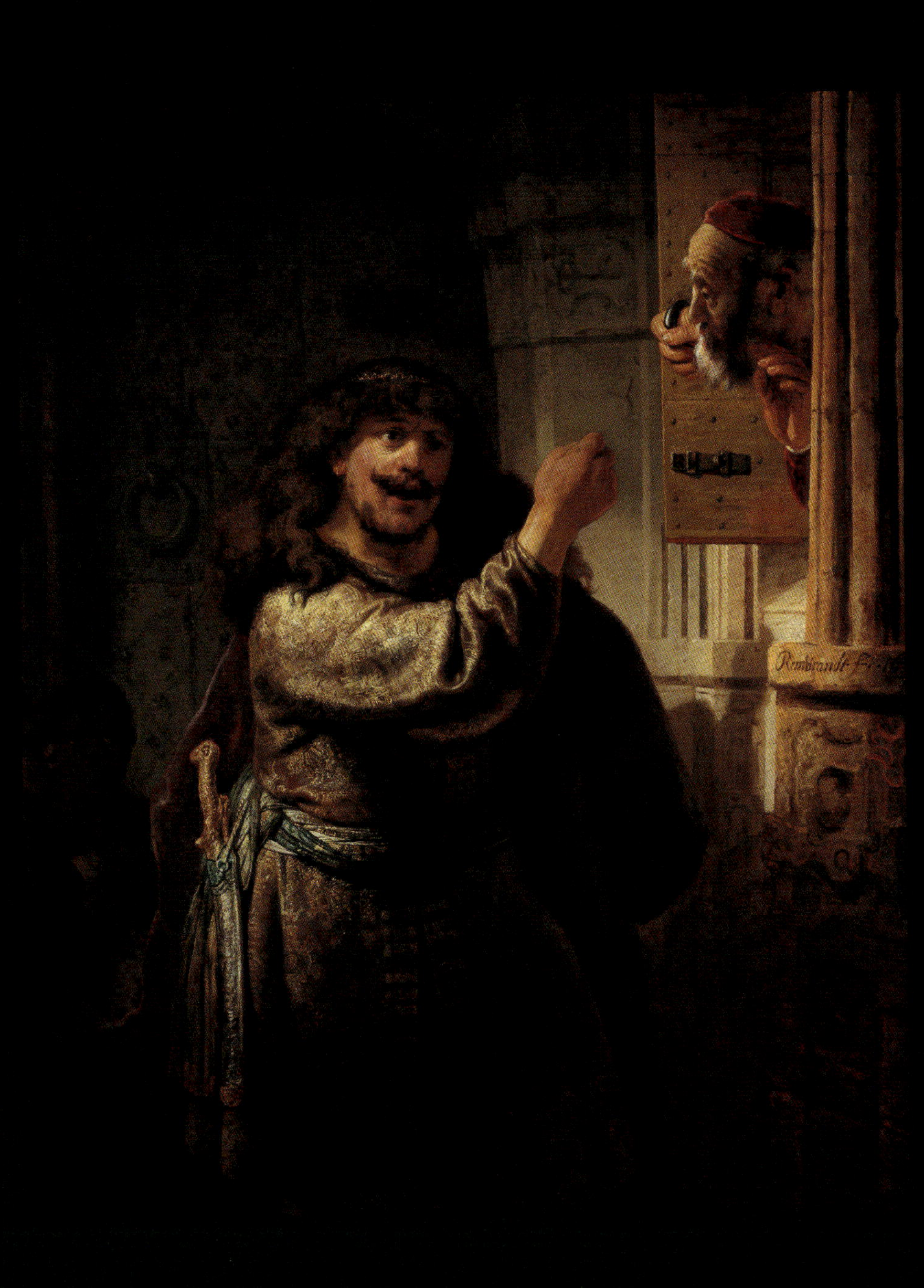
Rembrandt f.

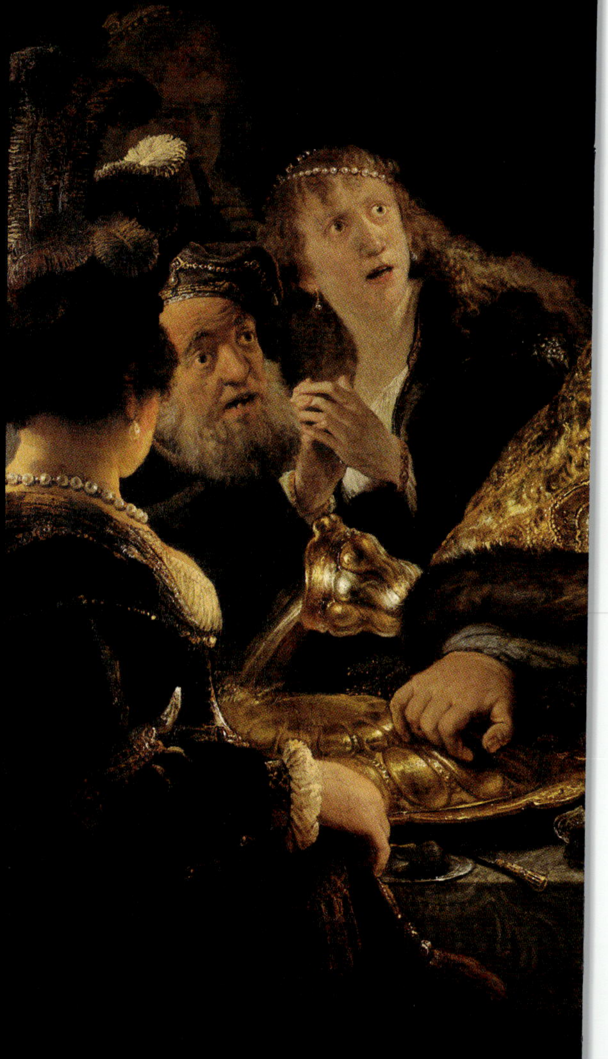

Belshazzar's Feast, *c.* 1635
Oil on canvas, 167.6 × 209.2 cm
(65 ¾ × 82 ⅜ in.)
London, The National Gallery

Pages 238/239
The Blinding of Samson, 1636
Oil on canvas, 206 × 276 cm
(81 ⅛ × 108 ⅔ in.)
Frankfurt am Main,
Städel Museum

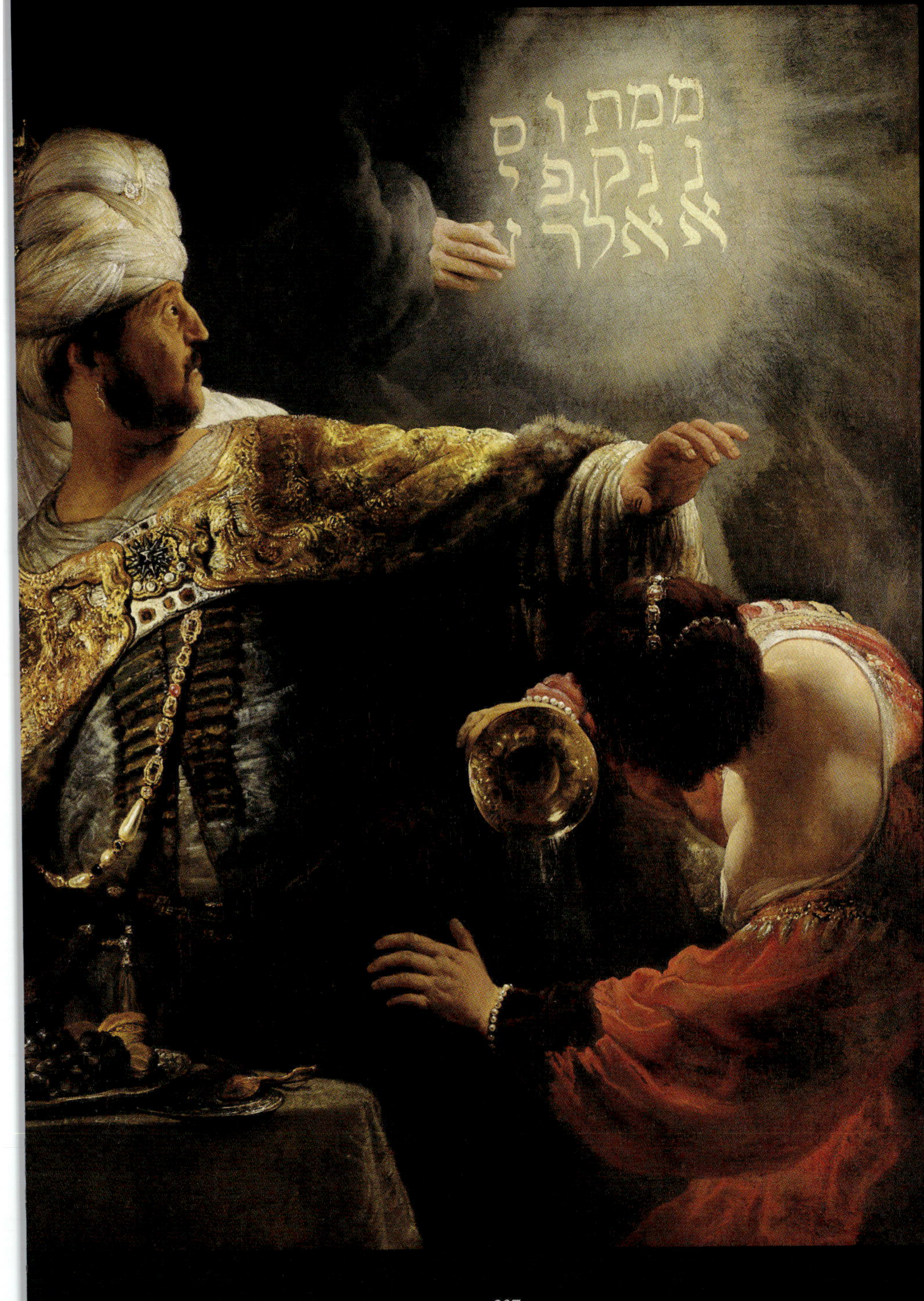
ממתוס
ננקפי
אאלרן

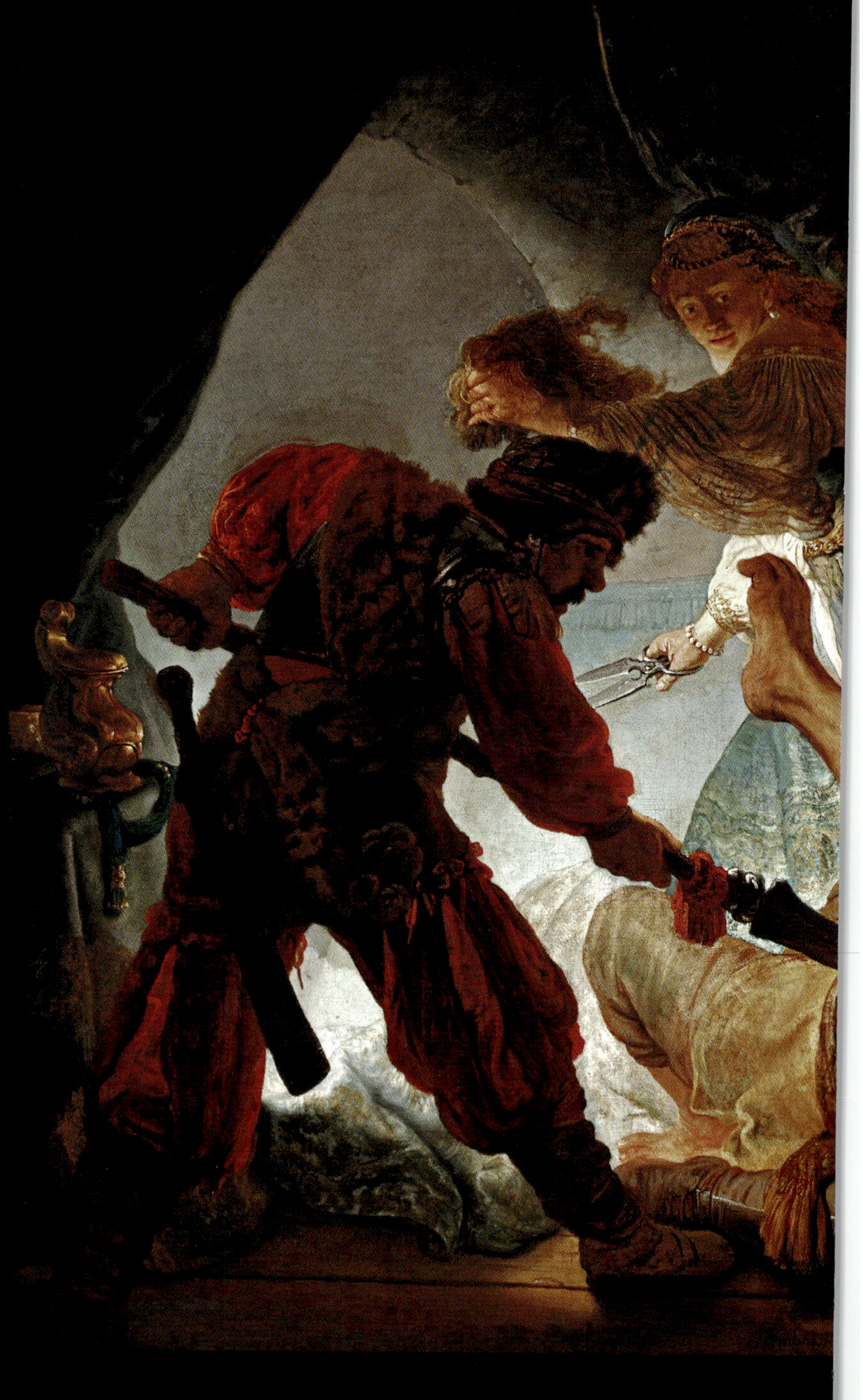

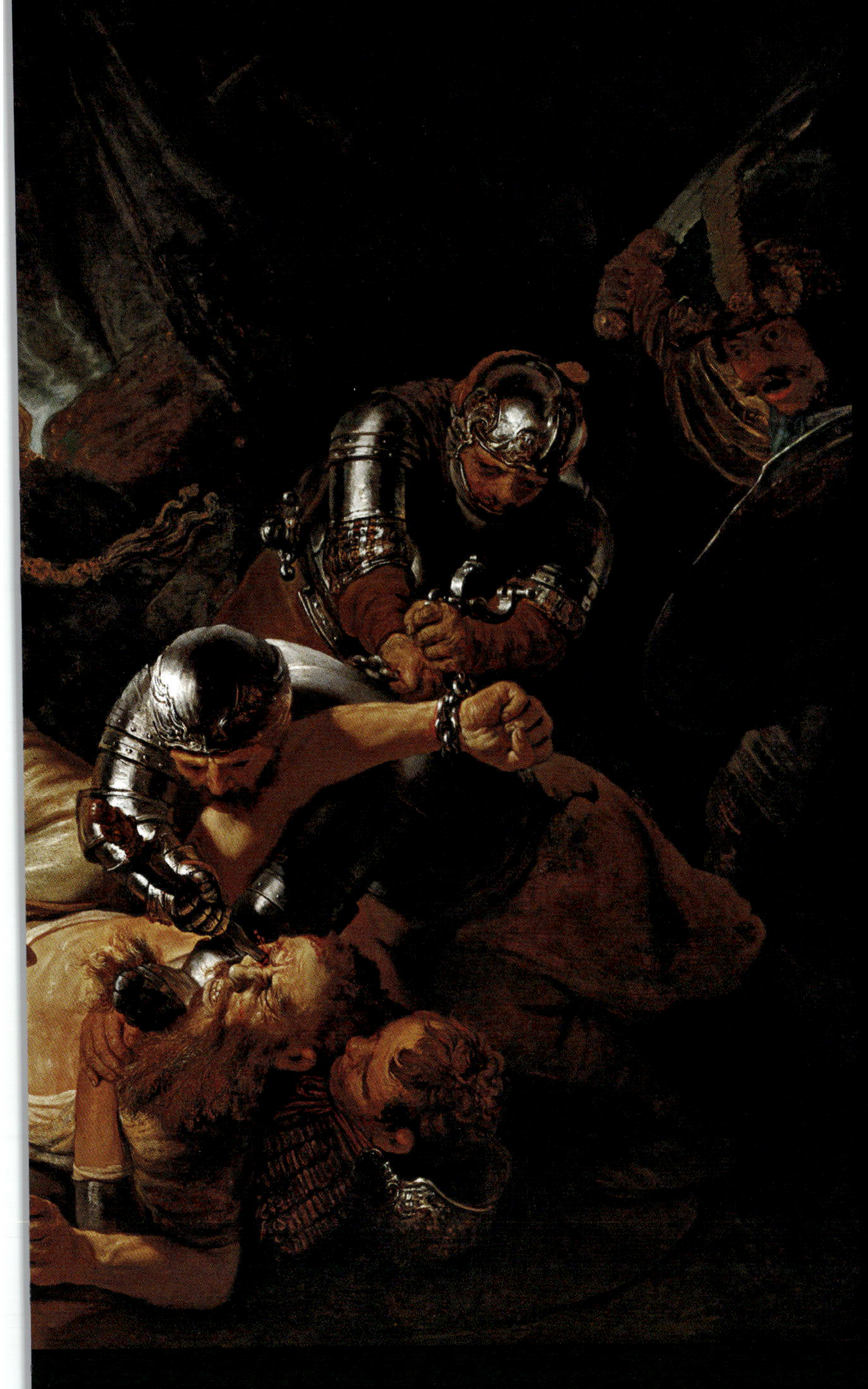

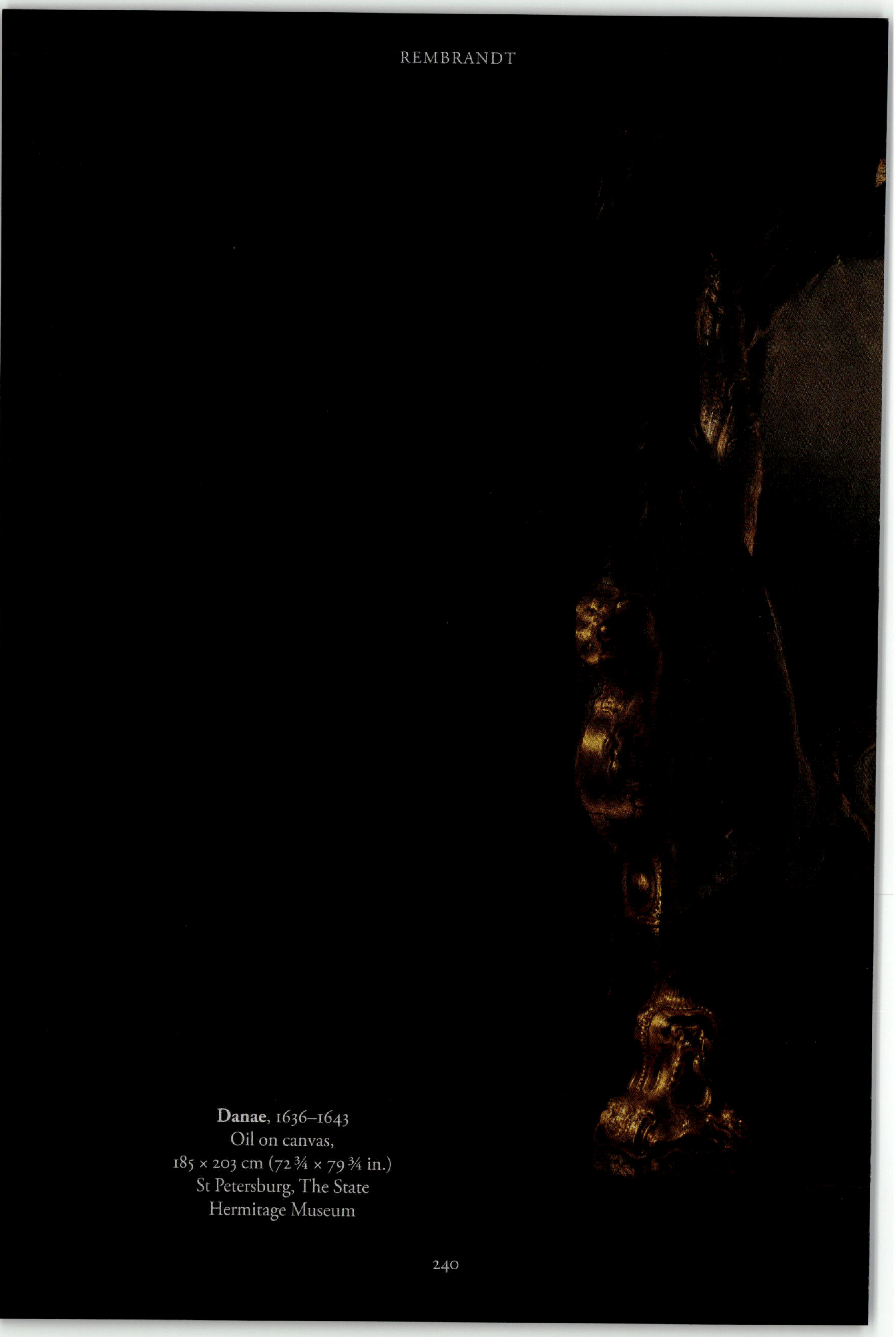

Danae, 1636–1643
Oil on canvas,
185 × 203 cm (72 ¾ × 79 ¾ in.)
St Petersburg, The State
Hermitage Museum

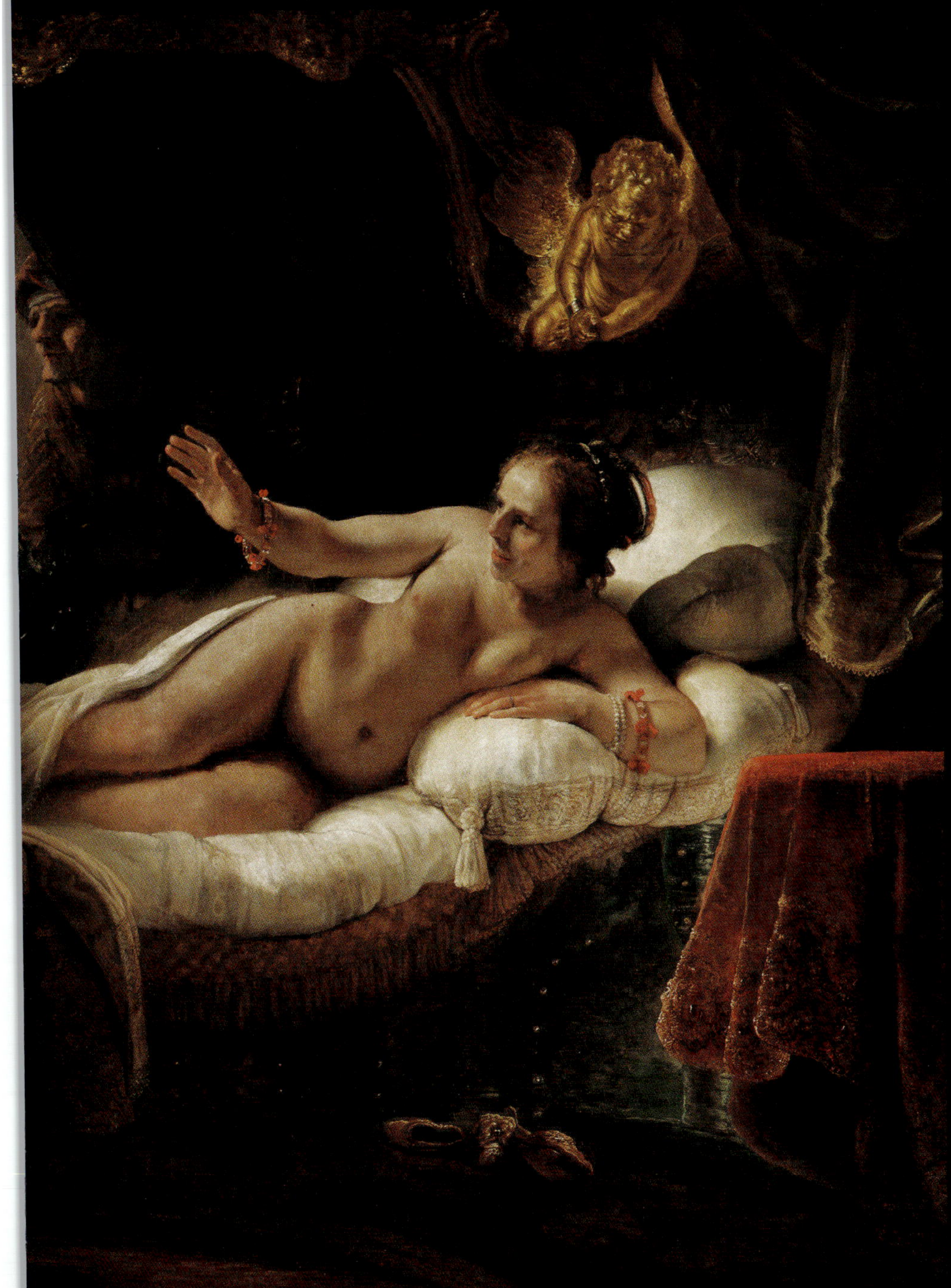

Lucas Vorsterman after Peter Paul Rubens
Susanna and the Elders, 1620
Copper engraving, 38.5 × 28 cm (15 ¼ × 11 in.)
Staatliche Museen zu Berlin, Kupferstichkabinett

Susanna at the Bath, 1636
Oil on panel, 47.4 × 38.6 cm (18 ⅔ × 15 ¼ in.)
The Hague, Mauritshuis

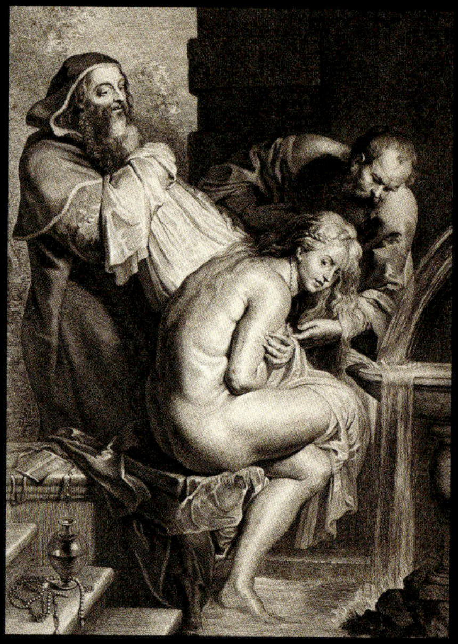

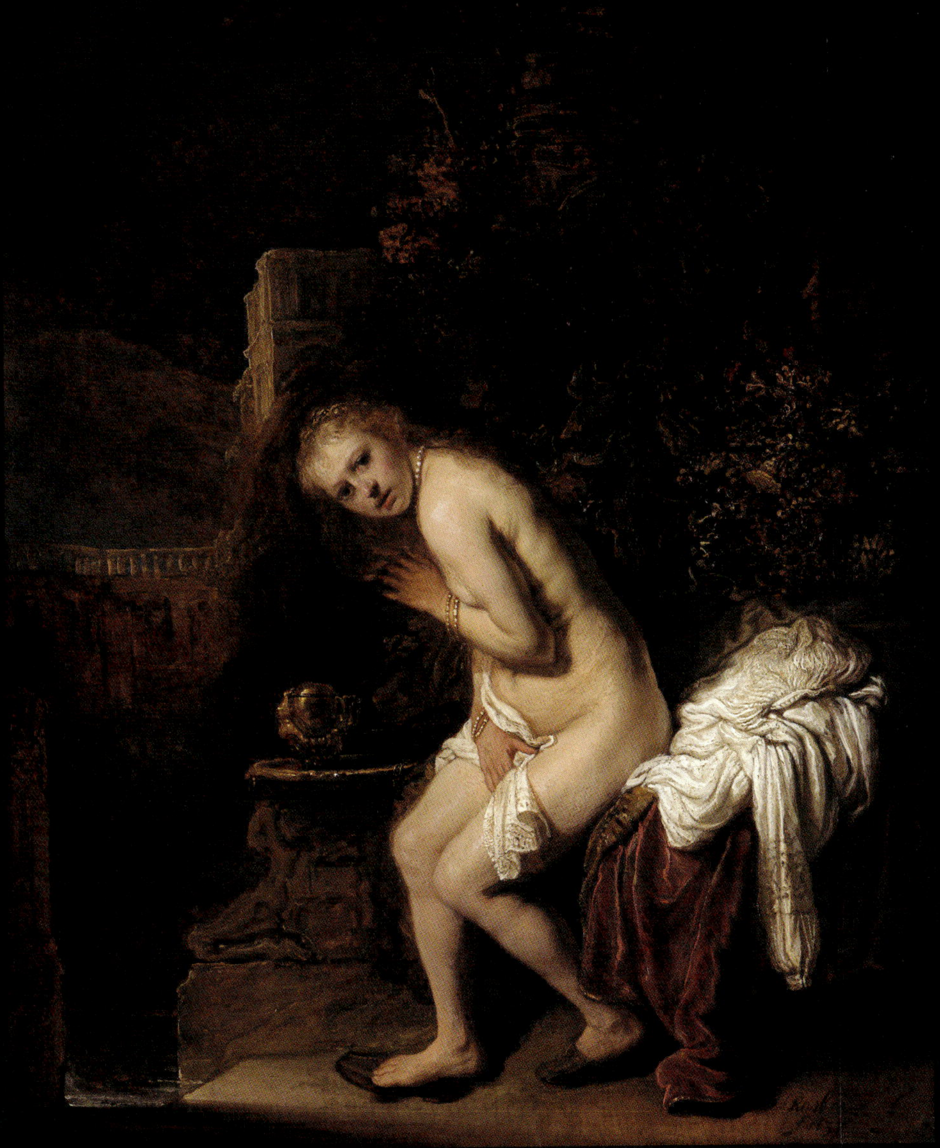

Susanna and the Elders, 1638–1647
Oil on panel, 76.6 × 92.8 cm
(30 ⅛ × 36 ½ in.)
Staatliche Museen zu Berlin,
Gemäldegalerie

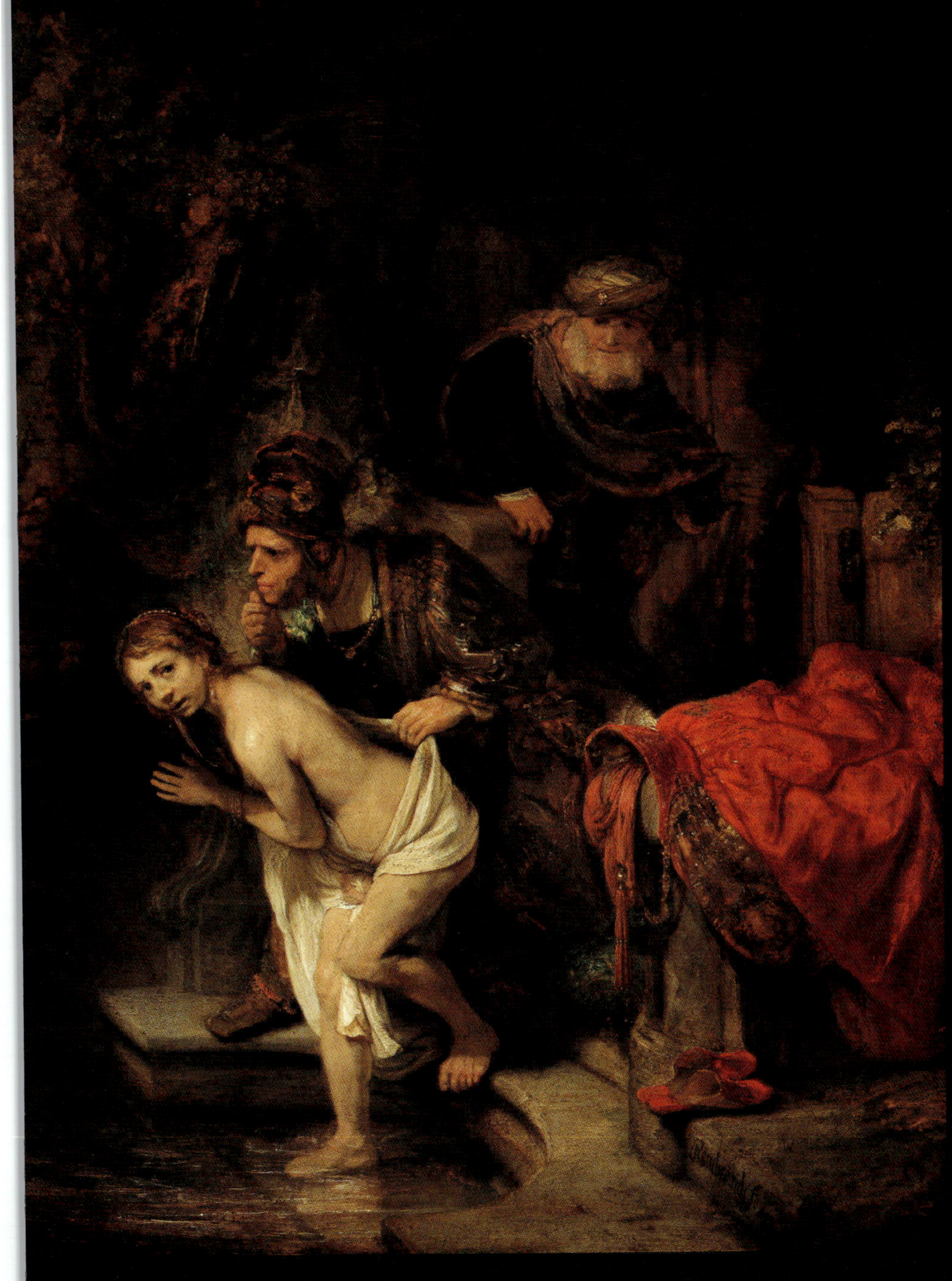

The Risen Christ Appearing to Mary Magdalene, 1638
Oil on panel, 61 × 49.5 cm (24 1/8 × 19 1/2 in.)
London, Royal Collection

Pages 248/249
The Wedding of Samson, 1638
Oil on canvas, 125.6 × 174.7 cm (49 1/2 × 68 3/4 in.)
Staatliche Kunstsammlungen Dresden,
Gemäldegalerie Alte Meister

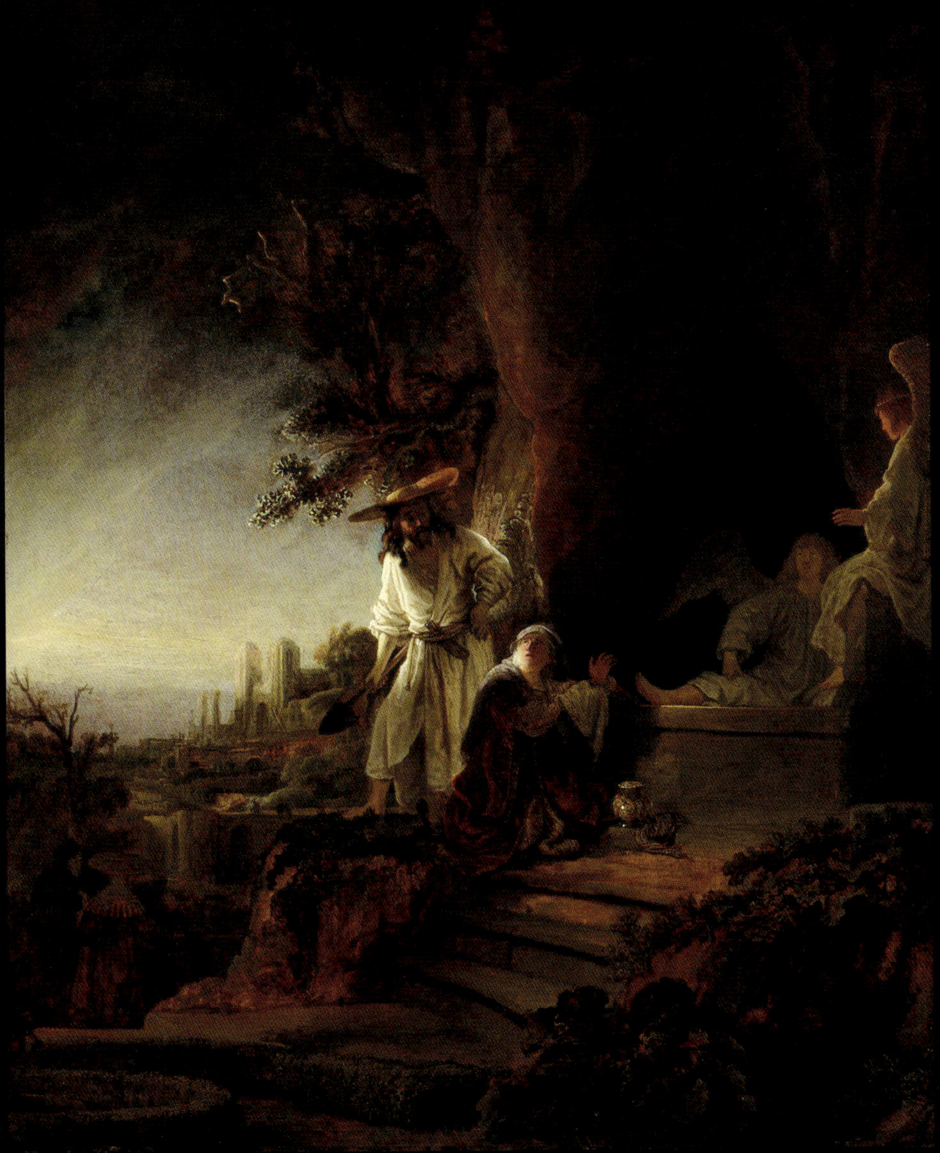

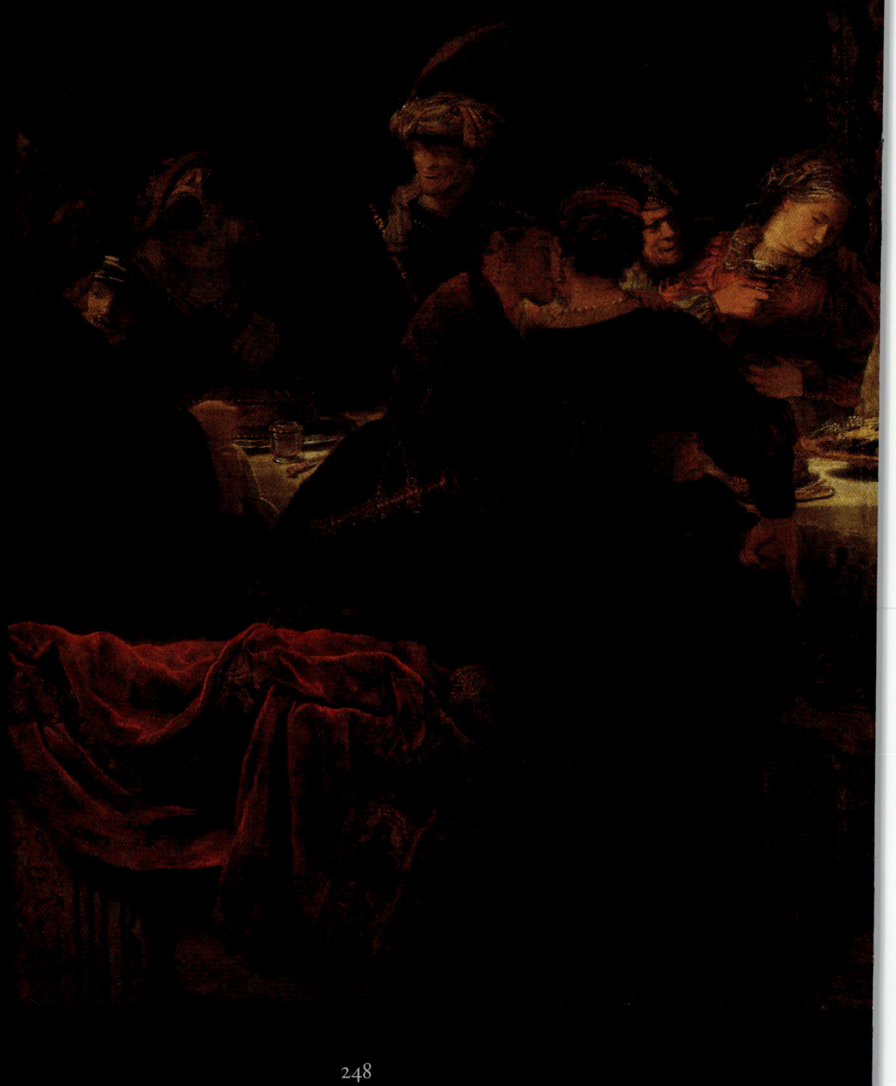

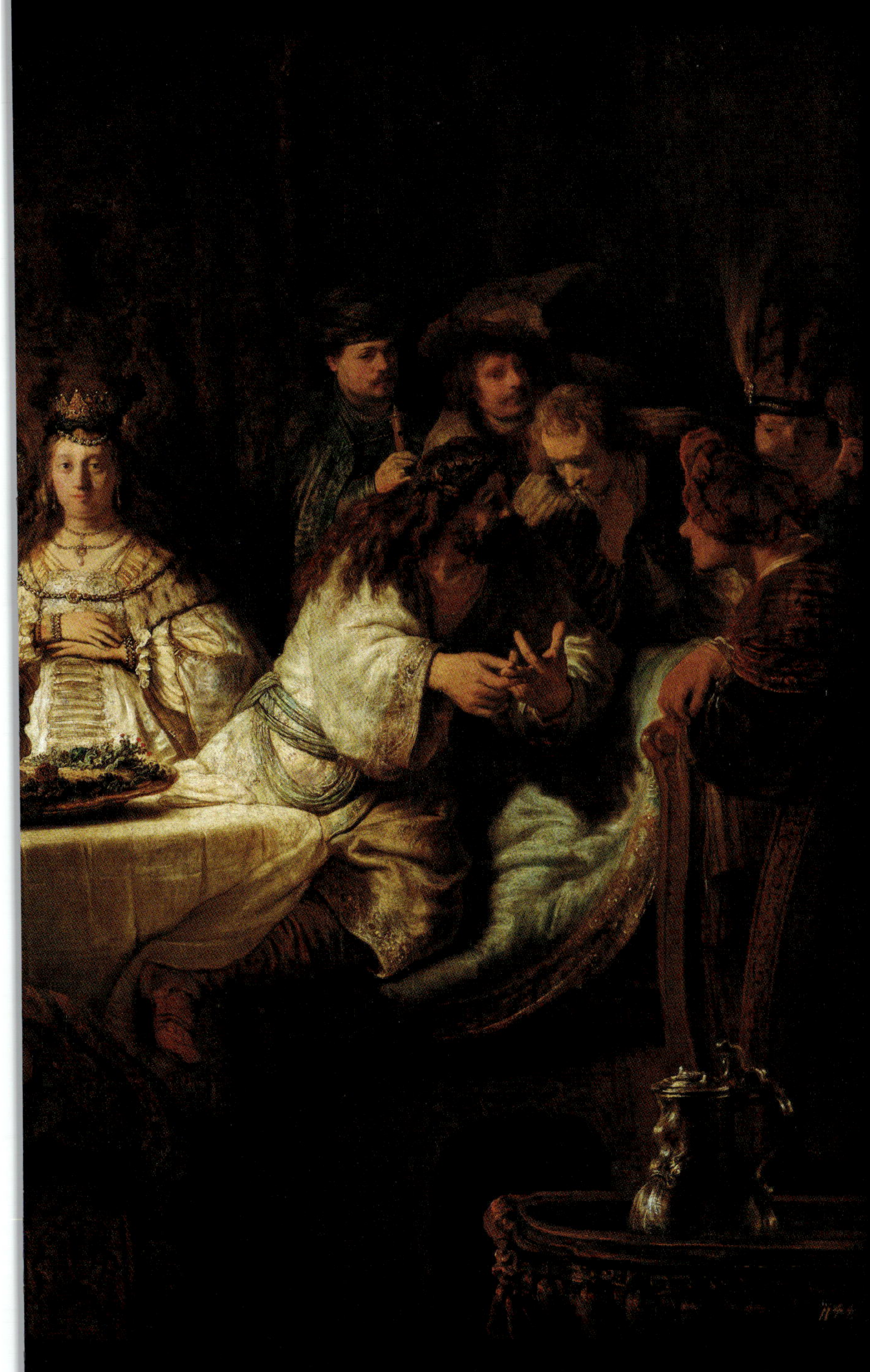

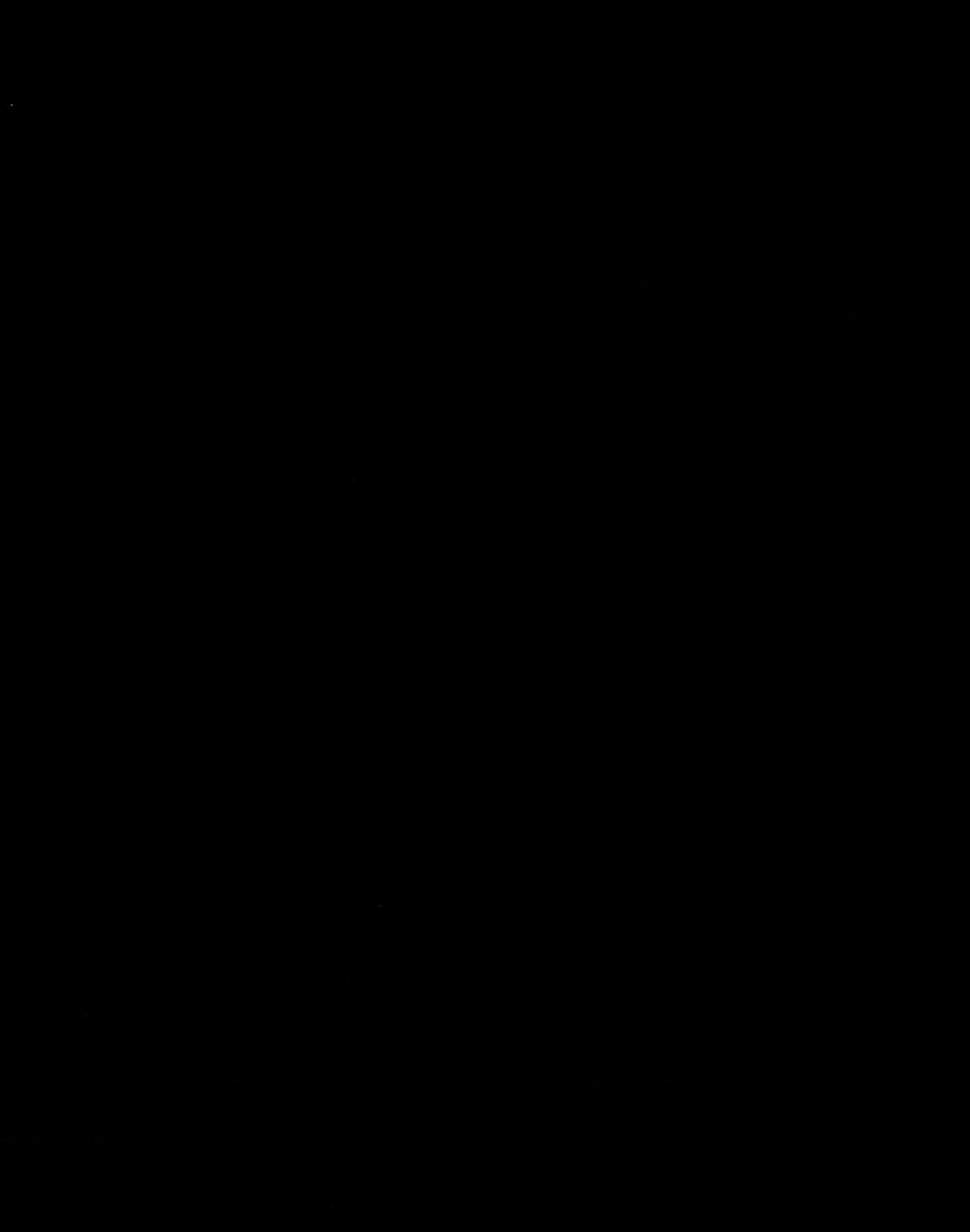

Scholar in His Study, 1634
Oil on canvas, 141 × 135 cm (55 ½ × 53 ¼ in.)
Prague, Národní Galerie v Praze

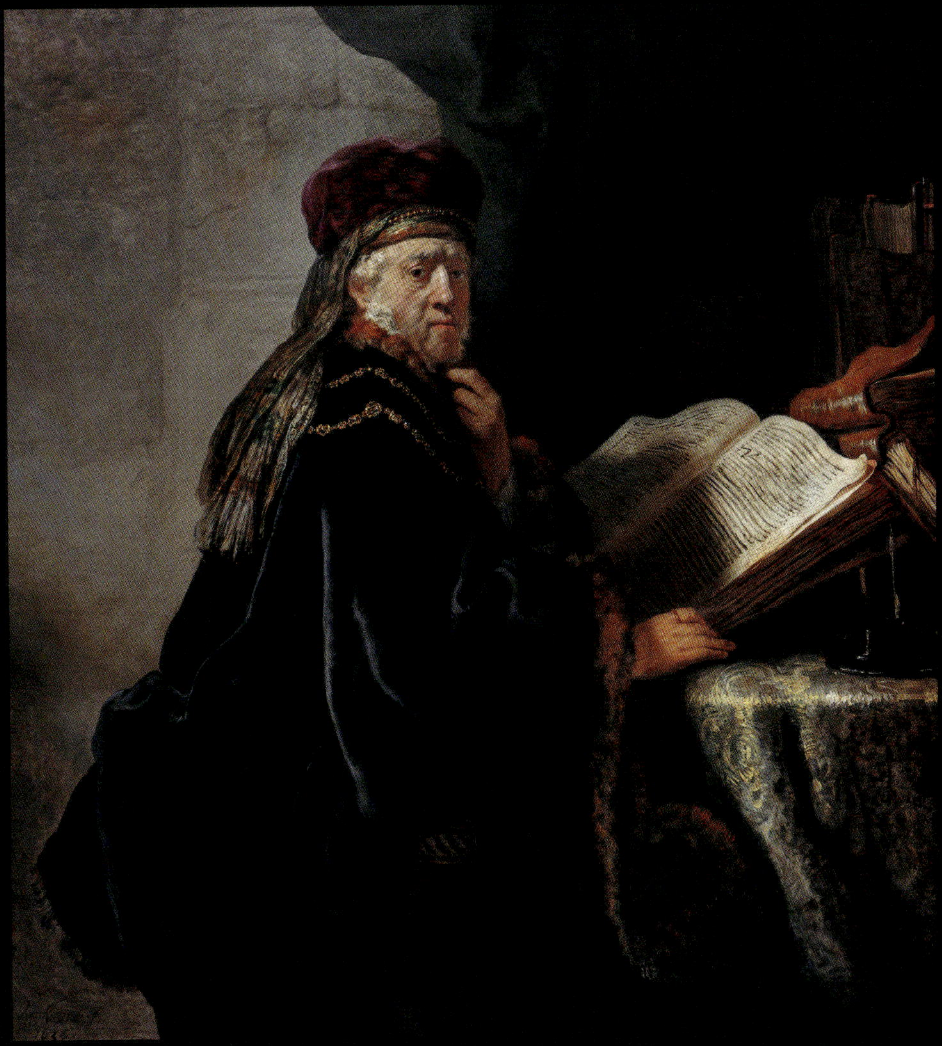

Jan Lievens
Man in Oriental Costume, 1629–1631
Oil on canvas, 135 × 100 cm (53 ¼ × 39 ⅜ in.)
Potsdam, Bildergalerie von Sanssouci

Man in Oriental Costume (so-called **Noble Slav**), 1632
Oil on canvas, 152.7 × 111.1 cm (60 ⅛ × 43 ¾ in.)
New York, The Metropolitan Museum of Art,
Bequest of William K. Vanderbilt 1920

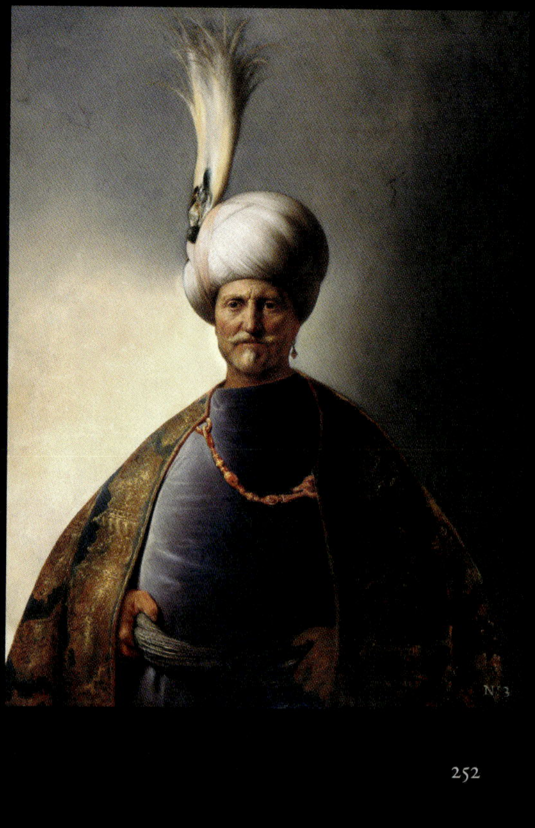

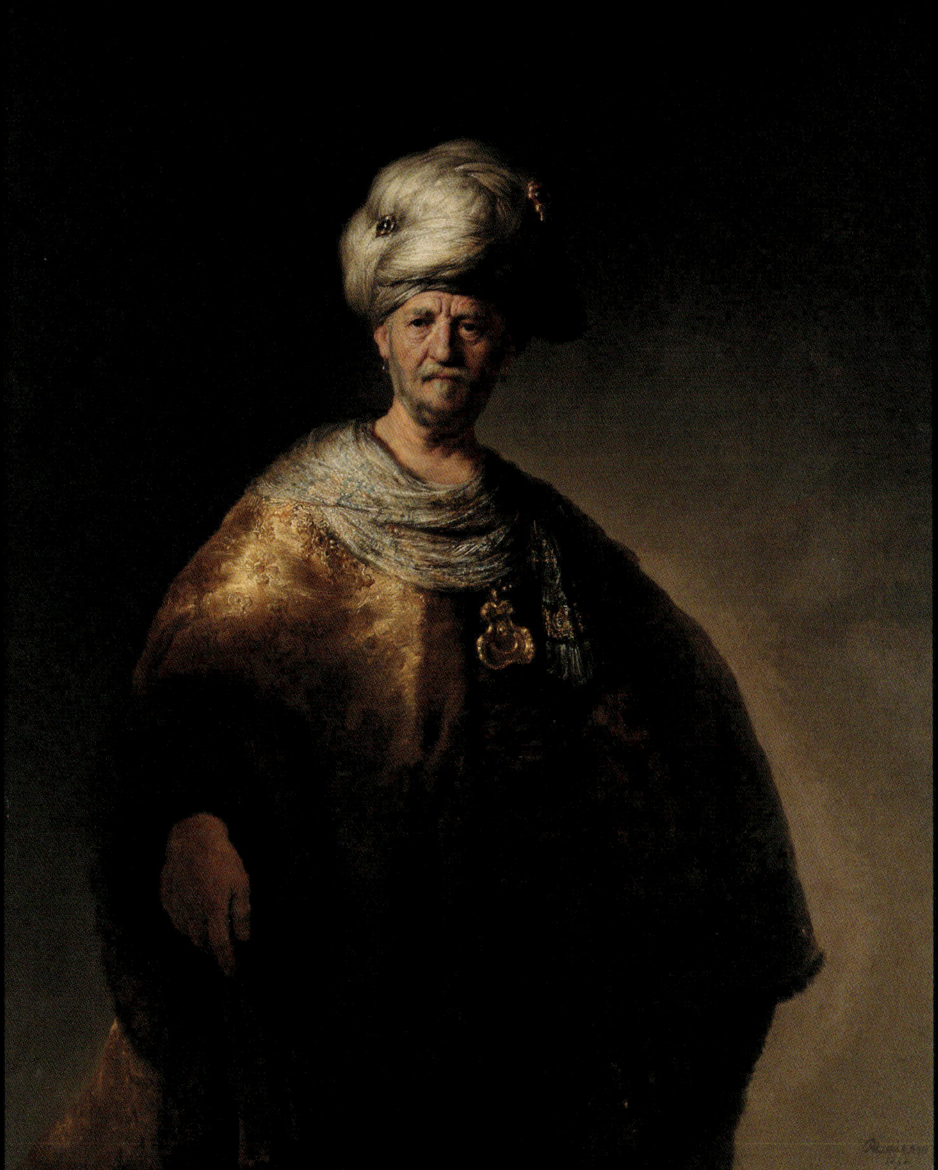

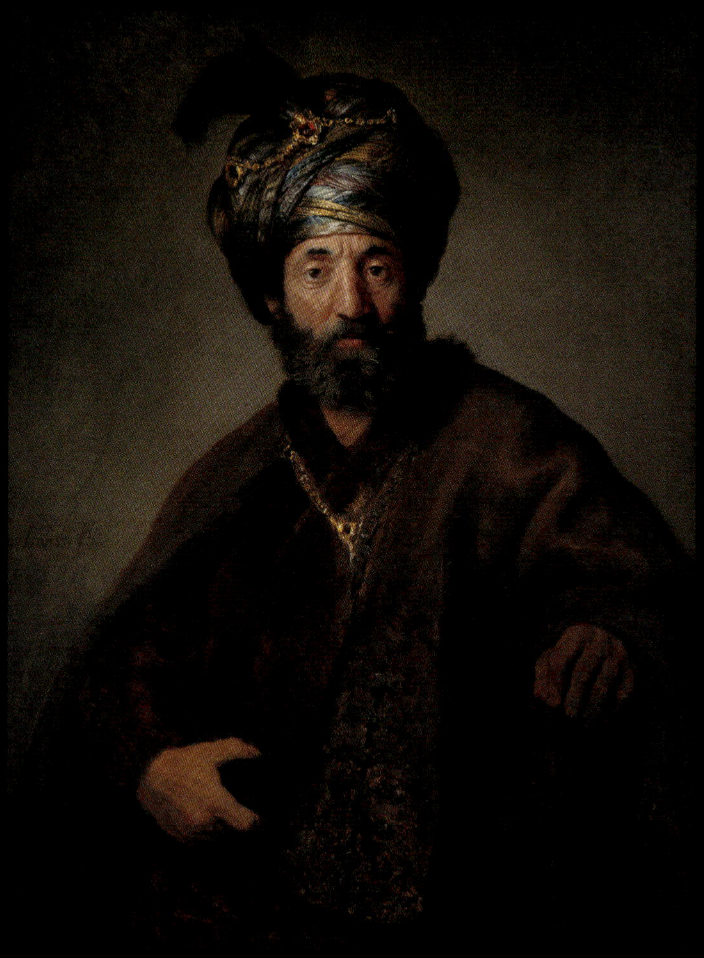

Man in Oriental Costume, 1633/34
Oil on canvas, 98.2 × 74.5 cm (38 ⅔ × 29 ⅓ in.)
Washington, DC, National Gallery of Art,
Andrew W. Mellon Collection

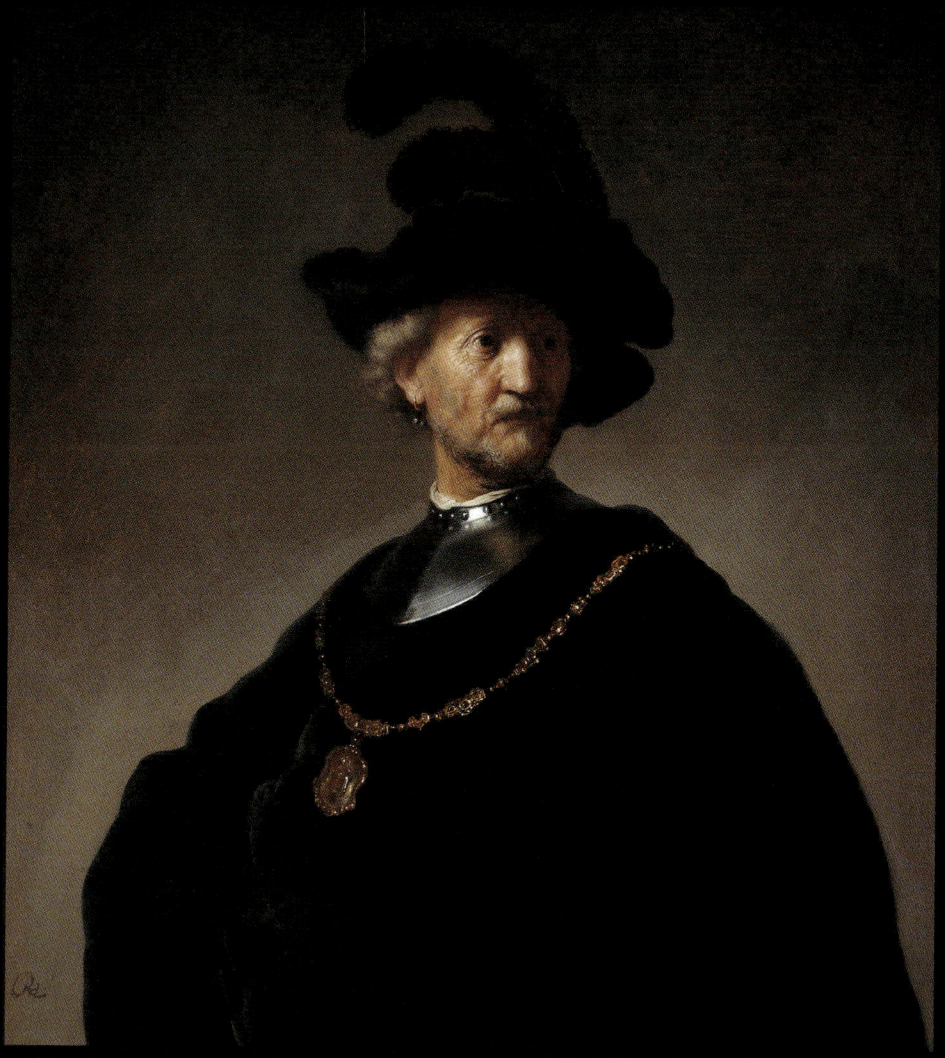

Old Man with a Gold Chain, 1631/32
Oil on panel, 83.5 × 75.6 cm (32 ¾ × 29 ¾ in.)
The Art Institute of Chicago,
Mr and Mrs W. W. Kimball Collection

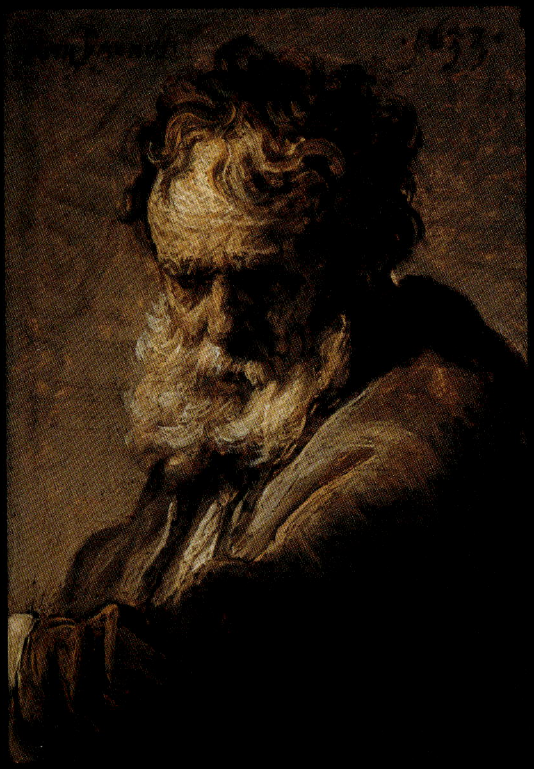

Bearded Old Man, 1633
Oil on paper, mounted on panel, 8.9 × 6.4 cm (3½ × 2½ in.)
New York, The Leiden Collection

Old Man with a Gold Chain, *c.* 1632
Oil on panel, 59.7 × 49.3 cm (23½ × 19⅜ in.)
Hessen Kassel Heritage, Gemäldegalerie Alte Meister

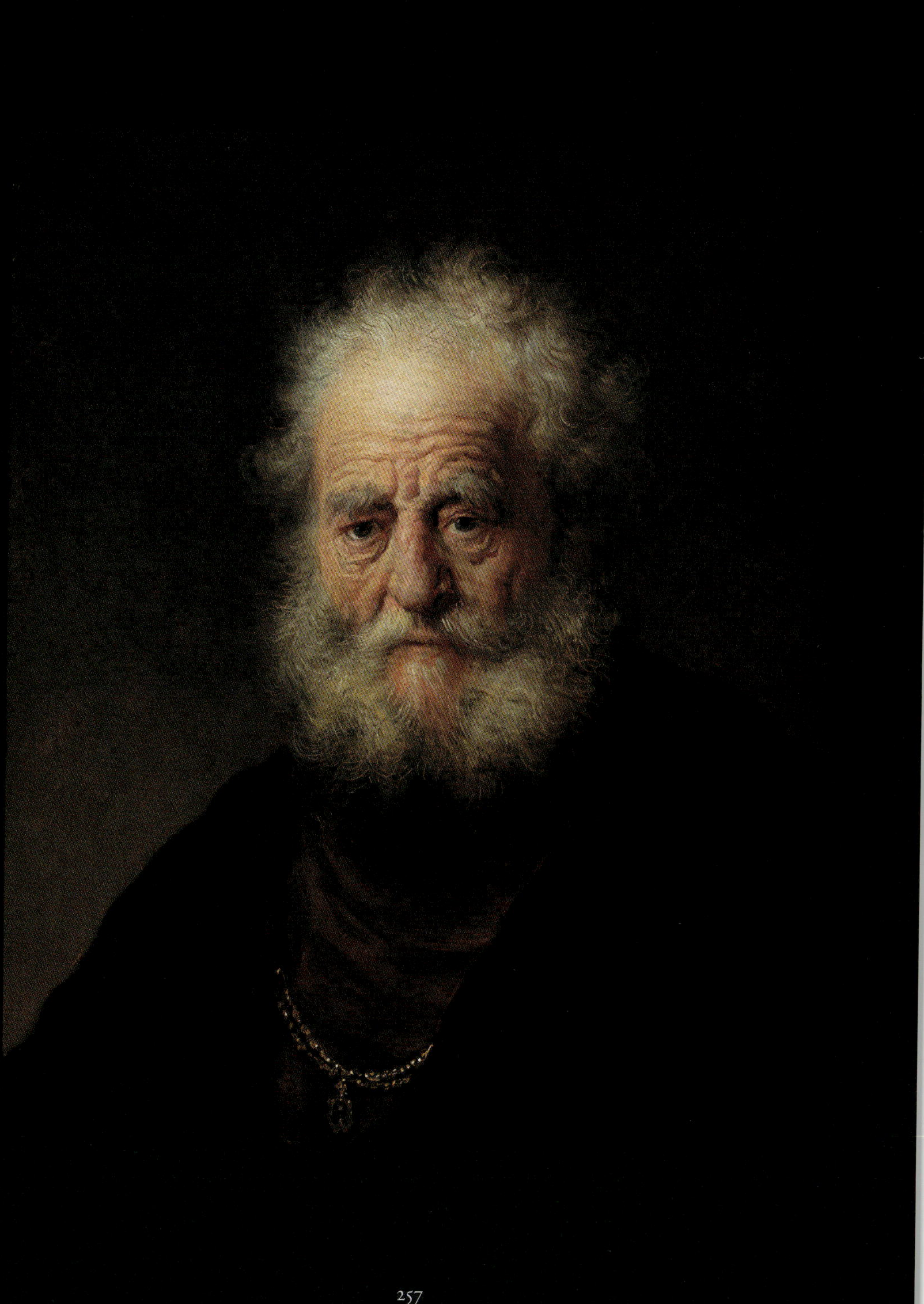

Woman with a Veil, *c.* 1640
Oil on panel, 62.5 × 49 cm (24 ⅝ × 19 ¼ in.)
Washington, DC, National Gallery of Art,
Widener Collection

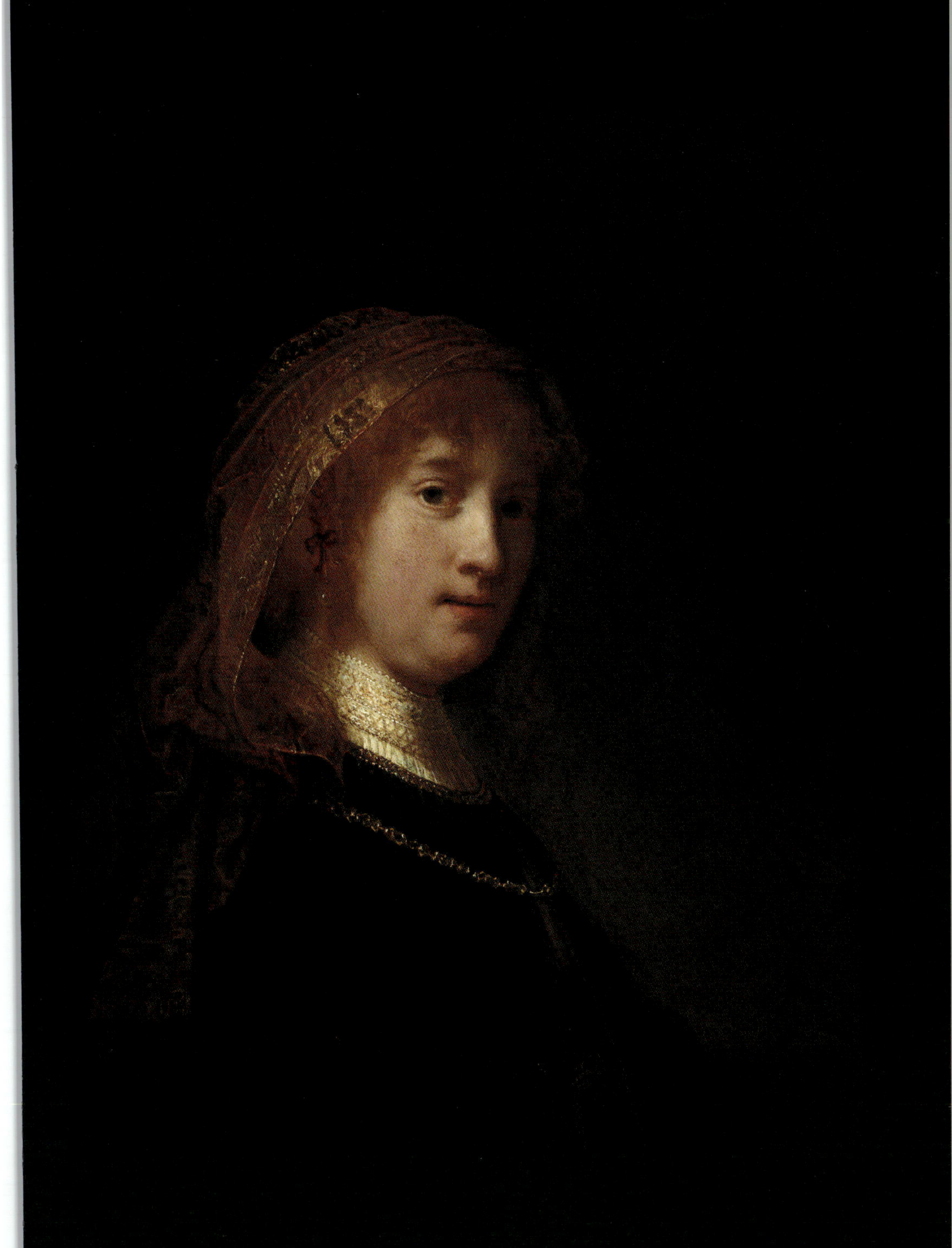

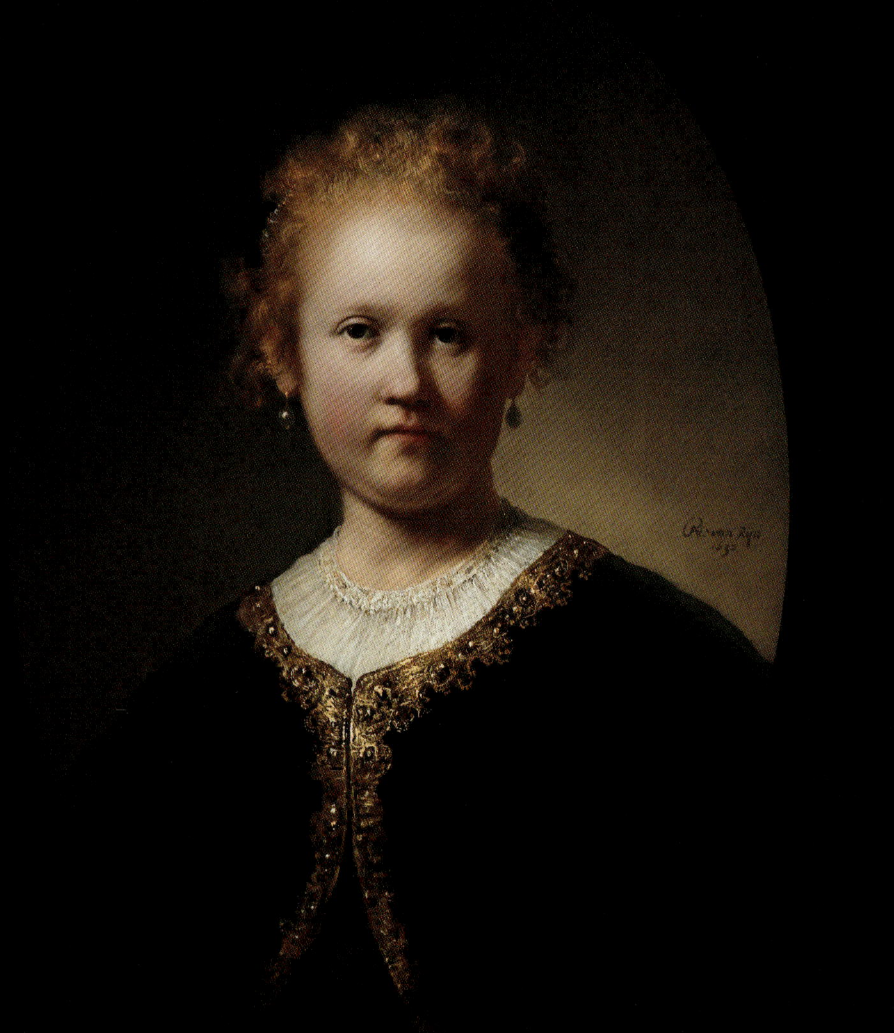

Young Woman with Pearl Earrings, 1632
Oil on panel, 59 × 44 cm (23 ¼ × 17 ⅓ in.)
New York, The Leiden Collection

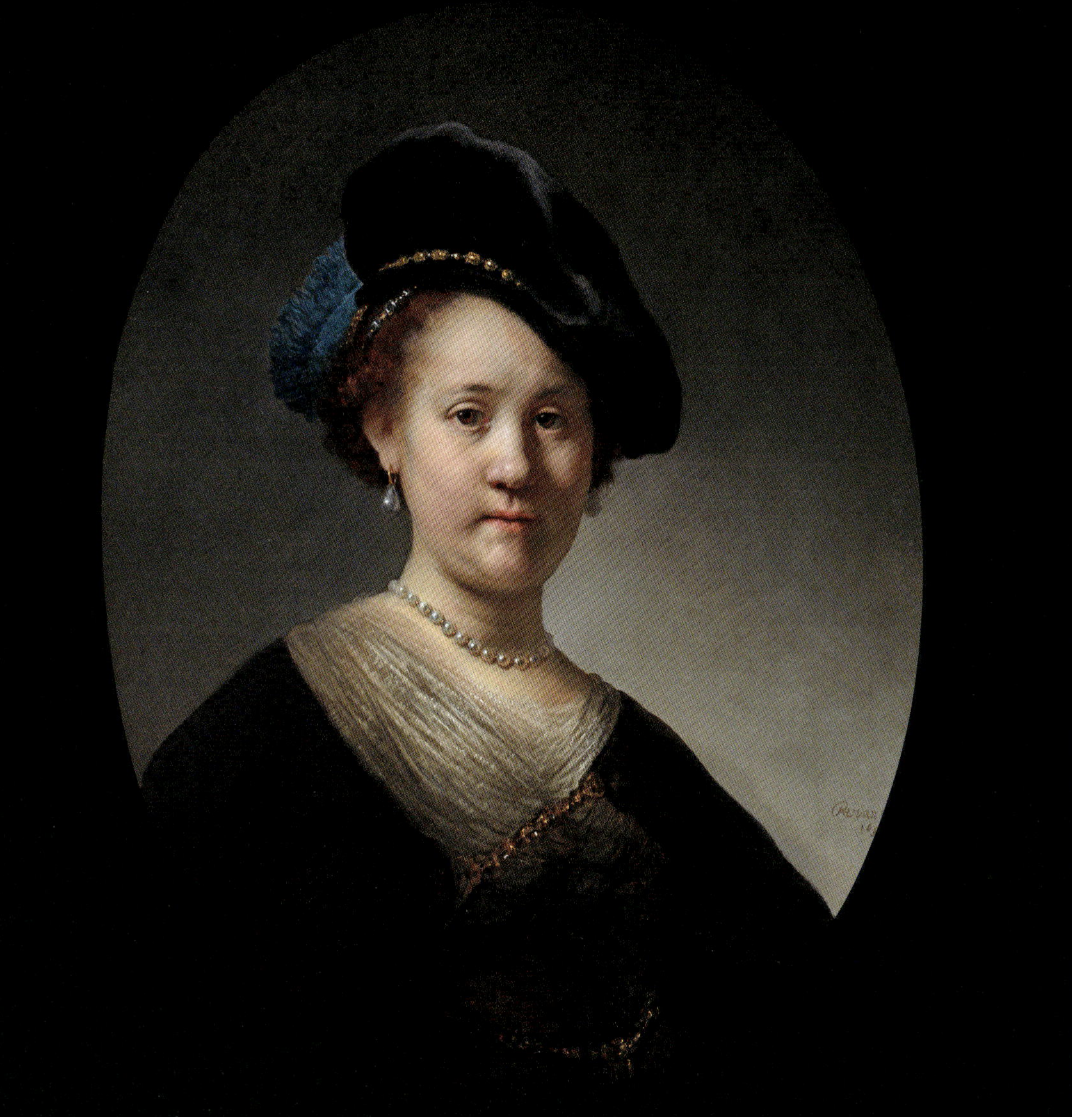

Young Woman with Pearl Earrings and Cap, 1632
Oil on canvas, mounted on panel, 68.6 × 53.5 cm (27 ⅛ × 21 ⅛ in.)
Madrid, Abelló Collection

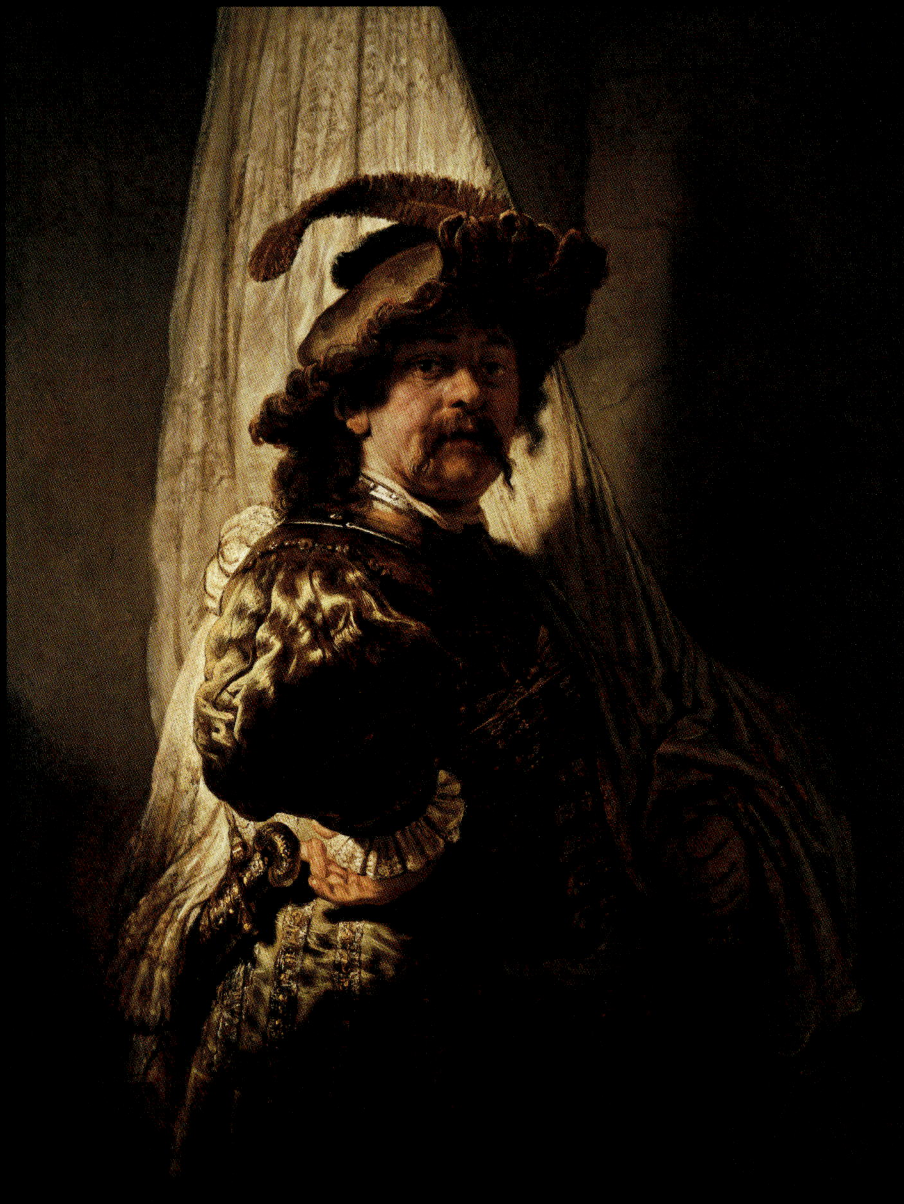

The Standard Bearer, 1636
Oil on canvas, 118.8 × 96.8 cm (46 ¾ × 38 ⅛ in.)
Amsterdam, Rijksmuseumn

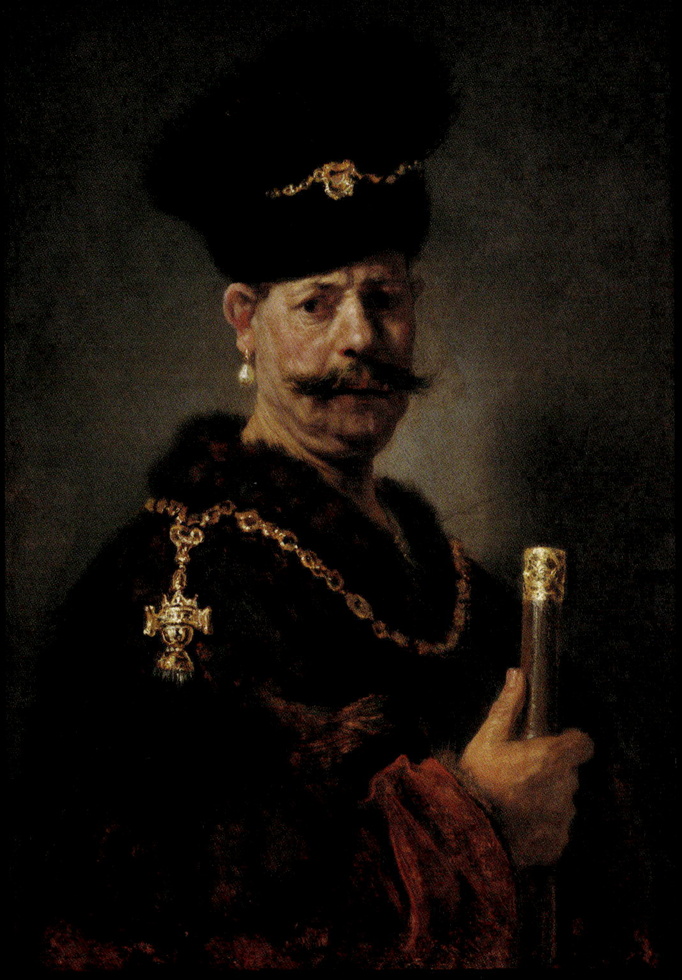

Russian Boyar, 1637
Oil on panel, 96.8 × 66 cm (38 1/8 × 25 3/4 in.)
Washington, DC, National Gallery of Art, The Andrew W. Mellon Collection

III.

Illusionism and Reorientation

1640–1651

*"Compare me with Rembrandt! What sacrilege!
With Rembrandt, the colossus of Art!
What are you thinking of, my friend!
We should prostrate ourselves before Rembrandt
and never compare anyone with him!"*

AUGUSTE RODIN, 1911

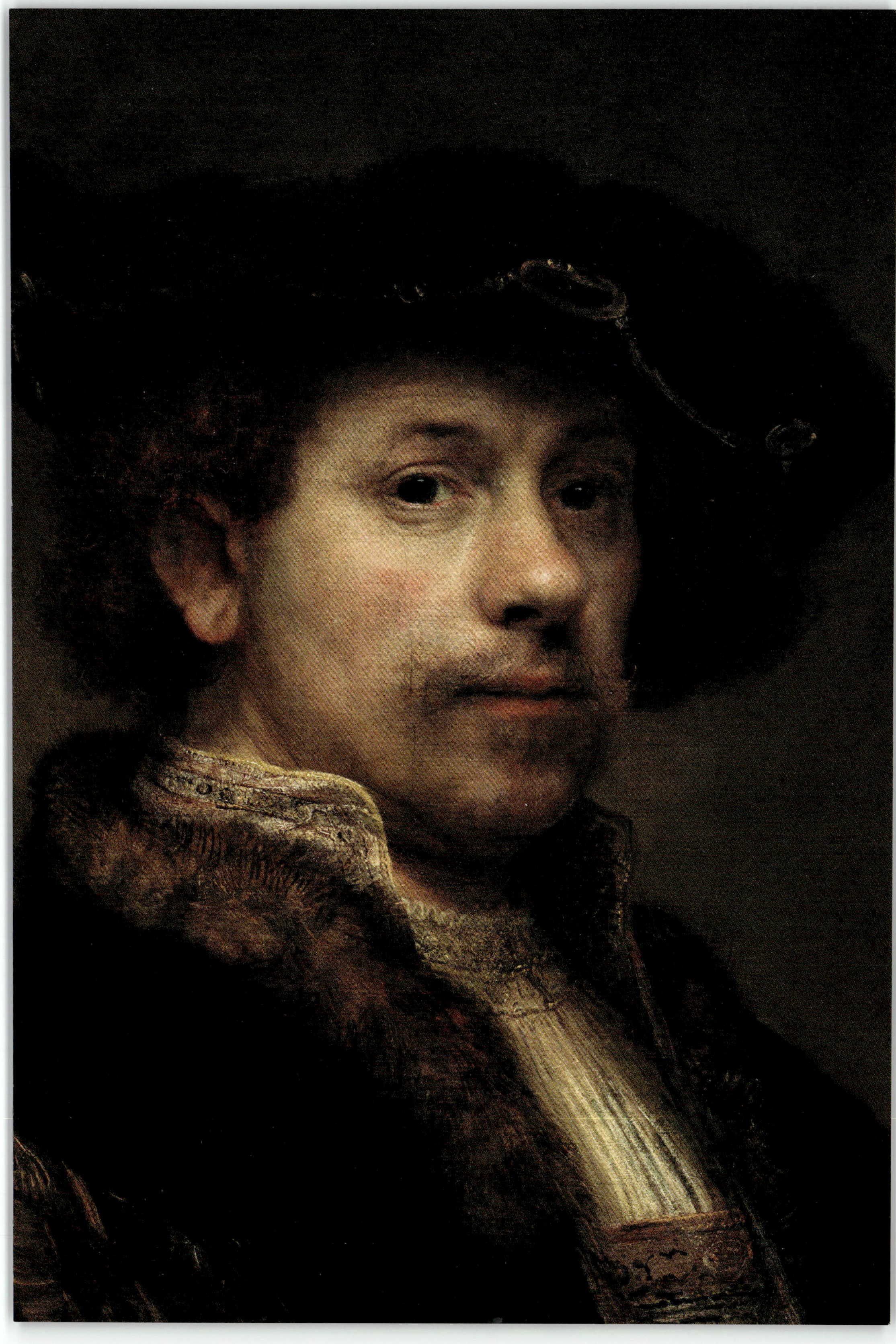

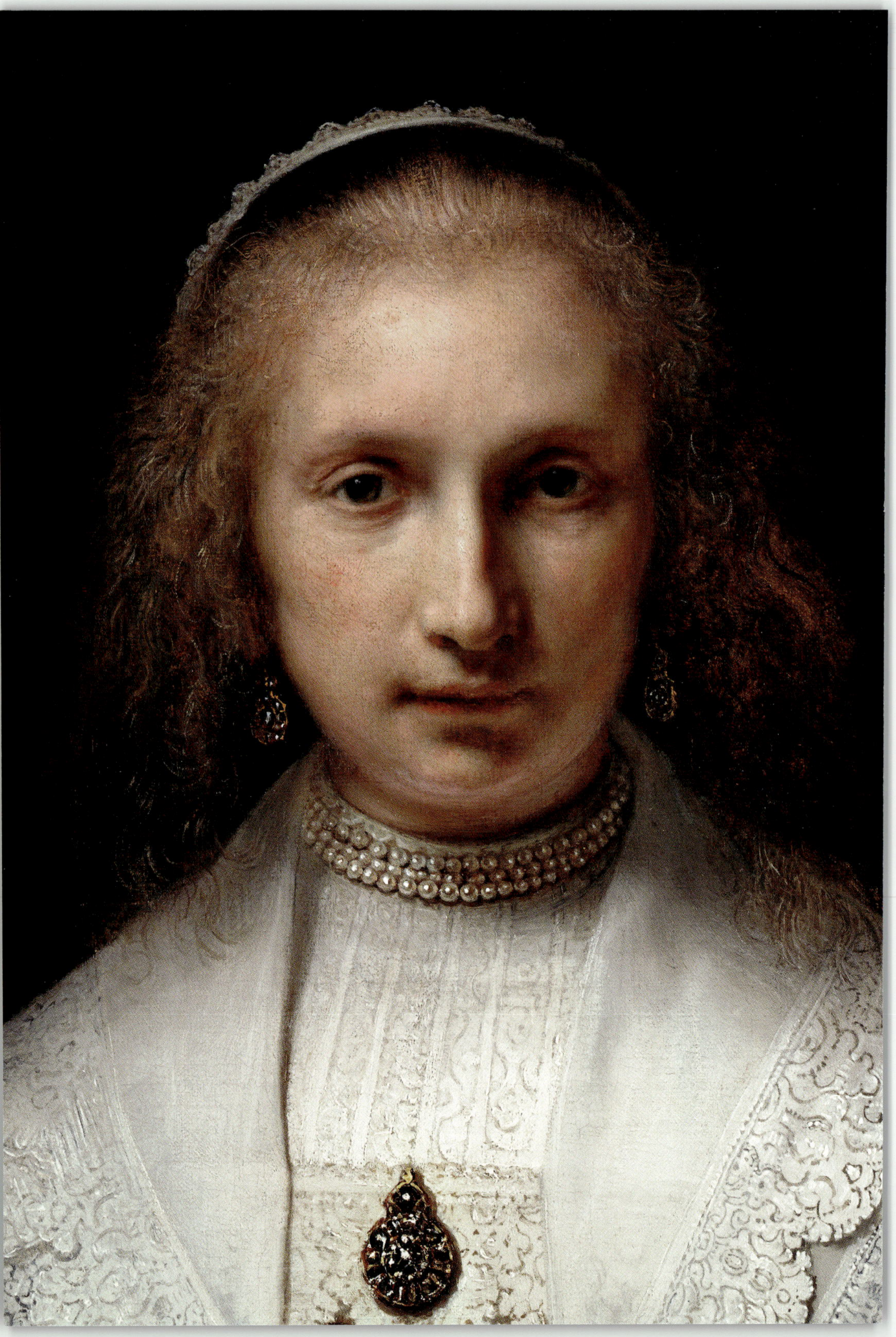

Portraits 1639–1642

Following his departure from Uylenburgh's workshop in 1635, Rembrandt stopped painting portraits until 1637. After the large and ambitious history paintings of 1635 and 1636, there followed two years during which he created only a handful of paintings (and etchings), including the *Portrait of Eleazar Swalmius* (p. 307, Cat. 187) from 1637. Two years later, he suddenly started accepting portrait commissions again. This increased production (also of other paintings) was undoubtedly linked to the down payment for the house which he had purchased at the beginning of that year. He probably expected to earn a considerable amount of money with the life-size, full-length portrait of Andries de Graeff (1611–1678), the youngest scion of one of the most powerful regent families of Amsterdam (p. 306, Cat. 188). Hendrick Uylenburgh later stated that he had acted as a mediator in a dispute lasting until 1642 between Rembrandt and De Graeff concerning the payment (RD 1659/21). Uylenburgh judged that the work was worth 500 guilders. That was still a large amount, but Rembrandt had apparently demanded even more. In the likeness, dated 1639, Andries de Graeff is standing elegantly in front of a semi-circular door opening. Some elements in this portrait are new: the light is distributed more evenly so that there are fewer sharp chiaroscuro contrasts; instead of stretching his arm out to one side, De Graeff is supporting his elbow on a sort of pedestal, with his arm extended forward directly towards the viewer. The ungloved hand is worked out in detail and forms a notable light accent, while the other hand, by means of a dark glove, vanishes in the shadow. Rembrandt uses this artistic device, designed to create the impression of greater depth, with even more emphasis than in his earlier *Portrait of Jan Harmensz. Krul?* from 1633 (Cat. 185). The second glove, lying ostentatiously at the feet of the unmarried De Graeff, has prompted a wide variety of different interpretations. This unusual motif was seen as a challenge to a duel, or, in contrast, as an invitation to a possible marriage partner.[113] In Rembrandt's oeuvre, however, fashion accessories rather served as aids in his compositions than as symbols. Thus the glove dangling elegantly from Marten Soolmans' fingers (p. 154, Cat. 241) served not so much as a marriage symbol but rather as a means of emphasising and extending optically his expansive gesture.[114] In the portrait of Andries de Graeff, the glove serves another compositional purpose. From 1639 onwards, Rembrandt experimented in the foregrounds of his compositions with steps or sills, as, for example, in *Girl with Dead Peacocks* (p. 205, Cat. 133). The little puddle of blood and the peacock's head heighten the illusionistic effect of the stone sill.

Page 265
Detail of: **Self-Portrait**, 1640 (see ill. p. 331)

Detail of: **Portrait of Agatha Bas**, 1641 (see ill. p. 313)

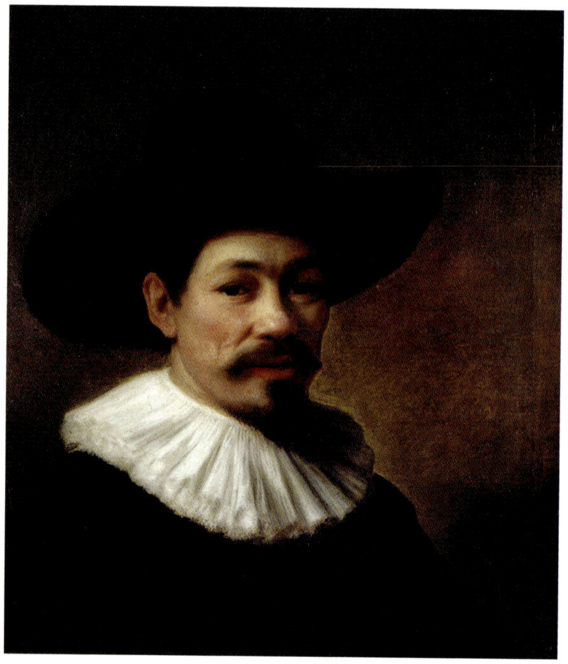

In the portraits between 1639 and 1641, fashion accessories or fingers extending over the edge serve this purpose. De Graeff's glove, which has apparently fallen carelessly to the ground – near the step – is a first manifestation of this artistic device. Later generations often failed to appreciate these visual tricks, which is the reason why the little puddle of blood beside the peacocks remained painted over for a long time. Something similar happened to the *Portrait of Aletta Adriaensdr.* (p. 165, Cat. 214), also dated 1639. This painting was drastically cleaned in the past and during the process the illusionistically painted fingers resting on the red tablecloth in the foreground were removed. Thus the fingers that can be seen today are a reconstruction on the basis of the remnants of the original paint.

In addition to these wealthy clients, in 1640 Rembrandt also portrayed the ebony worker Herman Doomer (*c.* 1595–1650; p. 308, Cat. 249) and his wife Baertje Martens (*c.* 1596–1678; p. 309, Cat. 250). Doomer was probably an acquaintance of Rembrandt and the supplier of his ebony frames. We know from sources that Rembrandt generally delivered his paintings already framed (RD 1639/3; 1659/18), and also that most of these picture frames are described either as black or made from ebony. The Doomers are simply dressed and their sympathetic faces with a gentle smile are depicted in remarkable detail. Their son Lambert Doomer (1624–1700) probably came to Rembrandt as an apprentice around 1644. During that same year, Lambert painted free copies of the portraits of his parents (p. 268, 271). Later, his mother determined in various wills that Lambert was to inherit the originals by Rembrandt if he made further copies for his brothers and sis-

Lambert Doomer, **Portrait of Herman Doomer**, 1644
Oil on panel, 65 × 54 cm (25 5/8 × 21 3/8 in.)
Chatsworth, Trustees of the Duke of Devonshire

ters (RD 1654/13; 1662/3; 1668/7). Lambert's versions from 1644 differ considerably from Rembrandt's originals with regard to the resemblance; in particular, his mother's face is much narrower. On the assumption that the son was more familiar with his mother's features, this could support the notion that Rembrandt was not always successful in striking the likeness of his sitters. Lambert also changed his parents' pose by omitting their hands and turning them towards each other in a more conventional way. Rembrandt on the other hand, as we frequently observe in his oeuvre, turned the man towards the woman, who is shown almost frontally.

Herman Doomer's sideward pose gave Rembrandt the opportunity to show him with his elbow bent and his lower arm parallel to the picture plane. Rembrandt used this pose, which had originated in the sixteenth century, in the majority of his male portraits and his self-portraits (see pp. 290–293) during the period between 1639 and 1642. In *Portrait of a Man Holding a Hat* (p. 311, Cat. 189) from about 1640, the unknown man is also shown turned towards the right with a bent elbow. He is holding his hat in front of him with both hands. The hat serves as a sort of barrier which seems to rule out a possible companion piece. The shiny gold and grey suit made of watered silk is unusual and led to the erroneous assumption that the fashionably dressed man was a foreign aristocrat.[115] Because in the past the panel was reduced considerably (on all sides), the original signature and the year have disappeared. However, the style of the collar, the hat and the lace pattern suggest a dating around 1640. The use of the unusual poplar wood panel also supports this dating. Rembrandt evidently had a batch of about ten such poplar panels measuring about 105 × 80 cm (41 3/8 × 31 1/2 in.) at his disposal in the period between 1639 and 1642.[116]

The pendant portraits of the merchant Nicolaes van Bambeeck (1596–1661; p. 312, Cat. 251) and his wife, Agatha Bas (1611–1658; p. 313, Cat. 252), from 1641 represent a high point in the way Rembrandt used optical illusions and subtle *sfumato* effects during these years in order to suggest an exceptional impression of depth.[117] The painted picture frames, over which the gloves and fan jut out, look deceptively real and create the impression that the lifelike figures are in the same space as the viewer. Rembrandt used this same trompe-l'oeil device in *Girl in a Picture Frame* (p. 319, Cat. 320) from the same year. The faces of the van Bambeecks are painted so thinly that the weave of the canvas shows through the layers of paint. The atmospheric lighting and the gradual contrasts lend the faces and the cloudy hair an almost luminous *sfumato* effect. The paint is applied somewhat more thickly in the clothing, for example in the little strokes of granular paint which make the texture of Agatha's partlet (the cloth beneath the neckerchief) almost tangible, or in the pastose brushstrokes of white paint in her sleeve. The gloves of van Bambeeck and the fan of Agatha Bas, which extend over the painted frame, are rendered with the most thickly applied *impasto*.

The *Portrait of a Woman from the van Weede Family* (p. 321, Cat. 215) lends itself to a comparison with the portraits of the van Bambeecks. The wealthy young lady is standing in an arched passage, and here, too, the figure has been painted in a very smooth manner and with gradual transitions from light to dark. The architectural elements in the background are indicated in a much more sketch-like manner. Here, too, the extreme foreground is reserved on the right-hand side for a strongly illusionistic element. The head of a greatly foreshortened fan which seems to jut out of the painting can be seen emerging from the plastically modelled hand. It was only during the painting process that Rembrandt had the idea of introducing this element. The X-ray of the picture shows that he had originally placed the woman behind a sort of decorated balustrade. In a drawing (p. 273, Cat. D636) he tried another solution, in which he shortened the balustrade considerably showing the woman's hand resting on a stair railing. It looks like a final stage in the use of continuous barriers in the foreground of his portraits: the balustrade literally dissolves. We can see the same effect in *Portrait of a Woman* (p. 317, Cat. 216) from 1641, in which, according to the X-ray the woman was initially shown standing behind a similar balustrade in the foreground. During this period, Rembrandt's interest evidently shifted to other illusionistic effects. In the drawing referred to above, the woman's fan is still flat and slightly opened like that of Agatha Bas. But in the course of the painting process, Rembrandt decided to turn the closed fan with its head pointing out of the picture towards the viewer. The same striking effect of foreshortened hands or protruding objects can be seen both in *"The Night Watch"* from 1642 (pp. 324/325, Cat. 265) and in the *Double Portrait of Cornelis Claesz. Anslo and His Wife Aeltje Gerritsdr. Schouten* from 1641 (pp. 322/323, Cat. 264). The similarities with these works from 1641/42 gives reason to suppose that *Portrait of a Woman from the van Weede Family* was also painted during this period. Another argument for this dating is the existence of a companion piece, *Man in an Arch-Shaped Niche*, which is dated "*164*[.]", whereby the last figure would probably have been a 1 or possibly a 2.[118] The two portraits doubtless belong together, because they are both painted on poplar panels of the same size. What is surprising, however, is that the man's portrait was largely overpainted by another hand. The fairly detailed layout of the figure underneath, however, appears to have been painted by Rembrandt himself. Probably the woman's portrait was already completed but the companion piece was still unfinished when it left Rembrandt's workshop to be finished by another artist. The reasons for this remain a mystery and cannot be explained without further technical examination of the companion piece.

The well-thought-out composition of the *Double Portrait of Cornelis Claesz. Anslo and His Wife Aeltje Gerritsdr. Schouten* has a lot in common with *"The Night Watch"*, on which Rembrandt was also working at that time. A relatively detailed drawing from

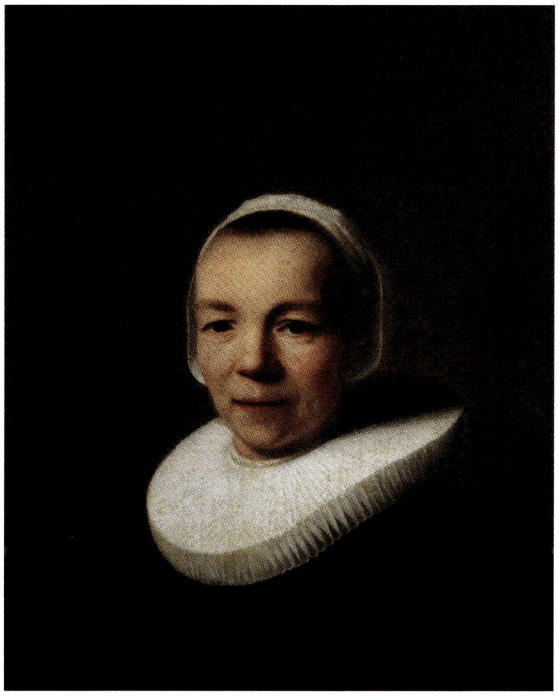

1640 shows Cornelis Claesz. Anslo (1592–1646) in a similar seated pose, but full-length (Cat. D638). The drawing allows us to surmise that Rembrandt originally imagined producing separate pendants of the couple. Possibly the ink drawing *Seated Woman with a Book on Her Lap* (p. 274, Cat. D637), which is executed much less precisely, was a study for the pendant of Aeltje Gerritsdr. Schouten (1589–1657). In any case, the seated woman in the drawing is wearing exactly the same (typical Mennonite) dress as Aeltje. The decision to paint a double portrait gave Rembrandt the opportunity of increasing the interaction between the sitters. The Mennonite preacher Anslo lends emphasis to his words with a rhetorical gesture, while his wife appears to be listening intently. Because Rembrandt arranged the still life on the table and the preacher and his wife at various heights, there is a great variety in light and colour. The table with the book still life takes up almost the entire left half of the picture, while the sitters are both grouped in the right half. A similar asymmetrical positioning of the figures is visible in *Woman from the van Weede Family* (p. 321, Cat. 215) and its companion piece, and also in *"The Night Watch"* (Cat. 265) in its original form. In the double portrait, the foreshortened, extended hand of the preacher plays the main role. Even with the naked eye, we can recognise how Rembrandt changed the contours of the fingers in his search to depict the gesture in the most convincing way. Captain Frans Banninck Cocq (1605–1655) makes the same gesture in *"The Night Watch"*. About the same time, Rembrandt must have painted another double portrait which has been lost. Abraham Wilmerdoncx (1605–1668) declared in 1659 that during Saskia's

Lambert Doomer, **Portrait of Baertje Martens**, 1644
Oil on panel, 65 × 54 cm (25 5/8 × 21 3/8 in.)
Chatsworth, Trustees of the Duke of Devonshire

illness and before her death in 1642 he had paid Rembrandt 500 guilders for the double portrait of himself and his wife and another 60 guilders for the canvas and the frame (RD 1659/18). It seems likely that Rembrandt would have charged Cornelis Anslo the same high price.

After *"The Night Watch"* Rembrandt painted no more portraits for a long time. The only exception was a little portrait sketch of Ephraim Bueno (1599–1665) from around 1647 (p. 329, Cat. 190), which he probably painted as a preliminary study for the etching (p. 328, Cat. E227). The gap in the portrait market which Rembrandt left was filled by his former assistants Bol and Flinck, but the elegant portraits by newcomers like Bartholomeus van der Helst (*c.* 1613–1670) and Abraham Lambertsz. van den Tempel (1622–1672) also found great favour with the Amsterdam elite.

The Night Watch

In 1642 Rembrandt completed his most famous painting, *The Militia Company of Captain Frans Banninck Cocq* (pp. 324/325, Cat. 265), better known as *"The Night Watch"*. This lucrative commission must have represented a particular challenge for Rembrandt, for the work was to be hung in a public place, surrounded by the militia pieces of his contemporaries with whom he entered into direct competition. His former student van Hoogstraten was of the opinion that this confrontation had turned out to Rembrandt's advantage.[119] According to him, in the other militia pieces, the individual heads were simply lined up in a row next to each other, while the true master ensured that his group composition was "eenwezich", a unity. Such unity would only be accomplished when the master arranged the individual figures in his imagination in such a way that they formed "a single image", like a history painting. "Rembrandt has taken [this principle] into account very well – in the opinion of many, however, too much – in his painting in the *Doelen* in Amsterdam, in that he took more trouble to create his own large image of his choice rather than the individual portraits he had been commissioned to paint." [120]

Rembrandt's main innovation was to arrange the militiamen in such a way that they appeared to be taking part in a history piece, united in a single common action. Captain Banninck Cocq indicates with a gesture that he is handing over the command to Wilhem van Ruytenburch (1600–1652). The latter shows the direction of march by pointing forward with his thrusting weapon, a partisan or spontoon, while the militiamen prepare to set off. Because of the great variety of activity in the ranks, the painting acquires the character of a snapshot. It is also noticeable that the marksmen of the lower ranks are portrayed in very different ways. Most of them are pushed into the dark background, so that their faces are not evenly illuminated, as was usually the case in portraits of the time. Rembrandt's decision to portray the militiamen in action and the strong chiaroscuro

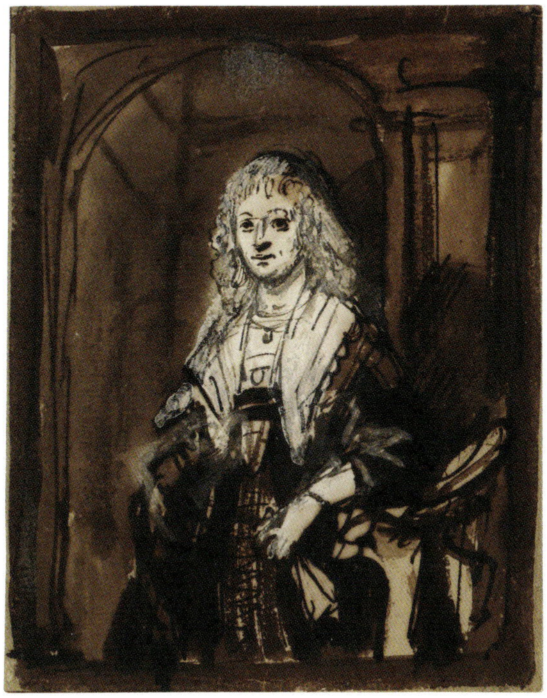

lend the composition an extraordinary liveliness and a dramatic character. The consequence, however, was that some of the marksmen were literally placed into the shadows and are thus less easy to recognise. This will doubtless have caused discontent, although there is no evidence to prove it. Filippo Baldinucci (1624–1697) was of the opinion – as related by the painter Bernhard Keil (1624–1687), who had been a student of Rembrandt's between 1642 and 1644 – that the composition was confusing because it was difficult to distinguish between one figure and another ("confuso in modo, che poco si distinguevano l'altre figure fra di loro").[121] Baldinucci, or rather Keil, nonetheless expresses amazement at the rendition in perspective of the partisan in van Ruytenburch's hand, which "although this measured no more than an arm's length *(braccio)*, nevertheless seemed to be full-length from every angle".

Van Hoogstraten countered the argument that Rembrandt had laid too much emphasis on the "eenwezichheid" (unity) at the expense of the recognisability of the individual portraits by commenting that the painting was "so picturesque in its conception, so graceful in '*sprong*' and so powerful that some had the impression that beside it all other pictures looked like playing cards in comparison". He, however, wished that Rembrandt "had ignited more light in it".[122]

Rembrandt's "picturesque conception" was expressed above all in numerous picturesque details; like the amalgam of contemporary, military and historical costumes and additions such as the little dog and other imaginative subsidiary figures, including the intriguing luminous girl in yellow. These subsidiary figures like dogs or children also gave

Portrait of a Woman, *c.* 1639
Pen and brown ink, brushwork in brown and white, 16 × 12.9 cm (6⅜ × 5 in.)
London, British Museum

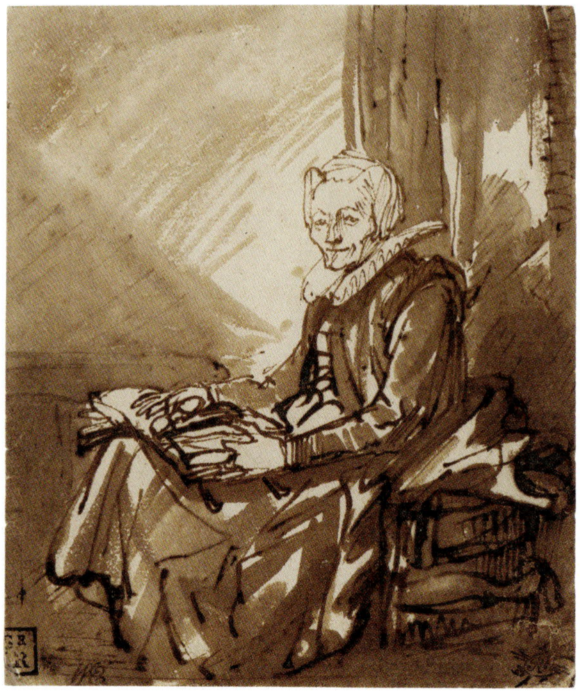

Rembrandt's history pictures a "graceful *sprong*"; Hoogstraten understood this to mean an agreeable variety of levels.[123] In order to achieve this variation in height, Rembrandt frequently used steps – not only in *"The Night Watch"*, but also in his other compositions (Cat. 62; Cat. 63, p. 247).

Hoogstraten's sigh of regret that it would have been better if Rembrandt "had ignited more light in it", led to the persistent misunderstanding that the patrons had rejected *"The Night Watch"* because they found it too dark. There is no evidence of this. The shadows in the painting structure the effect of depth, for example in the case of the partisan, which Baldinucci praises precisely because of its lifelike quality. The dark tip of the thrusting weapon seems to protrude because it is outlined against the yellow jerkin. This representation also corresponds to van Hoogstraten's observation that areas with rough surfaces appear closer than smooth ones (corresponding to the principle of *kenlijkheyt*). In the tassel of the partisan, the strands of cord that are closer are darker and are also defined in more granular paint than the end, where the colours seem increasingly to fade.[124]

Completed in 1642, the group portrait of the civic militia of District II was intended for the banqueting hall of the *Kloveniersdoelen*, the headquarters of the Amsterdam arquebusiers. Before 1578, Amsterdam had three marksmen's guilds, established to defend the city: the archers, the crossbowmen and the "Kloveniers", the arquebusiers (derived from *clover*, a gunpowder fireweapon). These guilds were divided into divisions and subdivisions known as squads, with the corresponding officers. In 1578, when the Roman

Seated Woman with a Book on Her Lap, *c.* 1639
Pen and brush in brown, 12.6 × 11 cm (5 × 4⅜ in.)
Rotterdam, Museum Boijmans Van Beuningen, Collectie Franz Koenigs

Catholic city government was deposed by the Calvinists, the marksmen's guilds merged into civic militia companies *(vendels)* divided up by city district, each commanded by a captain. During the course of the seventeenth century, the militia's acts became increasingly ceremonial in character because of the reduced risk of war. The firing ranges *(doelens)* also gradually lost their function as practice ranges and over time began to serve primarily as meeting places for officials, rather like a club. Nonetheless they continued to hold military marches, for example in the form of parades. According to alderman Hans Bontemantel (1613–1688), 20 militiamen "armed handsomely", paraded regularly, adding that this took place every Sunday in summer and every day during the annual fair.[125] Rembrandt's scene does not depict the normal marching of the guard. Nor does it seem to record a specific event.[126] The painting has often been characterised as a procession of the militiamen or a ceremonial parade.[127] In addition to this anecdotal aspect, various procedures are portrayed in the picture which are an expression of the corporate identity of the militiamen, such as the handling of the muskets *(clover)*.

The banqueting hall of the civic militia, the so-called Doelenzaal, for which Rembrandt painted *"The Night Watch"*, was constructed during the course of an extension project. In the mid-1620s, the *Kloveniersdoelen* was extended by the addition of a new building beside the *Swygh Utrecht* bastion, which had formed part of the parade ground since 1522. The large hall on the first floor, which was probably delivered in 1627, served as a banqueting and reception hall.[128] Six militia pieces were commissioned from various artists to adorn the new building, which was designed in classical style. Apart from Rembrandt, the artists who executed the works were Joachim von Sandrart, Govert Flinck, Nicolaes Eliasz. Pickenoy (1588–1650/56), Jacob Adriaensz. Backer (1608–1651) and Bartholomeus van der Helst.

It is not known exactly when the pictures for the *Doelenzaal* were commissioned, but it seems likely that they were not all ordered at the same time. We know with certainty that Jan Claesz. Leydeckers (1597–1640), whom Rembrandt portrayed in *"The Night Watch"*, was buried on 27 December 1640 in the Nieuwe Kerk, so we can surmise that the commission had been placed before this date. The place in the main hall which was allocated to the militiamen of District II for their group portrait was on the far left on the long wall. The present state of Rembrandt's militia piece gives only an incomplete impression of the original composition, because in 1715 the canvas was trimmed on all sides, but especially on the left, because it had to fit between two doors in the Amsterdam Town Hall on the Dam. The original composition has been retained in a small copy which Gerard Lundens (1622–1686) made about 1650 for Frans Banninck Cocq (p. 285). Banninck Cocq was clearly very satisfied with the way he was portrayed in Rembrandt's militia piece, because in addition to the copy by Lundens he also had a watercolour drawing after the painting made in 1653 for his family album (p. 281).[129] As the captain, and as one of the wealthiest men in District II, he was probably very influential in the choice of Rembrandt as the painter of the militia piece. That is remarkable inasmuch as his brother-in-law, Andries de Graeff, had had a life-size portrait painted by Rembrandt in 1639 (p. 306, Cat. 188), which had led to a dispute regarding the payment (RD 1659/21). Banninck Cocq was evidently impressed by the portrait of his brother-in-law and it must have been clear to him that the artist charged high prices for his work.

Rembrandt's militia piece does not have a single generally accepted title. It was occasionally maintained that the earlier title which was frequently adopted, "The Corporal's Command of Captain Banninck Cocq" was "completely incorrect" because two sergeants and a lieutenant are also shown on the canvas.[130] Nonetheless, the title "Corporal's Command" is not incorrect historically. Thus Jan Pietersz. Bronckhorst (1587–1666) in a notarial declaration of 1659 stated that on Rembrandt's militia piece "in addition to other persons of his company and corporal's command, up to sixteen in number, had been painted and portrayed" (RD 1659/16). He is the man with the helmet and sword on the right beside the halberd. The old name can be explained by the fact that in *"The Night Watch"* almost 30 men can be seen, which corresponds approximately to the strength of a corporal's command.[131] A company or rank, on the other hand, consisted of about 120 men, of whom, however, clearly not everybody was prepared to pay for their own portrait. Bronckhorst's explanation proves that each marksman had to pay for his own portrait. Each had to pay about 100 guilders, "some a little more and some a little less", depending on his position in the painting (RD 1659/16). It was confirmed in a declaration by Claes van Cruysbergen (1613–1663) in 1659 that *"The Night Watch"* cost a total of 1,600 guilders; he is probably the helmeted *rondassier* (shield-bearer) to the right of the standard bearer (RD 1659/19). Rembrandt made allowances for the fact that the painting was to be hung in a corner, where it would be concealed, at least in part, by the protruding fireplace on the narrow side of the room. Because this part of the canvas was lost to view of the spectator, he positioned the sergeant with the halberd not on the far left edge (which is the case with the picture in its present state) and placed the two principal figures, the Captain and the Lieutenant, further to the right of the centre. The major trimming in 1715 not only resulted in the loss of two portraits, but it also fundamentally changed the space concept and the suggestion of movement.

The man dressed in black with the red sash in the foreground is Frans Banninck Cocq, Lord of Purmerland and Ilpendam. From about 1639 to 1646 he was Captain

Detail of: **Portrait of a Woman from the van Weede Family**, *c.* 1641
(see ill. p. 321)

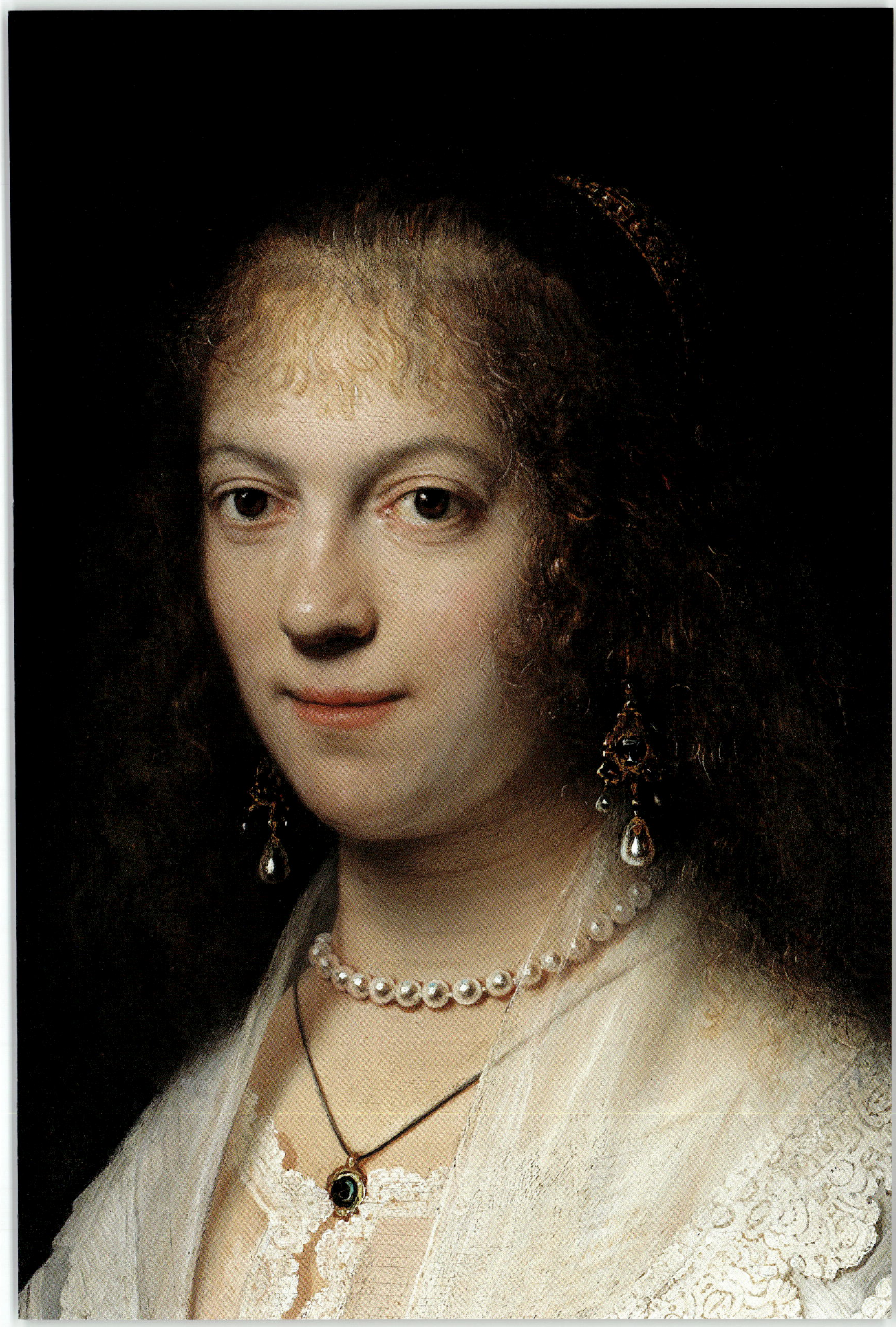

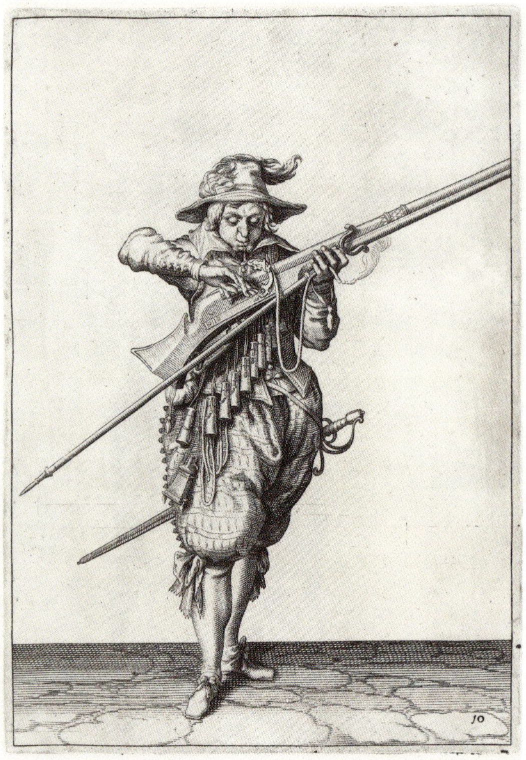

of City District II (Damrak and Nieuwendijk). He had held a number of important positions in Amsterdam since 1632, including commissioner for Matrimonial Affairs and in 1650 he even became burgomaster. Beside him, dressed in golden yellow and with a buff coat, stands Lieutenant Wilhem van Ruytenburch, Lord of Vlaardingen. During the same year in which Rembrandt painted him as an officer, he also joined the council for matrimonial affairs. Thereafter, his political career advanced no farther, though he succeeded Banninck Cocq as captain in 1646.[132]

The company was subdivided into four corporal's commands, two of which were led by a sergeant. This explains why two sergeants are to be seen on the painting: Rombout Kemp (1597–1653) with his right arm outstretched on the left beside the drummer, and Reynier Jansz. Engelen (1588–1651), shown as a halberd-bearer in a cuirass on the far left, seen in rear view. Usually all officers were shown on a militia piece, including the ensign. Here Jan Cornelisz. Visscher (1610–1650) is the standard bearer. The drummer Jacob Jorisz. (1591–after 1646) probably did not have to pay for his portrait, because unlike the militiamen he was paid for his job.[133]

The poses and movements of the three musketeers correspond with the illustrations which Jacques de Gheyn II (*c.* 1565–1629) produced for the weapons manual *Wapenhandelinghe van Roers Musquetten ende Spiessen* (pp. 278, 279). The man dressed in red on the captain's left, who is just loading his weapon, is Jan Aertsz. van der Heede (1610–1655). He is wearing a so-called bandolier or baldric, from which the little horns filled with gunpowder are hung. The bent figure behind Banninck Cocq is firing his weapon, as the flash at the end of the barrel to the left of van Ruytenburch's head betrays. The musketeer who is standing to the right behind the lieutenant, probably Leydeckers, is blowing the gunpowder pan of his weapon clean. These everyday activ-

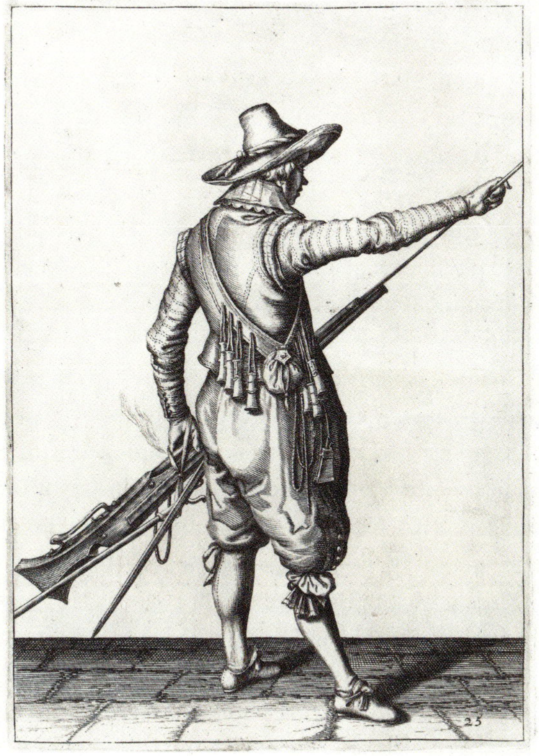

ities are highly instructive here, and the attributes serve to distinguish between the ranks and functions. Banninck Cocq can be recognised as a captain on account of his cane or commander's staff, and van Ruytenburch's thrusting weapon shows him to be a lieutenant. All the officers on the painting are wearing a sash. Those worn by Banninck Cocq, van Ruytenburch and Visscher are red, white and blue, possibly a reference to the flag of the Dutch Republic. The inventories of Visscher and Kemp confirm that they really did wear sashes of blue or white *armoisin* (taffeta).[134] Red sashes, on the other hand, are very rarely mentioned in inventories in Amsterdam. The red and black of Banninck Cocq's dress refers instead to the (black-red-white) coat of arms of Amsterdam, just as van Ruytenburch's yellow suit with the blue contrasts corresponds to the colours of the *Kloveniers*.[135] Banninck Cocq's red sash echoes the red of the clothing of the musketeer van der Heede. In the years after the creation of *"The Night Watch"*, red colour accents like these begin to play an increasing role in Rembrandt's compositions. There are also other heraldic symbols in the painting. Thus the shadow of the captain's hand falls onto the embroidered coat of arms of Amsterdam on van Ruytenburch's coat, which has been painted with thick *impasto*.[136] Jan van Dyck (*c.* 1690–1769) commented with amazement in 1758 on the differentiation in the paint application: "In the embroidery on the vest

Jacques de Gheyn II
A soldier blowing the match to keep the flame alive,
while covering the priming pan of his musket with two fingers to avoid flying sparks
and **A soldier pulling out the ramrod from the holder**
both from: *Wapenhandelinghe van Roers Musquetten ende Spiessen*, 1597–1607
Copper engraving, 25.5 × 18.5 cm (10 × 7 3/8 in.). Amsterdam, Rijksmuseum

or buff coat of the lieutenant the paint has been applied so thickly that you could grate a nutmeg on it."[137]

Banninck Cocq, van Ruytenburch, Visscher and Kemp are depicted wearing contemporary clothing. Like the helmeted militiamen in the background, the captain and the lieutenant are both wearing metal gorgets. When the canvas was trimmed, two fashionably dressed militiamen on the left-hand side, probably Jan Brughman (1614–1652) and Jacob Dircksz. de Roy (1601–1659), were cut off. The man behind van der Heede, probably Harman Jacobsz. Wormskerck (1590–1653), is wearing a broad-brimmed hat in the fashion of the time, together with a gorget. The remaining figures are fitted out in military or imaginary style. In accordance with their rank, the sergeants are armed with halberds. While Kemp is shown in relatively plain dress, Engelen is wearing a cuirass and has an imaginative helmet on his head which seems to be based on painterly models (Cat. 98).[138] Several militiamen are equipped with weapons of the type that were in common use during the time of the Dutch Revolt against Spain. The marksman between Banninck Cocq and van Ruytenburch, who is pointing the barrel of the weapon he has just fired away from him, is wearing a beret with slits in the style of the sixteenth century. This is probably Rembrandt's portrait of Jan Adriaensz. Keyser (1594–1664), who later became the castellan of the archers, the *Handboogdoelen*. In particular, the men carrying lances and pikes are imaginatively equipped. The man with the tall hat towards the back in the middle is holding a sort of cavalry spear; he is probably Jan Ockers (1599–1652). To his right, the pikeman with the helmet with a plume is Walich Schellingwou (1613–1653); the pikeman with the feathered beret behind Leydeckers is thought to be Barent Hermansz. Bolhamer (1589–1661). The man with the Spanish helmet on the far right is probably Paulus Harmensz. van Schoonhoven (1595–1679) and the helmeted musketeer to the left of the flag is Elbert Willemsz. Swedenrijck (1589–1644). He is also holding a fuse as well as a "furket", a forked pole used as a support for muskets. The two helmeted shield-bearers are Claes van Cruysbergen on the right of the standard bearer and Jan Pietersz. Bronckhorst on the right of Engelen's halberd.

In comparison to other militia pieces, it is noticeable that, in addition to the two officers, three sergeants and 13 men there are at least 16 additional, subsidiary figures who did not pay to be included. These include two girls, for apart from the conspicuous child in yellow we can also just catch a glimpse of a small, brown-haired girl in blue. During the military parades, children did indeed accompany the troops on occasion as a sort of mascot. Here they are dressed in the colours of the flag: yellow and blue. The girl is carrying the company's ceremonial drinking horn. The bird's claws on her belt are a clear reference to the word "Clauweniers/Cloveniers"; the claw is the emblem of the Amsterdam *Kloveniers* and can be seen on the guild silver, the glass dishes and on the gable of the

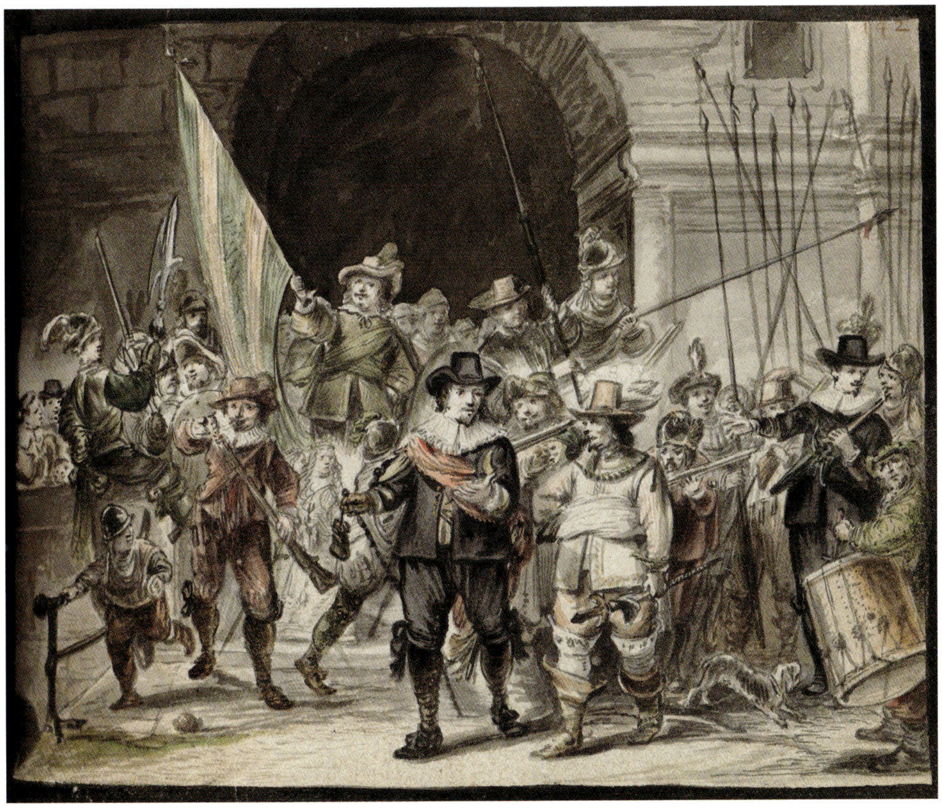

Jacob Colijn after Rembrandt, **The Militia Company of Captain Frans Banninck Cocq ("The Night Watch")**, *c.* 1650
Sketch from the family album of Frans Banninck Cocq
Watercolour, 14.2 × 18 cm (5 5/8 × 7 in.). Amsterdam, Rijksmuseum

Doelen. The young man behind the captain has decorated his helmet with oak leaves, a sign of strength which can be seen like the claw on the silver militiamen's chain which was presented every year.[139] The little boy on the left is carrying a powder horn and thus can be interpreted as the powder boy who was essential to the arquebusiers. In this manner, Rembrandt combined real elements of the parading militia with their symbols.

Around 1653, Banninck Cocq had a watercolour of *"The Night Watch"* painted for his family album. It bore the title *Sketch of the Painting in the Banqueting Hall of the Arquebusiers showing the Young Lord of Purmerlandt as Captain who is Ordering his Lieutenant, Lord of Vlaerdingen, to Make his Militia Company March Off* (p. 281).[140] In 1758 Jan van Dyk characterised Rembrandt's painting as "A militia company setting off",[141] and

Jan Wagenaar (1709–1773) spoke in his *Amsterdam in zyne opkomst* (1765) of a "Corporal's Command from the Rank of Captain Frans Banning Kok Setting Out".[142] These sources justify the frequently-used title "The Company of Captain Frans Banninck Cocq and Lieutenant Wilhem van Ruytenburch Prepares to March Off". It was not until 1808 that reference was first made in official documents to the "*Nagwagt*" (Night Watch) and the "*Nagt Patroelje*" (Night Patrol).[143] During that year, the painting was moved into the Trippenhuis, where it hung from 1815 until 1885. It is therefore not correct to claim that the English painter Joshua Reynolds (1723–1792) introduced the name *Nightwatch* in his *Journey to Flanders and Holland* (1781).[144] The nickname was mentioned for the first time in the prologue to the tragedy *Stephanus* (1790) by Pieter Pypers (1749–1805), where reference is made to the "dashing Night Watch by the bold Rembrand".[145] The painting probably acquired its name because it was thought, on account of the darkened layers of varnish, to show a night scene. This occurred, according to some, because of a coating of soot from the fireplace near where the work was hung in the Doelenzaal. The painting was cleaned in 1758 by Jan van Dyck. He revealed the cartouche with the names and wrote: "Because of the large quantities of baked oil and varnish, with which it had been coated from time to time, it was no longer possible to see which company it was, much less the names of the principal officers."[146]

For Rembrandt, *"The Night Watch"* represented an artistic high point but in some respects also a dead end. His composition is characterised by great variety and the "most agility", and the dramatic lighting and suggestion of depth are heightened to the utmost degree. In the course of the 1640s, he experimented with his stylistic idiom and sense of form, and finally decided on a new approach.[147]

Famous Examples: Albrecht Dürer and Lucas van Leyden

A genius like Rembrandt draws on himself and is largely independent of other artists. Statements about Rembrandt's relationship to the art of his predecessors formulated in this or a similar manner long prevented an adequate appreciation of his great interest in the works of previous generations of painters. Only slowly did the realisation begin to prevail that Rembrandt, too, was not only interested in the artistic achievements and successes of his predecessors, but also that he was thoroughly familiar with them and that he found inspiration in their works. His objective was not merely copying entire works or even parts of them. Already in 1604, Karel van Mander made clear in his so-called *Leerdicht* (didactic poem) which prefaces the *Schilder-Boeck*, that copying formed part of

Detail of: **Portrait of Nicolaes van Bambeeck**, 1641
(see ill. p. 312)

the training of the younger generation of artists.[148] He advised them to use parts of bodies derived from works by other artists in their own compositions. In a play on words, he uses here a comparison with a soup whose ingredients are no longer identifiable after cooking (chap. 1, fol. 5, verse 46). He plays with the dual meaning of the Dutch word "rapen" when he writes: "Wel ghecoockte rapen is goe pottage" (Well-boiled turnips/gleanings make a good soup). Even more worth pursuing, however, and expressly permitted even for advanced painters was the borrowing from works of famous artists, because this also brought honour to these distinguished examples.[149] Here it was not a matter of mere imitation, but rather of a dialogue with the artistic tradition as an act which was both receptive and creative. *Imitare* (to imitate) was opposed to the more demanding *aemulare* (emulate). Here the aim was even to surpass the example chosen.

The inventory of Rembrandt's property that was drawn up in 1656 on the occasion of his bankruptcy (RD 1656/12) shows that at that time he owned an extensive and wide-ranging collection of prints and drawings.[150] The many illustrious names of Italian artists include those of Michelangelo, Raphael, Titian, Antonio Tempesta, Guido Reni (1575–1642) and Annibale and Agostino Carracci. The reproduction prints after their works enabled Rembrandt, who never travelled to Italy, to study the works of the outstanding masters of the Italian Renaissance. For example, three drawings have survived in which Rembrandt studied Leonardo's *Last Supper* from about 1496 from Santa Maria delle Grazie in Milan (Cat. D658–660). The starting point was the engraving by Giovanni Pietro da Birago (*c.* 1471–1513) after the original. The three drawings by Rembrandt demonstrate how intensively he examined the moment in the narrative that Leonardo had chosen. He, too, does not choose the revelation of Judas as the traitor, but rather the moment before, in which Jesus announces the betrayal: "And as they did eat, he said, Verily I say unto you, that one of you shall betray me" (Matthew 26: 21). The words of Christ plunge the Apostles into disbelief and confusion, which is expressed above all in the gestures of the men as they discuss the news in animated fashion. In his drawings, Rembrandt heightens this aspect by concentrating on the emotional state of the apostles, whom he also individualises more strongly. In comparison with Da Birago's engraving after Leonardo, Rembrandt emphasises the movement of the Apostles towards the centre of the picture and Christ, whose announcement of the betrayal is the cause of their agitated behaviour. In emulation with Leonardo's famous model and the pictorial tradition of the scene, Rembrandt succeeds in reformulating the subject. In his paintings, too, we can clearly see that Rembrandt studied the model of Leonardo's *Last Supper*, as for example in *The Wedding of Samson* (pp. 248/249, Cat. 17).

The artists from northern Europe listed by name and of whom Rembrandt owned prints, included, for example, Martin Schongauer (*c.* 1448–1491), Israhel van Meckenem

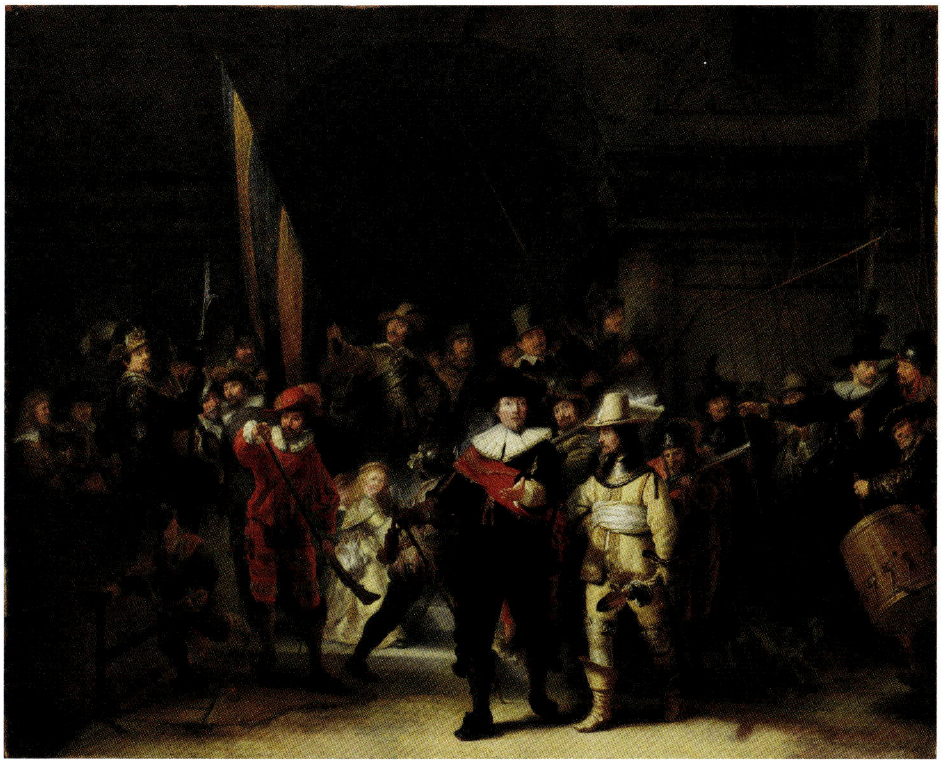

Gerard Lundens after Rembrandt, **The Militia Company of Captain Frans Banninck Cocq ("The Night Watch")**, copy, after 1642
Oil on oak, 66.8 × 85.4 cm (26 3/8 × 33 5/8 in.). London, The National Gallery

the Younger (*c.* 1445–1503), Hans Brosamer (1495–1554), Hans Holbein the Younger (1497/98–1543) and Lucas Cranach the Younger (1515–1586). Rembrandt apparently acquired most of his collection of prints at auctions in Amsterdam, where there was a flourishing market for "art on paper" (drawings, woodcuts, engravings and etchings). We know from documents that as early as 1635 he purchased graphic works at the auction of the painter and innkeeper Barend van Someren (1572–1632; RD 1635/1). At further auctions during the 1630s Rembrandt purchased a remarkable number of woodcuts and engravings (including complete series) by Lucas van Leyden and Albrecht Dürer. On 18 March 1637, Rembrandt's pupil Leendert Cornelisz. van Beijeren acquired at the Amsterdam auction of Jan Bassé (*c.* 1571–1637) for the enormous price of 637.10 guilders "1 konstboech [art book] van Lucas [i. e. Lucas van Leyden]" (RD 1637/2). In view of the high price, it must have contained the more or less complete printed graphics of Lucas van

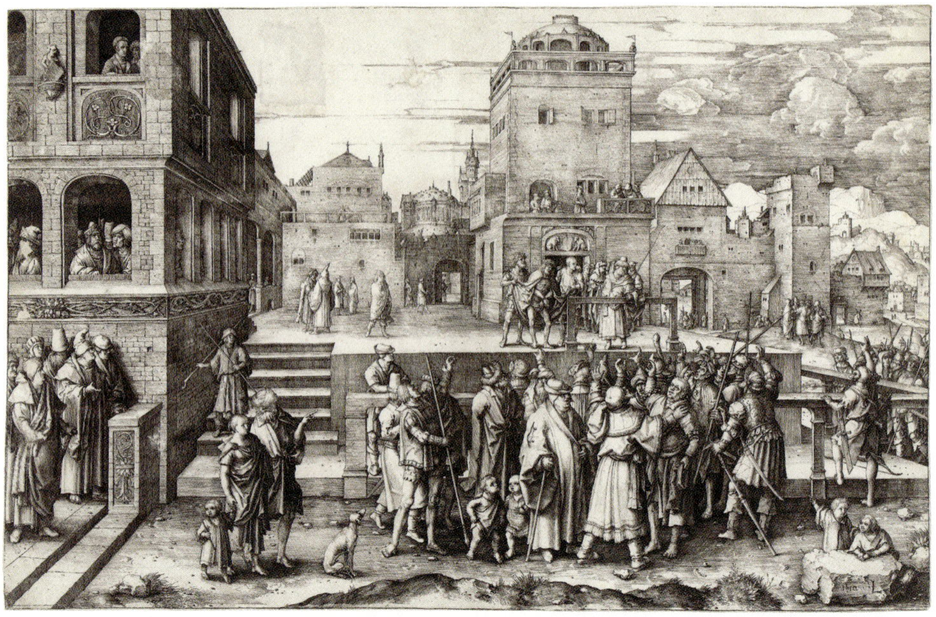

Lucas van Leyden, **Ecce homo**, 1510
Copper engraving, 28.8 × 45.4 cm (11 3/8 × 17 7/8 in.)
Amsterdam, Rijksmuseum

Leyden. Rembrandt himself had purchased engravings and drawings during the auction, which lasted for several weeks. Rembrandt's collection of prints by his famous fellow-citizen was further increased after this purchase. He also acquired single sheets by Lucas van Leyden at very high prices. Thus the burgomaster of Harderwijk, Ernst Brinck (1582–1649), wrote in 1642 that Rembrandt had recently bought a small engraving by Lucas van Leyden showing the "Ulenspiegelken" (little Eulenspiegel), having paid 179 guilders for it (RD 1642/10).[151] Samuel van Hoogstraten would later confirm this fact.[152] And Johann Ulrich Mayr (1630–1704) from Augsburg, who must have been in Rembrandt's workshop around 1645/47, mentioned according to Joachim von Sandrart that Rembrandt had paid 1,400 guilders for 14 high-quality states of engravings by Lucas van Leyden.[153] In Rembrandt's inventory from 1656, in addition to an album of woodcuts, another with engravings by Lucas van Leyden is also mentioned, with both single engravings and double specimens. Rembrandt's great predilection for the art of Lucas van Leyden is understandable in view of the quality of the works and the international reputation of his fellow-citizen. Both Vasari and van Mander saw Lucas van Leyden as the most important representative of Netherlandish art in their time.[154] And so it is not surprising that Rembrandt, too, found inspiration in the prints of Lucas van Leyden. Even in Rembrandt's early works we find references to Lucas van Leyden's works, for example in the painting *Two Old Men Disputing, Probably the Apostles Peter and Paul* from 1628 (p. 48, Cat. 37). The way one of the two figures is pointing to a passage in the text in the open book derives from Lucas van Leyden's engraving from 1527 showing the two Apostle princes in conversation in a landscape.[155] Another example is Rembrandt's etching from 1655 *Christ is Presented to the People* (Cat. E69). The central dais surrounded by buildings with people watching the scene from the windows, the staircase beside the dais on which Pilate presents the shackled Christ to the people, and the passionate gestures of the spectators had their origin in Lucas van Leyden's engraving with the Ecce Homo scene from 1510 (p. 286). Rembrandt doubtless owned a copy of the engraving and will also have been familiar with the passage in Karel van Mander's biography of Lucas van Leyden, in which he emphasises the inventiveness of the artist, who was only 16 years of age when he made the engraving.[156] How scrupulously Rembrandt studied the works of Lucas is evident from the etching *The Triumph of Mordecai* (Cat. E8) from the Book of Esther, which can be dated to around 1641.[157] Rembrandt owed two figures in his etching to Lucas van Leyden: the man on the right who is just removing his cap in a gesture of respect for Mordecai as he rides past, and the other man holding his hat in his hands.[158]

It is known that even in Dürer's lifetime his printed works were very widely distributed. The Nuremberg artist's disputes with Marcantonio Raimondi (*c.* 1480–1534) about the copyright of his engravings and woodcuts, recorded by Giorgio Vasari and also mentioned by Karel van Mander in his *Schilder-Boeck* from 1604, provide an indication of the flood of Dürer imitations and copies in the field of printed graphics, which began at an early stage.[159] The extremely perfected technique of Dürer's prints, remained a constant challenge to the following generations of artists. This was especially the case in the Netherlands. Thus, for example, Jan (1549–*c.* 1620), Anton (1555/59–1604) and Hieronymus Wierix (1553–1619) in Antwerp engraved no fewer than 50 sheets after Dürer's model. In addition to his prints, Dürer's theoretical works were also widely distributed. Mathias Quad von Kinkelbach (1557–1613) writes in his *Teutscher Nation Herligkeit* from 1609 that they were regarded "von den Künstnern *[sic]* und andern admiratoribus für Heiligthumb" (by the artists and other admirers as holy).[160] Rembrandt also owned a copy of Dürer's books on human proportions (RD 1656/12, 273).

In the years between about 1635 and 1640, Rembrandt was intensively occupied with Dürer's art. He copied, for example, individual figures from an identical iconographical context, such as the figure of Christ in the etching *Christ Driving the Money Changers from the Temple* from 1635 (p. 291, Cat. E33) after Dürer's woodcut from 1508/09 (p. 292). But Rembrandt also found inspiration in works by Dürer illustrating different subject matter. The dragon-like creature above the first parents in Rembrandt's etching of *Adam and Eve* from 1638 (Cat. E7) probably derives from a similar model above the archway in Dürer's engraving *Christ in Purgatory* from 1512. Dürer's series of woodcuts on the *Life of the Virgin* evidently left a lasting impression on Rembrandt. Vasari had judged this series to be executed "so well that it would not be possible, whether in invention, in the composition of the perspective-views, in the buildings, in the costumes, or in the heads of old and young, to do better".[161] Rembrandt's etching *The Death of the Virgin* (Cat. E38) dated 1639 reveals itself to be a compilation from at least two scenes from Dürer's *Life of the Virgin*. The youth with the long staff on the left of the etching must have been inspired by the kneeling Apostle in Dürer's *Death of the Virgin*, while the hovering angel by contrast can be traced back to the woodcut showing Dürer's *Birth of the Virgin Mary*. In his painting showing *The Visitation* (p. 345, Cat. 64) from 1640, Rembrandt took as his starting point Dürer's scene from the *Life of the Virgin* showing the same subject (p. 344), but combined it with motifs from an engraving after a design by Maerten van Heemskerck (1498–1574) showing the return of young Tobias in which he is being greeted by his parents.[162]

Rembrandt acquired woodcuts and engravings in large numbers whenever the opportunity arose, for example at the auction of Gommer Spranger (1577–1637) in February 1638 in Amsterdam.[163] Judging by the graphic works which were offered for auction, the sale must have been a sensational event for all lovers of Dürer's works. At any rate, Rembrandt took advantage of the opportunity and acquired an extraordinary number of works by Dürer at the auction. Drawings, woodcuts and engravings from the property of Gommer Spranger came under the hammer. Spranger was the nephew and principal heir of the painter Bartholomeus Spranger (1546–1611). Gommer died in 1637 in Amsterdam, and the auction of his estate in February 1638 was a major public attraction (RD 1638/2).[164] He had owned works by Raphael, Michelangelo, Polidoro da Caravaggio (1492–1543), Hendrick Goltzius (1588–1617) and Bartholomeus Spranger, to list just a few prominent names. More numerous than everything else, however, were the graphic works by Dürer that were on offer. About 300 individual prints by Dürer were auctioned, five copies of his Passion series, about 150 copies of the so-called Large and Small St Christopher, about 80 prints of *The Dream of the Doctor*, an *Apocalypse*, and at least 80 complete woodcut series of the *Life of the Virgin*. Rembrandt purchased nine of

Detail of: **Portrait of a Woman**, 1641
(see ill. p. 316)

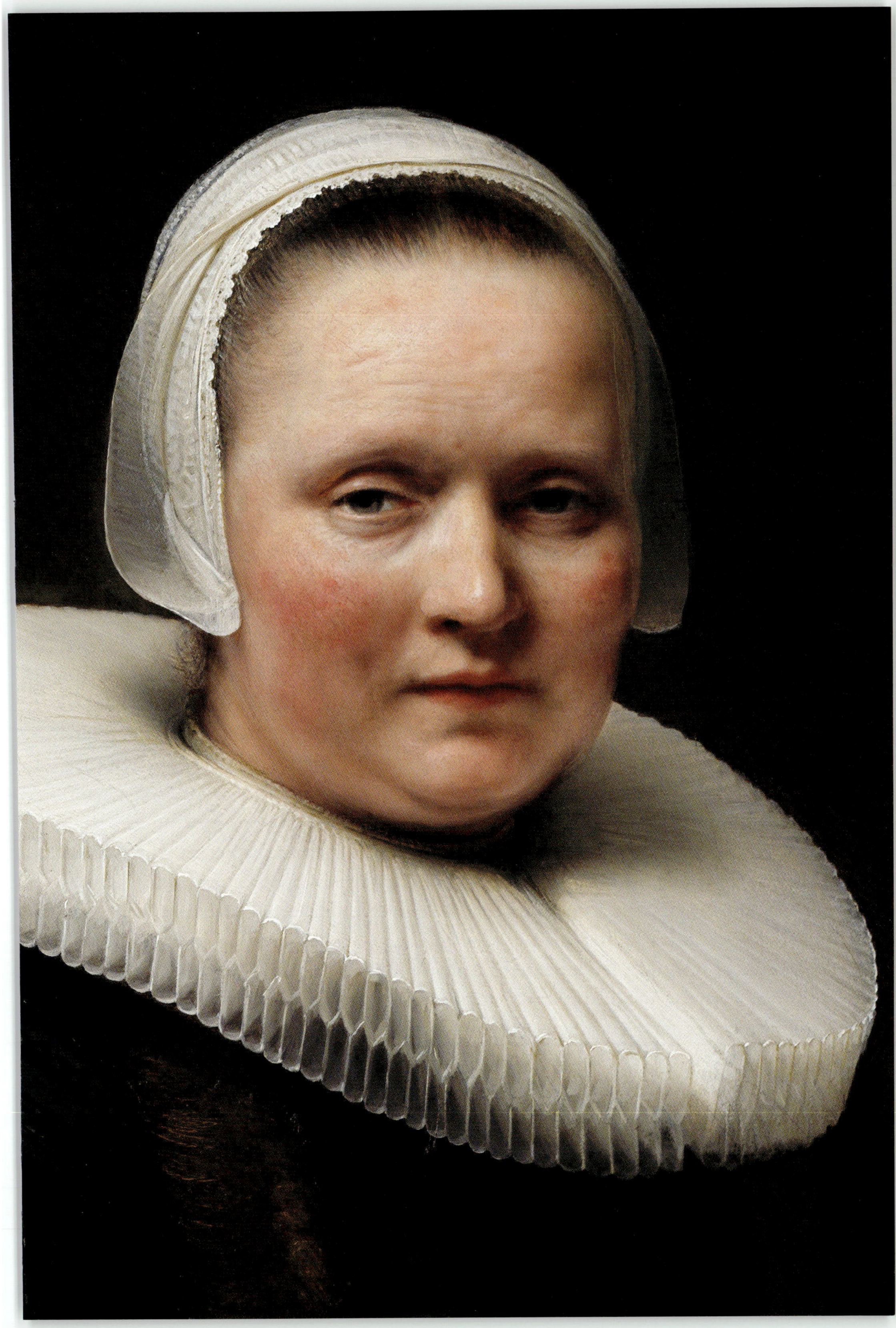

them, which sounds fairly modest in view of the total number. The enormous number of individual prints and series can be explained by the fact that Gommer Spranger owned Dürer's original woodblocks and copper plates. In addition to the blocks of the *Life of the Virgin*, 14 further copper plates were also offered for sale, including famous ones like the plate for the engraving *The Dream of the Doctor* from 1497/98.

With regard to the complete Dürer series which Rembrandt and other artists, collectors and dealers acquired at the auction, they will almost certainly have been prints in most cases made during Gommer Spranger's lifetime using the woodblocks and copper plates which he had taken over from the estate of his uncle Bartholomeus. It is also possible that Gommer's heirs made further prints from the woodblocks and copper plates shortly before the auction, in the justified hope of additional profit. Rembrandt will doubtless have acquired such large numbers of printed graphics of Dürer's works not only because he was an avid collector, but probably also in order to sell them as well. Surely, he also used part of the prints for instructing his large numbers of pupils, whom he could familiarise with the artistic tradition in this way.

Self-Portraits

Rembrandt must have regarded the time around 1640 as the zenith of his career. In the previous decades, his fame had spread rapidly and he was considered to be the most successful history and portrait painter in Amsterdam. Many of his paintings had found their way into the collections of princes and art connoisseurs, and he demanded (and received) exorbitantly high prices for his works. During the years 1637 and 1638, he painted relatively little and seems to have been mainly active in purchasing graphic works by his great predecessors. He evidently studied them with great intensity and his admiration for the art of the early sixteenth century was also reflected in the way he presented himself in his self-portraits. In what is possibly his most ambitious self-portrait (p. 331, Cat. 157), from 1640, he painted himself in a self-confident pose and dressed in the fashion of the sixteenth century, his arm resting on a wooden sill. Because of this pose, reference has frequently been made to the related pose both in Titian's portrait, supposed to depict the poet Ariosto (1474–1533) from about 1509, and also Raphael's portrait of the courtier Baldassare Castiglione (1478–1529) from 1514/15. Against this background, Rembrandt's self-portrait has been interpreted as an expression of his ambitions as a poet, courtier or aristocratic "gentiluomo".[165] This interpretation draws a false picture of Rembrandt's intentions, because he never showed even the slightest signs of any ambitions (or talents) in these fields. Throughout his entire life his ambitions lay purely in the field of art, and he strove to go down in history as the best painter of his age. Rembrandt had doubtless seen and admired

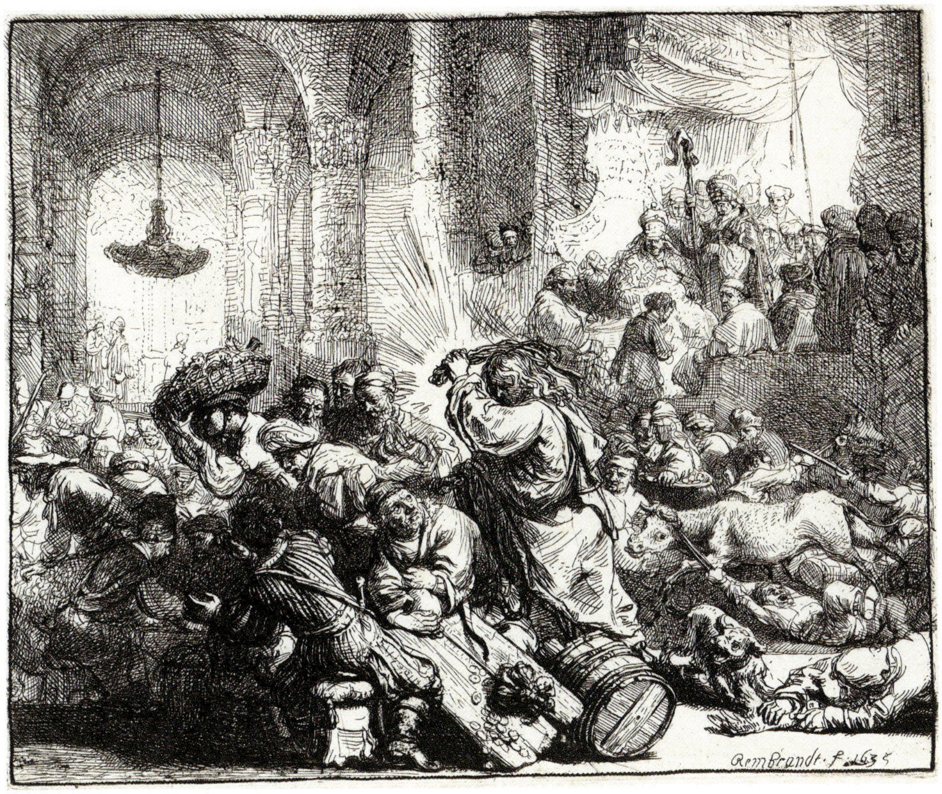

Christ Driving the Money Changers from the Temple, 1635
Etching, 13.6 × 16.9 cm (5 ⅜ × 6 ¾ in.). Amsterdam, Rijksmuseum

the works of Titian and Raphael, but it is most unlikely that he ever had the intention of identifying personally with their sitters. The self-portrait is, rather, an expression of his intense preoccupation with Northern art from the period between 1520 and 1535. The motif of the arm leaning on the sill was not restricted to Italian art, but was primarily a characteristic of the Northern portrait tradition, for which Dürer's *Self-Portrait* from 1498 in Madrid is one of the earliest examples (p. 330).[166] The X-ray of the London painting shows that initially Rembrandt, like Dürer, had positioned both hands on the sill.[167] The emphasis on the hands and the illusionistic depiction of the fingertips extending over the edge were a typical characteristic of Northern portraiture in the first half of the sixteenth century which is missing in Italian references (in Titian and Raphael, the hands are hardly visible). Other typical characteristics which Rembrandt adopted from the Northern tradition were the arched top and the painted

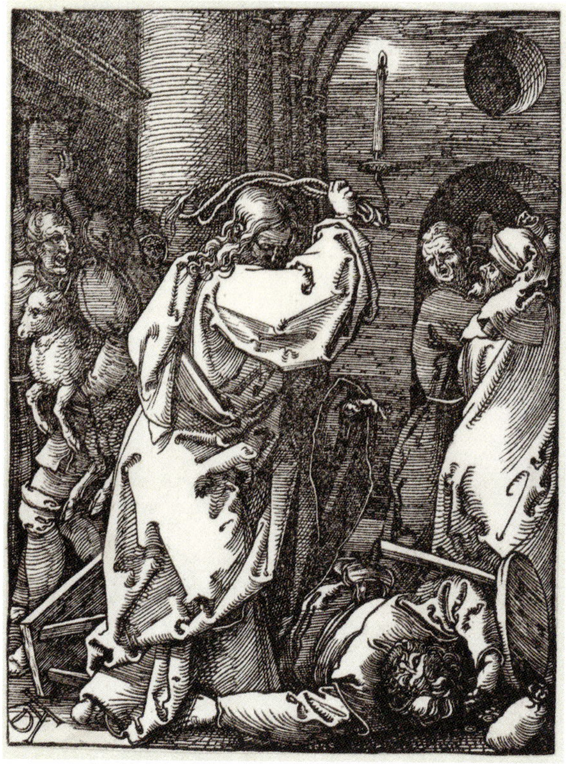

trompe-l'oeil frame which can be seen in various portraits by Jan van Scorel (1495–1562), Joos van Cleve (1485–1541) and Jan Gossaert (*c.* 1478–1532; p. 297). Rembrandt frequently used precisely such trompe-l'oeil frames, sills and fingers extending over the edge in his portraits during the years between 1639 and 1641. The highly detailed, smooth painting style and the relatively even lighting during this period also appear to bear witness to his efforts to create portraits with the same qualities as the Old Netherlandish masters. In his self-portrait, Rembrandt even goes one step further by portraying himself in sixteenth-century dress. This is neither a disguise nor a theatrical costume, as has occasionally been claimed, but rather a highly accurate, almost antiquarian reconstruction of a costume from the sixteenth century.[168] It is composed from elements which Rembrandt knew from a print after the portrait of Lucas van Leyden which Dürer had drawn.[169] The use of colour in the clothing reveals that Rembrandt was familiar not only with prints, but also with paintings from this time. The painting style, which is unusually smooth for him, and the soft, atmospheric tonality are also hints that here Rembrandt's aim was to "re-create" a painting of the early sixteenth century. In any case, in this self-portrait in the style of the sixteenth century he seems to want to place himself consciously in the tradition of the famous Northern painters of (self-) portraits; not as a courtier or a poet, but as a painter who was modelling himself on his illustrious Northern predecessors. In another self-portrait (p. 305, Cat. 158) from about

Albrecht Dürer
Christ Driving the Money Changers from the Temple, 1508/09
Woodcut, 12.8 × 9.7 cm (5 × 3 7/8 in.). Amsterdam, Rijksprentenkabinet

1640, Rembrandt wears a doublet in the fashion of the late fifteenth century, with fur trimming. The source for this was probably the portrait of Dieric Bouts (*c.* 1410/20–1475) from a series of portrait engravings of famous artists which Hieronymus Cock (1510–1570) had published in 1572.[170]

Geertje Dircks

Saskia was probably still alive when the young widow Geertje Dircks (*c.* 1613–1656) from Edam came to live with the family as a housekeeper and later to take care of Titus as a dry nurse (a nursemaid who did not breastfeed). Rembrandt apparently started a relationship with her soon after Saskia's death, because on 1 November 1642 he paid a large amount (1,200 guilders) to purchase the freedom of a certain Cornelis Jansz. from Edam, who had been captured by North African pirates (RD 1642/8). Jansz. was probably a relative of Geertje's. Rembrandt and Geertje lived as man and wife for several years, which is why his later biographer Houbraken assumed that Rembrandt had been married to "a little peasant woman from Raarep or Ransdorp in Waterland", who was small of stature, "but of a well-formed appearance and with a plump body".[171] The source of this information was doubtless Houbraken's own teacher, Samuel van Hoogstraten, who was apprenticed to Rembrandt during precisely this time (from about 1642 until 1646). Before Geertje moved to Amsterdam, she did indeed live with her brother in Ransdorp. She was not a peasant (she came from a seafaring family), but she did give that impression because in Amsterdam she probably continued to wear her regional dress, like most maid servants from Waterland. This included a tightly laced bodice which emphasised the advantages of her figure.[172] It is therefore tempting to recognise Geertje in the two Rembrandt drawings showing a woman in the traditional dress from Waterland (p. 300, Cat. D294, 295). One drawing is only a fragment but showed, according to an old description, a "Boerin en een slapend vrouwtje [Saskia?] met een kindtje aan de borst" (Peasant woman and a sleeping woman [Saskia?] with a child at her breast). On the back of the other drawing is written: "de minnemoer van Titus, soon van Rembrandt" (the nursemaid of Titus, Rembrandt's son).[173] Rembrandt is sure to have painted Geertje: we have proof that in 1647 a silk merchant exchanged a number of paintings by Rembrandt himself, including a portrait of Saskia, a self-portrait and "Rembrant's nursemaid" (RD 1647/1); in the next year, Geertje left in her will a portrait of herself, which was very probably also by Rembrandt (RD 1648/2). To date neither portrait of Geertje has been identified. It has been suggested that Geertje was the model for the inviting *Sarah waiting for Tobias?* (*A Young Woman in a Bed*; p. 356, Cat. 22) from 1647.[174] The intimate mood of the scene seems to suggest this, but without a portrait of Geertje to compare with, this remains conjecture.

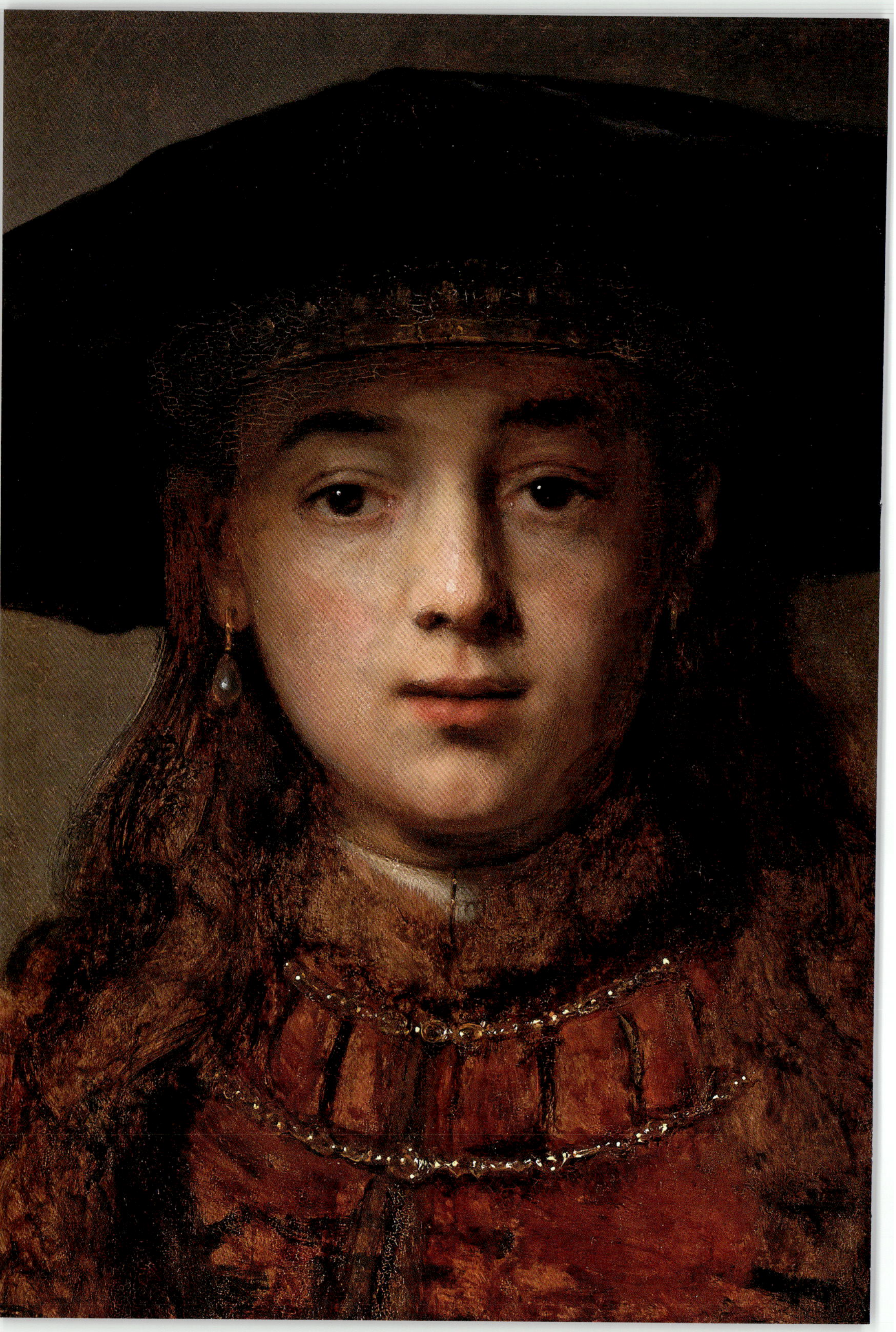

In January 1648, when Geertje was ill, she appointed the six-year-old Titus as her sole heir (RD 1648/2). Rembrandt had apparently given her Saskia's jewellery, for she now bequeathed it to Titus. Soon afterwards things went wrong, and the settlement of the separation from Rembrandt escalated into a drama. The probable cause was that Rembrandt had fallen in love with the young Hendrickje Stoffelsdr. Jegers (1626–1663) from Bredevoort in Gelderland, whom Geertje had engaged as a maid.[175] Hendrickje testified at Rembrandt's request that Geertje had left the house in June 1649 and was living in lodgings. It was agreed at the kitchen table that Geertje would receive 160 guilders alimony if she would redeem Saskia's pawned jewellery (RD 1649/4). Geertje was furious and had Rembrandt summoned before the Chamber of Matrimonial Affairs because she said he had "slept with her" and promised to marry her (RD 1649/3; 8). Rembrandt replied that there had been no talk of marriage (RD 1649/6; 1649/7). The magistrates did not force Rembrandt to marry Geertje. They generally did not do this when there was such a large class difference; however, they did sentence the artist to pay her an alimony amounting to 200 guilders "every year, for the rest of her life" (RD 1649/9).

This was not the end of the matter, however, because shortly afterwards Geertje was confined to a "Spinhuis" (bridewell) in Gouda because there were allegedly doubts about her state of mind, but in fact probably above all because she was harassing Rembrandt and had pawned Saskia's jewellery contrary to the agreement in their contract (RD 1650/5). There must have been declarations regarding her behaviour, which no longer exist, but which must have been highly incriminating, because a judge would not agree to such an arrangement upon demand for a period of at least eleven years without good cause. The application was officially lodged by her family, but Rembrandt would also have been involved behind the scenes. When Geertje was taken into custody and forcefully transported to Gouda, Rembrandt paid the (high) costs of the case (RD 1656/4). Eventually, a friend of Geertje's from Edam, Trijn Jacobs, succeeded in getting her released from the bridewell in May 1655, ahead of time (RD 1655/2). When Trijn informed Rembrandt about her plan of getting Geertje released, he warned her, "wagging his finger threateningly", that she would live to regret it (RD 1656/17). It is possible that Geertje Dircks was already ill at this point, but she is still listed in Rembrandt's bankruptcy proceedings in 1656 as a creditor (because of the alimony). That is the last trace we have of Geertje. She probably died soon afterwards.

Detail of: **Girl in a Picture Frame**, 1641
(see ill. p. 319)

Landscapes

At the end of the 1630s, after Rembrandt had occupied himself with painting autonomous landscapes (see pp. 111–113), from about 1640 onwards he also started to go on excursions out into the countryside with his sketchbook in order to record the surroundings of Amsterdam in a series of etchings and drawings of almost topographical accuracy (Cat. E165–191; Cat. D479–624). Unlike the dramatic and fanciful works of the 1630s, the landscape paintings which he made in the mid-1640s, such as *The Windmill* from 1645/46 (Cat. 140*) and the *Winter Landscape* from 1646 (pp. 334/335, Cat. 141), convey a more Dutch mood. Surprisingly, Rembrandt then gave up painting autonomous landscapes again. One exception is *Nocturnal Landscape with Flight into Egypt* from 1647 (pp. 336/337, Cat. 71), which displays the character of a landscape but takes as its subject a New Testament scene. The approach to the religious subject was quite different in the *Landscape with the Good Samaritan* from 1638 in Krakow (Cat. 136), in which the small sketch-like biblical figures clearly play a subordinate role and may even have been introduced as an afterthought.

For a long time, Rembrandt's landscapes were regarded as an anomaly in his oeuvre and as an isolated phenomenon in Dutch landscape painting. The fact that his landscapes nonetheless made a great impression is proved by paintings which were originally attributed to Rembrandt, but which in the meantime are thought to be the work of his assistants and followers. Thus, for example, Govert Flinck's signature was discovered on the rembrandtesque *Landscape with Obelisk* from 1638, today preserved in the Isabella Stewart Gardner Museum in Boston. The source of inspiration for this painting was Rembrandt's *Landscape with the Good Samaritan*, while his *Landscape with a Stone Bridge* from about 1638 in Amsterdam (pp. 218/219, Cat. 137) served as starting point for Flinck's painting with the same title in the Staatliche Museen zu Berlin. The landscapes by Jan Lievens, Ferdinand Bol and Philips Koninck (1619–1688) were undoubtedly also indebted to the works of Rembrandt.[176]

The fact that from 1638 Rembrandt took an increasing interest in the landscape setting of his biblical scenes can be seen in paintings such as *The Risen Christ Appearing to Mary Magdalene* from 1638 in London (p. 247, Cat. 63), *The Visitation* in Detroit from 1640 (p. 345, Cat. 64) and *David's Parting from Jonathan* from 1642 in St Petersburg (p. 339, Cat. 19). In *Susanna and the Elders* in Berlin, a painting on which Rembrandt worked between 1638 and 1647 (pp. 244/245, Cat. 18), the entire left half is taken up by a landscape. Here there is a clear distinction between Rembrandt's approach to landscape in mythological scenes from the 1630s (pp. 210, 214/215, 216/217, Cat. 96, 97, 99), which mostly focused on the foliage and less on horizons with fanciful architecture and atmospheric contrasts.

A Time of Transition and Reorientation

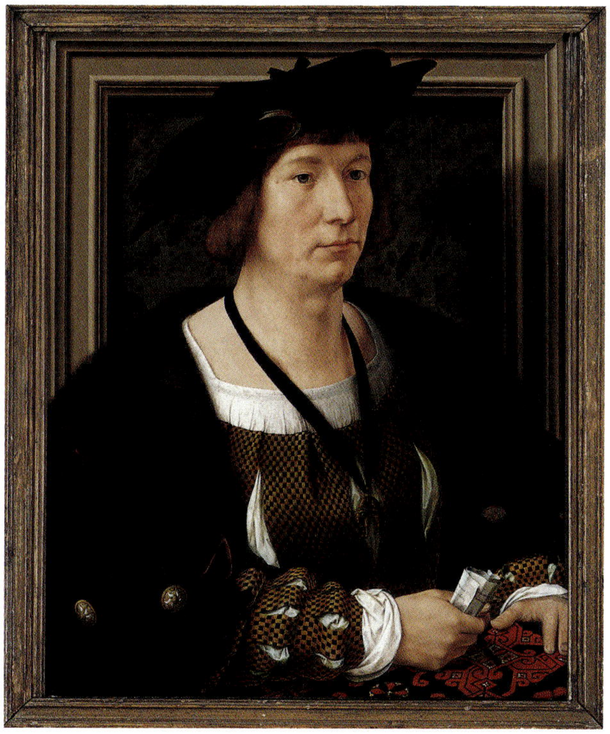

The years after *"The Night Watch"* marked a time of transition. During these years, Rembrandt reached the peak of his fame and material prosperity. In notarial deeds, he is described as the "far-famed painter Rembrant van Rhijn" (RD 1649/6; 1649/7). Already in 1641 a first biography of the artist appeared written by his former fellow-citizen Jan Jansz. Orlers, in which Rembrandt is described as a famous son of Leiden and "currently the most celebrated painter of our century" (RD 1641/8). In the same year, Philips Angel spoke in glowing terms about the "far-famed Rembrant" (RD 1641/5). Therefore, the sudden drop in his painting production at this very time poses one of the biggest riddles of Rembrandt's artistic career.[177] Moreover, during these years, each painting has the character of a highly personal experiment and there seems to be no logical development. The previously mentioned misconception that the clients had rejected *"The Night Watch"* because the picture was too dark, led to the assumption that Rembrandt's reputation deteriorated quickly and that he no longer received any portrait commissions. Thus, the myth was born that the misunderstood and ignored genius got into financial difficulties and died in poverty and forgotten by the world. Contemporary documents, however, do not give any indication that Rembrandt's fame ever diminished during his lifetime. Already in his early Leiden years he was a famous artist and he would remain so until the end of his life.

Jan Gossaert, **Hendrik III, Count of Nassau-Breda**, *c.* 1516/17
Oil on panel, 57.2 × 45.8 cm (22 ⅝ × 18 in.)
Fort Worth, Texas, Kimbell Art Museum

Also, Saskia's death in 1642 was seen as the reason why the grieving widower had stopped painting, and fell into oblivion. We do not know how Rembrandt felt about the loss of Saskia, but in the time around her death, he reworked a large, ambitious portrait of her (p. 201, Cat. 317), which he had already started in 1633/34. It shows Saskia in profile and in half-length in a red costume from the early sixteenth century.[178] As in his self-portrait from 1640, this is not just some theatrical costume or a picturesque disguise; but it betrays Rembrandt's almost archaeological knowledge of dress from the time around 1530, which he must have acquired by studying German sixteenth-century prints. Like the (self-)portraits from this time, the painting is highly detailed and originally arched at the top in imitation of the paintings of the sixteenth century.[179]

Still, the image persists that in the years between 1642 and 1651 because of the change in taste, the market for rembrantesque works became saturated and his style was no longer in demand amongst connoisseurs.[180] The opposite view explaining Rembrandt's fall in production is that he would have concentrated on the creation of only a few exclusive works for a select audience of art lovers.[181] Indeed, his *Christ and the Woman Taken in Adultery* (p. 349, Cat. 66) from 1644 was offered for the large sum of 1,500 guilders by the art dealer Johannes de Renialme (*c.* 1593–1657; RD 1657/2). The work was later admired in the cabinet of Hinlopen and in the collection of Willem Six (1662–1733), in whose auction of 1734 it was described as "the best by him [Rembrandt] ever seen, f. 2510". Six also owned *Saskia Uylenburgh in Sixteenth-Century Costume* (p. 201, Cat. 317), which Rembrandt had completed in 1642 and which is described as "as artful as seen by him". Indeed, particularly these detailed works from the 1640s seem to have been highly prized by (later) art lovers. But exactly because of this the question remains as to why Rembrandt painted so few of these pictures between 1642 and 1651, and why he changed them so radically.

As van de Wetering explained, it seems plausible that Rembrandt's "crisis" was more of an artistic nature.[182] In *"The Night Watch"*, he had achieved the "greatest motion" and heightened his spotlight effects to a maximum. It must have been clear to him that he had reached his goal in these respects and that it was time for a change. In *The Holy Family* from 1645 (p. 341, Cat. 67), we can observe a transition to much quieter compositions with figures who are more reflective and without the strong emotions or gestures of his former works. Restlessness can be detected only in the angels flying in the top left-hand corner. Instead of the strong, isolated spotlights, various light sources have been introduced. The light is reflected into the room lending the figures an almost mysterious aura. Also, Rembrandt introduced more colour into the picture by means of the little cover in warm red in the foreground. Hitherto, he had always favoured the strong lighting contrasts at the expense of colourfulness in his paintings.

His painting *Christ and the Woman Taken in Adultery*, which was so highly admired by his contemporaries, also shows a greater colourfulness and reflected light illuminating the space with a sort of supernatural glow. The small figures are worked out in great detail and seem like a return to the small-figured compositions of the early 1630s, but here the restrained protagonists stand quietly next to each other; there are neither violent emotions nor wild gestures. During the painting process, Rembrandt undertook a large number of changes to the composition which show that he was striving for a frontal rather than a diagonal composition. Notwithstanding the fact that the work with its small, detailed figures was offered at an extravagant price and clearly appealed to the taste of art lovers, it remained a one-off experiment and Rembrandt never returned to this solution again. This indicates that his experimentation with new artistic solutions rather had the character of a personal quest than that he was solely aiming to satisfy the wishes of an audience of potential buyers.

The striking aspect about Rembrandt's experiments towards new pictorial solutions is that he apparently questioned what was considered to be the essence of his art: the display of the most (e)motion and the strongly bundled light effects. This shift in his core values can be clearly seen in the fact that he drastically revised at least three important paintings which he had begun during the 1630s (Cat. 18, 105, 317). *Susanna and the Elders* (p. 245, Cat. 18), for example, was already largely finished around 1638, but it was revised in some important aspects by Rembrandt in 1647. From the composition, which was based on a work by his old teacher Lastman, he removed all the elements that captured a fleeting moment, such as the startled swans flying away in alarm or the overturned vase from which a liquid is pouring. This can be seen in the X-rays of the painting as well as in a pupil's drawing after it. Also, the aggressive gesture of Susanna's attacker has been mitigated.

In works like *Abraham's Sacrifice* from 1635 (p. 231, Cat. 11) and *Belshazzar's Feast* (pp. 236/237, Cat. 13), which was produced around the same time, it had been Rembrandt's aim to capture precisely such fleeting moments: Abraham's knife and the spilt wine are suspended in mid-air, as if frozen in time.[183] The tempered emotions and movements would become a characteristic of Rembrandt's late paintings, in which feelings are indicated rather than depicted. He also increased the colourfulness of his paintings: Susanna's cloak (in the right foreground) was initially cream-coloured but was overpainted in a deep red lacquer.[184] Also the *Danae* (pp. 240/241, Cat. 105), which was signed by Rembrandt in 1636 was drastically reworked by him around 1643.[185] The god Jupiter comes to Danae in the form of a supernatural light that no longer shines down on her in a single beam, but that seems to be reflected from her, so that the entire bed with its curtains are bathed in a mysterious glow.

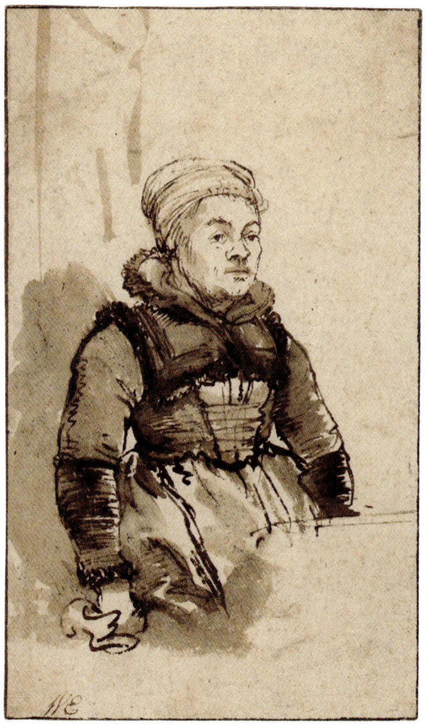

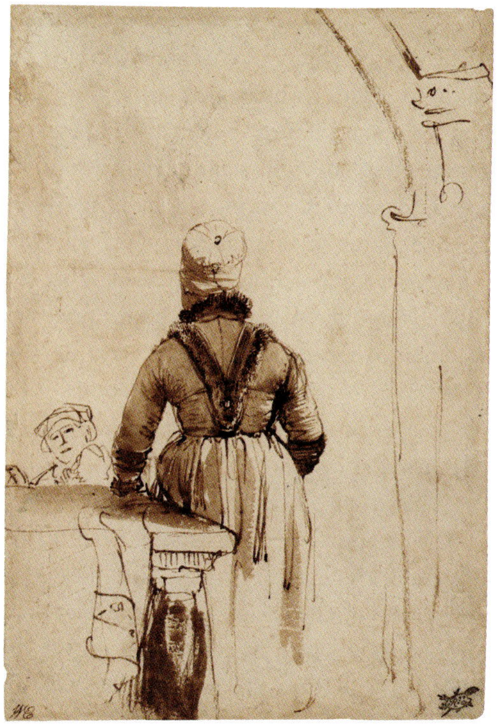

In the mid-1640s, Rembrandt's earlier fascination with illusionism and trompe-l'oeil effects still played an important role, albeit in a different fashion. In *Girl Leaning on a Stone Sill* (p. 357, Cat. 322) from 1645 and *Sarah Waiting for Tobias? (A Young Woman in a Bed*; p. 356, Cat. 22) from 1647, it looks as if the life-size figures are actually leaning out of the picture. In the eighteenth century, Roger de Piles (1635–1709) related that Rembrandt had placed a portrait of his servant girl in the window to mislead the passers-by.[186] Although the figures look deceptively real from a distance, they lack the detailed, meticulous execution of the trompe-l'oeil portraits of the early 1640s. From 1645, Rembrandt made use of broader, more lively brushwork, which shows similarities to the Venetian painting style of which Titian was the most important representative (see pp. 372–373, 375–379).

Woman in North Holland Dress, Half-Figure, Seen from the Front, *c.* 1637
Pen and brush in brown, 13 × 7.8 cm (5 1/8 × 3 in.). London, British Museum

Standing Woman in North Holland Dress, Seen from the Back, *c.* 1637
Pen and brush in brown, 22.2 × 15.4 cm (8 3/4 × 6 in.). Haarlem, Teylers Museum

Another factor which possibly contributed to the fall in Rembrandt's production may have been his increased activity as a teacher. Joachim von Sandrart, who lived in Amsterdam between 1637 and about 1645, even reports of "almost innumerable distinguished children who learned from him."[187] Each paid about 100 guilders a year to Rembrandt, which, together with the sale of their works, will have brought him, according to von Sandrart, an additional income of at least 2,500 guilders a year. Houbraken reports that Rembrandt had to rent a warehouse on the Bloemgracht in order to provide room in which the numerous pupils could practise.[188] During the 1640s, Rembrandt's apprentices included, amongst others, Samuel van Hoogstraten, the highly talented Carel Fabritius (1622–1654) and Willem Drost (1633–1659).[189]

In addition, Rembrandt focused on etchings and drawings more intensely. Many of his etchings exist in several states, and ambitious etched works like *Christ Preaching* (*"The Hundred Guilder Print"*; Cat. E51) took just as long to complete as a painting. Many drawings and etchings from this period testify to the fact that Rembrandt (with or without apprentices) regularly went on excursions out into the countryside around Amsterdam in order to draw the landscape. In the past, this renewed attention to the countryside has sometimes been interpreted as a flight from personal problems – that Rembrandt was seeking comfort and relaxation in nature. Edmé-François Gersaint (1694–1750), who published the first catalogue raisonné of Rembrandt's etchings (1751), presented a very different story in the 1730s. He pointed out that from 1645 Rembrandt had been a close friend of the young art lover Jan Six (1618–1700); of whom he made an ambitious portrait etching in 1647 (p. 389, Cat. E229). According to Gersaint, most of the landscapes were created during Rembrandt's excursions to the country house owned by Six in the vicinity of Amsterdam. Rembrandt was always so absorbed by his work that he experienced none of the usual pleasures of country life. In order to satisfy his desire to work, he always carried small prepared etching plates with him so that he could also continue working outdoors.[190] This story was always dismissed as an anecdote, but it illustrates the extraordinary intensity with which Rembrandt worked – of which already his contemporaries reported. Even during his Leiden years, Huygens was concerned about the health of the young artists Rembrandt and Lievens, because they both spent all their time painting and did not permit themselves any normal pleasures by way of recreation. This obsessive drive had clearly not lessened in the 1640s. Also Baldinucci reports that Rembrandt worked constantly "without taking a rest", and Von Sandrart also wrote that he was "a very hard working and untiring man".[191]

Detail of: **Self-Portrait**, *c.* 1645
(see ill. p. 333)

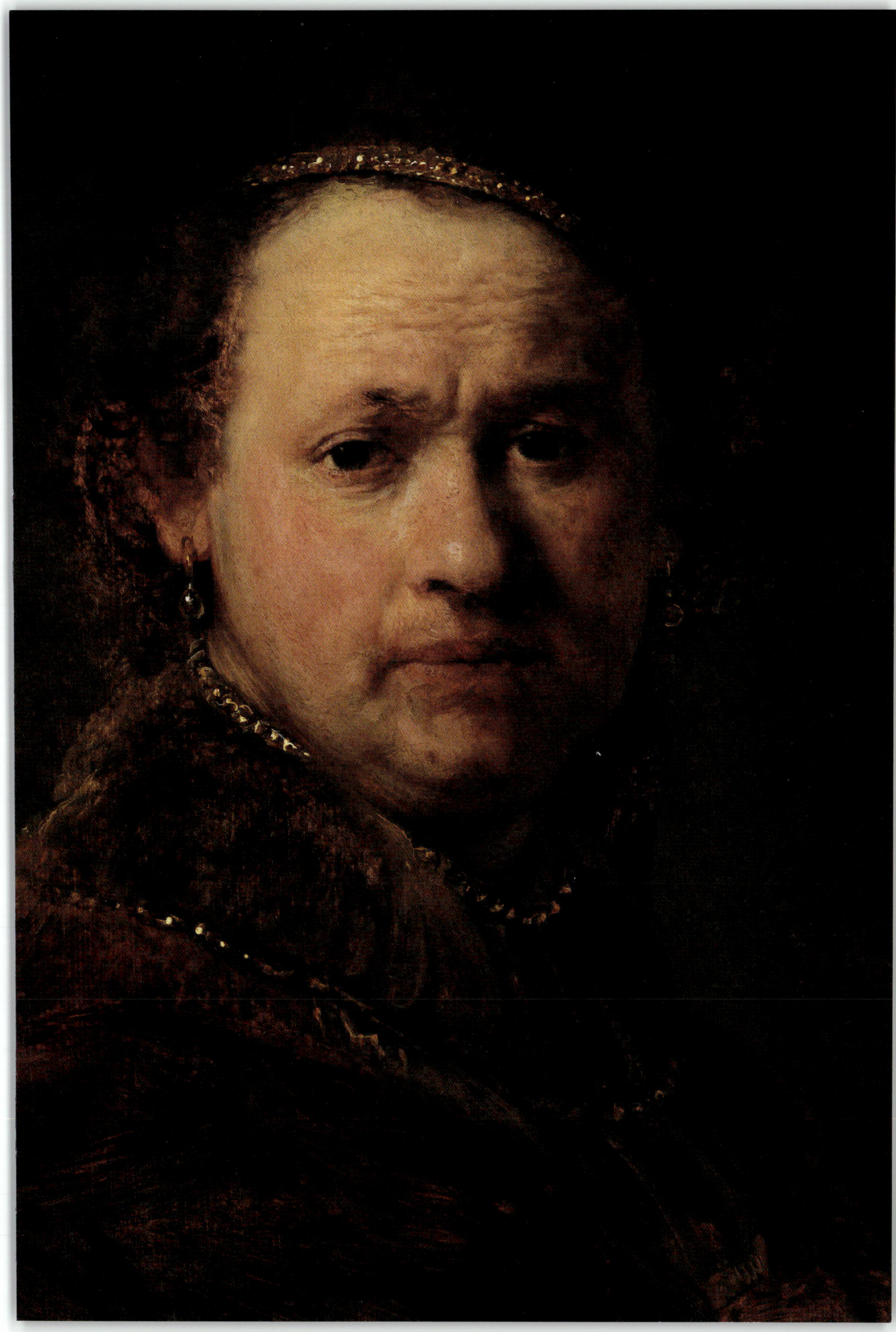

Self-Portrait, *c.* 1640
Oil on panel, 72.2 × 58.3 cm (28 3⁄8 × 22 3⁄4 in.)
Madrid, Museo Nacional Thyssen-Bornemisza

Page 306
Portrait of Andries de Graeff, 1639
Oil on canvas, 199 × 123.4 cm (78 1⁄3 × 48 5⁄8 in.)
Hessen Kassel Heritage, Gemäldegalerie Alte Meister

Page 307
Portrait of Eleazar Swalmius, 1637
Oil on canvas, 132 × 109 cm (51 3⁄4 × 42 3⁄4 in.)
Antwerp, Koninklijk Museum voor Schone Kunsten

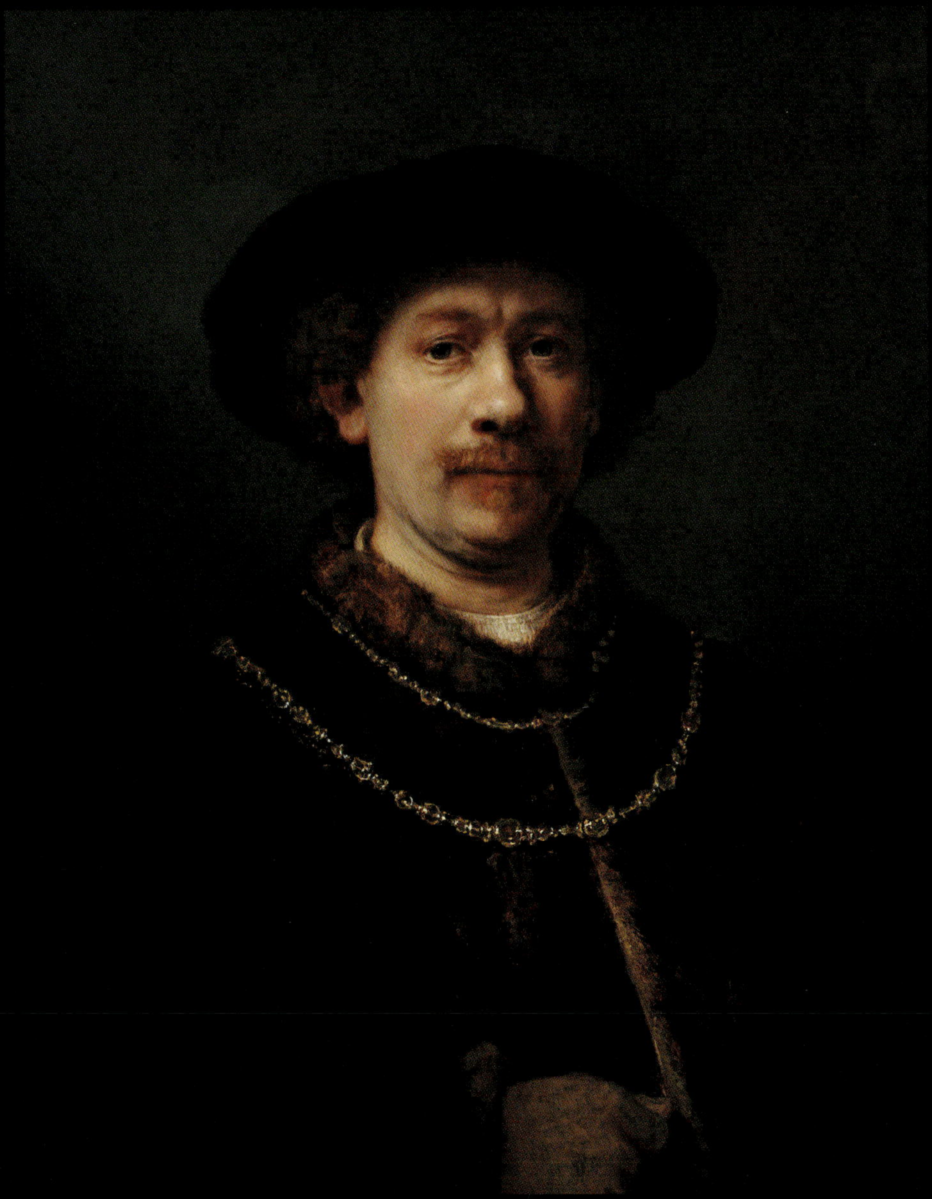

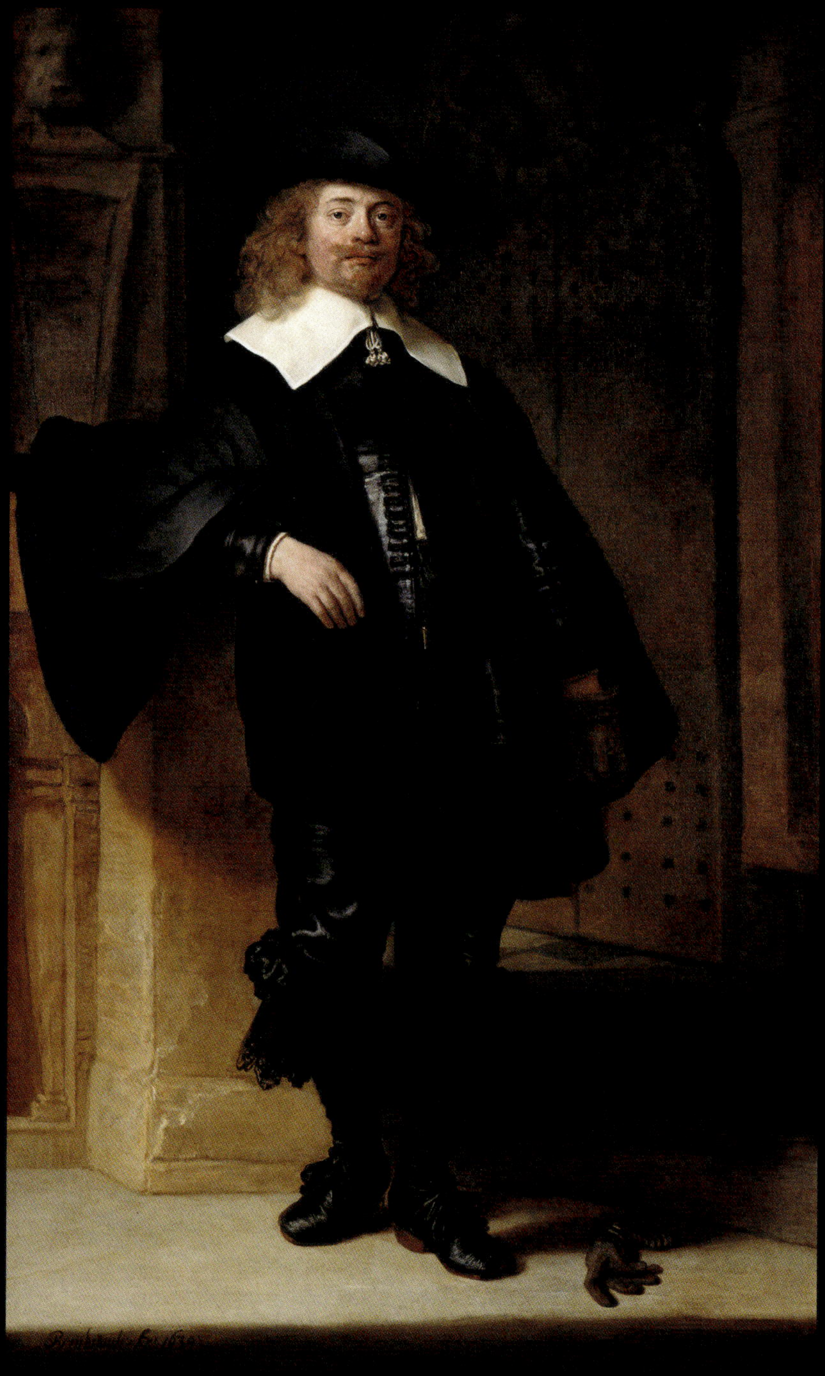

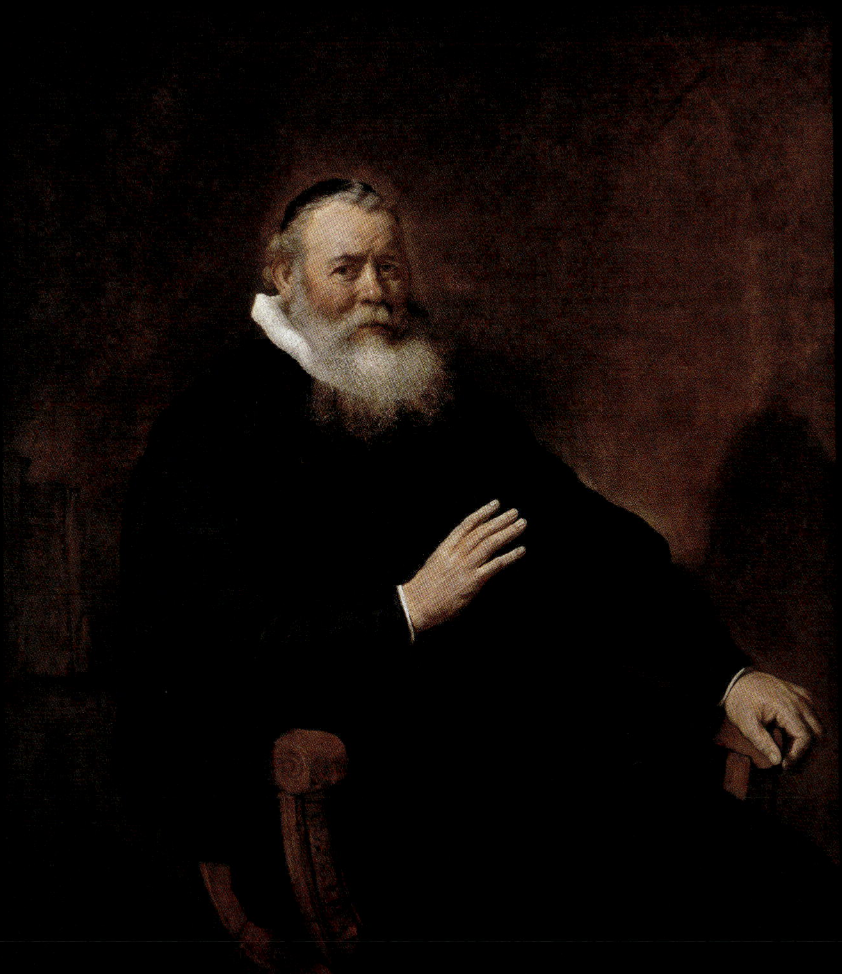

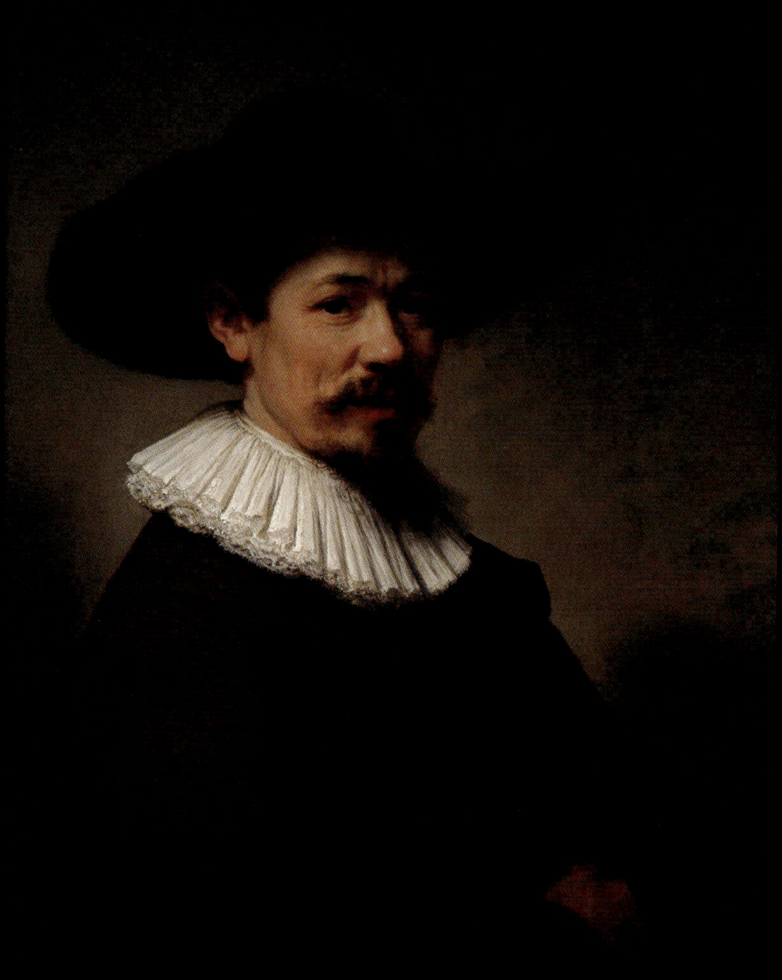

Portrait of Herman Doomer, 1640
Oil on panel, 75.2 × 55.2 cm (29 5/8 × 21 3/4 in.)
New York, The Metropolitan Museum of Art,
Bequest of Mrs H. O. Havemeyer, 1929

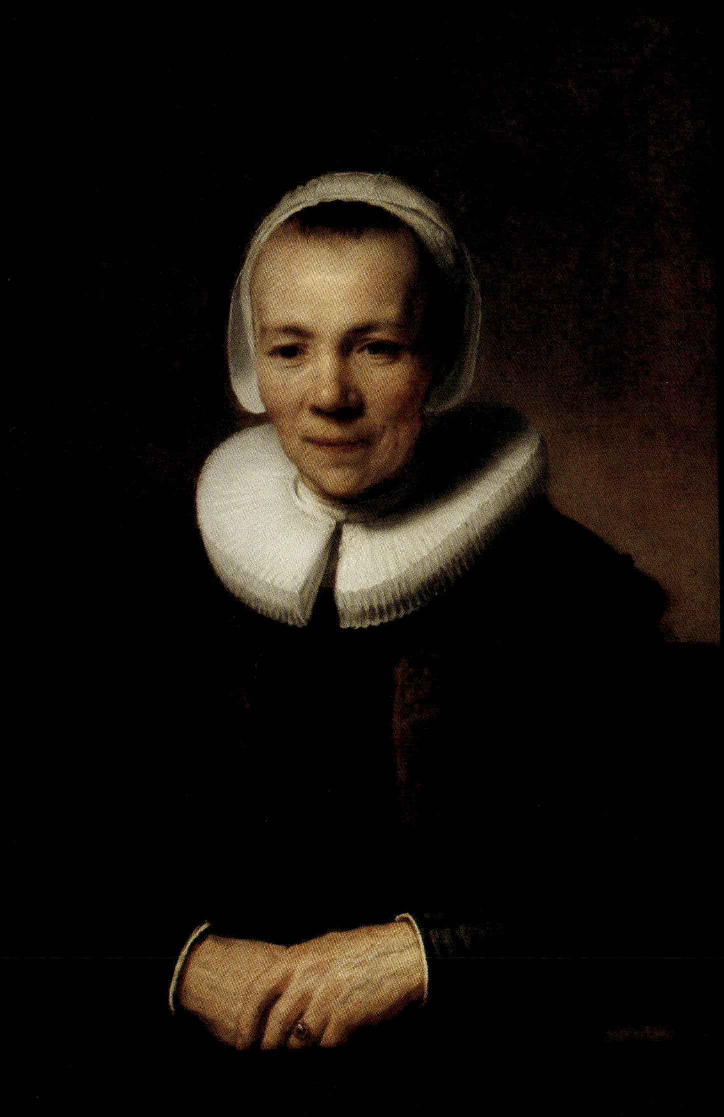

Portrait of Baertje Martens, 1640
Oil on panel, 75.1 × 55.9 cm (29 ⅝ × 22 ⅛ in.)
St Petersburg, The State Hermitage Museum

Portrait of a Man Holding a Hat, *c.* 1640
Oil on panel, 79.5 × 69.4 cm (31 ¼ × 27 ⅓ in.)
Los Angeles, The Armand Hammer Collection,
Gift of the Armand Hammer Foundation

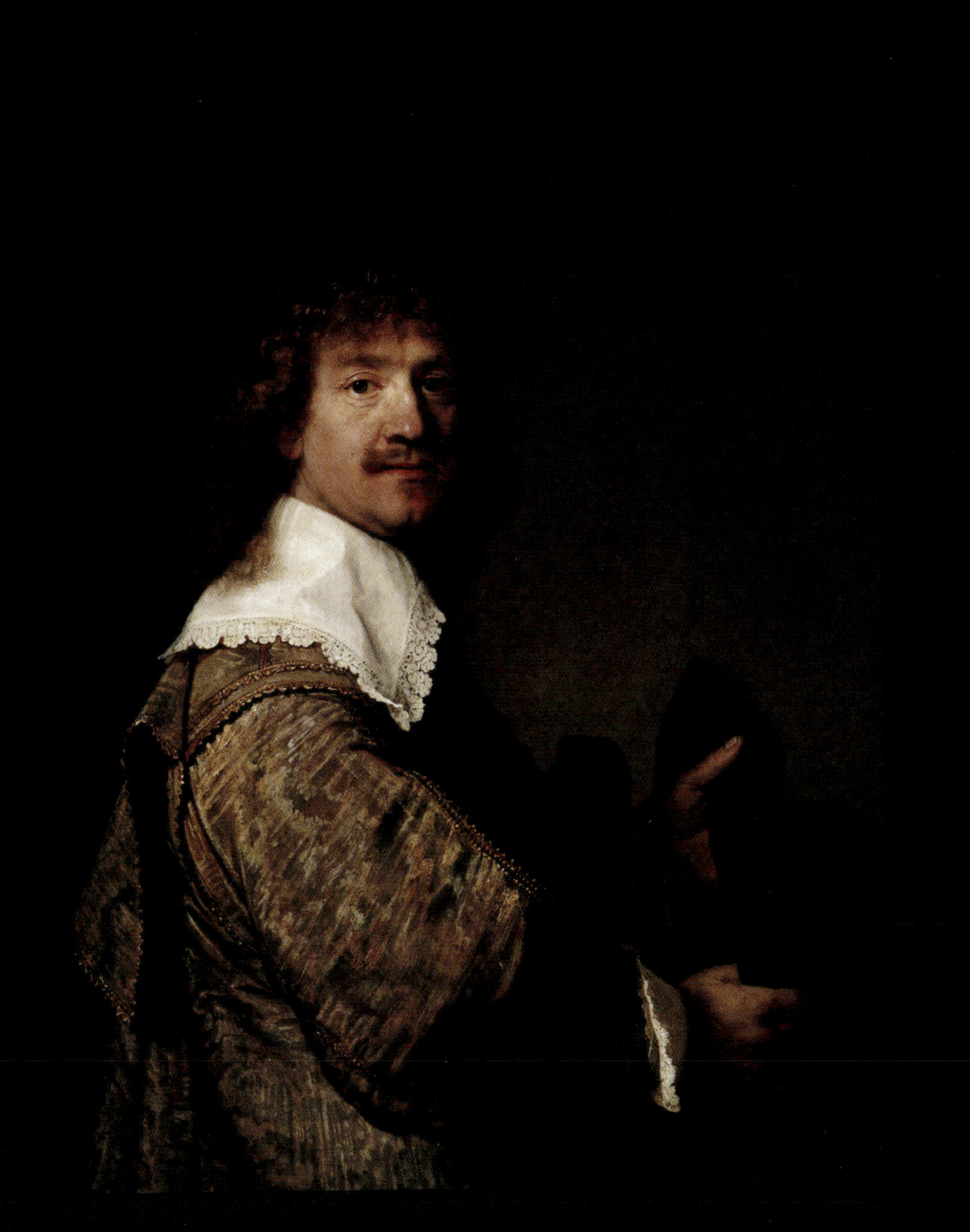

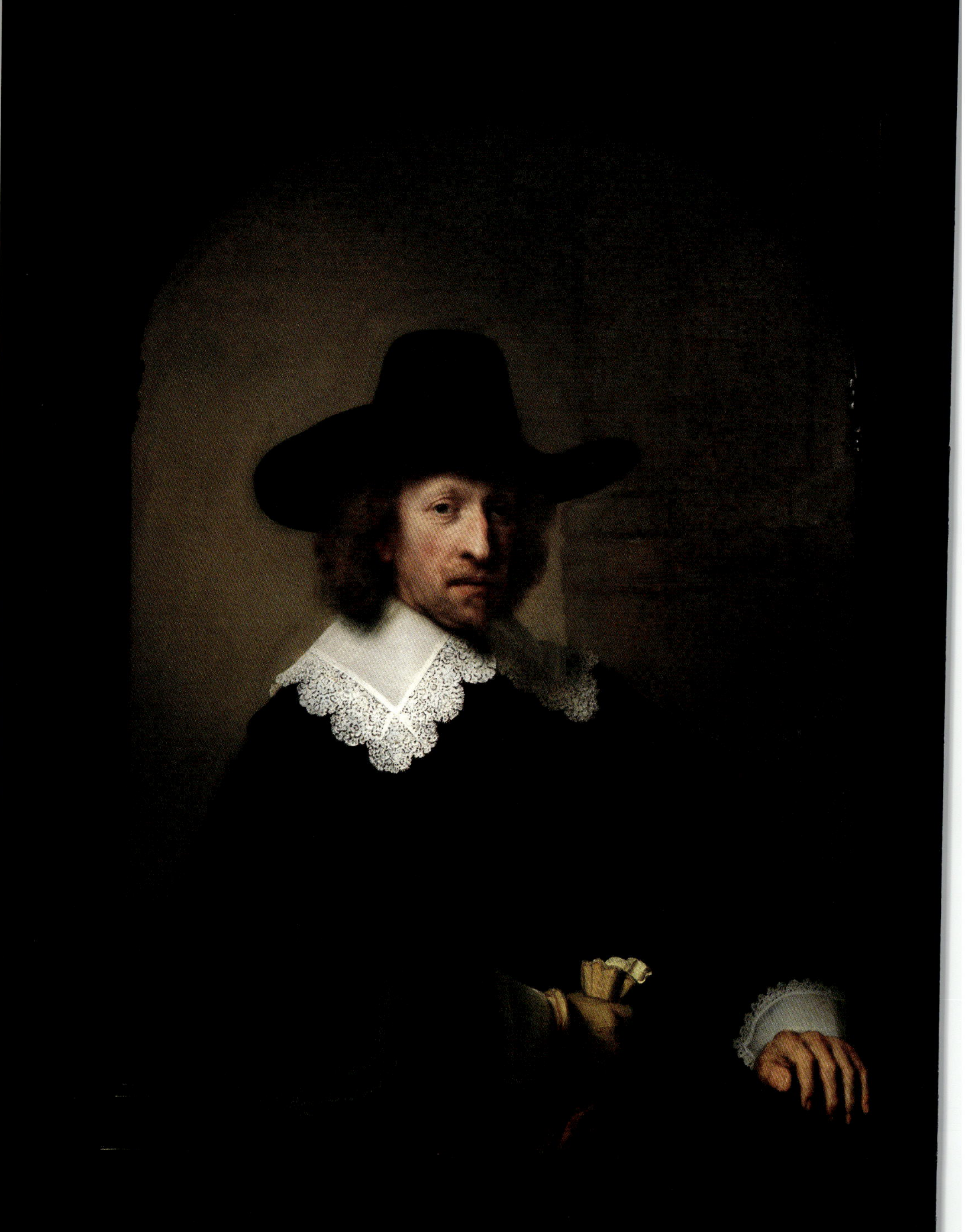

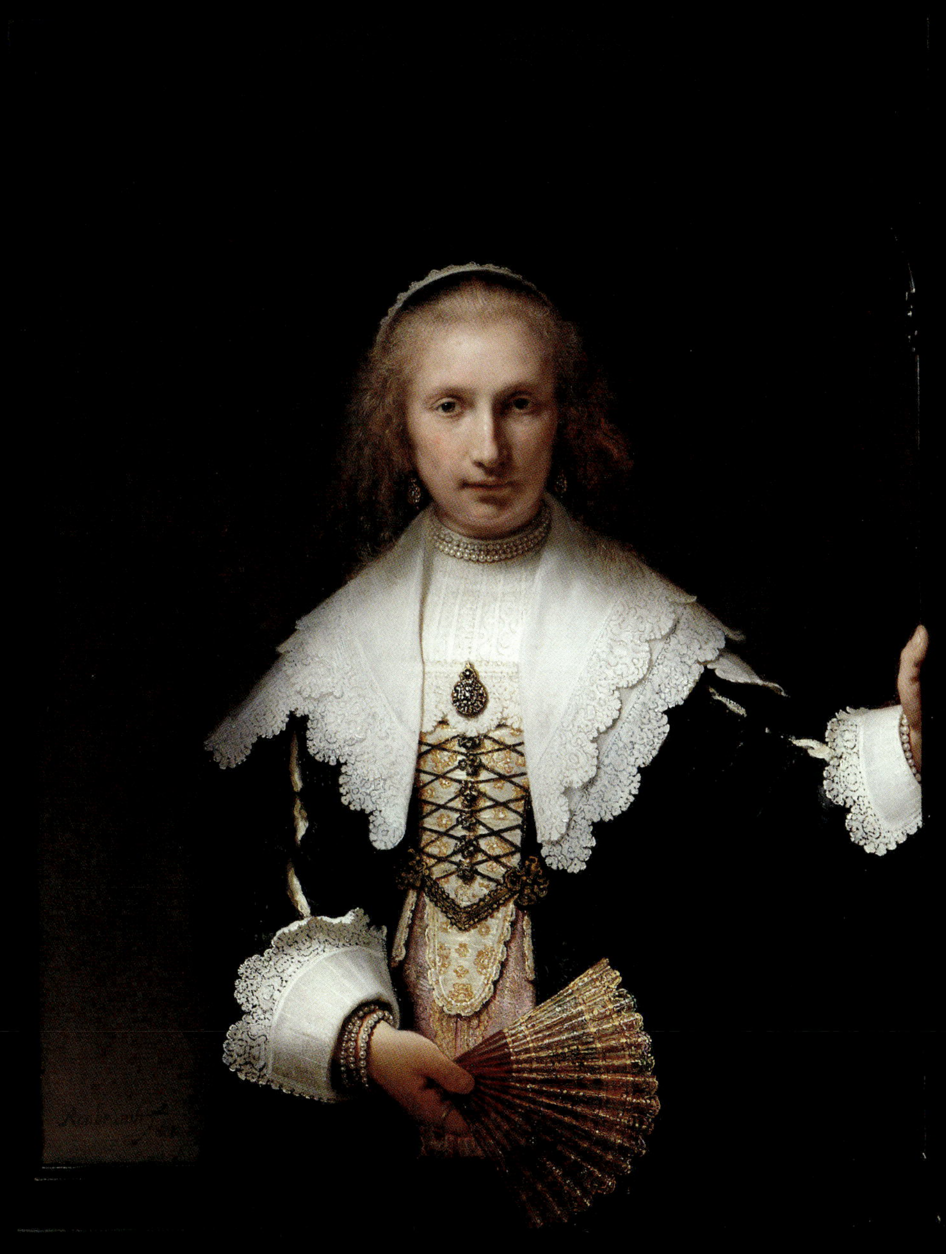

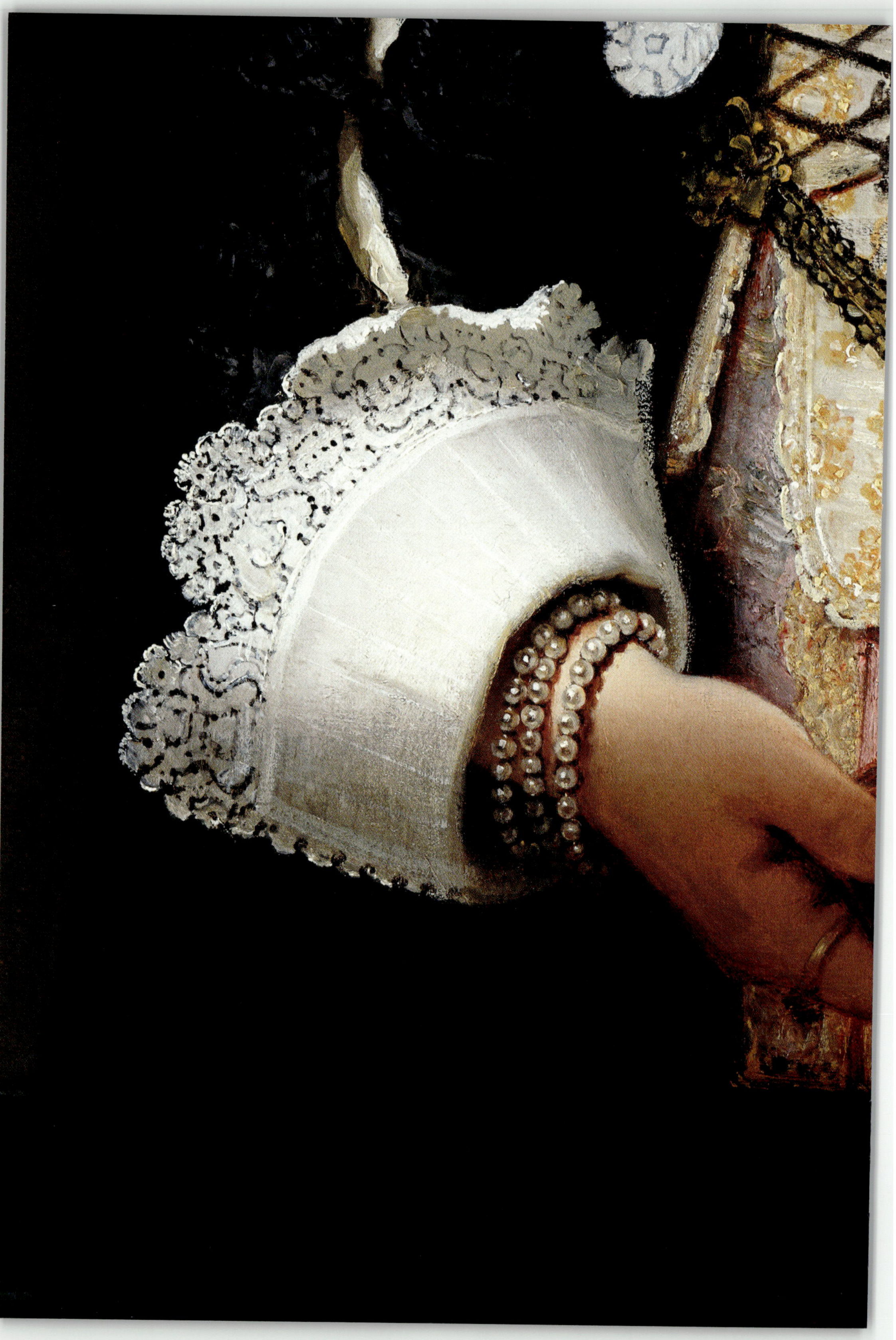

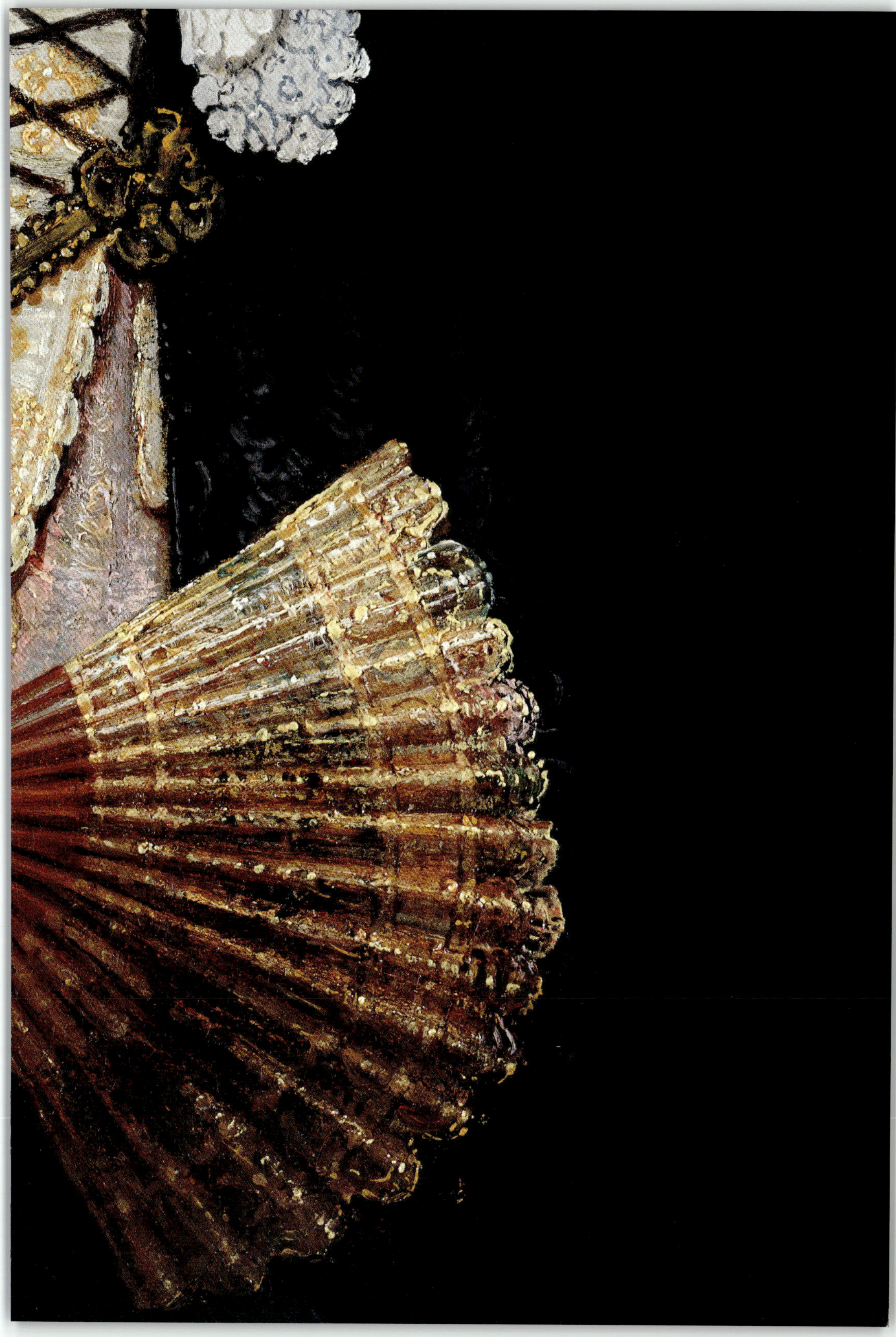

Page 312
Portrait of Nicolaes van Bambeeck, 1641
Oil on canvas, 105.5 × 84 cm (41 ½ × 33 ⅛ in.)
Brussels, Koninklijke Musea voor Schone Kunsten van België

Page 313
Portrait of Agatha Bas, 1641
Oil on canvas, 105.4 × 83.9 cm (41 ½ × 33 ⅛ in.)
London, Royal Collection
(detail pages 314/315)

Portrait of a Woman, 1641
Oil on panel, 99.5 × 81.5 cm (39 ⅛ × 32 ⅛ in.)
Amsterdam, Collectie Six

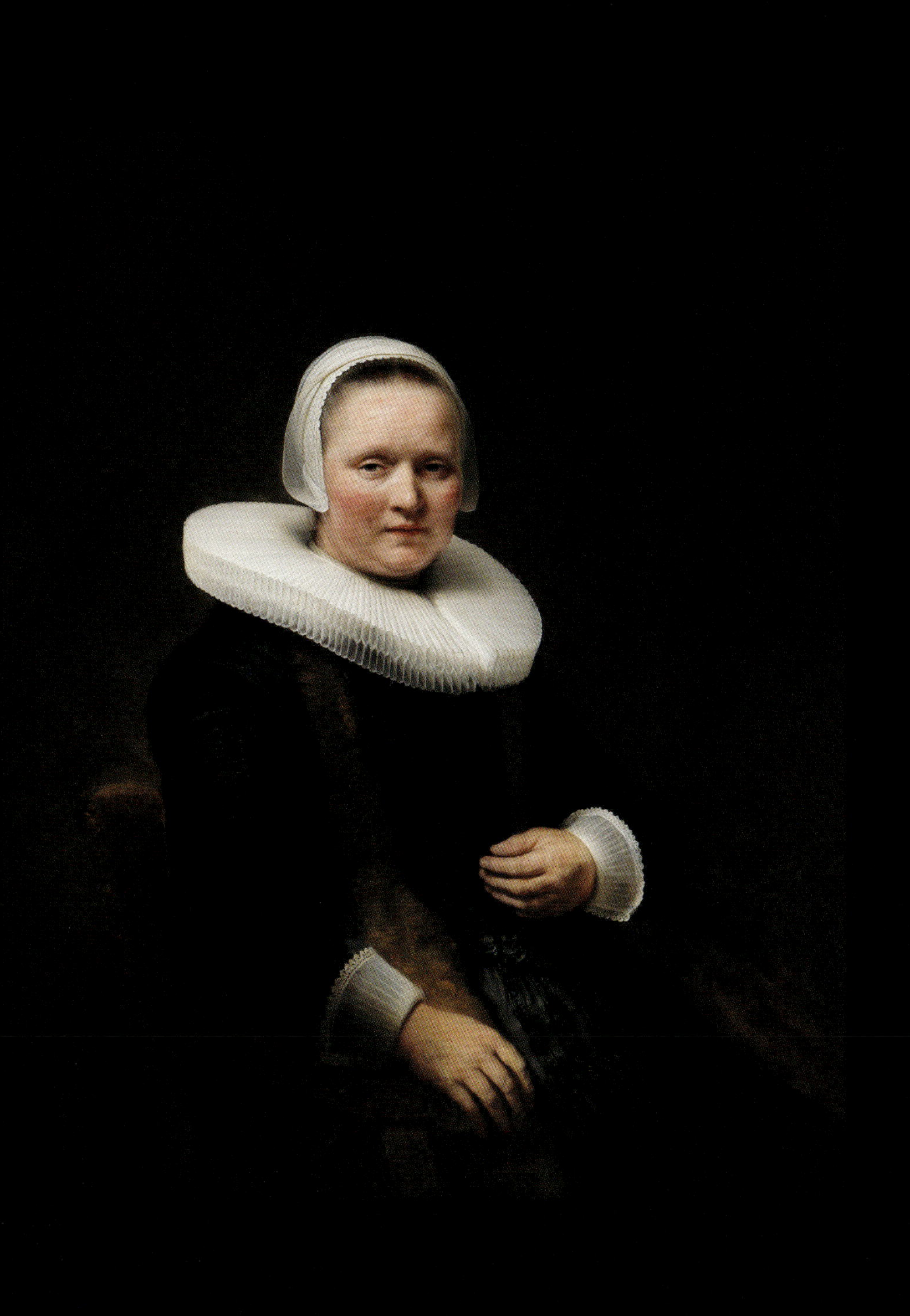

Girl in a Picture Frame, 1641
Oil on panel, 105.5 × 76.3 cm (41 ½ × 30 ⅛ in.)
Warsaw, Zamek Królewski w Warszawie

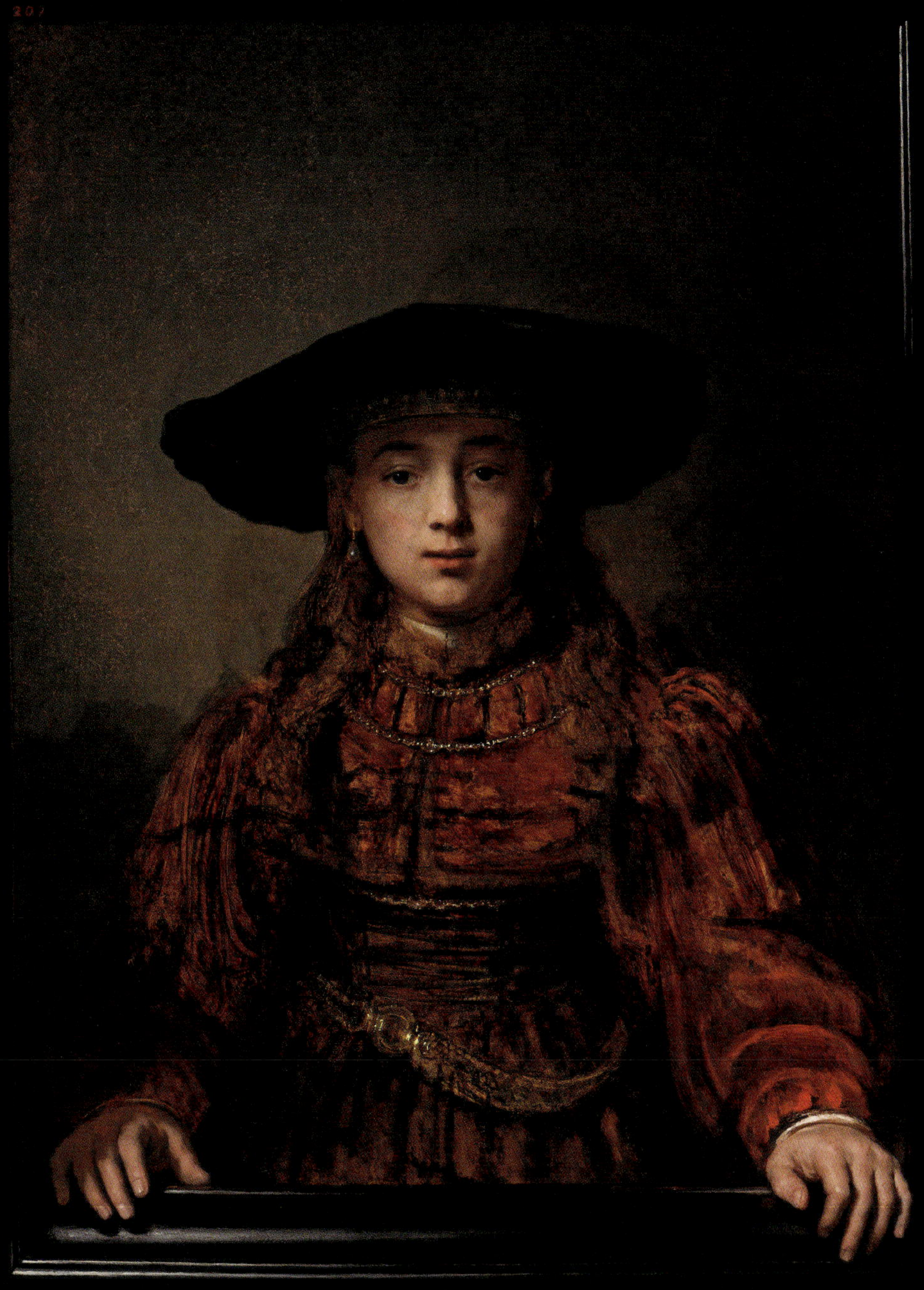

Portrait of a Woman from the van Weede Family, *c.* 1641
Oil on panel, 107 × 82 cm (42 ⅛ × 32 ¼ in.)
Amsterdam, Rijksmuseum, on loan from the van Weede Family Foundation

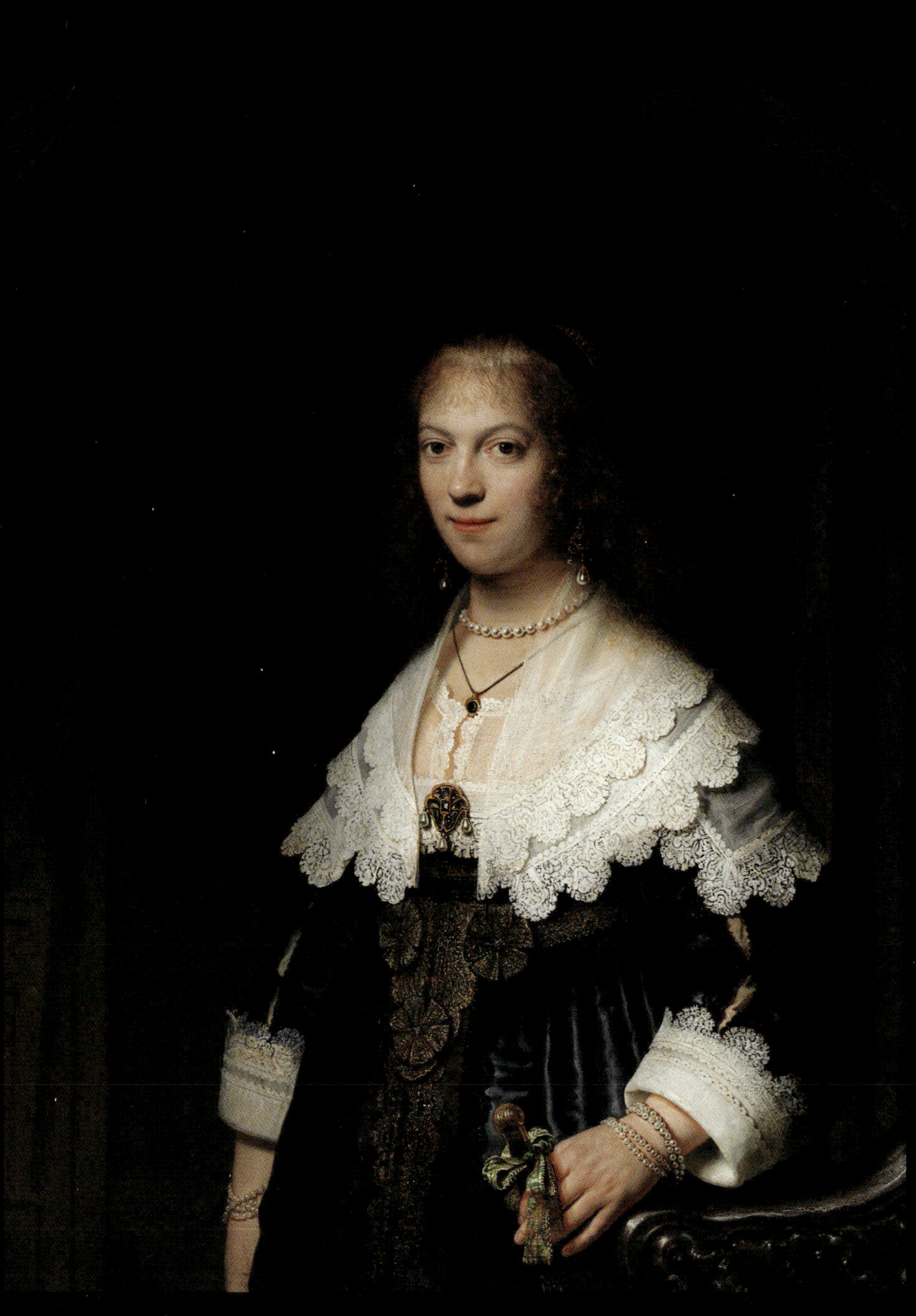

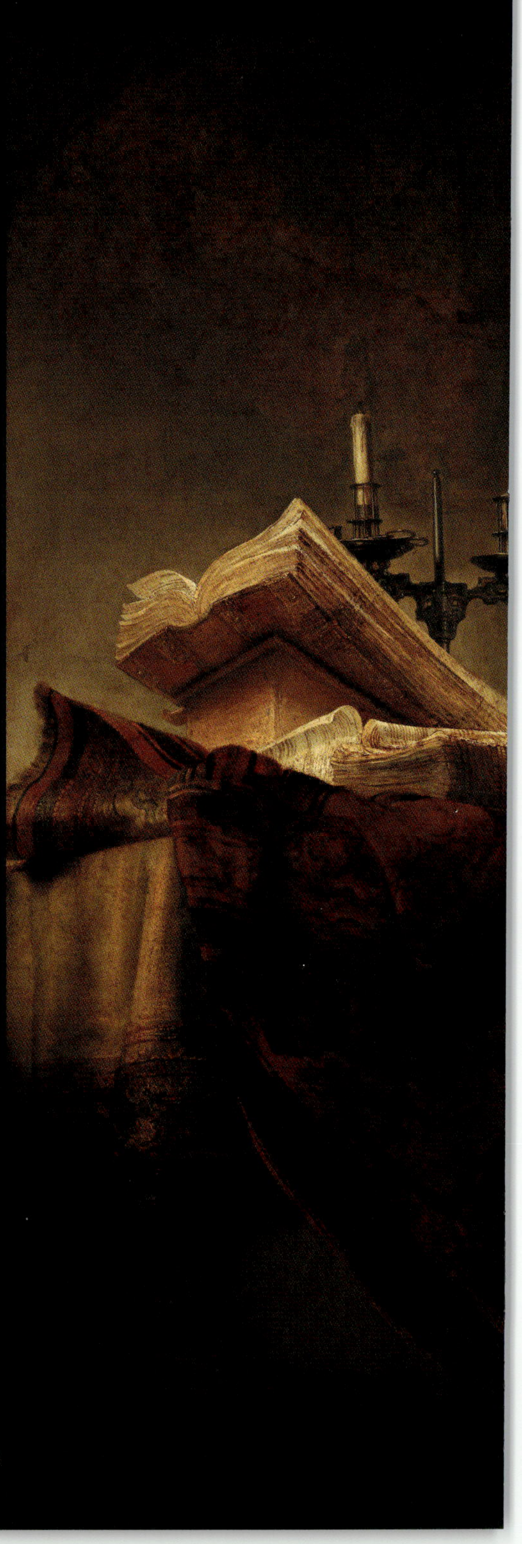

Double Portrait of Cornelis Claesz. Anslo and His Wife Aeltje Gerritsdr. Schouten, 1641
Oil on canvas, 173.7 × 207.6 cm
(68⅜ × 81¾ in.)
Staatliche Museen zu Berlin,
Gemäldegalerie

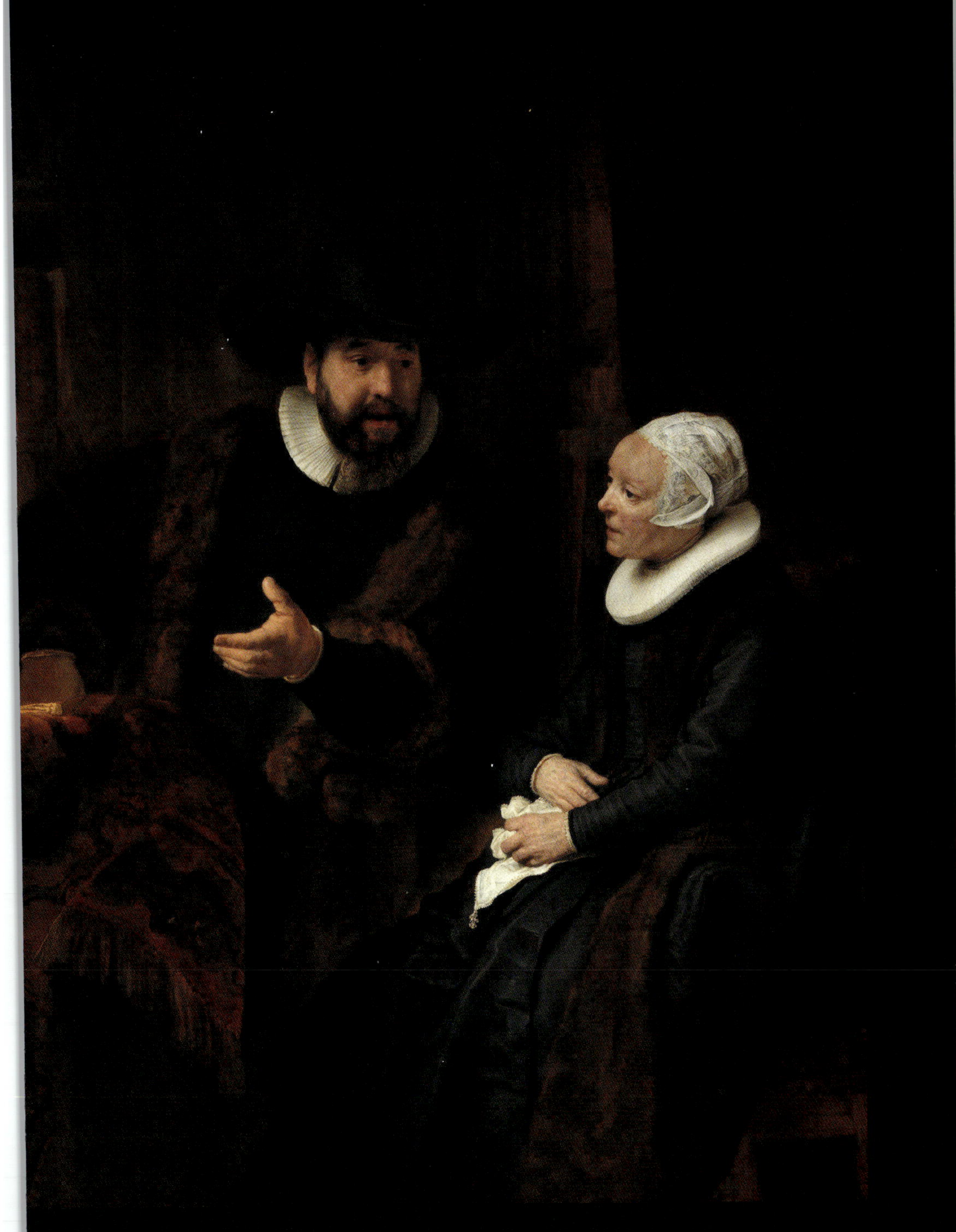

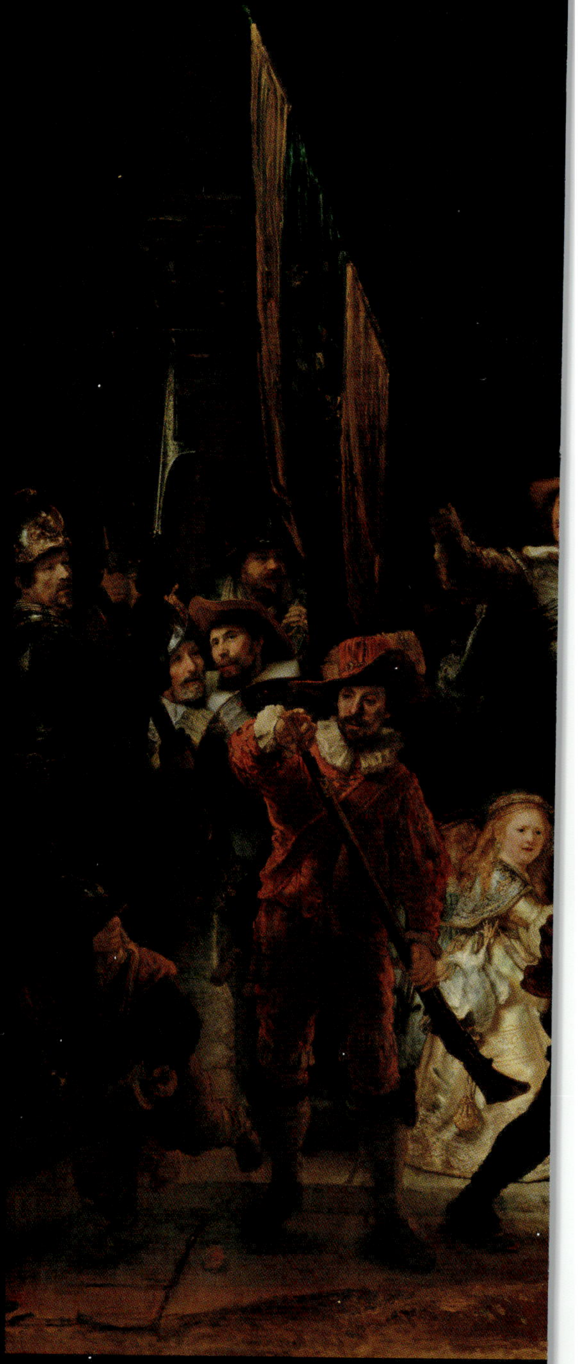

The Militia Company of Captain Frans Banninck Cocq ("The Night Watch"), 1642
Oil on canvas, 363 × 438 cm
(142 ¾ × 172 ½ in.)
Amsterdam, Rijksmuseum,
on permanent loan from the
City of Amsterdam
(detail pages 326/327)

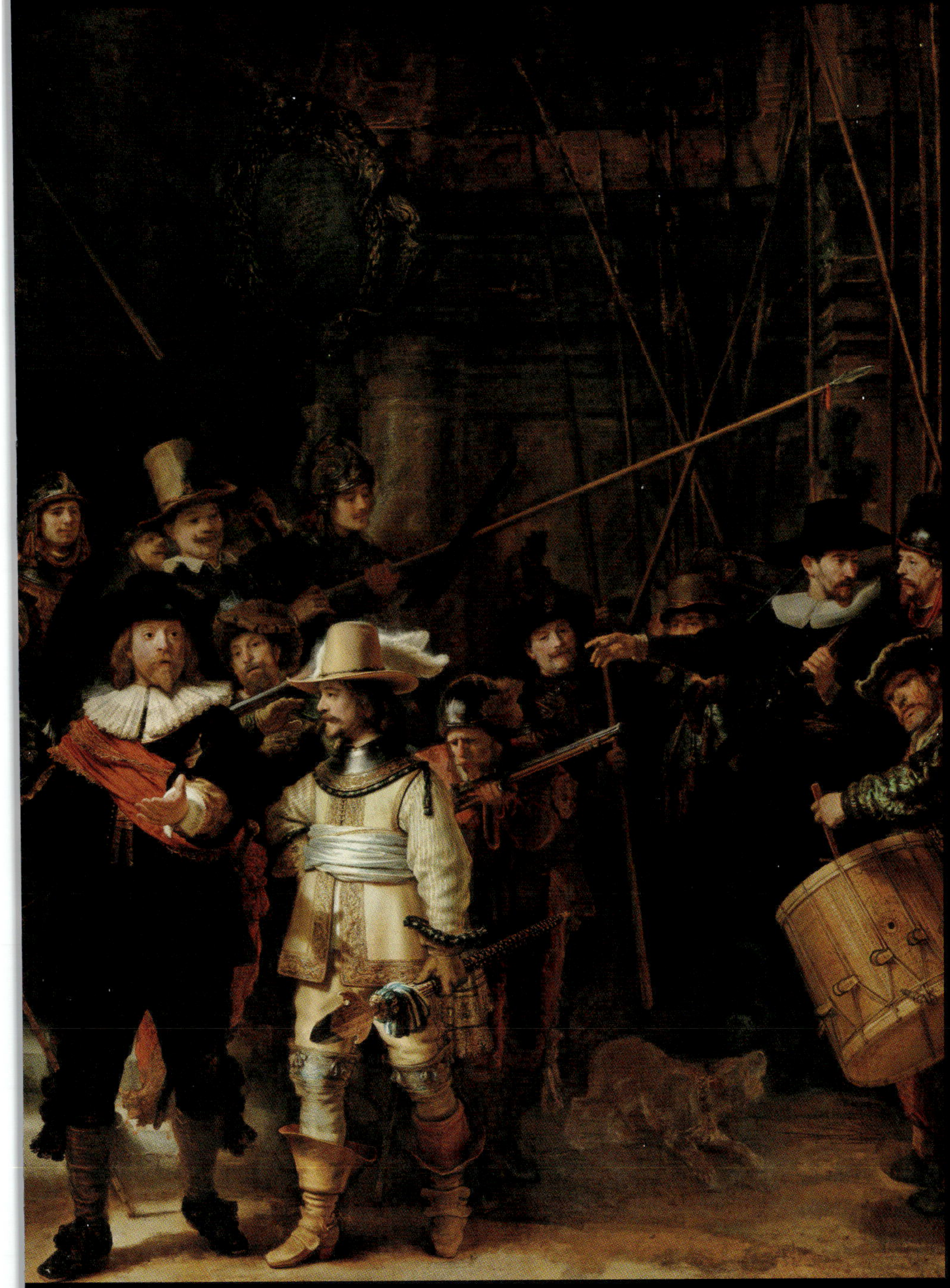

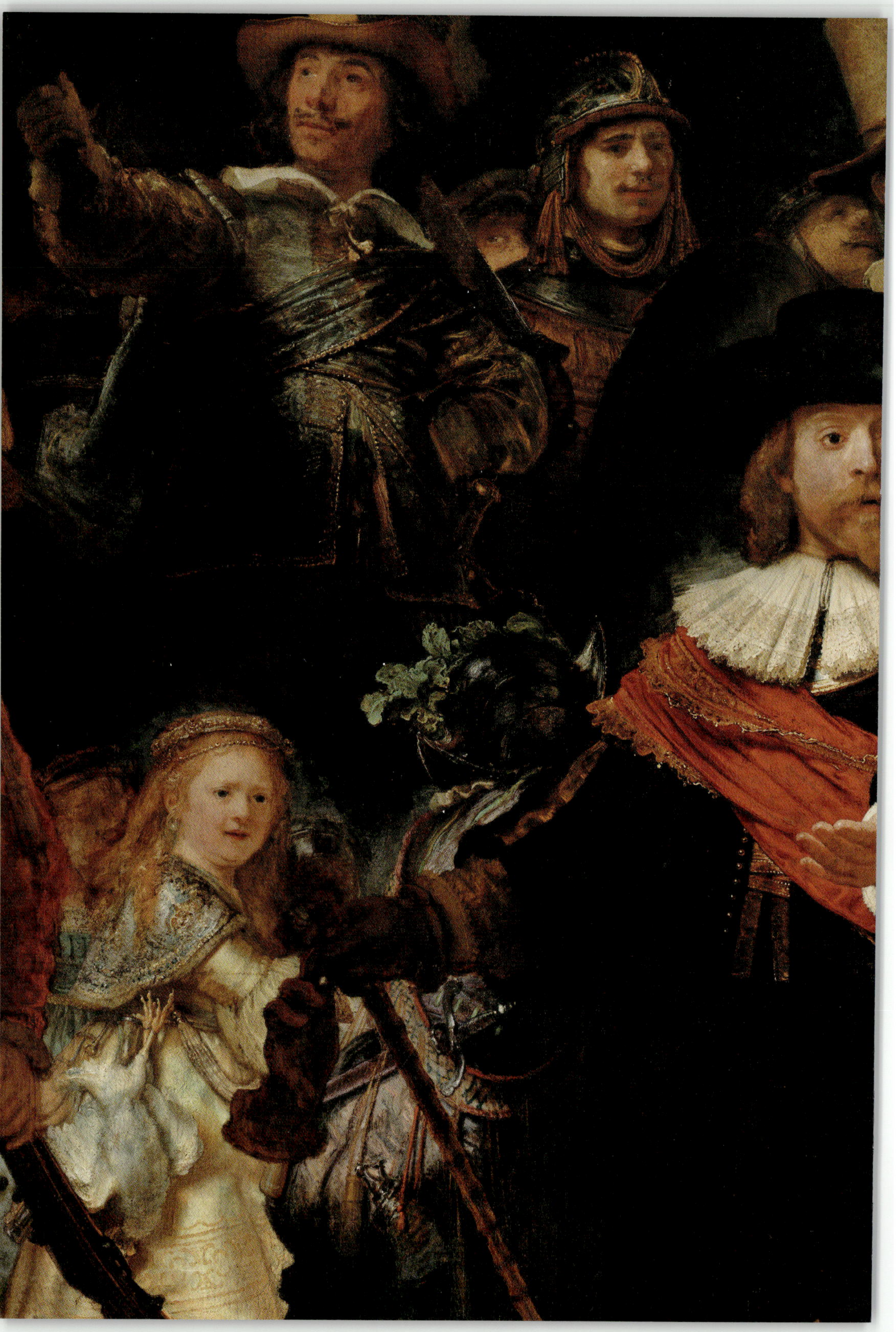

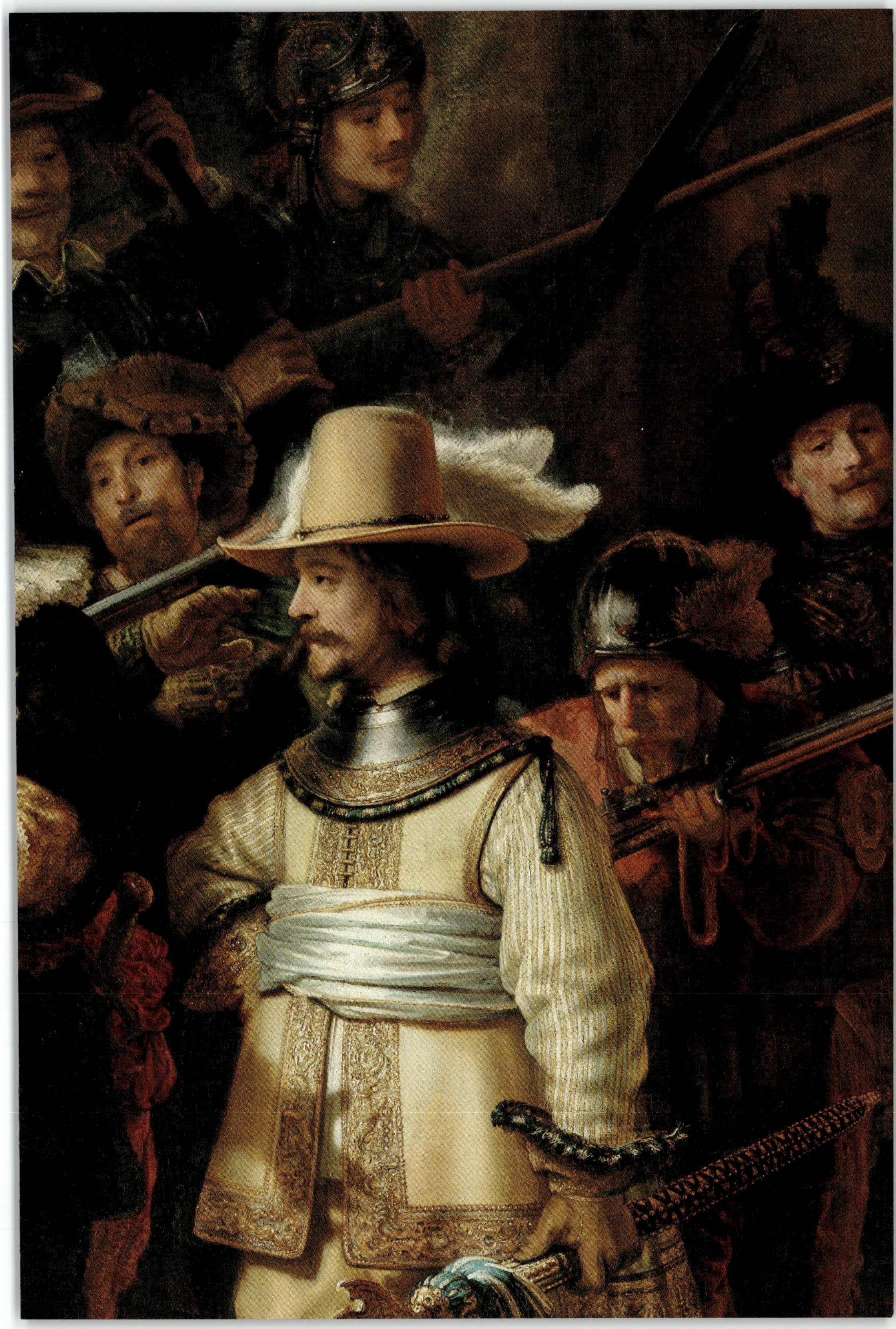

Ephraim Bueno, Jewish Physician, 1647
Etching, drypoint and burin, 24.1 × 17.7 cm (9 ½ × 7 in.)
Vienna, Albertina

Portrait of Ephraim Bueno, *c.* 1647
Oil on panel, 19 × 15 cm (7 ½ × 5 ¾ in.)
Amsterdam, Rijksmuseum

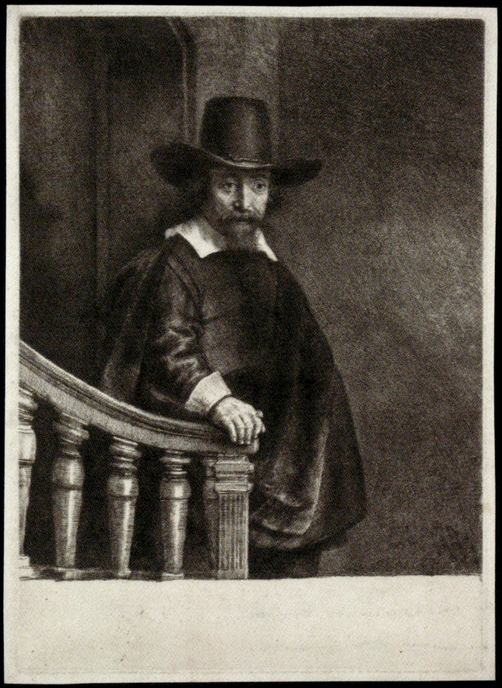

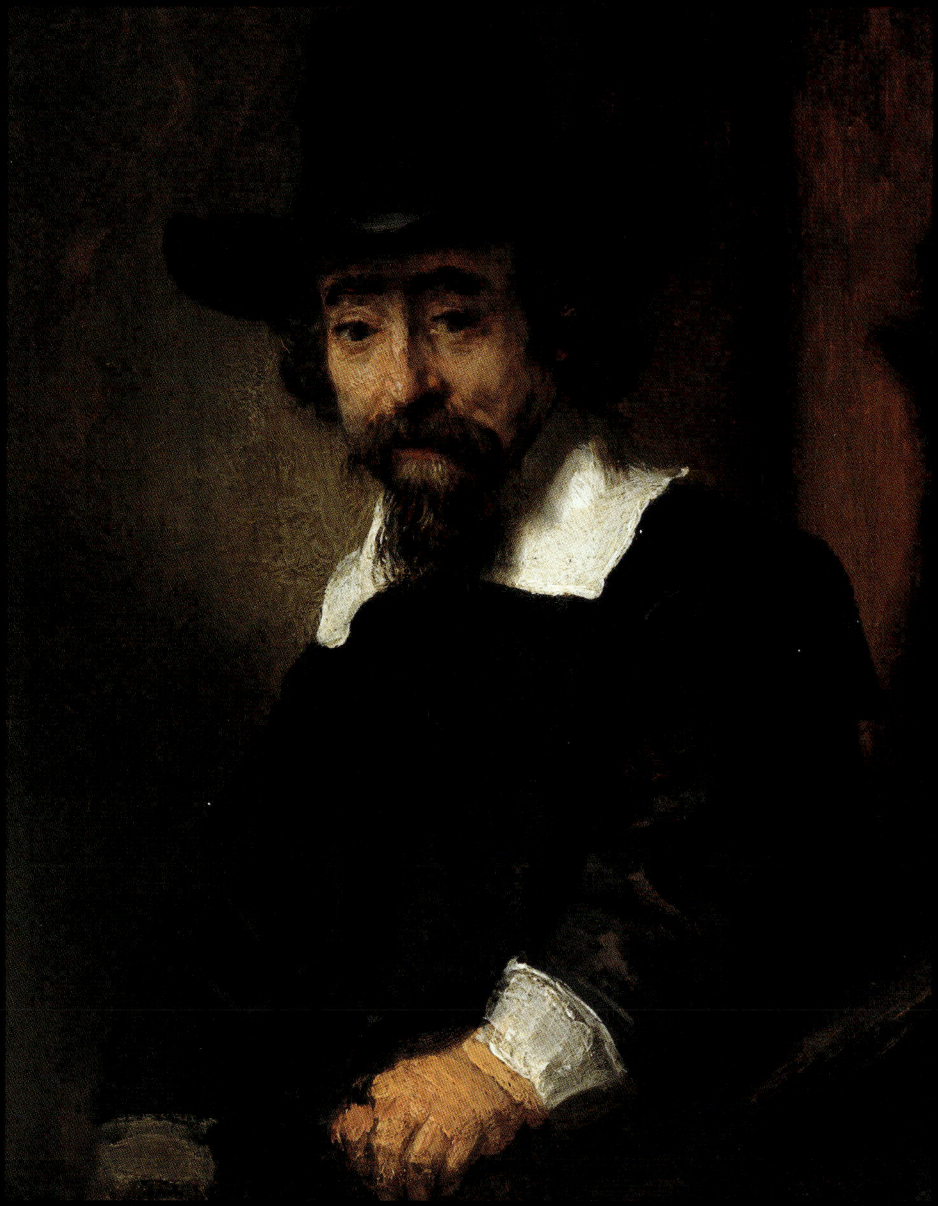

Albrecht Dürer
Self-Portrait, 1498
Oil on panel, 52 × 41 cm (20 ½ × 16 ¼ in.)
Madrid, Museo Nacional del Prado

Self-Portrait, 1640
Oil on canvas, 102 × 80 cm (40 ⅛ × 31 ½ in.)
London, The National Gallery

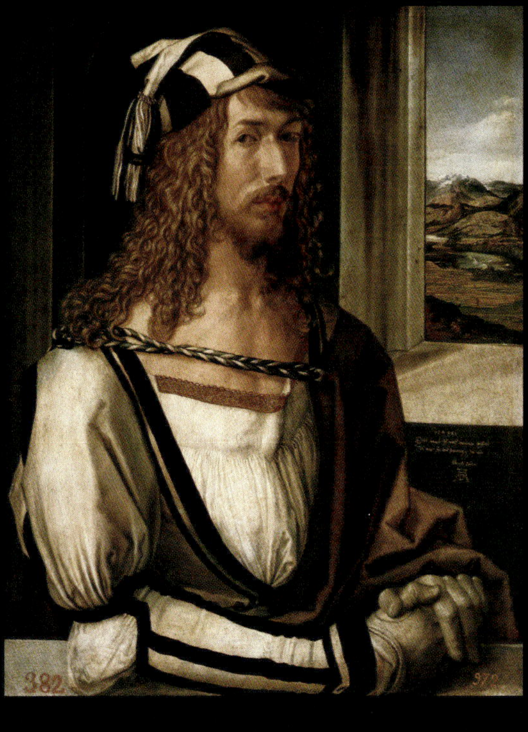

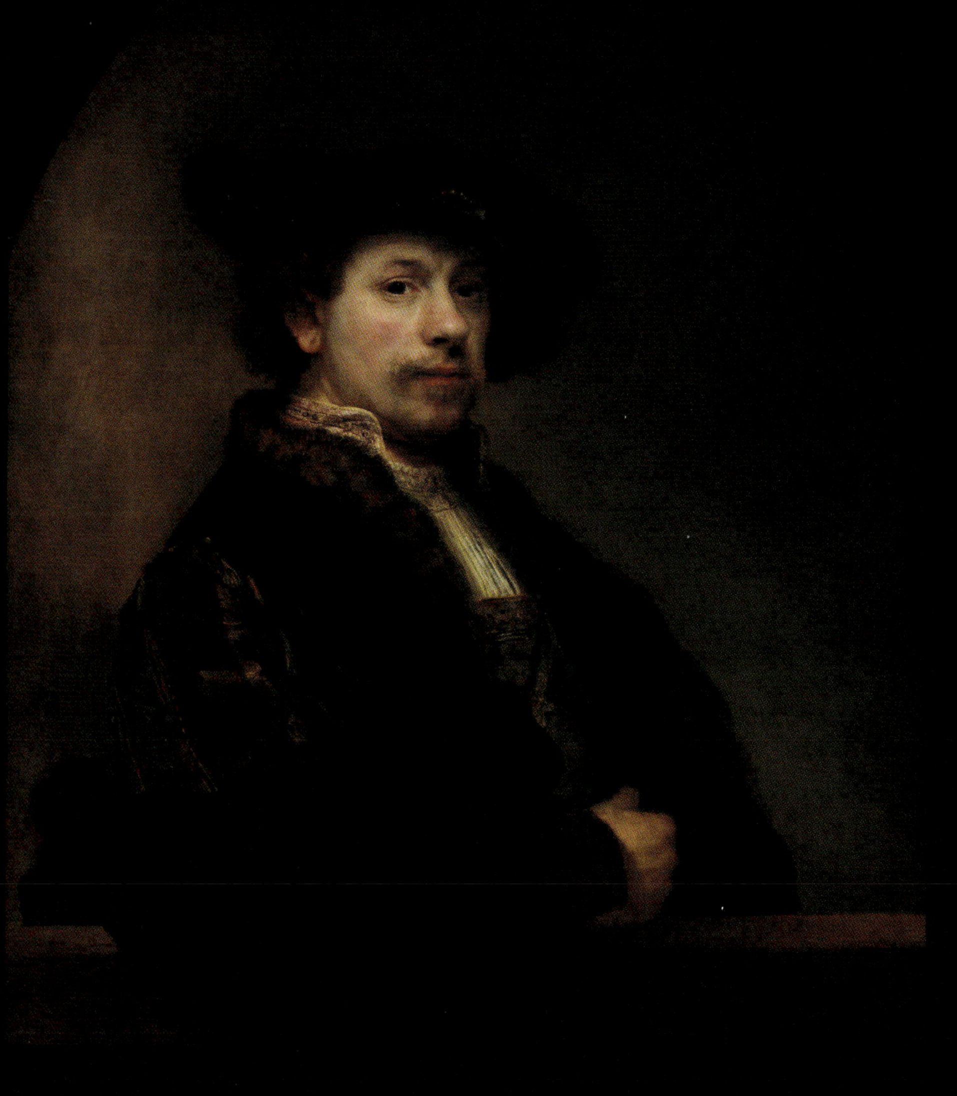

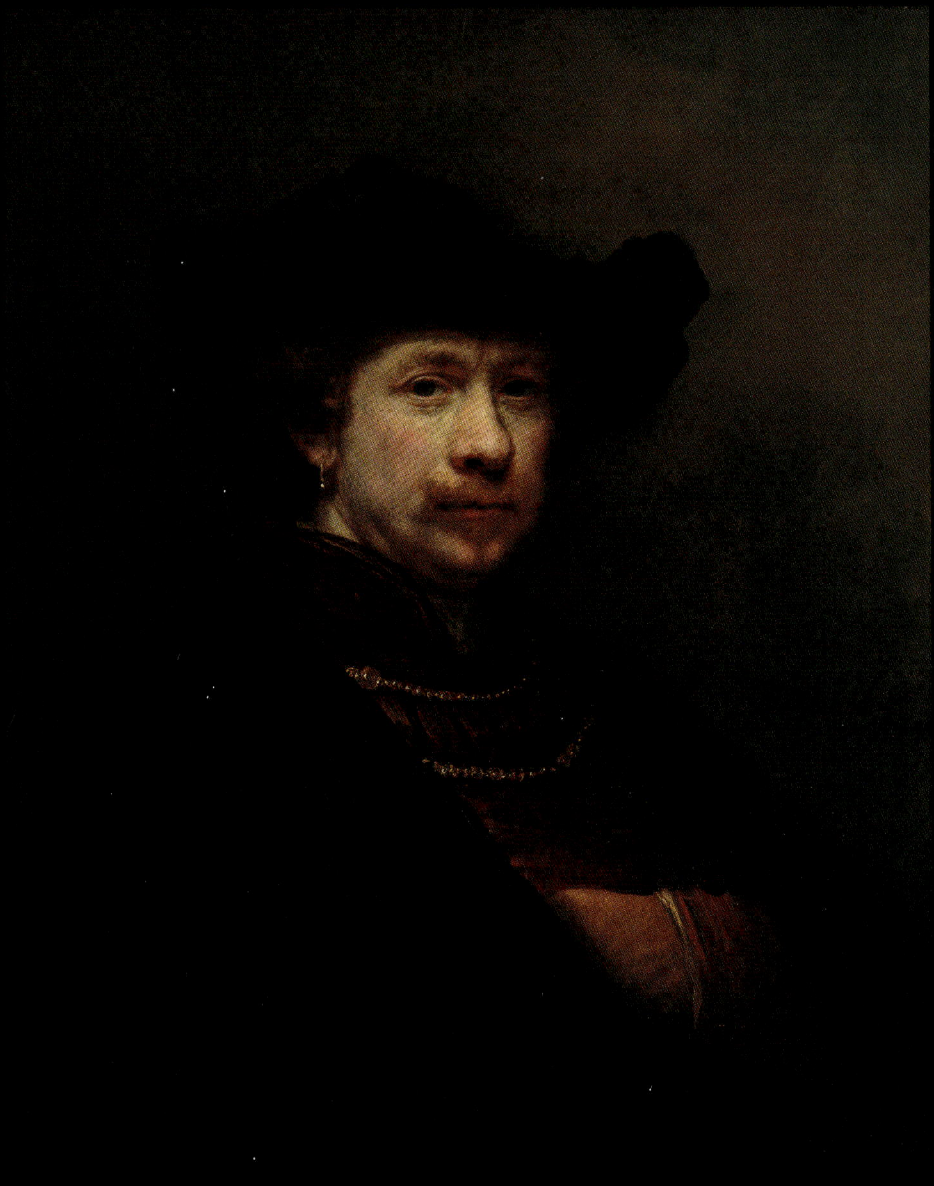

Self-Portrait, 1642
Oil on panel, 70.4 × 58.8 cm (27 ¾ × 23 ⅛ in.)
London, Royal Collection

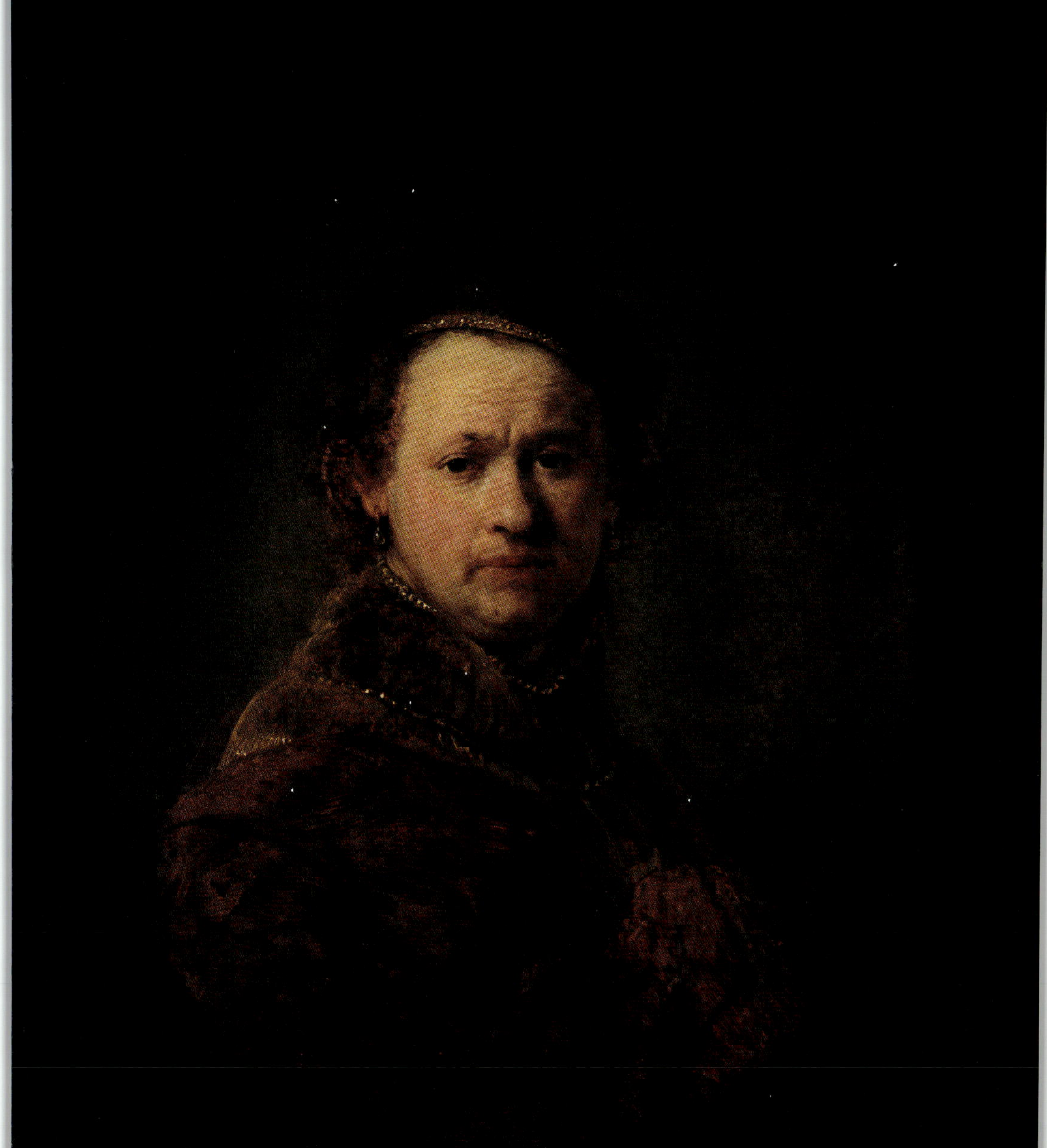

Self-Portrait, *c.* 1645
Oil on panel, 73.5 × 59.6 cm (28 ¾ × 23 ½ in.)
Staatliche Kunsthalle Karlsruhe

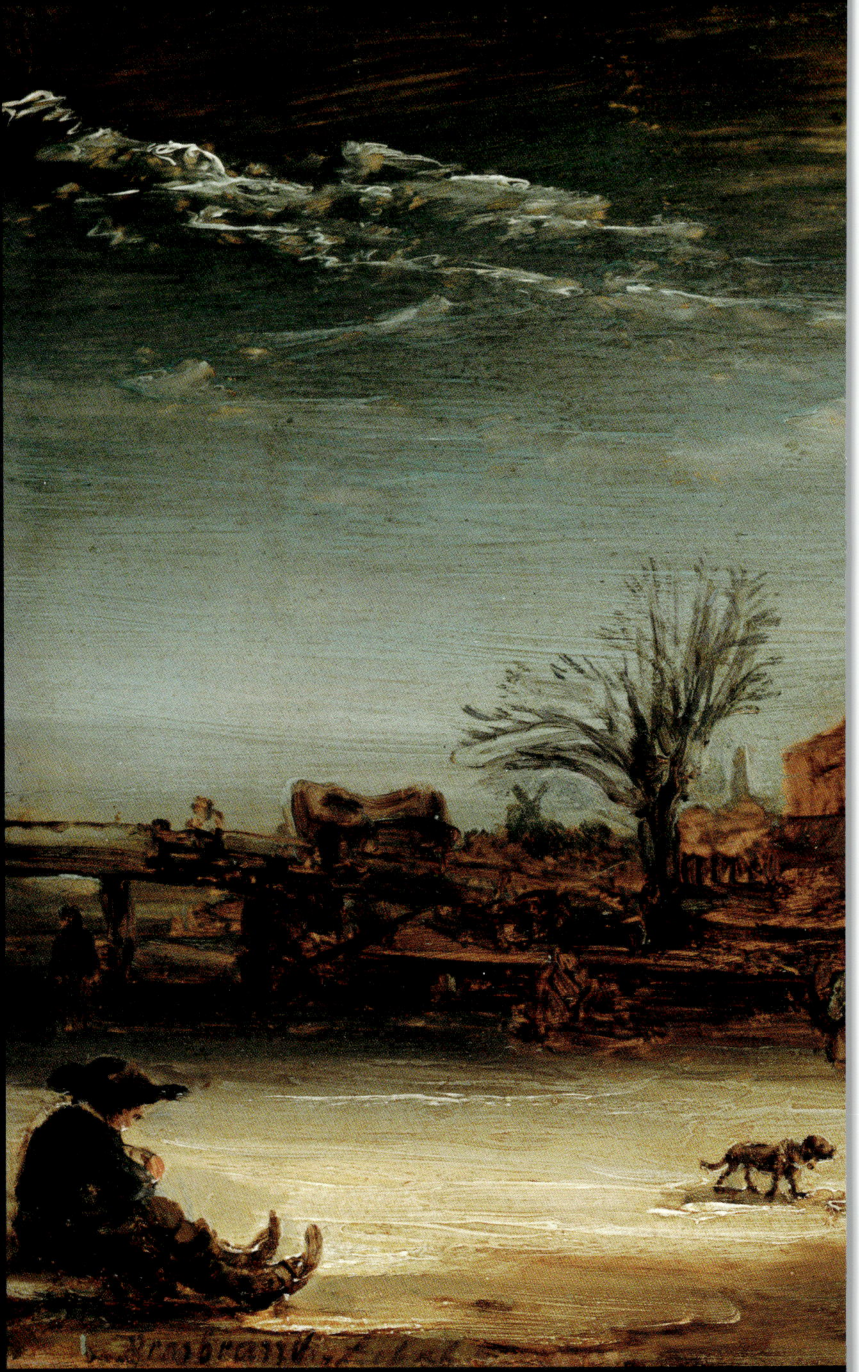

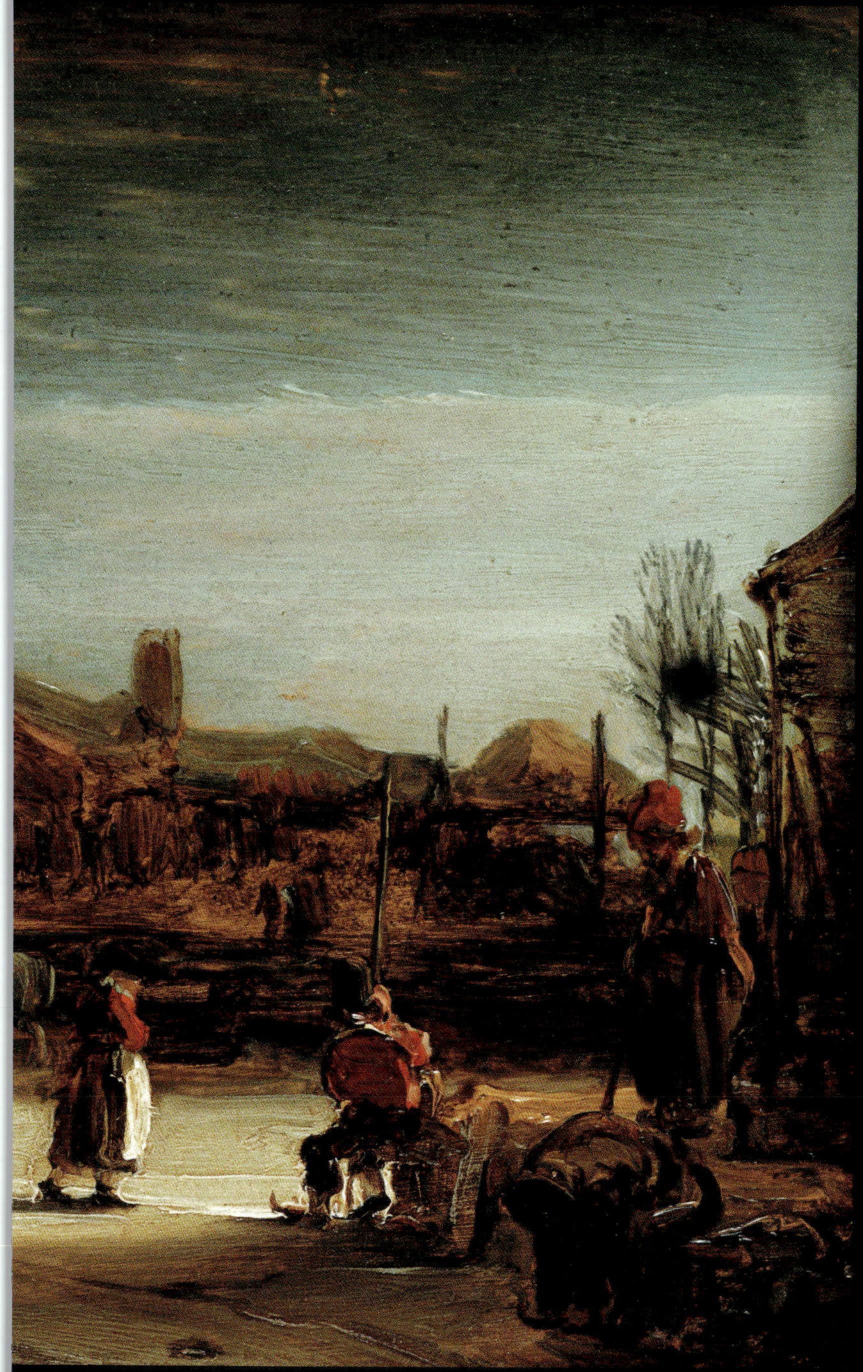

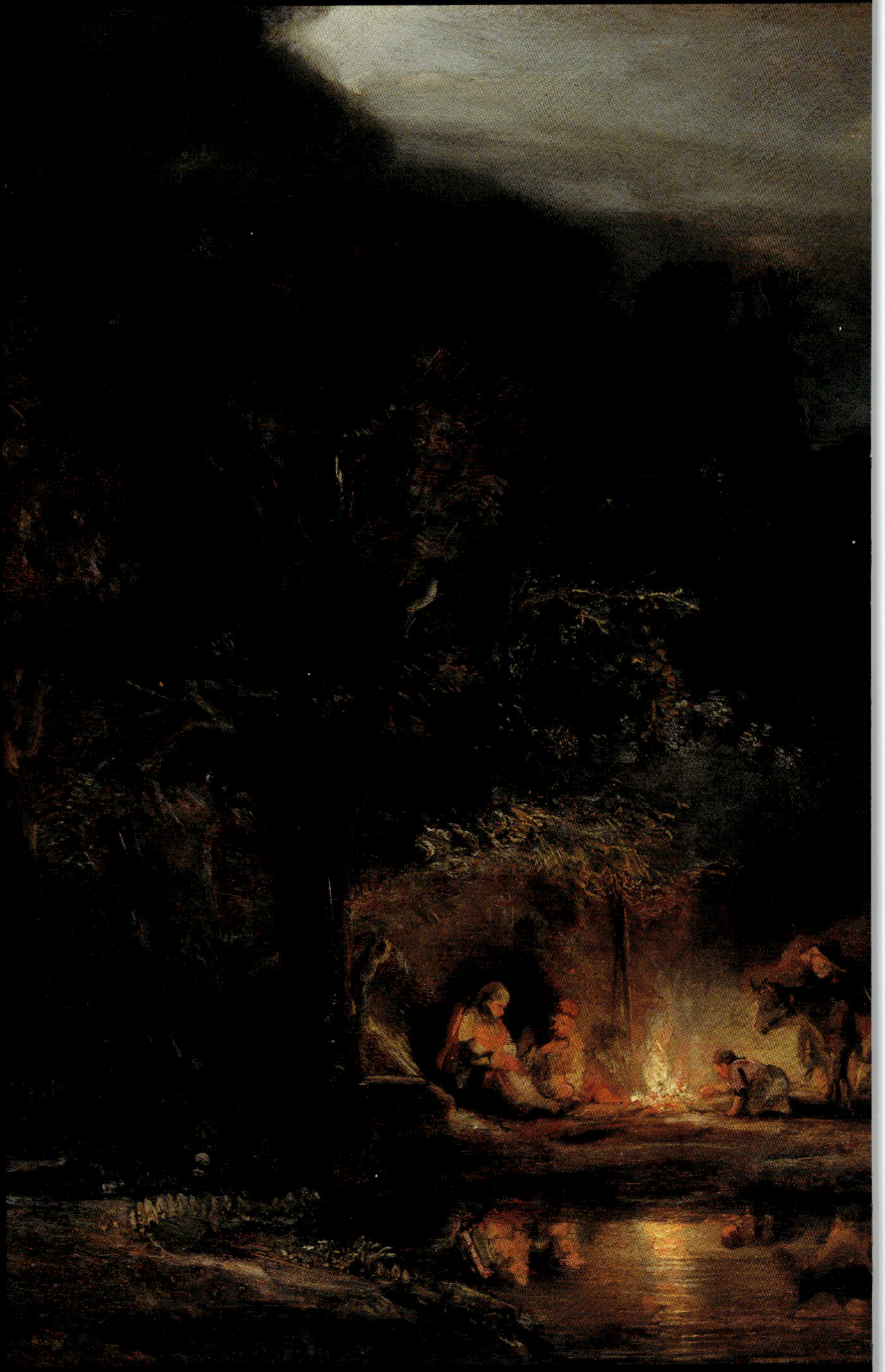

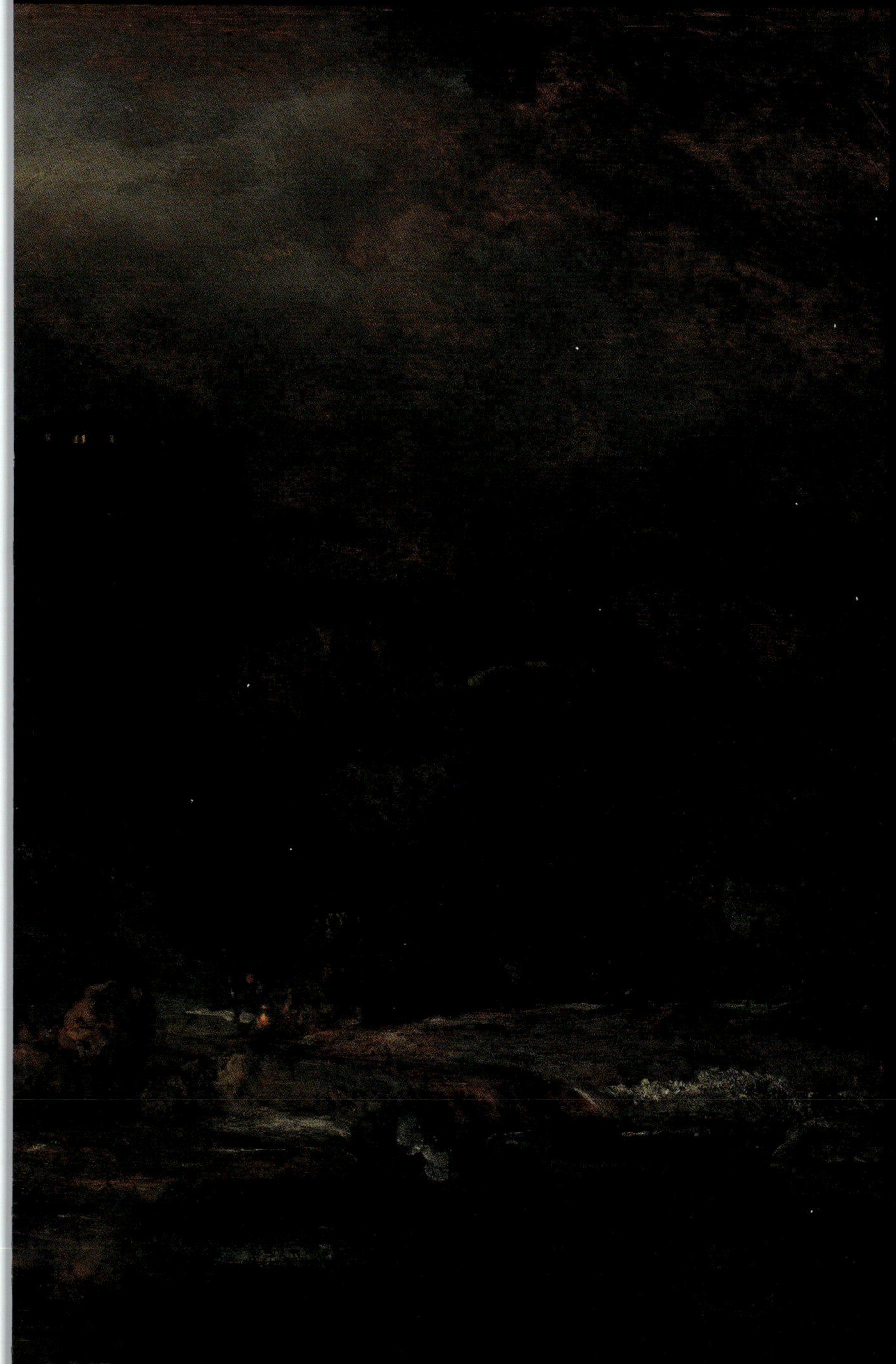

Pages 334/335
Winter Landscape, 1646
Oil on panel, 16.7 × 22.4 cm (6 5⁄8 × 8 3⁄4 in.)
Hessen Kassel Heritage, Gemäldegalerie Alte Meister

Pages 336/337
Nocturnal Landscape with Flight into Egypt, 1647
Oil on panel, 33.8 × 47.8 cm (13 1⁄4 × 18 3⁄4 in.)
Dublin, National Gallery of Ireland

David's Parting from Jonathan, 1642
Oil on panel, 73 × 61.5 cm (28 3⁄4 × 24 1⁄4 in.)
St Petersburg, The State Hermitage Museum

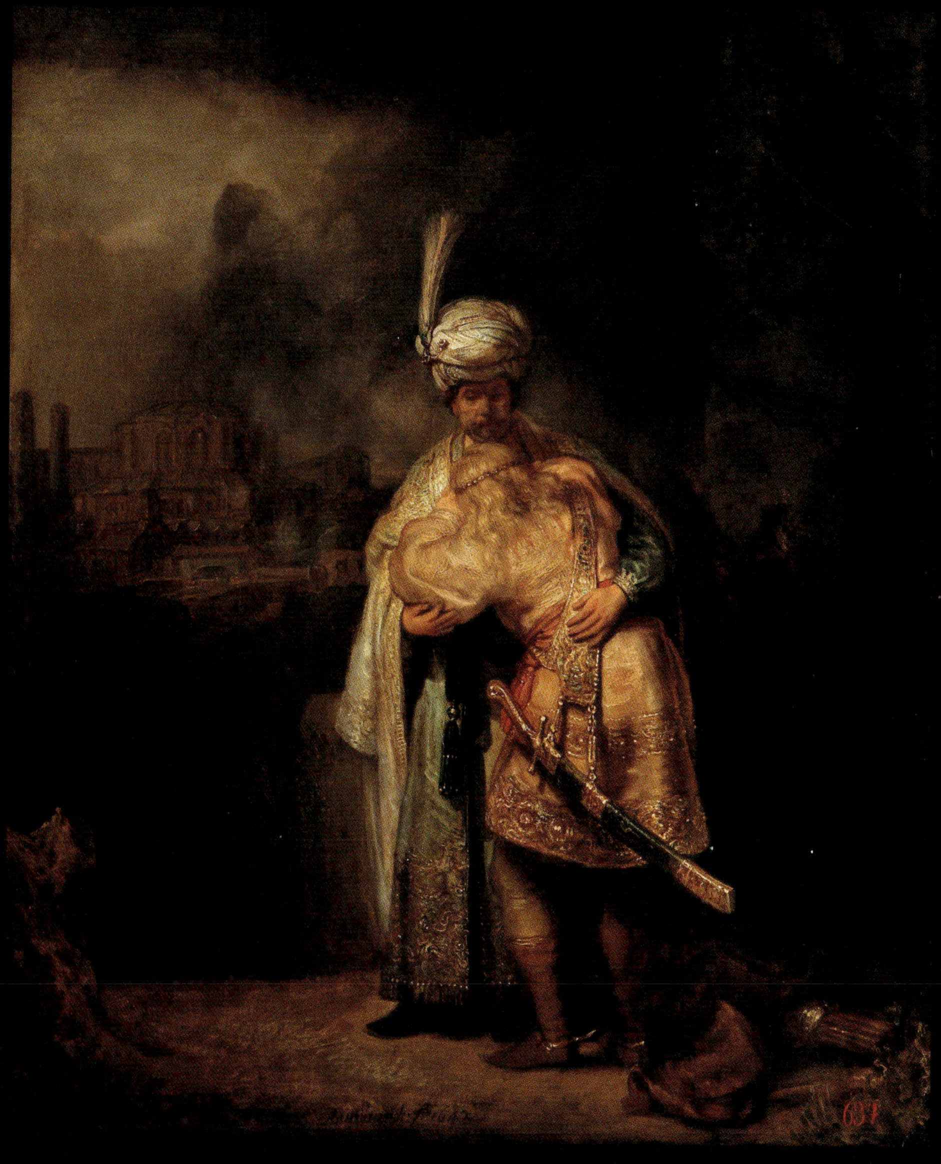

The Holy Family, 1645
Oil on canvas, 116.4 × 91 cm (45 ¾ × 35 ¾ in.)
St Petersburg, The State Hermitage Museum

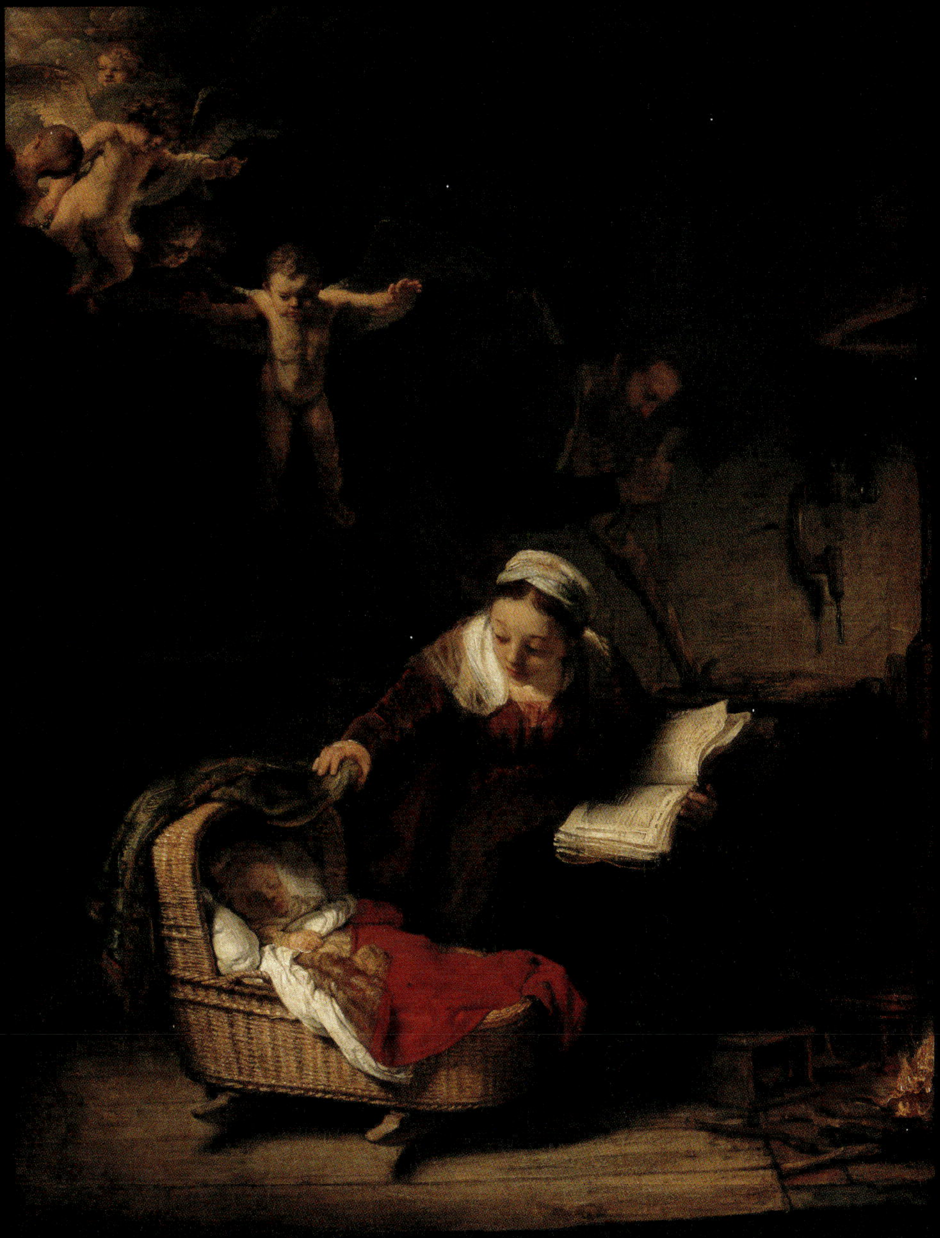

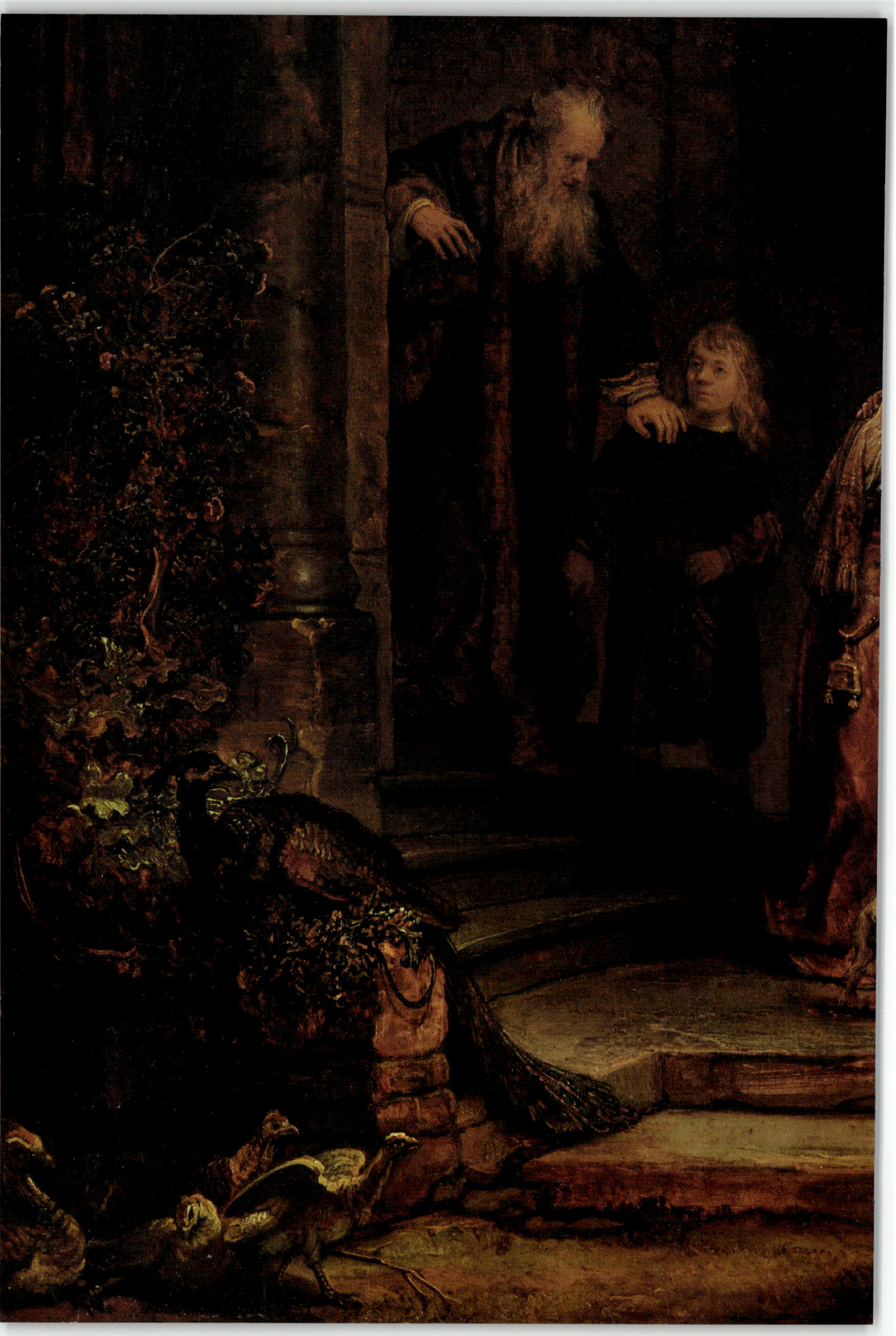

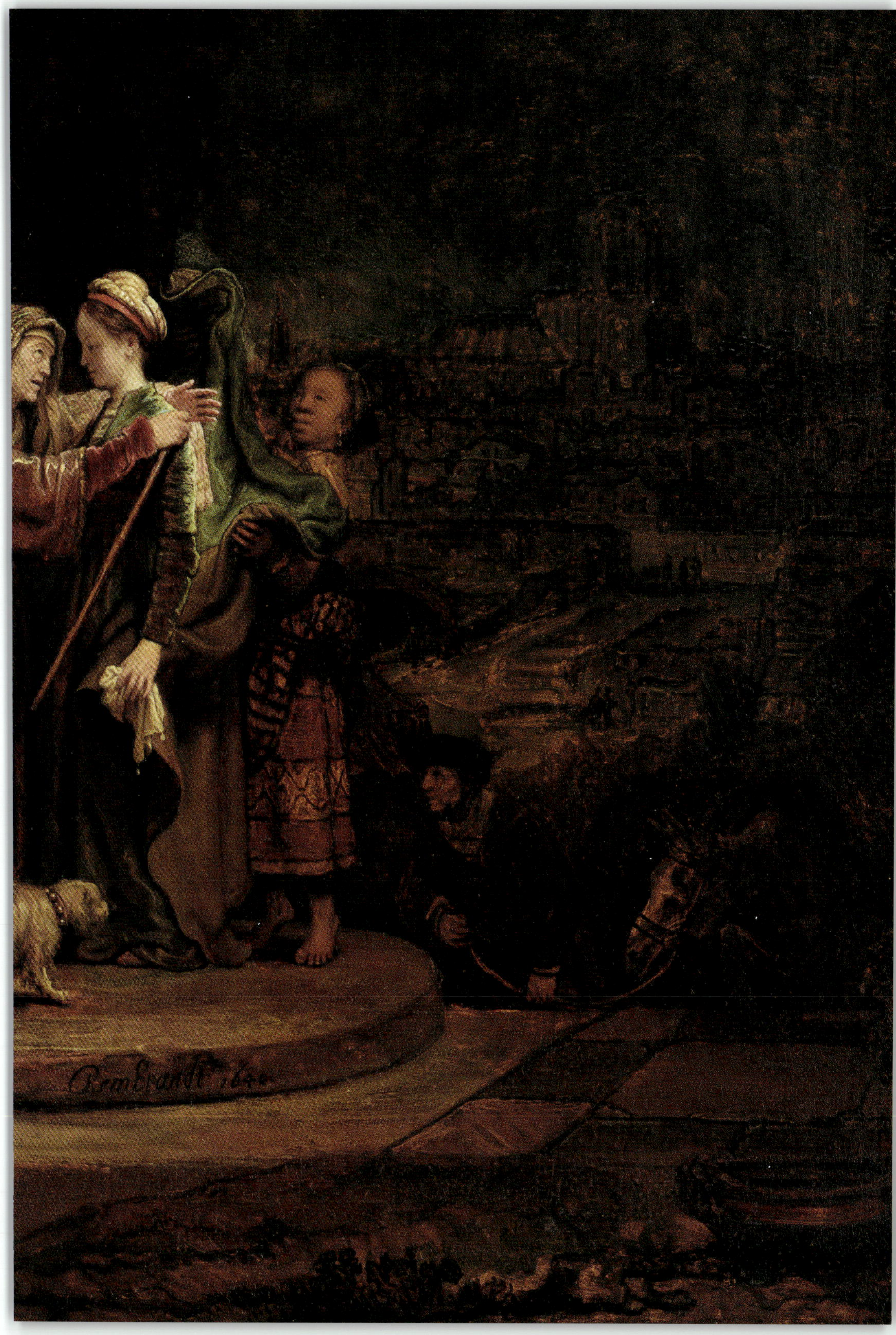

Albrecht Dürer
The Visitation, 1503/04
Woodcut, 29.9 × 21.1 cm (11 7/8 × 8 3/8 in.)
Amsterdam, Rijksmuseum

The Visitation, 1640
Oil on panel, 56.5 × 47.9 cm (22 1/4 × 18 3/4 in.)
Detroit, Michigan, The Detroit Institute of Art
(detail pages 342/343)

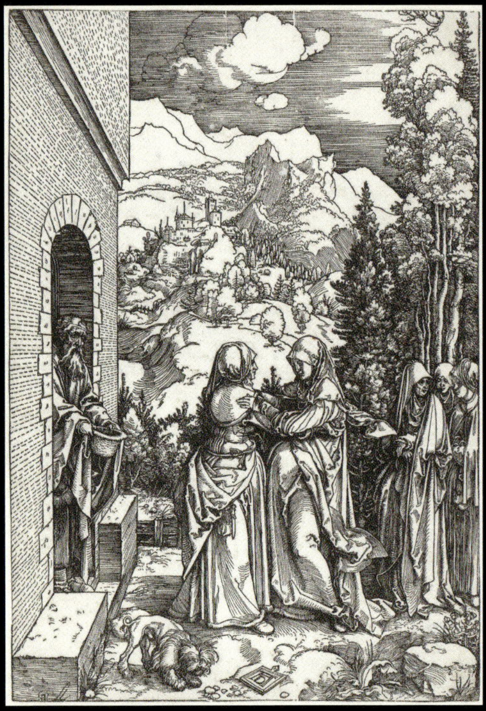

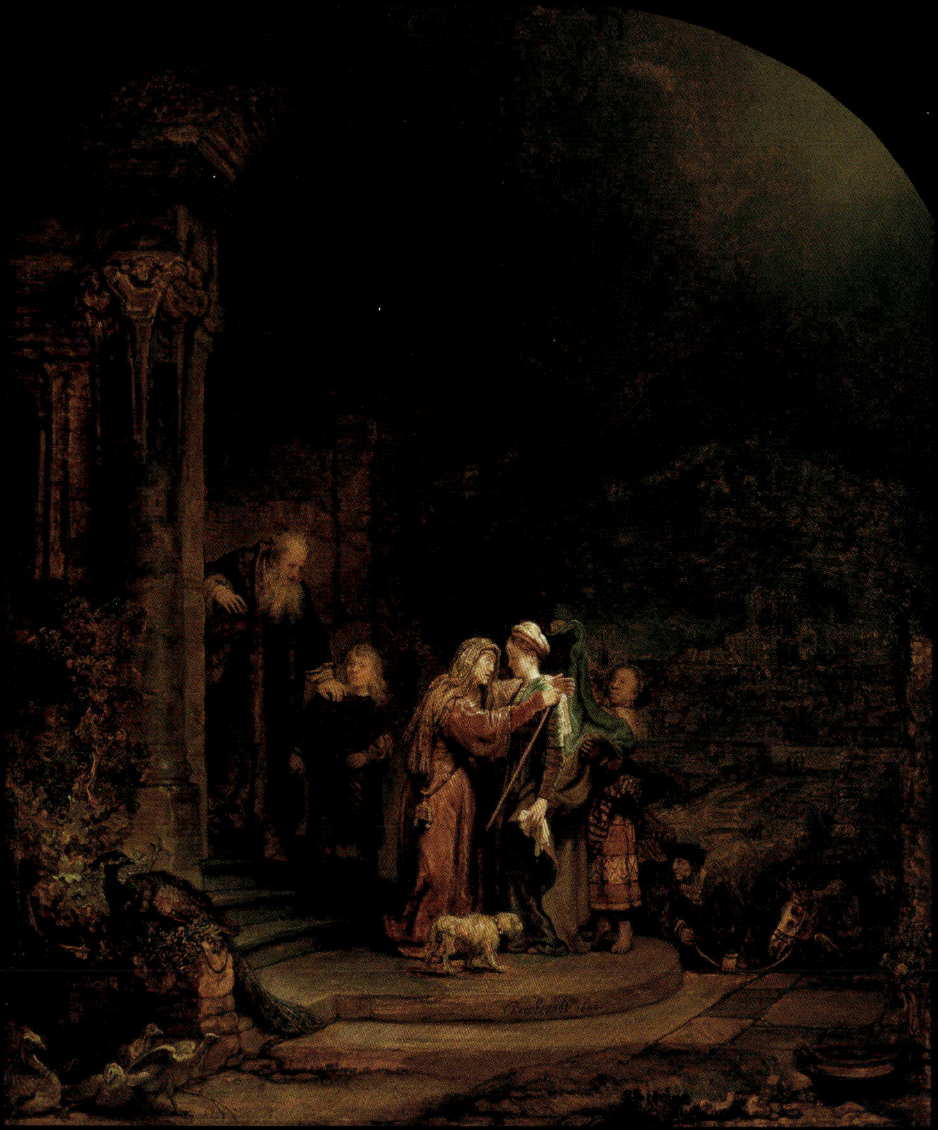

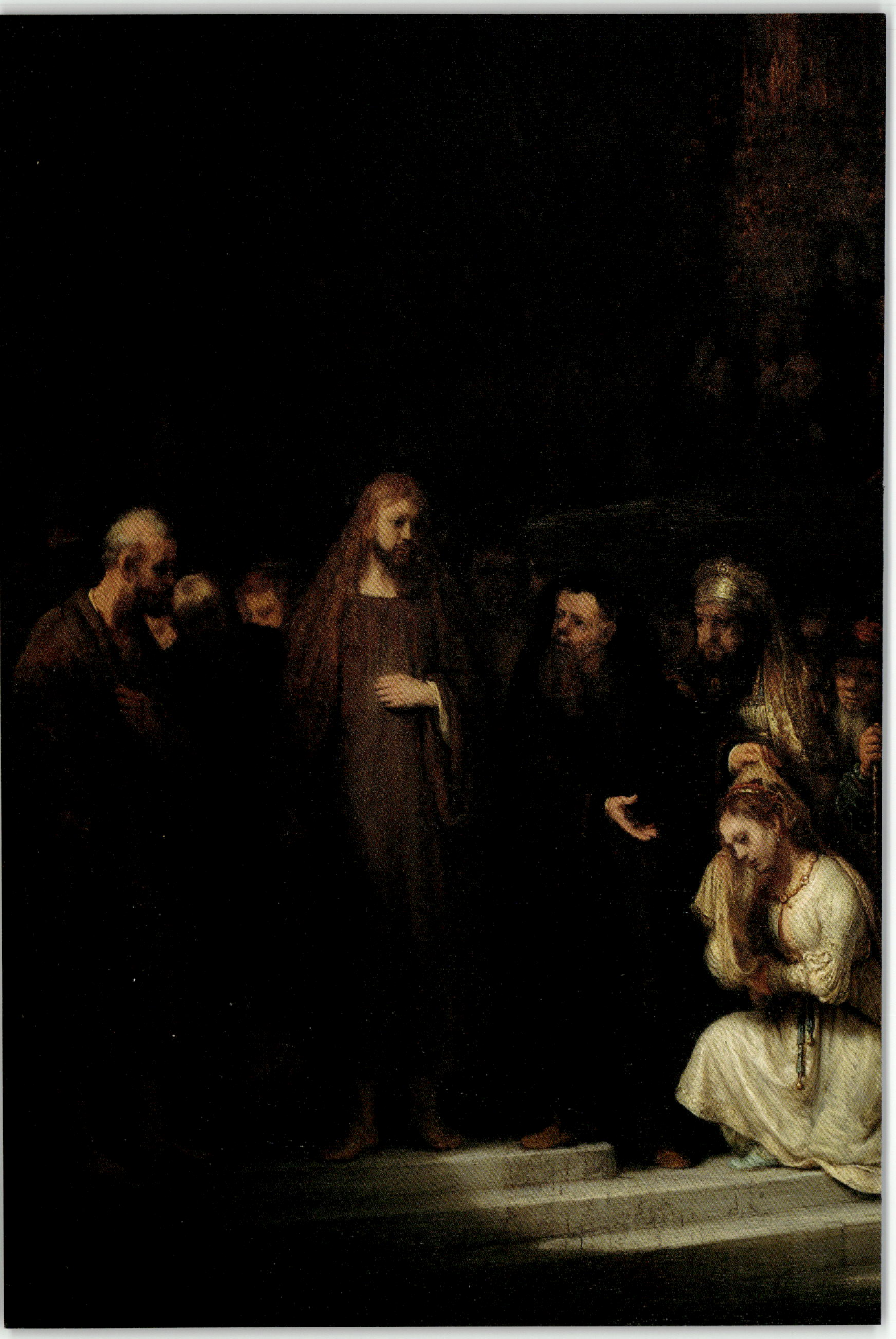

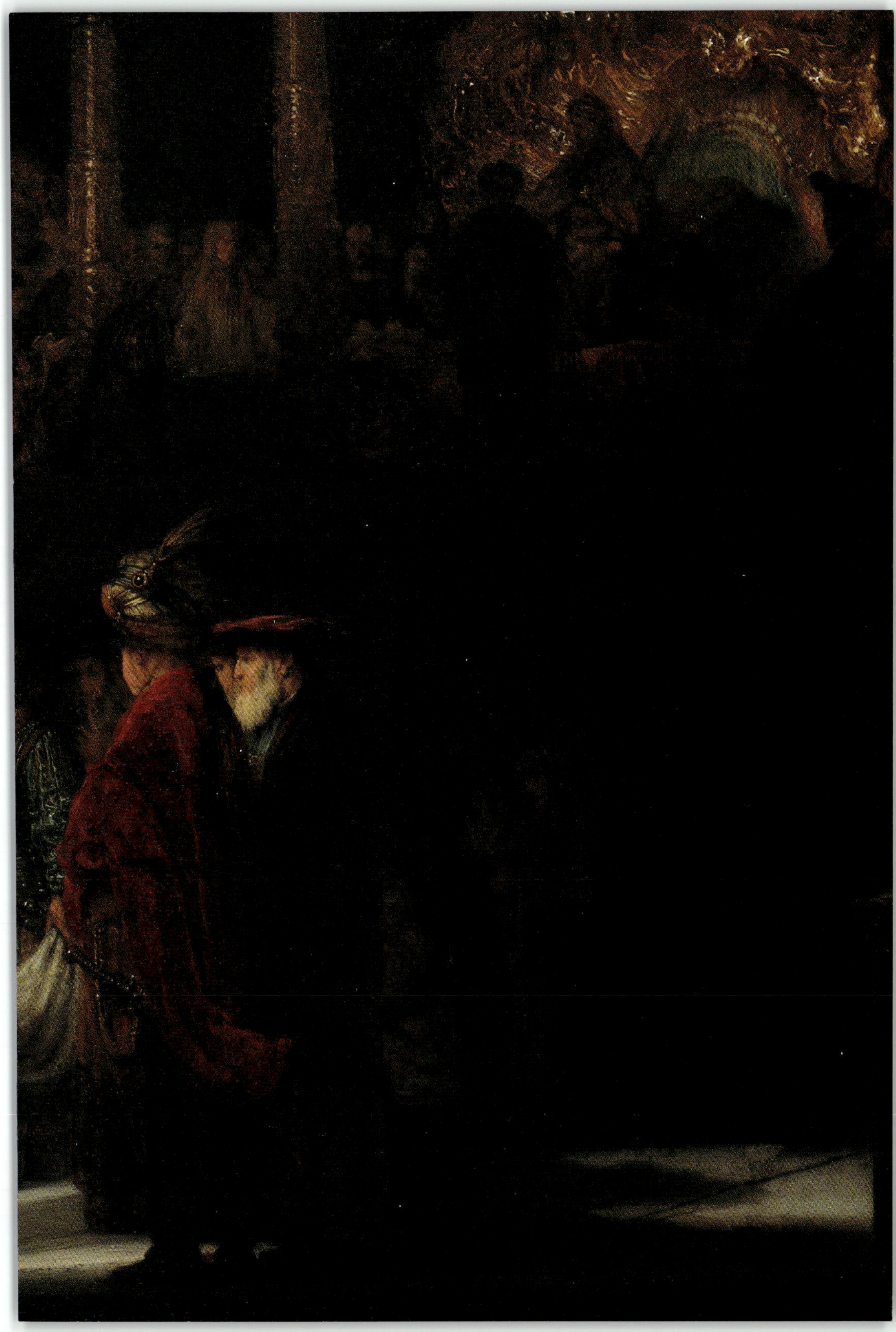

Christ and the Woman Taken in Adultery, 1644
Oil on panel, 83.8 × 65.4 cm (32 ¾ × 25 ¾ in.)
London, The National Gallery
(detail pages 346/347)

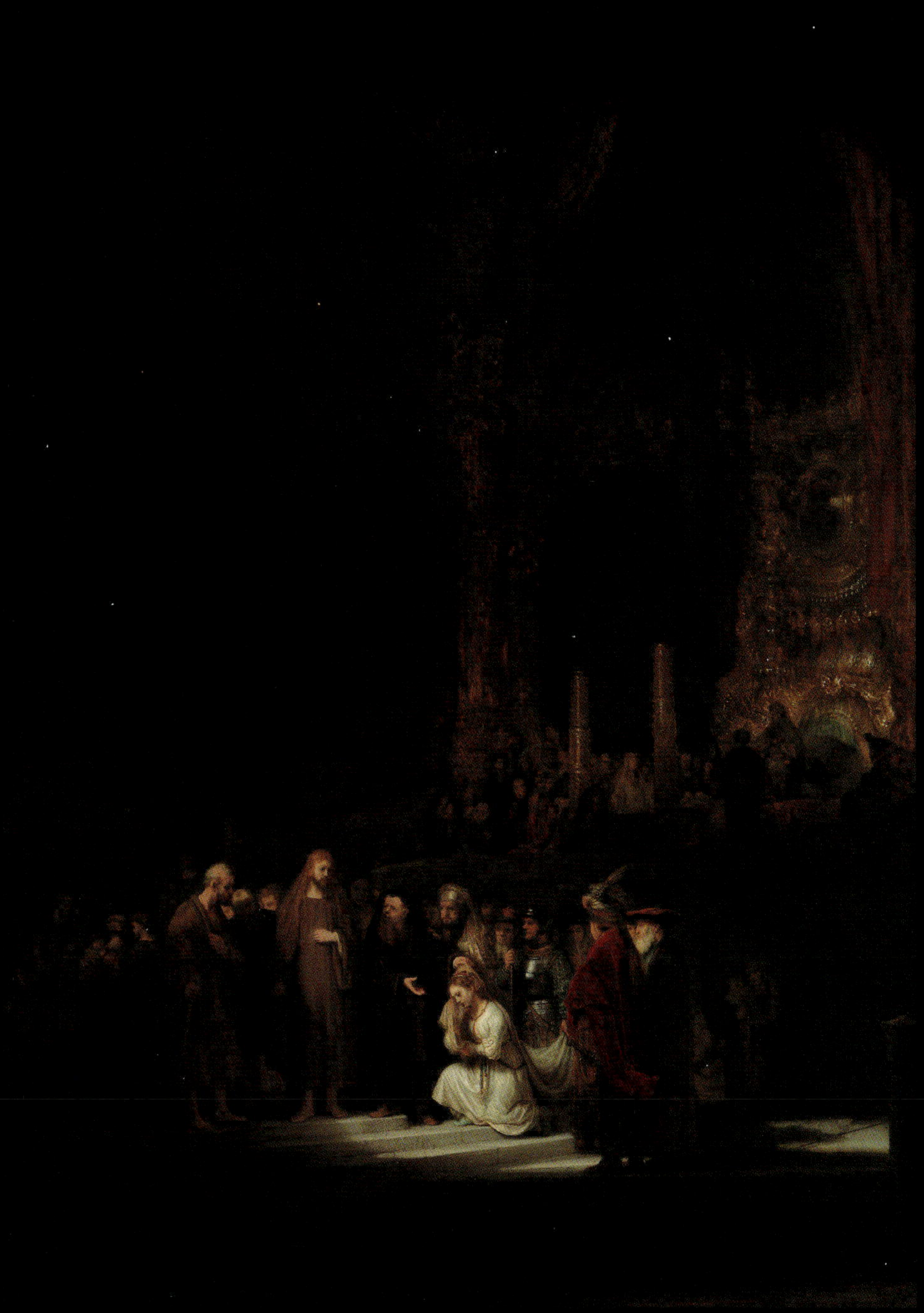

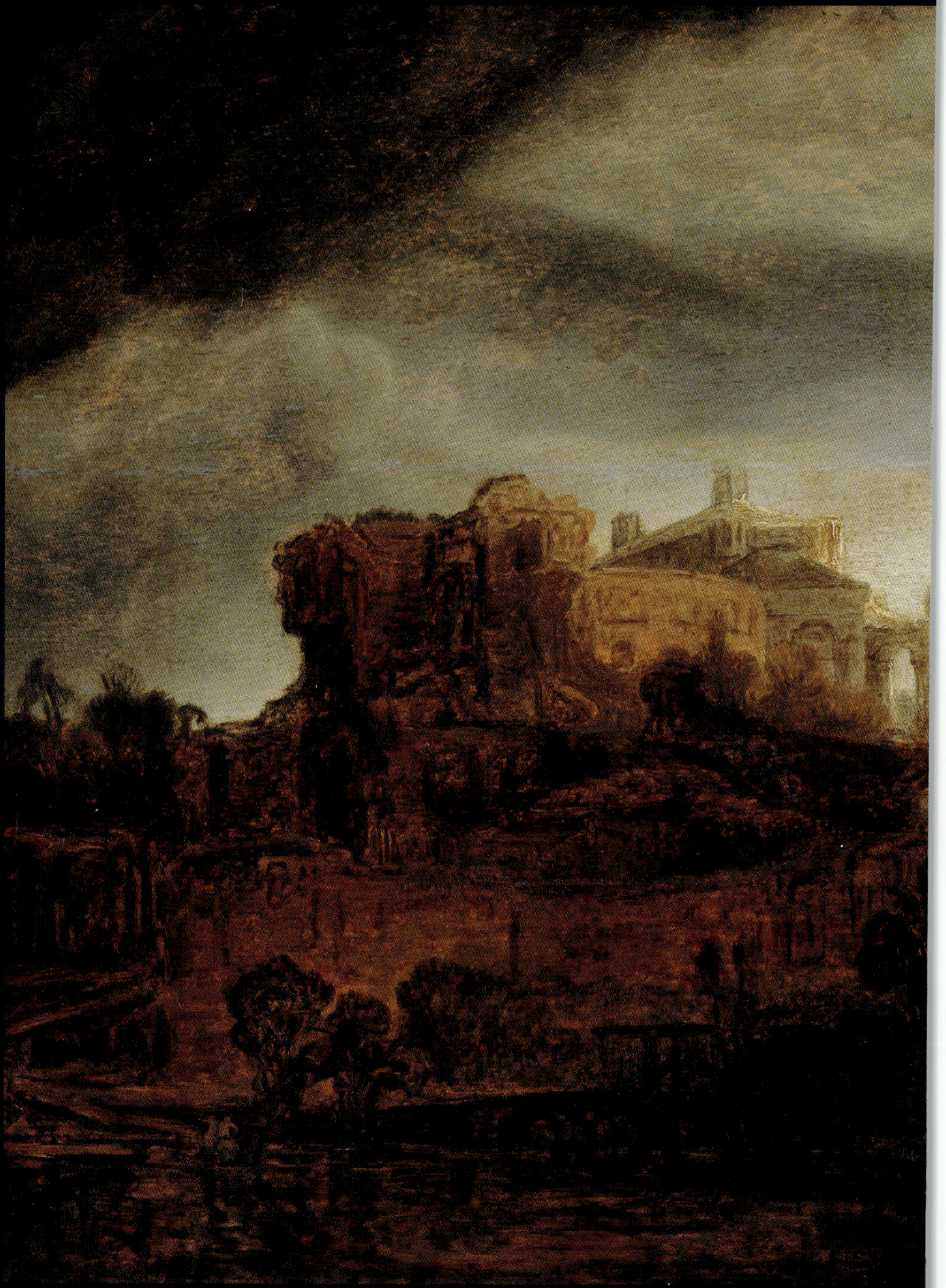

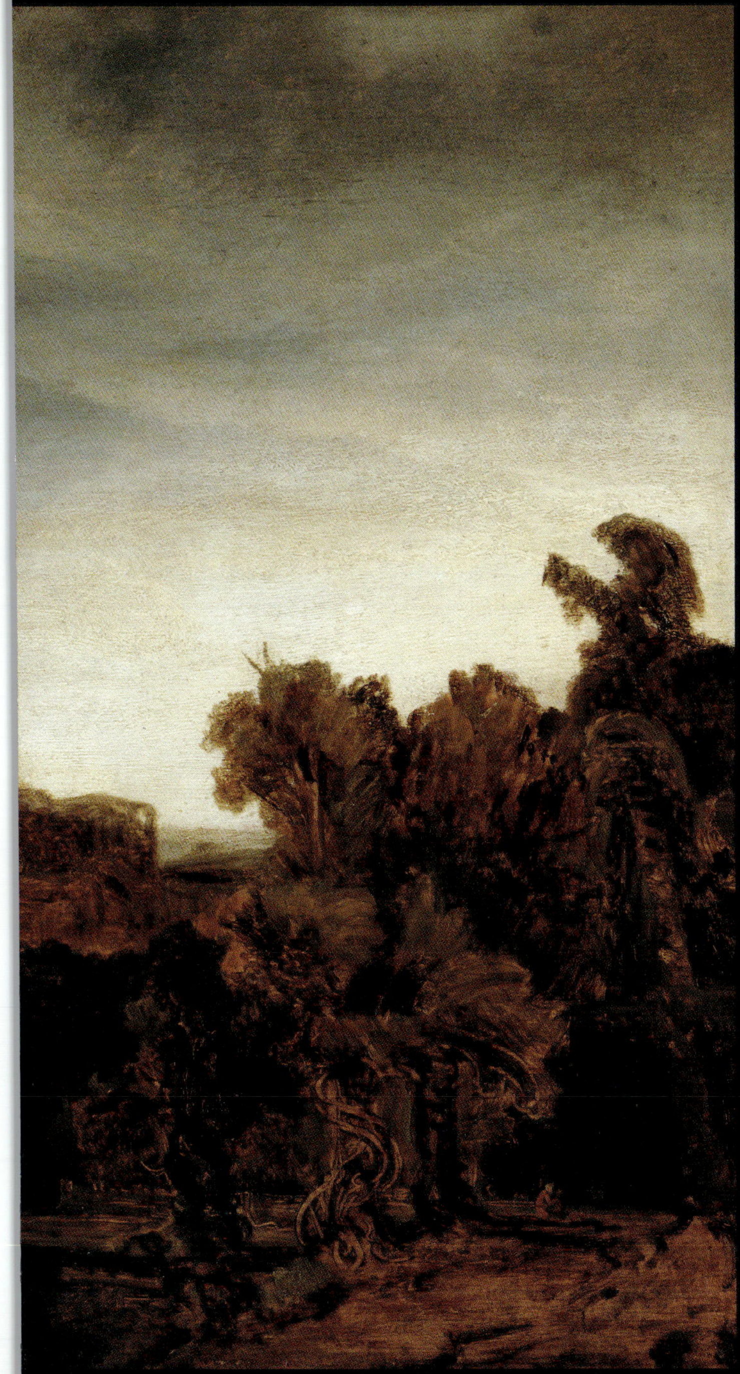

Pages 350/351
Landscape with a Castle, *c.* 1645
Oil on panel, 44.5 × 70 cm (17 ½ × 27 ½ in.)
Paris, Musée du Louvre, Gift of Étienne Nicolas

Flora, 1641
Oil on panel, 98.5 × 82.5 cm (38 ¾ × 32 ½ in.)
Staatliche Kunstsammlungen Dresden,
Gemäldegalerie Alte Meister

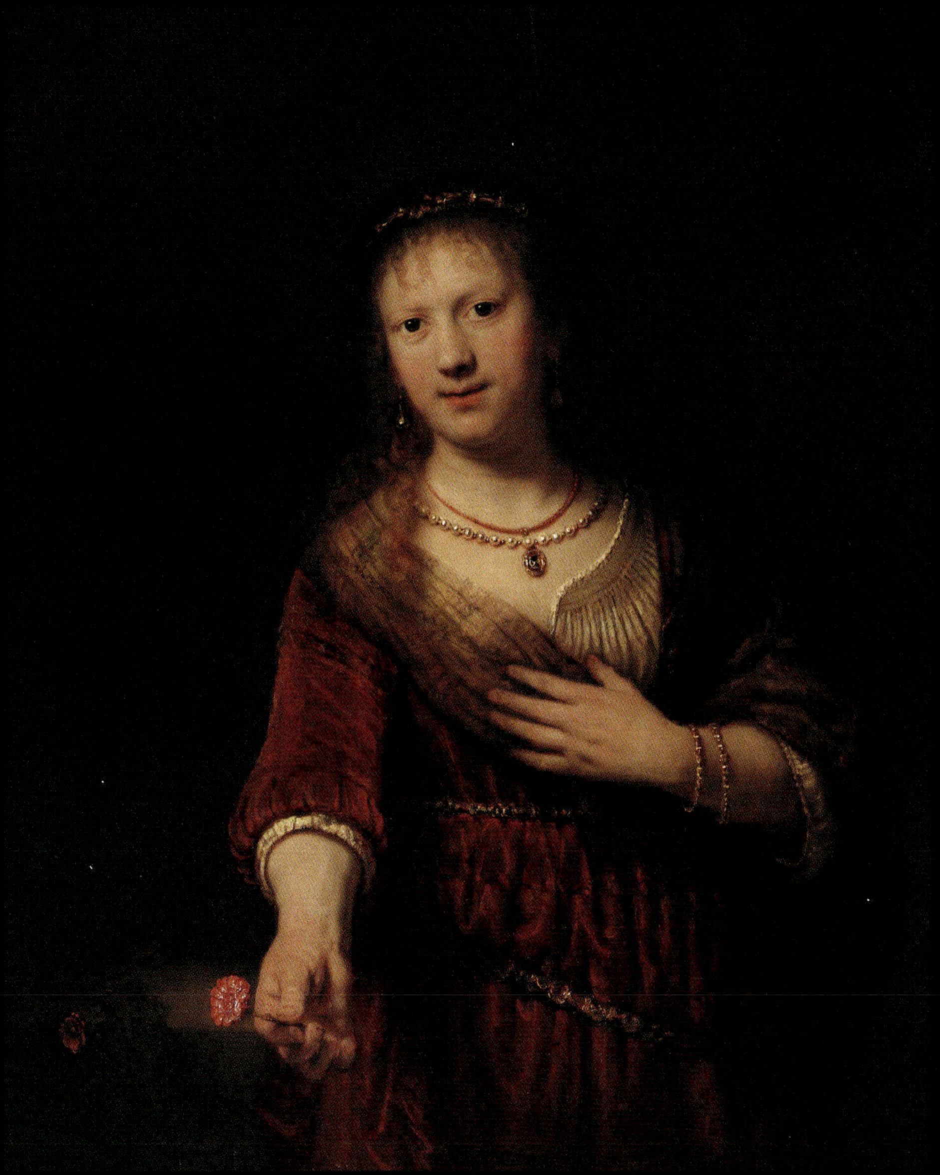

Man in Armour (Mars?), 1655
Oil on canvas, 137.4 × 104.4 cm (54 ⅛ × 41 ⅛ in.)
Glasgow, Kelvingrove Art Gallery and Museum

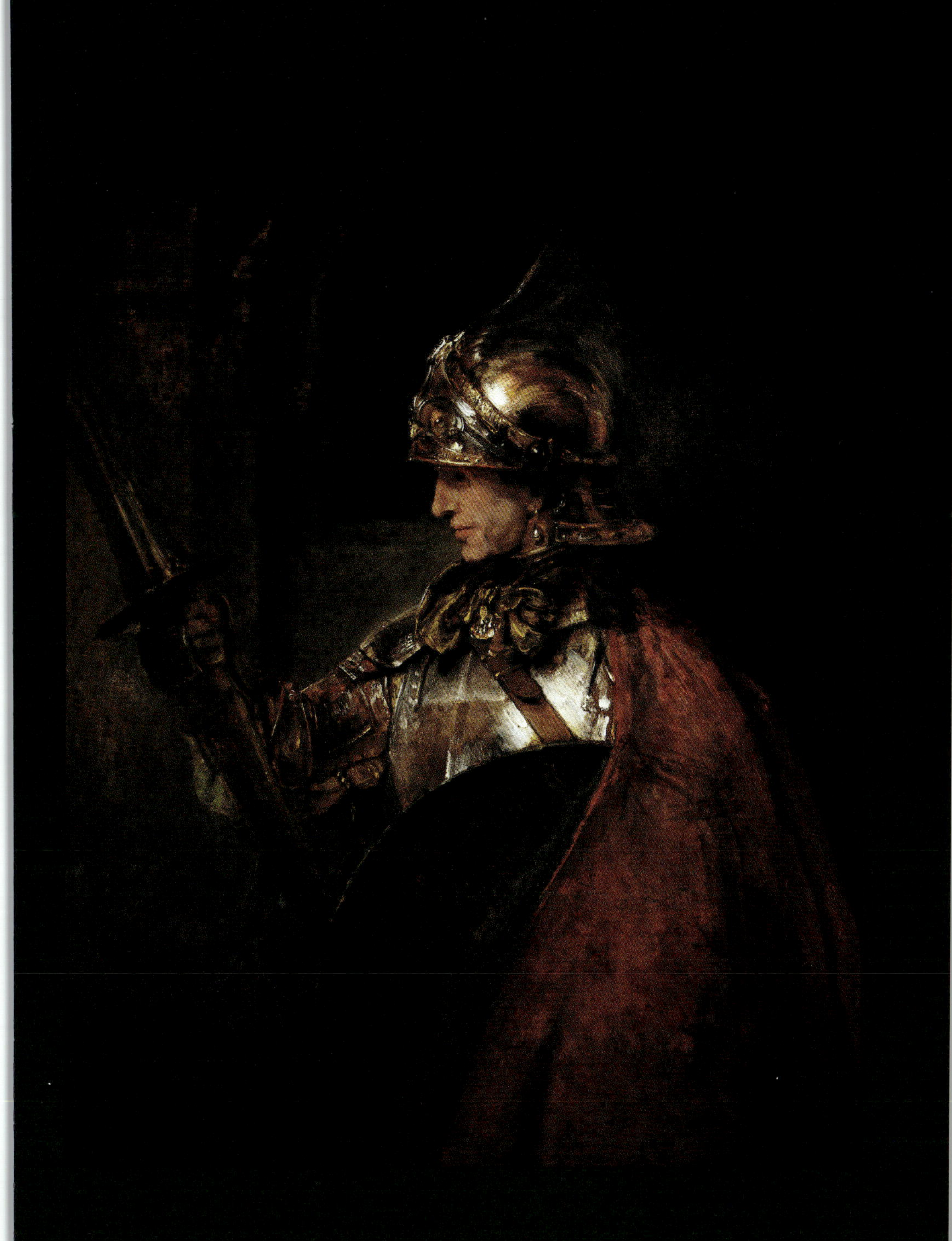

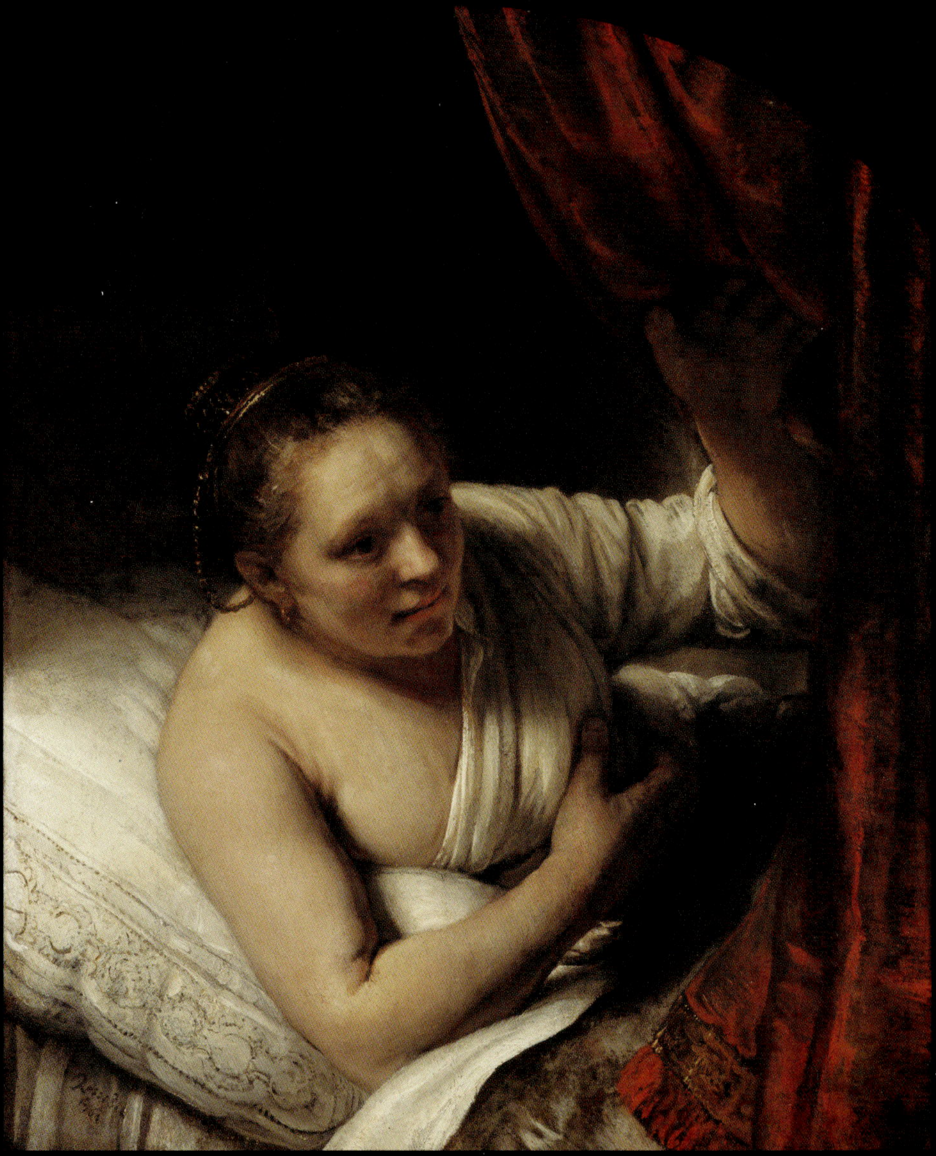

Sarah Waiting for Tobias? (A Young Woman in Bed), 1647
Oil on canvas, 81.1 × 67.8 cm (31 ¾ × 26 ¾ in.)
Edinburgh, Scottish National Gallery

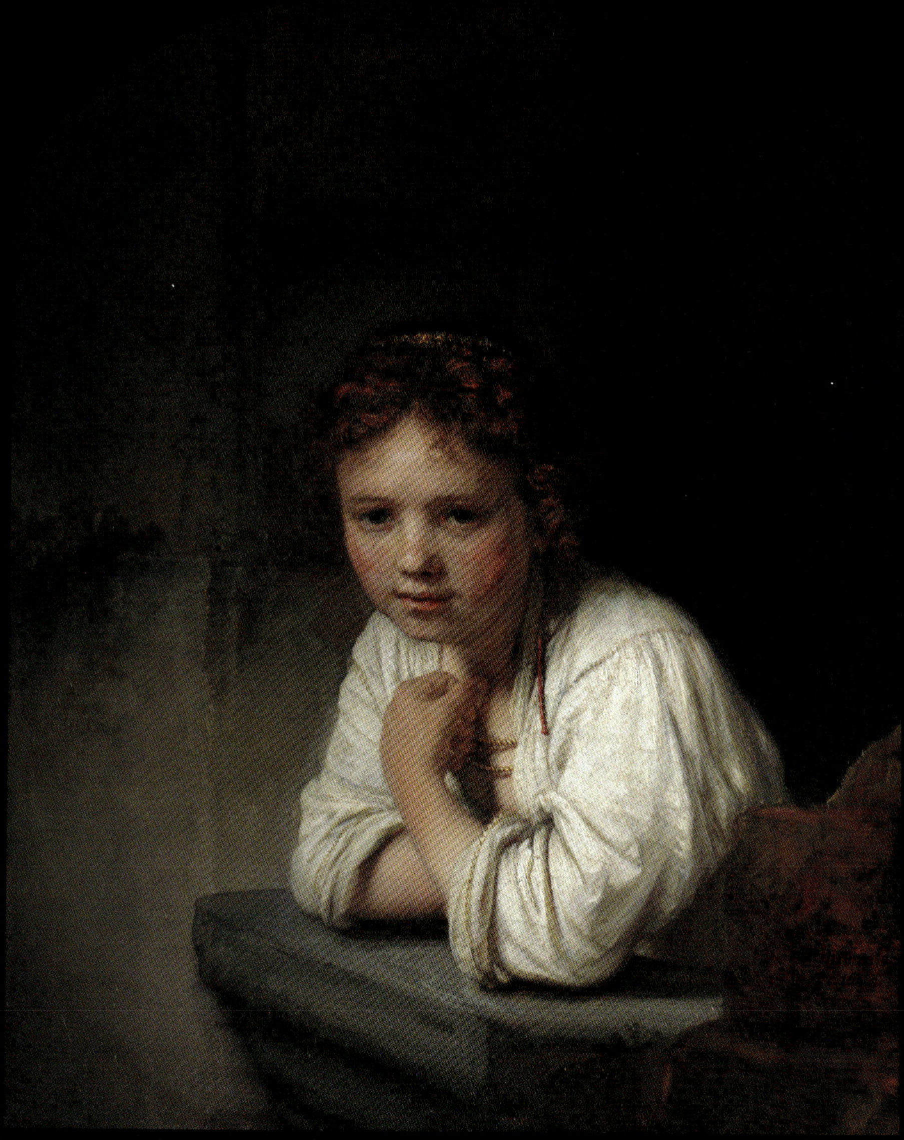

Girl Leaning on a Stone Sill, 1645
Oil on canvas, 81.6 × 66 cm (32 1/8 × 25 3/4 in.)
London, Dulwich Picture Gallery

Girl at a Window, 1651
Oil on canvas, 78 × 63 cm (30 ¾ × 24 ¾ in.)
Stockholm, Nationalmuseum

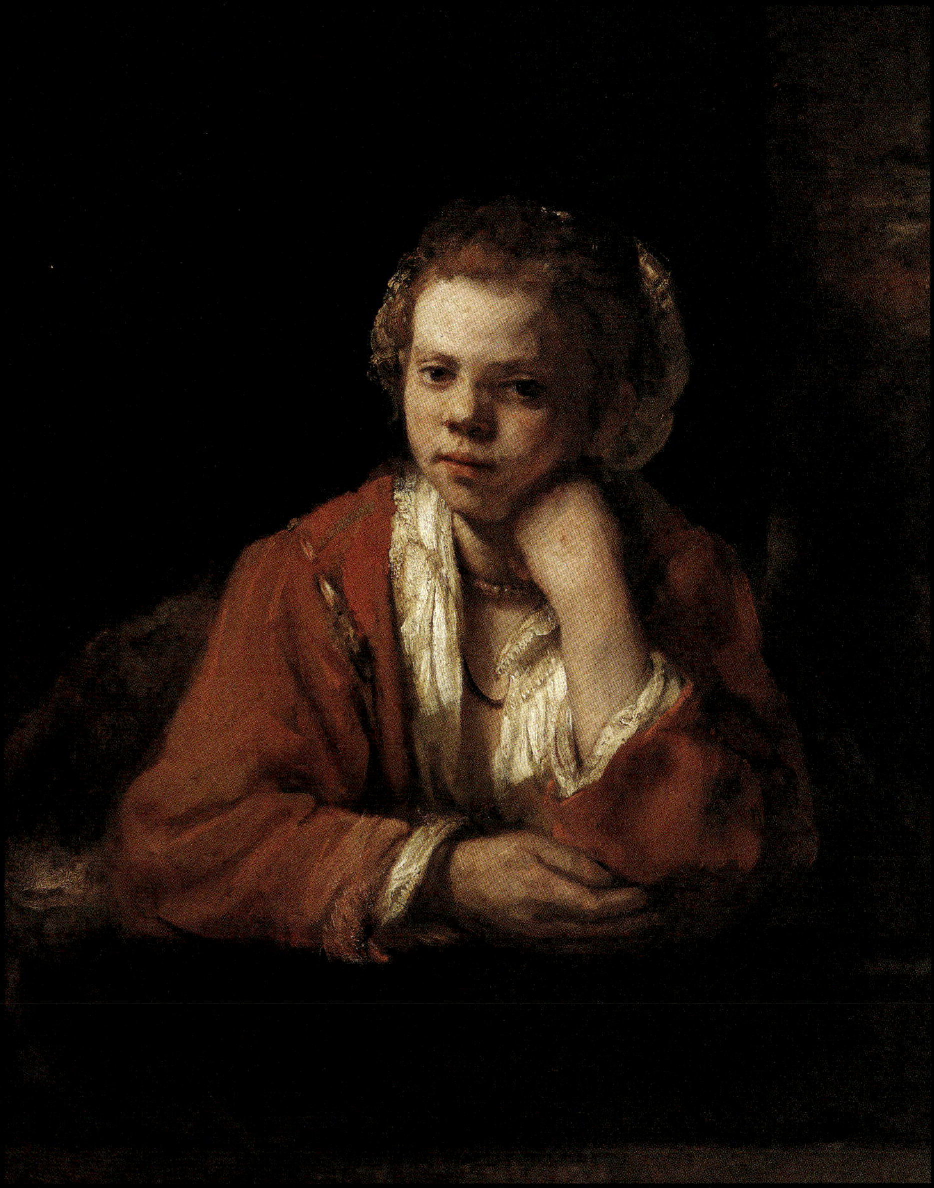

IV.

Rembrandt's Late Work

1652–1669

"But in Rembrandt's great portraits we feel face to face with real people, we sense their warmth, their need for sympathy and also their loneliness and their suffering. Those keen and steady eyes that we know so well from Rembrandt's self-portraits must have been able to look straight into the human heart."

ERNST GOMBRICH, 1951

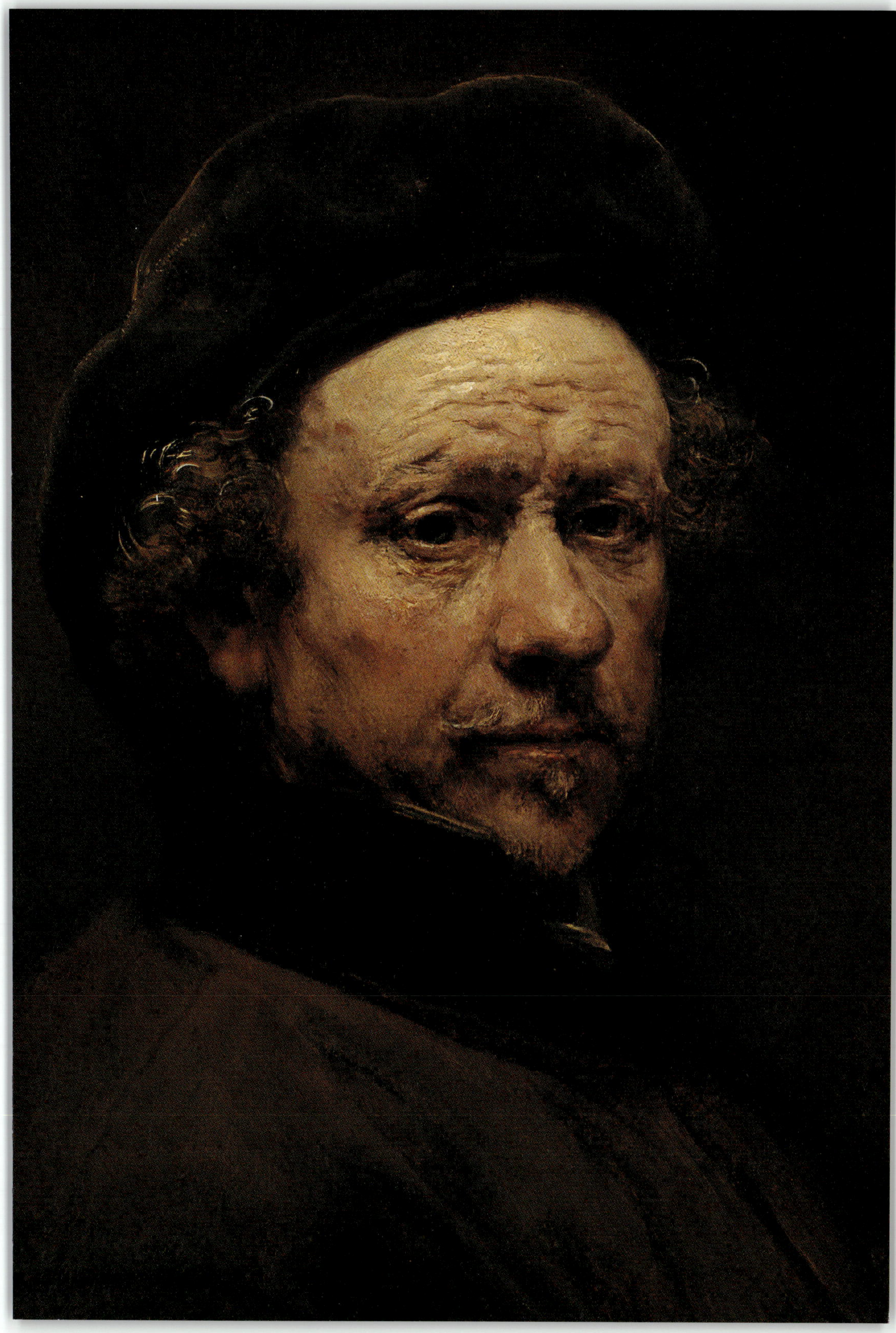

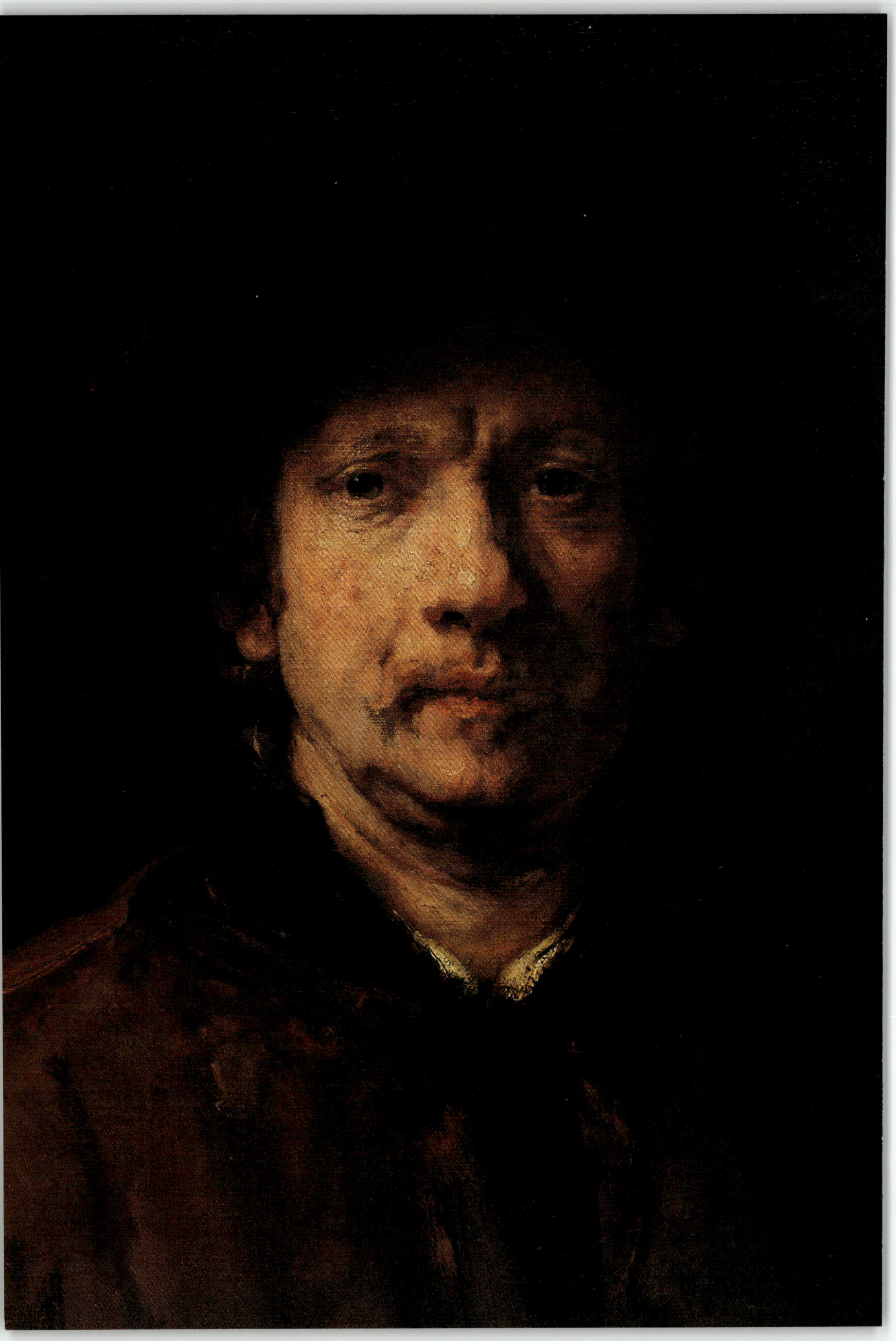

Financial Problems

After years of prosperity, it became clear in the spring of 1653 that Rembrandt was in financial difficulties. This is indicated by the fact that he took out large loans from acquaintances such as Cornelis Jansz. Witsen (1605–1669; RD 1653/5), Jan Six (RD 1653/11) and Isaac van Hertsbeeck (*c.* 1590–1668; RD 1653/12). He had already sold Jan Six a number of paintings in 1652, including *Saskia Uylenburgh in Sixteenth-Century Costume* (p. 201, Cat. 317) from 1633/34–1642 and *John the Baptist Preaching* (pp. 174/175, Cat. 57) from 1634/35 (RD 1658/18). He evidently cared greatly about these two paintings, because he had retained them for decades. About 1653, he must also have parted with his etching plates, because a few years later most of them were in the possession of the print dealer Clement de Jonghe (1624/25–1677).[192]

The house in Sint Antoniesbreestraat, which he had purchased in 1639 from Christoffel Thijs for 13,000 guilders, was signed over to Rembrandt in January 1653 (RD 1653/1). However, that year Rembrandt paid only the various taxes due after several payment reminders (RD 1653/2; RD 1653/3). He paid the principal of the purchase price with the loans from his friends. The outstanding interest remained as a loan from Thijs (RD 1653/6). Rembrandt was evidently still convinced at the time that he would be able to repay the loans, because he agreed with most of his creditors that he would pay back his debts during that same year. This did not happen, however, and in 1655 he started to look for a less expensive place to live.

In December 1655, he signed a contract with Otto van Cattenburch that he would purchase a house in Handboogstraat from him for 7,000 guilders, 4,000 guilders of which was to be in the form of a loan from the vendor that would be subject to interest. The remaining amount was to be paid in etchings and paintings (RD 1655/8). This transaction, a lucrative one for Rembrandt, was never realised for unknown reasons.[193] At the same time he decided to realise funds by selling part of his art collection in a public sale in the "Keyserskroon" inn (RD 1655/7).[194] It must have been quite a considerable part because the sale lasted two weeks, up to and including New Year's Day 1656. The proceeds must have been disappointing. In May 1656, possibly in an attempt at least to secure Titus' inheritance, Rembrandt had the house in Sint Antoniesbreestraat signed over to his son's name at the Amsterdam Orphans' Chamber (RD 1656/6). Since he could no

Page 361
Detail of: **Self-Portrait**, 1657
(see ill. p. 481)

Detail of: **Self-Portrait in Working Dress**, 1652
(see ill. p. 478)

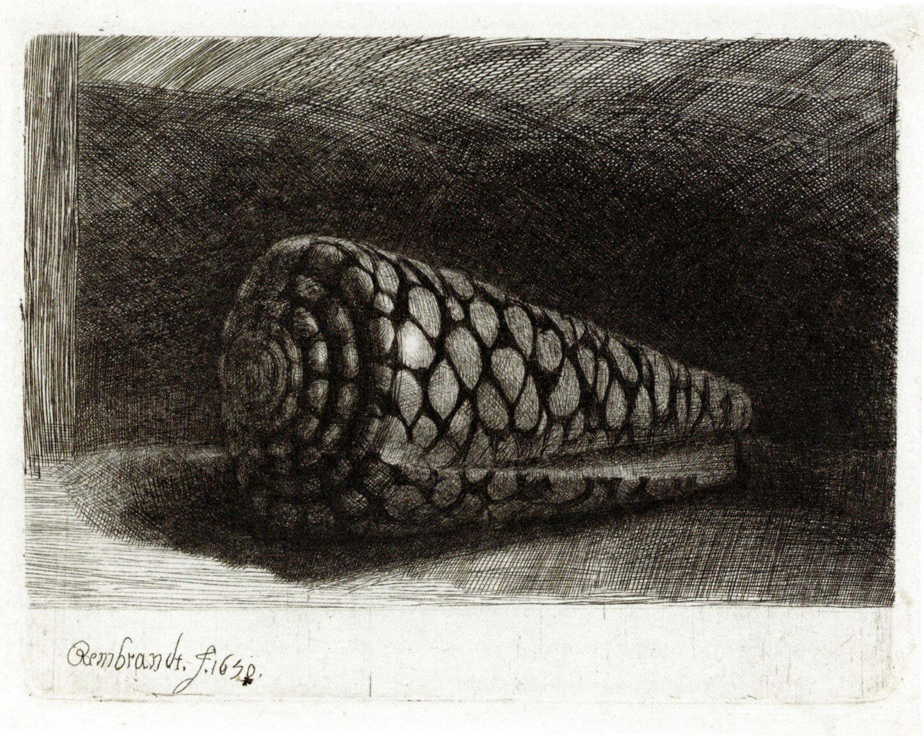

The Shell Conus Marmoreus, 1650
Etching, drypoint and burin, 9.7 × 13.2 cm (3 7/8 × 5 1/4 in.)
Amsterdam, Rijksmuseum

longer offer his creditors any mortgageable securities, bankruptcy was inevitable and he must have been aware of this. On 14 July 1656 Rembrandt applied to the *Hoge Raad*, the Supreme Court in The Hague, for a so-called *cessio bonorum* (RD 1656/10), an "honourable insolvency" on his own initiative. This was only granted to those who could prove that they had become bankrupt through no fault of their own. The Council granted permission for this on 8 August (1656/13).

Since Rembrandt surrendered his possessions voluntarily, his unpaid debts were thereafter dealt with by the civic *Desolate Boedelskamer*, the Amsterdam Bankruptcy Chamber. As a result of this decision in favour of the "honourable" bankruptcy, Rembrandt remained a free man and was spared the disgrace of an enforced bankruptcy. The consequence, however, was that all his possessions would be sold in public. On 25 and 26 July, Rembrandt was required to draw up an inventory of all his property in the presence of an administrator from the *Desolate Boedelskamer* (RD 1656/12). The list was 20 pages long and will have described the core of Rembrandt's collection. It did not include personal items such as clothing and tools which he required in order to be able to practise his profession. Thereafter, his furniture and paintings were auctioned in sessions lasting for several days. Unfortunately, the proceeds were not sufficient to pay all Rembrandt's debts, and so the administrator also sold the house in Sint Antoniesbreestraat. Legally, Titus was entitled to the proceeds, as was decided after almost 20 years of legal wrangling (RD 1665/15, 1665/22) – with the result that a number of Rembrandt's creditors never received their money. The house was sold on 1 February 1658 (RD 1658/3), and Rembrandt and his family moved into a rented house on the Rozengracht. In the autumn of 1658, public notices in Amsterdam were posted announcing the final sale (RD 1658/29), and on 20 December 1658 the large collection of drawings and prints which Rembrandt had assembled over the years at such cost and effort was sold. Its value was estimated at 4,000 guilders but despite their high quality, these fabulous works raised no more than 470 guilders and nine stuivers in all (RD 1658/30).[195]

It is difficult to say what precisely was the cause for Rembrandt's catastrophic financial situation. It is frequently claimed that he consumed too much of his fortune during the 1640s, because he did not take on any portrait commissions during this time. This explanation is not entirely convincing, however. The various periods in his career in which he did not accept any portrait commissions were the times when he had sufficient financial reserves to be able to afford to make such a decision. As mentioned, according to von Sandrart, the artist received an income of 2,500 guilders per year in tuition fees from his apprentices alone during these years. After Saskia's death in 1642, Rembrandt estimated the value of their joint possessions at more than 40,000 guilders (RD 1662/14). The main part of this fortune will have consisted of the house, which had not yet been paid off, and his stock of artworks which had been purchased at high prices. There are no indications that Rembrandt had also invested in property, land or securities. The fact that he had invested most of his money in works of art became a major problem after the outbreak of the First Anglo-Dutch War in 1652. This lasted until 1654 and led to a surge of bankruptcies as a result of the English blockade. The demand for luxury goods declined dramatically and prices hit rock bottom.[196] In his application for permission for the *cessio bonorum*, Rembrandt himself claimed that "losses suffered in trade and damages and losses at sea" were the reason for his inability to pay back his creditors (RD 1656/10).

Without doubt, the sale of his extensive collection must have been an enormous professional blow to Rembrandt. The obligation of drawing up an inventory provides, however, an insight into the nature of his collection. Contrary to previous assumptions, it was by no means just an accumulation of rags or a random cabinet of curiosities filled with exotic objects. Nor did it have the encyclopaedic character of a collection owned by a *collectionneur* or a *gentleman virtuoso*; it was a true artist's collection containing a large amount of study material and the odd curiosity such as shells (p. 364, Cat. E160) or oriental weapons which Rembrandt only occasionally used for his works.[197] One of the finest pieces from classical antiquity was the bust of Homer which can be seen in his *Aristotle with the Bust of Homer* (pp. 430/431, Cat. 114). The main focus of Rembrandt's collecting practice lay especially on art objects, but he did not simply assemble studio props. The most important part of Rembrandt's collection consisted of graphic works by other artists, especially old masters like Albrecht Dürer and Lucas van Leyden. He had acquired these, for example, at the auctions of the collections of Jan Bassé in 1637 and Gommer Spranger in 1638 (RD 1637/2, 1638/2), in times when he was still earning well (see pp. 283–288, 290). Part of his art collection was probably also intended as trade stock.

Rembrandt assembled his paper art in almost 90 "art books" and owned what was probably one of the most important collections of prints in Amsterdam, both in quantity and in quality. The classification system which he used in arranging his collection of prints and drawings is remarkable. Generally, works were kept according to subject and then arranged within the collection hierarchically according to genre. History, the genre with the highest prestige, was generally subdivided thematically, while portraits were classified according to the rank of the sitters, for example popes, kings, dukes or poets. Rembrandt, by contrast, generally arranged his prints according to artist. His aim was to collect complete oeuvres by artists and his system virtually anticipates the classification principle adopted by modern art historians. He classified prints according to the country of origin of the artist and separated German, Flemish and Italian artists from each other. He kept "kopere printen" (copper engravings) separately from "hout printen" (woodcuts). Rembrandt stored his own drawings in separate portfolios in categories such as figural studies, nudes and animal studies, and also landscapes "nae 't leven" (from life) and drawings of sculptures ("statuen"). It was probably thanks to his education at grammar school that he arranged the busts of the Roman emperors in strict chronological order.

Rembrandt kept erotic sheets, referred to as "de bouleringe" (lovemaking) separate from everything else. They were kept in their own portfolio and included, amongst other works, engravings after Raphael and Annibale Carracci. He frequently purchased complete series, and he even possessed several copies of some prints, such as the "copper engravings by Lucas van Leiden, both double and single" (RD 1656/12: fol. 34r). These were possibly not only study material for practical use in the workshop but also private

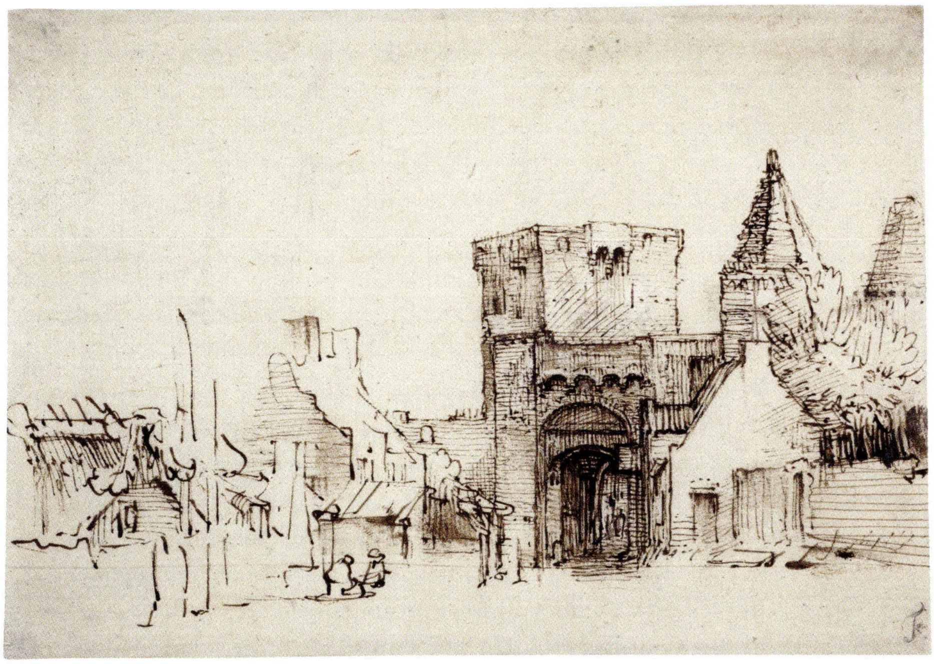

The Rijnpoort Town Gate in Rhenen, 1650–1652
Pen and brush in brown, 11.9 × 17.5 cm (4 ¾ × 7 in.)
Chatsworth, The Duke of Devonshire and the Trustees of the Chatsworth Settlement

collector's pieces, or possibly duplicates for resale. In the case of two albums, by Titian and Maerten van Heemskerck, Rembrandt had the clerk note in the inventory that he owned almost the complete oeuvre of both. In many cases, comments praising the work were added, such as "very fine print". Although most of his collection was auctioned during the 1650s, Rembrandt must have retained a few valuables of which he was especially fond or which were of essential significance for his creative work. It is known, for example, that on 23 July 1668 he still had in his possession a book containing the work of "Lucas van Leyden, as well as several drawings by the same Lucas van Leyden", which he used as security for a loan (RD 1668/5).

However, the consequence of his difficult financial circumstances was, that Rembrandt, after a period during which he had primarily focused on etching, took up painting again and also began to accept portrait commissions.

Hendrickje Stoffels

About 1648, the young Hendrickje Stoffelsdr. Jegers from the garrison town of Bredevoort in Gelderland was engaged by Rembrandt as a maidservant and to look after Titus. Her father, the sergeant and huntsman Stoffel Stoffelsz. Jeger, had probably died in 1646, and it may have been her mother's remarriage in 1647 that prompted the 21-year-old Hendrickje to seek her fortune in Amsterdam. It was probably not long before she took her predecessor Geertje Dircks' place as Rembrandt's companion in the artist's household. Immediately after Geertje had left the house in Sint Antoniesbreestraat in June 1649, Rembrandt accompanied Hendrickje on a journey to Bredevoort (RD 1649/1). He made drawings of the town gate in Rhenen (p. 367, Cat. D605), a small town halfway between Bredevoort and Amsterdam.

In 1654, Hendrickje was summoned to appear before the Reformed Church Council, where she was required to justify the fact that she was living together with the painter Rembrandt in a common-law marriage (RD 1654/11). Initially she did not respond to these or further summons, but eventually she did appear before the Council. As was usual in such cases, she was strongly admonished and banned from attending The Lord's Supper (RD 1654/15). Rembrandt was not summoned because he was evidently not a member of the Reformed Church. The immediate cause for this admonition was the fact that Hendrickje was pregnant. Three months later in the Oude Kerk their daughter Cornelia (1654–1678), was baptised, named after Rembrandt's deceased mother (RD 1654/18). The baptismal register did not record that the child was illegitimate, probably because the father himself presented her at the baptismal font. Frequently, an illegitimate child was later made legitimate by the marriage of the parents, but this was evidently not possible. If Rembrandt were to remarry he would have been obliged to pay Titus his share of his mother's inheritance – estimated as being in excess of 20,000 guilders. That would have been difficult in view of Rembrandt's precarious financial situation. The fact that no marriage took place, however, was highly disadvantageous to Hendrickje and Cornelia, both legally and financially, especially if Rembrandt were to die.

To the outside world, the couple lived as husband and wife. In 1661, Hendrickje was respectfully referred to as "Juffrouw Hendrickyen Stoffels, huysvrouw van Sr. Rembrant van Reyn" (Mistress Hendrickyen Stoffels, wife of sir Rembrandt van Reyn; RD 1661/12) in a neighbourhood matter, and Rembrandt himself also later called her "his late wife" (RD 1664/4). After they moved to Rozengracht in May 1658, Hendrickje

Detail of: **Self-Portrait**, 1658
(see ill. p. 485)

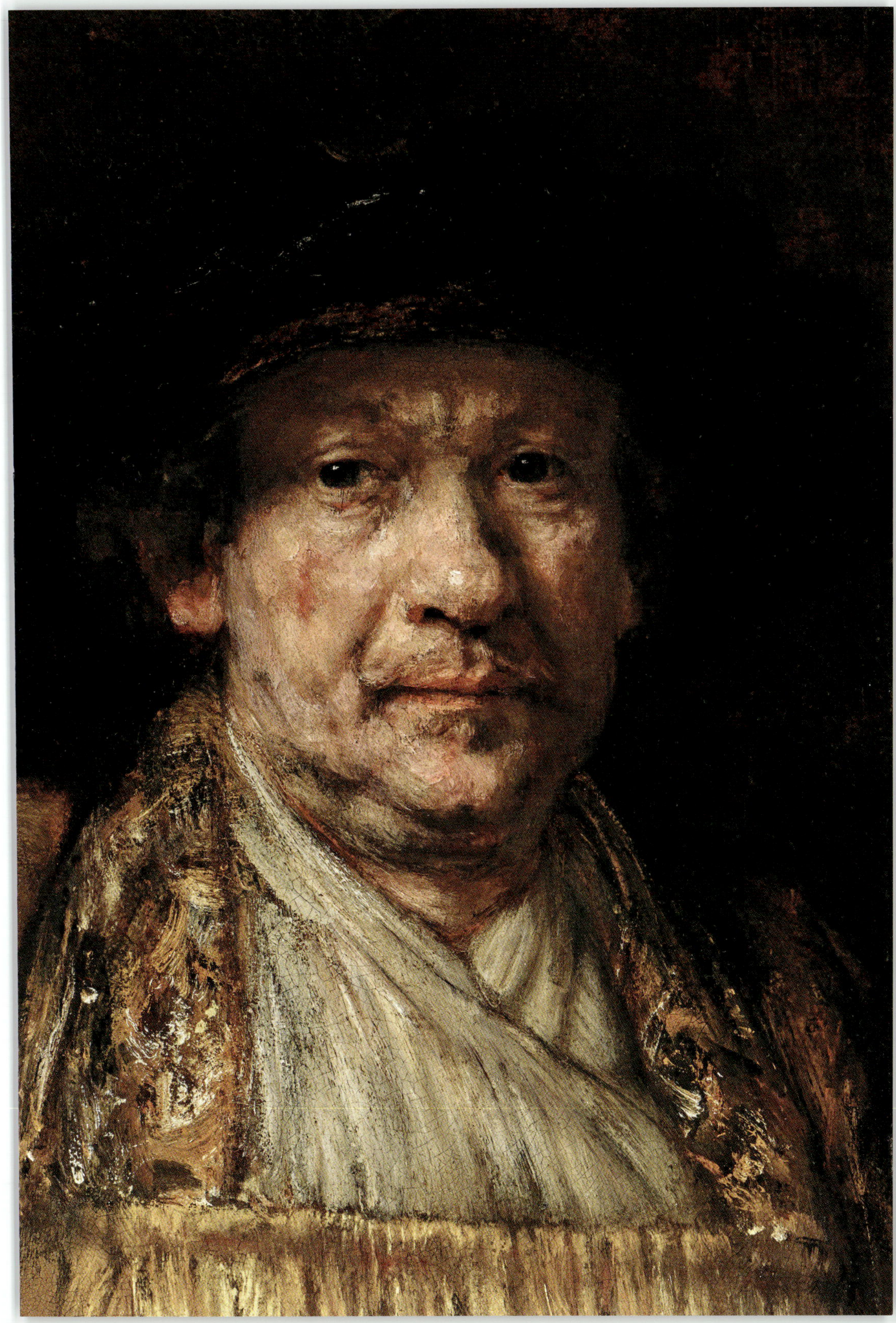

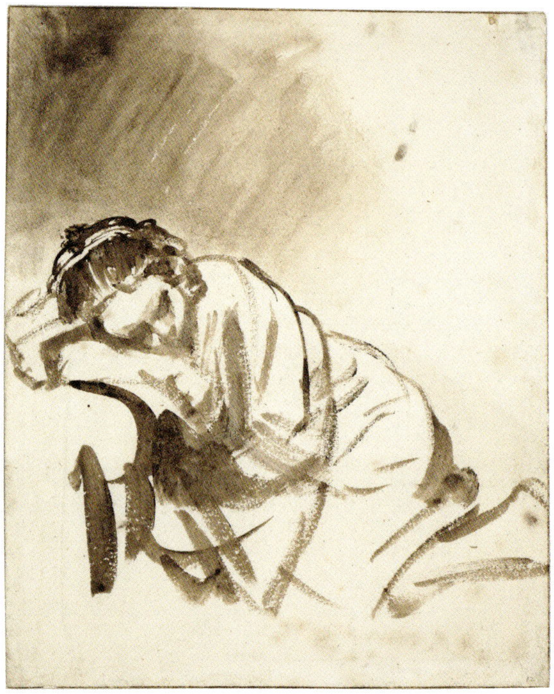

and the 17-year-old Titus started "a certain company or trading business" in which the two of them sold paintings, prints and curiosities. In December 1660, this became an official trading partnership (RD 1660/20), in which the equal partners engaged Rembrandt as an unpaid employee in return for food and board. Hendrickje invested the sum of 800 guilders in the firm as business capital, and Titus contributed 950 guilders. Titus declared that the money consisted of his earnings and his baptismal gifts; it was not clear, however, where Hendrickje's capital came from. The company created by Hendrickje and Titus has frequently and undeservedly been dismissed as a vehicle on paper only, designed to protect Rembrandt from the demands of his creditors. However, although he may have been the driving force behind this legal construct, here his motives were not entirely selfish. In this way it was possible to secure both Hendrickje's and Cornelia's financial future. As an illegitimate child, according to the laws of the time Cornelia was able to inherit only from her mother but not from her father.[198] It was therefore important that Hendrickje should have property of her own, at least on paper. Nonetheless, she seems not to have been a mere sleeping partner within this legal arrangement; she was actually active in the art trade.[199] Thus the connoisseur Edmé-François Gersaint commented that Rembrandt had married a wife who "was very skilful in selling his works and who demanded very high prices for them".[200] This can only refer to Hendrickje, because neither Saskia nor Geertje seems to have been involved in the art trade in any way.

Hendrickje Sleeping, *c.* 1654
Brushwork in brown and white, 24.6 × 20.3 cm (9¾ × 8 in.)
London, British Museum

On 7 August 1661, Hendrickje drew up a will in which she named Rembrandt as the sole guardian of Cornelia (RD 1661/6). Cornelia was her sole heir, which she would have been even if Hendrickje had not made a will. If Cornelia were to die earlier, Titus was to inherit Hendrickje's possessions. Hendrickje died during the summer of 1663, probably as a victim of a plague epidemic, which was particularly virulent in Amsterdam during that year. She was buried on 24 July 1663 in a leased grave in the Westerkerk (RD 1663/4).

There are no documented portraits of Hendrickje, but from the early 1650s a model appears in Rembrandt's history paintings and single figures with a round forehead, brown eyes and curls who probably bears her features (p. 370, Cat. D 441; p. 423, Cat. 108, 109; p. 421, Cat. 112; p. 414, Cat. 324; p. 417, Cat. 325; p. 415, Cat. 327; Cat. 328, 329). On the one hand, the woman seems to be a general idealised female type, like the "Saskia" type who frequently recurs in his works from the 1630s, including the blonde girl in *"The Night Watch"* (pp. 324/325, Cat. 265).[201] Similarly, all the women in Rembrandt's portraits from the time around 1665 (Cat. 220; pp. 424/425, Cat. 268; pp. 470/471, Cat. 269) not only resemble each other to a great extent but also look like the "Hendrickje" type, despite the fact that it was already two years since she had died. Yet, the woman in Rembrandt's work, believed to be Hendrickje, is always wearing a contemporary hairstyle and earrings irrespective of the different costumes and roles in which she is portrayed – which indeed seems to indicate that Rembrandt was painting an existing model.

In 1782 a painting by Rembrandt was auctioned in London. It was described as "His wife in the character of Queen Bathseba, a very noble and masterly performance in point of effect and colouring".[202] Although it is by no means certain that this is the work in question, the description makes us think involuntarily of Rembrandt's *Bathsheba with King David's Letter* from 1654 (pp. 418/419, Cat. 23). With the message in her hand, her head slightly lowered, Bathsheba appears totally lost in thought and oblivious of the old maidservant who is tending to her foot. By placing her close to the picture plane and putting her in dramatic light, Rembrandt has especially emphasised Bathsheba's naked vulnerability. In contrast to his predecessors or contemporaries, Rembrandt concentrated on Bathsheba's inner emotional state, which has never before been as poignantly portrayed as it is here. The artist records the moment of her moral dilemma in having to decide in favour of obedience to her king or loyalty towards her husband, realising that the end would be fateful, whichever way she decides. Her beauty had evoked this tragedy. The intimate mood of the painting – which shows one of Rembrandt's rare nude figures – led to the assumption even at an early stage that it was Hendrickje who had posed for the future biblical queen. Did she pose as a nude model for Rembrandt?[203] Since we see

Bathsheba's face only in profile, it is difficult to ascertain whether she does indeed bear a resemblance to the other possible "Hendrickjes".

An equally intimate and mysterious mood can be observed in *Bathing Woman* (*Hendrickje?*; p. 417, Cat. 325) from the same year. Thanks to its spontaneous execution, the little panel almost has the character of an oil sketch and is a typical example of Rembrandt's new painting style. In contrast to the hair and face – which are both executed subtly and with great care – the chemise is indicated with thick, rapid brushstrokes. The hand is even more summarily rendered, so that for a long time it was believed that the work was unfinished. And yet this impression of spontaneity is partly superficial, because the painting consists of various layers which had to dry before Rembrandt could continue to work. At the end he added his signature, which indicates that he considered the work to be finished. It shows a young woman who is holding up her chemise as she wades through a stream. Believing herself to be unobserved, she seems to be enjoying the cool water. The gleaming red and gold robe behind her (comparable with that of Bathsheba or Susanna) and the dark setting arouse the impression that this is not an ordinary scene, but rather a biblical or mythological history painting. Since, however, all other iconographical references are absent, it impossible to identify the woman with any precision. Perhaps Rembrandt intentionally left the question of her identity open. In this way, the picture remains a mysterious image of a woman wading through water, completely absorbed in her own world.

It is not surprising that Hendrickje was seen as the model for the woman. The apparently spontaneous execution, the iconographical ambiguity, but above all the informal pose and the intimate mood make this assumption tempting. In this context it is notable that the hair of the bathing woman, like that of Bathsheba, has been pinned up in a fashionable style, unlike that of Rembrandt's earlier bathing historical heroines, for example the two Susannas, whose hair is loose (pp. 243, 244/245, Cat. 14, 18). This strengthens the impression that Rembrandt wanted to portray the model –thought to be Hendrickje – in a recognisable way.

Rembrandt and Titian

Throughout Rembrandt's career, the works of Titian were an important source of inspiration. This applied not only to his use of certain motifs but also to composition and style. In the inventory of Rembrandt's possessions drawn up in 1656 on the occasion of his bankruptcy, mention is made of a large album with prints after "almost all the works of Titian". He also owned a book with "contrefijtsels" (likenesses) by Titian and other artists (RD 1656/12). These were reproduction engravings after portraits by the Venetian artist. There are numerous indications that Rembrandt knew Titian's

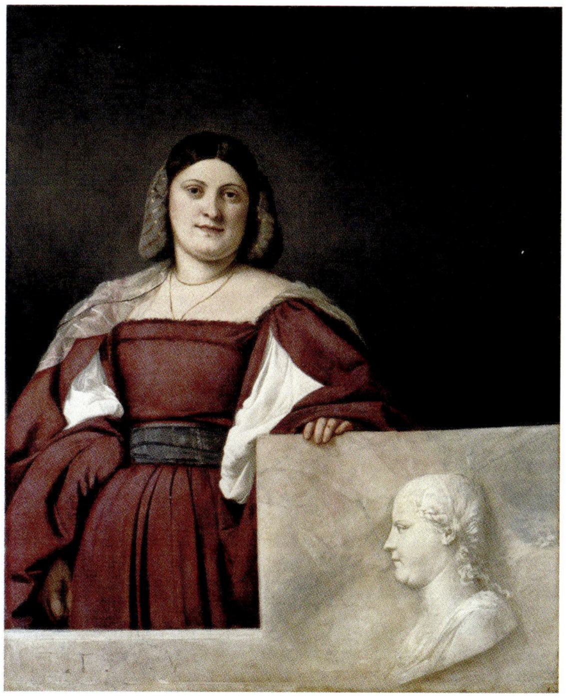

compositions through engravings.[204] There is little doubt that *The Ascension* from 1636 (p. 187, Cat. 61) was based on Titian's *Assumption of the Virgin Mary (Assunta)* from 1516–1518 in Santa Maria Gloriosa dei Frari in Venice (p. 186).

It is very likely that Rembrandt was familiar with the engraving which Theodoor Matham (1605/06–1676) had made of Titian's altarpiece in Venice.[205] Furthermore, the group of figures around Callisto in Rembrandt's *Diana Bathing, with Actaeon and Callisto* (pp. 214/215, Cat. 99) is derived from the engraving by Cornelis Cort dated 1566 after Titian's painting *Diana and Callisto* from 1556–1559 in Edinburgh (Scottish National Gallery).[206] What is remarkable is that Titian also painted the encounter between Actaeon and Diana as a companion piece for his Callisto painting (Edinburgh, Scottish National Gallery). Since Rembrandt combined the two scenes in a single painting it is not clear how he could have known about Titian's scene showing Actaeon and Diana, since we do not know of an engraving after it. It is very likely that he remembered van Mander's biography of Titian, in which the painting is mentioned as being in the possession of King Philip II of Spain (1527–1598).[207] Rembrandt also made use of two etchings by Antonio Tempesta showing the two scenes separately but in a forested setting comparable with that in Rembrandt's painting, and with small figures.

Rembrandt knew Titian's paintings not only through the prints in his collection. He was evidently also familiar with painted or drawn copies which were in Amsterdam and occasionally even originals by the Venetian artist. Both Rembrandt's *Flora*

Titian, **Portrait of a Lady ("La Schiavona")**, *c.* 1510–1512
Oil on canvas, 119.4 × 96.5 cm (47 × 38 in.)
London, The National Gallery

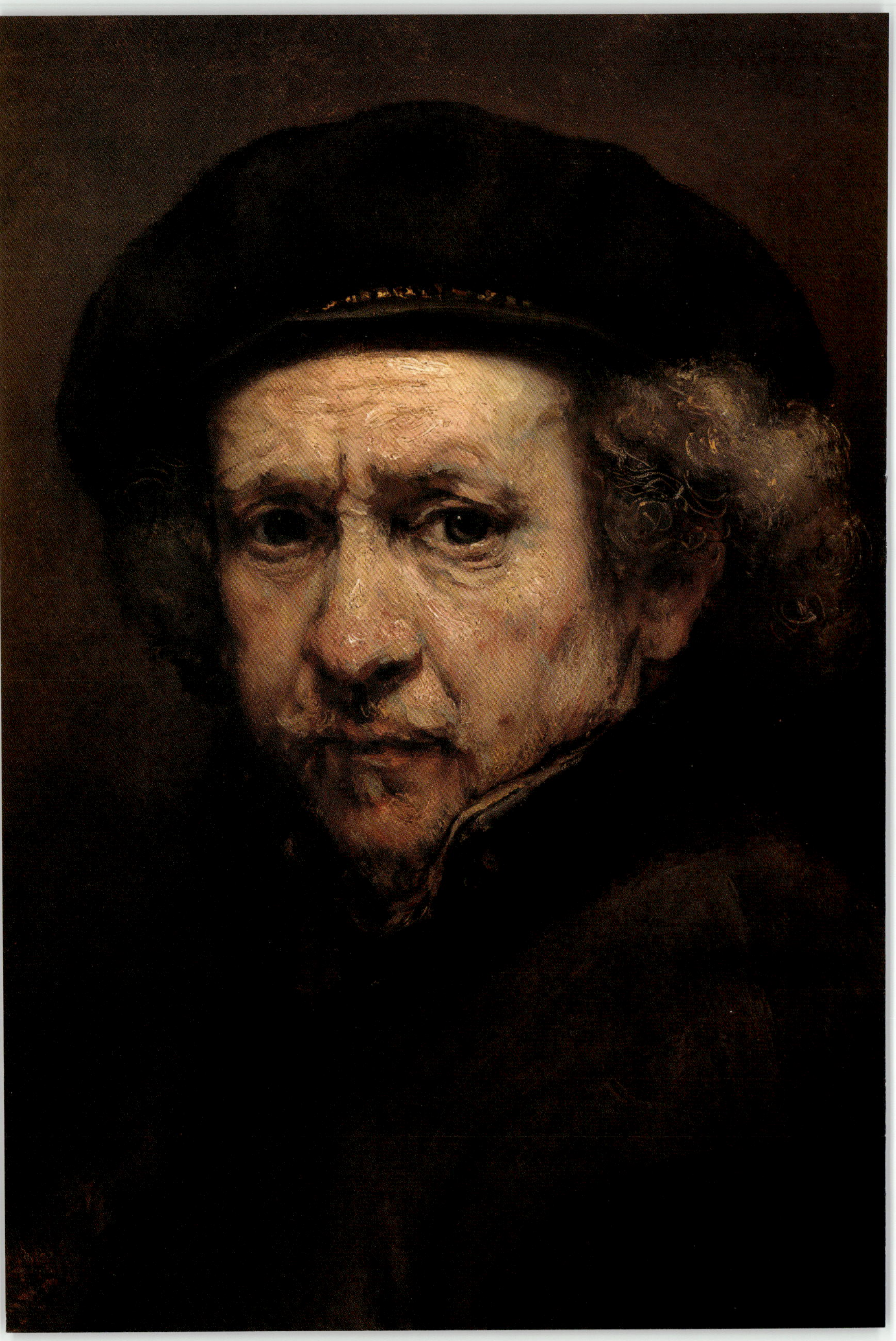

(p. 353, Cat. 106) from 1641, and his painting with the same subject from about 1660 (p. 421, Cat. 112), contain clear references to Titian's *Flora* (p. 420) from around 1515–1520 in the Uffizi in Florence. Between 1637 and 1641 the painting was in the Amsterdam collection of the Portuguese diplomat, collector and art agent Alfonso López (1572–1649) before he moved to Paris. Joachim von Sandrart made a drawing of the painting in Amsterdam around 1640 and commissioned Reinier van Persijn (1614–1668) to make an engraving which Rembrandt surely knew. It provided him with inspiration for his late *Flora*, although Titian's original had long since left Amsterdam.[208] Alfonso López's collection also included Titian's *Portrait of Gerolamo (?) Barbarigo* (London, The National Gallery), which in the seventeenth century was thought to be a portrait of the poet Ariosto. Rembrandt also knew this painting, as can be seen in his etched self-portrait from 1638 (Cat. E214) and the painted self-portrait dated 1640 (Cat. 157). In both works, the pose with the arm positioned parallel to a sill resembles the portrait by Titian as well as Raphael's *Portrait of Baldassare Castiglione* in the Louvre, created 1514/15. Regardless of the general similarity to the portraits by Titian and Raphael, other details indicate that Rembrandt deliberately identified in his self-portrait with the Northern European portrait tradition of the first three decades of the sixteenth century (see pp. 290–293).

In the 1630s and 1640s, Rembrandt still referred explicitly to Titian as a source through the selection and adoption of certain motifs. During the 1650s and later years, Rembrandt made less use of specific pictorial elements from Titian's oeuvre. Less often he chose the same subject matter and the references to Titian are of a more general nature. The supposed link between Rembrandt's *Juno* (p. 423, Cat. 108) and Titian's *Portrait of a Lady ("La Schiavona")* from about 1510–1512 in London (p. 373), for example, is a problematic one.[209] Related are for instance the frontality of the figure, the horizontal neckline and the hairnet with its decoration of pearls. There are differences, however, especially in the positioning of the figure in the picture space and its proportions. Titian's portrait remained in the possession of the Martinengo Family in Brescia from about 1640 until the mid-nineteenth century, and there is no known reproduction print after it. It therefore cannot be considered as a direct model for Rembrandt's work. More likely, Rembrandt took other Venetian three-quarter-length women's portraits as models, for example a portrait attributed to Bonifazio de' Pitati Veronese (1487–1533).[210] Other possible models would also be portraits by Giovanni Cariani (1485–1547), Paris Bordone (1500–1571) and Francesco Montemezzano (*c.* 1540–after 1602).

Detail of: **Self-Portrait**, 1659
(see ill. p. 487)

There is no doubt that Rembrandt's late style is amongst the most spectacular aspects of his oeuvre. It differs considerably from his style of the early years and has contributed in no small measure to his fame. In his early years, he painted in a predominantly smooth and not infrequently highly detailed manner with forms determined by contour lines. Admittedly, even during this time he experimented with a spontaneous and less detailed style, as we can see for example in some of his early self-portraits (p. 79, Cat. 146; p. 80, Cat. 142) and *tronies* (Cat. 272; p. 77, Cat. 275; p. 256, Cat. 283). However, only during the further course of his career did Rembrandt change his style fundamentally, choosing a much freer manner characterised by clearly visible brushstrokes which were not blended: the so-called "rough" manner. Examples of this include, amongst other works, the *Family Portrait* from about 1665 (pp. 424/425, Cat. 268) and *Portrait of a Young Woman with a Lapdog* (p. 427, Cat. 219), painted at around the same time. This style of Rembrandt's has frequently been connected with Titian's sketch-like and blotched late style (*pittura di macchia*).[211] Paintings executed in this style frequently give the impression of being unfinished. This applies, for example, to Rembrandt's painting *Moses Breaking the Tablets of the Law* (p. 428, Cat. 27), which is signed and dated 1659. The artist's biographer Arnold Houbraken makes clear in his biography of Rembrandt that, according to the artist, a work does not need to be executed down to the last detail in order to be regarded as completed. He puts the following saying into Rembrandt's mouth: "dat een stuk voldaan is als de meester zyn voornemen daar in bereikt heeft" (that a work is finished when the master has achieved his intention in it).[212]

In art history Rembrandt's "rough" manner is often related to Titian's late style. Titian's late work was expressly praised by Giorgio Vasari – contrary to the frequently negative assessment of the manner of artists in old age, that their style is supposedly characterised by a decline of artistic skills. Rembrandt and his artist colleagues doubtless knew Vasari's biography of Titian, because Karel van Mander followed it almost word for word in his *Schilder-Boeck* from 1604.[213] What was doubtless important for Rembrandt was the fact that Vasari's positive assessment of Titian's late works was explicitly shared by van Mander. In his didactic poem "Den Grondt der Edel vry Schilder-const" at the beginning of the *Schilder-Boeck*, he reports in his address to young artists that the young Titian had executed his paintings in a fine technique with great neatness ("netticheyt"). Later, however, he had adopted a style with blotches and rough brushstrokes ("met vlecken en rouw' streken"), which only achieved the desired effect when the works were seen at a distance and not at close quarters.[214] Moreover, van Mander warned of the pitfalls of this technique, which had resulted in particularly clumsy and awkward paintings by some of Titian's imitators, because these painters had thought that he had executed his works without putting any effort into them. According to van Mander, the

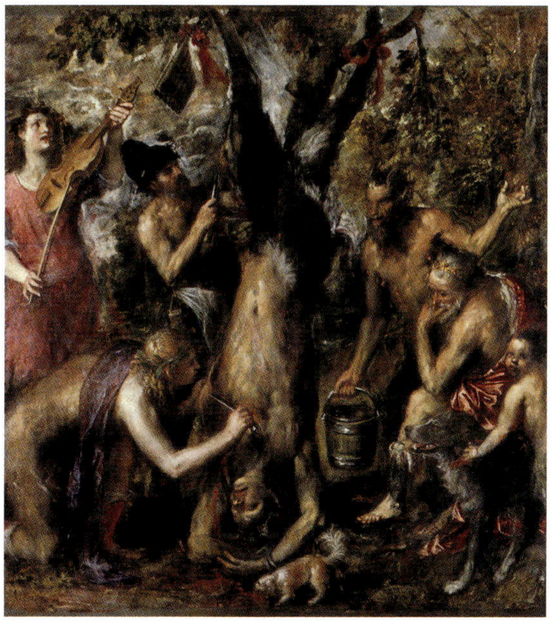

fact that this was by no means the case could be seen in the numerous overpaintings which Titian had undertaken in order to make corrections. Finally, he advised young painters to decide between the "fine" and the rough manner, but in any case to begin with the former.[215]

Rembrandt began his works by applying the paint directly onto the panel or the canvas. Only occasionally did he make precise preliminary studies on paper. As a consequence, he undertook various modifications during the painting process. Corrections in the form of *pentimenti* by the artist were an inevitable side effect of Titian's late style. According to Vasari, the latter was convinced that painting with paint only without drawn preliminary studies on paper was the best working method and represented true art.[216] Rembrandt, who no doubt shared this opinion, used a similar approach. However, his habit to make modifications in the course of the painting process was not restricted to his late work but already prevalent in his early works.

It is not possible to answer the question as to how many of Titian's late works Rembrandt knew and could study in the original in order to gain an authentic impression of the Venetian artist's painting style. Drawings and engravings are not a satisfactory substitute in this case. There were collections of paintings containing Venetian works in the Northern Netherlands, assembled by merchant families who maintained intensive business contacts with Venice and who had agents on the spot to advise them about art purchases. Amongst the most important collectors, who also dealt in art and who had excellent contacts in Venice, were Daniel Nijs (1572–1647), Jan Niquet (1539–1608), Lucas van Uffelen (1586–1638) and the brothers Gerard (1599–1658) and

Titian, **The Flaying of Marsyas,** *c.* 1570–1576
Oil on canvas, 212 × 207 cm (83 ½ × 81 ½ in.)
Kroměříž, Archbishop's Palace

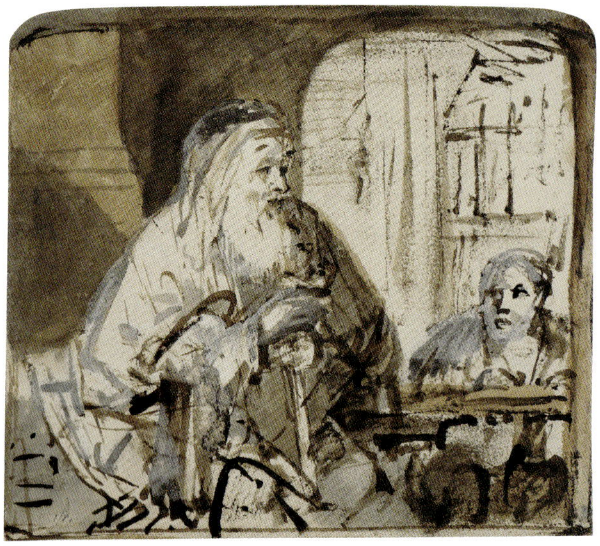

Jan (1601–1646) Reynst, the grandsons of Jan Niquet.[217] The lion's share of the collection of the Reynst brothers was originally owned by the Venetian aristocrat Andrea Vendramin (1565?–1629) and was shipped to Amsterdam in the 1630s and kept in the brothers' house on the Keizersgracht (no. 209). The collection included a large number of works by Venetian artists, including Jacopo Bassano (*c.* 1510–1592), Paris Bordone, Lorenzo Lotto (*c.* 1480–1556/57), Jacopo Tintoretto (1518–1594), Paolo Veronese (1528–1588) and also Titian.[218] However, there were no works that were characteristic of Titian's late style in the Reynst collection, which Rembrandt doubtless knew.

What is certain, however, is that the widow of Thomas Howard, Earl of Arundel (1585–1646), whose painting collection contained some 600 works, owned at least one late work by Titian: *The Flaying of Marsyas*, which is preserved today in the Archbishop's Palace in Kroměříž (Czech Republic; p. 377).[219] The collection of the English aristocrat, who had lived in exile since 1642, shared the odyssey of its owner. After the death of his widow in Amsterdam in 1654, it was assembled there, an inventory was drawn up and it was prepared for sale. Rembrandt will certainly have had an opportunity to study the collection, which was held in temporary storage in a house on the Keizersgracht.[220] However, if we compare Titian's *The Flaying of Marsyas* stylistically with typical late works by Rembrandt, it seems hardly credible that contemporary art lovers would have found strong points of similarity between the two artists. What distinguishes Rembrandt's late works from Titian's is above all the great differentiation in the handling of paint depending on the texture of the objects and motifs depicted. The blotched paint application executed with coarse brushstrokes which both Vasari

Homer Dictates His Poetry to a Scribe, 1661/62
Pen and brown ink, brush in brown and white, yellow and grey,
14.9 × 16.8 cm (5 ⅞ × 6 ⅝ in.). Stockholm, Nationalmuseum

and subsequently van Mander saw as being typical of Titian's late work is used only locally by Rembrandt, and primarily where it can contribute to the heightening of the illusionism. This can be found occasionally even in Rembrandt's early works, for example when, in order to characterise the old age of the sitter of the portrait, he executes the skin either with delicate and carefully scumbled (p. 143, Cat. 224) or with short, heavy pastose brushstrokes positioned side by side (p. 164, Cat. 213). It is notable that Gerard de Lairesse (1640–1711; p. 451, Cat. 205) emphasises that the similarities between Rembrandt and Titian apply above all to their use of colour and that in this respect "Rembrandt did not yield to Titian".[221] Rembrandt studied Titian in great depth, but it was rightly pointed out that it was not so much the familiarity with the Italian artist's paintings itself that inspired him, but rather "the Titian *legend* that had the strongest impact on him", as van de Wetering writes.[222]

Commissions from Italy

Although, as the Italian biographer Baldinucci writes (1686), there were only a few paintings by Rembrandt in Italy, his fame had also spread to these regions by the middle of the century.[223] The clerk who kept Cosimo de' Medici's diary wrote of him in 1667 as a "pittore famoso" (famous painter). Especially the rarity of his works could have made them particularly desirable for Italian collectors. In 1668, he was likewise described in the list of paintings of the Ruffo Collection as "Pittore olandese stimatissimo e raro" (highly estimated, rare Dutch painter).[224]

During the last decades of his life, Rembrandt was approached by three aristocratic Italian art lovers to paint pictures for them. He received the first commissions, which were extensively documented, from Messina, from Don Antonio Ruffo (*c.* 1610–1678).[225] Around 1652 this Sicilian prince must have asked Rembrandt to paint a life-size, half-length figure. Rembrandt painted *Aristotle with the Bust of Homer* (pp. 430/431, Cat. 114) dated 1653 for him, for which, according to his invoice, he was paid the sum of 500 guilders (RD 1654/10). In 1654, the work was described as "a half-length figure of a philosopher made in Amsterdam by the painter called Rembrandt (it seems to be an Aristotle or Albertus Magnus)" (RD 1654/16). The uncertainty regarding the identity of the figure proves that the artist himself was responsible for the choice of subject. His rather melancholy rendition of the ancient philosopher lost in thought was unusual and contained not only references to Alexander the Great (356–323 BC), the pupil of Aristotle (384–322 BC), but also to the poet Homer, whom both greatly admired. Although it is questionable whether the ambitious iconography was recognised by the client, the latter was evidently so taken by the work that he asked the Italian artist Guercino (1591–1666) to paint a companion piece. Because the Bolognese artist erroneously interpreted the half-length figure as a physiognomist, he created a *Cosmographer* in 1660 as a counterpart. Over the years Ruffo commissioned four more Italian artists to paint half-length figures with the aim of creating a larger series around the *Aristotle*.[226]

About 1660 Rembrandt himself must have received a commission to paint two further single figures with the same measurements as the *Aristotle*. That, at least, can be gathered from a handwritten note in which he agreed to the measurements of the two new works to be painted, each of which was to be 6 (Sicilian) *palmi* wide and 8 *palmi* in height, approximately 154.8 × 206.4 cm (RD 1661/5).[227] Ruffo had evidently complained about the price, because Rembrandt assured him once more that his asking price for the paintings should not be considered too high. Taking up the references to Homer and Alexander the Great which were already present in the *Aristotle*, in 1661 Rembrandt painted a seated "Alexander the Great", a work for which he once more received the sum of 500 guilders (RD 1661/5). In the invoice enclosed on 30 July 1661, he already listed the costs for the canvas for a depiction of Homer which was still to be painted, and which today has survived only in the form of a fragment (p. 432, Cat. 116). Over a year later, Rembrandt sent the prince the half-finished *Homer* for his approval. Ruffo was evidently satisfied with this layout, because he requested Rembrandt via his agent in a letter dated 1 November 1662 to complete the picture (RD 1662/11). In the same letter he also complained, however, that the Alexander which he had received the previous year consisted of four pieces of canvas and that the seams were annoyingly visible. He expressed the suspicion that Rembrandt had enlarged a previously painted head to make a half-length figure by adding pieces of canvas, and he suggested that Rembrandt should therefore grant him a discount of 250 guilders on the *Homer* (for which Rembrandt was again asking 500 guilders), or else that he should send him a completely new version of the Alexander.

Remarkably, the relatively detailed Ruffo documents in the literature have given rise to contradictory interpretations and misunderstandings. For example, attempts have been made to identify both *Man in Armour* (*Mars?*; p. 355, Cat. 107) and *Minerva* in Lisbon (Cat. 110*) as Ruffo's "Alexander the Great".[228] Giltaij convincingly disproved this assumption, however, on the grounds of the differing measurements, contemporary inventory descriptions and the divergent provenances of the two paintings.[229] In a list of the paintings in the Ruffo collection, drawn up from 1668 onwards, the Alexander is moreover described as "a sedere col suo spadone e lancia a lato" (seated, with his two-handed sword and lance at his side).[230] Since no work by Rembrandt matching this description has sur-

Detail of: **Self-Portrait**, 1660
(see ill. p. 486)

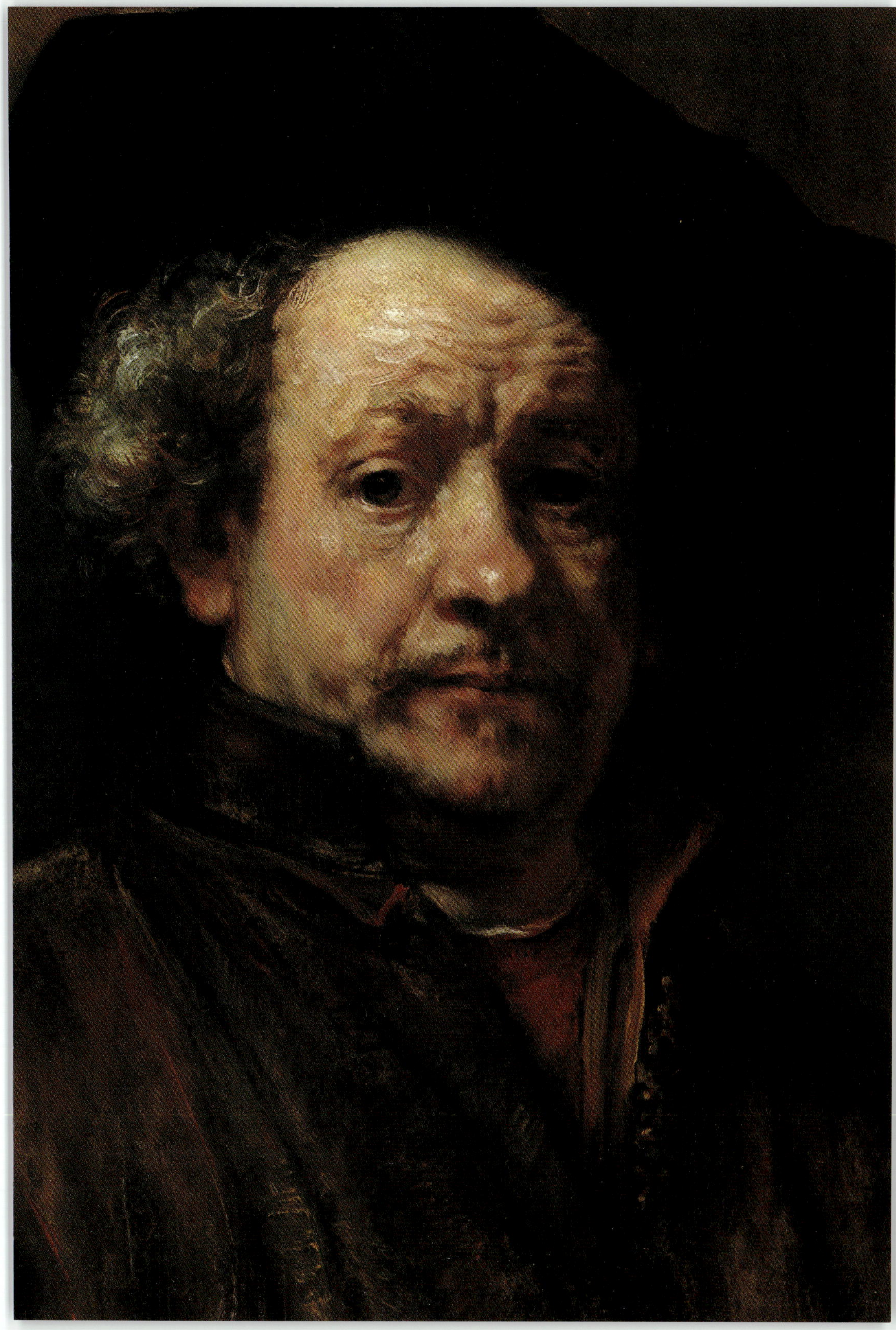

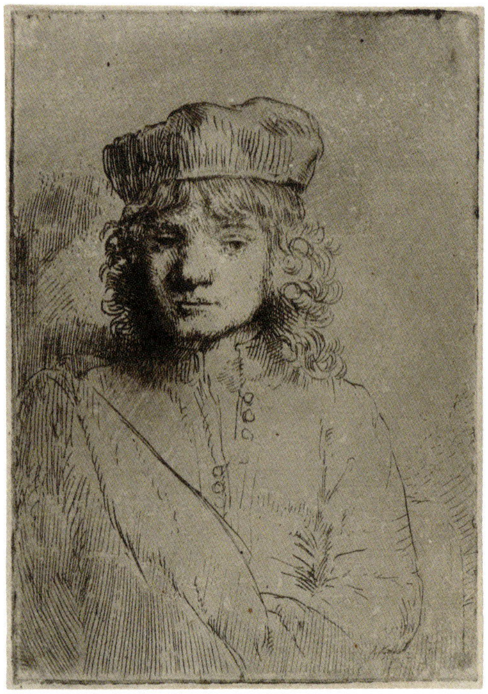

vived, the Alexander, therefore must be regarded as lost.

It is often incorrectly surmised that Ruffo was disappointed not only with the Alexander, but also with the Homer which – according to Broos – Rembrandt had even foisted onto him unasked.[231] He claims that Ruffo sent the painting back because he was dissatisfied with Rembrandt's late painting style which was "mezzofinito" (half-finished).[232] There is no indication of this in Ruffo's letter, however: the painting itself, not its style, was half-finished and it was duly returned to Amsterdam for completion according to the client's wish. What is more, Rembrandt himself confirms that he regarded the Homer at this point only as a "schizzo" (sketch) and not as a finished painting (RD 1662/12). Nor is the thought tenable that the picture had been sent to Ruffo at the same time as the Alexander (RD 1662/12), since on the invoice for the painting of "Alexander" from 1661, Rembrandt announces that he has yet to start painting the Homer.[233] The delivery of the half-finished Homer must have taken place some time in 1662, and the letter from 1 November 1662 mentioned above was presumably the response to that. From the final words of the letter, incidentally, we gather that Ruffo was not as dissatisfied as he had appeared to be in the beginning. He wrote that if Rembrandt accepted his proposal he would order three further half-length figures, for which Rembrandt could send him sketches on paper.

A letter by Mattia Preti (1613–1699) written over one year previously also confirms that Ruffo was initially very satisfied with the Alexander, saying that he even liked it better than the first half-length figure, i. e. the Aristotle (RD 1661/15). It is therefore justified to ask whether it was in fact Ruffo's prime aim to negotiate a substantial discount

Portrait of Titus, the Artist's Son, *c.* 1656
Etching with surface tone on Japan paper, 9.9 × 7 cm (4 × 2 7/8 in.)
Amsterdam, Rijksmuseum

for the as yet unfinished Homer. After all, he informed Rembrandt (repeatedly) that he found his asking prices exorbitantly high, asserting that Rembrandt demanded four times as much as Italian masters. In his reply to Ruffo's letter from 1 November 1662, Rembrandt showed himself to be resentful and unwilling to compromise (RD 1662/12). He was surprised at Ruffo's criticism and was almost insulting with his remark that he believed there must be very few art lovers in Messina, and the seams which Ruffo criticised would not be visible if the picture was hung in the right light. In the end, however, he accommodated the prince, because his Homer (finished in 1663) joined Ruffo's collection on 20 May 1664 for the sum of 300 guilders – virtually half of the original asking price.[234] Rembrandt's series of half-length figures formed a highly prized part of the collection and they remained together at least until 1783, when all three works were rescued from the ruins of the palace in Messina following an earthquake and the subsequent fire.[235]

Less well documented but no less honourable was the visit which Prince Cosimo III de' Medici (1642–1723), the later Grand Duke of Tuscany, paid to "the famous painter Rembrandt" in his studio on the Rozengracht on 29 December 1667 (RD 1667/6).[236] The latter had no finished painting in stock at the time, so that Cosimo will not have purchased anything on this occasion. The prince was probably searching for a self-portrait for his extensive collection of artists' self-portraits in the Uffizi. Since a self-portrait by Rembrandt from 1669 is still in this collection to this day (p. 497, Cat. 174), it is tempting to assume that Cosimo purchased the work during his second visit to Amsterdam on 29 June 1669, on which occasion he succeeded in acquiring a series of paintings by "very excellent masters".[237]

The previously unknown material which Lauro Magnani discovered in the archives of the patrician Sauli family in Genoa caused a surprise.[238] From the correspondence of the future Doge Francesco Maria Sauli (1620–1699), we learn that he had approached Rembrandt in 1666 with the request that he paint two large altarpieces to adorn the Sauli family's church, Santa Maria Assunta di Carignano in Genoa. A certain Giovanni Lorenzo Viviano, captain of a ship which travelled to Holland on Sauli's behalf, established contact with Rembrandt through two commercial agents. These were the prominent Catholic merchant Gian Battista Benzi (1602–1674) and his son-in-law and co-partner, Jean Gabriël Voet (1635–1681).[239] From 18 June 1666 the two Amsterdam agents reported regularly to Sauli about the progress of the negotiations. Rembrandt agreed immediately to paint two small *modelli* by the end of the month. One was to show the Assumption of the Virgin, to whom the church was dedicated. Rembrandt admitted that his asking price was very high; however, since he had a great understanding of painting ("persona intelligente di pittura"), he was not prepared to lower his price. Sauli replied coolly that

Rembrandt would have to be satisfied with what was fair and usual and that he would only be able to decide on this when the *modelli* were presented. The delivery date for the sketches was repeatedly postponed, however, and the agents became increasingly nervous and complained about the artist's difficult character. They said that he worked very slowly, and moreover that Rembrandt was "stravagante" (eccentric), "as is usually the case with painters", and could not be relied on to keep his word. They feared that the matter might turn out to be very expensive and that it might drag on.

In October Rembrandt said that he regarded the commission to paint a large religious picture for an important Italian church as a stroke of luck and that "he aimed to acquire honour and fame in our (i.e. Italian) regions with this commission". He declared that he had immersed himself in his work with "tutto il suo spirito" (his entire spirit) but that it was simply not possible to complete the *modelli* in such a short time. By about December, Captain Viviano was in despair and did not know what he should do with this "unpredictable" painter. Rembrandt was suddenly demanding 3,000 guilders for the two paintings, though he had originally asked for 1,200 guilders. Eventually, in February 1667, Benzi and Voet were relieved to be able to tell their master that the *modelli* were finally ready to ship and that after protracted negotiations they had agreed on a price of 1,023 guilders. Paid invoices for the shipping, packaging, customs duties and Rembrandt's fee confirm that the sketches must actually have reached Genoa, but the documents are silent as to what happened to the commission after that. Nor are the *modelli* known today. Did the sketches fail to meet Sauli's expectations or was he deterred by Rembrandt's slow working methods and the high costs?

The relatively well documented Italian commissions show clearly how Rembrandt treated his aristocratic clients; here we can observe the same pattern as with his earlier commission for the series for Prince Frederik Hendrik (see pp. 98–99, 101–104; p. 183, Cat. 49; p. 185, Cat. 50; p. 187, Cat. 61; p. 188, Cat. 70; p. 189, Cat. 59; p. 191, Cat. 60). At the time, he initially demanded 1,200 guilders apiece for these (relatively small) history pieces. Exactly as he had done then, he justified the long delays and high prices with the extraordinary mental efforts which he put into the creative process. His tone towards his nobly-born clients is remarkably offhand, and Rembrandt dispensed with the usual courtesies. It is evident that he saw himself as a great artist and the only one who was truly knowledgeable about art. He expressed doubt as to whether there were any art connoisseurs in Messina and insisted initially on his high asking price because of his "great understanding of art". In the end, however, he did agree to a compromise with his clients as regards the price.

Behind Rembrandt's high asking prices lay not (only) desire for profit; he was convinced of the direct link between the prestige of art and its financial value.[240] Baldinucci

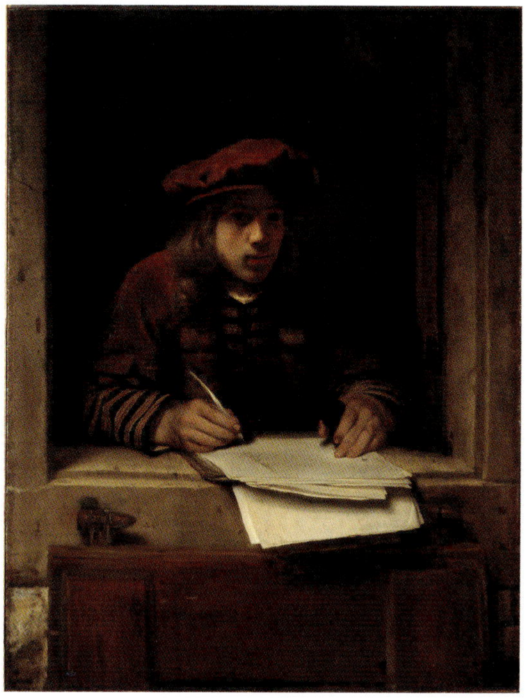

praises Rembrandt's extraordinarily high regard for the art of his famous Northern predecessors, which was expressed in the extravagantly high sums which he was prepared to pay for their works. During the 1630s and 1640s, he did indeed spend large sums on works by Albrecht Dürer and Lucas van Leyden (RD 1638/2, 1642/10).[241] And even after his financial problems it was said that "Master Rembrandt of Amsterdam" had offered at least 1,000 guilders for a "principael" (original) by Holbein (RD 1666/3). Baldinucci reports that he even forced up the prices for great art at auctions intentionally, "per mettere in credito il professione", in order to raise the prestige of the profession, as he himself said.[242]

The pattern is clear: Rembrandt's concern was the fame and honour of art (and also his own as an artist), and that justified both his high asking prices and the protracted delays. Houbraken confirms that clients would have to beg and pay additional money in order to get a work from him. Especially during his last years he had received so many commissions that "people had to wait for their pictures for a long time, despite the fact that he worked diligently".[243] His stature as a great artist also justified the unconventional, unpredictable behaviour towards his clients. Sauli's agents actually did not expect anything different: after all, all artists were more or less "stravagante" (eccentric). Baldinucci, too, described Rembrandt as "molto diverso di cervello" (very non-conformist in the head) and "stravagantissimo" (very extravagant) as a painter.[244] This acceptance of the notion of the unconventional artist, prevalent at the time, also explains the remarkable patience and the (partial) willingness to make concessions of his Italian clients.

Samuel van Hoogstraten
Self-Portrait, *c.* 1650
Oil on canvas, 102 × 79 cm (40 ¼ × 31 ⅛ in.)
St Petersburg, The State Hermitage

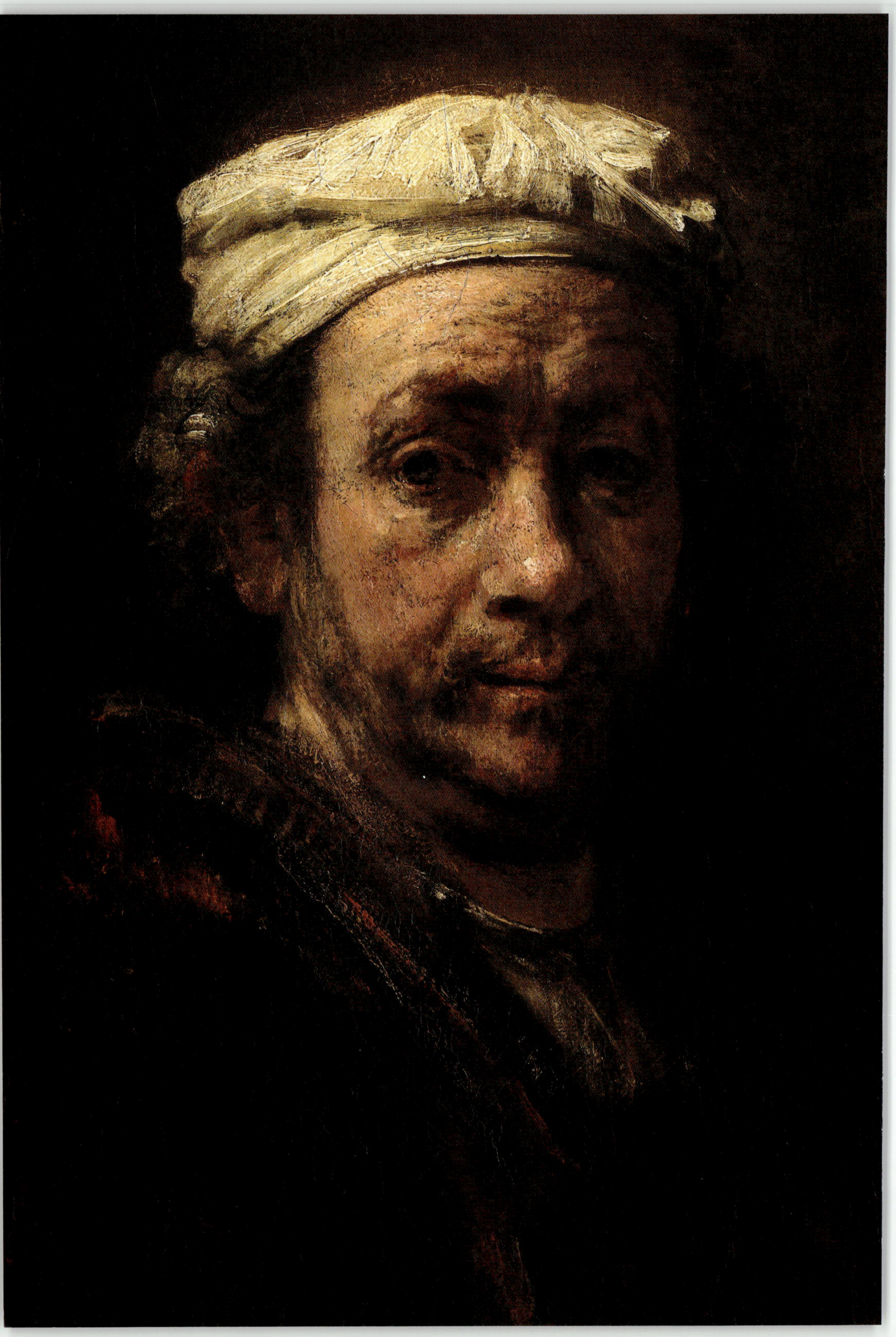

Titus

Titus was born in September 1641 as the fourth and last child of Rembrandt and Saskia. He would be the only one to reach adulthood. He owed his unusual first name to Saskia's sister, Titia, after whom he was named. Titia died shortly before he was born, and his mother, Saskia, would also not live for much longer: she died when Titus was only nine months old. The child was brought up until he was seven by Geertje Dircks, and thereafter by her successor, Hendrickje Stoffels, who had also taken over Geertje's position as his father's companion. Titus evidently had a good relationship with both stepmothers. His father trained him as an artist and he was painted by him on a number of occasions (p. 435, Cat. 85; p. 433, Cat. 297; p. 434, Cat. 300; p. 436, Cat. 303; Cat. 305, 308; p. 438, Cat. 309).

Around 1656 Rembrandt created the etching of a boy with a painter's beret perched on his blond curls whom we can regard as being Titus; he was 15 years of age at the time (p. 374, Cat. E234). Although the boy portrayed there looks considerably younger than 15, his identification as Titus is confirmed by a mention in the inventory of the art dealer Clement de Jonghe, who knew both Rembrandt and Titus well. The etching is listed in his stocks as a " Titus' likeness".[245] In 1655 Rembrandt painted his son drawing and gazing intently into the distance, leaning over a wooden railing or a broad writing desk (p. 433, Cat. 297). Titus is shown in close-up, and this directness is heightened further by the inkwell and the leather portfolio with the loose papers which project over the edge in an illusionistic way. We have the impression that Rembrandt has recorded his son in a moment when Titus is utterly immersed in his thoughts. The spontaneous character of the work is underlined by the sketch-like portrayal of the boy. The surface of the "writing desk", which occupies almost half of the picture's surface, has been painted with broad brushstrokes which have partly been smoothed out using a palette knife. Nonetheless, this spontaneity is only superficial. The artist's beret with which Titus is almost always shown in his portraits was not worn in everyday life; Rembrandt had turned it into the distinguishing mark of the artist. Following their master, Rembrandt's apprentices also began to portray themselves – and each other – wearing a beret. Samuel van Hoogstraten, for example, painted himself around 1650 as a young artist wearing a beret and drawing, leaning on an illusionistic window sill (p. 385).

The beret seems to indicate that Rembrandt also wanted to show Titus as a young artist.[246] At the age of 14 he would have already learned the basic skills of the artist's trade from his father. These were acquired through endless drawing, both from plaster casts and "from life". It is noticeable that both Titus and van Hoogstraten drew with a

Detail of: **Self-Portrait at the Easel**, 1660
(see ill. p. 489)

quill and ink. Since a drawing in ink can hardly be corrected, this technique requires a certain experience. In his treatise on the art of drawing from 1668, Willem Goeree (1635–1711) calls it a technique for advanced artists and too "difficult a torture instrument for apprentices"[247]. Rembrandt was obviously more demanding as a teacher and seems to have required that his pupils draw with pen and ink for this very reason. His former student van Hoogstraten likewise found that a quill pen of "swan" or "goose feather" was well suited to the task.[248]

Rembrandt was probably proud of his son's progress, because his inventory from 1656 lists three small paintings executed by Titus (RD 1656/12, no. 298–300). Only one of his drawings, a *Flora* from 1659 executed in pen and ink, has survived (RD 1659/6). Since it is difficult to assess the artistic talent of Titus on the basis of a single drawing, we can only speculate as to what his other works must have looked like. It is feasible that from the late 1650s Titus will have contributed to a greater or lesser degree to the painting production in his father's workshop. In any case, from 1658 he was responsible for the sale of Rembrandt's works in the art dealer's shop which he initially managed with Hendrickje and then ran alone after her death (RD 1660/20). Arnold Houbraken attested – a little disparagingly – that Rembrandt had his etchings "peddled by his son Titus […]", and Joachim von Sandrart also remarked on Rembrandt's "son, who is likewise said to have an understanding of art".[249]

About 1660 Rembrandt painted a number of large religious half-length figures (see p. 390–391), including a Franciscan monk lost in contemplation (p. 435, Cat. 85). It was unmistakably the 19-year-old Titus who acted as model for the young Minorite, dressed in a brown habit with the hood pulled well down over his head. The monk's habit, sewn with coarse stitching, and the dark background are painted in different shades of brown, which makes Titus' pale face stand out. It is a mystery why Rembrandt should have painted Titus as a monk or as St Francis of Assisi. In any case, the contemplative expression of the young man is very appropriate for St Francis and his visions. We know little about the character of Titus. It is evident from his estate, however, that financially he was in better shape than Rembrandt.[250] He seems to have been loyal to his father and it is moving to learn how he praised him as an engraver to a potential client, especially because Rembrandt, who was an outstanding etcher, never produced any engravings (RD 1665/6).

In contrast to his father, Titus seems to have strengthened the ties with relatives and old friends. He retained friendly contacts with Karel van der Pluym (1625–1672), his second cousin in Leiden and also with the family of Rembrandt's old acquaintance, Jan van Loo, the brother of his uncle and godfather, Gerrit van Loo. In February 1668 Titus married Jan's daughter, Magdalena van Loo (1641–1669; RD 1668/1). Four months after

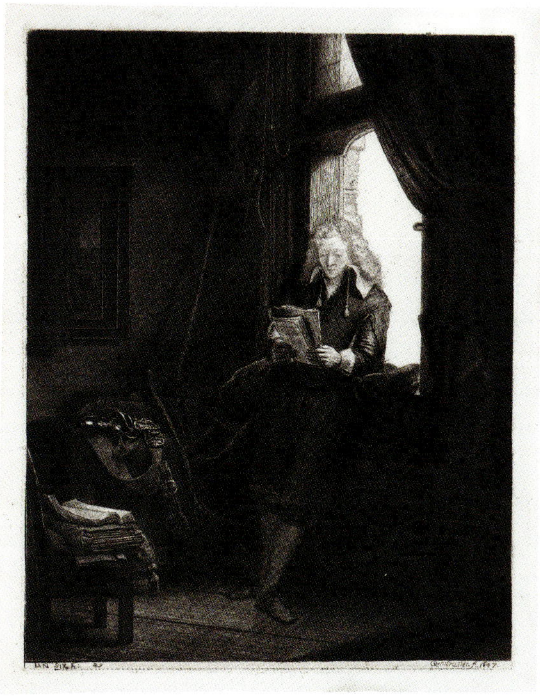

the wedding, Titus was suddenly taken ill and died during a visit to Leiden with Magdalena. He was buried in the Westerkerk in Amsterdam on 7 September 1668 (RD 1668/8d). Six months later his daughter Titia was baptised, with Rembrandt standing witness at the baptismal font (RD 1669/1). In October of the same year, both Rembrandt and Magdalena van Loo died within a short time of each other. The inventory of the estate of Titus and Magdalena gives the impression that his artistic activities were relatively limited. "Fifteen small paintings without frames and a number of albums filled with many simple drawings and small sketches" and "a small copper plate" are listed, whereby it is unclear who the artist was.[251] Titus also owned four paintings which were hung together as a group: a (self-)portrait of his father, a portrait of his mother, Saskia, and then a third of himself, "where he is leaning over the railing", and finally "a hooded monk".[252] These paintings were most probably painted by Rembrandt. It is tempting to assume that the two last-mentioned works are the pictures described above, for which Titus had acted as model in his youth. In that case the paintings evidently had a special personal significance both for Rembrandt and for his prematurely deceased son.

Religious Tronies and Single Figures

In Rembrandt's bankruptcy inventory from 1656, we find three paintings which are described as "Een Cristi tronie van Rembrant" (RD 1656/12, no. 115), "Cristus tronie van Rembrant" (RD 1656/12, no. 116) and "Een Cristus tronie nae 't leven" (RD 1656/12,

Jan Six, 1647
Etching, drypoint and burin, 24.4 × 19.1 cm (9 5/8 × 7 5/8 in.)
Amsterdam, Rijksmuseum

no. 326). The three paintings belong to a larger group of similar heads of Christ, not all of which were painted by Rembrandt himself.

The subject was apparently popular and successful. Variations of one or more prototypes by Rembrandt were evidently produced by apprentices and workshop assistants. The heads of Christ of p. 439, Cat. 79; Cat. 80, 81* and 82* are probably by Rembrandt himself.[253] The versions in Philadelphia, Cambridge (Massachusetts) and Amsterdam on the other hand probably originate from Rembrandt's workshop.[254] One or two of the heads of Christ have occasionally been linked to the figures of Christ in his history paintings and etchings.[255] However, none of them come into question as direct preparatory studies. It seems as if Rembrandt had quickly recognised the popularity of these *tronies* and correspondingly painted several versions, or had them painted in his workshop. There has been much discussion as to whether Rembrandt and painters from his circle made use of a Jewish model for these heads of Christ. Art-historical literature on this problem is closely linked with the rather romanticised ideas of Rembrandt's relationship with his Jewish fellow-citizens. People wanted to see an expression of his sympathy for the Jews of Amsterdam in the circumstance that Rembrandt used Jewish models. There is no doubt that he made portraits and etched book illustrations for Jewish clients (p. 329, Cat. 190; pp. 110, 113, Cat. E13, 122).

The fact that Rembrandt and probably other painters used models for the heads of Christ can possibly be derived from the entry in his inventory mentioned above where it is maintained that a *tronie* of Christ had been painted "from life" (nae 't leven).[256] A poem by Jan Vos (1610–1667) is relevant regarding the question as to whether the models really were Jewish. Its title was "Christus, voor Jooris de Wyze, door Govert Flinck, naar een Joodt, geschildert" (Christ, for Jooris de Wyze, painted by Govert Flinck, after a Jew). Vos praises Flinck, Rembrandt's former apprentice, for the lively portrayal of the model, but then declares, in an anti-Jewish manner, that Flinck did not portray his Christ "speaking", because "this Christ would curse as he spoke of Christ", because he had been "painted after a Jew".[257] The painting referred to by Vos has repeatedly been identified with *Christ with the Cross* by Flinck, dated 1649 and preserved in the Suermondt-Ludwig-Museum in Aachen.[258] Whatever the circumstances, it is at least possible that Rembrandt also used a Jewish model for his Heads of Christ. The explanation for this might not necessarily lie in Rembrandt's sympathy for members of the Jewish community in Amsterdam, but rather in his striving for a historically accurate portrayal of the historical persons and circumstances in the Holy Land at the time of Christ.

In the second half of the 1650s, and especially in the first half of the 1660s, Rembrandt painted a number of half-lengths showing religious figures. The subjects were various Apostles and an Evangelist. *The Apostle Bartholomew* (p. 441, Cat. 83) dates

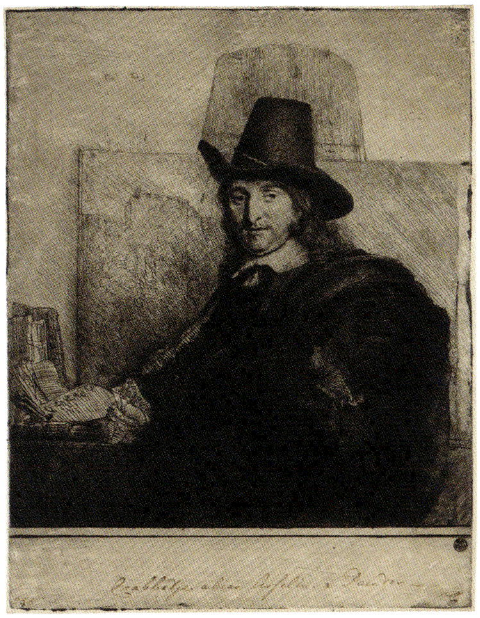

from 1657. *The Apostle Paul* (Cat. 84) must date from about the same time, but did not belong to a series that included Bartholomew, since the X-ray image shows that the sword (the attribute of St Paul) was added later, presumably with the intention of transforming an anonymous scholar or philosopher into an Apostle. Four additional half-length figures of bearded men were created in 1661. Their attributes point to their martyrdom and identify them as *The Apostle Bartholomew* (Cat. 88), *The Apostle James the Greater* (Cat. 89), *The Apostle Simon* (p. 444, Cat. 90) and *The Apostle James the Lesser* (*Christ?*; p. 445, Cat. 91). This distinguishes them from *The Evangelist Matthew and the Angel*, also dated 1661 and of approximately the same size (p. 440, Cat. 87). The latter, however, is clearly portrayed in his role as the author of the Gospel of the same name and not as an Apostle.[259] This is evident in the standard attribute of the Evangelist, a man or the Son of Man in the form of an angel who whispers the words inspired by God to Matthew as he writes the Gospel. Rembrandt dispenses with the wings and gave the youthful figure features which display a certain resemblance to those of his son, Titus, who was 20 years old at the time.

It is uncertain whether the half-length figures created in 1661 were originally painted as independent pictures or as parts of a series. At any rate, there is no proof that they were ever part of the same collection. Not all the Apostle paintings display black markings or scratched lines as an indication that they were to be framed in same-size frames, as has been claimed.[260] They are not present, for example in *The Apostle Bartholomew* (Cat. 88).[261] Moreover, iconographically the Evangelist Matthew accompanied by the Angel does not fit into a series of Apostles. Also problematic is the relationship of this presumed "series" to Rembrandt's *Mater Dolorosa* from 1661 (Cat. 92*) and the

Jan Asselijn, Painter ("Krabbetje"), *c.* 1647
Etching and drypoint, with surface tone on Japan paper, 21.6 × 17 cm (8 ⅝ × 6 ¾ in.)
Amsterdam, Rijksmuseum

painting *The Risen Christ* (p. 442, Cat. 86), which, however, no longer has its original format and which must have been painted around 1660.

It is quite conceivable that Rembrandt devised the half-length figures of the Apostles as independent pictures and on his own initiative. At the time he painted them, he also received other commissions for paintings without a prescribed subject, which he chose himself. For example, Don Antonio Ruffo just ordered half-length figures from him without specifying the subject matter (pp. 430/431, Cat. 114; p. 432, Cat. 116; see pp. 379–380, 382–385).

Although in his rejection of pictorial representations in a religious context Calvin (1509–1564) had not made an exception for the Apostles, they played an important role in the Reformed Church as the companions of Christ and the preachers of his teachings.[262] He had appointed and instructed them: "Go ye therefore, and teach all nations, baptizing them in the name of the Father, and of the Son, and of the Holy Ghost: teaching them to observe all things whatsoever I have commanded you: and, lo, I am with you always, even unto the end of the world" (Matthew 28: 19–20). The Twelve Apostles played an important role not only within the Reformed Church but also within the other denominations which formed part of the multi-confessional society in the Northern Netherlands during Rembrandt's time. The patrons or buyers of Rembrandt's half-length Apostle figures are unknown, but the paintings – regardless of their religious connotations – were also stylistic manifestations of the late Rembrandt. At the time they were painted, there was without doubt a market for such works both in Amsterdam and beyond.

Portraits

Probably because of his precarious financial situation, from 1652 Rembrandt once more began to accept portrait commissions. Different from his earlier portraits, now his sitters tended to be people to whom he had a personal or professional link, for example poets (Cat. 196), art lovers (p. 448, Cat. 193; Cat. 206*; p. 468, Cat. 259), art dealers (p. 463, Cat. 209) and colleagues (p. 451, Cat. 205). This seems to confirm Houbraken's observation that: "In the autumn of his life he mostly kept the company of common people and those who practised art."[263] During his late years Rembrandt had no shortage of portrait commissions, but his clientele had changed. His idiosyncratic and increasingly dark painting style probably differed too greatly from the changing taste of the average client for portraits. Certainly Houbraken mentions that Rembrandt's former pupil Nicolaes Maes (1634–1693) soon stopped painting in the style of the master, because

Detail of: **Self-Portrait as the Apostle Paul**, 1661
(see ill. p. 488)

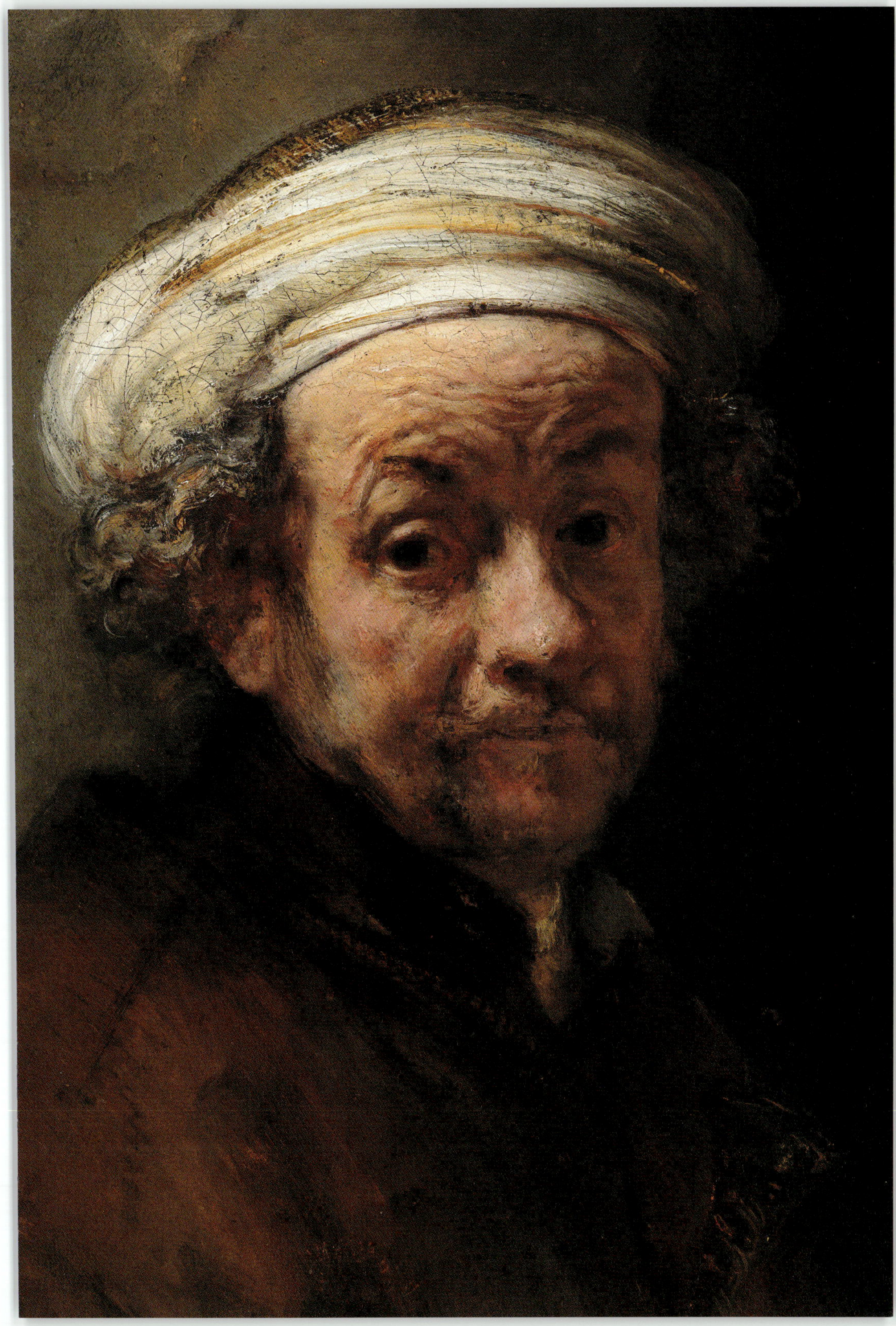

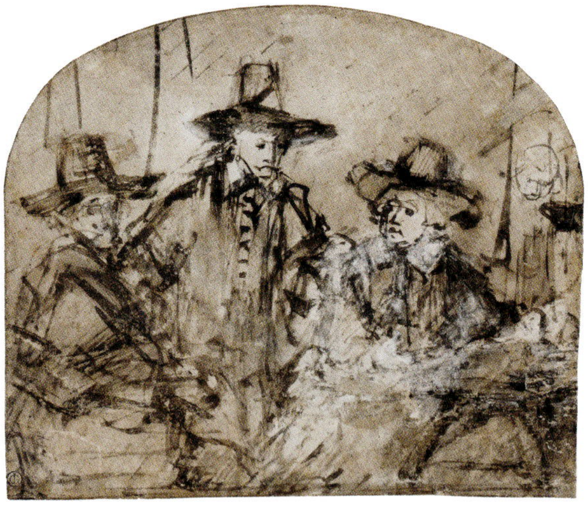

he "realised that especially the young ladies felt more comfortable with white than with brown".[264] The darling of the Amsterdam elite, his former student Govert Flinck, had also "gone to great lengths as regards both effort and work to give up [Rembrandt's] painting style [...]" when "bright painting became fashionable again".[265] Rembrandt on the other hand had never conformed to the fashionable, smooth, neo-classical portrait style. He went against the current and single-mindedly continued to search for artistic solutions which he himself found interesting and which were probably valued especially by his colleagues and other art lovers. The connoisseur Roger de Piles, actually a supporter of the classical style, nonetheless admired Rembrandt's portraits because of their "surprising power, charm and truthfulness".[266]

Rembrandt's intriguing *Portrait of a Man* (p. 446, Cat. 191) from about 1651/52 already shows a number of characteristics of this new portrait style. The face and the blond hair are painted in great detail. The black suit seems almost to fuse with the dark background, and also the hand and the cuff are toned down with brown paint so that the eye is automatically drawn towards the face. The mysterious landscape in the background forms a unique feature in this portrait. Possibly the unknown fair-haired man belonged to Rembrandt's circle of acquaintances. The unusual landscape in the background invites speculation that Rembrandt could possibly have painted a portrait of the landscape painter Jan Asselijn (1600/16–1652). He had already made a portrait etching of this artist with an easel behind him on which a landscape with a castle can be seen (p. 391, Cat. E228).

According to Houbraken, Asselijn was known as "Krabbetje" (Little Crab), because he had burned his left hand and as a consequence his fingers remained so bent that he

Three Syndics (The Wardens of the Amsterdam Drapers' Guild), *c.* 1662
Pen and brown ink, brushwork in brown and white,
on brownish paper, probably ledger paper, 17.3 × 20.5 cm (6 7/8 × 8 in.)
Staatliche Museen zu Berlin, Kupferstichkabinett

could hardly hold a palette. Although "he was small in stature [...], in art he was a great master", observes Houbraken.[267] Asselijn was famous for his poetical Italianate landscapes with towers and bright blue skies. Although today the details on the portrait painted by Rembrandt are difficult to make out because of the thick layer of yellow varnish, a patch of bright blue sky is visible at the top left, a background colour which otherwise Rembrandt never uses in his portraits. Whether the Asselijn in the etching and the man in the painted portrait are the same person is difficult to judge. Both are wearing the same style of clothing and the collar, beard and hairstyle match, and so even does the slightly crooked nose. In the etching, of course, the colour of Asselijn's hair is difficult to determine. After Jan Asselijn's premature death in 1652, Rembrandt remained in contact with the former's younger brother, the poet and dramatist Thomas Asselijn (*c.* 1620–1701). In 1655, the latter appeared as a witness on his behalf (RD 1655/8). In 1667, Thomas Asselijn pawned a "portrait by Rembrandt" (RD 1667/3). Although further evidence is lacking here, it is tempting to speculate in this context that this could have been the portrait of his elder brother.

The portrait of Nicolaes Theunisz. Bruyningh (1629/30–1680; p. 447, Cat. 192), aged about 22, from 1652 looks casual and relaxed in every respect, as a result of the free brushwork, the sitter's relaxed pose and his casual open collar. The bachelor is leaning with one arm on the armrest. His amused interest seems to have been aroused by something which is happening outside the picture, so that his attitude attains a fleeting quality. From the X-ray of the painting we can gather that Rembrandt initially portrayed Bruyningh with one hand on top of the other and with the wide billowing shirt-sleeves which were very fashionable at that time.[268] At second sight, however, Rembrandt evidently found that this relatively large bright patch in the middle of the dark composition drew too much attention away from the face, so that he decided to tone down the cuffs and hands to a large extent with brown paint. According to Houbraken, Rembrandt was so rigorous in sacrificing certain details in order to draw the eye to one part of the painting that he "would tone down with tan pigments a beautiful Cleopatra, just to make a single pearl stand out more strongly".[269] He also remarks that Rembrandt only rarely painted a good hand, because he "scumbles them away into the shadows, especially in his portraits".[270]

The looseness that characterises the Bruyningh portrait is also a distinctive feature in his *Portrait of Jan Six* (p. 448, Cat. 193) from about 1654. The portrait of the wealthy art lover, whom Rembrandt knew well, is an impressive example of what is generally characterised as Rembrandt's "late style". Lost in thought, Six is standing frontally close to the picture plane. Rembrandt conveys the impression of a fleeting snapshot in the way Six looks up from underneath his hat while putting on his gloves. This vitality is heightened by his cloak hanging casually over one shoulder. Six appears as it were to have emerged suddenly from the darkness and to be stepping forwards because of the gloomy background, against which the figure stands out: a suggestion of deceptive proximity, strengthened by the use of the warm red of the cloak. The painting technique is highly differentiated in places – subtle, for example, in the face and sketch-like and rough in the brown glove. The yellow braiding of the cloak was quickly drawn wet-in-wet (using a finger), and the white cuffs are painted with fluent brushstrokes. The yellow cuff has been applied almost grazingly, using a dry flat brush. What is new in this painting is that the hands are no longer banished to the shadows, but – like the face – have been strongly emphasised, thereby shifting the viewer's attention to their interplay.

Six looks much older than 36 in this portrait, but that can be due to the faintly melancholy facial expression. In this portrait, too, the question arises as to what extent Rembrandt let his artistic aims prevail at the cost of a convincing resemblance. In the same year, 1654, a client complained that Rembrandt was either unable or unwilling to create a satisfactory portrait likeness (RD 1654/4). The Jewish merchant Diego d'Andrade (1608–1660) had Rembrandt notified by a notary that the portrait "did not resemble" his relative "at all", and that the artist should modify the picture immediately, otherwise he, Rembrandt, would have to return the down payment.[271] The accused reacted to this as if stung by an adder. He would not return the down payment, and he refused to even touch the picture again until the purchase price – probably 150 guilders – had been paid in full. If this did not happen, he would finish the portrait as he thought best and then sell it off at the next public sale. A commission from the guild was to judge the resemblance to the sitter.

Rembrandt adopted a similar injured attitude, with the same inflexibility in reaction of criticism a few years later in 1662, in his dealings with the aristocratic Italian patron Don Antonio Ruffo (RD 1662/11). The striking virtuosity of the ambitious and yet personal *Portrait of Jan Six* clearly left a deep impression in the client's circle. During that same year, the standard bearer Floris Soop (1604–1657; p. 450, Cat. 194) had an even larger, knee-length portrait painted by Rembrandt; the bachelor, an enthusiastic art lover, lived next-door to Jan Six. Two years later, in 1656, Six's older brother-in-law, Arnout Tholinx (1607–1679), placed a commission for a painted bust-length portrait and a portrait etching (Cat. 195; Cat. E235). Tholinx was a prominent doctor, like his father-in-law, Nicolaes Tulp, and the Inspector in charge of the Collegium Medicum in Amsterdam. His successor to that post was Dr Jan Deyman (1619–1666) in 1653; he, too, commissioned Rembrandt – also in 1656 – to paint an *Anatomy Lesson* (pp. 464/465, Cat. 266), of which, unfortunately, only a small fragment has survived.

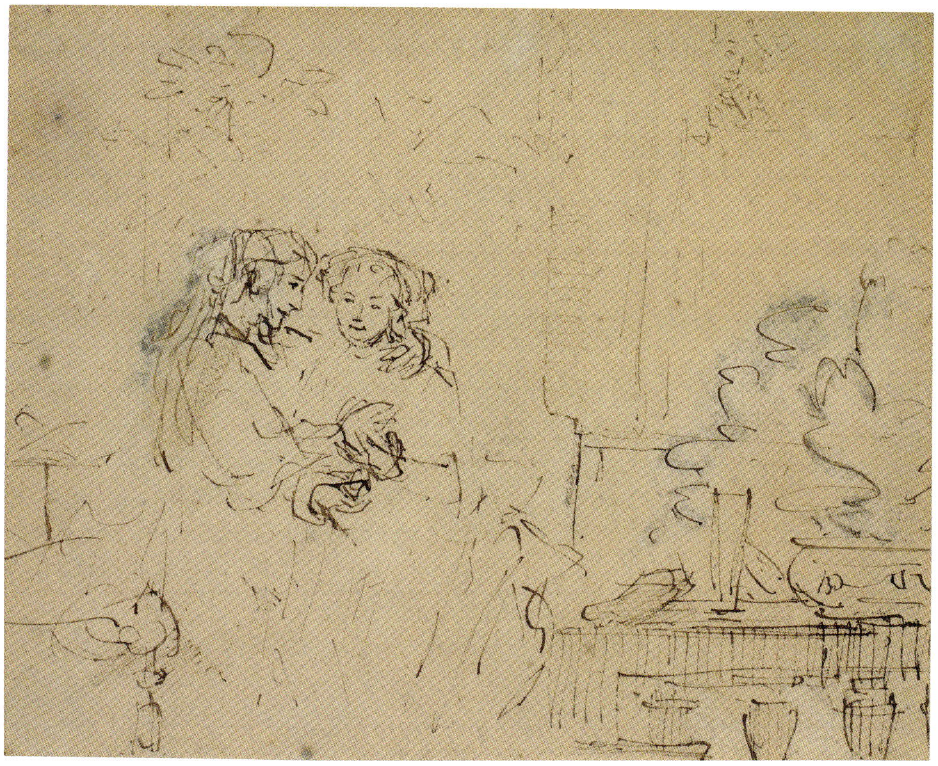

Isaac and Rebecca, Overheard by Abimelech, *c.* 1663
Pen and brown ink, brushwork in white, 14.5 × 18.5 cm (5 ¾ × 7 ⅜ in.)
New York, Private Collection

Particularly intriguing are the two life-size companion pieces, *Portrait of a Man with a Hat and Gloves* (p. 452, Cat. 255) and *Portrait of a Woman with an Ostrich-Feather Fan* (p. 453, Cat. 256) from about 1655. As in Rembrandt's pendants from the 1630s and 1640s, the man is facing to the right and gestures with an outstretched hand towards his female companion. The woman, on the other hand, is depicted almost frontally with her hands placed lightly on top of each other. While the man appears to seek direct eye contact with the viewer, the woman is gazing past him in a melancholy fashion. Compared with the loosely painted portrait of the man, the likeness of the woman has been worked out in much greater detail, especially the impasto of the jewellery and the fluffy ostrich feather in her hand. As in the *Portrait of Jan Six* (p. 448), the faces and the interplay of the hands are emphasised in these likenesses. Rembrandt made skilful use of the fact that in the fashion of the time, the face and hands were framed, so to speak, by white

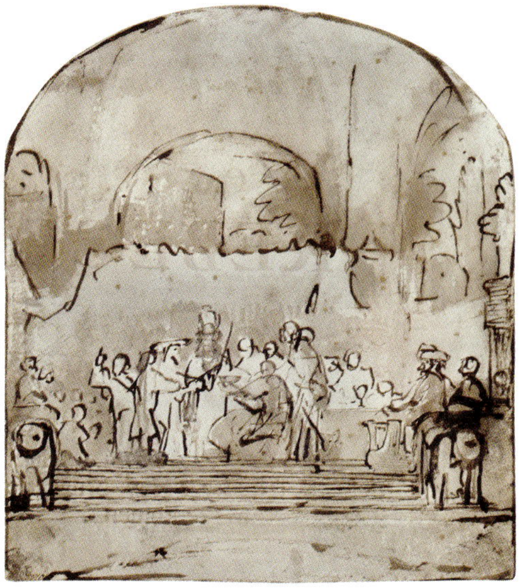

linen collars and cuffs, so that they stood out almost luminously against the black costume. Rembrandt also made use of this device in his portrait of the 78-year-old Margaretha de Geer (1583–1672; p. 455, Cat. 258) from about 1661. Here, too, the male sitter in the companion piece, *Portrait of Jacob Trip* (p. 454, Cat. 257), is facing to the right, while the woman is shown frontally. The light is reflected on the white linen accessories, making Margaretha's finely detailed facial features and her hands shine out in an almost supernatural manner. The rest of the costume is "sacrificed" as it blends into the dark background and as a result of the sketch-like painting style.

As had been the case even during the 1630s, during the 1650s and 1660s the portraits of women are often more finely detailed in their execution than the portraits of men. This is particularly evident in the portrait of the eccentric Catharina Hoogsaet (1607–1685; p. 457, Cat. 217), a Mennonite woman who was separated from her husband and who had her portrait painted by Rembrandt in 1657. The face of the *Boy in Sixteenth-Century Costume* (p. 456, Cat. 302) from about 1658 is also painted remarkably detailed. The delicate face forms a strong contrast to the clothing and the arm, which seem to have been executed so rapidly that this time we really must assume that the painting is unfinished.[272] On the breast and the right shoulder, the even brown ground layer has remained entirely uncovered.

Besides their typically smooth painting style, Rembrandt's portraits from the 1650s have other characteristics in common. During this period, Rembrandt seems to have developed a certain predilection for standing three-quarter-length figures, which were depicted more or less frontally (p. 448, Cat. 193; Cat. 194; Cat. 197; p. 452, Cat. 255; p. 453, Cat. 256; p. 456, Cat. 302). In his male portraits from around 1655, it is noticeable that the eyes are shaded by the broad rim of their hats (pp. 448, 450 and 452;

The Conspiracy of Claudius Civilis, 1661
Pen and brown ink, brush in brown and white, 19.2 × 18.1 cm (7 5/8 × 7 1/4 in.)
Munich, Staatliche Graphische Sammlung

Cat. 195, 196). In contrast, for the portraits of the 1660s, Rembrandt more often opts for a seated pose and a prominent light accent on the forehead.

Rembrandt's largest portrait is the unusual *Portrait of Frederick Rihel on Horseback* (p. 459, Cat. 203*), completed in 1663. A wealthy man, Rihel was a horse lover and clearly wanted to be shown on horseback. This resulted in a rather curious equestrian portrait in which Rembrandt himself clearly painted the rider, while he left the execution of the large dappled horse to one of his workshop assistants. We do not know much about the assistants who were employed in Rembrandt's workshop at this time. Titus will certainly have been responsible for part of the workshop production, and about 1661 a young painter from Dordrecht, Arent de Gelder (1645–1727), came to Rembrandt as an apprentice. De Gelder would retain Rembrandt's style and technique for the rest of his life.

One of the most conspicuous characteristics of Rembrandt's late portraits is that they differ greatly from each other in execution. The figure of Frederick Rihel (1621–1681), for example, is executed in great detail, while the *Portrait of an Old Man* (p. 463, Cat. 209) from 1667 is painted so loosely that for a long time it was not recognised as a work by Rembrandt but was thought to be a pastiche from the nineteenth century. The loose painting style, the casual pose and clothing give the portrait a remarkable informal impression. This led to speculation as to whether the old man was an acquaintance of the artist, perhaps Lodewijk van Ludick (*c.* 1606/07–1669), a neighbour and "lover and experienced connoisseur of painting"; or the collector and print-seller Pieter de la Tombe (1593–1677), with whom Rembrandt had also maintained business relations for a long time.[273]

About 1661 Rembrandt received a commission from the wardens of the Amsterdam Drapers' Guild to paint a group portrait which resulted in the painting known as *The Wardens of the Amsterdam Drapers' Guild* (*"The Syndics"*; pp. 466/467, Cat. 267). Once again, he was faced with the challenge of producing a group composition, which had to fit into a conventional formula and – like *"The Night Watch"* (pp. 324/325, Cat. 265) – had to become "eenwezich" (a unity), or, to put it differently, in which the individual portraits were united in a shared activity. Here he shows the wardens gazing at the viewer as if they have been interrupted during their discussion. The X-ray and various drawings (Cat. D653–655) show that Rembrandt made major changes in the arrangement of the different figures during the course of the painting process. The sitters have been placed close to the picture plane and the red tablecloth serves as a sort of repoussoir which seems extend beyond the picture plane because of the low view point. Also in this painting, the way in which the paint has been applied is extremely differentiated. The rich pattern of the rug on the table has partly been worked out using a palette knife. The hand on the book and the texture of the paper are almost tangible and the fringes of the glove have been scratched out of the wet paint. In 1699, the well-informed art connoisseur Roger de Piles related that whenever anyone spoke to Rembrandt about his "singular" treatment of the paint, because it made the structure of his paintings so "bumpy", the artist would reply that he was a painter and not a dyer![274]

About 1665 Rembrandt painted a group of portraits which stand out for their colourfulness (p. 427, Cat. 219; p. 468, Cat. 259; p. 469, Cat. 260; pp. 424/425, Cat. 268; pp. 470/471, Cat. 269). These last portraits are his most famous and at the same time his most puzzling works. Some parts, like the costumes and the background, are generally rendered in a summary manner, while the faces and hands are worked out much more smoothly and with greater precision. Houbraken was amazed by this exceptionally varied painting technique, so that within a single painting "some things were executed to the utmost degree and the rest was smeared on as if with a coarse tar brush, without any consideration to the drawing".[275] Rembrandt used a palette knife in order to indicate the cuff of the mother in the *Family Portrait* (pp. 424/425, Cat. 268) with a few grazingly applied white blotches as he did in the dappled red sleeve in *Portrait of a Young Woman with a Lapdog* (p. 427, Cat. 219). These late works were often seen as unfinished. Like Houbraken, who sighed that Rembrandt was "so inclined to sudden change or driven to do something else, that he left many things only half-finished".[276] However, from the fact that Rembrandt signed most of his late works, it can be deduced that he regarded them as finished.

Apart from the fashionably dressed young woman with the lapdog (Cat. 219), most of the sitters of his portraits in these years were dressed in opulent fantasy costumes which were based on historical clothing styles going back at least one hundred and fifty years. Until then, Rembrandt had used costumes of this kind only for his self-portraits and for paintings which portray his closest family – his mother, Saskia, Hendrickje and Titus. Is the use of the same type of costume an indication that the people portrayed in this group of works also belonged to his circle of close friends or acquaintances? Although most of them have not yet been identified, it may be possible to name the couple who sat for the *Portrait of a Man with a Magnifying Glass* (p. 468, Cat. 259) and *Portrait of a Woman with a Pink Carnation* (p. 469, Cat. 260). They probably depict the auctioneer Pieter Gerritsz. Haringh (1609–1685) and his wife Lysbet Jansdr. Delft (*c.* 1620–1679).[277] Rembrandt will certainly have known this "Young Haringh" through the auctions of his household goods and probably even before that, because he already made a portrait etching of him in 1655 (Cat. E232).

We do not know the identity of the couple portrayed in the *Portrait of a Couple as Isaac and Rebecca* (*"The Jewish Bride"*; pp. 470/471, Cat. 269). Rembrandt's painting

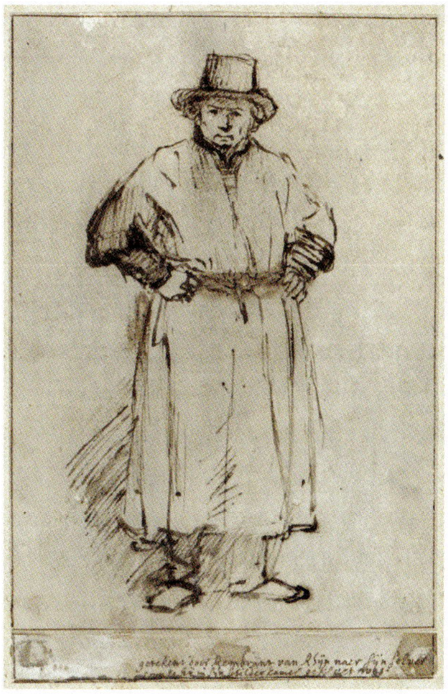

technique in this intimate picture is as astonishing as it is unfathomable.[278] The hands, for example, are painted in a pastose, almost granular paint which lends the skin a texture which is almost tangible. The small furrows in the paint, drawn with the hairs of the paintbrush, capture the light, creating the impression that the finger is detaching itself from the smooth, dim background. One of the most spectacular parts of the work is the radiant yellow sleeve of the man. The artist achieved the characteristic structure not with a palette knife, but by mixing small pieces of dried paint into the yellow. The red skirt, by contrast, has been made in quite a different way: various thin layers of transparent red paint have been laid on over an orange ground, thereby giving the skirt its deep red colour. De Piles was right in concluding that Rembrandt "was master of his paints and possessed the skill of handling them to the highest degree".[279]

Perhaps as unfathomable as the technique in this painting is its subject matter. Although it has been known for many years as "*The Jewish Bride*", it shows a loving couple of whom the man has put his arm around the shoulder of the woman. As in many other portraits painted by Rembrandt the man is reaching out towards the woman, who seems to be lost in thought. His other hand rests gently on her breast. He looks smilingly down at her. The woman's hand lies in her lap and the fingertips of the other hand are lightly touching those of the man. Both are sitting on a stone balustrade with a plant in a pot in front of a stone wall. Unlike their clothing, the man and the woman's jewellery and hairstyle agree with contemporary fashion. This forms a strong indication that this is a so-called *portrait historié*, a type of portraiture in which the sitters are shown as if they were playing a role in a story from the Bible or mythology. Here the unknown couple are shown as Isaac and his wife Rebecca in an episode from Genesis 26: 8. Driven by

Pupil of Rembrandt (Willem Drost)
Full-Length Portrait of Rembrandt in Working Clothes, 1652
Pen and brown ink on brownish paper, 20.3 × 13.4 cm (8 × 5 3/8 in.)
Amsterdam, Museum Het Rembrandthuis

a famine, they had journeyed to the land of the Philistines. As Rebecca was exceptionally beautiful, Isaac was afraid of being murdered and pretended to be her brother. One day Abimelech, the King of the Philistines, watched the couple exchanging secret caresses in the palace garden, whereupon he gathered that they were husband and wife. He chastised them for this lie but ordered his people that they were not to be harmed. Rembrandt portrayed the moment before the discovery, when the couple believed to be unobserved.

In a rapid sketch (p. 397, Cat. D180), which possibly served him as a preliminary study, Rembrandt had laid down the main features of the composition: the gestures of the seated couple on the balustrade, the plant in the pot and the palace wall in the background. In this sketch, he also provides a clear reference to the Old Testament by showing the king spying on the lovers from the window. In the painting, Rembrandt concentrated on the two main figures by "zooming in" on them and omitting the figure of King Abimelech. This extreme focus on the main figures and their state of mind is characteristic of Rembrandt's habit to choose the decisive key moment from the story to increase the dramatic load of the scene still further. He obviously took for granted that the subject might not be immediately or unequivocally comprehensible to the viewer for lack of additional iconographic clues. The carefully painted interplay of the hands of the protagonists thus acquires the principal role in the painting. Here, the gestures of the sitters express their feelings much more clearly than their facial expressions.

History Pieces

Rembrandt's impressive painting *Jacob Blessing the Sons of Joseph* from 1656 (pp. 472/473, Cat. 25) illustrates all the aspects of his changed artistic ideas. The light no longer falls in a narrow beam but reflects in the enclosed space and makes the protagonists light up in an almost supernatural manner. The red blanket at the bottom edge of the picture acts as a sort of repoussoir in the foreground in the same way as the rug on the table in the *"Syndics"* (pp. 466/467, Cat. 267), in order to suggest depth. The striking colouring consists of yellow, white and red. The painting shows the moment in which the dying patriarch Jacob blesses his grandsons (Genesis 48: 14–20). Joseph, the father of the children, thinks that his blind father is mistaken and attempts to move his right hand, placed in blessing on the head of the younger son, Ephraim, over to his first-born son, Manasseh. Jacob refuses, however, and declares that the eldest son will found a great people, but that the descendants of the youngest son will surpass them in greatness.

Detail of: **Self-Portrait**, *c.* 1669
(see ill. p. 497)

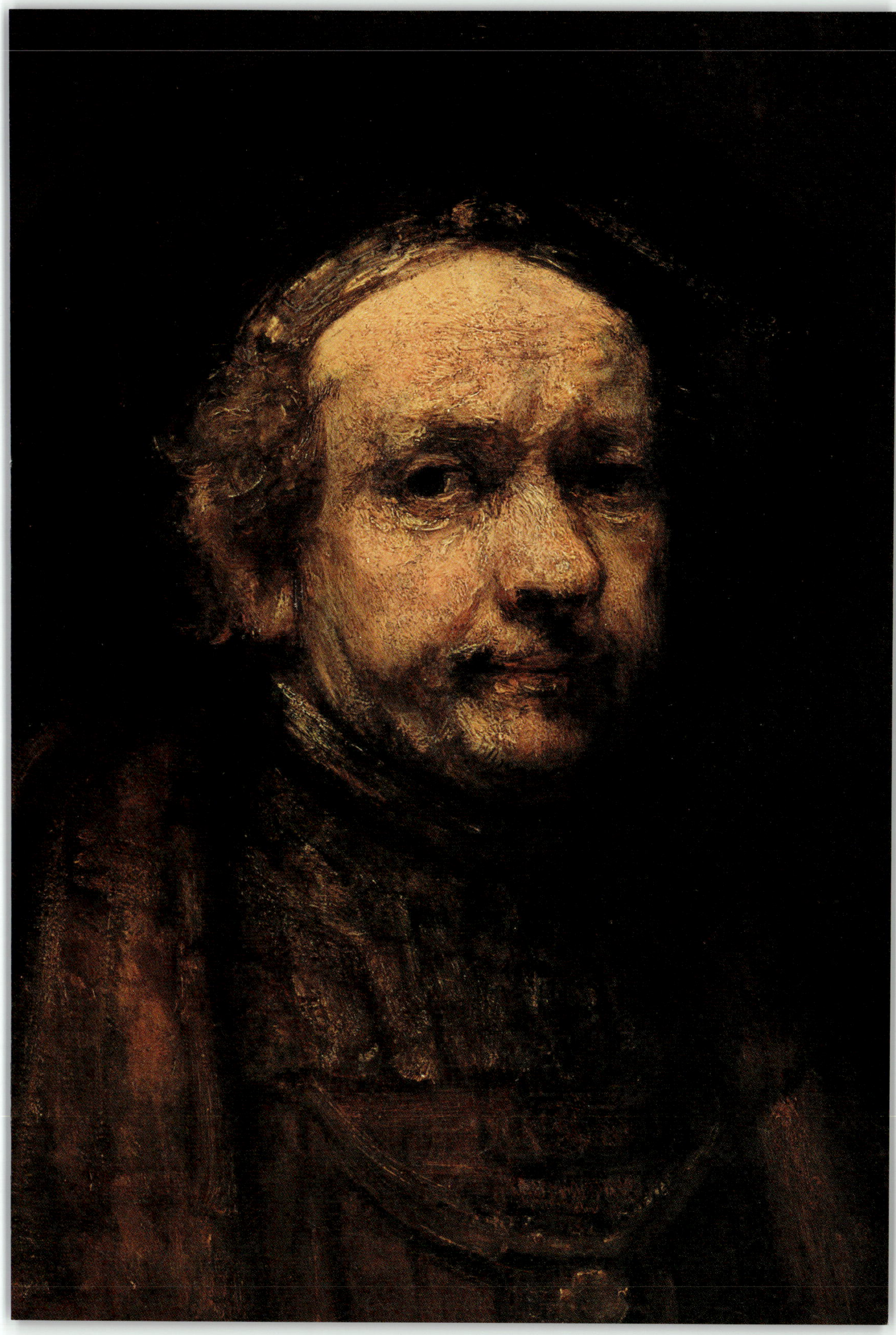

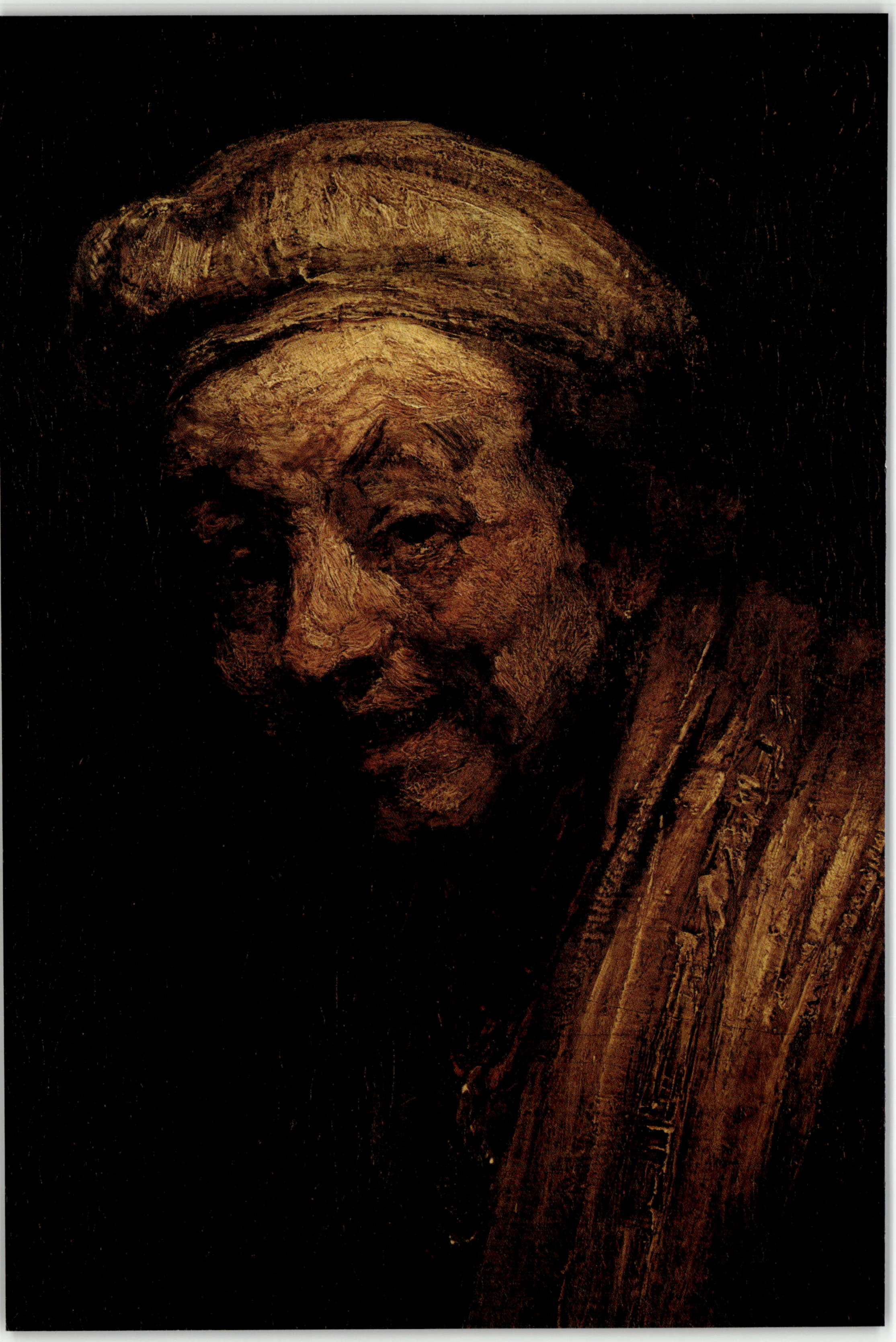

Rembrandt's good habit of researching the sources of a story scrupulously and then adding his own "nagedachten" (reflections) can also be seen in this history painting. The Bible speaks of Joseph, "and he held up his father's hand", which is precisely what Joseph is doing in the picture. In the X-rays, we can recognise that in an earlier stage Rembrandt had positioned Joseph more or less opposite to his father, suggesting he was in conflict with him. The artist had already studied the subject at an earlier date, in a lost drawing from 1636, which, however, has survived in the form of a copy. Here Joseph reacts by gesticulating wildly with his arms and looking angrily, or with "the most natural [e]motion", so to speak, as Rembrandt had described it in another context (RD 1639/2). Previously Rembrandt had preferred to depict the high point, the most intense or violent moment of a story. Here, however, the more mature Rembrandt decided during the painting process, on a later, quieter moment in which the patriarch's decision is accepted in resignation.[280] The serene pose of the beautiful Asnath, the children's Egyptian mother, who is watching the events, heightens the mood of calm and acceptance. In the Bible, her presence is not mentioned, but Rembrandt has added her as a natural amplification to the scene of blessing. Another result of such "profound reflections" or empathy for the story can be seen in the fact that in the painting the fingertips of the patriarch seem to caress the face of the astonished Manasseh almost in a gesture of comfort. As in the *Bathsheba* from 1654 (pp. 418/419, Cat. 23), Rembrandt now no longer depicted the outer but rather the inner emotions and the moment of realisation and the restrained acceptance of the unexpected turn of fate.

Rembrandt's last major commission, *The Conspiracy of the Batavians under Claudius Civilis* of 1661/62 (pp. 474/475, Cat. 115), ended in a fiasco. He received this prestigious commission for a monumental painting for the new Amsterdam Town Hall only at a later stage. Earlier, on 28 November 1659, Govert Flinck had been given the commission as part of a series of twelve large history paintings. The project was initiated by the powerful burgomaster, Cornelis de Graeff (1599–1664), possibly in agreement with Jan Six, the Commissioner for Marital Affairs, who acted as an advisor for the decoration of the Town Hall. The decision in favour of Flinck is not surprising. In contrast to his teacher, Rembrandt's former student was pleasant to deal with and extremely accommodating to his clients. After work and on Sundays, he paid courtesy visits to both De Graeff and Six, with whom he cultivated a friendly acquaintance.[281]

When Flinck unexpectedly died of a fever on 2 February 1660, the burgomasters decided in early 1661 to divide the major commission between several artists. They chose

Detail of: **Self-Portrait as Zeuxis**, 1662/63
(see ill. p. 491)

Rembrandt for the most important scene with the nocturnal conspiracy of the Batavian hero Claudius Civilis, and Rembrandt set to work with "studious diligence". He depicted Civilis exactly as he is described by the Roman historian Tacitus (*c.* 56–117 CE) in his *Historiae*: blind in one eye, with a beard and with long hair, because he had sworn not to cut it until the Roman legions had been overcome. The conspirators underlined their oath according to "barbaro ritu" (barbarian rite), in other words with their swords rather than by shaking hands.[282] Rembrandt worked on the painting for a long time. While Jacob Jordaens (1593–1678) and Jan Lievens had finished their paintings already after six months, he was still busy with the composition in October 1661, as the sketch proves which he made while he was working (p. 398, Cat. D179). The result was a mysterious, intimate scene in a dark setting, in which a hidden source of light illuminates the faces of the conspirators.

The poet Melchior Fokkens saw the painting in July 1662 hanging in the south-east corner of the Great Gallery of the Town Hall. In contrast to Lievens and Jordaens, who received the agreed payment of 1,200 guilders promptly, Rembrandt's fee was obviously the subject of a dispute. He probably expected the burgomasters to pay him more, and he apparently also wanted to make changes to his work. That at least is what he told the art dealer Lodewijk van Ludick in August 1662 (RD 1662/6). Rembrandt owed van Ludick money and he was promised a quarter of what the painter "would profit from the work delivered to the Town Hall", and furthermore he would "benefit from the [income] from the changes". But Rembrandt miscalculated here, because the burgomasters had agreed that under no circumstances would they pay any extra for alterations.[283] Moreover, they were running out of time, because the painting had to be finished before the visit of the Elector Maximilian Heinrich (1621–1688), who was also Archbishop of Cologne, in September. As a stopgap measure, they had the wall filled with a sketch by Flinck, which was hurriedly touched up by Jürgen Ovens (1623–1678) for 48 guilders and which is still there today.[284]

In line with the myth that Rembrandt's late work found little favour with the elite, in the literature on this matter it is mostly assumed that the burgomasters found Rembrandt's painting offensive or too dark and that they therefore refused it. Yet, the burgomasters must have known what they were letting themselves in for when they ordered a night piece from Rembrandt. In view of the unbending and demanding attitude which he demonstrated in such matters when dealing with his clients – and especially when it was a matter of money – it is also quite feasible that he had demanded the work back himself. He then rigorously reduced the size of his largest painting (originally approximately 550 × 550 cm / 216 5⁄8 × 216 5⁄8 in.) so that he could sell it. Such were his financial straits one month later, in October 1662, that he was forced to sell Saskia's grave (RD 1662/9).

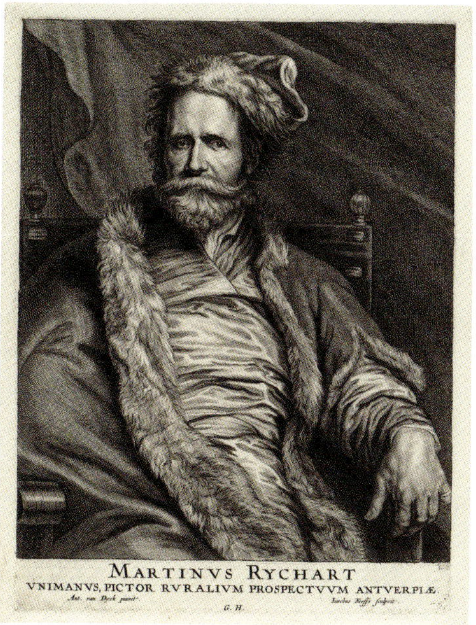

During the 1660s, Rembrandt mostly painted historical half-length single figures (see pp. 389–392). In the case of two paintings, *Lucretia* of 1666 (p. 477, Cat. 117) and *Juno* from 1657–1665 (p. 423, Cat. 108), he seems to have had recourse to the type of life-size female half-length figures which he had created during the 1630s, such as *Flora* (p. 353, Cat. 103) and *Bellona* (Cat. 98). In *Lucretia*, he deviated from the pictorial tradition in which Lucretia is shown holding the raised dagger, ready to kill herself with a deadly blow. Rembrandt showed the moment after she had wounded herself, as testified by the dramatic bloodstain on her white chemise. Her raised arm is painted with broad strokes applied with a palette knife. The painting gives the impression of being unfinished. The majestic *Juno* was probably painted for Herman Becker (*c.* 1617–1678), an art lover and one of Rembrandt's creditors. According to a notarial declaration dated 9 August 1665, he rejected the repayment of a loan in cash from Rembrandt with the words: "Let Rembrandt first finish the Juno" (RD 1665/17). Here the question arises as to whether Becker gave him the commission or whether he saw the unfinished painting in Rembrandt's workshop asked him to finish it for him. The X-ray of the picture reveals that Rembrandt had spent a long time working on it and had made many changes during the process.[285]

The Late Self-Portraits

In 1652, after an interval of seven years, Rembrandt turned once more to painting self-portraits. In the meantime, he had been mostly occupied with the production of etchings and landscapes. Maybe it is significant that in a print from 1648 (Cat. E217), he depicted himself etching by a window that opens onto a landscape. Here Rembrandt

Jacobus Neeffs after Anthony van Dyck, **Martin Rijckaert**, 1626/41
Copper engraving, 24.1 × 20.3 cm (9 ½ × 8 in.)
Washington, DC, National Gallery of Art

showed himself for the first time as an artist at work – not dressed in an opulent and imaginative manner or in a historical or fashionable dress as in earlier portraits, but quite simply in his working clothes. A drawing by an anonymous pupil which was made some two years later shows him dressed in similar fashion, but here as a full-length figure and with his hands on his hips (p. 401). Under the drawing, in seventeenth-century handwriting, is written: "drawn by Rembrant van Rhijn, after himself as he was dressed in his studio." Rembrandt is clad in a gown reaching almost to the ground, known at the time as a *tabbaard*, which he has tied at the waist with a sash. He is also wearing slippers and a hat. The (night)gown was a popular form of house dress worn by men, and slippers are also a comfortable form of footwear for use in the house. We know from the inventories of artists that most painters worked at home in a gown; Rembrandt's inventory from 1656 also lists "two fur(lined) gowns".

In his impressive *Self-Portrait in Working Dress* (p. 478, Cat. 161) from 1652, Rembrandt also depicts himself in a similar *tabbaard*, self-assured and again with his hands on his hips. Instead of a contemporary hat, he is wearing a beret in the fashion of the sixteenth century that had become his personal trademark. This first self-portrait that he painted after a long interval is also one of the first manifestations of his new style. He is standing close to the picture plane, frontally and life-size. The hands and the brown artist's gown are rendered in a sketch-like manner with thin brown paint, while the face is composed of carefully placed pastose brushstrokes. The dark clothing and background direct our full attention to the face and the penetrating gaze. With his gaze, pose, the simple working dress and the artist's beret Rembrandt seemed to have wanted to express that he was first and foremost an artist – no more, but most certainly no less either.

The tendency to read Rembrandt's large oeuvre of self-portraits as an autobiography is tempting but also misleading. Thus in 1658 (p. 485, Cat. 166) he again depicted himself in a life-size portrait and frontally, but here he is sitting straddle-legged and wearing a remarkable colourful costume. The almost triumphant pose looks so majestic that he has on occasion be compared with the "Painter Prince" or Zeus, the ruler of the gods, sitting enthroned.[286] In reality he was confronted in this year with possibly his greatest professional loss: he was forced to sell first his house (RD 1658/3), his furniture (1658/5) and finally even the collection of graphic art which he had so carefully assembled and preserved (RD 1658/30; see pp. 363–367). Rembrandt borrowed some pictorial elements, such as the frontal seated pose and the costume, from an engraving in his collection: Anthony van Dyck's portrait of the landscape painter Martin Rijckaert (1587–1631; p. 407). Rembrandt will have known the engraving from van Dyck's *Iconographie*, a famous series of portraits of artists which had been published in 1645. Rembrandt also based his self-portrait from the last year of his life (p. 495, Cat. 173) on a model from another series of portraits of famous artists. The pose and the doublet in the style of the fifteenth century, with a high small fur collar and a button, are the same as those in Hieronymus Cock's *Portrait of Dieric Bouts* in the series which Cock's widow published in 1572. In the X-ray of the painting, we can see that the resemblance in the earlier version was even greater, because Rembrandt initially, like Bouts, was shown holding a paintbrush in his right hand.

From 1660 Rembrandt started to depict himself for the first time with his painting tools in his hand and a work on his easel, as in *Self-Portrait at the Easel* from 1660 (p. 489, Cat. 168) and in the impressive *Self-Portrait with Palette and Maulstick* from 1665–1669 (p. 494, Cat. 172). The sketch-like rendering of the white artist's cap and the hand with the painting utensils has been heightened to the extreme here. The face, on the other hand, was worked out in much greater detail, with numerous little scratchings in the wet paint, for example in the eyebrow and moustache. Rembrandt has aged visibly: his hair is grey, and his prominent features have drooped. But his gaze and attitude are undaunted. As in other late self-portraits, Rembrandt depicts himself here in something that we could describe as historicising working clothes. He portrays himself as a painter, not of his own time but as an artist of a time that is long past.

About 1662/63, he painted himself with a face contorted into a grin in the role of Zeuxis (5th century BC; p. 491, Cat. 171), the painter from classical antiquity. Van Mander reports that in his old days the latter had literally died of laughter while painting the portrait of a "wrinkled, droll old woman".[287] The fact that Rembrandt painted himself in this unusual way may perhaps have derived from the fact that – according to van Mander – Zeuxis, just like Rembrandt, was famous for being able to portray emotions accurately.[288] It is puzzling, however, why he should have portrayed himself as the Apostle Paul in 1661 (p. 488, Cat. 170). The number of contemplative religious half-length figures which he painted in 1660 may have prompted him to do so. It was also during this year that he painted Titus as a pensive monk (p. 435, Cat. 85), but the role of the pugnacious Apostle Paul, chastened by adversity, suited Rembrandt better. Earlier (p. 59, Cat. 40; p. 61, Cat. 37; p. 67, Cat. 40; Cat. 84), he had been particularly fascinated by this Apostle, the most important for Protestants, because of the emphasis he placed on the direct and personal relationship of the believer to God.[289] In contrast to Saskia's sisters, and also Rembrandt's later companions Geertje and Hendrickje, who were official members of the Reformed Church, Rembrandt and Saskia had never taken the decision to become official church members – despite their friendly contacts with Saskia's cousin, the orthodox minister Sylvius.[290] This did not mean, however, that Rembrandt and Saskia were not religious: after all, they had made their marriage vows in the Reformed Church, and their children were also baptised there.

In *Self-Portrait as the Apostle Paul* the light falls from above onto Rembrandt's wrinkled brow and the masterfully painted turban, which consists of a few strokes of white and yellow paint drawn wet-in-wet. The brown coat and St Paul's traditional attributes, the sword and the scroll, are in deeper shadow and only recognisable at second glance. It is questionable whether the probable first owner, the prominent Parisian collector Everhard Jabach (1618–1695), recognised the Apostle in this work at all. According to his inventory of 1696, he saw the painting primarily as a self-portrait of the artist.[291]

Rembrandt was aware of the fact that his self-portraits were popular collectible items amongst art lovers. In 1669, the last year of his life, he painted no fewer than three self-portraits (p. 494, Cat. 175; p. 495, Cat. 173; p. 497, Cat. 174), one of which (p. 497) was probably purchased during the course of the same year by Prince Cosimo III de' Medici for his famous gallery of artists' self-portraits. It is a suitable self-portrait for the collection. Once again Rembrandt painted himself in a costume from the sixteenth century and thus placed himself intentionally in the tradition of the self-portraits of his illustrious predecessors. His likeness in The Hague (p. 494) is regarded as his final self-portrait. It looks unfinished in some places, and the execution seems hesitant.[292] Also Rembrandt's grey hair is longer, and his features look more flaccid. Nonetheless, the vigorous and effective brushwork in the cap does not exactly point to diminished artistic strength or powers of observation. In view of the numerous alterations he made to the picture, this self-portrait – like almost all his other works – is the result of his unceasing search during the painting process. And in spite of its unfinished character the work is signed, an indication that the painting (in Houbraken's words) was "voldaan" (finished), because "the master has achieved his intention in it".

The Final Years

We are mistaken if we believe that Rembrandt had to spend his final years misunderstood and in poverty because of a lack of commissions. The financial situation at the end of his life is more accurately characterised as highly fluctuating. On the one hand, during these years there was an upsurge in his painting production, and he will have earned well at times. He had also started collecting again, because by the time he died his inventory lists at least three rooms full of "paintings, drawings, curiosities and antique objects" (RD 1669/5). On the other hand, after Hendrickje's death he sometimes had difficulty paying the rent and on occasion borrowed Cornelia's savings (RD 1666/2, 1658/9). He clearly found it difficult to manage money. He was a compulsive collector who was willing to pay large sums for art and who often robbed Peter to pay Paul.

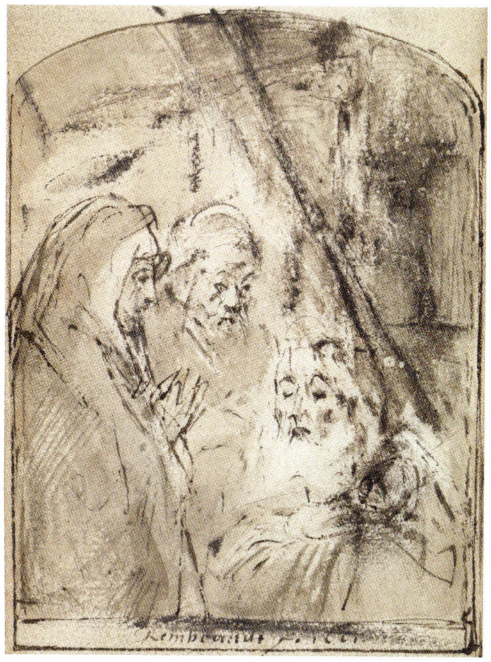

Rembrandt died on 4 October 1669, just over a year after Titus – probably rather unexpectedly (RD 1669/4), because in the months before his death two artists saw him still working on *Simeon's Song of Praise* from around 1668/69 (p. 499, Cat. 76), "which was still unfinished".[293] Because of the poor condition in which the painting is today, we cannot say with certainty whether the figure of the Virgin Mary is by Rembrandt's own hand or not. It is quite possible that it was completed by another artist. It seems particularly appropriate that this painting was on Rembrandt's easel when he died, because it shows the moment when the pious Simeon recognises the Messiah in the little boy who has been brought to the temple by his parents. When Simeon takes the child into his arms he praises God with the words "Lord, now lettest thou thy servant depart in peace", thus alluding to his imminent death (Luke 2: 29–32).

Rembrandt's estate contained a remarkable number of unfinished works: "Four paintings, unfinished" and "twenty-two finished and unfinished paintings" (RD 1669/5). As her mother's heir, Rembrandt's daughter, Cornelia, was entitled to inherit half the works. On 3 May 1670, exactly six months after Rembrandt's death (the minimum period of mourning), she married, aged just 16 years, her young neighbour, Cornelis Suijthof (*c.* 1646–after 1689), who was also a painter. After the wedding, the couple emigrated to Batavia. Probably they sold the works she had inherited.[294]

Rembrandt certainly sought fame during his lifetime. But he never aspired to belong to the higher echelons of society. And so it seems unlikely that he strove – like Rubens – to become a cultivated gentleman and courtier. Instead, it was rather his ambition to go down in history as a great artist. Unlike his former apprentices, including Govert Flinck

The Presentation in the Temple, 1661
Pen and brush in brown, 12 × 8.9 cm (4 ¾ × 3 ⅝ in.)
The Hague, Koninklijke Bibliotheek

and Ferdinand Bol, Rembrandt demonstrated a remarkable lack of respect towards the rich and powerful. His artistic independence was important to him, and the countless conflicts with his clients reveal that he would brook no criticism or interference. Houbraken's famous remark (earlier made by de Piles), that during the autumn of his life Rembrandt "mostly [associated] with common people and those who practised art", seems to have been accurate. Rembrandt justified this decision thus: "If I want to give my mind relaxation, it is not honour that I seek but freedom."[295] For him, his work always occupied first place, and when he was working he did not want to be disturbed even by a king.[296] Von Sandrart also described him as an untiring and hard worker, who earned very well with his art. Especially because, according to Houbraken, Rembrandt "was not a man who consumed a great deal in taverns or in company, and [...] he only lived a bourgeois life, and when he was working, his meal often consisted of bread and a piece of cheese or a salted herring".[297] Huygens and Gersaint also report that Rembrandt was so absorbed by his work that he did not even allow himself time to relax.

Indeed, we can deduce from Rembrandt's extraordinarily extensive oeuvre that he never tied himself down to a single successful formula. Instead he searched unceasingly and restlessly for new solutions to the artistic problems which he was working on at any time, such as the effect of light and shadow, the arrangement of space or the observation of his own surroundings. As a result, during the course of his long career he continually changed his style, his use of colour, his technique and his choice of subject matter.

Detail of: **Self-Portrait**, 1669
(see ill. p. 495)

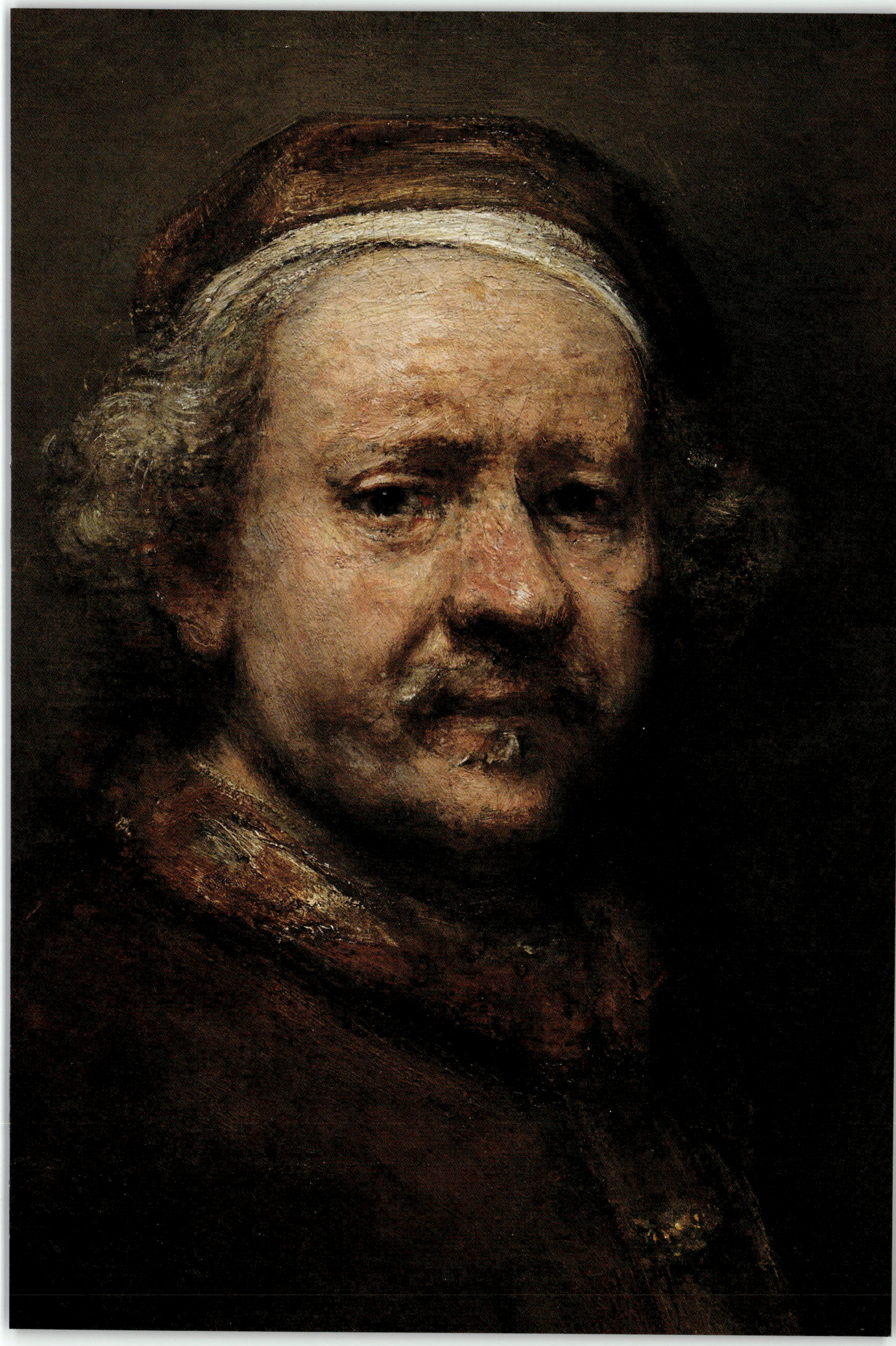

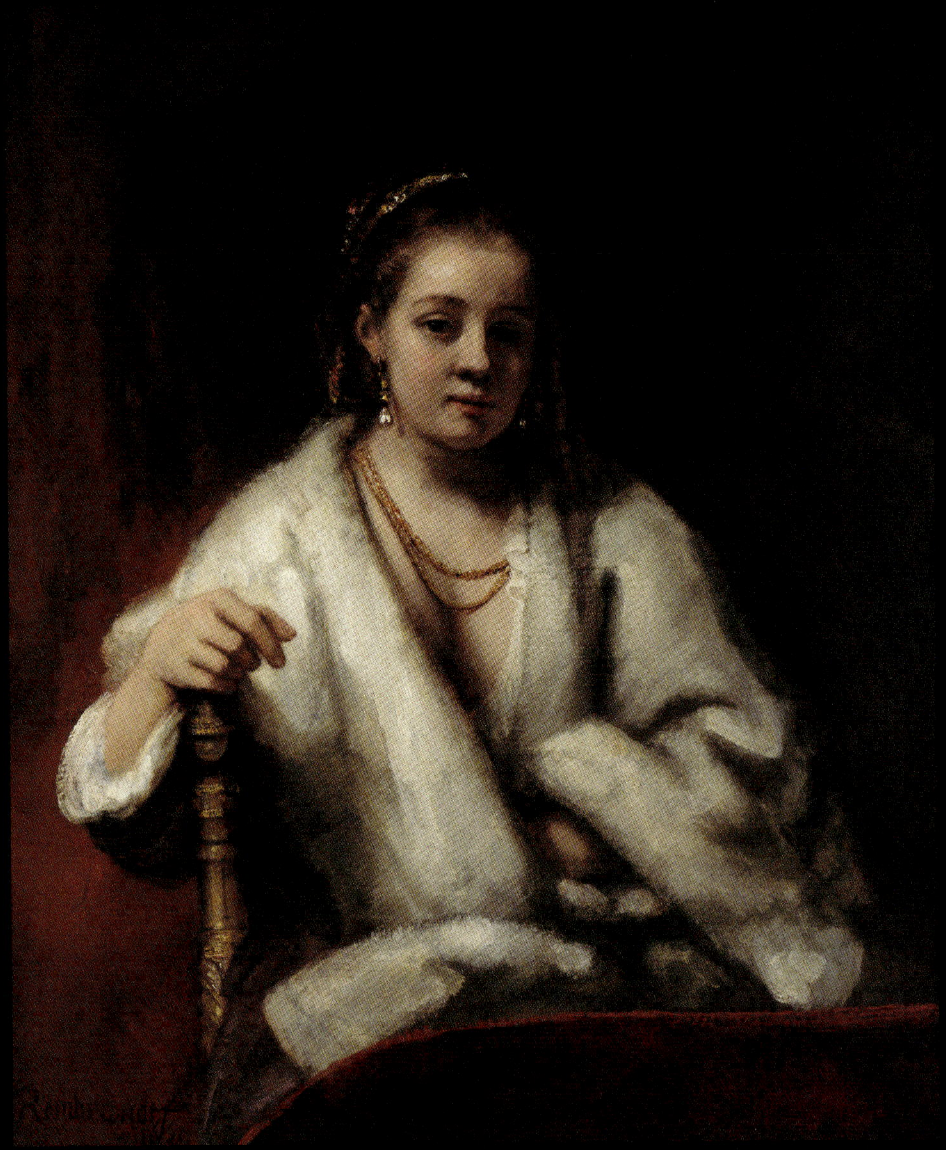

Woman with a White Wrap (Hendrickje?), *c.* 1653/54
Oil on canvas, 101.9 × 83.7 cm (40 1/8 × 32 3/4 in.)
London, The National Gallery

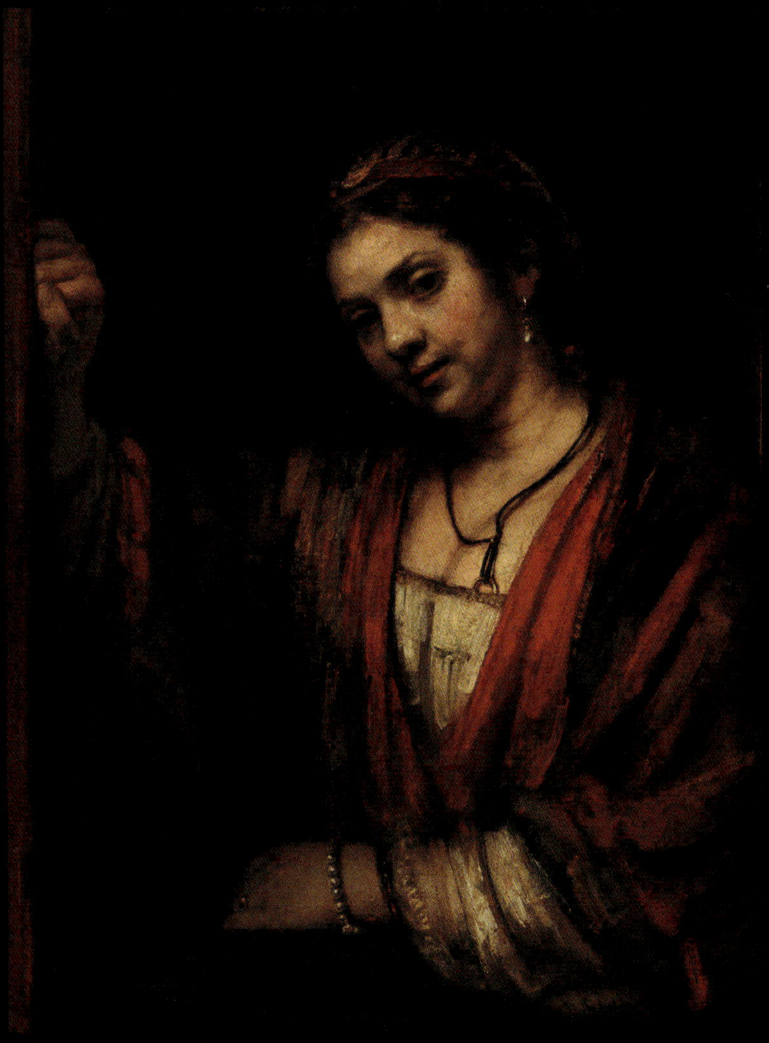

Woman at an Open Doorway (Hendrickje?), 1656/57
Oil on canvas, 88.5 × 67 cm (34 ¾ × 26 ⅜ in.)
Staatliche Museen zu Berlin, Gemäldegalerie

A Woman Bathing (Hendrickje?), 1654
Oil on panel, 61.8 × 47 cm (24 ⅓ × 18 ½ in.)
London, The National Gallery

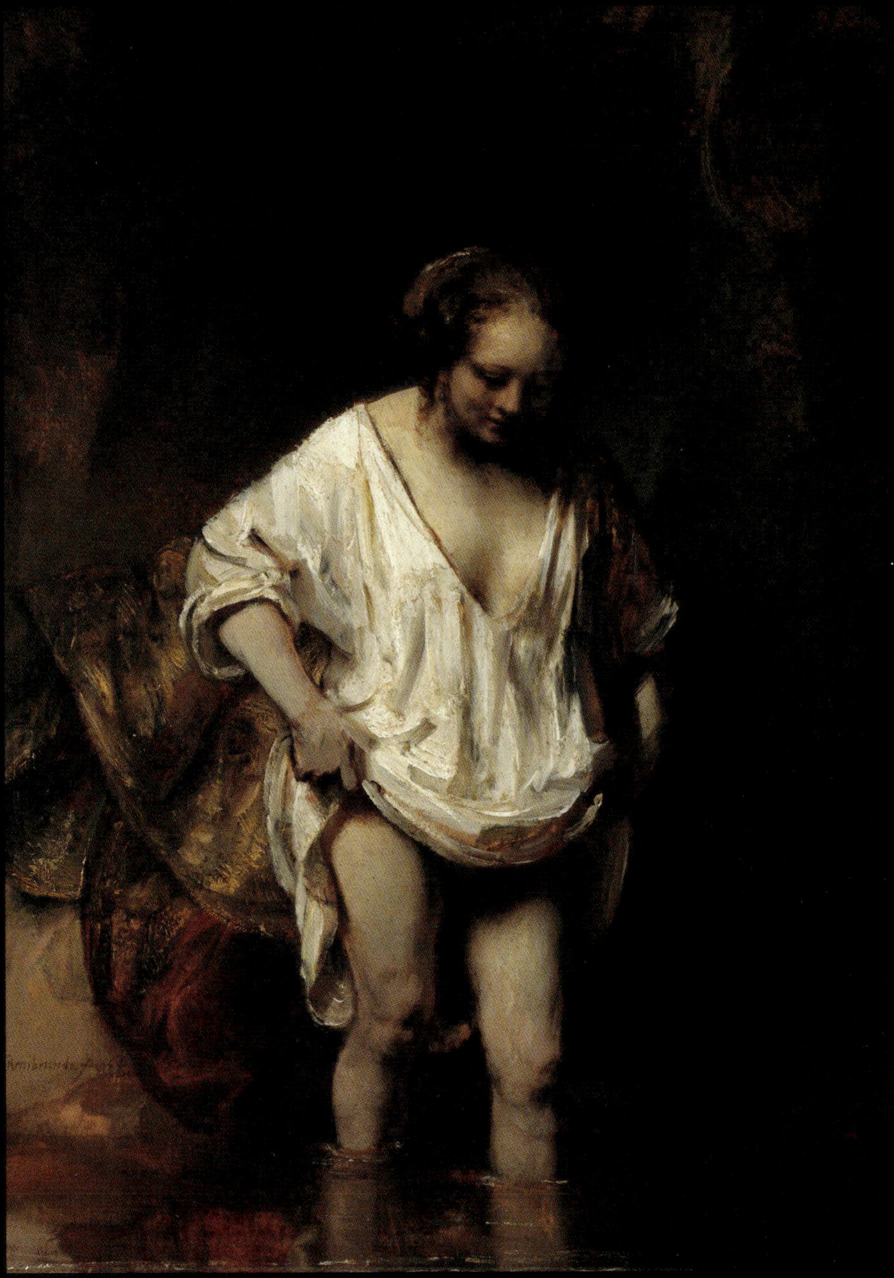

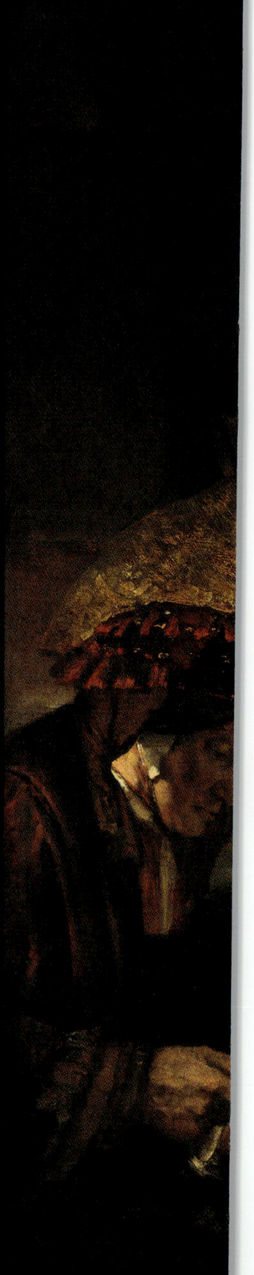

Bathsheba with King David's Letter, 1654
Oil on canvas, 142 × 142 cm (55 ¾ × 55 ¾ in.)
Paris, Musée du Louvre

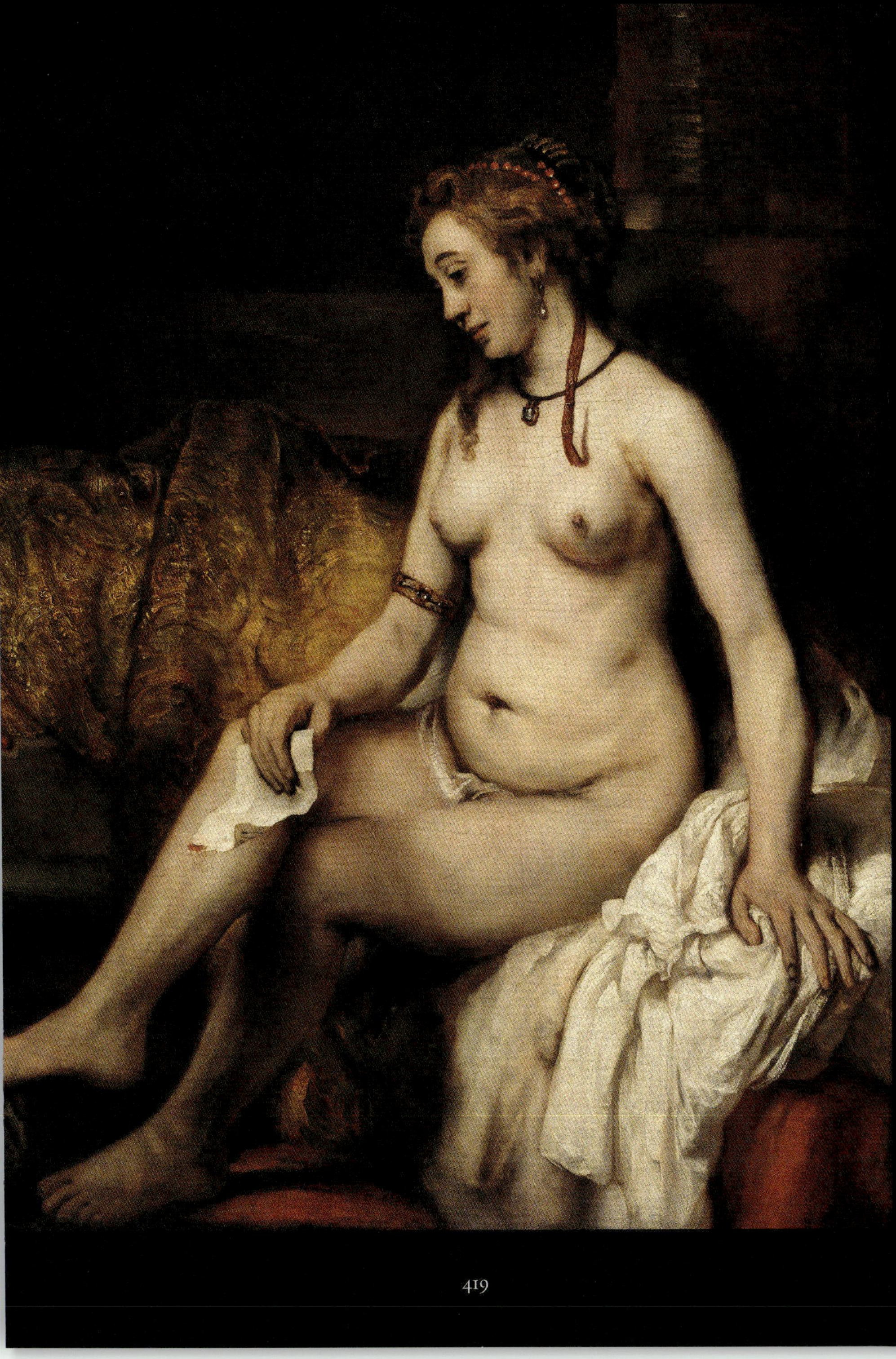

Titian
Flora, *c.* 1515–1520
Oil on canvas, 79.7 × 63.5 cm (31 ½ × 25 in.)
Florence, Galleria degli Uffizi

Flora, *c.* 1660
Oil on canvas, 100 × 91.8 cm (39 ⅜ × 36 ⅛ in.)
New York, The Metropolitan Museum of Art,
Gift of Archer M. Huntington in memory of his father,
Collin Potter Huntington, 1926

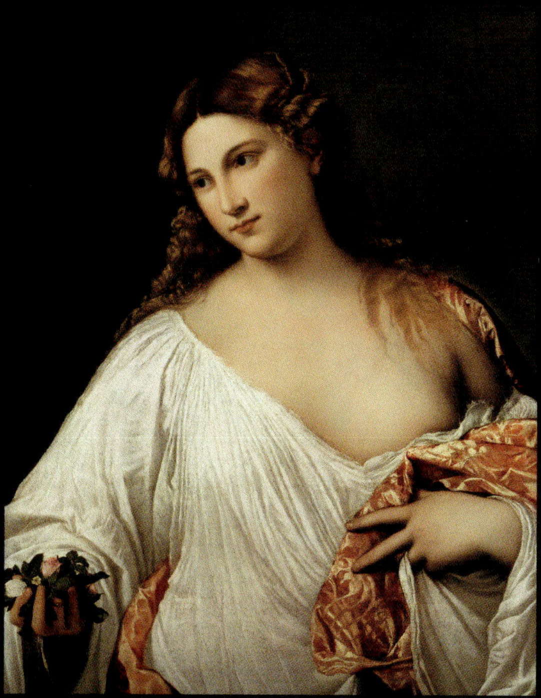

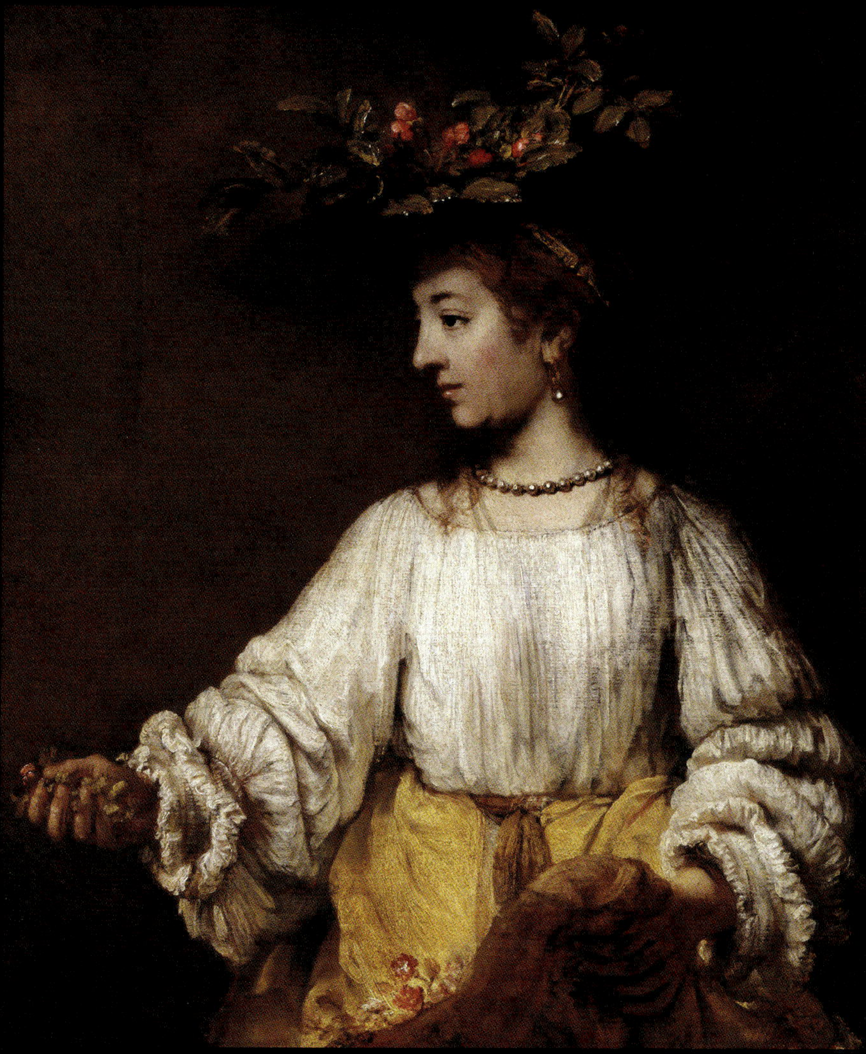

Juno, *c.* 1657–1665
Oil on canvas, 127 × 107.5 cm (50 × 42⅓ in.)
Los Angeles, Hammer Museum, The Armand Hammer Collection,
Gift of The Armand Hammer Foundation

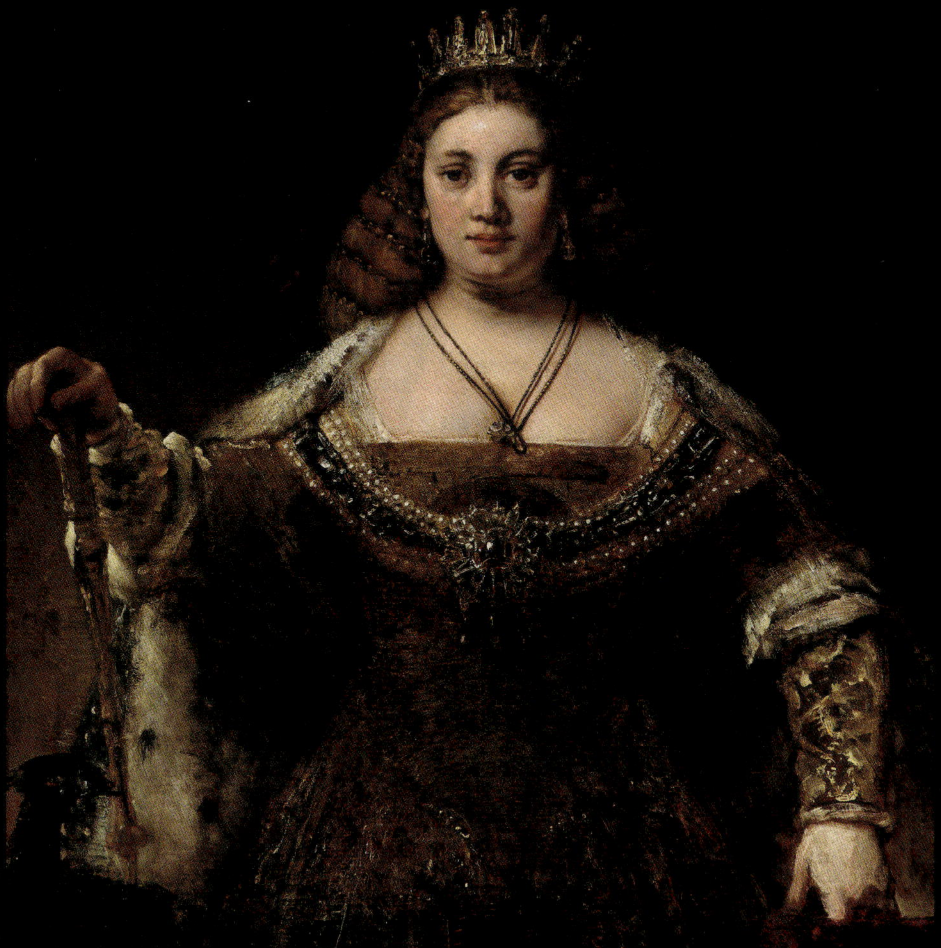

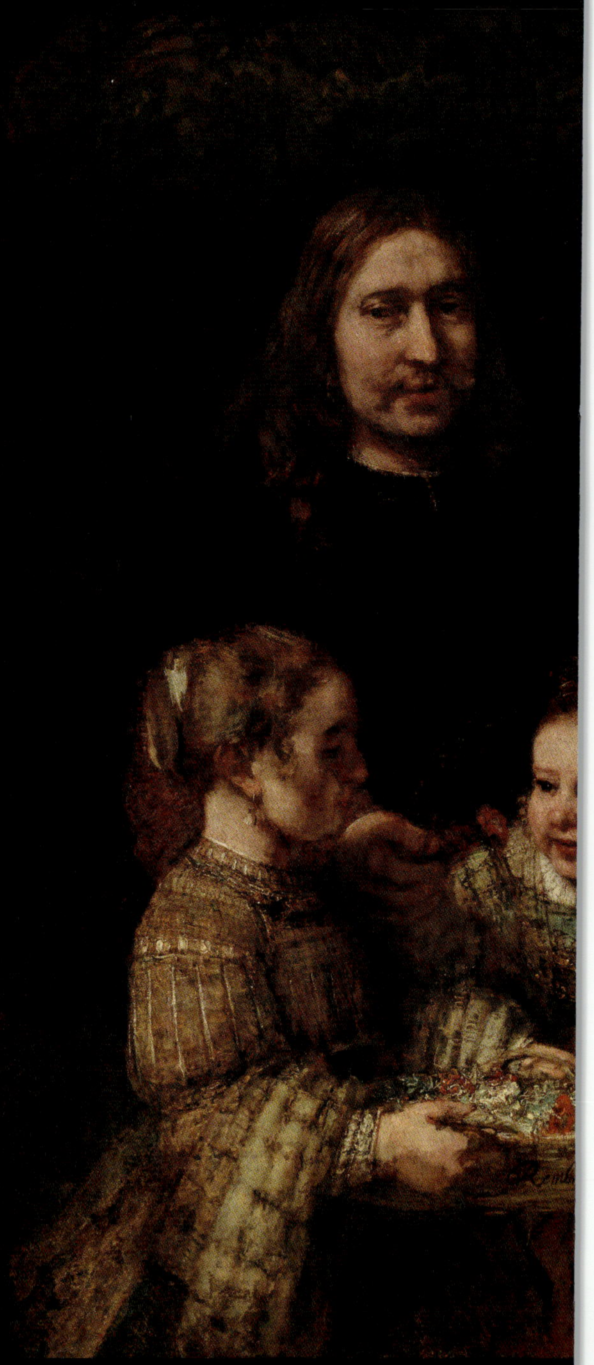

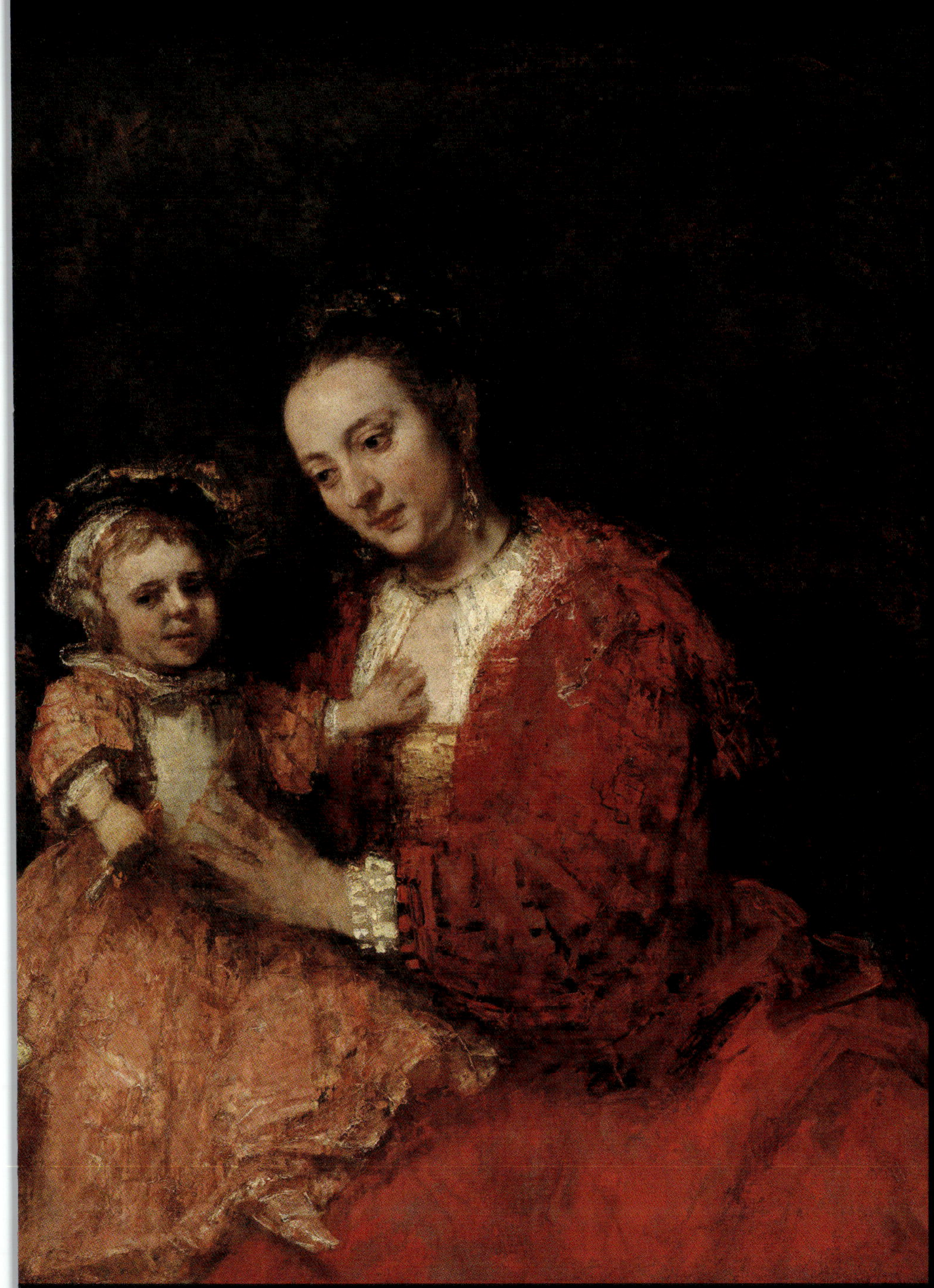

Pages 424/425
Family Portrait, *c.* 1665
Oil on canvas, 126 × 167 cm (49 ⅝ × 65 ¾ in.)
Braunschweig, Herzog Anton Ulrich-Museum

Portrait of a Young Woman with a Lapdog, *c.* 1665
Oil on canvas, 81.3 × 64.1 cm (32 ⅛ × 25 ¼ in.)
Toronto, Art Gallery of Ontario, Bequest of Frank P. Wood 1955

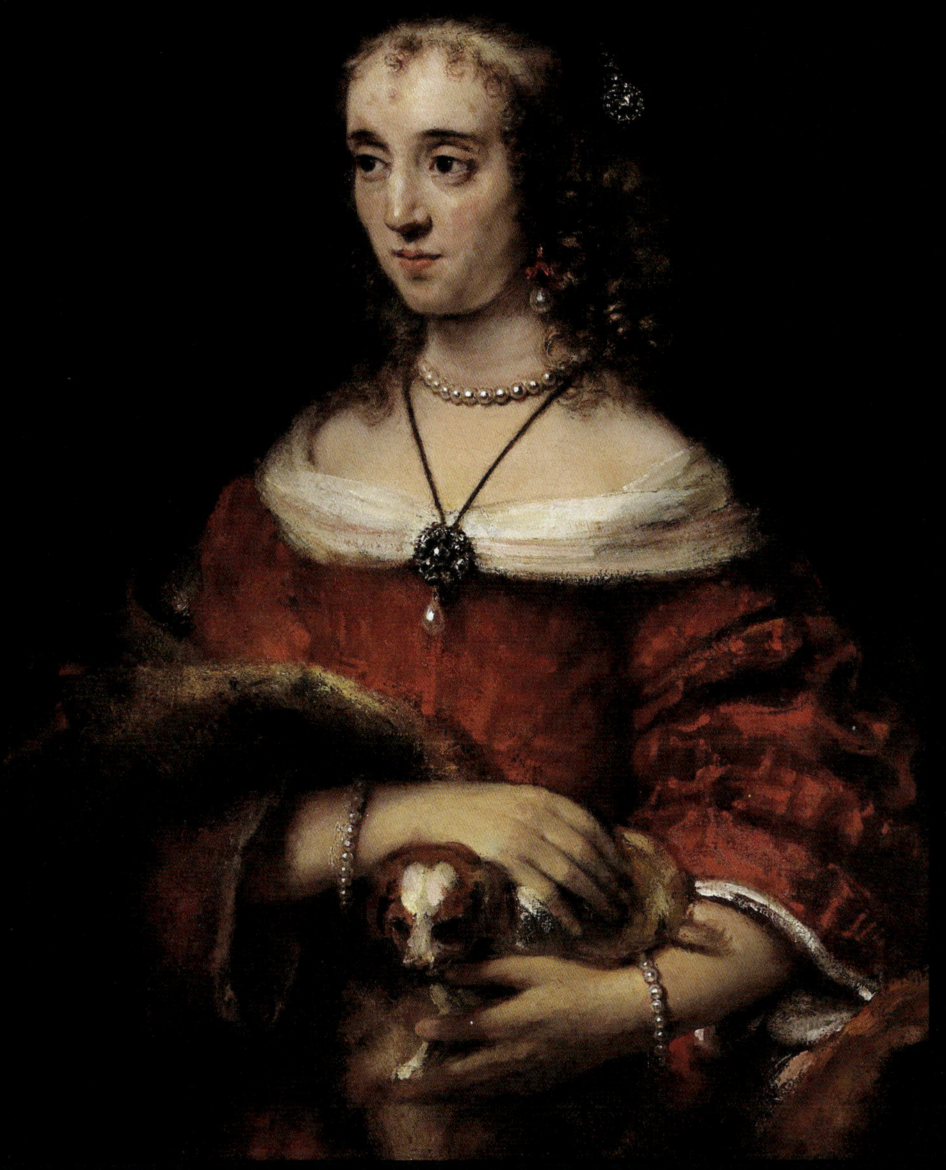

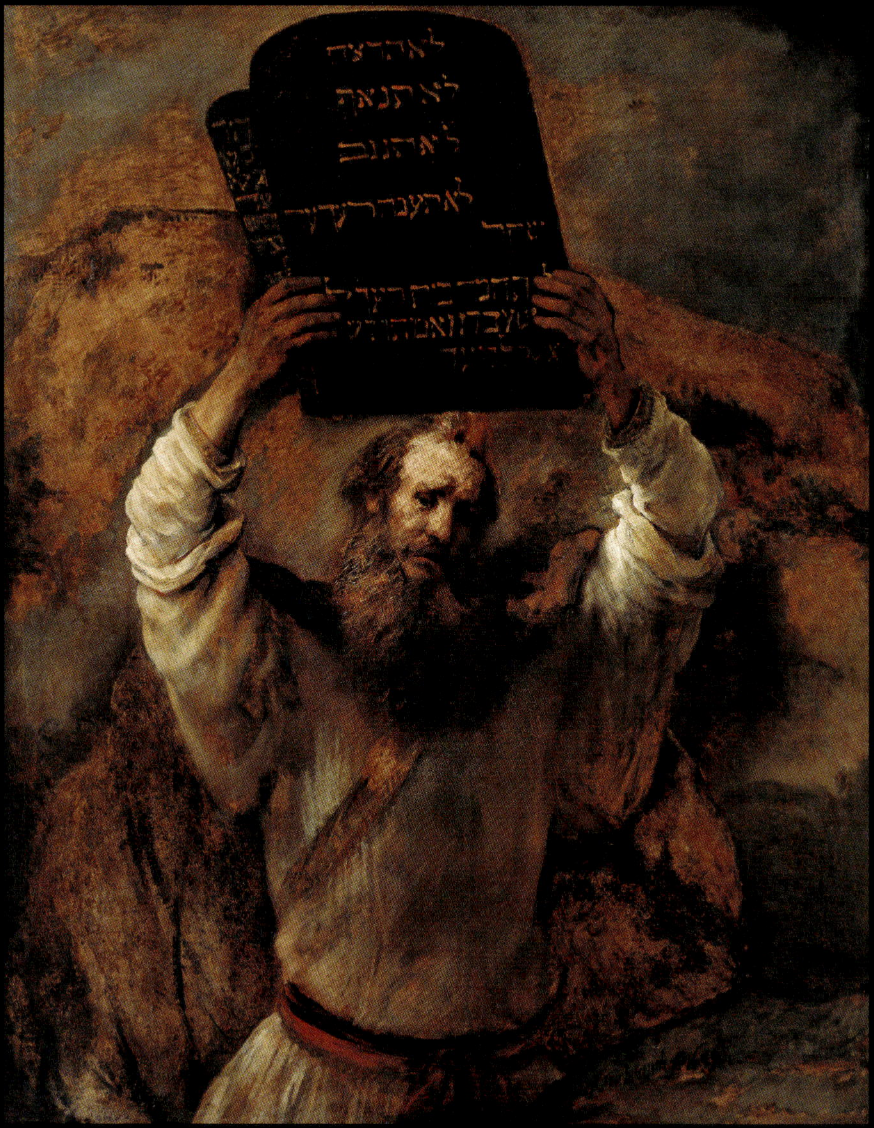

Moses Breaking the Tablets of the Law, 1659
Oil on canvas, 168.5 × 136.5 cm (66 ⅓ × 53 ¾ in.)
Staatliche Museen zu Berlin, Gemäldegalerie

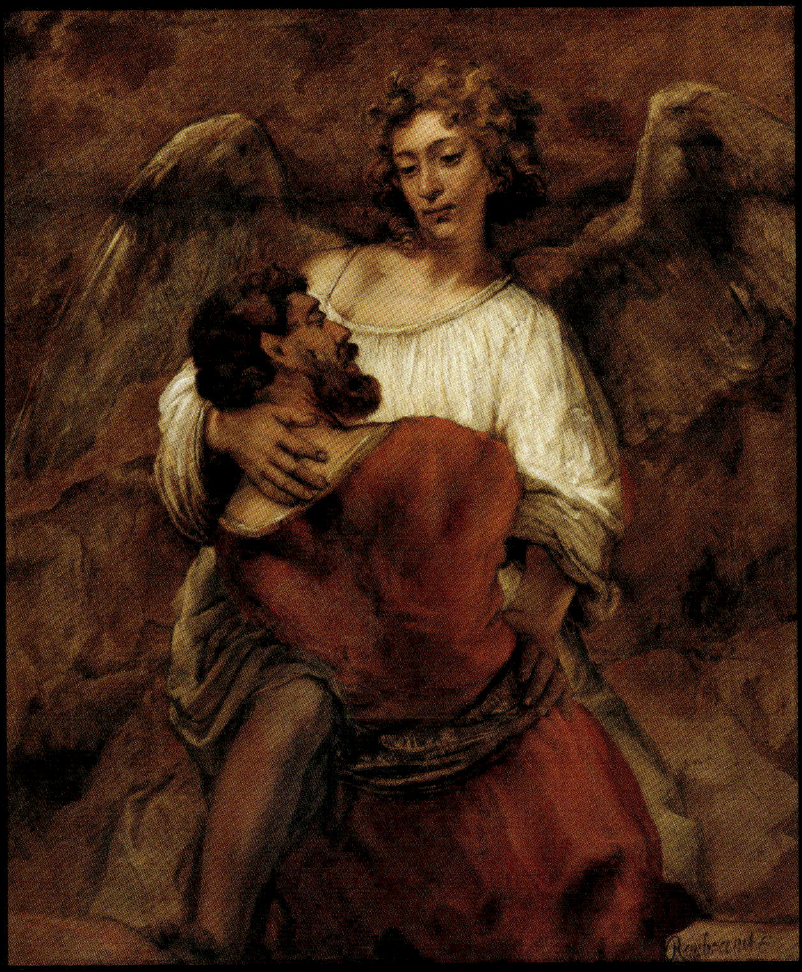

Jacob Wrestling with the Angel, *c.* 1659
Oil on canvas, 137 × 116 cm (53 ¾ × 45 ⅔ in.)
Staatliche Museen zu Berlin, Gemäldegalerie

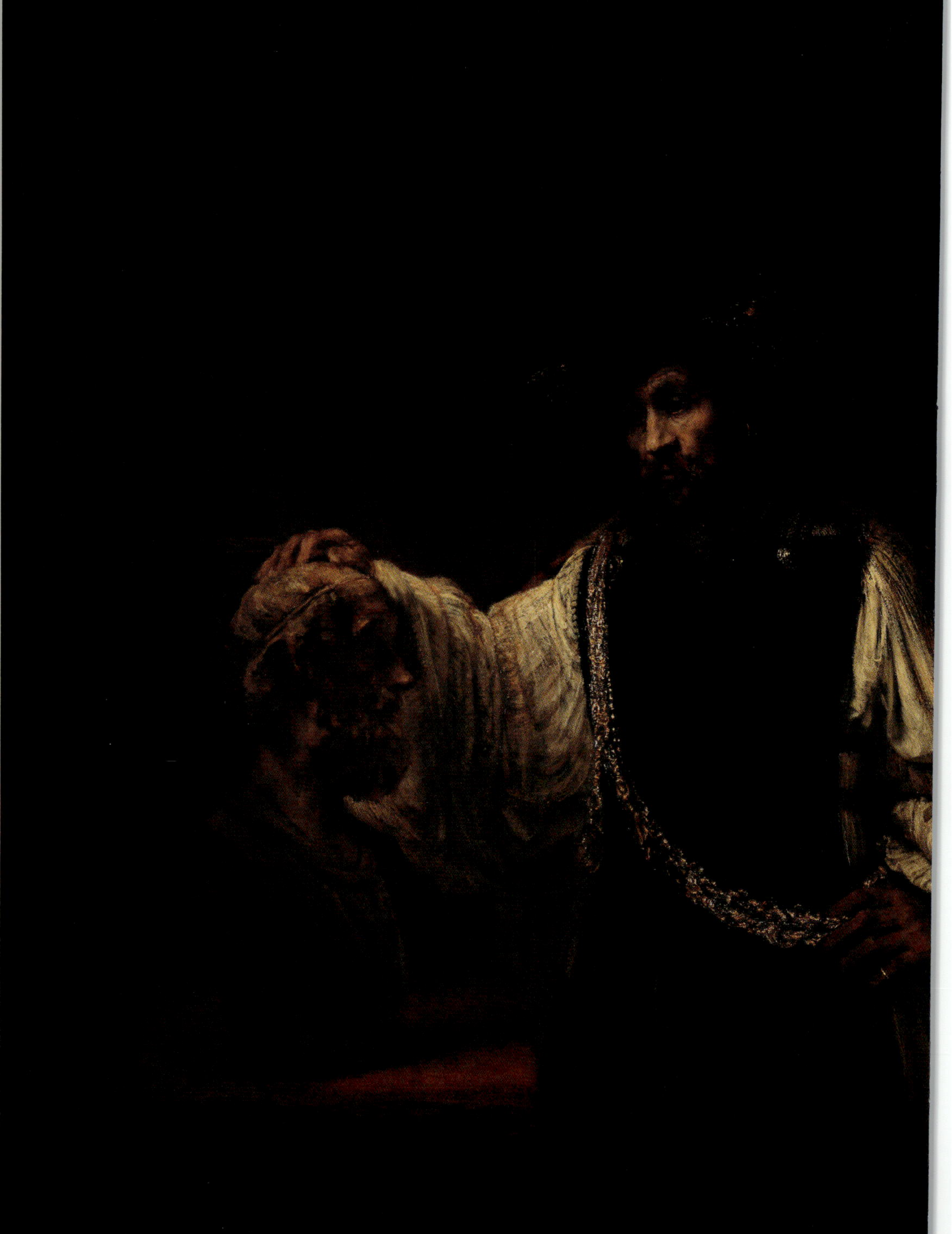

Aristotle with the Bust of Homer, 1653
Oil on canvas, 143.5 × 136.5 cm (56 ½ × 53 ¾ in.)
New York, The Metropolitan Museum of Art

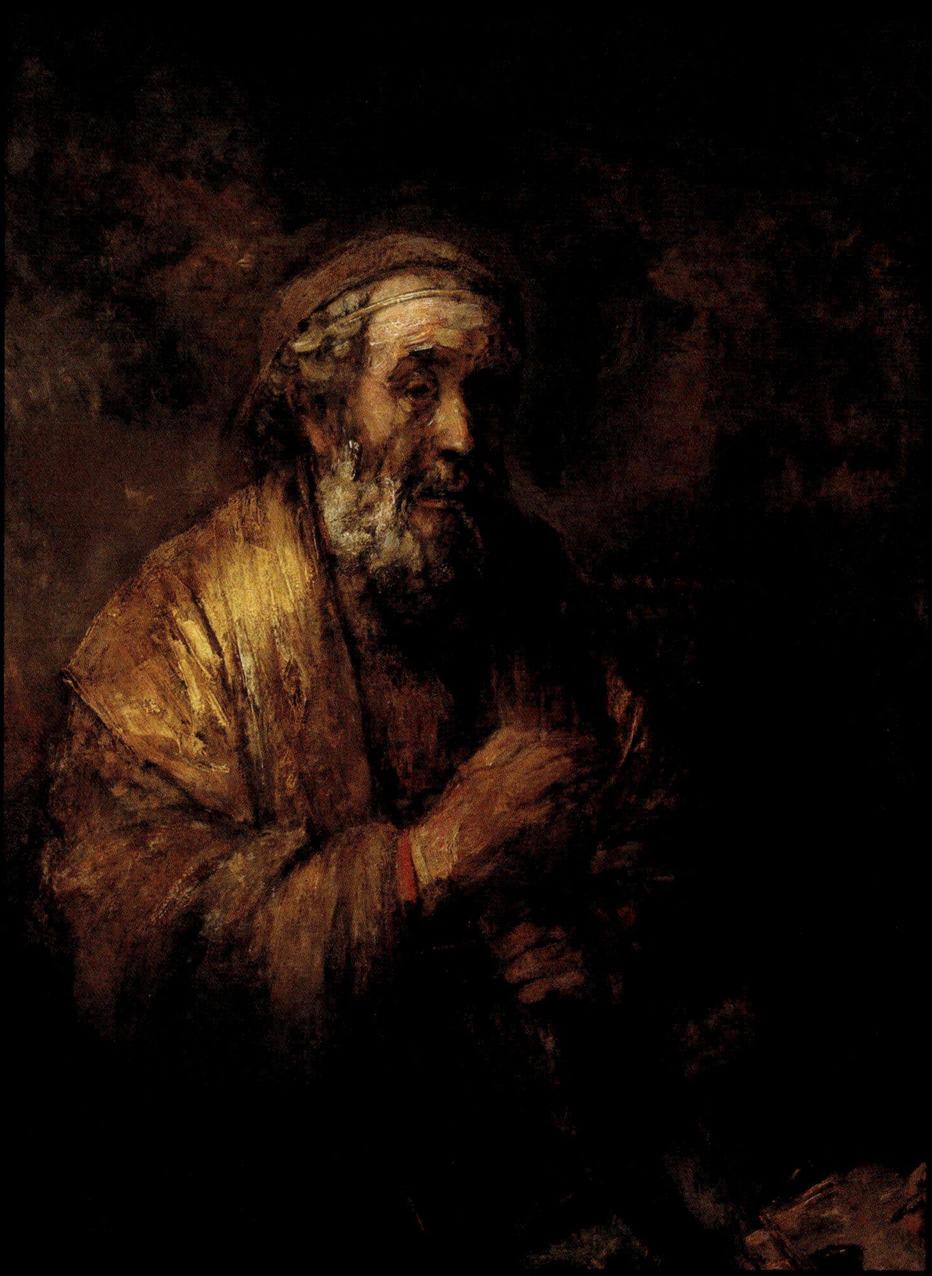

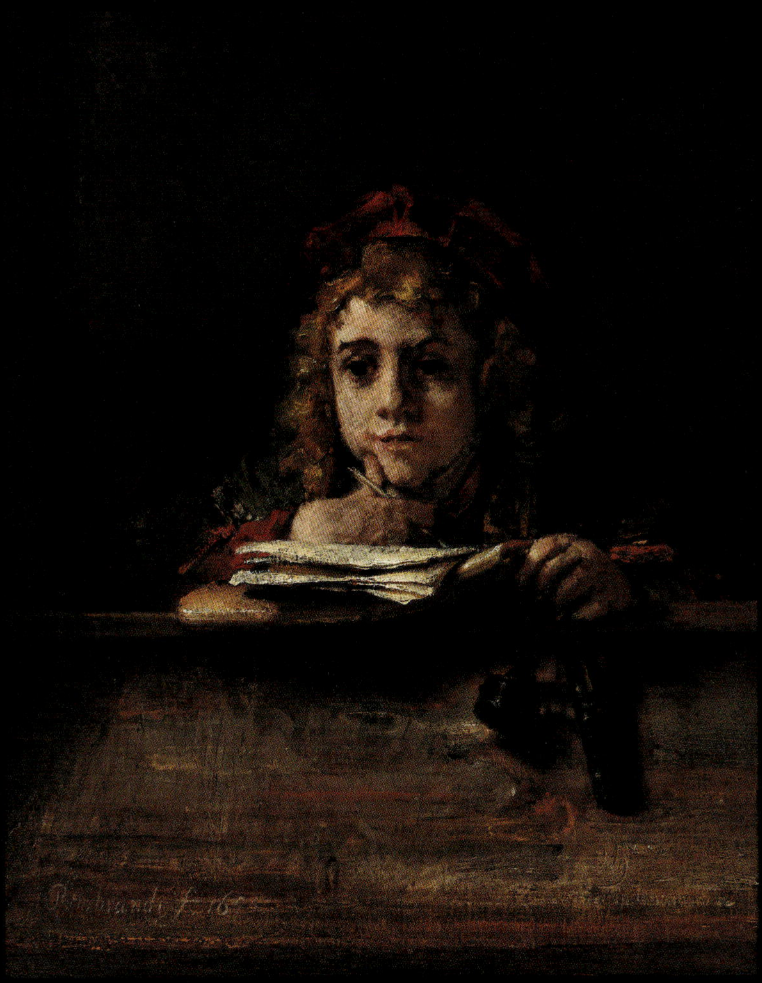

Homer, 1663
Oil on canvas, 108 × 82.4 cm (42 ½ × 32 ½ in.)
The Hague, Mauritshuis

Boy Drawing at His Desk (Titus?), 1655
Oil on canvas, 73 × 63 cm (28 ¾ × 24 ¾ in.)
Rotterdam, Museum Boijmans Van Beuningen

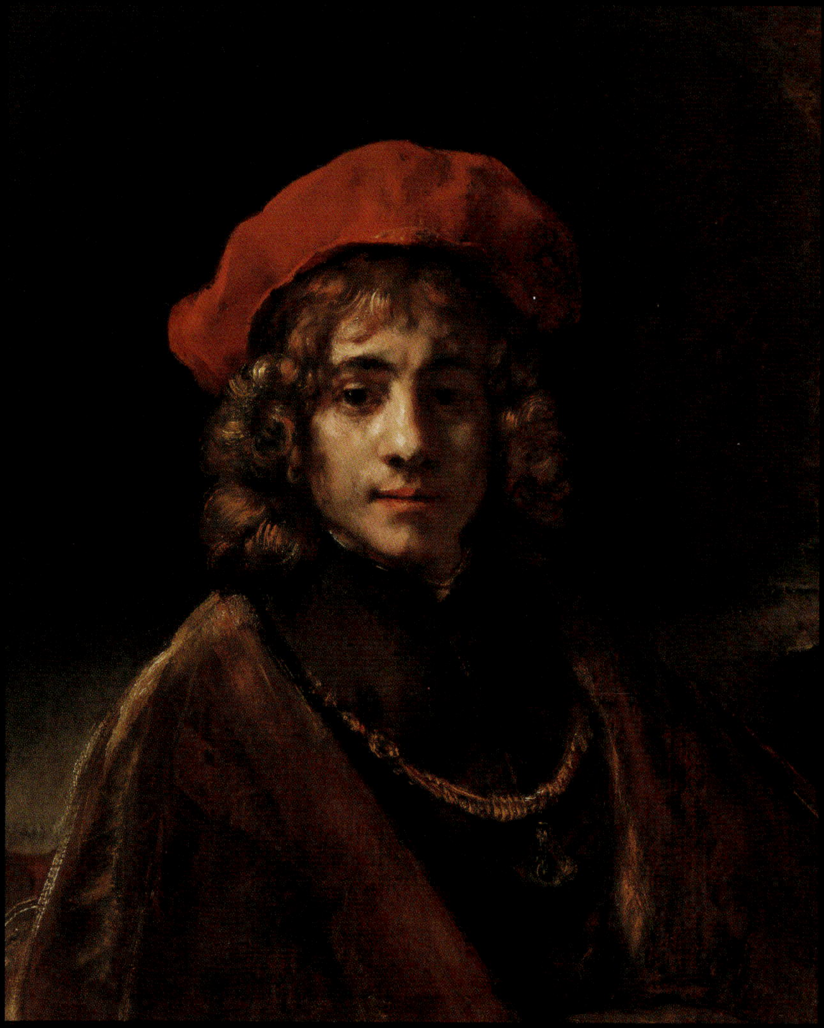

Young Man (Titus?), *c.* 1657
Oil on canvas, 68.5 × 57.3 cm (26 ¾ × 22 ½ in.)
London, Wallace Collection

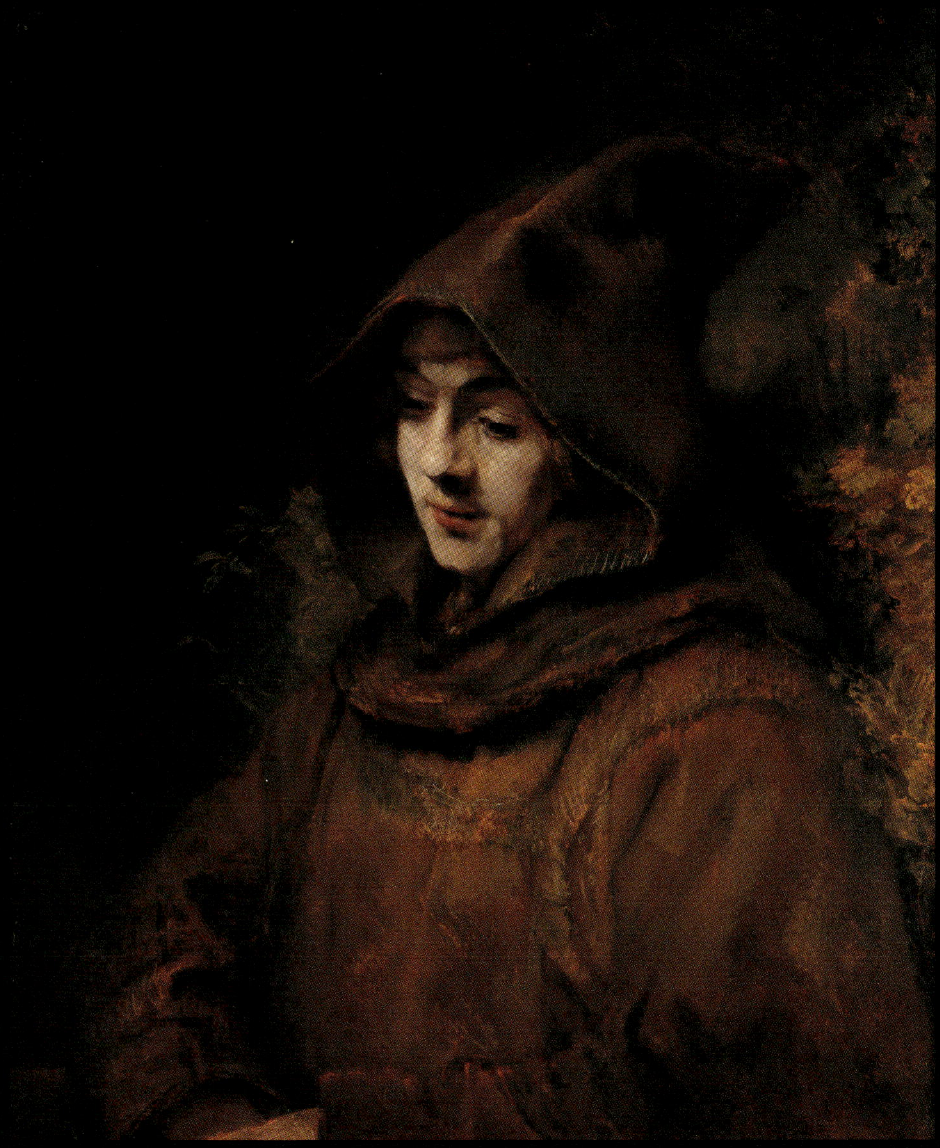

St Francis? (Titus as a Monk), 1660
Oil on canvas, 79.6 × 67.7 cm (31⅓ × 26⅔ in.)
Amsterdam, Rijksmuseum

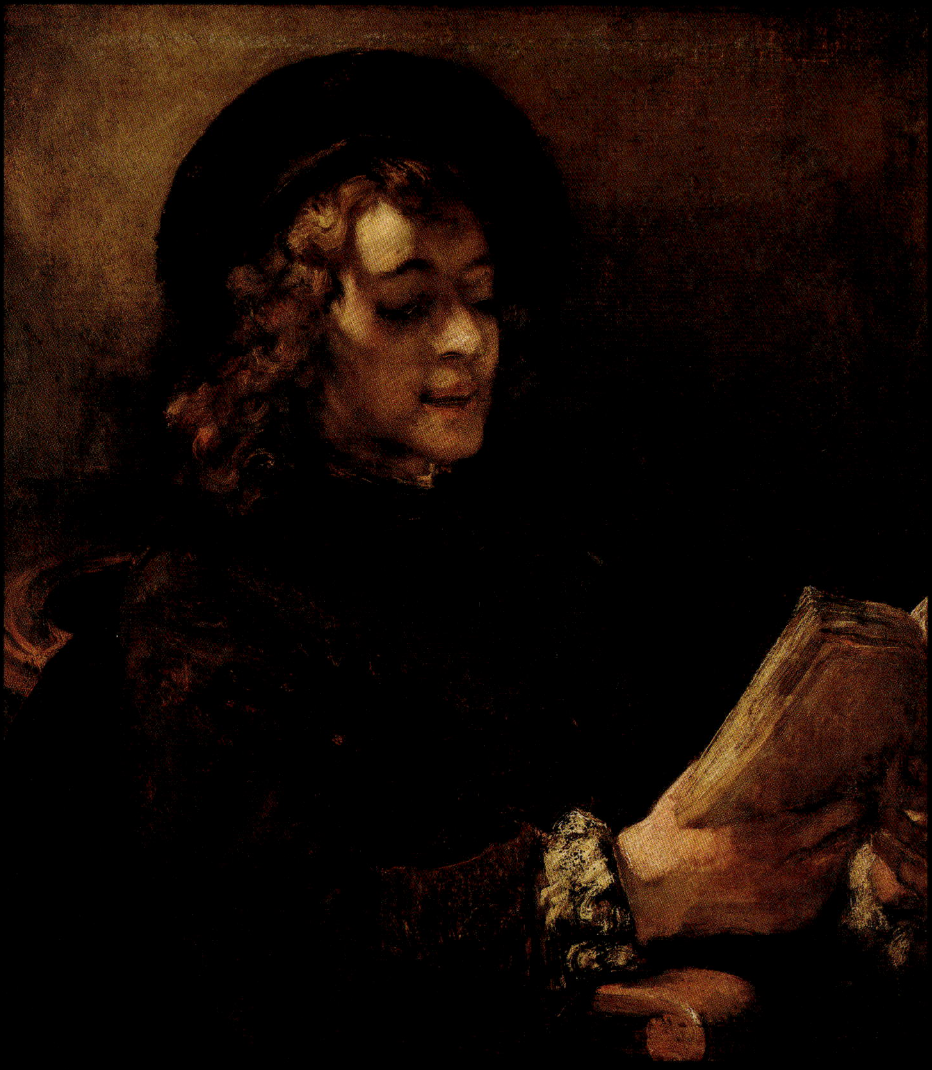

Young Man Reading (Titus?), *c.* 1658
Oil on canvas, 70.5 × 64 cm (27 ¾ × 25 ¼ in.)
Vienna, Kunsthistorisches Museum

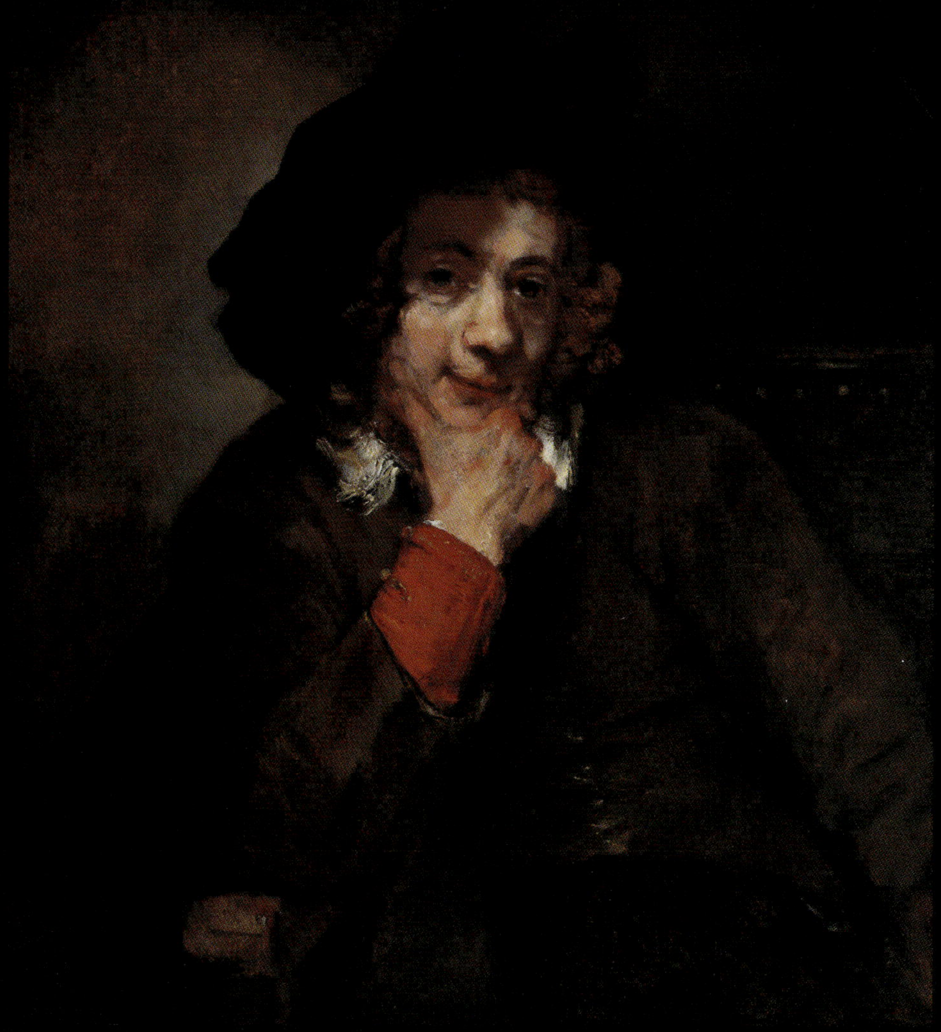

Young Man (Titus?), 1660
Oil on canvas, 81.3 × 68.7 cm (32 1/8 × 27 1/8 in.). Baltimore, Maryland, Baltimore Museum of Art, The Mary Frick Jacobs Collection

Young Man (Titus?), *c.* 1662
Oil on canvas, 72 × 56 cm (28 1/3 × 22 1/8 in.)
Paris, Musée du Louvre

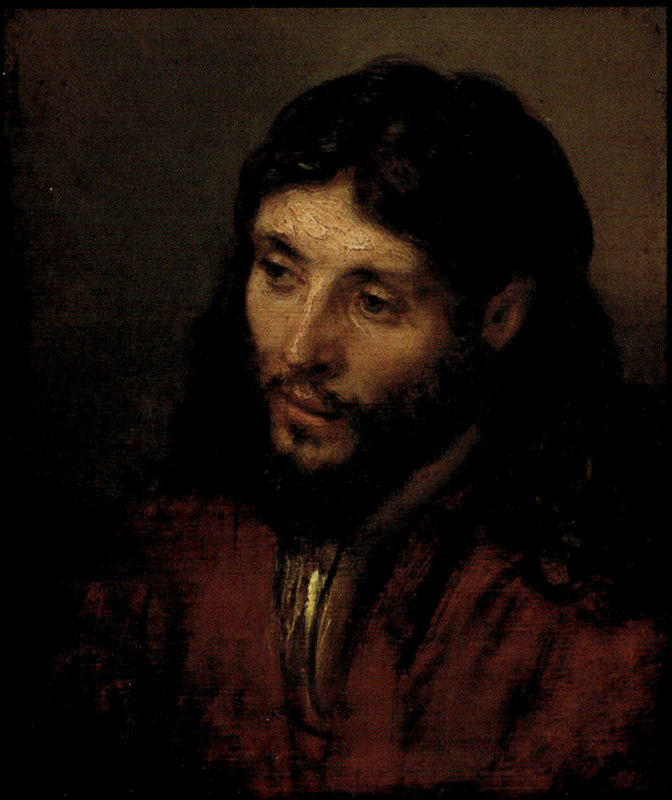

Christ, 1648–1650
Oil on panel, 25 × 21.5 cm (9 ¾ × 8 ½ in.)
Staatliche Museen zu Berlin, Gemäldegalerie

The Evangelist Matthew and the Angel, 1661
Oil on canvas, 96 × 81 cm (37 ¾ × 31 ¾ in.)
Paris, Musée du Louvre

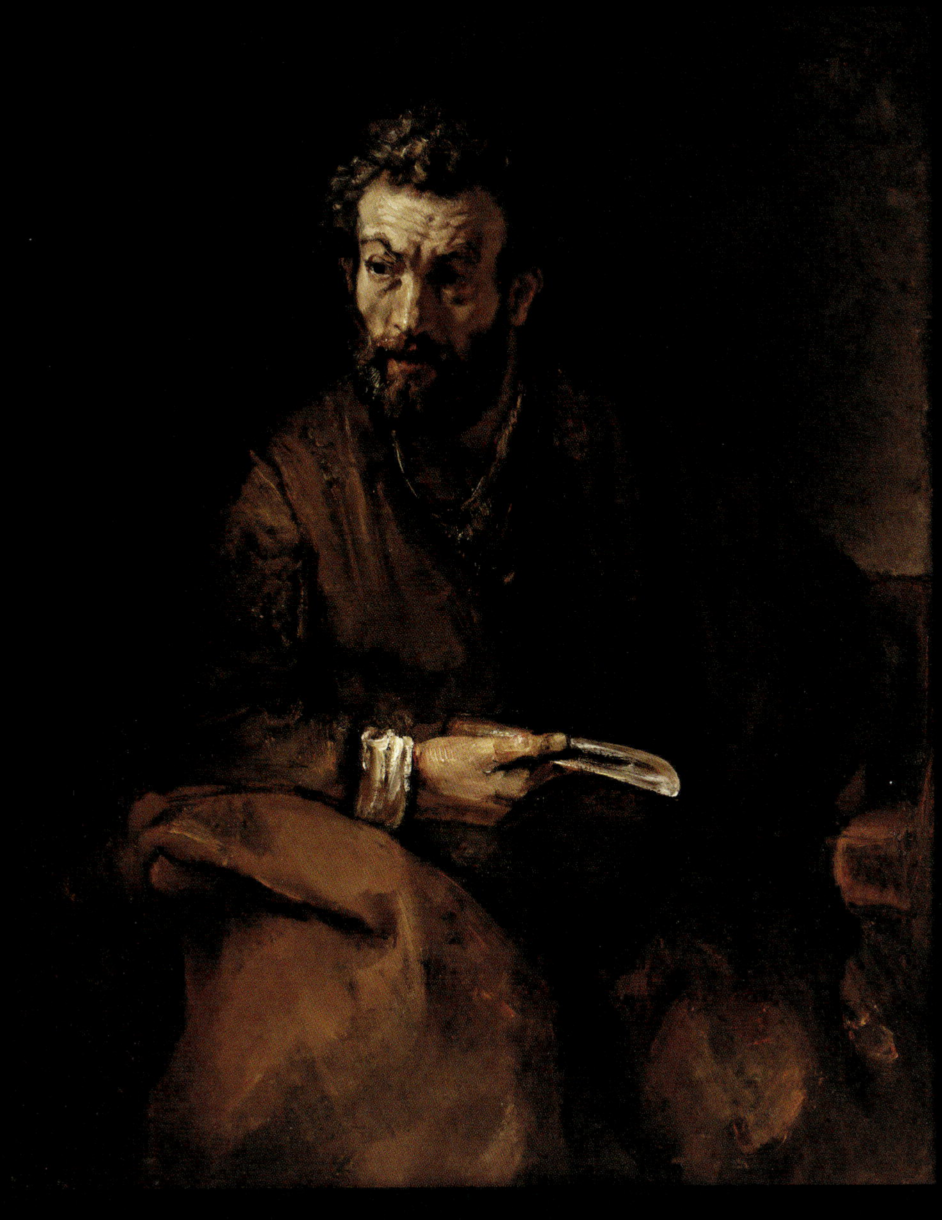

The Apostle Bartholomew, 1657
Oil on canvas, 122.7 × 99.7 cm (48 ¼ × 39 ¼ in.). San Diego, California, Timken Museum of Art, The Putnam Foundation

The Risen Christ, *c.* 1660
Oil on canvas, 78.5 × 63 cm (30 ¾ × 24 ¾ in.)
Munich, Bayerische Staatsgemäldesammlungen,
Alte Pinakothek

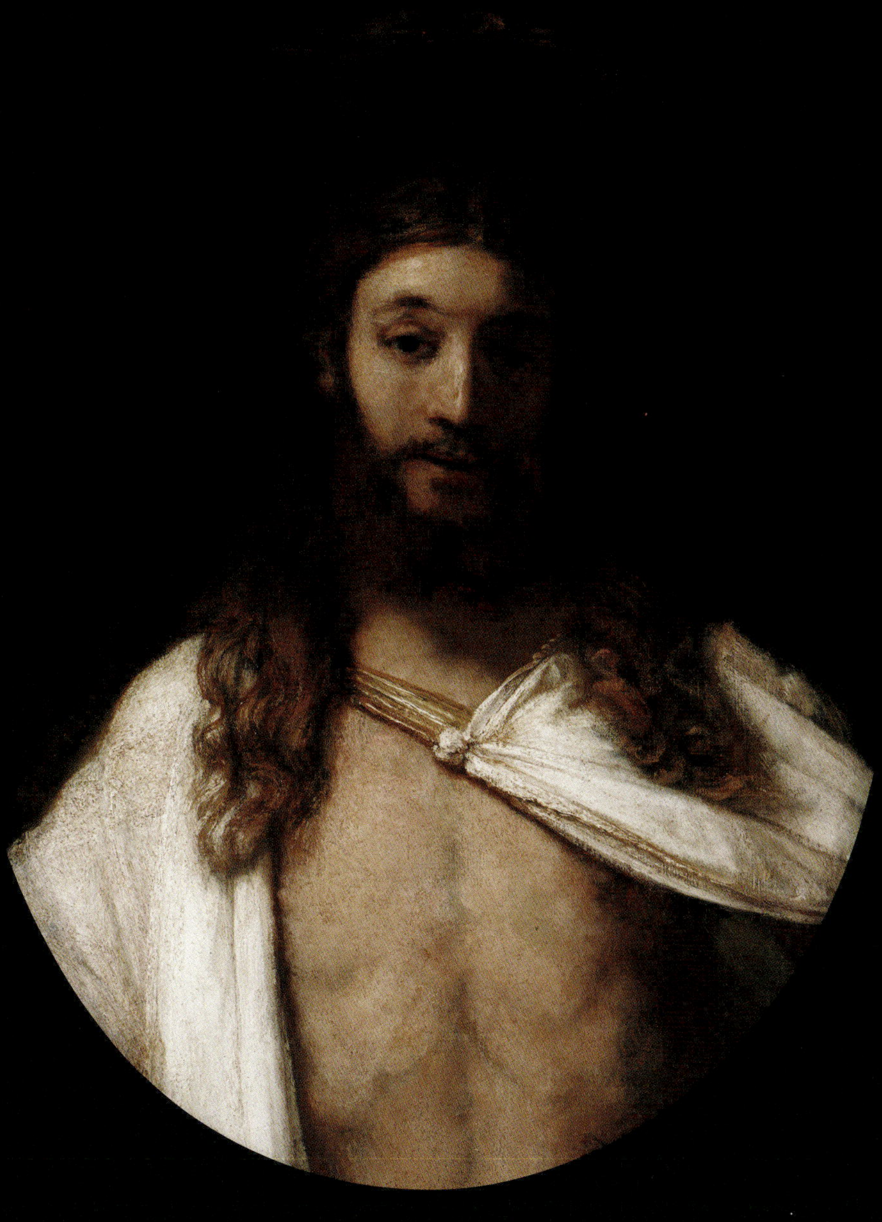

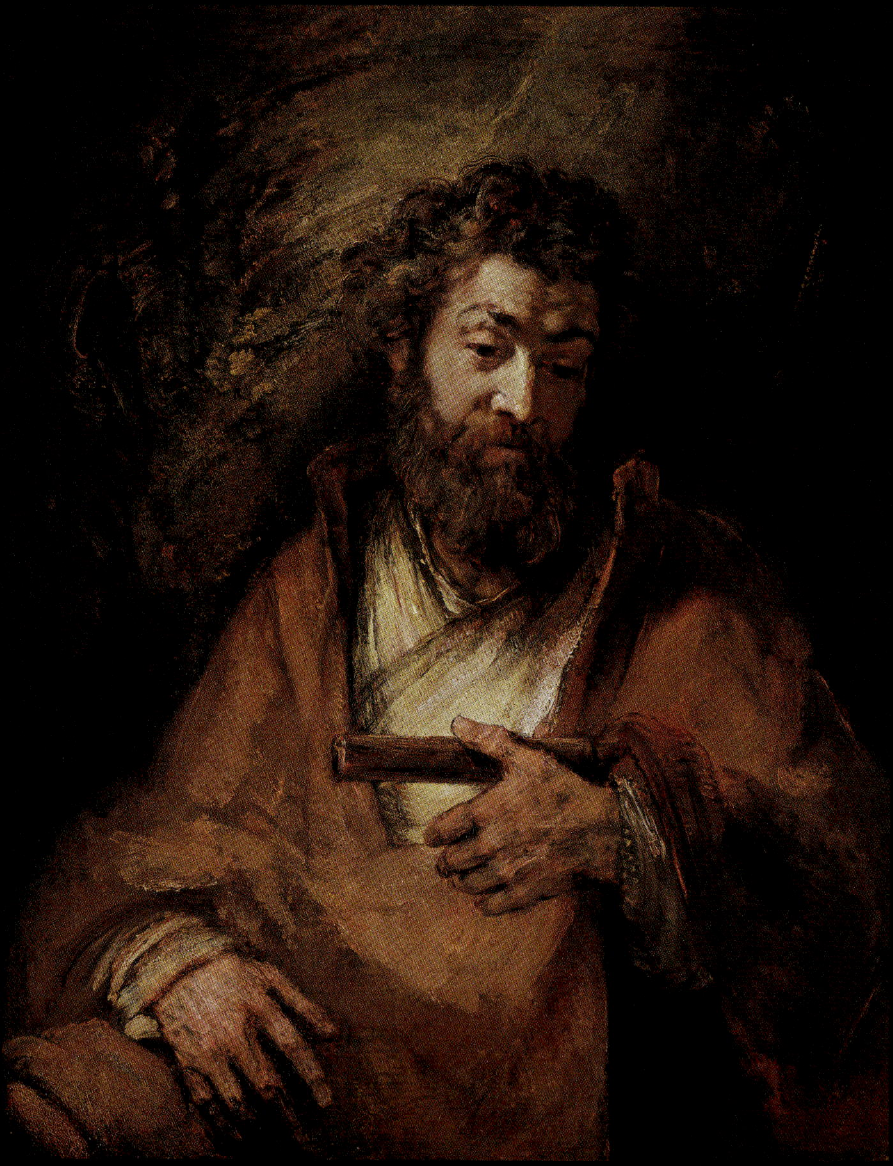

The Apostle Simon, 1661
Oil on canvas, 98.3 × 79 cm (38 ¾ × 31 ⅛ in.)
Zurich, Kunsthaus Zürich, Prof. Leopold Ruzicka Foundation

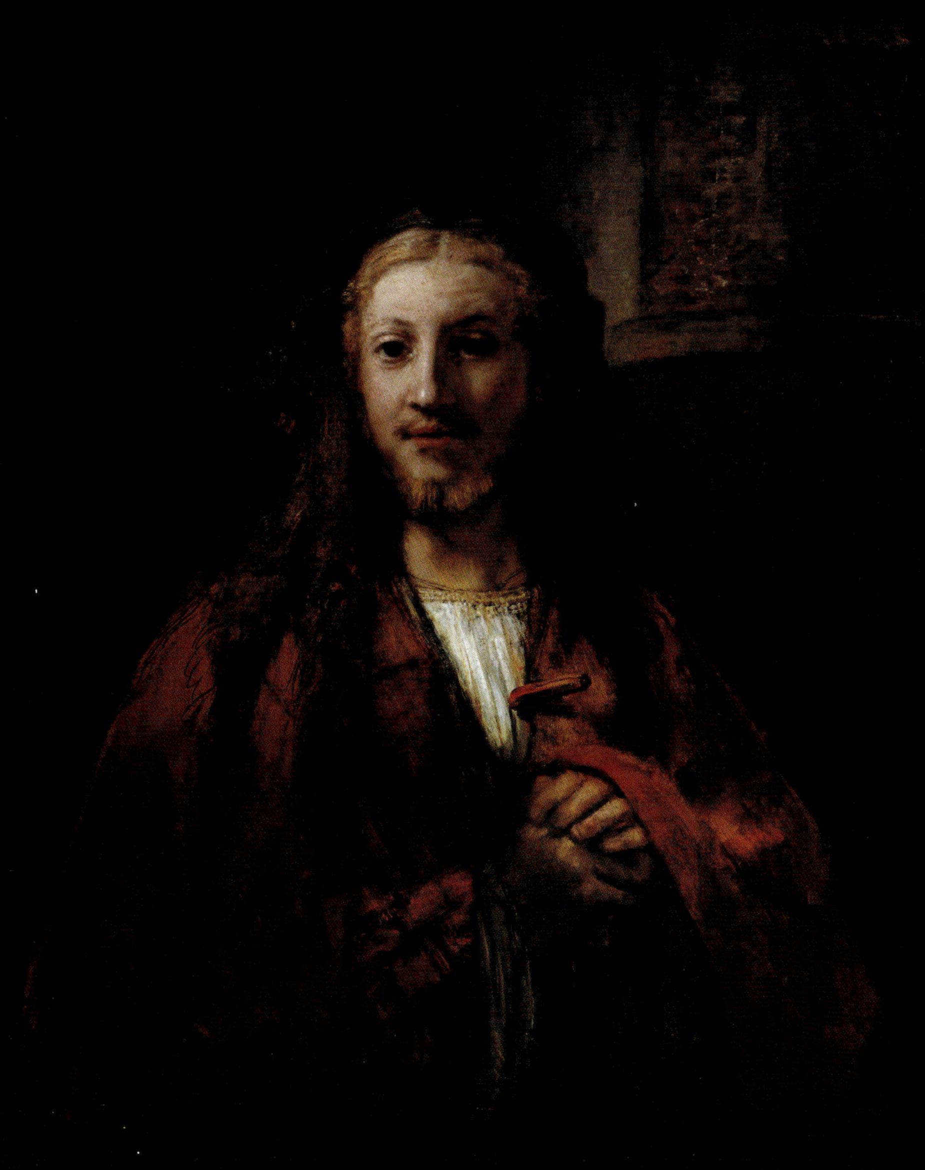

The Apostle James the Lesser (Christ?), 1661
Oil on canvas, 95.3 × 82.6 cm (37 ½ × 32 ½ in.)
New York, The Metropolitan Museum of Art, The Jules Bache Collection

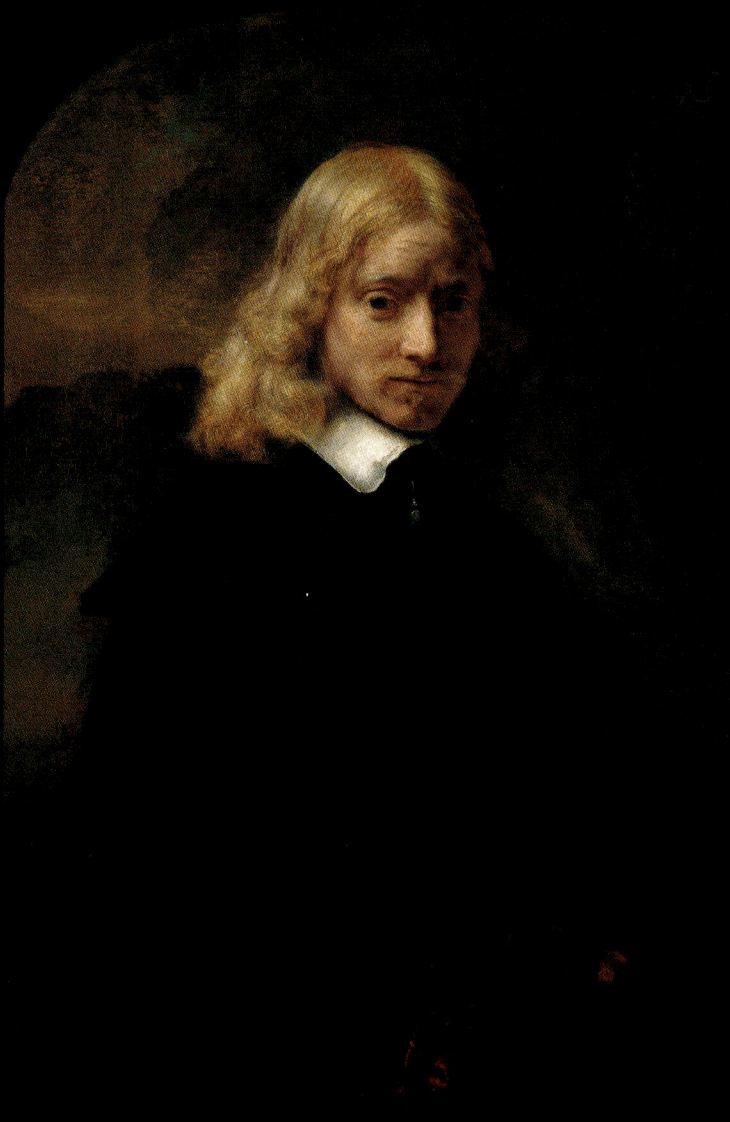

Portrait of a Man, *c.* 1651/52
Oil on canvas, 92.5 × 73.5 cm (36 ⅜ × 28 ¾ in.)
Faringdon, Oxfordshire, Buscot Park, The Faringdon Collection Trust

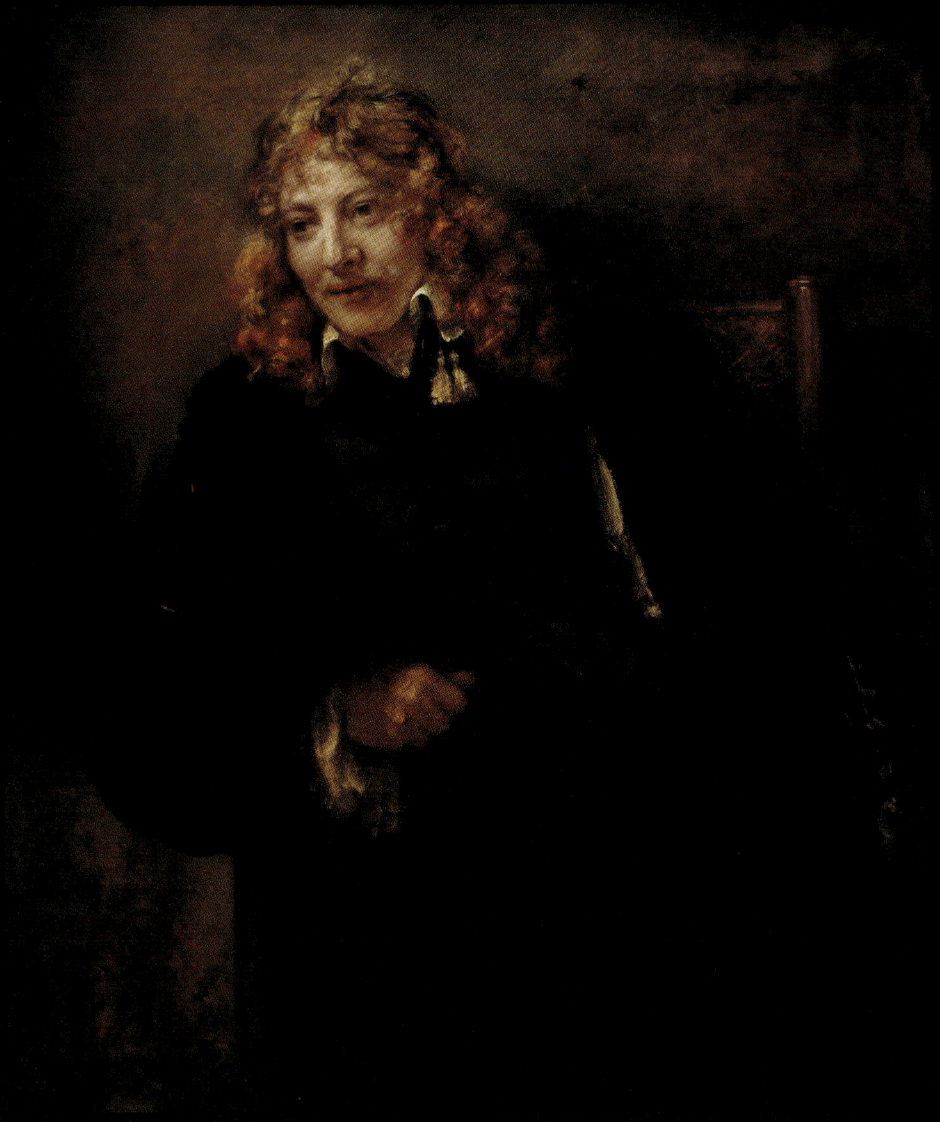

Portrait of Nicolaes Bruyningh, 1652
Oil on canvas, 106.8 × 91.5 cm (42 ⅛ × 36 ⅛ in.)
Hessen Kassel Heritage, Gemäldegalerie Alte Meister

Portrait of Jan Six, *c.* 1654
Oil on canvas, 112 × 102 cm (44 1/8 × 40 1/8 in.)
Amsterdam, Collectie Six

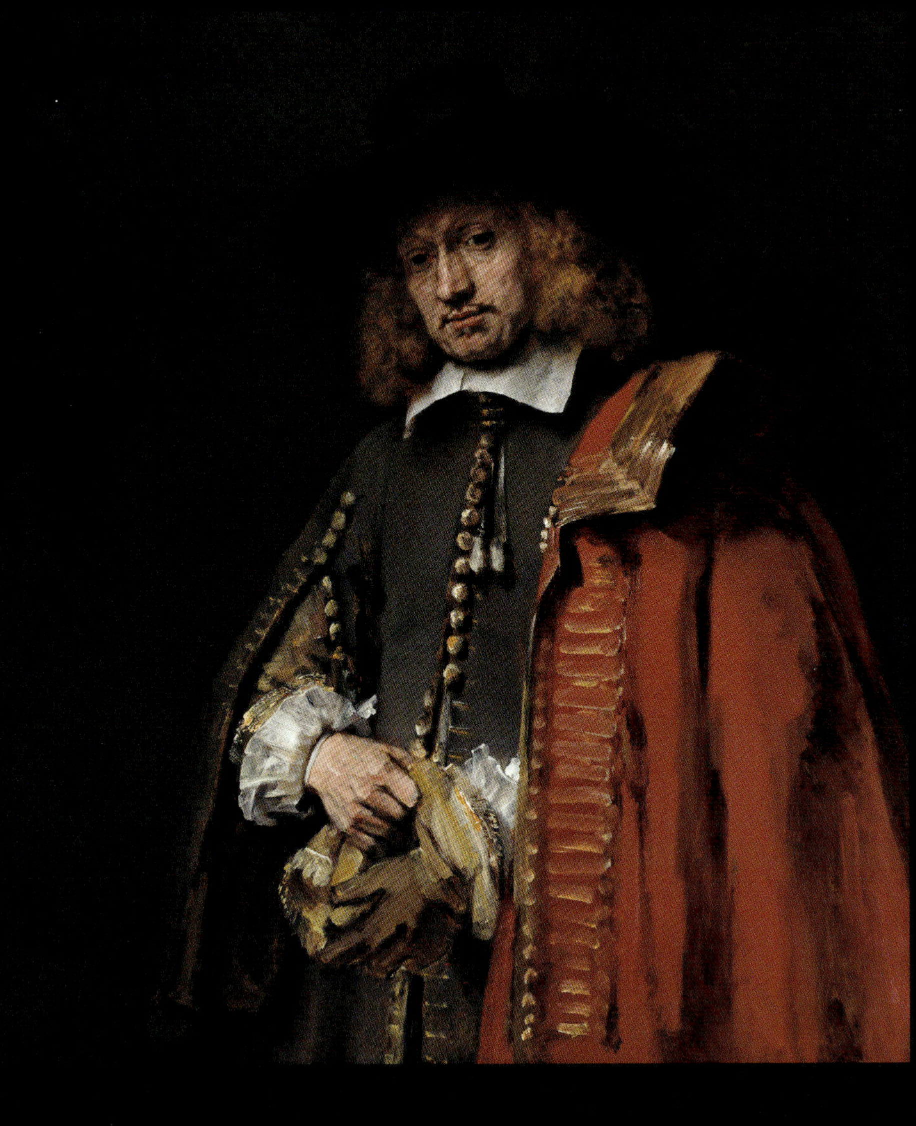

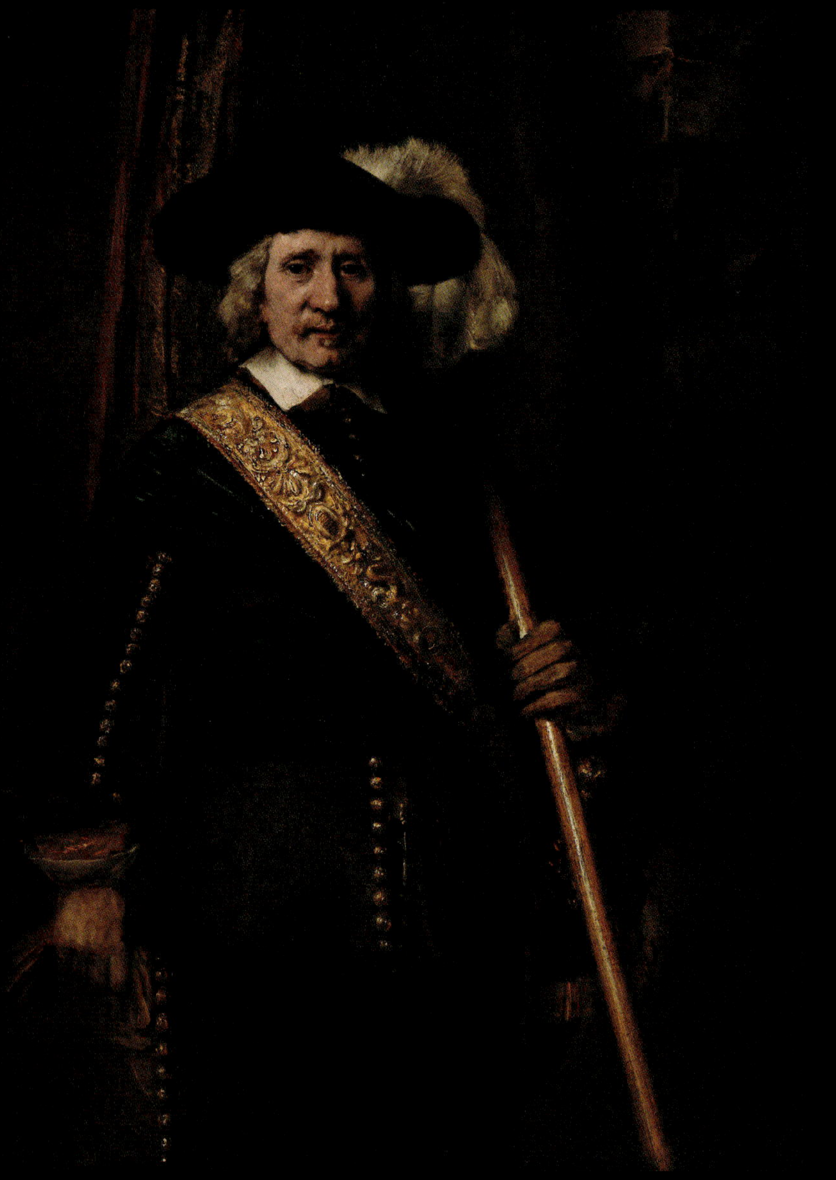

Portrait of Floris Soop, 1654
Oil on canvas, 140.3 × 114.9 cm (55 ¼ × 45 ¼ in.)
New York, The Metropolitan Museum of Art

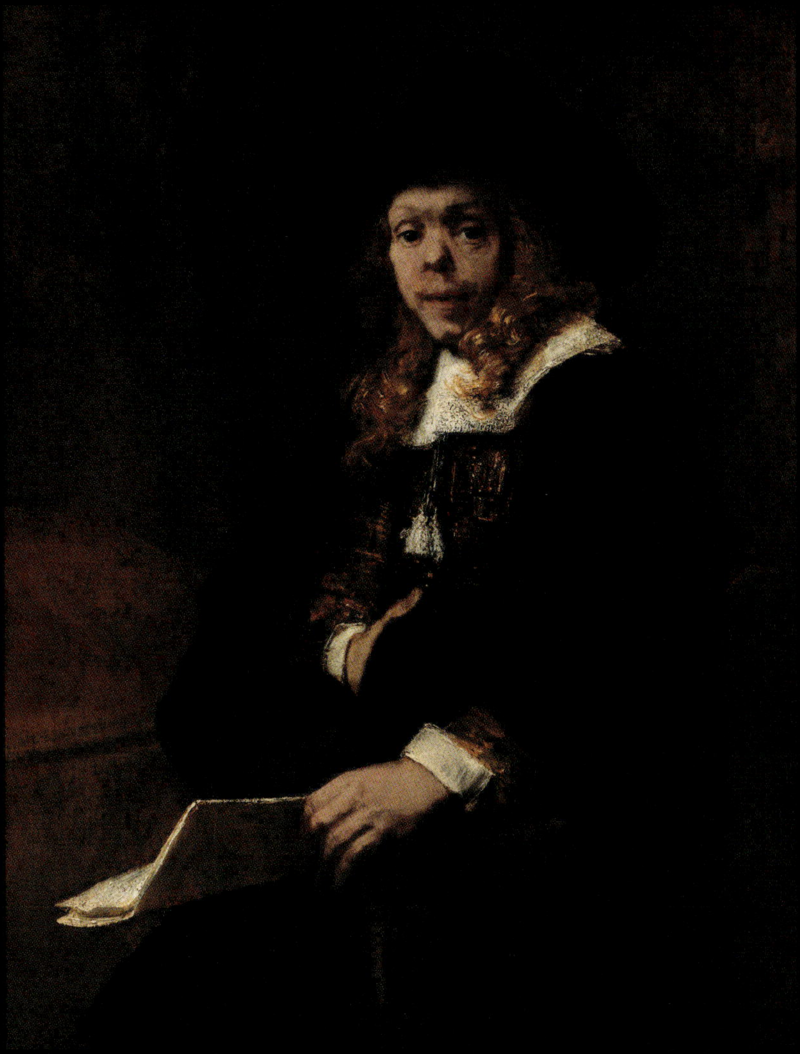

Portrait of Gerard de Lairesse, 1665–1667
Oil on canvas, 112.7 × 87.6 cm (44 3/8 × 34 1/2 in.)
New York, The Metropolitan Museum of Art, Lehman Collection

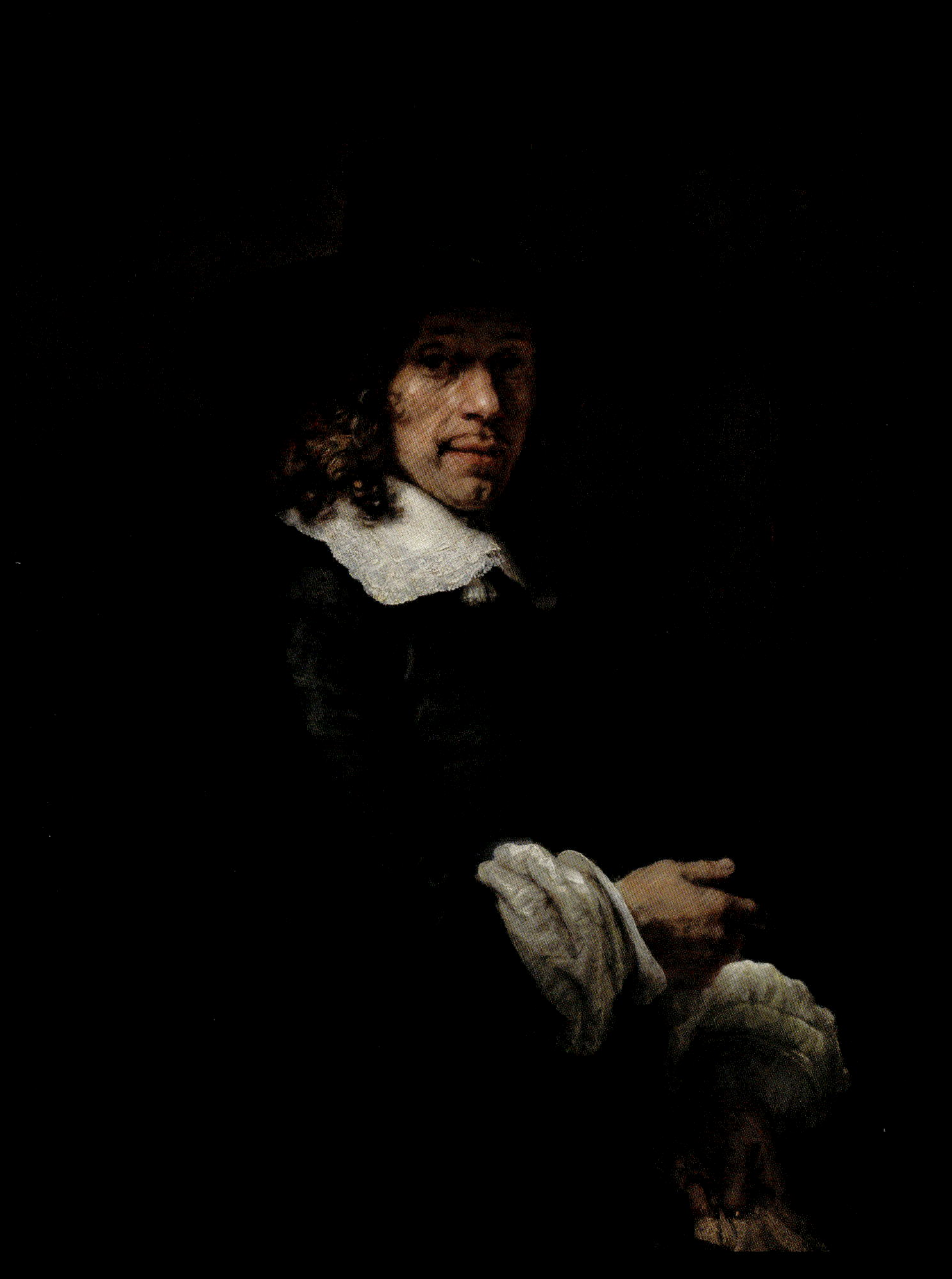

Portrait of a Man with a Hat and Gloves, *c.* 1655
Oil on canvas, 99.5 × 82.5 cm (39 ⅛ × 32 ½ in.)
Washington, DC, National Gallery of Art, Widener Collection

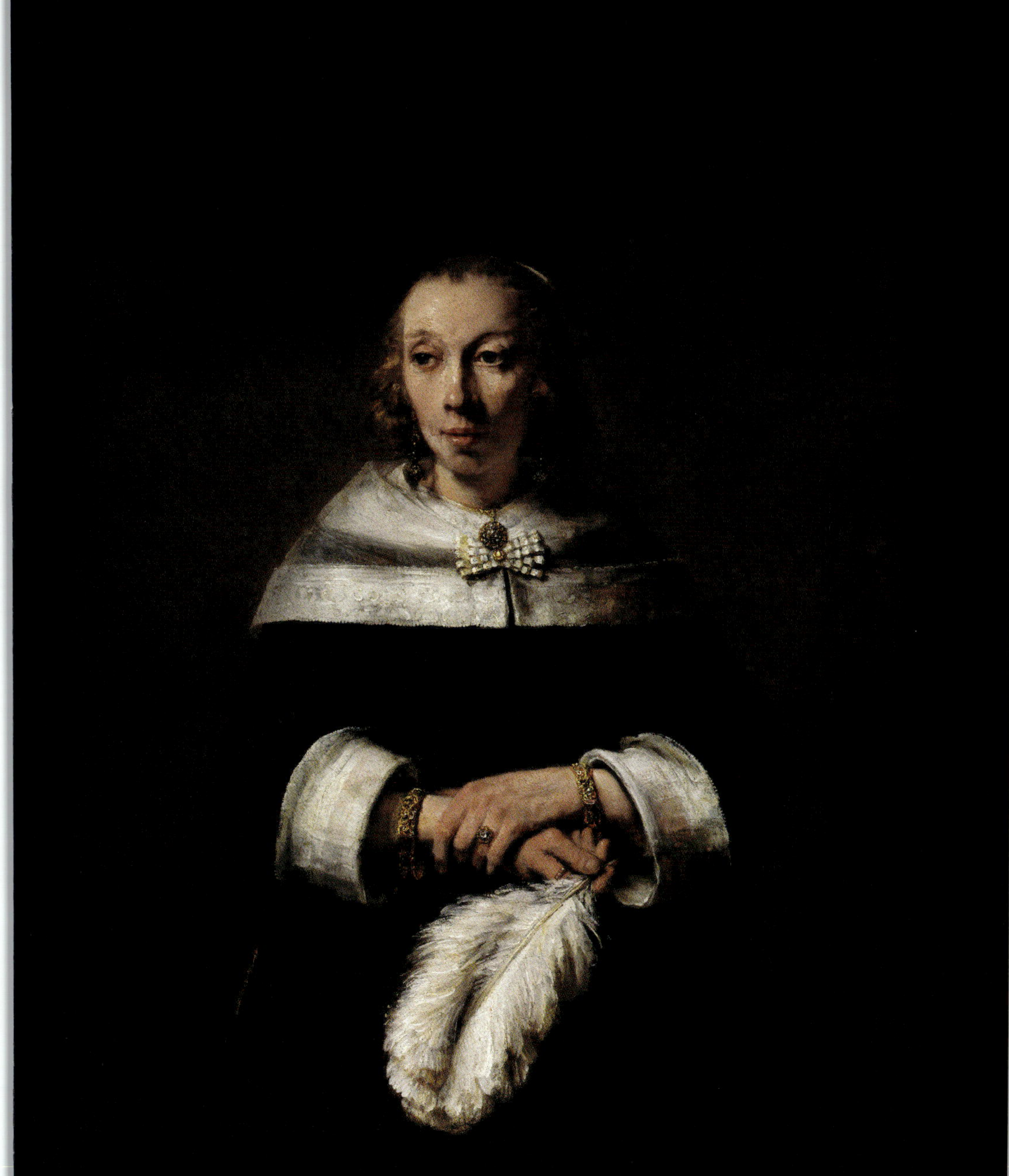

Portrait of a Lady with an Ostrich-Feather Fan, *c.* 1655
Oil on canvas, 99.5 × 83 cm (39 ⅛ × 32 ⅔ in.)
Washington, DC, National Gallery of Art, Widener Collection

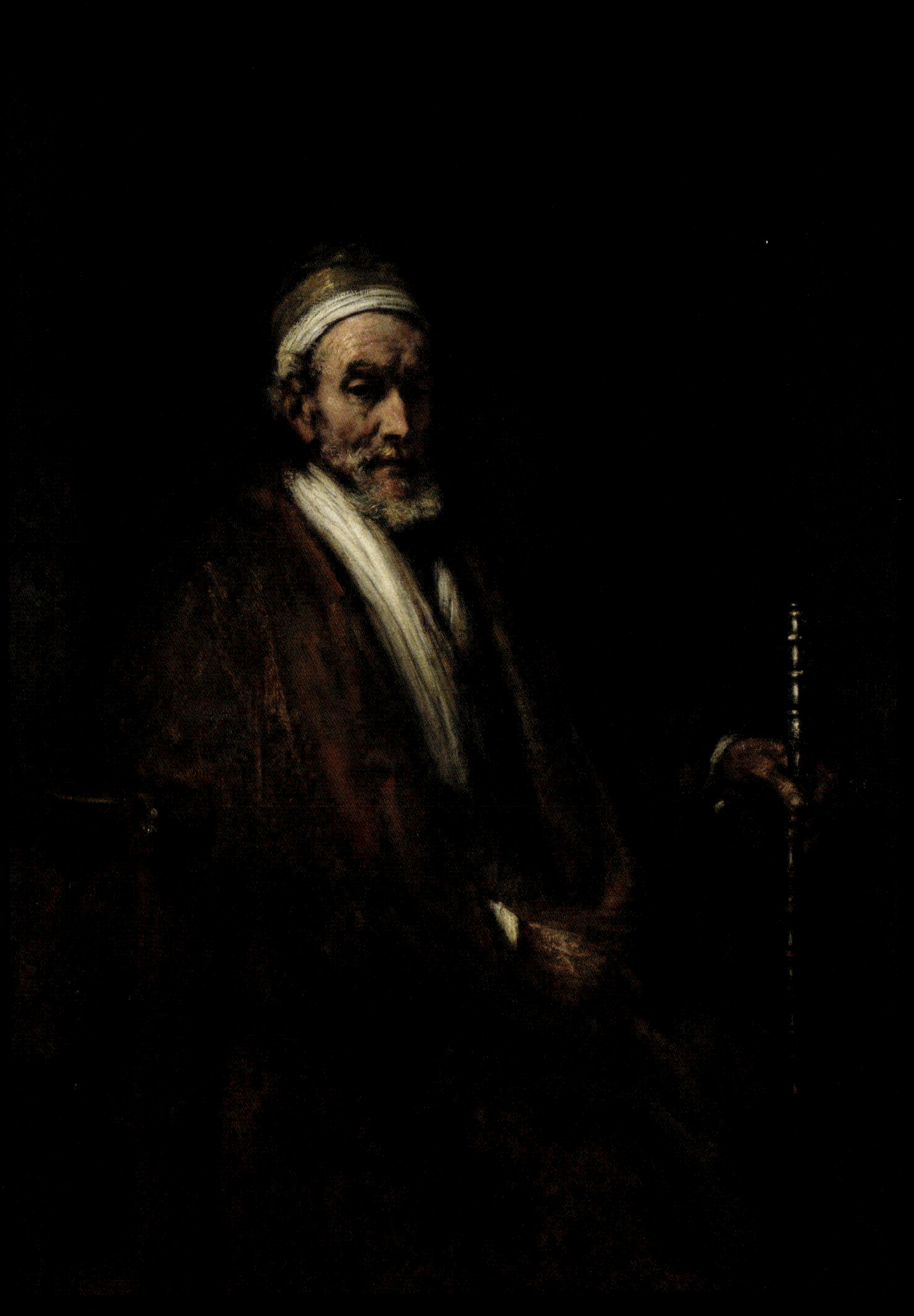

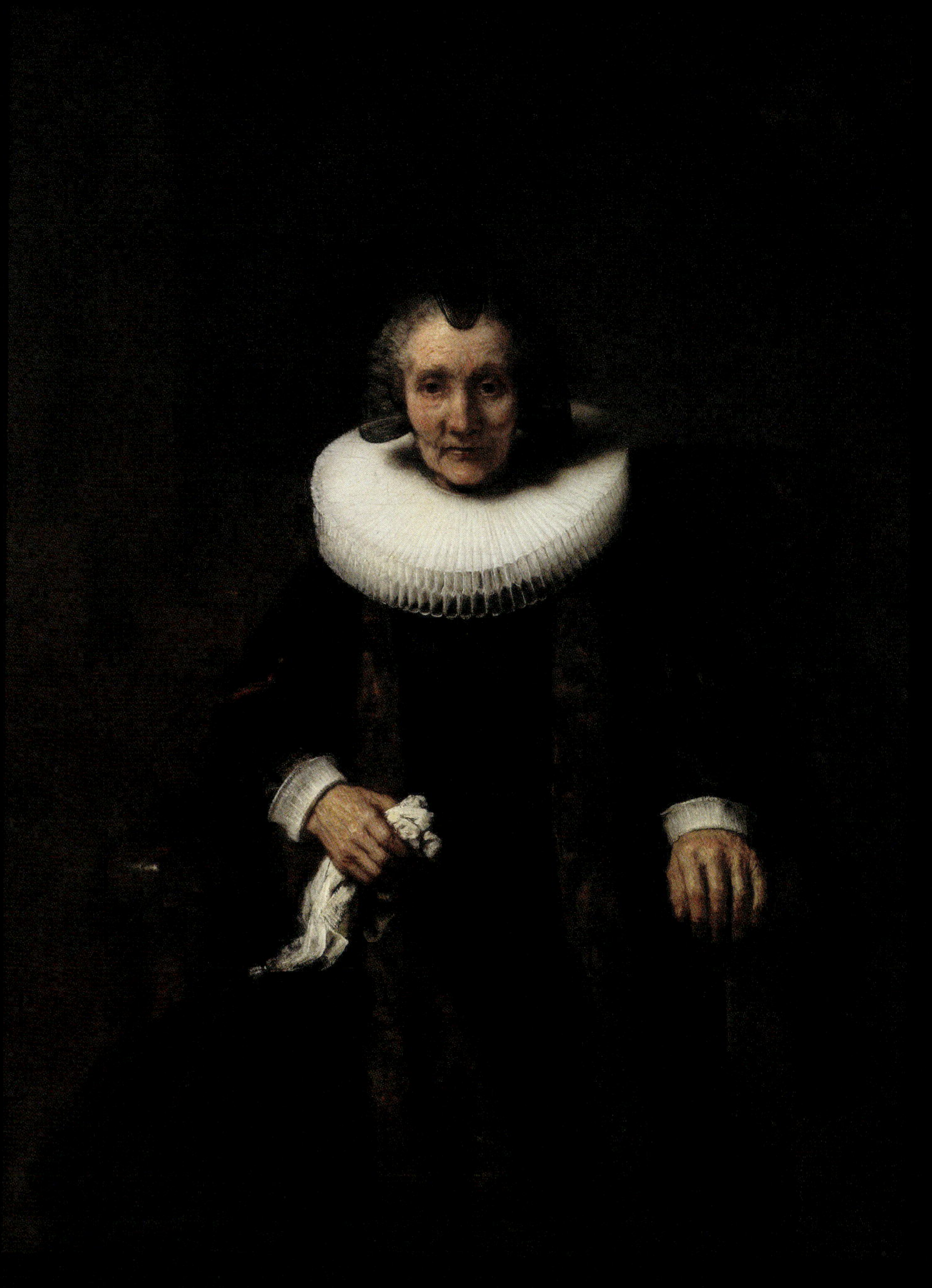

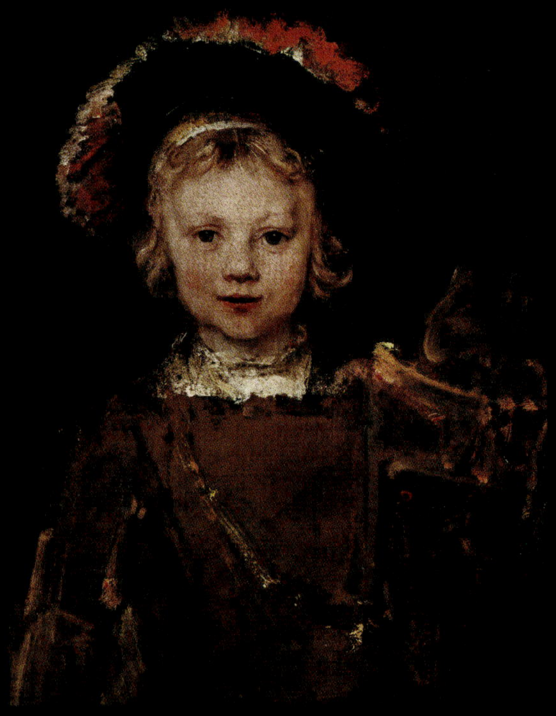

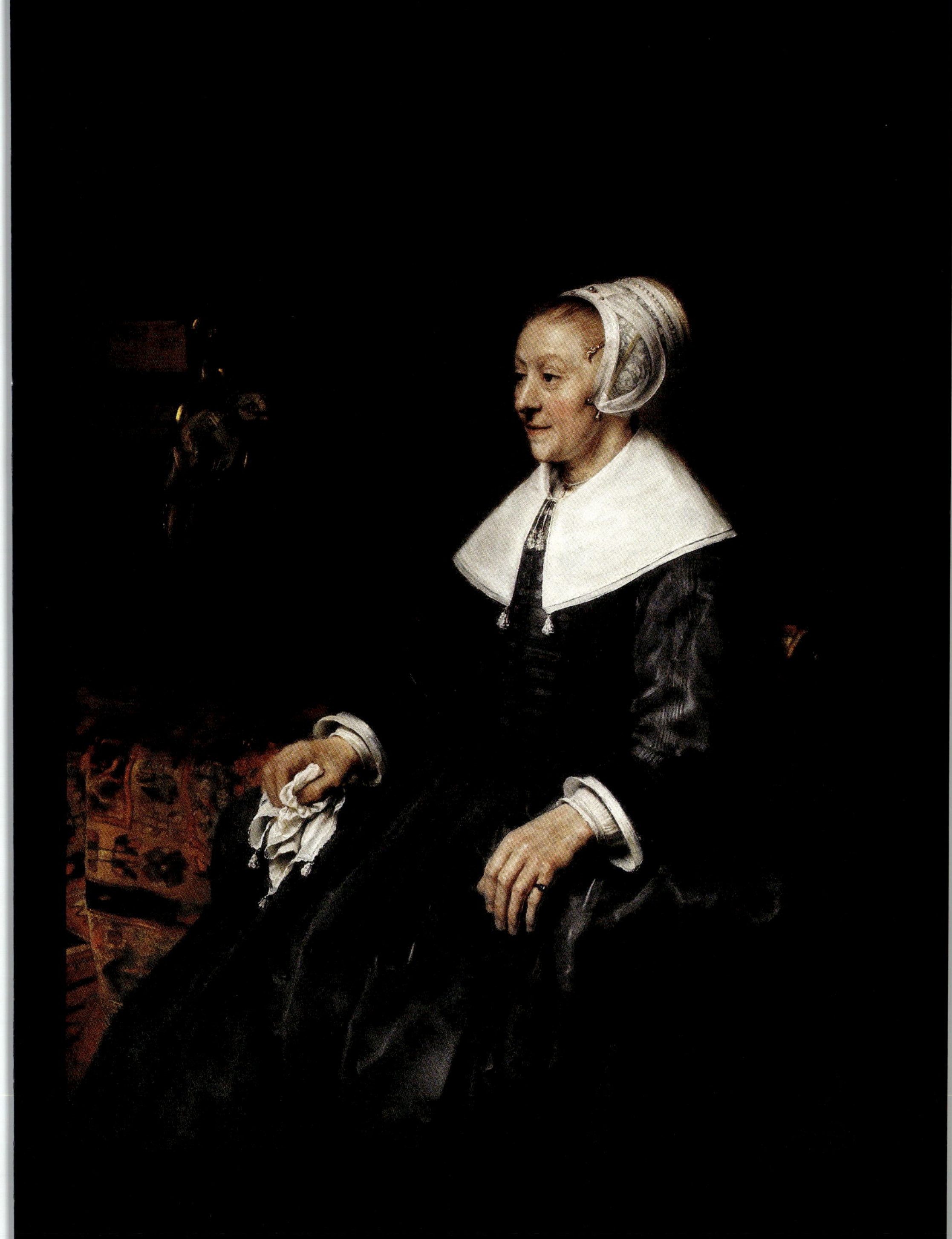

Page 454
Portrait of Jacob Trip, *c.* 1661
Oil on canvas, 130.5 × 97 cm (51 3/8 × 38 1/4 in.)
London, The National Gallery

Page 455
Portrait of Margaretha de Geer, *c.* 1661
Oil on canvas, 130.5 × 97.5 cm (51 3/8 × 38 3/8 in.)
London, The National Gallery

Page 456
Boy in Sixteenth-Century Costume, *c.* 1658
Oil on canvas, 64.8 × 55.9 cm (25 1/2 × 22 1/8 in.)
Pasadena, California, The Norton Simon Foundation

Page 457
Portrait of Catrina Hoogsaet, 1657
Oil on canvas, 126.5 × 98.5 cm (49 3/4 × 38 3/4 in.)
Private Collection, on permanent loan to the
National Museum Cardiff

Portrait of Frederick Rihel on Horseback, 1663
Oil on canvas, 294.5 × 241 cm (115 3/4 × 94 3/4 in.)
London, The National Gallery

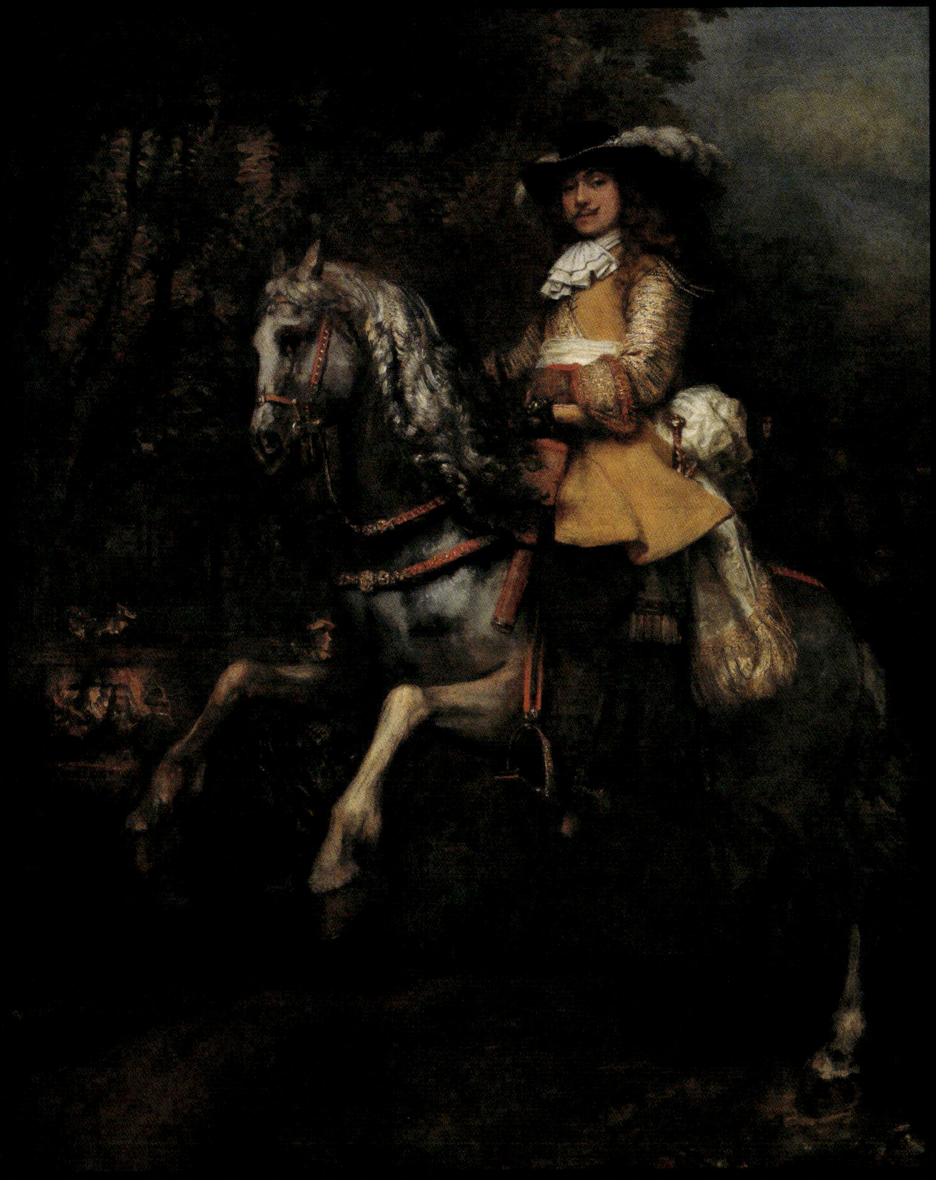

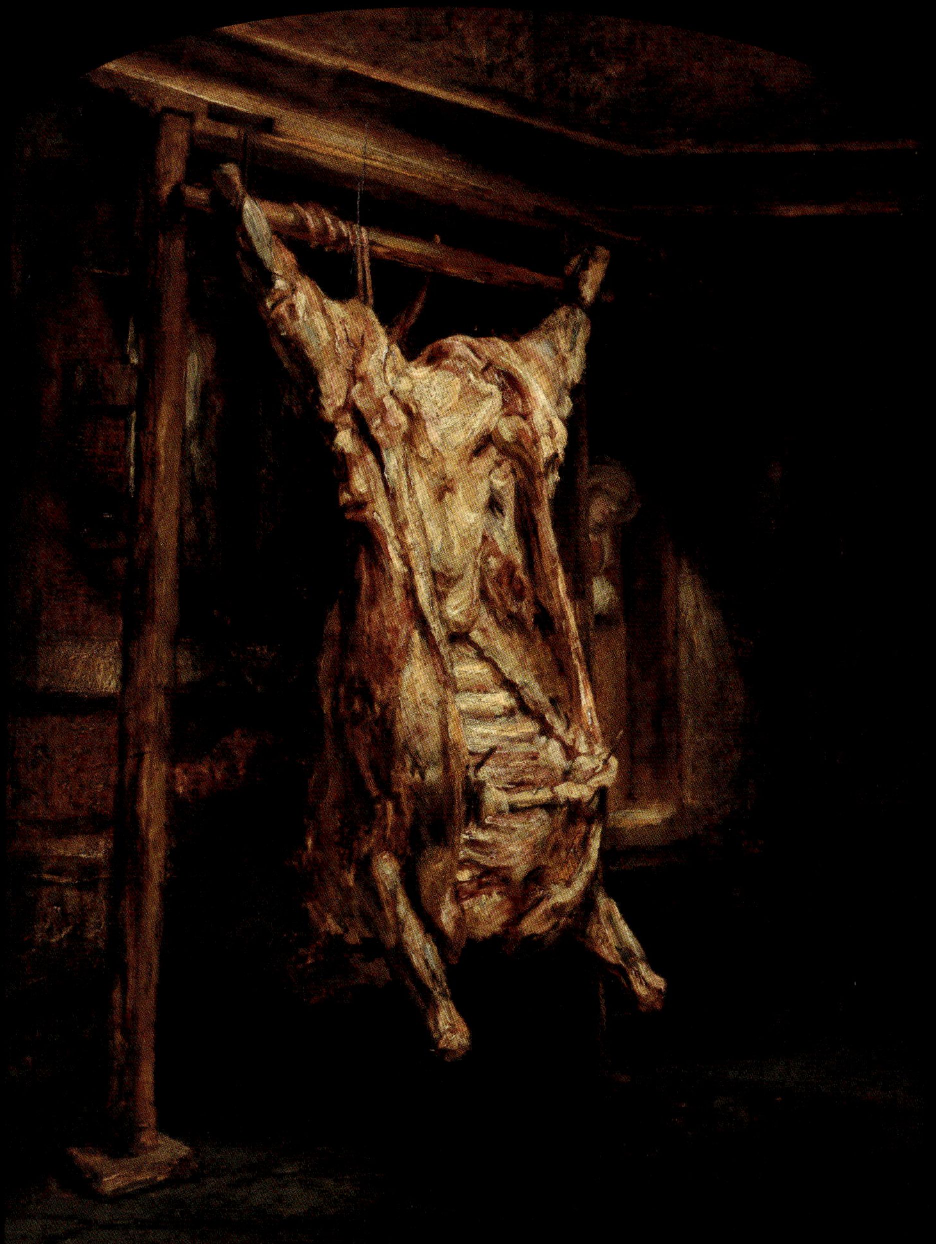

Slaughtered Ox, 1655
Oil on panel, 95.5 × 68.8 cm (37 5/8 × 27 1/8 in.)
Paris, Musée du Louvre

Philips Galle after Maerten van Heemskerck
The Killing of the Fatted Calf, 1562
From the series: *The Parable of the Prodigal Son*
Copper engraving, 20.1 × 25.1 cm (8 × 10 in.)
Wolfenbüttel, Herzog August Bibliothek

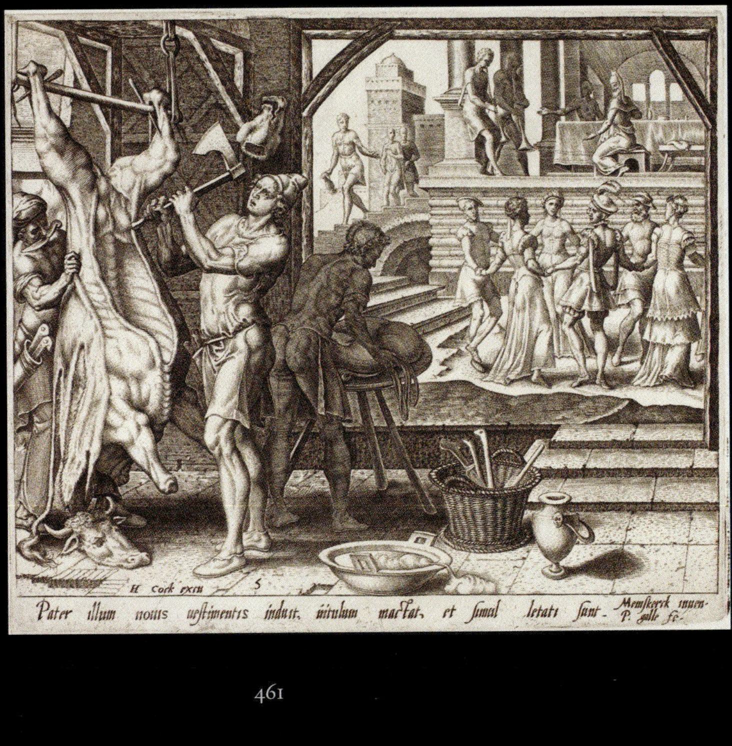

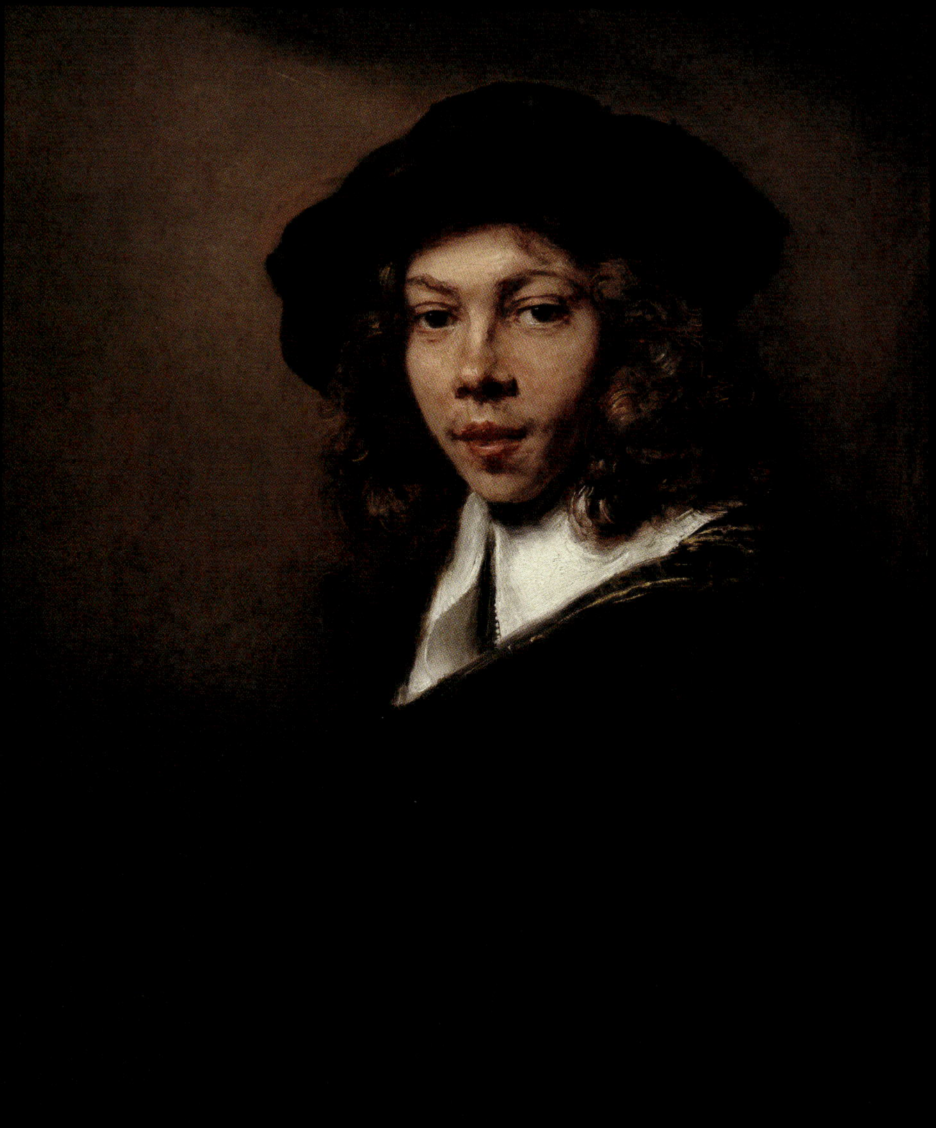

Portrait of a Young Man with a Black Cap, 1666
Oil on canvas, 71.6 × 62.8 cm (28 ¼ × 24 ¾ in.). Kansas City, Missouri,
The Nelson-Atkins Museum of Art, Purchase: William Rockhill Nelson Trust, 31-75

Portrait of an Old Man, 1667
Oil on canvas, 81.9 × 67.7 cm (32 ¼ × 26 ⅔ in.)
The Hague, Mauritshuis

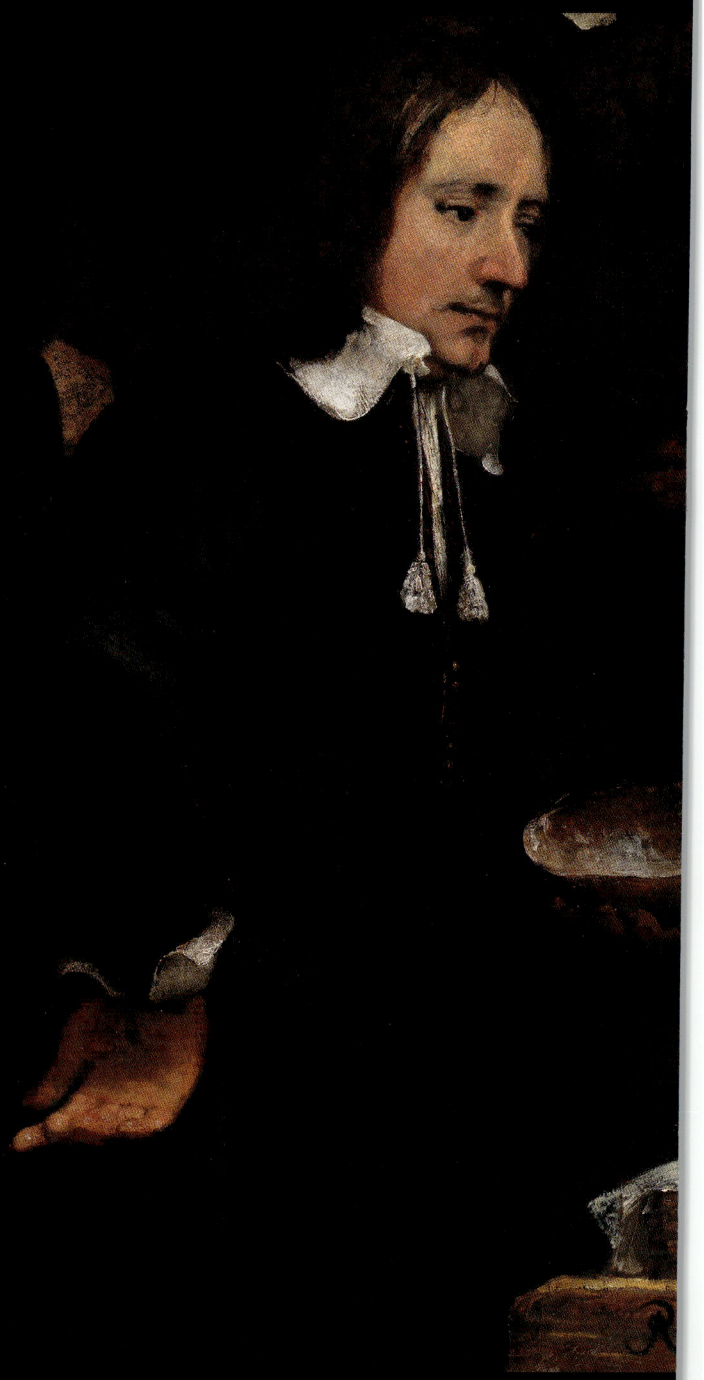

The Anatomy Lesson of Dr Jan Deyman, 1656
Oil on canvas (fragment), 100 × 134 cm (39⅜ × 52¾ in.); without later additions: 98.5 × 132.5 cm (38¾ × 52⅛ in.)
Amsterdam Museum

Pages 466/467
The Wardens of the Amsterdam Drapers' Guild ("The Syndics"), 1662
Oil on canvas, 191.5 × 279 cm (75⅜ × 109¾ in.)
Amsterdam, Rijksmuseum

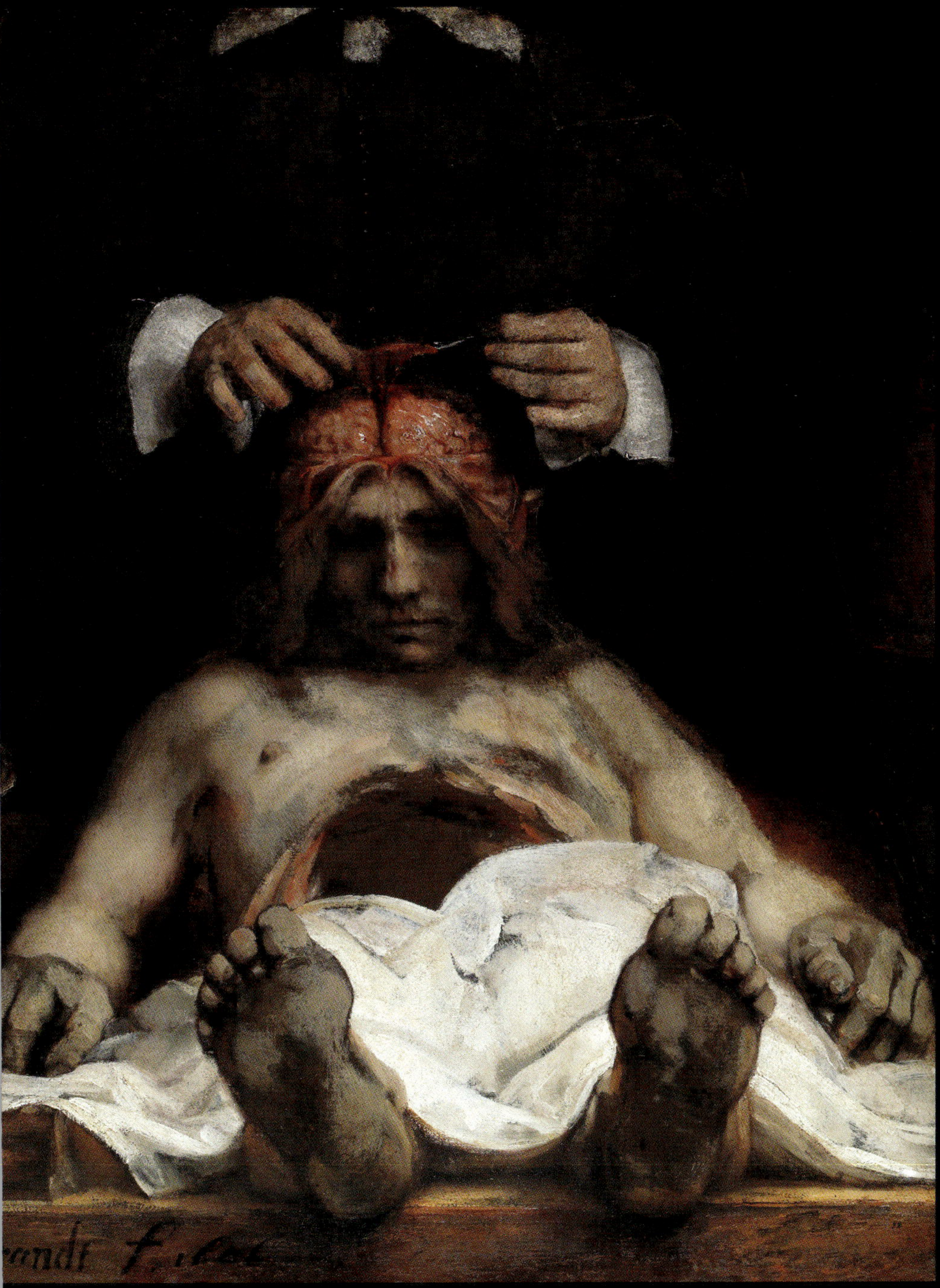

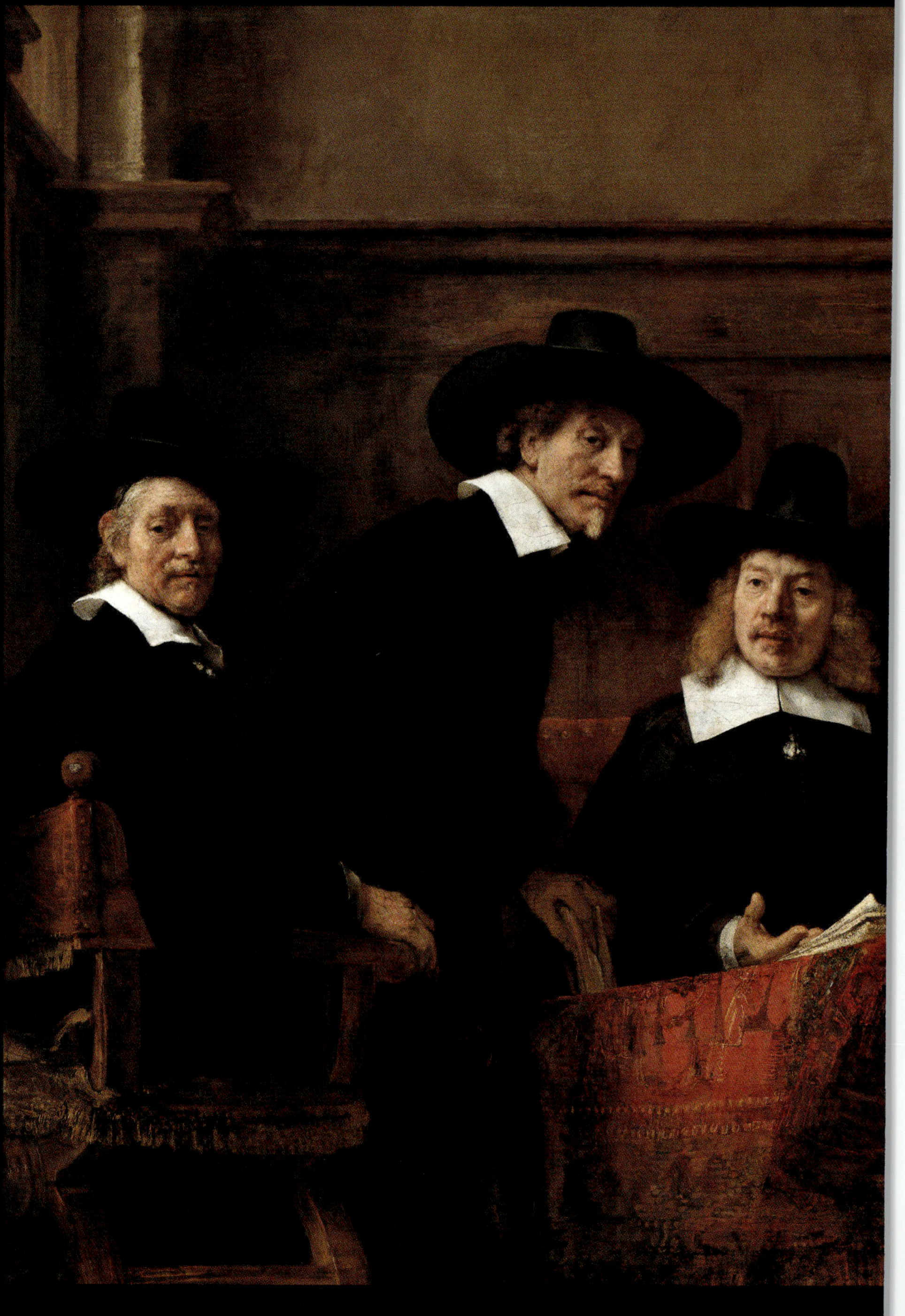

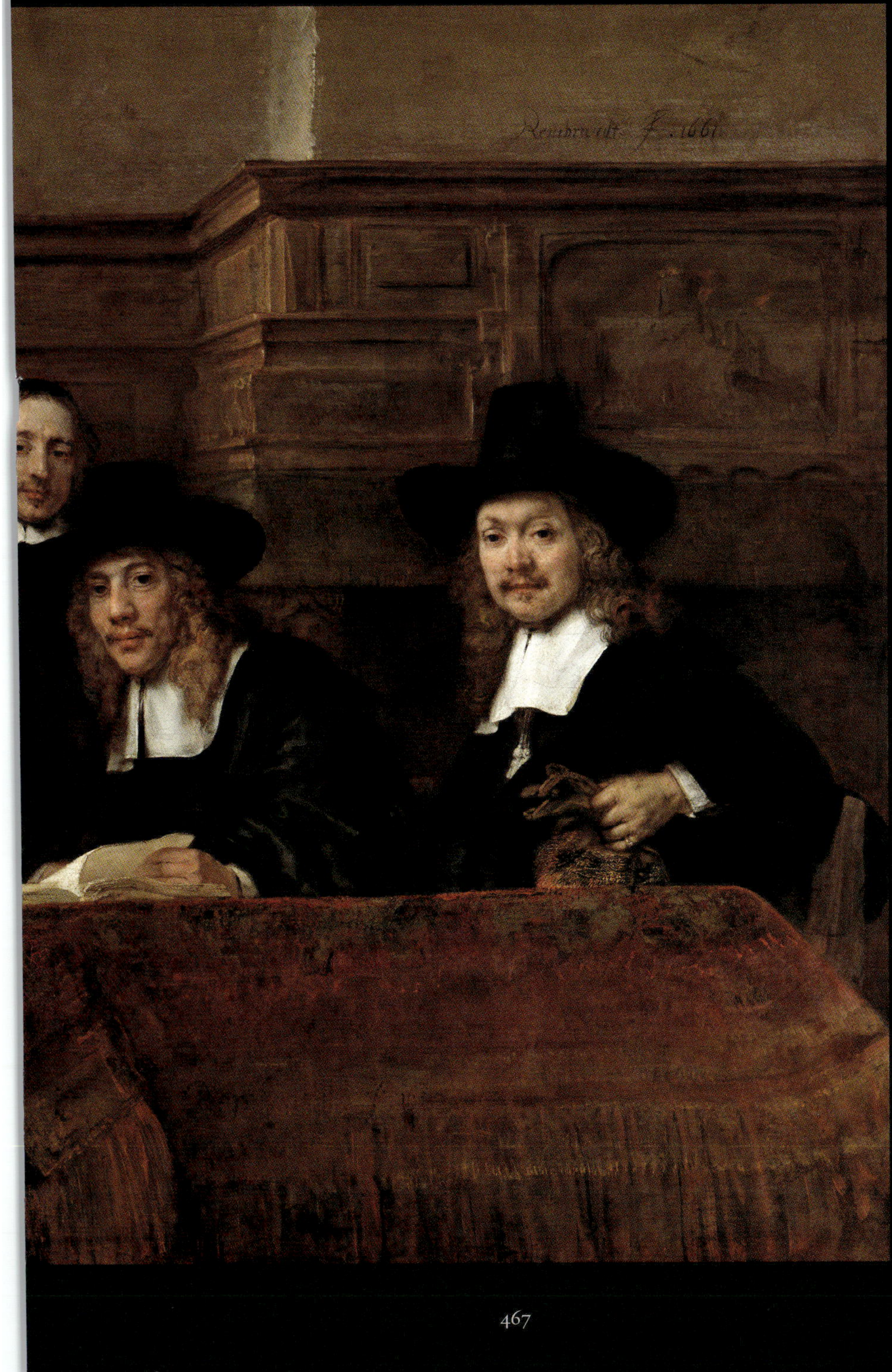
Rembrandt f. 1661

Portrait of a Man with a Magnifying Glass (Pieter Haringh?), *c.* 1665
Oil on canvas, 91.4 × 74.3 cm (35 ¾ × 29 ¼ in.)
New York, The Metropolitan Museum of Art, Bequest of Benjamin Altman, 1913

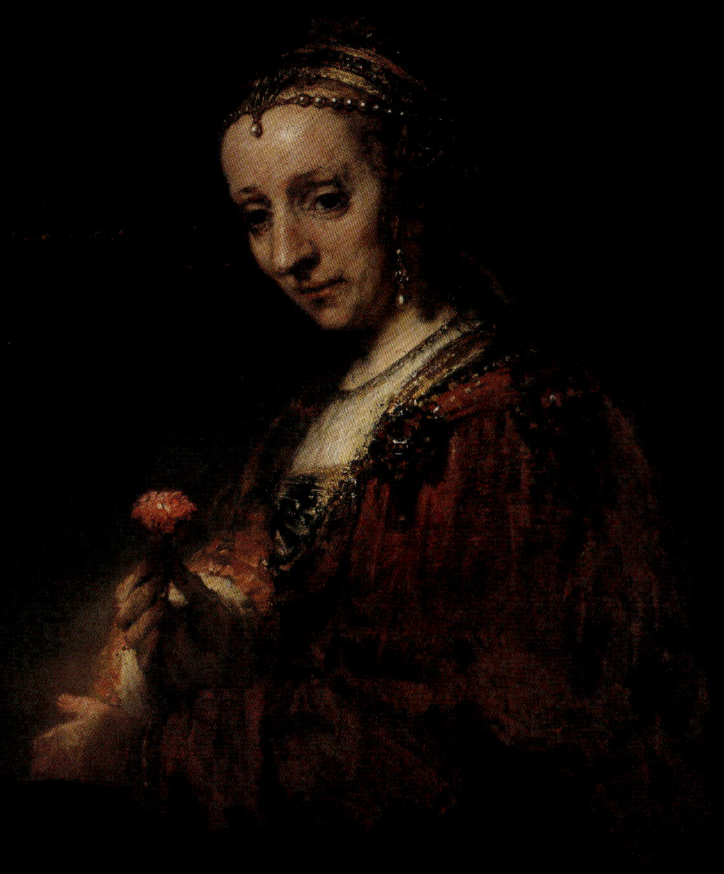

Portrait of a Woman with a Pink Carnation (Lysbet Jansdr. Delft?), *c.* 1665
Oil on canvas, 92.1 × 74.6 cm (36¼ × 29⅜ in.)
New York, The Metropolitan Museum of Art, Bequest of Benjamin Altman, 1913

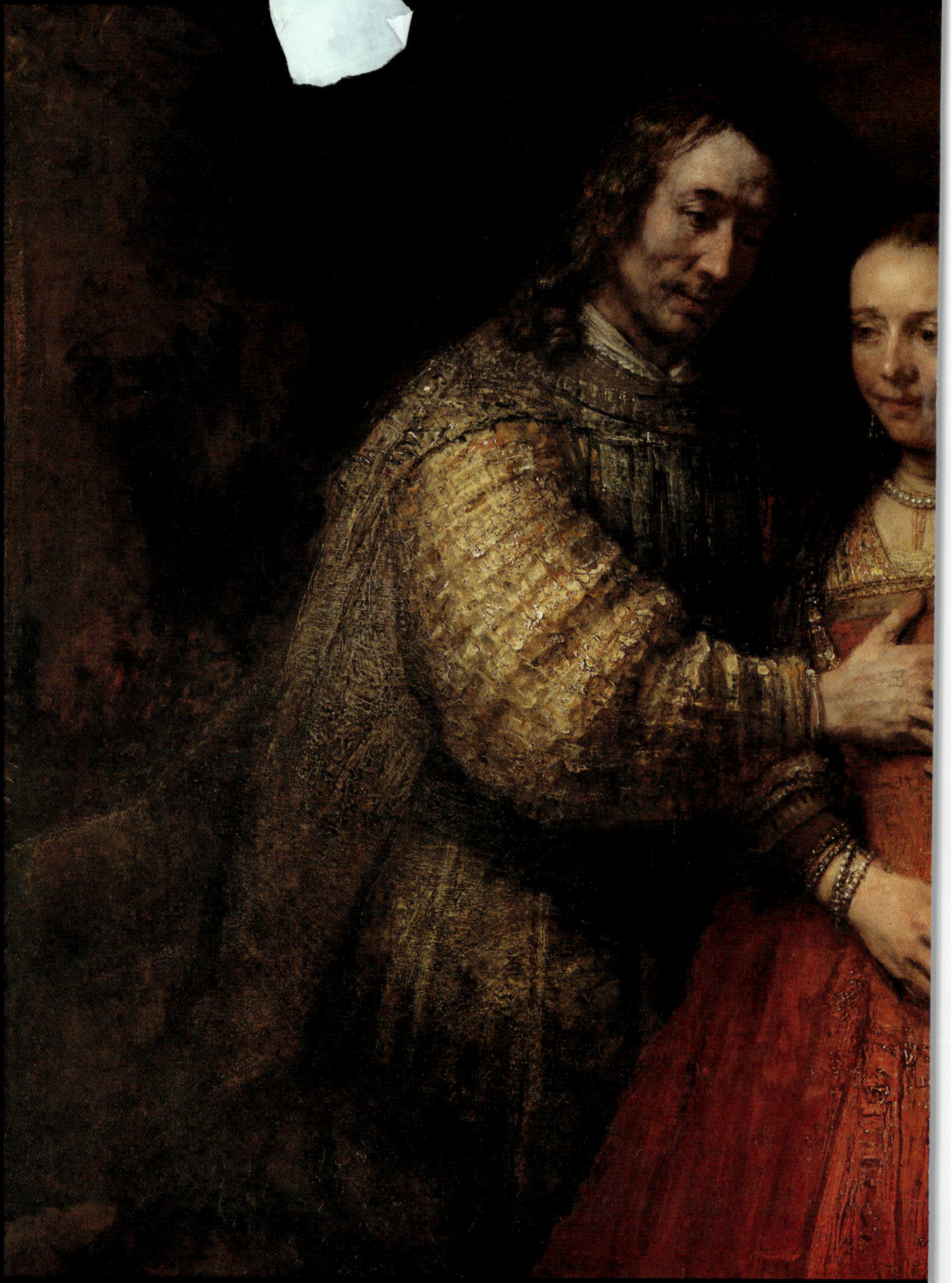

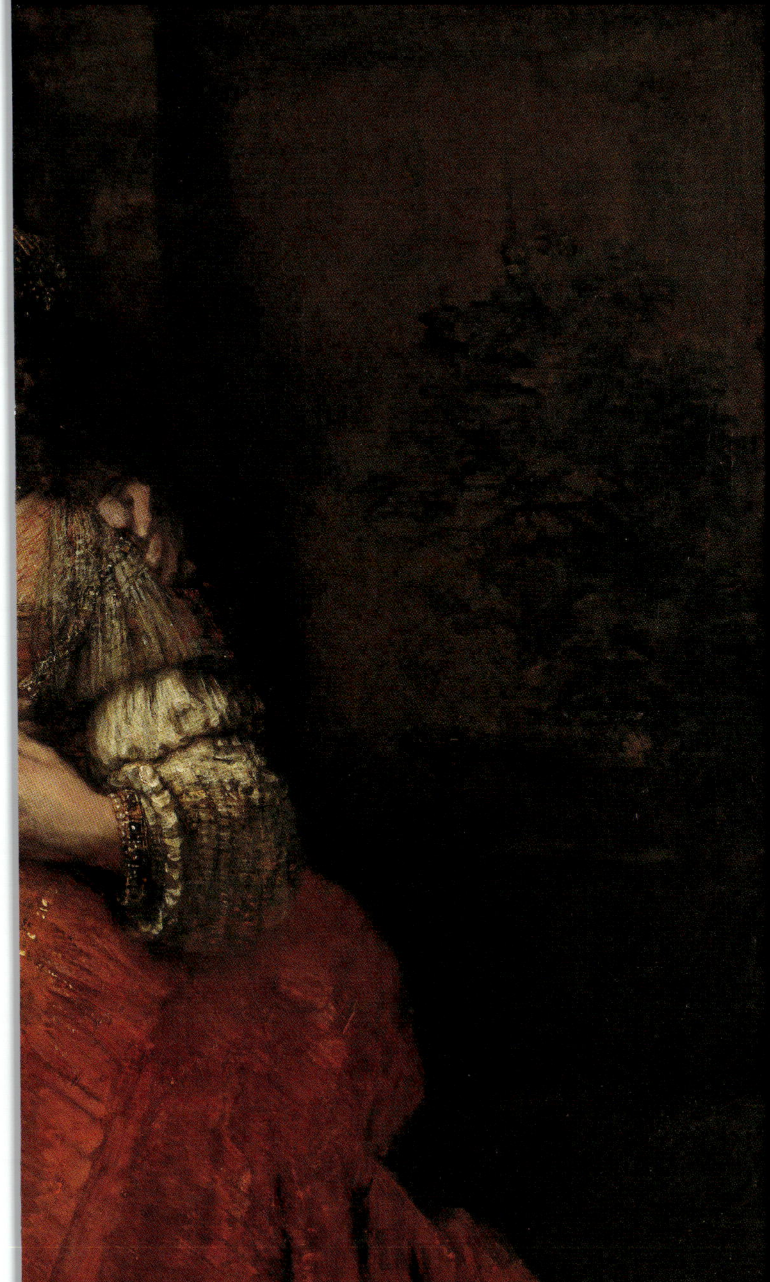

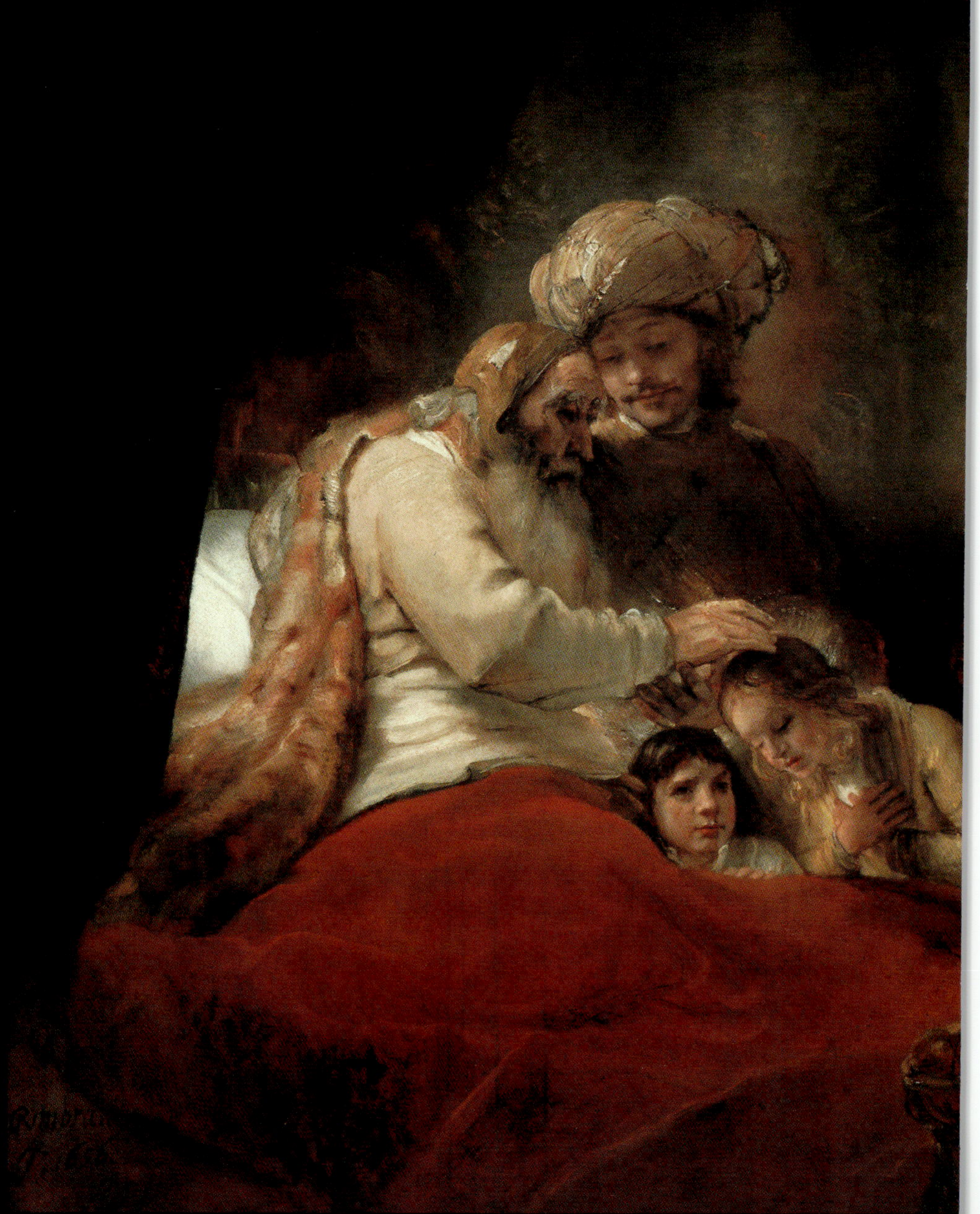

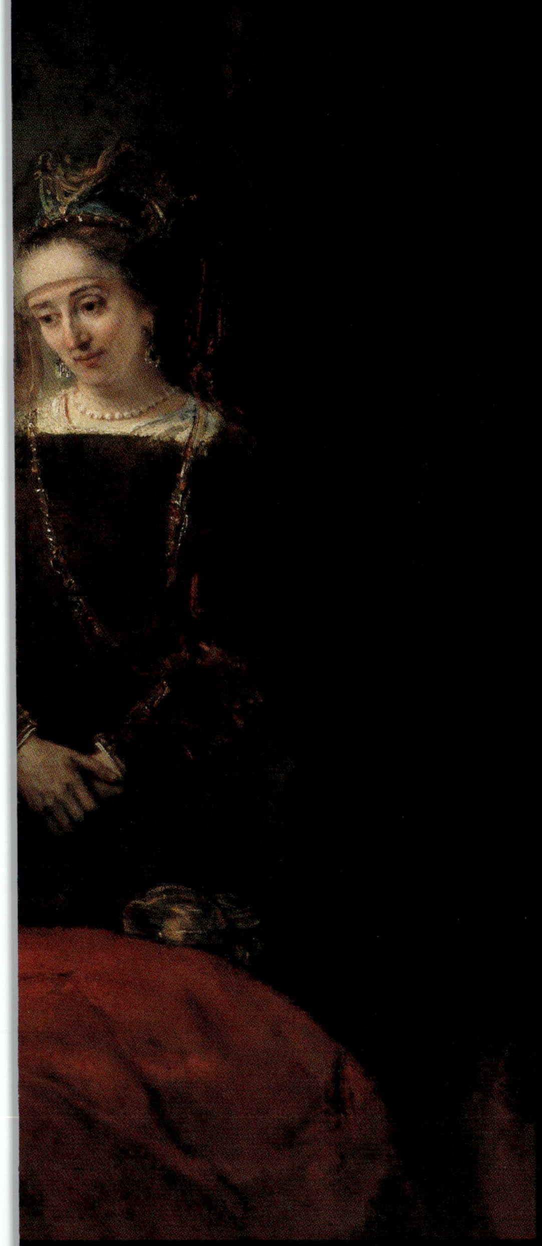

Pages 470/471
Portrait of a Couple as Isaac and Rebecca ("The Jewish Bride"), *c.* 1665
Oil on canvas, 121.5 × 166.5 cm
(47 ¾ × 65 ½ in.)
Amsterdam, Rijksmuseum, on loan from the City of Amsterdam
(A. van der Hoop Bequest)

Jacob Blessing the Sons of Joseph, 1656
Oil on canvas, 175.2 × 210.5 cm
(68 ¾ × 82 ¾ in.)
Hessen Kassel Heritage, Gemäldegalerie Alte Meister

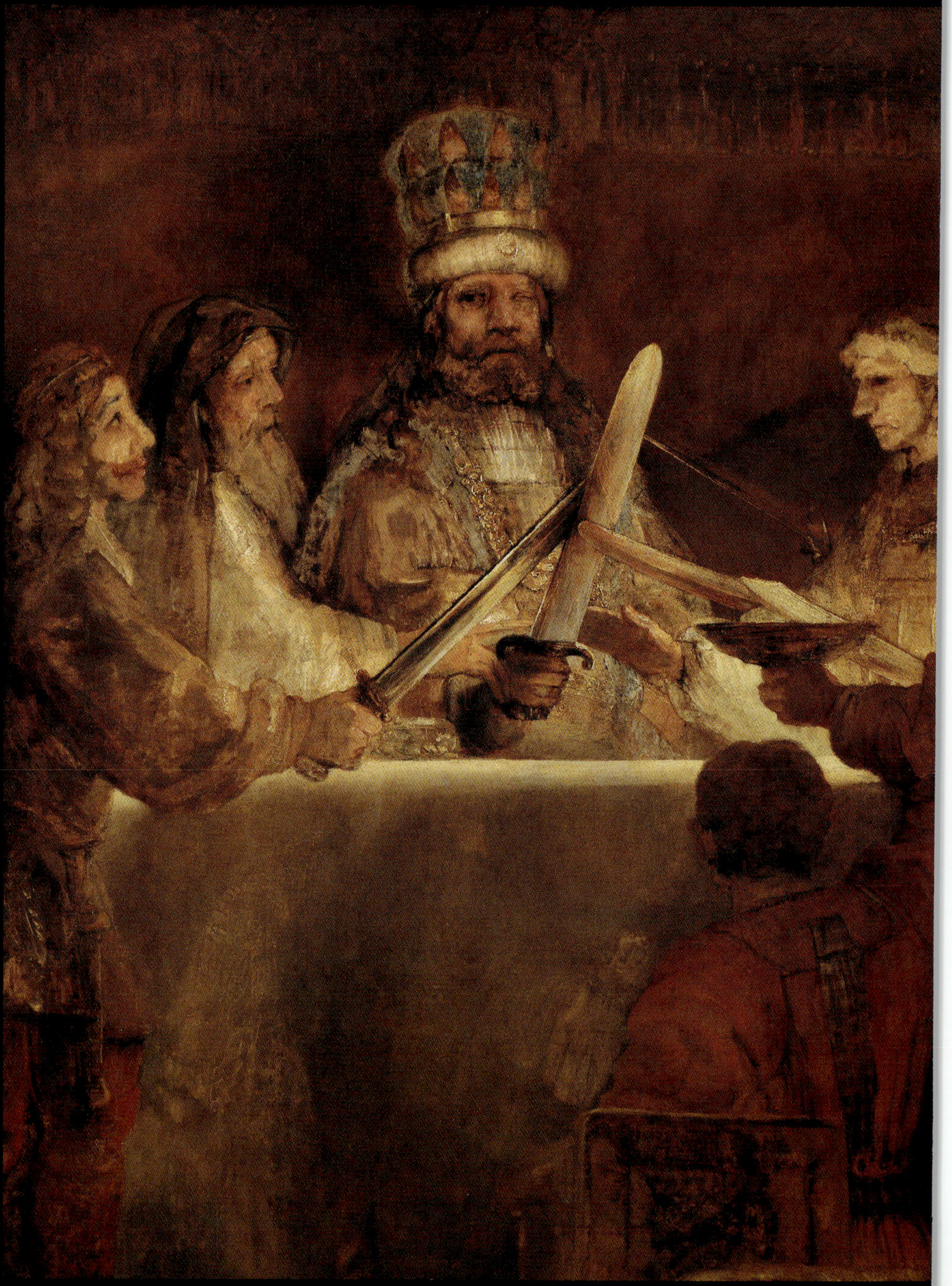

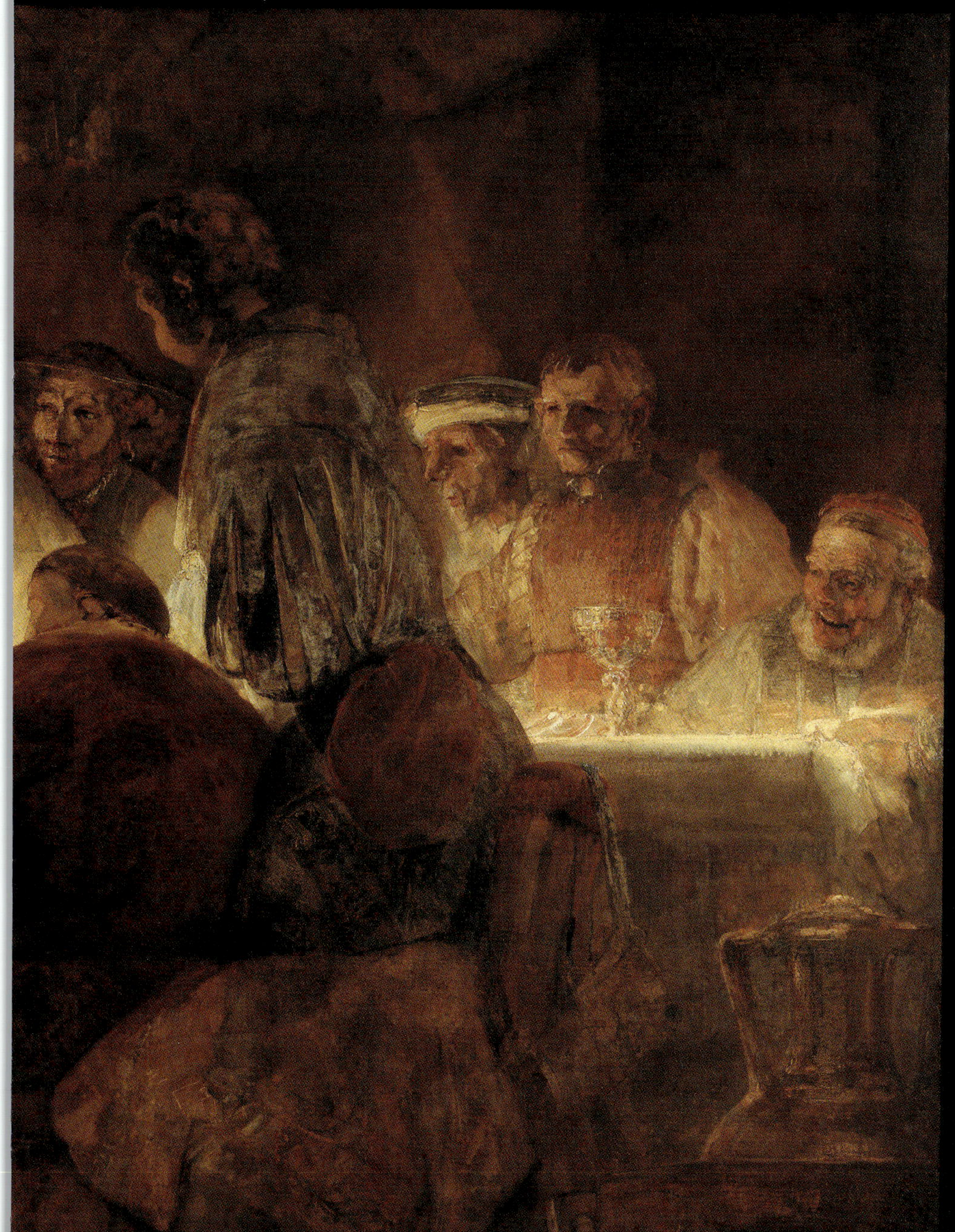

Pages 474/475

The Conspiracy of the Batavians under Claudius Civilis, 1661/62
Oil on canvas, 196 × 309 cm (77 ⅛ × 121 ⅔ in.)
Stockholm, Nationalmuseum, on permanent loan from The Royal Academy of Fine Arts, Sweden, donated in 1798 by Mrs Anna Johanna Peill, born Grill, widow of Mr Henrik Wilhelm Peill in memory of her late husband

Lucretia, 1666
Oil on canvas, 110.2 × 92.3 cm (43 ⅜ × 36 ⅓ in.)
Minneapolis, Minnesota, Minneapolis Institute of Art, The William Hood Dunwoody Fund

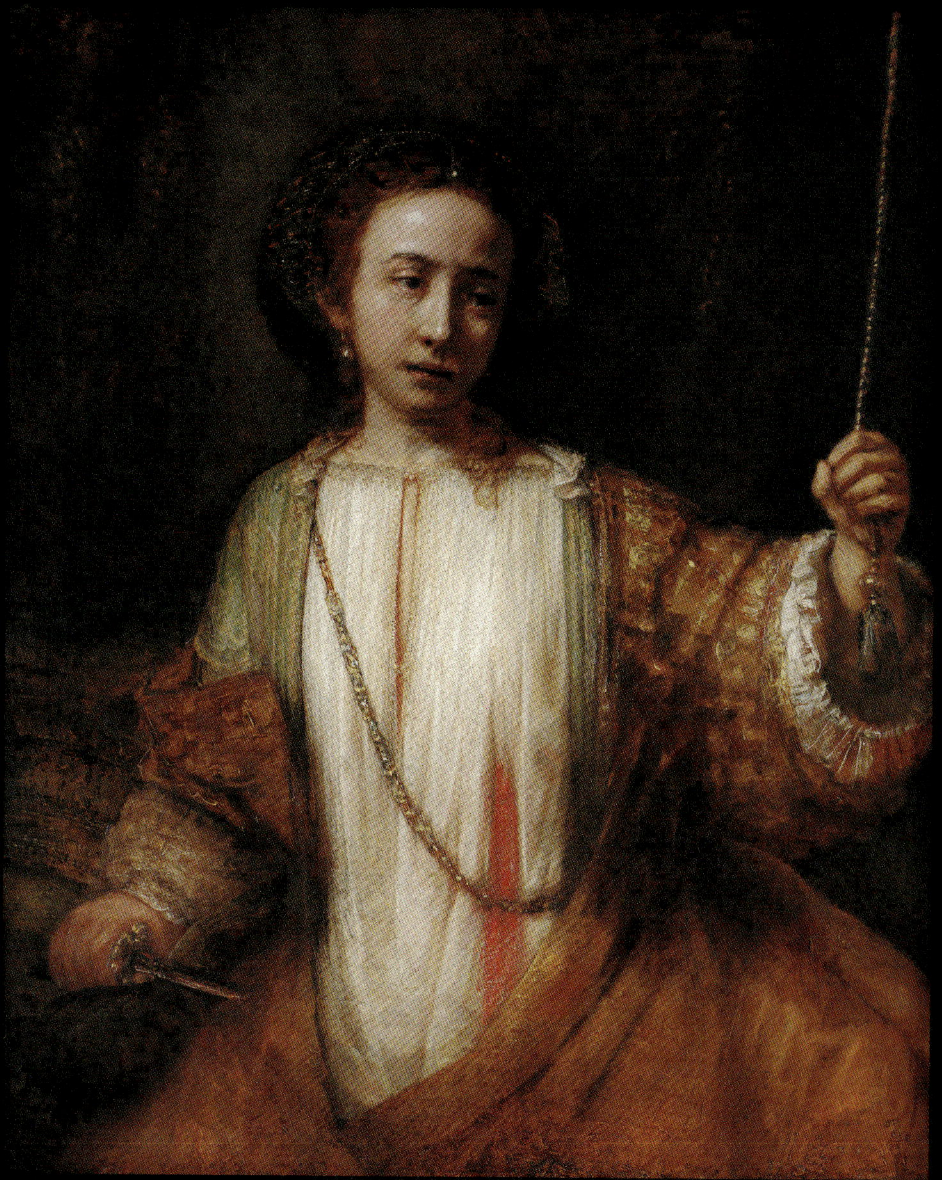

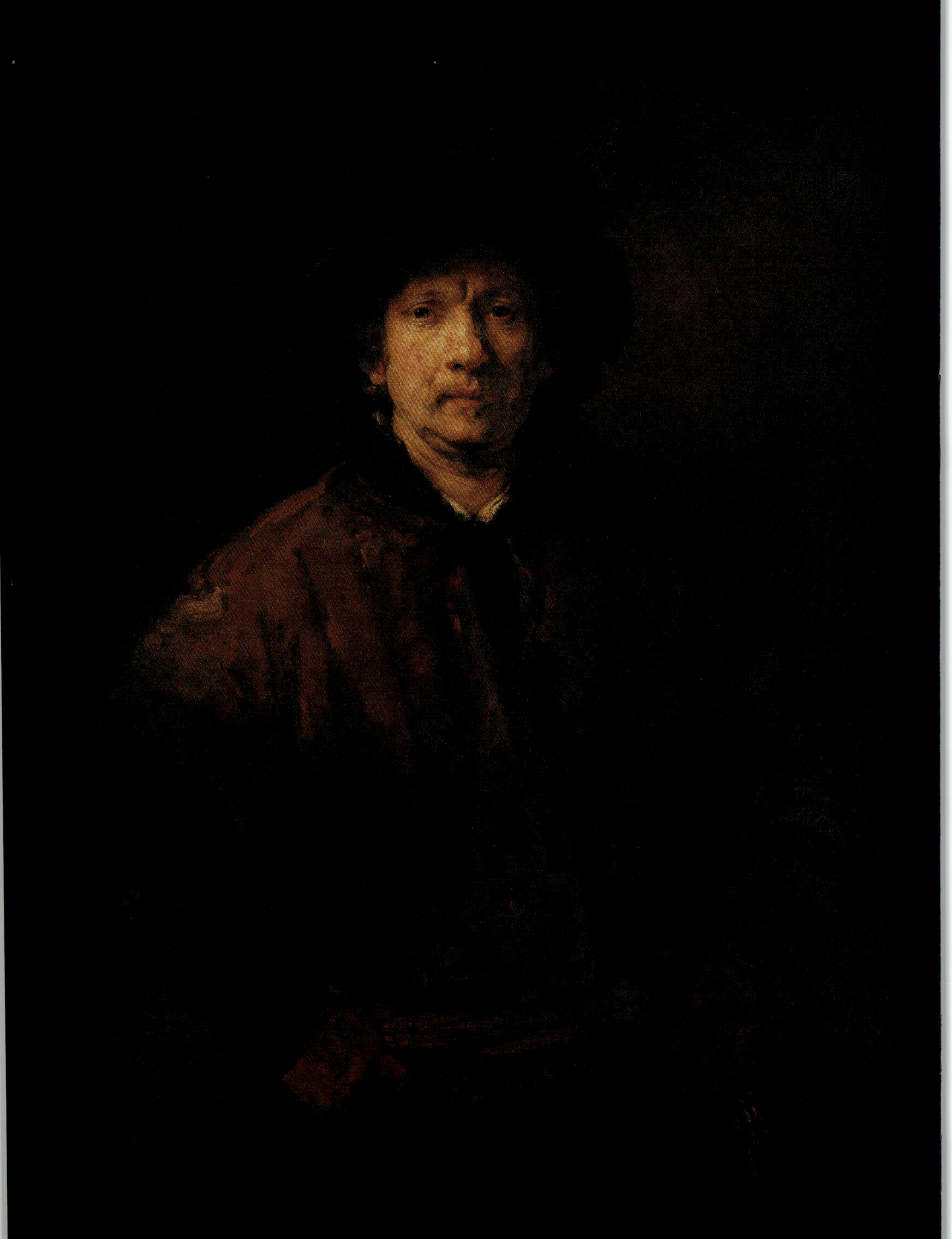

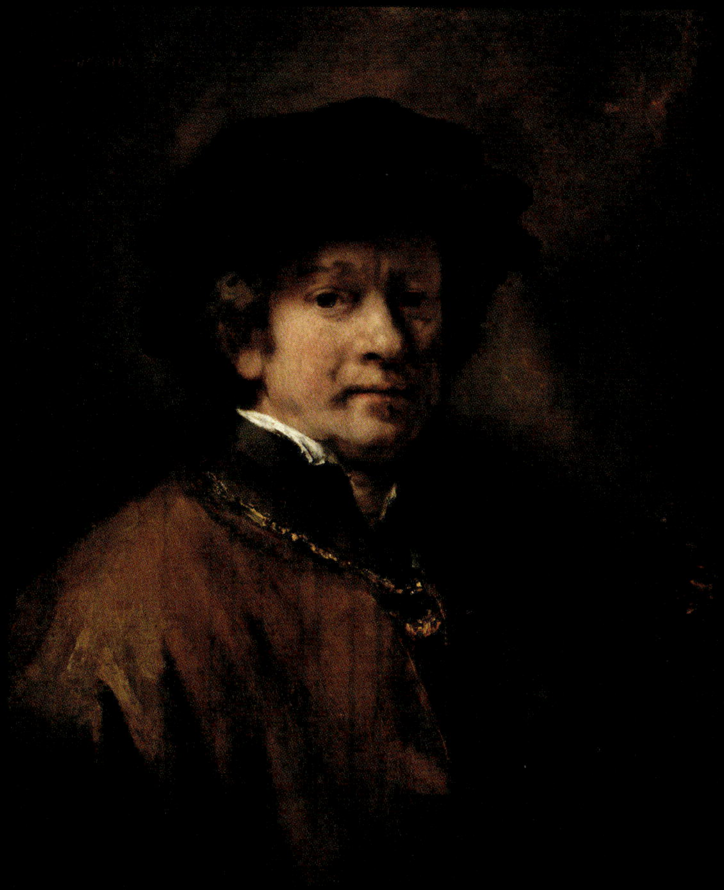

Self-Portrait in Working Dress, 1652
Oil on canvas, 112.1 × 81 cm (44 ⅛ × 31 ¾ in.)
Vienna, Kunsthistorisches Museum

Self-Portrait, 1654
Oil on canvas, 72.5 × 59.3 cm (28 ½ × 23 ⅓ in.)
Hessen Kassel Heritage, Gemäldegalerie Alte Meister

Self-Portrait, 1657
Oil on canvas, 52.7 × 42.7 cm (20 ¾ × 16 ¾ in.)
Edinburgh, Scottish National Gallery
(Bridgewater Loan, 1945)

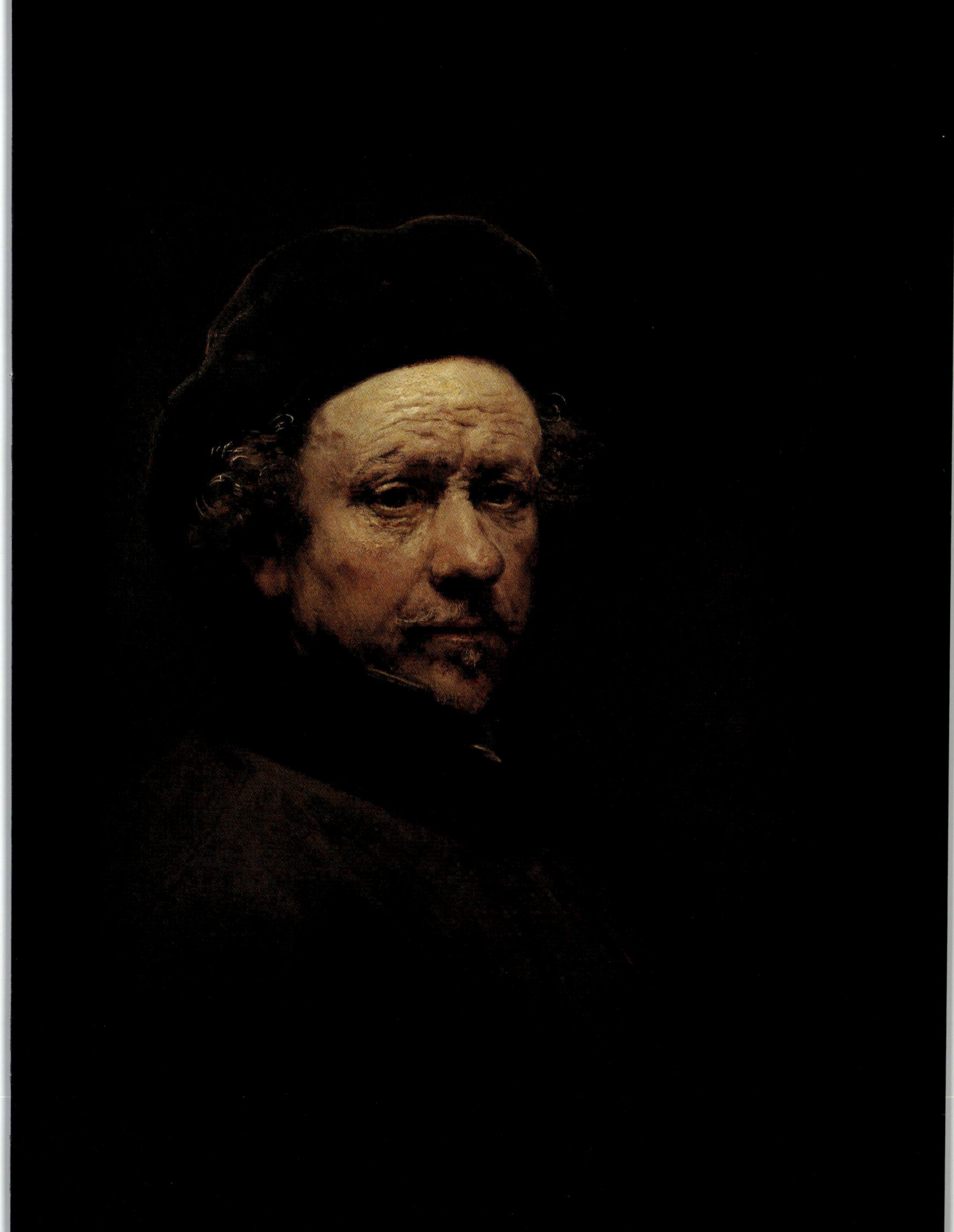

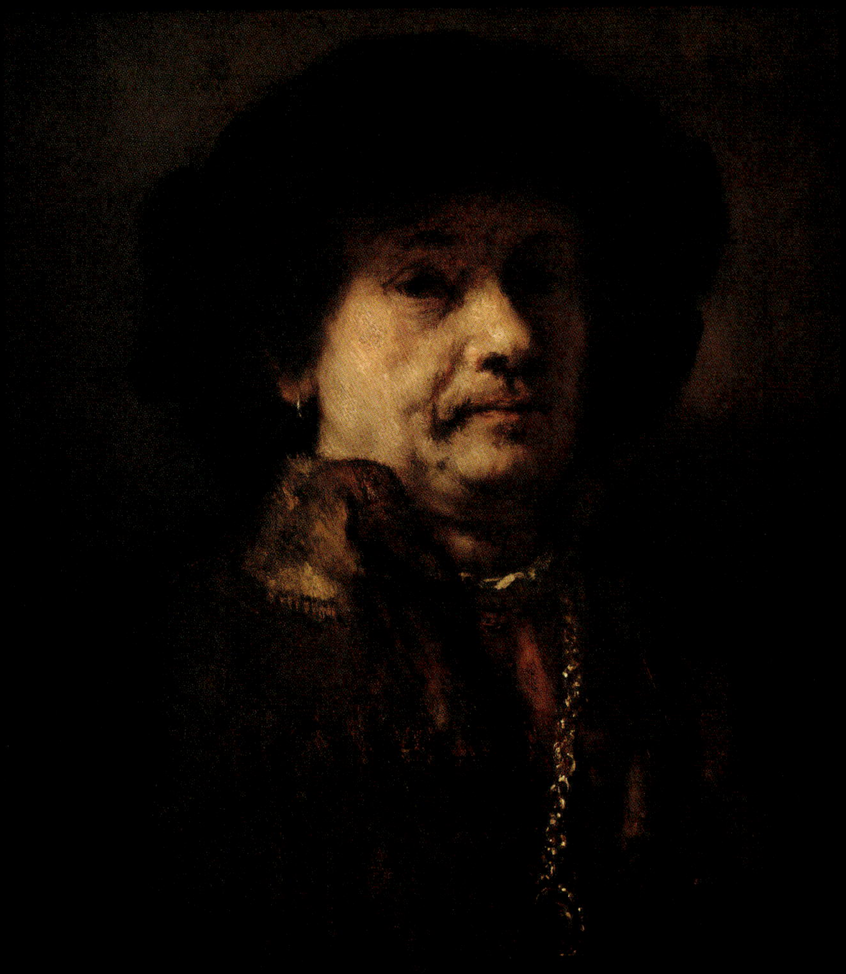

Self-Portrait with a Gold Chain, 1655
Oil on panel, 64.3 × 50.8 cm (25 1/3 × 20 in.)
Vienna, Kunsthistorisches Museum

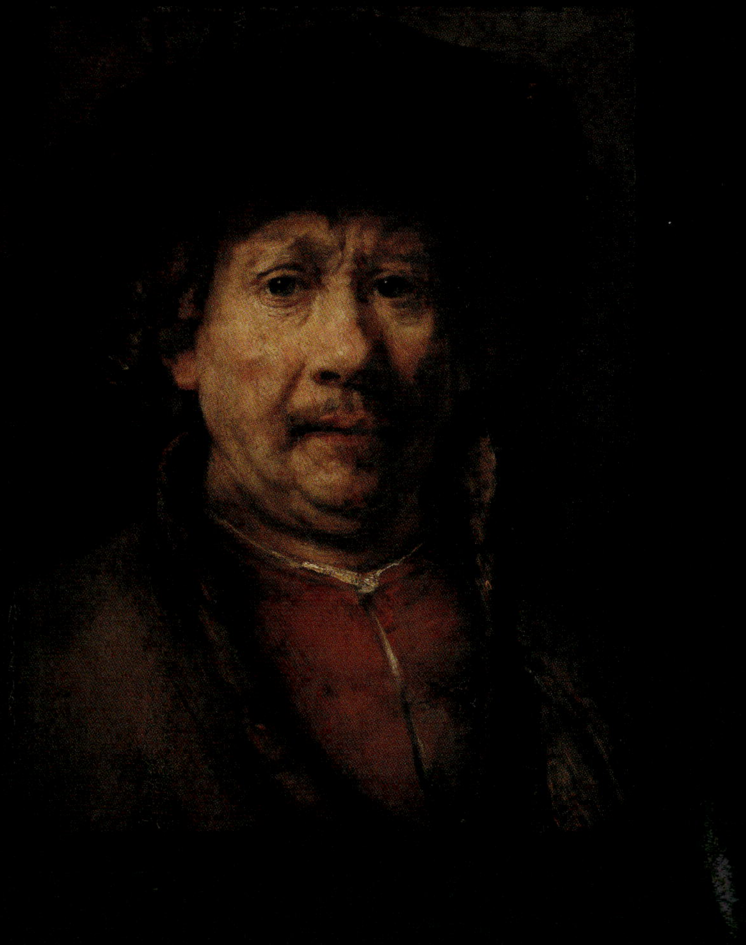

Self-Portrait, *c.* 1657/58
Oil on panel, 48.9 × 40.2 cm (19 ¼ × 15 ¾ in.)
Vienna, Kunsthistorisches Museum

Self-Portrait, 1658
Oil on canvas, 133.7 × 103.8 cm (52 5⁄8 × 40 3⁄4 in.)
New York, The Frick Collection

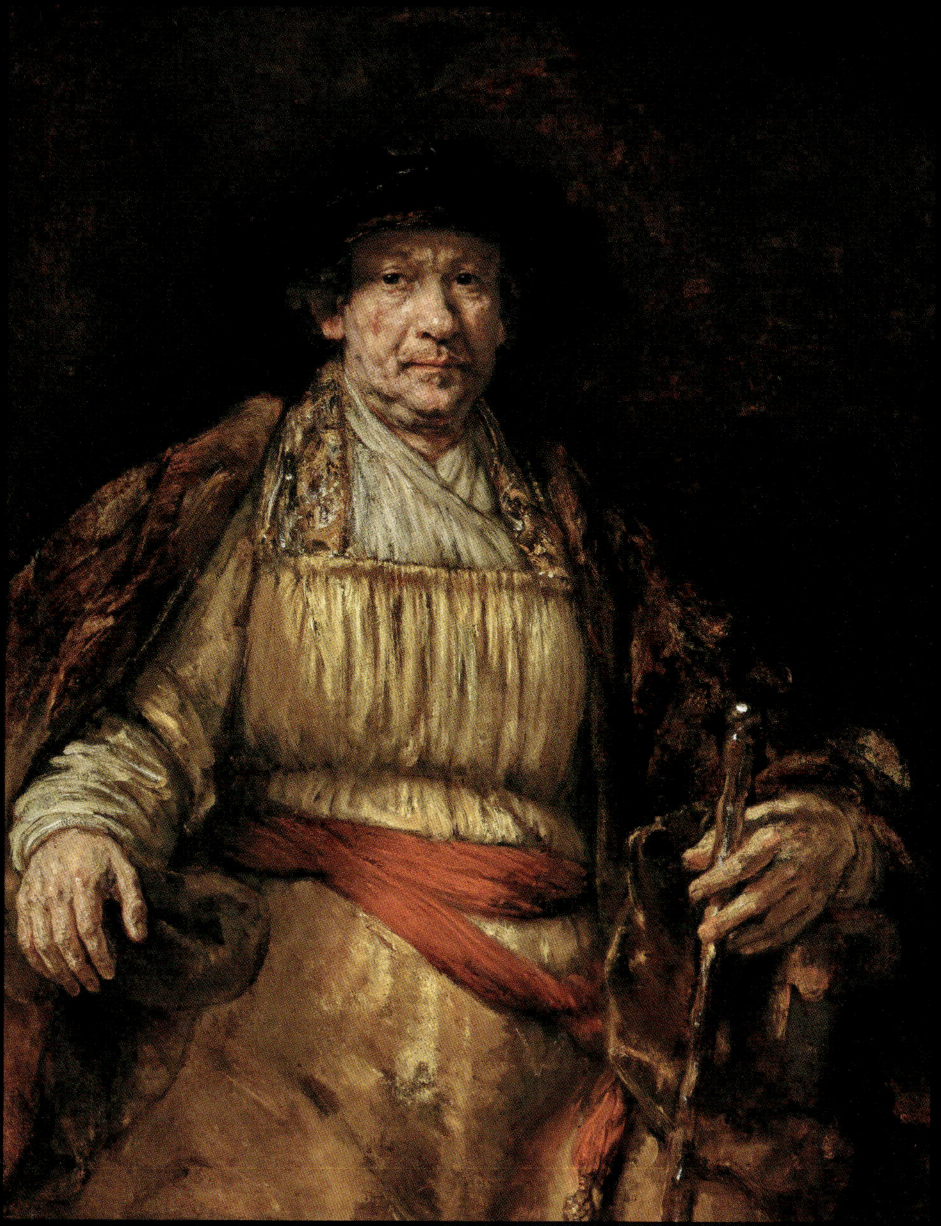

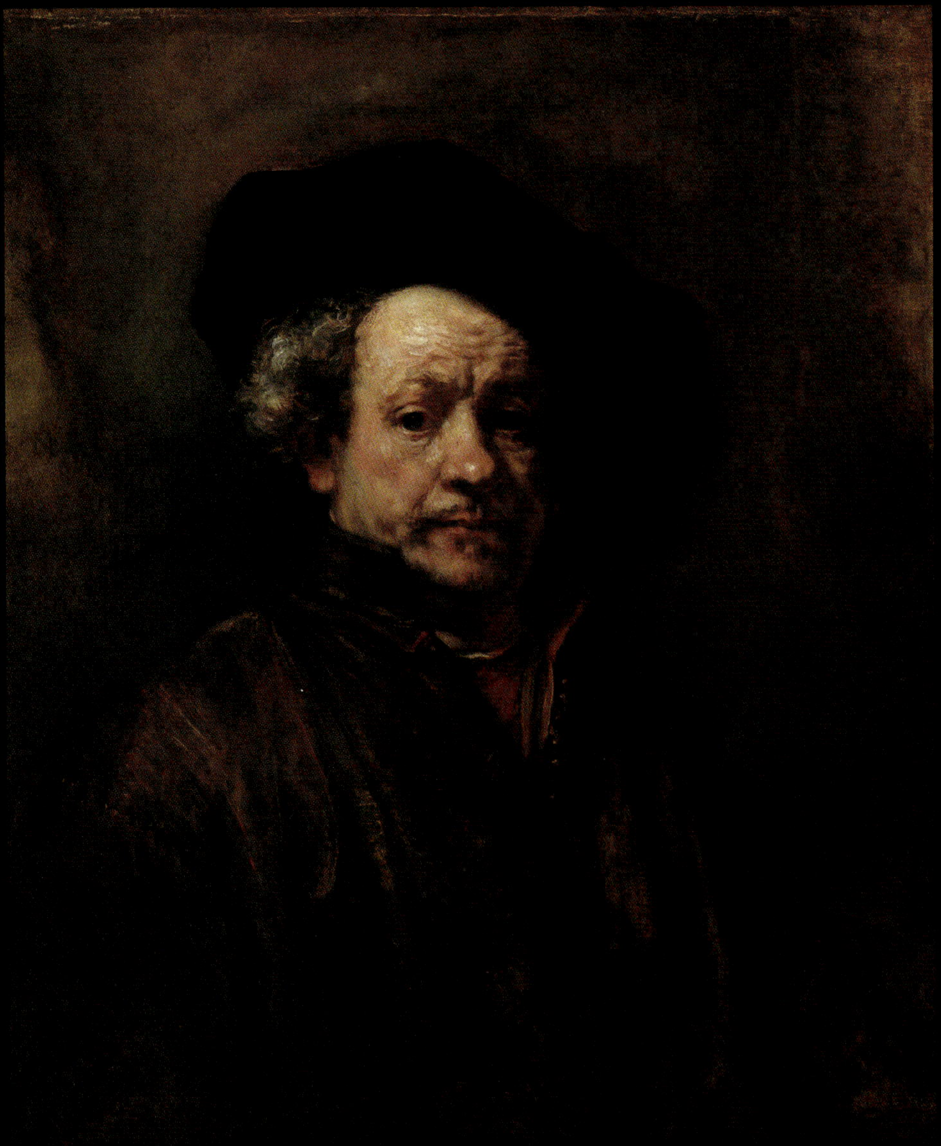

Self-Portrait, 1660
Oil on canvas, 80.3 × 67.3 cm (31 ⅝ × 26 ½ in.). New York,
The Metropolitan Museum of Art, Bequest of Benjamin Altman, 1913

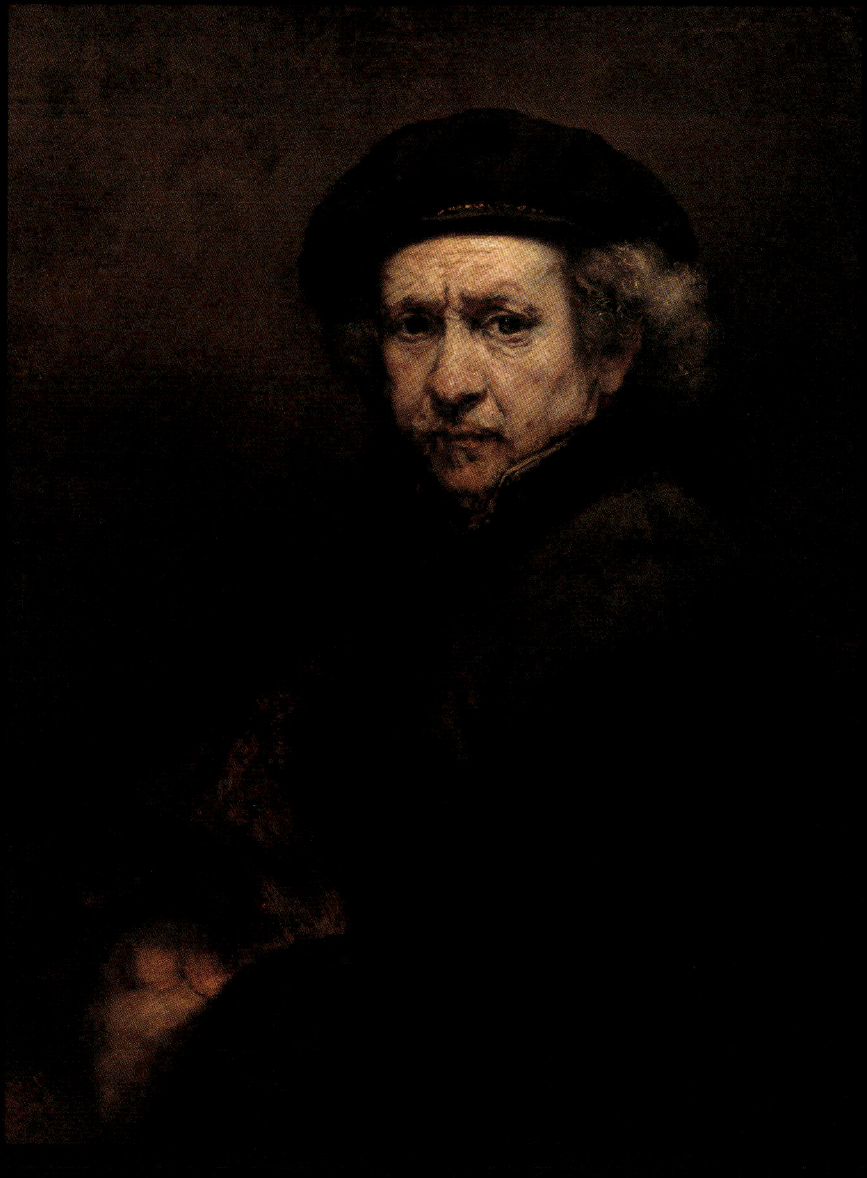

Self-Portrait, 1659
Oil on canvas, 84.4 × 66 cm (33 ¼ × 25 ¾ in.). Washington, DC, National Gallery of Art, Andrew W. Mellon Collection

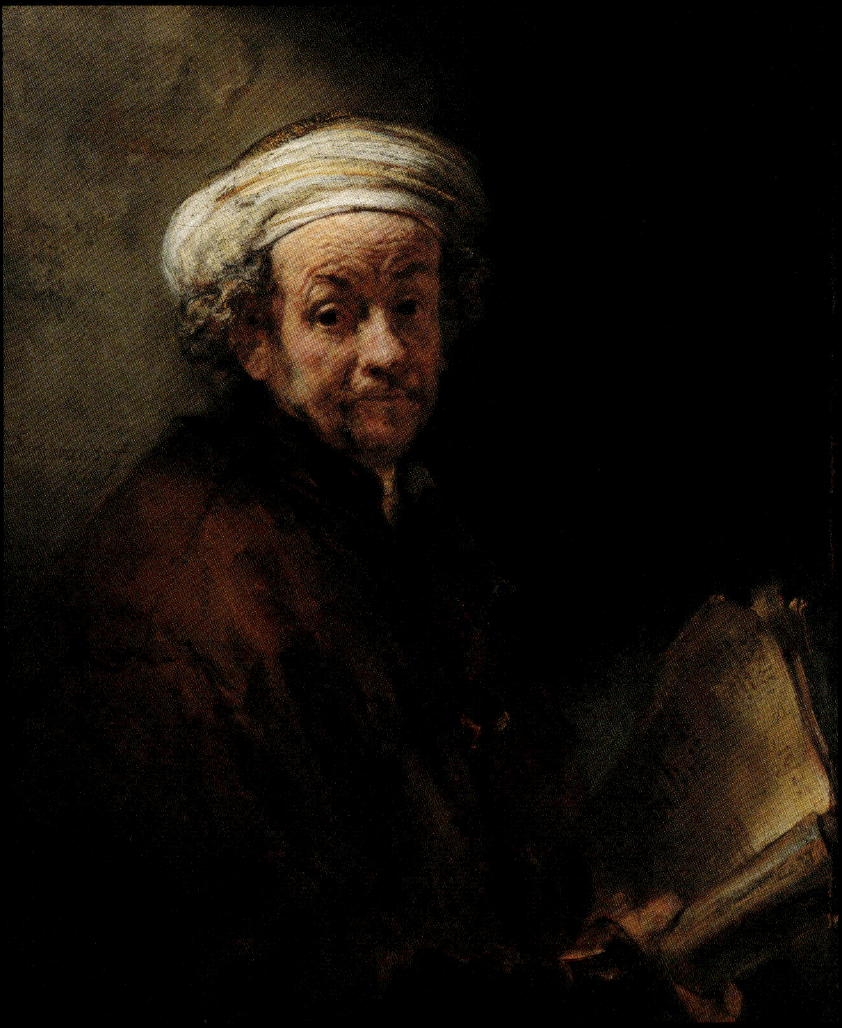

Self-Portrait as the Apostle Paul, 1661
Oil on canvas, 91 × 77 cm (35¾ × 30⅓ in.). Amsterdam, Rijksmuseum, Bequest of Mr and Mrs De Bruijn-van der Leeuw, Muri, Switzerland

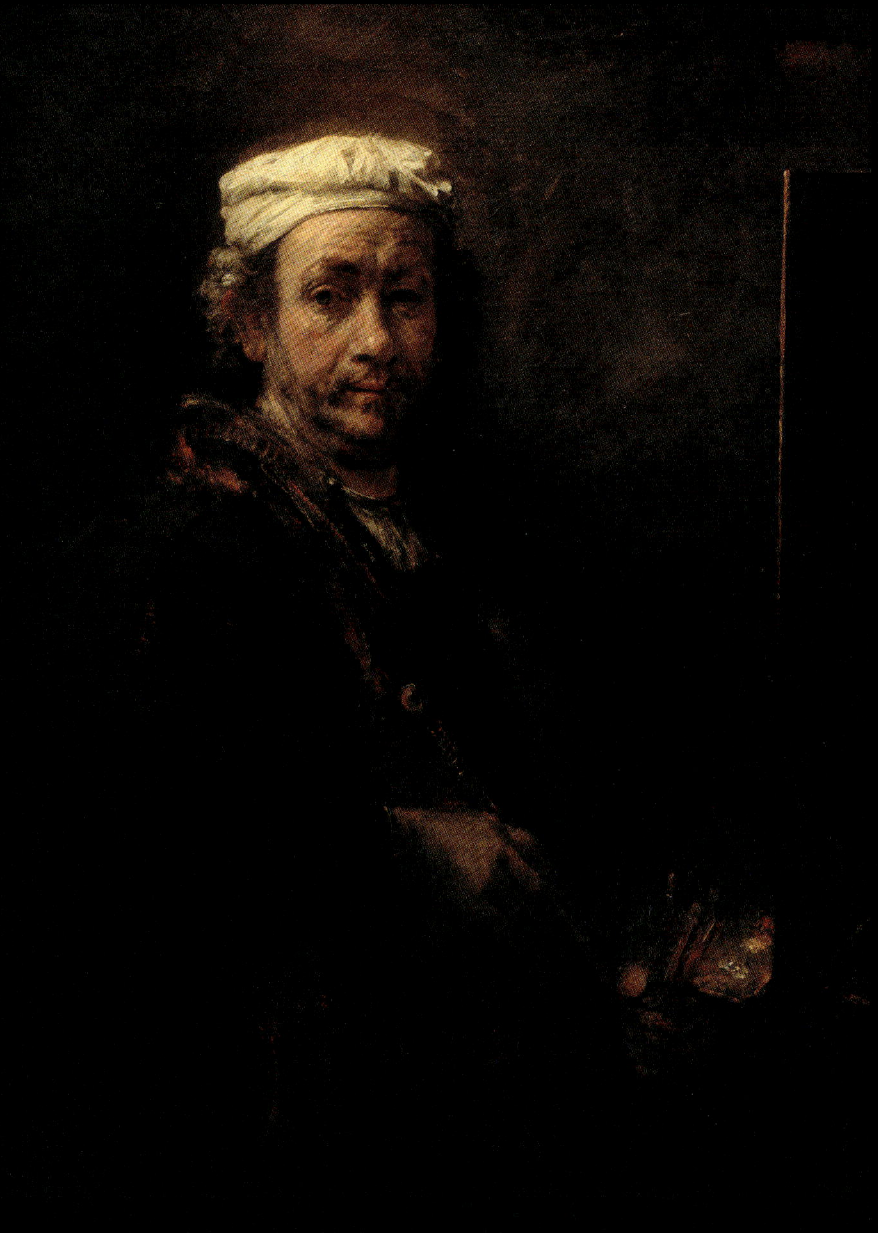

Self-Portrait at the Easel, 1660
Oil on canvas, 111 × 90.6 cm (43 ¾ × 35 ⅔ in.)
Paris, Musée du Louvre

Self-Portrait as Zeuxis, 1662/63
Oil on canvas, 82.5 × 65 cm (32 ½ × 25 ⅝ in.)
Cologne, Wallraf-Richartz-Museum & Fondation Corboud

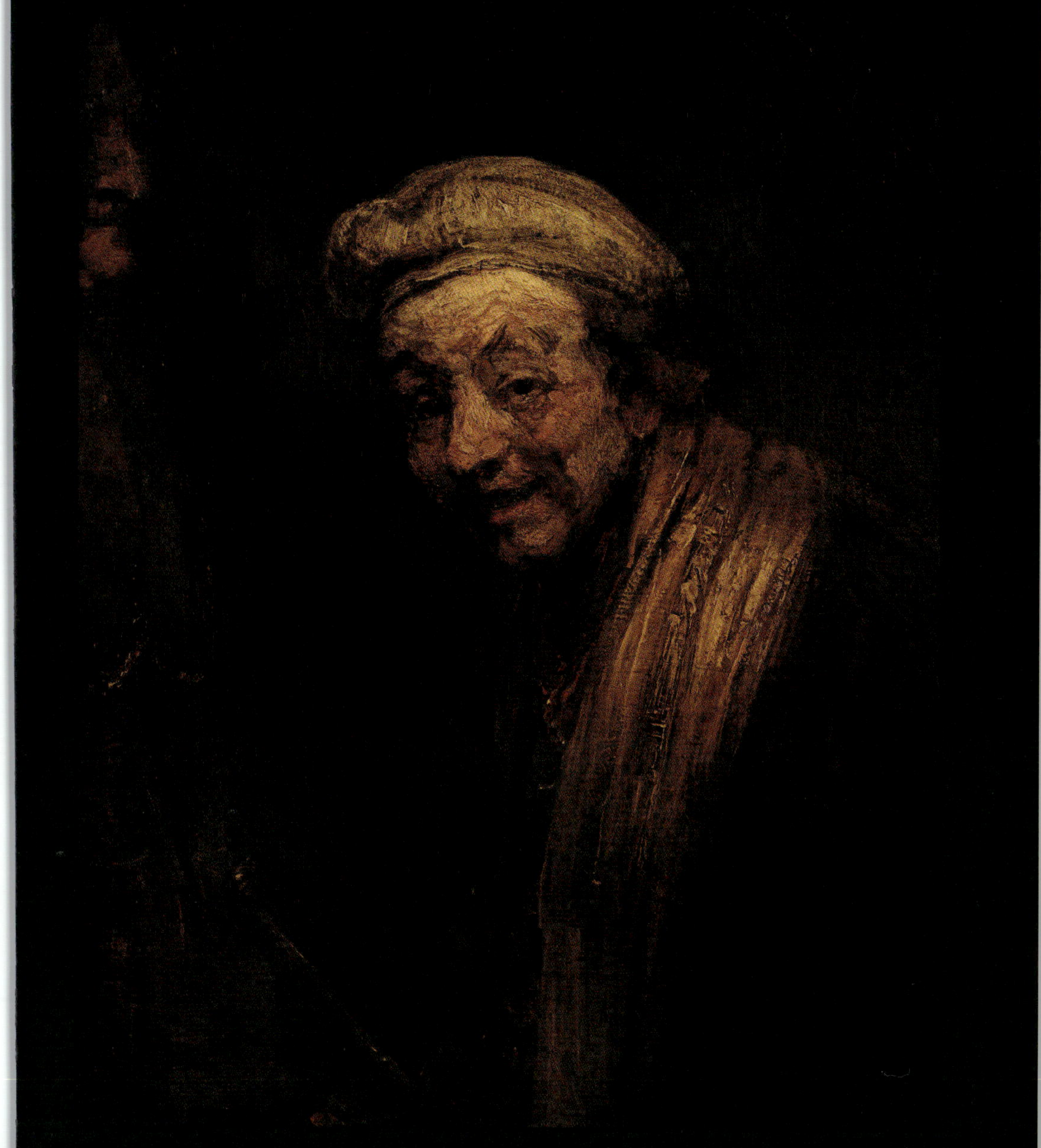

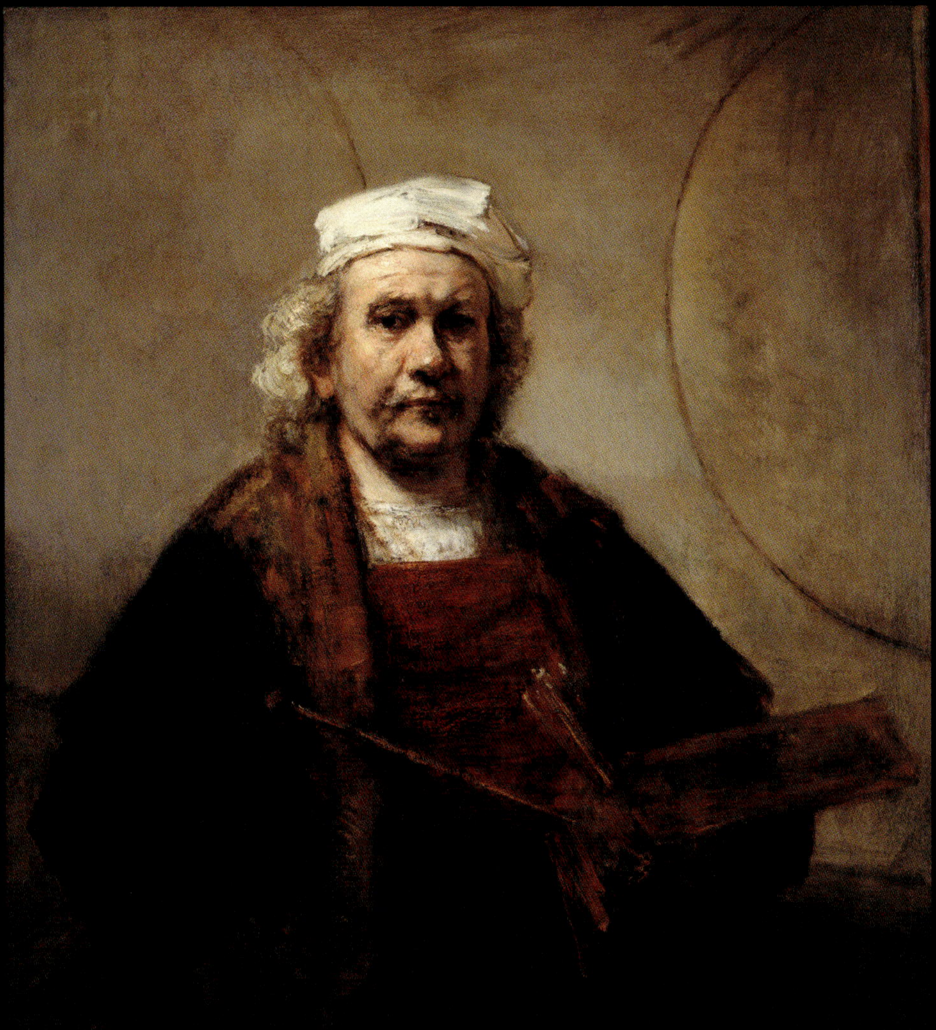

Self-Portrait with Palette and Maulstick, 1665–1669
Oil on canvas, 114.3 × 94 cm (45 × 37 ⅛ in.)
London, Kenwood House, The Iveagh Bequest

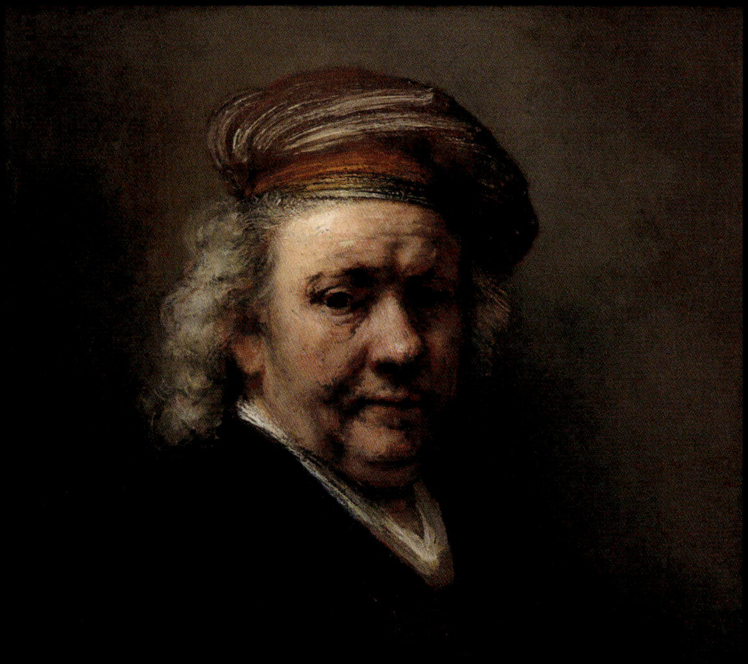

Self-Portrait, 1669
Oil on canvas, 65.4 × 60.2 cm (25¾ × 23¾ in.)
The Hague, Mauritshuis

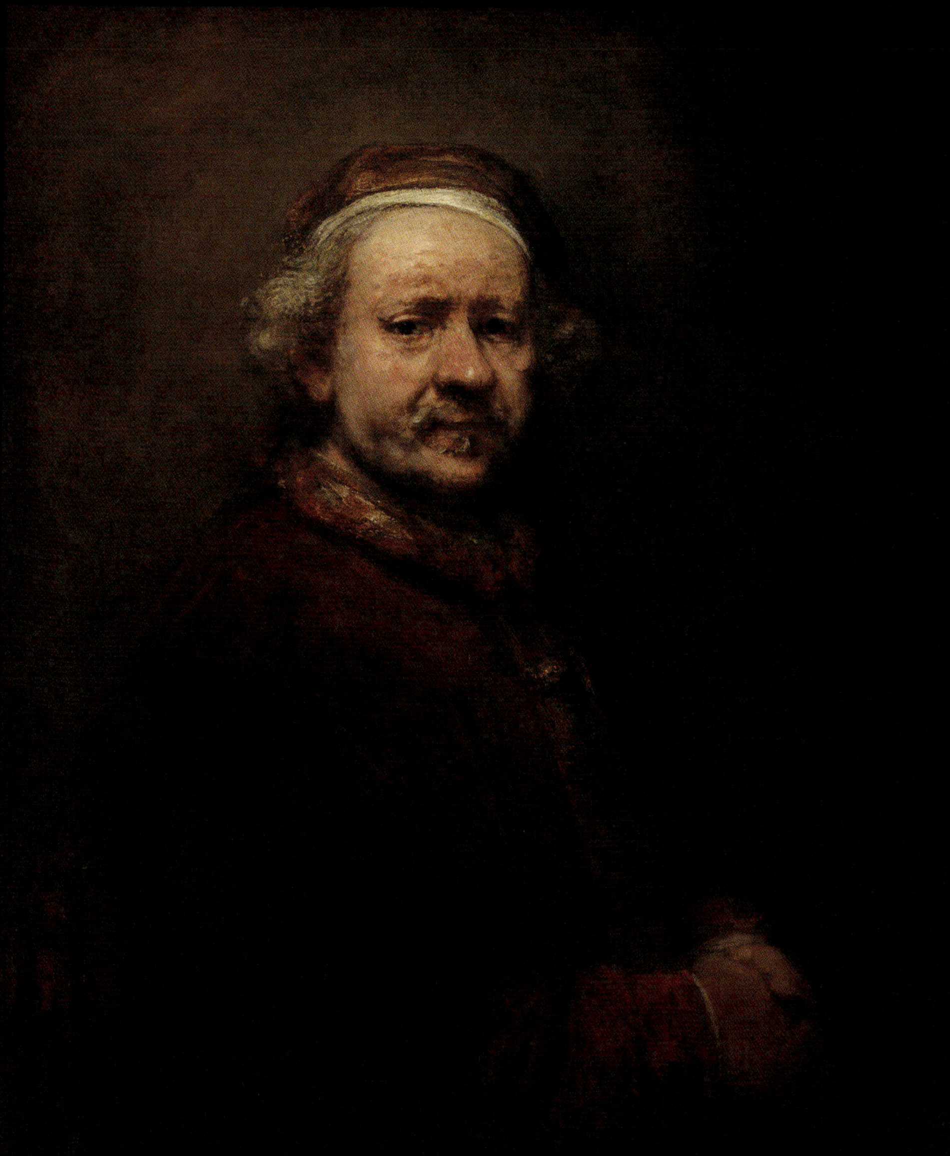

Self-Portrait, 1669
Oil on canvas, 86 × 70.5 cm (33 ¾ × 27 ¾ in.)
London, The National Gallery

Self-Portrait, *c.* 1669
Oil on canvas, 71 × 54 cm (27 ¾ × 21 ¼ in.)
Florence, Galleria degli Uffizi

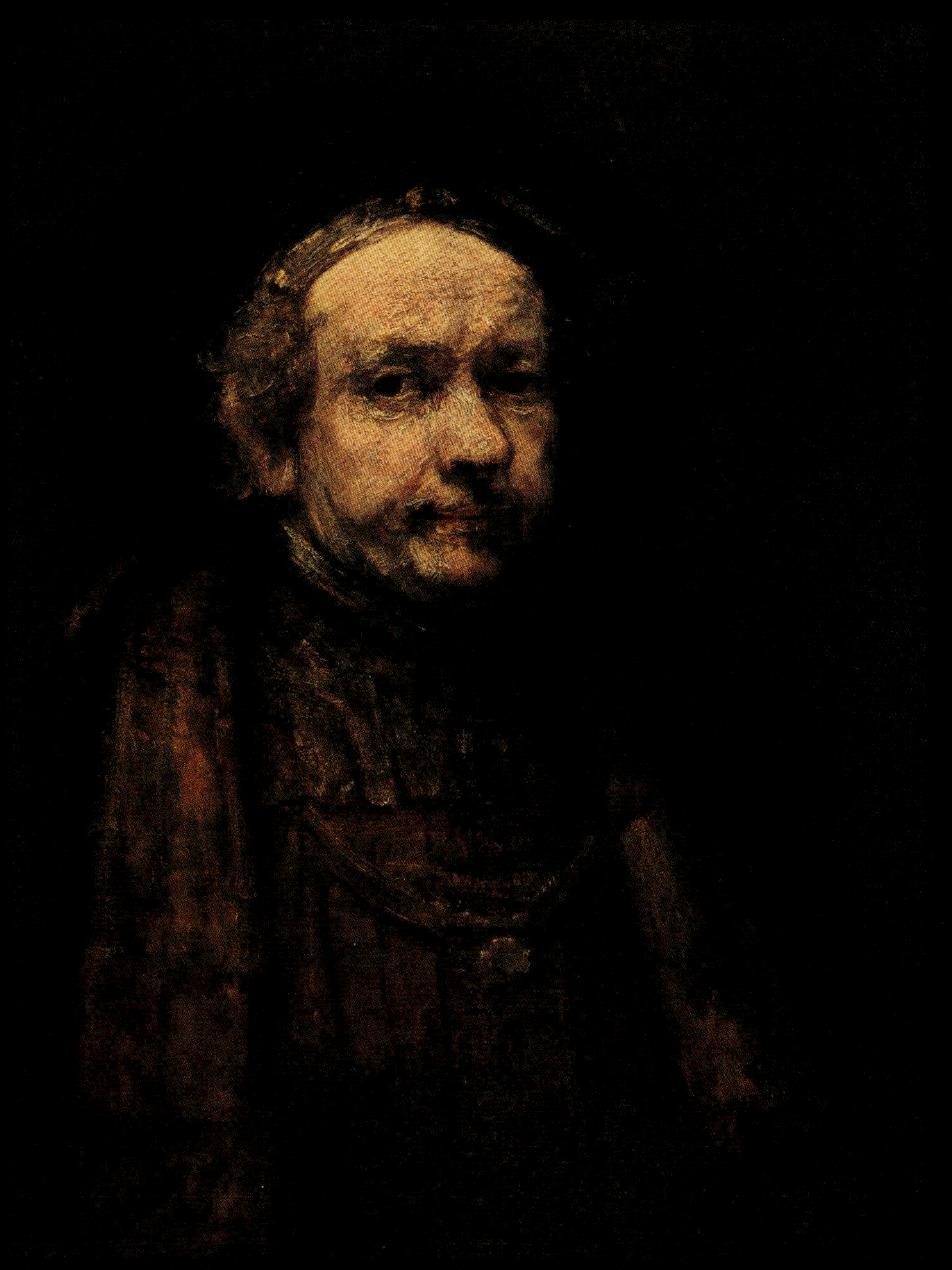

Simeon's Song of Praise, *c.* 1668/69
Oil on canvas, 98.5 × 79.5 cm (38 ¾ × 31 ¼ in.)
Stockholm, Nationalmuseum

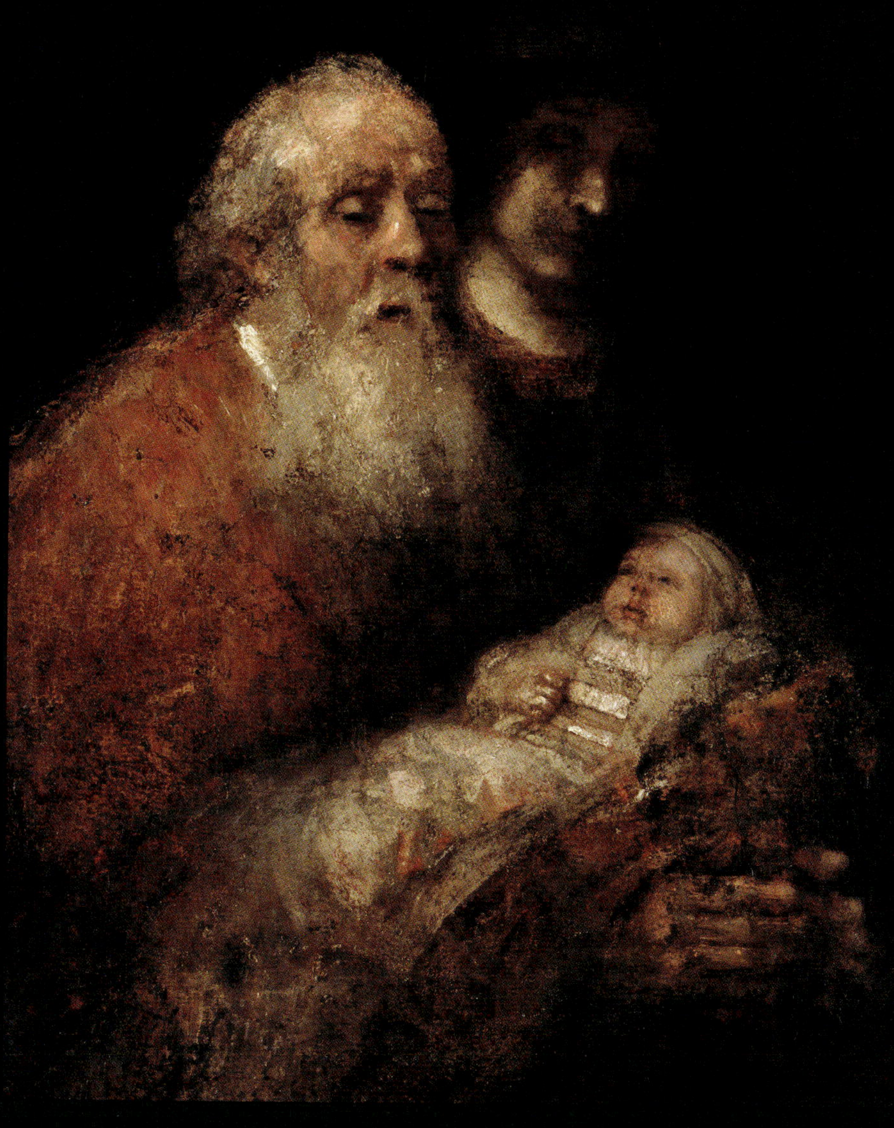

Notes

Rembrandt's Early Years in Leiden 1606–1631

1 Orlers 1641, p. 375. See the text of Orlers' Rembrandt biography in: RD 1641/8.
2 On Rembrandt's biography, see Dudok van Heel 1991; De Baar/Moerman 1991; van de Wetering 2006b (van de Wetering 2006g) and Manuth 2018, pp. 213–215. The most exhaustive genealogy of Rembrandt's family can be found in De Baar 1992 and Dudok van Heel 2006, pp. 225–231.
3 Walle 2005.
4 Walle 2005, p. 74.
5 Walle 2005, p. 231, note 77.
6 De Baar 1992, p. 2.
7 Orlers 1641, p. 375.
8 Dudok van Heel 2006, p. 14.
9 On the curriculum of the grammar school, see van Doorninck/Kuijpers 1993, pp. 63–66 and Golahny 2003, pp. 51–58.
10 Van Gelder 1953, p. 273.
11 Van Straten 2005, p. 21.
12 "heeft daer toe gants geen lust ofte genegentheyt gehadt, dewijle zijne natuyrlicke beweginghen alleen streckten tot de Schilder ende Teycken Conste; waer omme zy luyden genootsaeckt geweest zijn, haren Soon uyt de Schole te nemen, ende volgende zijn begeeren te brengen ende te besteden, by een Schilder omme by de selve te leeren de eerste fundamenten ende beginselen van dien"; Orlers 1641, p. 375.
13 Ekkart 1998, pp. 13–24.
14 Ibid., pp. 94–112.
15 Van Straten 2005, pp. 24–25.
16 Ekkart 1998, pp. 126–128.
17 On Lastman, see Freise 1911; Dudok van Heel 1991, Dudok van Heel et al. 1991; Amsterdam 1991; Hamburg 2006; Golahny 2010 and especially Seifert 2011.
18 Van Mander 1604, fol. 293v.
19 See here most recently Seifert 2011, pp. 155–162.
20 Vondel 1660, p. 151.
21 Orlers 1641, part 1, p. 375.
22 Witt 2008, p. 255, no. 157.
23 Dudok van Heel 2006, pp. 146–147.
24 Tümpel, in: Amsterdam 1991, p. 60. The Bible quotation here is from the King James Bible (Authorised Version).
25 Van de Wetering 1997, pp. 174–175.
26 Held 1964.
27 Quotation based on the author's translation from the foreword to the Book of Tobit in the Dutch Authorised Version *(Statenvertaling)* from 1637; here, see Manuth 2004, p. 101.
28 Manuth 2004, pp. 88–106.
29 Here, see especially the pioneering contributions by Tümpel 1968, 1969 and 1971.
30 Here, see Washington/Milwaukee/Amsterdam 2008/09, pp. 3–12 and Schnackenburg 2016, pp. 42–52.
31 See primarily Tümpel 1971, pp. 27–30.
32 See Manuth 2006.
33 The original manuscript in Latin is preserved in the National Library of the Netherlands in The Hague and was first published by J.A. Worp (1891). Translation from Corpus I, p. 193.
34 Quoted after the translation by Lynne Richards, based on the Dutch translation of Heesakkers 1994, pp. 85/86, published in Kassel/Amsterdam 2001/02, pp. 396–398.
35 Baer 2000/01.
36 See van de Wetering 1983, pp. 59–69.
37 Sandrart 1675, as quoted in Peltzer 1925, p. 203.
38 See van der Veen 1997/98, Hirschfelder 2008, Gottwald 2011.
39 Chapman 1990; Corpus IV; London/The Hague 1999/2000.
40 De Winkel 2006, pp. 139–141.
41 Corpus II, p. 838: Chapman 1990, pp. 34, 36, 39–40.
42 Houbraken 1718–1721, II, pp. 178–179.

Amsterdam 1631–1639

43 Van der Veen 1997, pp. 69–80.
44 See Amsterdam/London 2006.
45 Ekkart, in: Amsterdam 2002/03, p. 32.
46 In Karel van Mander (1604, fol. 281r) and Samuel van Hoogstraten 1678 (pp. 44–47), and elsewhere. See Miedema 2017, pp. 150–152.
47 Van Hoogstraten 1678, p. 87.
48 Van der Veen, in: London/Amsterdam 2006.
49 Lambour, in: Eikema Hommes et al. 2016, note 99.
50 Corpus II, p. 397.
51 This is said by a prostitute. Anonymous, *D'openhertige Juffrouw, of d'ontdekte geveinsdheid*, Leiden 1680, p. 158.
52 Van Hoogstraten 1678, p. 265.
53 This principle, and the connection with the writing of Van Hoogstraten, were first noticed by Van de Wetering (1997, p. 187).
54 Bikker 2016, pp. 30–31.
55 Bikker (2016, p. 30) claims, incorrectly, that the couple first sat during the summer of 1634, because he is of the opinion that Oopjen is shown pregnant.
56 Houbraken 1718–1721, I, p. 269.
57 Dudok van Heel 2006, pp. 251–257; Dirkse 1994.
58 Edinburgh/London 2001, p. 86.
59 Kok 2011 and 2016; Amsterdam 2017.
60 Broos, in: The Hague 1997/98, pp. 132–141.
61 Anthony van Dyck, *Portrait of Amalia of Solms*, 1631/32, oil on canvas mounted on wooden panel, 105 × 91 cm, Madrid, Museo Nacional del Prado, Inv. P01483. See The Hague 1997/98, pp. 119–123.
62 For a related observation in Rembrandt's *Christ on the Cross* (Cat. 46) from 1631, see Manuth, in: Berlin 2006, pp. 54–55.
63 Tümpel 1986a, p. 136; Chapman 1990, pp. 112–113.
64 Van de Wetering, in: Corpus IV, pp. 178–179.

65 Between the Buitenhof wing and the Vijver wing. Thus the series was not intended for Huis Noordeinde as was long assumed. The seven paintings were not brought to Noordeinde until after Frederik Hendrik's death in 1647. Van der Veen, in: The Hague 1997/98, p. 193.
66 According to Van de Wetering 2016, pp. 245–248.
67 Hoogstraten 1678, p. 75.
68 Broos, in: The Hague 1997/98, p. 196, note 16.
69 Houbraken 1718–1721, I, p. 255.
70 As proposed by R. E. O. Ekkart, in: Liedtke 2007, p. 576.
71 Huygens, *Mijn jeugd*, in: Heesakkers 1994, p. 88.
72 According to the files in the Stadsarchief Rotterdam, Notary Jan van Aller, Nr. 93, acts 145, 146 and 147, d.d. 12. and 13.-10.-1632, Nr. 99, act 23, d.d. 5 April 1633.
73 Van Dorp, who had a dubious reputation himself, was portrayed by Rembrandt in 1634. This oval bust portrait was lost and is only known from an engraving by Salomon Saverij.
74 Van der Veen, in: London/Amsterdam 2006, pp. 135–136.
75 Hoogstraten 1678, pp. 306–309. Developed in: Van de Wetering 1997, pp. 184–186; Van de Wetering 2016, pp. 76–78, 104, 206, 216, 221, 278.
76 On this development see Corpus II, pp. 99–106; Corpus VI, p. 66.
77 Schwartz 1984, p. 134.
78 For an overview and a commentary in the biographical facts relating to Saskia and her family, see: Broos 2012.
79 De Winkel 2006, p. 62.
80 See: Dudok van Heel, in: Berlin/Amsterdam/London 1991/92, pp. 55–56.
81 This in contrast to his earlier assistants Flinck and Bol. Both married women from a more genteel background, which was clearly reflected in the commissions which they received after their marriages. See Kok 2011 and Kok 2016.
82 See Broos 2005.
83 Dickey 2002.
84 Bomford et al. 2006, pp. 89–99, no. 6.
85 Bruyn 1987.
86 Corpus II, pp. 96–97.
87 Angel 1642, p. 47. Translation from Miedema and Hoyle 1996, p. 245.
88 Miedema 2017, p. 47.
89 Corpus V, pp. 166–167.
90 Hoogstraten 1678, p. 116; Van de Wetering, in: Corpus V, pp. 51–52.
91 Van Mander 1604, fol. 17v.; Van de Wetering, in: Corpus V, p. 166.
92 The term was introduced by Tümpel (1968, pp. 113–114).
93 Angel 1642, p. 55.
94 Van Mander 1604, fol. 28r.
95 Haussherr 1963.
96 Corpus III, p. 128.
97 Manuth 1990.
98 Neumann 1906, pp. 315–316 and De Winkel 2006, pp. 107, 311.
99 Weisbach 1926, p. 184.
100 Manuth 1990, pp. 174–181.
101 See here Broos 1977, p. 52; Manuth 1990, p. 195, note 36 and most recently Sluijter 2015, p. 48.
102 *Wtleggingh op den Metamorphosis*, Haarlem 1604, Book 4, fol. 33v.
103 Manuth 1990, pp. 188–193.
104 Lenz 1985, p. 150 and Manuth 1990, pp. 188–189 with fig. 18.
105 Van Rijckevorsel 1932, p.126, Figs. 149 and 150.
106 Angel 1642, p. 55. Translation in Hoyle and Miedema 1996, p. 245.
107 Huygens, in: Heesakkers 1994, p. 88.
108 Corpus III, p. 227.
109 Delft 2011.
110 Thus Corpus II, chapter III.
111 Houbraken 1718–1721, pp. 20–21.
112 Sluijter 2015; Amsterdam 2017; Dickey et al. 2017.

Illusionism and Reorientation 1640–1651

113 Dudok van Heel 2002, p. 54; Schnackenburg 1996, p. 241.
114 Van Thiel, in: Berlin/Amsterdam/London 1991/92, p. 175. Gloves were indeed a wedding present, but these had a special form of decoration; moreover, they were worn by the bride. Soolmans is wearing ordinary men's gloves. De Winkel 2006, pp. 85–88.
115 Corpus III, p. 308.
116 Corpus VI, p. 565.
117 Corpus III, p. 420; Van de Wetering, in: Amsterdam 2006, p. 115.
118 Van de Wetering 2006b, p. 94; Corpus VI, no. 184A.
119 Van Hoogstraten 1678, p. 176.
120 Ibid.
121 Baldinucci 1686, p. 78; Documents 360.
122 Van Hoogstraten 1678, p. 176.
123 Van de Wetering 2016, pp. 135, 138, 140–142, 171, 179–180.
124 Van Hoogstraten 1678, pp. 307–308. Cf. Van de Wetering 1991/92, pp. 32–33; Van de Wetering 1997, pp. 187–188.
125 Bontemantel 1897, p. 215.
126 Hijmans/Kuiper/Vels Heijn 1976, p. 64.
127 Van Dillen 1934; Martin 1947.
128 Dudok van Heel 2009b, p. 12. Cf. On the other hand: Schwartz 2006, p. 170, under note 44.
129 *Het geslachtsregister der heren en vrouwen van Purmerlandt en Ilpendam,* Amsterdam, Rijksmuseum, Inv.-no. SK-C-1102. See Documents 139; Carasso-Kok et al. 1988, p. 209, no. 27.
130 Wijnbeek 1944, p. 44.
131 Cf. Wijnbeek 1944, p. 42; Knevel 1994, pp. 108, 379–380; Middelkoop 2013, p. 35.
132 Biographical details in this chapter are based on: Dudok van Heel 2009a and 2009b.
133 Carasso-Kok et al. 1988, p. 208, under no. 26.
134 Dudok van Heel 1993, p. 20; Haverkamp-Begemann 1982, p. 78, note 17.
135 Dudok van Heel 2009a, p. 29. Cf. Corpus III (1985), p. 461.
136 Haverkamp-Begemann 1982, pp. 76–77.
137 Van Dyck 1758, pp. 58–61.
138 Haverkamp-Begemann 1982, pp. 9, 89, 90; Carasso-Kok et al. 1988, p. 208; Kist 1988, pp. 16–17; Dudok van Heel 2009a, p. 34.
139 Hijmans/Kuiper/Vels Heijn 1976, p. 59.
140 *Het geslachtsregister der heren en vrouwen van Purmerlandt en*

Ilpendam, Amsterdam, Rijksmuseum, Inv.-no. SK-C-1102. See Documents 139; Carasso-Kok et al. 1988, p. 209, no. 27.
141 Van Dyck 1758, p. 58.
142 Wagenaar 1760–1768, II (1765), p. 26.
143 Schendel/Mertens 1947, p. 10, note 2, p. 18; Kuiper/Hesterman 1976, p. 10.
144 Slive 1953, p. 5. This error can be traced back to Thoré-Bürger 1858, p. 16; Vosmaer 1868, p. 149; Dyserinck 1890, p. 258.
145 Pypers 1790, p. iii. Cf. The use of the word in van Hoogstraten 1678, p. 176.
146 Van Dyck 1758, pp. 58–59
147 Van de Wetering 2016, p. 260.
148 *Grondt der edel vry schilder-const*, published in 1604 as part of the *Schilder-Boeck*, see Miedema 1973, vol. 1, p. 86, v. 46, vol. 2, p. 388, I 46, f–g.
149 Thus Angel 1642, p. 36; see also Miedema 1973, vol. 2, p. 389.
150 Amsterdam 1999/2000, pp. 147–152.
151 This refers to Lucas van Leyden's engraving (Bartsch 158) with the beggar and his family from 1520.
152 Hoogstraten 1678, p. 212.
153 Sandrart 1675, as quoted in Peltzer 1925, p. 86 (in the biography of Lucas van Leyden).
154 On the high regard in which the art of Lucas van Leyden was held during the 16th and 17th centuries, see Cornelis/Filedt Kok 1998.
155 Tümpel 1969, pp. 182–185.
156 Broos, in: Amsterdam 1985/86, p. 55, nos. 45 and 44.
157 See here Wheelock 1983 and Broos, in: Amsterdam 1985/86, pp. 20–21.
158 Broos, in: Amsterdam 1985/86, pp. 20–21, nos. 3 and 4.
159 See Nuremberg 1978 and London 2002.
160 Białostocki 1986, p. 23.
161 Quoted from the translation by De Vere 1912–1916, vol. VI, p. 94 (1913) (Vasari in the Life of Marcantonio Raimondi).
162 Tümpel 1986a, p. 244.
163 Montias 2002, pp. 172–179 and Schauerte 2006.
164 The document published in the Rembrandt Documents (1638/2) is incomplete, see Schauerte 2006.
165 De Jongh 1969; Brown 1980, p. 4; Raupp 1984, pp. 169, 175–181.
166 De Bussierre, in: Paris 1986, p. 100; Dickey 1998, pp. 123–127; Manuth 1999, pp. 43–44; Dickey 2004, pp. 92–93.
167 Corpus III, p. 377.
168 De Winkel 2006, pp. 176–179.
169 Ibid., 178–179.
170 Ibid., 188–189.
171 Houbraken 1718–1721, p. 272.
172 On maidservants from Waterland in Amsterdam see De Winkel 2015/16, pp. 62–64.
173 Plomp 1997, pp. 300–301.
174 Schwartz 1984, p. 240.
175 The woman of the house was always responsible for appointing servants.
176 Schneider 2006/07, pp. 28–33.
177 Van de Wetering 2006a, p. 48.
178 De Winkel 2006, pp. 246–248.
179 From documentary sources and also from the reconstruction by Van de Wetering in Corpus VI, p. 527.
180 Crenshaw 2006, p. 31.
181 Sluijter 2015, chap. IIA.
182 Van de Wetering 2006b, passim.
183 Hoogstraten 1678, p. 116, Weststeijn 2010, pp. 266–267.
184 Berlin 2015, p. 31.
185 Bruyn et al., in: Corpus III (1987), pp. 215–219.
186 Roscam Abbing, in: London 1993, pp. 22–23.
187 Von Sandrart 1675, I, p. 326.
188 Houbraken 1718–1721, I, p. 256.
189 Liedtke, "Rembrandt's Pupils of the 1640s and later", in: New York 1995/96, II, pp. 26–31.
190 Gersaint 1751, p. xxviii.
191 Baldinucci 1686, p. 78; von Sandrart 1675, I, p. 326.

Rembrandt's Late Work 1652–1669

192 Hinterding 2001, pp. 137–148, 1160.
193 Van Eeghen 1969b; Vos/Roscam Abbing 2006, pp. 246–247. On Rembrandt and the van Cattenburch family, see also Roscam Abbing/Vos 2010.
194 Van Eeghen 1969a.
195 See also Broos 1983, pp. 26–27.
196 Crenshaw 2002, pp. 163–164.
197 See van der Veen, in: Amsterdam 1999/2000.
198 De Groot 1631, vol. I, part 12: *Van wettigen en onwettigen.*
199 On Hendrickje and other female art dealers in the 17th century, see Waltmans 2006.
200 Gersaint 1751, p. xxviii.
201 Lloyd Williams, in: Edinburgh/London 2001, pp. 14–15.
202 The Earl of Halifax auction, Christie's, London, 19–20 April 1782 (first day), no. 69 (Lugt 3409).
203 Sluijter 2006, pp. 352–358, excludes this.
204 Meijer 1991.
205 Hollstein IX, p. 252, no. 8; see Corpus III (1989), p. 207.
206 Rijckevorsel 1932, pp. 117–119; Busch 1989; Grohé 1996, pp. 199–204; Sluijter 2006, pp. 165–193.
207 Van Mander 1604, fol. 176v.
208 Held 1961, fig. 16, and Bikker, in: London/Amsterdam 2014/15, pp. 75–76.
209 Bikker, in: London/Amsterdam 2014/15, pp. 77–80.
210 Held 1969, p. 97, fig. 11; Golahny 1984, pp. 207–208.
211 Here, see especially Van de Wetering 1991/92a, pp. 16–21; Van de Wetering 1997, pp. 160–169; Bikker/Krekeler, in: London/Amsterdam, 2014/15, pp. 14, 140.
212 Houbraken 1718–1721, I, p. 259.
213 Van Mander 1604, fol. 174v–177v.
214 Ibid., fol. 48, 21–22.
215 Ibid., fol. 48v, 24–26; Bikker/Krekeler, in: London/Amsterdam 2014/15, pp. 138–143.
216 Van de Wetering 1991/92a, p. 21.
217 See Lugt 1936; Logan 1979 and 1991; Meijer 1991.
218 Logan 1979, pp. 236–242; Logan 1991, pp. 148–155.
219 See here Bikker/Krekeler, in: London/Amsterdam 2014/15, pp. 140–141 with fig. 53.
220 Dudok van Heel 1975.
221 De Lairesse 1707, p. 18.
222 Van de Wetering 1991/92, p. 22.
223 See Giltaij 1999; Rutgers 2003 and 2008.
224 Giltaij 2005, p. 48.
225 Ruffo 1916; Hoogewerff 1917 and Ricci 1918 were the first to publish these sources.

226 Giltaij 1999, pp. 85–94.
227 This shows unequivocally that it was a matter of two works from the beginning and that Rembrandt did not force the Homer on Ruffo unasked, as is sometimes erroneously claimed (see also below).
228 Amongst others Hoogewerff 1917; Broos 1987, p. 303; Brown/Roy 1992.
229 Giltaij 1999, pp. 55–66.
230 Giltaij 2005, pp. 47–48, on the basis of De Gennaro 2003.
231 Broos 1987, pp. 303, 306; followed in this thereafter by Rutgers 2003, p. 11; Sluijter 2008, pp. 14–15.
232 Slive 1953, p. 63; Broos 1971, p. 183; Bredius/Gerson 1969, no. 483.
233 This important passage is missing in RD 1661/5. See the facsimile in Ricci 1918, pp. 21–23; Giltaij 1999, p. 66. Moreover the transport costs for the Homer were also listed here.
234 Rutgers 2003, p. 13.
235 Giltaij 2005, pp. 48–49, on the basis of the documents in: De Gennaro 2001.
236 See also Rutgers 2003, pp. 7–10.
237 Corpus VI, p. 368.
238 Magnani 2007. All the facts referred to here derive from this article, to date the only source on this commission.
239 Until this point nothing was known of these two go-betweens. The financially powerful Benzi (Bentio, Bencio) came from Como. He married the Catholic Isabella Bosmans from Amsterdam in 1640; who was a member of the Vondel circle. He lived on Herengracht and was a merchant for corn, skins, Spanish wool and weapons from Spain and Italy. In 1646, he also shipped paintings from Venice to Amsterdam and back. Nationaal Archives The Hague, 1.03.01, No. 264, fol. 30v, dd. 16 August 1646. Voet, a Catholic, came from Antwerp, lived on Keizersgracht and married Maria Catharina Benzi in Amsterdam in 1661. Biographical information from: Doop/Trouw/Begraafregisters of the Amsterdam City Archive.
240 Sluijter 2015, pp. 52–53.
241 Von Sandrart 1675, II, book 3, p. 240; van Hoogstaten 1678, p. 212.
242 Baldinucci 1686, p. 80, through Rembrandt's former pupil Bernhard Keil.
243 Houbraken 1718–1721, I, p. 269.
244 Baldinucci 1686, p. 79.
245 Rotterdam 2006, p. 213, supplement 3, no. 58.
246 As previously set out by Welcker 1938, p. 269, and van den Boogert, in: Berlin 2006, p. 370.
247 Goeree 1668, p. 79.
248 Van Hoogstraten 1678, p. 31.
249 Houbraken 1718–1721, I, p. 271; von Sandrart 1675, II, p. 327.
250 Van Eeghen 1985, p. 55.
251 Ibid.
252 Ibid., p. 67.
253 See Cat. 79.
254 Paris/Philadelphia/Detroit 2011/12, Cat. 40, 39, 60.
255 See Cat. 79.
256 Slive 1965; Kelch 1975, p. 343.
257 On the poem, see Schwartz 1984, p. 284; Weber 1991, pp. 186–187, and Van der Molen 2015, p. 41.
258 See van der Molen 2015, pp. 41, 122 and 134, no. 18.
259 Bikker, in: London/Amsterdam 2014/15, pp. 229–230.
260 Thus Van de Wetering, in: Corpus VI, p. 669.
261 Bikker, in: London/Amsterdam 2014/15, pp. 229, 279 with notes 50 and 51; see Cat. 87.
262 Manuth 2005, pp. 39–55.
263 Houbraken 1718–1721, I, p. 272.
264 Ibid., I, p. 274.
265 Ibid., II, p. 21.
266 De Piles 1699, p. 422: "[…] il a fait quantité de Portraits, d'une force, d'une suavite & d'une vérité surprenantes."
267 Houbraken 1718–1721, I, p. 64.
268 Corpus VI, no. 226.
269 Houbraken 1718–1721, I, p. 259.
270 Ibid., I, p. 261.
271 Van der Veen, in: Melbourne/Canberra 1997/98, p. 77.
272 Van de Wetering 1997, pp. 203–204
273 Edinburgh/London 2001/02, p. 26; Broos/van Suchtelen 2004, pp. 219–220; Van der Veen, in: Amsterdam 1999/2000, p. 143; Corpus VI, pp. 683/84.
274 De Piles 1699, p. 433: "Et comme on luy reprochoit un jour la singularite de sa mattiere d'employer les Couleurs qui rendoient ses Tableaux raboteux, il repondit qu'il etoit Peintre, & non pas Teinturier."
275 Houbraken 1718–1721, I, p. 272.
276 Houbraken 1718–1721, II, pp. 258–259.
277 Liedtke 2007, II, p. 698.
278 For a description of its technique, see van de Wetering 1991/92, pp. 13–16 and Bikker and De Krekelder, in: London/Amsterdam 2014/15, pp. 147–150.
279 De Piles 1699, p. 427: "il étoit maître de ses couleurs, & qu'il en possedoit l'art en souverain."
280 Weber 2014/15, pp. 253–254.
281 Houbraken 1718–1721, II, pp. 22–23.
282 De Waal 1974, p. 35; De Winkel 2006, p. 206.
283 Franken 2004; Van de Wetering 2011a.
284 Eikema Hommes/Froment 2011.
285 Houbraken 1718–1721, I, p. 271.
286 Chapman 1990, pp. 88, 94–95; Slatkes 1992, no. 272.
287 Van Mander 1604, p. 301; Blankert 1973.
288 Corpus IV, no. 25.
289 Manuth 2005, pp. 44–45.
290 Geertje Dircks appealed from Gouda to the Amsterdam Reformed Church Council in 1652 for help (RD 1652/4). This indicates that she was a member, otherwise she could not have expected any assistance from them.
291 Manuth 1999, p. 51.
292 Corpus VI, 323.
293 Bredius 1909, pp. 239–240.
294 Hofstede de Groot 1906, nos. 317 and 320.
295 Houbraken 1718–1721, I, p. 272.
296 Baldinucci 1686, p. 79: "Quando operava, non avrebbe dato udienza al primo monarca del mondo."
297 Houbraken 1718–1721, I, p. 272.

Selected Bibliography

On the website of the Rembrandt Documents Project (RemDoc) you will find source material on Rembrandt's life and work (up to 100 years after his death): remdoc.org (http://remdoc.huygens.knaw.nl/). For technical information and research material on Rembrandt's paintings in important museums see the website of the Rembrandt database (The Rembrandt Database): www.rembrandtdatabase.org.

Amsterdam 1985/86: *Rembrandt en zijn voorbeelden/Rembrandt and His Sources*, exh. cat., ed. by Ben Broos, Amsterdam 1985.

Amsterdam 1991: *Pieter Lastman: Leermeester van Rembrandt/The Man who Taught Rembrandt*, exh. cat., ed. by Astrid Tümpel and Peter Schatborn, with contributions by Christian Tümpel, Ed de Heer and Marijke Holtrop, Zwolle 1991.

Amsterdam 1999/2000: *Rembrandt schatkamer/Rembrandt's Treasures*, ed. by Bob van den Boogert, Zwolle/Amsterdam 1999.

Amsterdam 2002/03: *Kopstukken: Amsterdammers geportretteerd, 1600–1800*, exh. cat., ed. by Jan Baptist Bedaux and Norbert Middelkoop, Bussum 2002.

Amsterdam 2006a: *Rembrandt – Caravaggio*, exh. cat., ed. by Duncan Bull et al., Zwolle 2006.

Amsterdam 2006b: *Rembrandt: zoektocht van een genie [Rembrandt: Quest of a Genius]*, exh. cat., ed. by Bob van den Boogert, Zwolle 2006.

Amsterdam 2015: *Rembrandts late leerlingen: In de leer bij een genie*, exh. cat., ed. by David de Witt and Jaap van der Veen, Amsterdam 2015.

Amsterdam 2017: *Rembrandt en Jan Six: de ets, de vriendschap*, exh. cat., ed. by Menno Jonker and Mariëlla Beukers, Amsterdam 2017.

Amsterdam/Groningen 1983: *The Impact of a Genius: Rembrandt, His Pupils and Followers in the Seventeenth Century: Paintings from Museums and Private Collections*, exh. cat., ed. by Albert Blankert, Ben Broos, Ernst van de Wetering, Guido Jansen and Willem van de Watering, Groningen 1983.

Angel, Philips, *Lof der Schilder-Konst*, Leiden 1642.

Baar, P. J. M. de, *De Leidse verwanten van Rembrandt van Rijn en hun Leidse afstammelingen tot heden*, Leiden 1992.

Baer, Ronni, "The Life and Art of Gerrit Dou,", in: Ronni Baer, *Gerrit Dou, 1613–1675: Master Painter in the Age of Rembrandt*, exh. cat. Washington/London/The Hague 2000/01, ed. by Arthur K. Wheelock Jr., Zwolle 2001, pp. 26–52.

Baldinucci, Filippo, *Cominciamento, e progresso dell'arte dell'intagliare in rame: colle vite di molti de' più eccellenti maestri della stessa professione*, ed. by Piero Marini, Florence 1686.

Berlin 2006: *Rembrandt: Genie auf der Suche*, exh. cat., ed. by Katja Kleinert and Bernd W. Lindemann, Cologne/Berlin 2006.

Berlin 2015: *Rembrandts Berliner Susanna und die beiden Alten: Die Schaffung eines Meisterwerks*, exh. cat., ed. by Holm Bevers, Katja Kleinert and Claudia Laurenze-Landsberg, Berlin 2015.

Berlin/Amsterdam/London 1991/92: *Rembrandt, De Meester & Zijn Werkplaats: Schilderijen*, exh. cat., ed. by Christopher Brown, Jan Kelch and Pieter J. J. van Thiel, Zwolle 1991.

Białostocki, Jan, *Dürer and His Critics, 1500–1971*, Baden-Baden 1986 (Saecula spiritualia, 7).

Bikker, Jonathan, "Emulation", in: London/Amsterdam 2014/15, pp. 74–97.

Bikker, Jonathan, *Marten and Oopjen. Two Monumental Portraits by Rembrandt*, Amsterdam 2016.

Bikker, Jonathan/Krekeler, Anna, "Experimental Technique: The Paintings", in: London/Amsterdam 2014/15, pp. 133–151.

Blankert, Albert, "Rembrandt, Zeuxis and Ideal Beauty", in: *Album Amicorum J. G. van Gelder*, ed. by Josua Bruyn, Jan A. Emmens, Eddy de Jongh and Derk P. Snoep, The Hague 1973, pp. 32–39.

Bomford et al. 2006: *Art in the Making: Rembrandt*, ed. by David Bomford, London 2006.

Bontemantel, Hans, *De regeeringe van Amsterdam, soo in 't civiel als crimineel en militaire (1653–1672)*, ed. by G. W. Kernkamp, 2 vols., The Hague 1897.

Boston/Kansas City 2015/16: *Class Distinctions: Dutch Painting in the Age of Rembrandt and Vermeer*, exh. cat., ed. by Ronni Baer, Boston MA 2015.

Bredius, Abraham, "Uit Rembrandt's laatste levensjaar", in: *Oud Holland* 27, 1909, pp. 238–240.

Bredius, Abraham/Gerson, Horst, *Rembrandt: the Complete Edition of the Paintings*, London 1969.

Broos, Ben P. J., "The 'O' of Rembrandt", in: *Simiolus* 4, 1971, pp. 150–184.

Broos, Ben P. J., *Index to the Formal Sources of Rembrandt's Art*, Maarssen 1977.

Broos, Ben P. J., "De bronnen over Rembrandt anno 1983", in: *Kroniek van het Rembrandthuis* 35, 1983, pp. 1–31.

Broos, Ben P. J., *Meesterwerken in het Mauritshuis*, The Hague 1987.

Broos, Ben P. J., "Rembrandts Zeeuwse connectie: François Coopal en Titia Uylenburgh", in: *Kroniek van het Rembrandthuis* 57, 2005, pp. 24–33.

Broos, Ben P. J., *Saskia: De Vrouw van Rembrandt*, Zwolle 2012.

Broos, Ben P. J./Suchtelen, Ariane van, *Portraits in the Mauritshuis, 1430–1790*, The Hague/Zwolle 2004.

Brown 1980: Brown, Christopher, *Second Sight: Titian, Portrait of a Man, and Rembrandt, Self-Portrait at the Age of 34*, London 1980.

Brown, Christopher/Roy, Ashok, "Rembrandt's 'Alexander the Great'", in: *The Burlington Magazine* 134, 1992, pp. 286–298.

Bruyn 1987: Bruyn, Josua, "Towards a Scriptural Reading of Seventeenth-Century Dutch Landcape Painting",

in: *Masters of Seventeenth-Century Dutch Landscape*, exh. cat. Amsterdam/Boston/Philadelphia 1987/88, ed. by Peter C. Sutton, Amsterdam 1987, pp. 84–103.
Busch, Werner, "Das keusche und das unkeusche Sehen. Rembrandts 'Diana, Aktaion und Callisto'", in: *Zeitschrift für Kunstgeschichte* 52, 1989, pp. 257–277.
Carasso-Kok et al. 1988: Carasso-Kok, Marijke/Levy-van Halm, J. [Koos]/Bergh-Hoogterp, Louise E. van den, *Schutters in Holland: kracht en zenuwen van de stad*, Zwolle 1988.
Chapman, H. Perry, *Rembrandt's Self-Portraits: A Study in Seventeenth-Century Identity*, Princeton NJ 1990.
Cornelis, Bart/Filedt Kok, Jan Piet, "The Taste for Lucas van Leyden Prints", in: *Simiolus* 26, 1998, pp. 18–86.
Corpus I, II, III: Bruyn, Josua/Haak, Bob/Levie, Simon H./Thiel, Pieter J. J. van/Wetering, Ernst van de, *A Corpus of Rembrandt Paintings*, vol. I (1982: *Rembrandt Paintings*, I, 1625–1631); vol. II (1986: *Rembrandt Paintings*, II, 1631–1634); vol. III (1989: *Rembrandt Paintings*, III, 1635–1642), The Hague/Boston MA/London 1982–1989 (Stichting Foundation Rembrandt Research Project).
Corpus IV: Wetering, Ernst van de et al., *A Corpus of Rembrandt Paintings*, IV, *The Self-Portraits*, Dordrecht 2005 (Stichting Foundation Rembrandt Research Project: A Corpus of Rembrandt Paintings, IV).
Corpus V: Wetering, Ernst van de et al., *A Corpus of Rembrandt Paintings*, V, *Small-Scale History Paintings*, Dordrecht 2011 (Stichting Foundation Rembrandt Research Project: A Corpus of Rembrandt Paintings, V).
Corpus VI: Wetering, Ernst van de et al., *Rembrandt's Paintings Revisited: A Complete Survey*, Dordrecht 2015 [2014] (Stichting Foundation Rembrandt Research Project: A Corpus of Rembrandt Paintings, VI).
Crenshaw, Paul, "Rembrandt's Declaration of Bankruptcy", in: *Rethinking Rembrandt*, ed. by Alan Chong and Michael Zell, Boston MA/Zwolle 2002, pp. 159–171.
Crenshaw, Paul, *Rembrandt's Bankruptcy: The Artist, His Patrons, and the Art Market in Seventeenth-Century Netherlands*, Cambridge UK/New York 2006.
Delft 2011: *De portretfabriek van Michiel van Mierevelt (1566–1641)*, exh. cat., ed. by Anita Jansen, Delft/Zwolle 2011.
Dickey, Stephanie S., *Prints, Portraits and Patronage in Rembrandt's Work around 1640*, PhD thesis University of Michigan, Ann Arbor MI 1998.
Dickey, Stephanie S., "Rembrandt and Saskia: Art, Commerce, and the Poetics of Portraiture", in: *Rethinking Rembrandt*, ed. by Alan Chong and Michael Zell, Boston MA/Zwolle 2002, pp. 17–47.
Dickey, Stephanie S., *Rembrandt: Portraits in Print*, Amsterdam/Philadelphia PA 2004 (Oculi: Studies in the Arts of the Low Countries, 9).
Dickey et al. 2017: *Rembrandt and His Circle: Insights and Discoveries*, ed. by Stephanie Dickey, Amsterdam 2017.
Dillen, Johannes G. van, "De sergeants en schutters van Rembrandts schuttersoptocht", in: *Jaarboek Amstelodamum* 31, 1934, pp. 97–110.
Dirkse, Paul, "Portretschilderijen van 'Arminiaense Santen'", in: *Rekkelijk of precies. Remonstranten en contraremonstranten ten tijde van Maurits en Oldenbarnevelt*, exh. cat., ed. by T.G. Kootte, Utrecht 1994, pp. 82–101.
Van Doorninck/Kuijpers 1993: Doornick, G. A. M. van/Kuijpers, Hendrica M. E. P., *De geschoolde stad: onderwijs in Amsterdam in de Gouden Eeuw. Amsterdamse historische reeks*, Amsterdam 1993.
Dudok van Heel, Sebastien A. C., "De kunstverzamelingen Van Lennep met de Arundel-tekeningen", in: *Jaarboek Amstelodamum* 67, 1975, pp. 137–148.
Dudok van Heel, Sebastien A. C., "De familie van de schilder Pieter Lastman (1583–1633): een vermaard leermeester van Rembrandt van Rijn", in: *Jaarboek van het Centraal Bureau voor Genealogie* 45, 1991, pp. 111–132.
Dudok van Heel, Sebastien A. C., "Rembrandt en de vaandrigs van de Amsterdamse schutterij: diende Rembrandts Vaandeldrager uit 1636 als 'modello'?", in: *Kroniek van het Rembrandthuis* 45, 1993, pp. 15–25.
Dudok van Heel, Sebastien A. C., "Rembrandt: His Life, His Wife, the Nursemaid and the Servant", in: Edinburgh/London 2001, pp. 19–27.
Dudok van Heel 2002: Dudok van Heel, Sebastien A. C., "Toen hingen er burgers als vorsten aan de muur", in: Amsterdam 2002/03, pp. 46–63.
Dudok van Heel, Sebastien A. C., *De jonge Rembrandt onder tijdgenoten: Godsdienst en schilderkunst in Leiden en Amsterdam*, Diss. Universität Nimwegen, Rotterdam 2006 (Nijmeegse kunsthistorische studies, 14).
Dudok van Heel 2009a: Dudok van Heel, Sebastien A. C., "Frans Banninck Cocq's Troop in Rembrandt's Night Watch: the Identification of the Guardsmen", in: *The Rijksmuseum Bulletin* 57, 2009, pp. 43–86.
Dudok van Heel 2009b: Dudok van Heel, Sebastien A. C., "The Night Watch and the Entry of Marie de' Medici: a New Identification of the Guardsmen", in: *The Rijksmuseum Bulletin* 57, 2009, pp. 5–41.
Dyck, Jan van, *Kunst en historiekundige beschryving en aanmerkingen over alle de schilderyen op het stadhuis te Amsterdam*, ed. by Pieter Yver, Amsterdam 1758.
Dyserinck, Johannes, "De Nachtwacht van Rembrandt", in: *De Gids* 54, 1890, pp. 235–276.
Edinburgh/London 2001: *Rembrandt's Women*, exh. cat., ed. by Julia Lloyd Williams, Munich 2001.
Van Eeghen 1969a: Eeghen, Isabella H. van, "De Restauratie van het voormalige Anslohofje", in: *Maandblad Amstelodamum* 56, 1969, pp. 199–205.
Van Eeghen 1969b: Eeghen, Isabella H. van, "Handboogstraat 5", in: *Maandblad Amstelodamum* 56, 1969, pp. 169–176.
Eeghen, Isabella H. van, "Anna Wijmer en Jan Six", in: *Jaarboek Amstelodamum* 76, 1984, pp. 38–68.
Eeghen, Isabella H. van, "Rembrandt en de veilingen (Titus van Rijn, Clement de Jonghe en Samuel Smijters)", in: *Maandblad Amstelodamum* 77, 1985, pp. 54–69.
Eikema Hommes, Margriet van/Froment, Emilie, "'Een doek van geene beteekenis': De nachtelijke samenzwering van Claudius Civilis in het Schakerbos van Govert Flinck

en Jürgen Ovens technisch onderzocht", in: *Oud Holland* 124, 2011, pp. 141–170.

Van Eikema Hommes et al. 2016: Eikema Hommes, Margriet van et al., "A hidden portrait by Govert Flinck discovered", in: *The Rijksmuseum Bulletin*, 2016, pp. 4–61.

Ekkart, Rudolf E. O., *Isaac Claesz. van Swanenburg, 1537–1614: Leids schilder en burgemeester*, Zwolle 1998.

Ekkart, Rudolf E. O., "Amsterdamse portretschilders in de zeventiende en achttiende eeuw", in: Amsterdam 2002/03, pp. 28–45.

Franken, Michiel, "Changing Direction: The Reconstruction of the Genesis of Rembrandt's Conspiracy of the Batavians under Claudius Civilis Reconsidered", in: *Art Bulletin of Nationalmuseum Stockholm* 11, 2004, pp. 75–82.

Freise, Kurt, *Pieter Lastman. Sein Leben und seine Kunst*, Leipzig 1911.

Gelder, Jan Gerrit van, *Rembrandt's vroegste ontwikkeling*, Separate printing of (overdruk van): "Rembrandt's vroegste ontwikkeling", in: *Mededelingen der Koninklijke Nederlandse Akademie van Wetenschappen, Afd. Letterkunde Nieuwe Reeks* 16, 1953, no. 5, pp. 273–300.

Gennaro, Rosanna De, "Aggiunta alle notizie sulla collezione di Antonio Ruffo. 'Nota di quadri vincolati in primogenitura.' scampati al terremoto del 5 febbraio 1783", in: *Napoli Nobilissima* 2, 2001, nos. 5–6, pp. 211–215.

Gennaro, Rosanna De, *Per il collezionismo del Seicento in Sicilia: L'inventario di Antonio Ruffo Principe della Scaletta*, Pisa 2003.

Gersaint, Edmé-François, *Catalogue raisonné de toutes les estampes qui forment l'œuvre de Rembrandt*, Paris 1751.

Giltaij, Jeroen, *Ruffo & Rembrandt: Over een Siciliaanse verzamelaar in de zeventiende eeuw die drie schilderijen bij Rembrandt bestelde*, Zutphen 1999.

Giltaij, Jeroen, "Nieuws omtrent Ruffo en Rembrandt", in: *Kroniek van het Rembrandthuis*, 2005, pp. 47–49.

Goeree, Wilhelmus (Willem), *Inleydinge tot de Al-ghemeene Teycken-Konst*, Middelburg 1668.

Golahny, Amy, *Rembrandt's Paintings and the Venetians Traditions*, PhD thesis University of Michigan, Ann Arbor MI 1984.

Golahny, Amy, *Rembrandt's Reading: The Artist's Bookshelf of Ancient Poetry and History*, Amsterdam 2003.

Golahny, Amy, "Pieter Lastman: Moments of Recognition", in: *The Passions in the Art of the Early Modern Netherlands, NKJ: Nederlands Kunsthistorisch Jaarboek/Netherlands Yearbook for History of Art* 60, 2010, pp. 179–201.

Gottwald, Franziska, *Das Tronie – Muster, Studie und Meisterwerk: Die Genese einer Gattung der Malerei vom 15. Jahrhundert bis zu Rembrandt*, Berlin/Munich 2011.

Grohé, Stefan, *Rembrandts mythologische Historien*, Diss. Universität Bochum, Cologne/Weimar/Vienna 1996.

De Groot, Hugo, *Inleydinge tot de Hollantsche rechtsgeleertheit*, The Hague 1631.

Haak, Bob, *Rembrandt: zijn leven, zijn werk, zijn tijd*, Amsterdam 1968.

Hamburg 2006: *Pieter Lastman: In Rembrandts Schatten?*, exh. cat., ed. by Martina Sitt, Munich 2006.

Haussherr, Reiner, "Zur Menetekel-Inschrift auf Rembrandts Belsazarbild", in: *Oud Holland* 78, 1963, pp. 142–149.

Haverkamp-Begemann, Egbert, *Rembrandt: The Nightwatch*, Princeton NJ 1982.

Heesakkers, C. L., *Constantijn Huygens. Mijn Jeugd*, Amsterdam 1994.

Held, Julius S., "Flora, Goddess and Courtesan", in: *De artibus opuscula*, XL: *Essays in Honor of Erwin Panofsky*, New York 1961, pp. 201–218.

Held, Julius S., *Rembrandt and the Book of Tobit*, 1964.

Held, Julius S., *Rembrandt's "Aristotle" and Other Rembrandt Studies*, Princeton NJ 1969.

Hijmans, Willem/Kuiper, Luitsen/Vels Heijn, Annemarie, *Rembrandts Nachtwacht: het vendel van Frans Banning Cocq, de geschiedenis van een schilderij*, Leiden 1976.

Hinterding, Erik, *Rembrandt als etser: twee studies naar de praktijk van productie en verspreiding/Rembrandt as an Etcher: Two Studies into the Practice of Production and Distribution: with a Summary in English*, Diss. Universität Utrecht, 2 vols., Utrecht 2001.

Hirschfelder, Dagmar, *Tronie und Porträt in der niederländischen Malerei des 17. Jahrhunderts*, Berlin 2008.

Hofstede de Groot, Cornelis, *Die Urkunden über Rembrandt (1575–1721)*, The Hague 1906.

Hoogewerff, Godefridus Johannes, "Rembrandt en een Italiaansche Maecenas", in: *Oud Holland* 35, 1917, pp. 129–148.

Hoogstraten, Samuel van, *Inleyding tot de hooge schoole der schilderkonst: anders de zichtbaere werelt*, Rotterdam 1678.

Houbraken, Arnold, *De groote schouburgh der nederlantsche konstschilders en schilderessen…*, 3 vols., The Hague 1718–1721.

Jongh, Eddy de, "The Spur of Wit: Rembrandt's Response to an Italian Challenge", in: *Delta: A Review of Arts, Life and Thought in the Netherlands* 12, 1969, no. 2, pp. 49–67.

Jonker, Menno, "Rembrandt's Philosopher: Aristotle in the Eye of the Beholder", in: *Journal of Historians of Netherlandish Art* 9, 2017, no. 1. Online: DOI: 10 5092/jhna. 2017. 9.1.12 (Last accessed on 11.3.2019).

Kassel/Leiden 2006/07: *Rembrandts landschappen/Rembrandt's Landscapes/Rembrandts Landschaften*, exh. cat., ed. by Christiaan J. J. Vogelaar, Gregor J. M. Weber and Boudewijn Bakker, Zwolle 2006.

Kelch, Jan, *Katalog der Gemäldegalerie der Staatlichen Museen Preußischer Kulturbesitz Berlin*, Berlin 1975 (1978).

Kist, Bas, "Een curieus militair tafereel", in: *De kroniek van het Rembrandthuis* 40, 1988, no. 1, pp. 1–23.

Knevel, Paul, *Burgers in het geweer: de schutterijen in Holland, 1550–1700*, Haarlem 1994.

Kok, Erna E., "Zonder vrienden geen carrière: de succesvolle loopbanen van Govert Flinck en Ferdinand Bol", in: *De Zeventiende Eeuw* 27, 2011, pp. 300–336.

Kok, Erna E., *Netwerkende kunstenaars in de Gouden Eeuw: de succesvolle loopbanen van Govert Flinck en Ferdinand Bol*, Hilversum 2016.

Kuiper, Luitsen/Hesterman, W., "Beschadiging en herstel van Rembrandts Nachtwacht", in: *Bulletin van het Rijksmuseum* 24, 1976, pp. 14–51.

Lairesse, Gerard de, *Het groot schilderboek*, Amsterdam 1707.

Leeuwen, Rudie van/Ruhe, Lilian, "De receptie en reproductie van Rembrandts geëtste portret van Jan Six", in: Amsterdam 2017, pp. 37–46.

Lenz, Christian, "Rembrandts Auseinandersetzung mit Rubens: Die Blendung Simsons", in: *Intuition und Darstellung: Festschrift für E. Hubala*, ed. by Frank Büttner and Christian Lenz, Munich 1985, pp. 137–158.

Liedtke, Walter, *Dutch Paintings in The Metropolitan Museum of Art*, 2 vols., New York 2007.

Logan, Anne-Marie S., *The 'Cabinet' of the Brothers Gerard and Jan Reynst*, Amsterdam/Oxford/New York 1979.

Logan, Anne-Marie S., "Kunstenaars, kooplieden en verzamelaars. Venetiaans-Amsterdamse kunsthandel in de zeventiende eeuw", in: *Amsterdam: Venetië van het Noorden*, exh. cat., ed. by Margriet de Roever, 's-Gravenhage/Amsterdam 1991, pp. 137–155.

London 1993: *Rembrandt van Rijn: Girl at a Window, Dulwich Picture Gallery*, exh. cat., ed. by Kate Bomford et al., London 1992 (Paintings & Their Context, 4).

London 2002: *Albrecht Dürer and his Legacy. The Graphic Work of a Renaissance Artist*, exh. cat., ed. by Giulia Bartrum, London/Princeton 2002.

London/Amsterdam 2006: *Uylenburgh & Zoon: Kunst en commercie van Rembrandt tot De Lairesse, 1625–1675/Uylenburgh & Son: Art and Commerce from Rembrandt to De Lairesse, 1625–1675*, exh. cat., ed. by Friso Lammertse and Jaap van der Veen, Amsterdam/Zwolle 2006.

London/Amsterdam 2014/15: *Rembrandt: The Late Works*, exh. cat., ed. by Jonathan Bikker, Gregor J.M. Weber, Marjorie E. Wieseman et al., London 2014.

London/The Hague 1999/2000: *Rembrandt by Himself*, exh. cat., ed. by Christopher Wright and Quentin Buvelot, London/The Hague/Zwolle 1999.

Lüdecke, Heinz/Heiland, Susanne, *Dürer und die Nachwelt*, Berlin 1955.

Lugt, Frits, "Italiaansche kunstwerken in Nederlandsche verzamelingen van vroeger tijden", in: *Oud Holland* 53, 1936, pp. 97–135.

Magnani, Lauro, "1666. Een onbekende opdracht uit Genua voor Rembrandt", in: *Kroniek van het Rembrandthuis* 59, 2007, pp. 3–18.

Mander, Carel van, *Het Schilder-Boeck: waerin Voor eerst de leerlustighe Iueght den grondt der Edelvry Schilderconst in verscheyden deelen Wort voorghedraghen*, Haarlem 1604.

Manuth, Volker, "Die Augen des Sünders: Überlegungen zu Rembrandts 'Blendung Simsons' von 1636 in Frankfurt", in: *Artibus et Historiae* 11, 1990, no. 21, pp. 169–198.

Manuth 1999: Manuth, Volker, "Rembrandt and the Artist's Self-Portrait: Tradition and Reception", in: London/The Hague 1999/2000.

Manuth, Volker, "Rembrandts Beschneidung in München: Entstehung und Funktion", in: *Rembrandt-Zeichnungen in München/The Munich Rembrandt Drawings: Beiträge zur Ausstellung Rembrandt auf Papier – Werk und Wirkung*, ed. by Thea Vignau-Wilberg, Munich 2003, pp. 115–125.

Manuth, Volker, "Tobias, Anna und das Böckchen: Variationen über ein Thema aus dem Buch Tobias von Rembrandt und Gerbrand vanden Eeckhout", in: *Collected Opinions: Essays on Netherlandish Art in Honour of Alfred Bader*, ed. by Volker Manuth and Axel Rüger, London 2004, pp. 88–105.

Manuth, Volker, "Rembrandt's Apostles: Pillars of Faith and Witnesses of the Word", in: *Rembrandt's Late Religious Portraits/Rembrandts late religieuze portretten*, exh. cat. Washington/Los Angeles 2005, ed. by Arthur K. Wheelock Jr., Zwolle 2005, pp. 38–55.

Manuth, Volker, "'Michael Agnolo van Caravaggio, die te Room wonderlijkcke dinghen doet': Over Rembrandts kennis van het leven en werk van Caravaggio/'Michelangelo of Caravaggio, who Does Wondrous Things in Rome': On Rembrandt's Knowledge of Caravaggio", in: *Rembrandt – Caravaggio*, exh. cat., ed. by Duncan Bull et al., Zwolle 2006, pp. 180–193.

Manuth, Volker, "Jan Six als kunstverzamelaar", in: Amsterdam 2017, pp. 8–19.

Manuth, Volker, "Lemma Rembrandt", in: *SAUR Allgemeines Künstler-Lexikon: Die Bildenden Künstler Aller Zeiten und Völker*, vol. 98, Berlin/Boston MA 2018, pp. 213–215.

Manuth, Volker/Winkel, Marieke de, *Rembrandt's Minerva in Her Study of 1635: The Splendor and Wisdom of a Goddess*, New York 2002.

Melbourne/Canberra 1997/98: *Rembrandt: A Genius and His Impact*, exh. cat., ed. by Albert Blankert et al., Zwolle 1997.

Meijer, Bert W., *Rondom Rembrandt en Titiaan. Artistieke relaties tussen Amsterdam en Venetië in prent en tekening*, 's-Gravenhage 1991.

Middelkoop, Norbert, "'Met schutterschilderijen behangen': De Amsterdamse schutterstukken in de drie doelens", in: *De Amsterdamse schutterstukken: Inrichting en gebruik van de doelengebouwen in de zeventiende eeuw*, ed. by Norbert Middelkoop, Judith van Gent, Marten Jan Bok and Wouter Kloek, Amsterdam 2013 (= *Jaarboek Amstelodamum* 105, 2013, pp. 12–90).

Miedema 1973: *Karel van Mander. Den grondt der edel vry schilder-const*, ed. by Hessel Miedema, 2 vols., Utrecht 1973.

Miedema, Hessel, *Theorie en praktijk. Teksten over schilderkunst in de Gouden Eeuw van de Noordelijke Nederlanden*, Hilversum 2017.

Molen, Tom van der, *Govert Flinck: Reflecting History*, exh. cat., Kleve 2015.

Montias, John Michael, *Art at Auction in 17th Century Amsterdam*, Amsterdam 2002.

Neumann, Carl, "Ein orientalischer Dolch auf Rembrandts Gemälde der Blendung Simsons in Frankfurt am Main", in: *Studien aus Kunst und Geschichte. Friedrich Schneider zum siebzigsten Geburtstage gewidmet*, Freiburg im Breisgau 1906, pp. 315–316.

New York 1995/96: *Rembrandt/Not Rembrandt in the Metropolitan Museum of Art: Aspects of Connoisseurship*, exh. cat., 2 vols.

(I: *Paint-ings: Problems and Issues*, ed. by Hubertus von Sonnenburg; II. *Paintings, Drawings, and Prints: Art-Historical Perspectives*, ed. Walter A. Liedtke et al.), New York 1995.

Nuremberg 1978: *Vorbild Dürer*, exh. cat., ed. by Peter Strieder and Leonie von Wilkens, Nuremberg/Munich 1978.

Orlers, Jan J., *Beschreyvinge der Stadt Leyden*, Leiden 1641.

Paris 1986: *Rembrandt: Eaux-fortes*, exh. cat., ed. by Sophie de Bussierre, Paris 1986.

Paris/Philadelphia/Detroit 2011/12: *Rembrandt and the Face of Jesus*, exh. cat., ed. by Lloyd deWitt et al., Philadelphia PA 2011.

Piles, Roger de, *Abregé de la vie des peintres, avec des réflexions sur leurs ouvrages*, Paris 1699.

Plomp, Michiel, C., *The Dutch Drawings in the Teyler Museum: Artists Born between 1575 and 1630*, Doornspijk 1997.

Pypers, Pieter, *Stephanus, de eerste christen bloedgetuige: Treurspel (Tooneel- en dichtwerken van Pieter Pypers, Bd. XI)*, ed. by Matthys Schalekamp, Amsterdam 1790.

Raupp, Hans-Joachim, *Untersuchungen zu Künstlerbildnis und Künstlerdarstellung in den Niederlanden im 17. Jahrhundert*, Hildesheim/Zurich/New York 1984.

Ricci, Corrado, *Rembrandt in Italia*, Milan 1918.

Rijckevorsel, Joannes L. A. A. M. van, *Rembrandt en de traditie*, Rotterdam 1932.

Roscam Abbing, Michiel/Vos, Aart, "Een nieuwe Rembrandt-vermelding. De familie Van Cattenburch en Rembrandt", in: *Bossche Bladen* 1, 2010, pp. 14–23.

Rotterdam 2006: Waals, Jan van der, *Prenten in de Gouden eeuw: Van kunst tot kastpapier*, exh. cat., ed. by Peter van der Coelen, Rotterdam 2006.

Ruffo, Vincenzo, "Galleria Ruffo nel secolo XVII in Messina (con lettere di pittori ed altri documenti inediti)", in: *Bollettino d'Arte* 10, 1916, pp. 21–64, 95–128, 237–256, 284–320, 369–388.

Rutgers Jaco, "'Sijn' kunstfaem over 't spits der Alpen heen gevlogen? Rembrandts naam en faam in Italië in de zeventiende eeuw", in: *Kroniek van het Rembrandthuis* 2003, 1/2, pp. 2–19.

Rutgers, Jaco, *Rembrandt in Italië: Receptie en verzamelgeschiedenis*, Diss. Universität Utrecht 2008.

Sandrart, Joachim von, *Teutsche Academie der Bau-, Bild- und Mahlerey-Künste*, Nuremberg 1675.

Joachim von Sandrarts Academie der Bau-, Bild- und Mahlerey-Künste von 1675, ed. by A. R. Peltzer, Munich 1925.

Schauerte, Thomas, "Dürer und Spranger: Ein Autographenfund im Spiegel der europäischen Sammlungsgeschichte. Mit einer Transkription der Amsterdamer Auktionsliste vom Februar 1638", in: *Mitteilungen des Vereins für Geschichte der Stadt Nürnberg* 93, 2006, pp. 25–69.

Schendel, Arthur van/Mertens, H. H., "De restauraties van Rembrandt's Nachtwacht", in: *Oud Holland* 62, 1947, no. 1, pp. 1–52.

Schnackenburg, Bernhard, *Gemäldegalerie Alte Meister: Gesamtkatalog, Staatliche Museen Kassel*, 2 vols., Mainz 1996.

Schnackenburg, Bernhard, *Jan Lievens. Freund und Rivale des jungen Rembrandt*, Petersberg 2016.

Schneider, Cynthia P., "Rembrandts landschappen: de uitzondering die de regel bevestigt", in: Kassel/Leiden 2006/07, pp. 13–35.

Schwartz, Gary, *Rembrandt: zijn leven, zijn schilderijen: een nieuwe biografie met alle beschikbare schilderijen in kleur afgebeeld*, Maarssen 1984 (*Rembrandt: His Life, His Paintings: a New Biography with all Accessible Paintings Illustrated in Colour*, Harmondsworth 1985).

Schwartz, Gary, *De grote Rembrandt*, Zwolle 2006.

Seifert, Christian Tico, *Pieter Lastman. Studien zu Leben und Werk. Mit einem kritischen Verzeichnis der Werke mit Themen aus der antiken Mythologie und Historie*, Petersberg 2011.

Slatkes, Leonard J., *Rembrandt and Persia*, New York 1983.

Slatkes, Leonard J., *Rembrandt: Catalogo completo dei dipinti*, Florence 1992 (Gigli dell'arte, 23).

Slive, Seymour, *Rembrandt and His Critics*, The Hague 1953.

Slive, Seymour, "An Unpublished 'Head of Christ' by Rembrandt", in: *The Art Bulletin* 47, 1965, pp. 407–417.

Sluijter, Eric Jan, *Rembrandt and the Female Nude*, Amsterdam 2006.

Sluijter, Eric Jan, "Rembrandts Jeremia treurend om de verwoesting van Jeruzalem en een tragedie van Guilliam van Nieuwelandt", in: *De verbeelde wereld: Liber amicorum voor Boudewijn Bakker*, ed. by Jaap E. Abrahamse et al., Bussum 2008, pp. 127–140.

Sluijter, Eric Jan, *Rembrandt's Rivals: History Painting in Amsterdam, 1630–1650*, Amsterdam/Philadelphia 2015 (Oculi: Studies in the Arts of the Low Countries, 14).

Straten, Roelof van, *Rembrandts Leidse Tijd, 1606–1632*, Leiden 2005 (*Rembrandts Weg zur Kunst. 1606–1632*. Berlin 2006).

Strauss, Walter L./Meulen, Marjon van der, *The Rembrandt Documents*, New York 1979.

The Hague 1997/98: *Vorstelijk vertoon: Aan het hof van Frederik Hendrik en Amalia*, ed. by Marika Keblusek and Jori Zijlmans, Zwolle 1997.

Thoré-Bürger, Théophile E. [Burger, William], *Musées de la Hollande: Amsterdam et La Haye: Études sur l'ecole hollandaise*, Paris 1858 (1st edition "Rembrandt au musée d'Amsterdam", in: *L'Artiste: Journal de la littérature et des beaux-arts* 40, 1858, pp. 182–188.

Tümpel, Christian, "Ikonographische Beiträge zu Rembrandt: Zur Deutung und Interpretation seiner Historien", in: *Jahrbuch der Hamburger Kunstsammlungen* 13, 1968, pp. 95–126.

Tümpel, Christian, "Studien zur Ikonographie der Historien Rembrandts: Deutung und Interpretation der Bildinhalte", in: *NKJ: Nederlands Kunsthistorisch Jaarboek/Netherlands Yearbook for History of Art* 20, 1969, pp. 107–198.

Tümpel, Christian, "Ikonographische Beiträge zu Rembrandt: Zur Deutung und Interpretation einzelner Werke (II)", in: *Jahrbuch der Hamburger Kunstsammlungen* 16, 1971, pp. 20–38.

Tümpel 1986a: Tümpel, Christian/Tümpel, Astrid, *Rembrandt: Mythos*

und Methode, Königstein im Taunus 1986 (Dutche edition: *Rembrandt*, Antwerp 1986).
Tümpel 1986b: Tümpel, Christian, "Bild und Text: Zur Rezeption antiker Autoren in der europäischen Kunst der Neuzeit (Livius, Valerius Maximus)", in: *Forma et subtilitas. Feestbundel voor Wolfgang Schöne*, ed. by Wilhelm Schlink and Martin Sperlich, Berlin/New York 1986, pp. 198–218.
Tümpel, Christian, "Pieter Lastman en Rembrandt", in: *Pieter Lastman: Leermeester van Rembrandt/The Man who Taught Rembrandt*, ed. by Astrid Tümpel and Peter Schatborn, Zwolle 1991, pp. 54–84.
Veen, Jaap van der, "Faces from Life: *Tronies* and Portraits in Rembrandt's Painted Oeuvre", in: Melbourne/Canberra 1997/98, pp. 69–80.
Veen, Jaap van der, "Eenvoudig en stil: Studeerkamers in 17de-eeuwse woningen, voornamelijk te Amsterdam, Deventer en Leiden", in: *Wooncultuur in de Nederlanden, 1500–1800/The Art of Home in the Netherlands, 1500–1800*, ed. by Jan L.de Jong, Zwolle 2001 (= *NKJ: Nederlands Kunsthistorisch Jaarboek/Netherlands Yearbook for History of Art* 51, 2000), pp. 137–171.
Veen, Jaap van der, "Hendrick Uylenburgh's Art Business, Production and Trade between 1625 and 1655/Het kunstbedrijf van Hendrick Uylenburgh in Amsterdam. Productie en handel tussen 1625 en 1655", in: London/Amsterdam 2006, pp. 117–205.
Vondel, Joost van den, in: *Hollantsche Parnas, of verscheide gedichten gerijmt door J. Westerbaen, J v. Vondel, J. Vos, G. Brant, R. Anslo*, ed. by Tobias van Domselaar, Amsterdam 1660.
Vos, Aart/Roscam Abbing, Michiel, "The Cattenburch Family and Rembrandt", in: *Rembrandt 2006: Essays*, 2 vols., ed. by Michiel Roscam Abbing, Leiden 2006, I, pp. 239–250.
Vosmaer, Carel, *Rembrandt Harmens van Rijn: Sa vie et ses œuvres*, The Hague 1868 (2nd edition 1877).
Waal, Henri van de, *Steps towards Rembrandt: Collected Articles 1937–1972*, ed. by Rudi Fuchs, Amsterdam 1974.
Wagenaar, Jan, *Amsterdam, in zyne opkomst, aanwas, geschiedenissen, voorzegten ...*, 4 vols., Amsterdam 1760–1768.
Walle, Kees, *Buurthouden. De geschiedenis van burengebruiken en buurtorganisaties in Leiden (14e–19e eeuw)*, Leiden 2005.
Waltmans, Astrid, *Hendrickje Stoffels. Een meisje uit de provincie in een Amsterdams kunstenaarsmilieu*, IJzerlo 2006.
Washington/Milwaukee/Amsterdam 2008/09: *Jan Lievens: A Dutch Master Rediscovered*, exh. cat., ed. by Arthur K. Wheelock Jr., Zwolle 2009.
Weber, Gregor J. M., *Der Lobtopos des "lebenden" Bildes: Jan Vos und sein "Zeege der schilderkunst" van 1654*, Hildesheim 1991.
Weber Gregor J. M., "Reconcilation", in: London/Amsterdam 2014/15, pp. 252–269.
Weisbach, Werner, *Rembrandt*, Berlin/Leipzig 1926.
Welcker, Albertus, "Titus van Rhijn als teekenaar", in: *Oud Holland* 55, 1938, pp. 268–273.
Weststeijn, Thijs, "Between Mind and Body: Painting the Inner Movements According to Samuel van Hoogstraten and Franciscus Junius", in: *The Passions in the Arts of the Early Modern Netherlands/De hartstochten in de kunst in de vroegmoderne Nederlanden*, ed. by Stephanie S. Dickey and Herman Roodenburg, Zwolle 2010 (= *NKJ: Nederlands Kunsthistorisch Jaarboek/Netherlands Yearbook for History of Art* 60, 2010), pp. 261–281.
Wetering, Ernst van de, "Isaac Jouderville, a Pupil of Rembrandt", in: Amsterdam/Groningen 1983, pp. 59–69.
Van de Wetering 1991/92: Wetering, Ernst van de, "Rembrandts schilderwijze: techniek in dienst van illusie", in: Berlin/Amsterdam/London 1991/92a, pp. 12–39.
Wetering, Ernst van de, *Rembrandt: The Painter at Work*, Amsterdam 1997.
Van de Wetering 2006a: Wetering, Ernst van de, "Rembrandt, a Biography", in: Amsterdam 2006b, pp. 27–64.
Van de Wetering 2006b: Wetering, Ernst van de, "Rembrandt als zoekende kunstenaar/Rembrandt as a Searching Artist", in: Amsterdam 2006b, pp. 79–123.
Van de Wetering 2006c: Ernst van de, "Rembrandt, eine Biographie", in: Berlin 2006, pp. 21–49.
Wetering, Ernst van de, *Rembrandt: the Painter Thinking*, Amsterdam 2016.
Wheelock, Arthur K. Jr., "The Influence of Lucas van Leyden on Rembrandt's Narrative Etchings", in: *Essays in Northern European Art: Presented to Egbert Haverkamp-Begemann on His Sixtieth Birthday*, Doornspijk 1983, pp. 291–296.
Wijnbeek, David, *De Nachtwacht: De historie van een meesterwerk*, Amsterdam 1944.
Winkel, Marieke de, "Het kostuum in Rembrandts zelfportretten", in: *Rembrandt Zelf*, exh.-cat. London/The Hague 1999/2000, ed. Edwin Buijsen, Zwolle 1999, pp. 58–74.
Winkel, Marieke de, "De sieraden van 'Het Joodse Bruidje'", in: *Nieuw Israëlitisch Weekblad*, 8.12.2000, p. 25.
Winkel, Marieke de, "Fashion or Fancy? Some Interpretations of the Dress of Rembrandt's Women Re-Evaluated", in: London/Edinburgh 2001, pp. 55–63.
Winkel, Marieke de, "Rembrandt's Clothes – Dress and Meaning in His Self-Portraits", in: Ernst van de Wetering et al., *A Corpus of Rembrandt Paintings, IV, The Self-Portraits*, Dordrecht 2005 (Stichting Foundation Rembrandt Research Project: A Corpus of Rembrandt Paintings, IV), pp. 45–87.
Winkel, Marieke de, *Fashion and Fancy: Dress and Meaning in Rembrandt's Paintings*, Amsterdam 2006.
Winkel, Marieke de, "Rembrandt en Jan Six, een vriendschap in portretten", in: Amsterdam 2017, pp. 20–27.
Winkel, Marieke de, "Ambition and Apparel. Dress of Domestic Servants in 17th-century Holland", in: Boston/Kansas City 2015/16, pp. 55–71.
Witt, David de, *The Bader Collection: Dutch and Flemish Paintings*, Kingston (Ontario) 2008.

Photo Credits

The following abbreviations below stand for: l. = left, r. = right.

Agnes Etherington Art Centre, Queen's University, Kingston, Ontario, Photo: Paul Litherland: pp. 77, 125
akg-images/Erich Lessing: p. 143
Albertina, Vienna: pp. 110, 328
Collection Amsterdam Museum: p. 465
Archive of the publisher, the authors or collectors: pp. 68/69, 184, 186, 198, 230, 262, 297, 330, 363, 377, 397, 420, 442
Art Gallery of Ontario, Toronto, Kanada/Bequest of Frank P. Wood, 1955/Bridgeman Images: p. 427
Photography © The Art Institute of Chicago: p. 255
© ARTOTHEK: p. 177
© Ashmolean Museum, University of Oxford: p. 19
Aurora Trust/Bridgeman Images: p. 356
The Baltimore Museum of Art: The Mary Frick Jacobs Collection, Photography by Mitro Hood: p. 437
Bildergalerie von Sanssouci, Potsdam: p. 252
© Blauel Gnamm – ARTOTHEK: pp. 29, 79, 183, 185, 187–191, 443
Museum Boijmans Van Beuningen, Rotterdam. Loan: Museum Boijmans Van Beuningen Foundation/ Photographer: Studio Tromp, Rotterdam: pp. 274, 433
Museum Boijmans Van Beuningen, Rotterdam. Loan Willem van der Vorm Foundation: p. 165
bpk | Gemäldegalerie, SMB | Photo: Luciano Romano: pp. 174/175, 208–210, 213, 232/233, 235
bpk | Gemäldegalerie, SMB | Photo: Christoph Schmidt: pp. 62, 64/65, 242, 244/245, 322/323, 394, 415, 428–429, 439, bpk | Reinhard Görner: p. 489
bpk | Hamburger Kunsthalle: p. 66
bpk | Hamburger Kunsthalle | Elke Walford: p. 170
bpk | The Metropolitan Museum of Art: pp. 160, 253, 381, 421, 430/431, 445, 450, 451, 468–469, 486
bpk | The Metropolitan Museum of Art | Malcolm Varon: pp. 100, 149, 151, 308
bpk | Staatliche Kunstsammlungen Dresden | Elke Estel | Hans-Peter Klut: pp. 193, 204, 248/249, 353, 248/249
bpk | Staatliche Kunsthalle Karlsruhe | Wolfgang Pankoke: pp. 303, 333
bpk | Kupferstichkabinett, SMB | Jörg P. Anders: p. 107
Museum Catharijneconvent, The Netherlands/Tarker/Bridgeman Images: p. 47
Photo © Christie's Images/Bridgeman Images: p. 161
Detroit Institute of Arts, USA/ Bridgeman Images: pp. 342/343, 345
© Devonshire Collection, Chatsworth/ Reproduced by permission of Chatsworth Settlement Trustees/Bridgeman Images: pp. 273, 367
Dulwich Picture Gallery, London, UK/Bridgeman Images: pp. 171, 357
© Edinburgh, National Gallery of Scotland (Bridgewater Loan, 1945): pp. 361, 481
© The Faringdon Collection: p. 426
Fine Arts Museums of San Francisco: p. 173
Fondation Custodia, Collection Frits Lugt, Paris: pp. 46, 98
© The Frick Collection: pp. 105, 132, 369, 485
Isabella Stewart Gardner Museum, Boston, MA, USA/Bridgeman Images: pp. 40, 82, 227
Digital image courtesy of the Getty's Open Content Program: pp. 16, 75, 80, 216/217
Germanisches Nationalmuseum, Nuremberg: p. 59
Germanisches Nationalmuseum, Nuremberg. Loan Kunstsammlungen der Stadt Nürnberg. Photo: J. Musolf: back cover, pp. 30, 81
Getty Images/Hulton Archive: p. 129
© CSG CIC Glasgow Museums Collection/Bridgeman Images: pp. 87, 195, 355
The Armand Hammer Collection, Gift of the Armand Hammer Foundation. Hammer Museum, Los Angeles: pp. 311, 423
Photograph © The State Hermitage Museum/photo by Vladimir Terebenin, Pavel Demidov: pp. 141, 202, 231, 309, 339, 341, 385
Herzog Anton Ulrich-Museum, Braunschweig, Kunstmuseum des Landes Niedersachsen. Museums photographer: pp. 97, 424/425
Herzog August Bibliothek, Wolfenbüttel: p. 461
Hessen Kassel Heritag, Gemäldegalerie Alte Meister: pp. 122, 142, 201, 220/221, 257, 306, 334/335, 447, 472/473, 479
© Historic England: pp. 8–9, 492
Indianapolis Museum of Art, Courtesy of The Clowes Fund: p. 85
Innsbruck, Tiroler Landesmuseen: p. 76
The Israel Museum, Jerusalem, Israel/Gift of Michael and Judy Steinhardt/Bridgeman Images: pp. 33, 56
Photo Josse/Scala, Florence: p. 169
KHM-Museumsverband: pp. 362, 436, 476, 482–483
Koninklijke Bibliotheek, The Hague: p. 411
Kunsthaus Zürich, Zurich/Bridgeman Images: p. 444
Kunstmuseum Basel, Vermächtnis Max Geldner, Basel 1958: pp. 54/55
Digital Image Museum Associates/ LACMA/Art Resource NY/Scala, Florence: pp. 63, 133, 162
© Museum Associates/LACMA, Photo: p. 63
Museum De Lakenhal, Leiden; Loan from the Collection Cultural Heritage Agency of the Netherlands: pp. 48/49, 73 l.
Image courtesy of The Leiden Collection, New York: pp. 72, 73 r., 146, 229, 256, 260
© Lukas – Art in Flanders VZW/ Bridgeman Images: p. 307
Image © Lyon MBA – Photo: Alain Basset: p. 43
Mauritshuis, The Hague: pp. 136–139, 207, 211, 243

Mauritshuis, The Hague, on perman-ent loan from Stichting Historische Verzamelingen van het Huis Oranje-Nassau: p. 168 l.
Mauritshuis, The Hague/Bridgeman Images: pp. 10, 432, 463, 494
Minneapolis Institute of Arts, MN, USA/The William Hood Dunwoody Fund: p. 1
Minneapolis Institute of Arts, MN, USA/The William Hood Dunwoody Fund/Bridgeman Images: p. 477
Image Copyright Museo Nacional del Prado © Photo MNP/Scala, Florence: p. 228
Museo Nacional Thyssen-Bornemisza/ Scala, Florence: p. 305
Museum of Fine Arts, Boston, Massachusetts, USA/William K. Richardson Fund/Bridgeman Images: pp. 134–135
Museum of Fine Arts, Boston, Massachusetts, USA/Zoe Oliver Sherman Collection/Bridgeman Images: pp. 70/71
Photograph © The Museum of Fine Arts, Houston: pp. 121, 147
Museum Rotterdam: p. 103
Photograph © National Gallery in Prague 2015: pp. 2/3, 251
The National Gallery, London: pp. 164, 203, 236/237, 265, 285, 331, 346/347, 349, 404, 413, 414, 417, 454–455, 459, 491, 495
National Gallery of Art, Washington, DC: pp. 254, 259, 263, 374, 407, 452–453, 487
Photo National Gallery of Canada: p. 212
Photo © National Gallery of Ireland: pp. 336/337
National Gallery of Victoria, Melbourne, Felton Bequest: p. 61
© Photo Nationalmuseum, Stockholm: pp. 84, , 359, 378, 499
The Nelson-Atkins Museum of Art, Kansas City, Missouri. Purchase: William Rockhill Nelson Trust, 31–75: p. 462
North Carolina Museum of Art, Raleigh: p. 25
© Norton Simon Art Foundation: pp. 166, 456
© The Norton Simon Foundation: pp. 131, 199
Photo Art Media/Heritage Images/ Scala, Florence: pp. 240/241
Prince of Salm-Salm, Anholt: pp. 214/215
Pushkin Museum, Moscow: p. 42
The Putnam Foundation, Timken Museum of Art, San Diego, USA/ Bridgeman Images: p. 441
Photo: Rheinisches Bildarchiv, Cologne, Britta Schlier: p. 491
Museum Het Rembrandthuis, Amsterdam: p. 401
Rijksmuseum, Amsterdam: front cover, pp. 6/7, 15, 26 r., 35, 36, 39, 51–53, 60, 78, 88, 91–92, 95, 113, 117, 119, 159, 163, 194, 205, 218/219, 223, 224, 277, 278, 279, 281, 286, 291–292, 321, 324–327, 329, 344, 364, 382, 389, 391, 393, 435, 466/467, 470/471, 488
Photo © RMN-Grand Palais | Agence Bulloz: pp. 45, 83
Photo © RMN-Grand Palais (musée du Louvre) | Hervé Lewandowski: pp. 178/179, 181, 196, 386, 438, 489
Photo © RMN-Grand Palais (musée du Louvre) | Thierry Le Mage: pp. 350/351
Photo © RMN-Grand Palais (musée du Louvre) | René-Gabriel Ojéda: p. 197
Photo © RMN-Grand Palais (musée du Louvre) | Mathieu Rabeau: pp. 152–157, 418/419
Photo © RMN-Grand Palais (musée du Louvre) | Michel Urtado: p. 440
Photo © RMN-Grand Palais (musée du Louvre) | Tony Querrec: pp. 460, 489
The Royal Castle in Warsaw – Museum, Photo: Andrzej Ring, Lech Sandzewicz: pp. 294, 319,
Royal Collection Trust/© His Majesty King Charles III: pp. 144/145, 247, 266, 313–315, 332
© Royal Museums of Fine Arts of Belgium, Brüssel/image by Google: pp. 283, 312
Photo Scala, Florence – courtesy of the Ministero Beni e Att. Culturali e del Turismo: pp. 403, 497
© Scottish National Gallery: pp. 26 l., 358
© Six Collection, Amsterdam: pp. 4/5, 289, 316, 448
© Sotheby's 2019: p. 261
Collection of the Speed Art Museum, Louisville, Kentucky: p. 167
Staatliche Graphische Sammlung, Munich: p. 398
© Photo: Staatsgalerie Stuttgart: p. 67
© Städel Museum – ARTOTHEK: pp. 238/239
© Städel Museum – U. Edelmann – ARTOTHEK: p. 225
Stichting Historische Verzamelingen van het Huis Oranje-Nassau, The Hague: p. 168 r.
Stockholm, The Royal Academy of Fine Arts: pp. 474/475
Taft Museum of Art, Cincinnati, Ohio, USA/Bequest of Charles Phelps and Anna Sinton Taft/ Bridgeman Images: p. 148
Teylers Museum, Haarlem, The Netherlands: p. 300 r.
© The Trustees of The British Museum: pp. 273, 300 l., 370
Galleria degli Uffizi, Florence – Su concessione del Ministero dei Beni e delle Attività Culturali e del Turismo: p. 114
Reproduced by kind permission from the Board of the University of Dublin, Trinity College Dublin, Ireland: p. 20
Wallace Collection, London, UK/ Bridgeman Images: p. 434

Imprint

Authors' acknowledgements
Comprehensively representing an artist's work poses an enormous challenge, especially when the artist is as prominent and controversial as Rembrandt. The authors are gratefully aware that they have profited from the work of the many experts who have studied Rembrandt in the past – even when conclusions reached by some of them were different ones. We should like to thank in particular our friend and colleague David DeWitt, who informed us of the current whereabouts of some of the paintings. And we should like to thank Petra Lamers-Schütze and particularly Ute Kieseyer and Brigitte Beier for the close cooperation with the team at the publisher's offices. They have provided us with untiring help and support throughout the long journey to the finished publication.

Publisher's acknowledgements
The publishers would like to thank the museums, archives and institutions listed in the illustration captions for their kind support for this publication. Many curators and collectors as well as photographers and photo agencies have made a valuable personal contribution to the success of the project.

Page 1
Lucretia (detail), 1666
Oil on canvas, 110.2 × 92.3 cm (43 3/8 × 36 1/3 in.)
Minneapolis, Minnesota, Minneapolis Institute of Art, The William Hood Dunwoody Fund

Pages 2/3
Scholar in His Study (detail), 1634
Oil on canvas, 141 × 135 cm (55 1/2 × 53 1/4 in.)
Prague, Národní Galerie v Praze

Pages 4/5
Portrait of Jan Six (detail), *c.* 1654
Oil on canvas, 112 × 102 cm (44 1/8 × 40 1/8 in.)
Amsterdam, Collectie Six

Pages 6/7
The Wardens of the Amsterdam Drapers' Guild ("The Syndics"; detail), 1662
Oil on canvas, 191.5 × 279 cm (75 3/8 × 109 3/4 in.)
Amsterdam, Rijksmuseum

Pages 8/9
Self-Portrait with Palette and Maulstick
(detail), 1665–1669
Oil on canvas, 114.3 × 94 cm (45 × 37 1/8 in.)
London, Kenwood House, The Iveagh Bequest

EACH AND EVERY TASCHEN BOOK PLANTS A SEED!
Each year, we offset our annual carbon emissions with carbon credits at the Instituto Terra, a reforestation program in Minas Gerais, Brazil, founded by Lélia and Sebastião Salgado. To find out more about this ecological partnership, please check: www.taschen.com/institutoterra.
Inspiration: unlimited. Carbon footprint: (almost) zero.

Want to see more? Visit taschen.com to view our current publications, browse our latest magazine, and subscribe to our newsletter.

Hohenzollernring 53, D–50672 Köln
www.taschen.com

Translation: Jane Michael, Munich; Abigail Prohaska, Henndorf am Wallersee
Design: Andy Disl, Los Angeles; Claudia Frey, Cologne

Printed in Bosnia-Herzegovina
ISBN 978-3-8365-9175-1